CLARK
2008

THE
STRONG
MAN

THE STRONG MAN

JOHN MITCHELL
and the SECRETS of
WATERGATE

James Rosen

DOUBLEDAY

New York London Toronto Sydney Auckland

PUBLISHED BY DOUBLEDAY

Copyright © 2008 by James Rosen

All Rights Reserved

Published in the United States by Doubleday, an imprint of The Doubleday Broadway Publishing Group, a division of Random House, Inc., New York.
www.doubleday.com

Excerpts from MARTHA: THE LIFE OF MARTHA MITCHELL by Winzola McLendon, copyright © 1979 by Winzola McLendon. Used by permission of Random House, Inc.

Excerpts from MAXINE CHESHIRE: REPORTER by Maxine Cheshire with John Greenya. Copyright © 1978 by M & M, Inc., and John Greenya. Reprinted by permission of Houghton Mifflin Company. All rights reserved.

The author gratefully acknowledges the permission granted by author Len Colodny for the use of quotations from his numerous interviews with John Mitchell and other relevant individuals, dated 1985–1990.

The author gratefully acknowledges the permission granted by Robert Gettlin for the use of his interview with John Mitchell dated May 1985.

The author gratefully acknowledges the permission granted by historian Stanley Kutler for the use of quotations from his two interviews with John Mitchell, dated February and April 1988.

The author gratefully acknowledges the permission granted by Tom Wells for the use of interviews with relevant individuals in the 1980s.

Library of Congress Cataloging-in-Publication Data

Rosen, James.
    The strong man : John Mitchell and the secrets of Watergate / James Rosen. — 1st ed.
      p.   cm.
    Includes bibliographical references and index.
    1. Mitchell, John N. (John Newton), 1913–1988. 2. Attorneys general—United States—Biography. 3. Watergate Affair, 1972–1974. 4. United States–Politics and government—1969–1974. I. Title.
    KF373.M5349R67 2008
    973.924092—dc22
    [B]   2007049430

ISBN 978-0-385-50864-3

PRINTED IN THE UNITED STATES OF AMERICA

10 9 8 7 6 5 4 3 2 1

First Edition

For my beloved mother and father,

Regina and Mike Rosen,

who gave me life—

mine and theirs

CONTENTS

John Mitchell I love.

—*Richard Nixon, 1973*

I think that the current time in the affairs of men are to the point where these stories are now out, they should be fully explored. . . . I think, however, that great care should be taken to ascertain who was involved and how they were involved, instead of just lumping it into a catchphrase of "Watergate" or "cover-up" or things like that. I think it is time that the individual activities be properly parceled out.

—*John Mitchell, 1973*

PROLOGUE

History means the endless rethinking—and reviewing and revisiting—of the past. History, in the
broad sense of the word, is revisionist. History in-
volves multiple jeopardy that the law eschews: People and events are retried and retried again.

—*John Lukacs, 1998*[1]

ON JUNE 22, 1977, the sixty-seventh attorney general of the United
States, John Newton Mitchell, strode onto the grounds of the Federal
Prison Camp at Maxwell Air Force Base in Montgomery, Alabama,
and began serving his sentence for convictions on conspiracy, obstruction of justice, and perjury charges in the Watergate cover-up.
"It's nice to be back in Alabama," Mitchell told reporters with defiant
jocularity.

With his next step, he became the highest-ranking U.S. government official ever to serve time: Federal Prisoner No. 24171-157. Inmates lined Maxwell's walkways for a glimpse of their new neighbor.
They got you now, Big John! they jeered. *You're nothing but another convict with a number now!* On the winding path to his cell, Mitchell visited offices where his own signature hung on the wall, conferring
power on the same individuals who now welcomed him into federal
custody.[2]

Many lives were ruined in the Watergate maelstrom. However, ex-President Richard Nixon, disbarred but pardoned, and ex–Vice President Spiro Agnew, who pleaded nolo contendere to tax evasion charges, both escaped the public servant's ultimate shame: incarceration. Not so John Mitchell. Like many of his fellow Watergate defendants, the former attorney general could have traded evidence, real or fabricated, against a more senior official—Nixon himself, in Mitchell's case—in exchange for leniency, perhaps even avoided prison altogether. But Mitchell did not do that. Instead, he asked Watergate prosecutors to cease their pursuit of the president in exchange for his own guilty plea; the prosecutors refused.[3]

Equally unlike his fellow Watergate convicts, Mitchell never published a book about his years in power, never sold his soul to pay lawyers' fees, never dished dirt on Richard Nixon to delight university audiences on the lecture circuit or viewers of *The Mike Douglas Show*. He never "found God." In electing to tough it out, one columnist wrote, Mitchell stood "up to his hips in midgets among the other Watergate characters . . . divided the men from the boys." "Among the WASP Westchester country club Mafia," another columnist observed of Mitchell's behavior in Watergate, "the code of *omertà* holds." Richard Nixon, toasting his former attorney general at a post-prison party he threw for Mitchell in San Clemente, put it simplest: "John Mitchell has friends—and he stands by them."[4]

This stoicism and loyalty exacted enormous costs: personal, professional, financial. Mitchell's criminal convictions made it fashionable to regard his tenure as attorney general, the capstone to a brilliant legal career on Wall Street, as merely a prelude to scandal; his stewardship of the Department of Justice, from 1969 to 1972, a lawless dress rehearsal in the dark theater of repression. Critiquing the Senate Watergate hearings for *The Observer* of London, novelist Mary McCarthy saw in Mitchell "shades of the late Senator Joe McCarthy . . . an old-style, coarse, crony-type law-and-order politician and backroom mouthpiece . . . a proto-fascist mentality" who "brought evil into the Caucus Room." Former U.S. Attorney Whitney North Seymour Jr., who unsuccessfully prosecuted Mitchell on influence-peddling charges in New York in 1974, wrote the following year, after his guilty verdict in the Watergate cover-up trial, that Mitchell "acted in a fashion totally inconsistent with the standards of integrity and impartiality required of the chief legal officer of a great nation." "The idea of Mitchell as the United States' constitutional guardian staggers the imagination," agreed historian Stanley Kutler in 1991. "Mitchell apparently never understood the American Revolution, let alone the Constitution."

Many on the left had always seen him this way. Mark Rudd, a founder of the radical subversive group the Weathermen, contemptuously dismissed Mitchell as "a Wall Street Nazi." The *New Republic* fumed in 1970 that "John Mitchell personifies and encourages some of the worst tendencies of this administration." *The Nation* worried that "so great is the current preoccupation with crime and 'law and order' that we are in danger of permitting, by default, this grim-lipped attorney general to fashion the legal structure of a new-style police state." "Liberty under the law is under the most severe attack in America since Joe McCarthy's hey-day," fretted the *New York Times'* Tom Wicker, a few months after Woodstock. Yale Law School professor Alexander Bickel complained to *Newsweek* that Mitchell was advancing "the most breath-taking claim for untrammeled executive authority since Lincoln"; the *New Yorker* interpreted his every act as a "signal from the administration that it believes a nation of laws is no longer workable."[5]

Yet many others, from both sides of the political aisle—particularly those who knew Mitchell well, worked with him on Wall Street, in the Department of Justice, and at the Committee for the Re-Election of the President (CRP)—drew a starkly different portrait. "He was a great man," lamented Brent Harries, Mitchell's friend of twenty-five years from the municipal bond business. "A tremendous worker, loyal, nice to people, good to [them]—he made probably millionaires out of those lawyers he worked with. He rewarded people well, they worked hard, and they'd bust their ass for him, but he took care of them."

Rob Odle, a young aide at the White House and CRP who first met Mitchell prior to the '68 campaign, encountered a man far different from the image that preceded him. "He was so unpretentious, so plain, so nice, so at ease that he made you feel at ease. That wasn't quite what I expected; I expected a mean, tough, gruff guy, and he wasn't that at all." Michael Raoul-Duval, who worked under John Ehrlichman as associate director of the Domestic Council and later served as special counsel to President Ford, told a symposium audience in the mid-1980s: "John Mitchell is one of the most misunderstood public figures that I've ever known. He is one of the most gentle, unassuming, humble men that I've met who got to the level of the Cabinet."

Even John Dean, who served as an associate deputy attorney general under Mitchell before becoming White House counsel, and who later proffered the most damning testimony against his former boss, told an interviewer in 1977: "The John Mitchell I know is far different from the man the public perceives. I saw him more as a restraining influence on Nixon and some of the people in the White House. . . . If not for Mitchell, Nixon might have been even more forward in his actions."

Finally, and most compelling, was the word of Erwin N. Griswold, the revered dean of the Harvard Law School for twenty-two years who was named solicitor general of the United States by President Johnson and continued in that office for the entirety of President Nixon's first term. Griswold's stature in the legal fraternity was unrivaled. "Dean Griswold has, in the world of law and learning, become a legend in his own time," said Senator Edward Kennedy. "He has earned a position of respect and renown for his ability as an attorney, scholar, teacher and educational leader, as well as a public-spirited citizen and family man." As solicitor general, it was Griswold's duty to argue the positions of the federal government in all cases before the U.S. Supreme Court. In such cases, with nothing less than the future of American jurisprudence and society at stake, surely an attorney general determined to use the Justice Department as "a partisan instrument for pursuing presidential policies," as one Oxford-educated historian has charged Mitchell, or who "had no respect for rule of law," as the leading scholar of American attorneys general has written of him, would have taken extraordinary pains to prejudice Griswold's work and actions; yet Mitchell did just the opposite.

"All I can say," wrote Griswold in 1992, "is that Mr. Mitchell was always fair and square with me. I never saw anything in our association in the Department of Justice which gave me concern about his integrity. Generally speaking, the attorney general left me alone. He understood that I wanted to act professionally, and he did not seek to interfere with that." Indeed, Griswold recalled that Mitchell "shielded me from several matters . . . [and] served to protect me from a good deal of direct pressure" exerted by political appointees in the Nixon White House.[6]

When Mitchell emerged from Maxwell, on January 19, 1979, the oldest and last of the president's men to leave prison, a ghost from the era of the Chicago Eight and Kent State disgorged, incongruously, into the age of *Star Wars*, disco, and designer jeans, he wryly told the assembled news media: "From henceforth, don't call me, I'll call you." But no biographer ever did. Yet by that same year, the world had three books about Mitchell's late ex-wife, Martha, an emotionally disturbed alcoholic whose late-night crank calls splashed her face across the front pages of every newspaper and magazine in America. Stunningly, no one bothered to chronicle the life of John Mitchell: child of the Great Depression; World War II combat veteran; Wall Street innovator; gray-flannel power broker to governors and mayors in all fifty states; Richard Nixon's law partner, consigliere, and winning campaign manager in 1968 and 1972; America's top cop, as attorney general, during the Days of Rage, the May Day riots, and the Pentagon Papers; and Public Enemy Number One when, in the words of a

British observer, "the great black cloud of Watergate seemed to settle over America like a kind of grand judgment, not just on Nixon himself, but on the whole of post-war America."[7]

To understand this "grand judgment," to ensure the facts and lessons of the Watergate scandals are properly recorded, requires a revisiting of John Mitchell, and his extraordinary life and times, that the man himself, with his penchant for privacy, would surely have discouraged. If America truly aspires to be "a nation of laws," it can ill afford to leave unexamined the conduct, and treatment, of its highest-ranking government official ever to be convicted on criminal charges—especially when that same figure was the nation's chief law enforcement officer. *The Strong Man: John Mitchell and the Secrets of Watergate* aims to fill this unacceptable gap in the sprawling literature of the Nixon presidency, and in our understanding of American society in the second half of the twentieth century.

Mitchell's life raises questions both simple and profound: Was he centrally a part of, or did he somehow stand fundamentally apart from, the criminality of the Nixon administration? Were his problems, as one of his lawyers later rued, simply Nixon's problems—or was it vice versa, as one of Nixon's biographers would claim after both men were dead? Which association contributed more to the attorney general's demise: his political alliance with Nixon, as Martha Mitchell sobbed in her final years, or his ill-starred marriage to Martha, as Nixon argued from 1973 onward? To all who knew and respected him, however, one question loomed above all others: Was Mitchell guilty in Watergate—and if so, guilty of what?

The great scandal began, as a matter of public record, in the early morning hours of June 17, 1972, when plainclothes Washington police officers, responding to a call placed by a private security company, arrested five men inside the headquarters of the Democratic National Committee in the Watergate office complex. Unlike most local burglars, these men were found in business suits and rubber gloves, carrying cameras, sophisticated electronics equipment, and crisp hundred-dollar bills. Within days, police and FBI investigators, joined by reporters for the *Washington Post*, established direct ties between the arrested men, their flimsy aliases notwithstanding, and the Nixon White House and reelection committee. James McCord, a longtime FBI and CIA operative and the covert team's expert on electronic surveillance, was employed as chief of security for Nixon's reelection committee; the other burglars, veterans of the Cuban Bay of Pigs invasion, were swiftly linked to E. Howard Hunt, a longtime CIA officer listed on the White House payroll as a consultant to Nixon's special counsel, Charles Colson. Mitchell, having resigned from Justice to spearhead Nixon's reelection drive, was then the head of the campaign committee.

Over the next nine and a half months, during which period President Nixon was reelected by one of the greatest landslides in American history, the arrested men, Hunt, and his chief coconspirator in the break-in, G. Gordon Liddy, the reelection committee's general counsel, were indicted and began receiving secret, sporadic, and invariably incomplete cash payments. Left in phone booths at National Airport and other ingenious drop spots, the payments were designed—depending on whom one asked—either to buy the defendants' silence or to honor the first rule of the spy game: *When your men get caught, they and their families get taken care of, and they, in turn, keep their mouths shut.*

During this same period, members of the White House and reelection committee staffs, led by Jeb Magruder, Mitchell's deputy at the campaign, destroyed evidence, perjured themselves before a federal grand jury, and conspired in myriad other ways to obstruct the multiple investigations that were gleefully launched, in a capital controlled by Democrats, to probe the origins and financing of the break-in. The admitted "ringleader" in this multifarious undertaking was John Dean, the ambitious young White House counsel who scrambled to find ways to raise the "hush money" that kept the cover-up together; kept close tabs on the FBI investigation and civil litigation that threatened to unravel it; and coached Magruder in his perjury.

The cover-up came crashing down in March 1973, when

McCord broke ranks with his fellow burglars—all of whom had dutifully pleaded guilty—and wrote a bombshell letter to the judge in the case, John J. Sirica. The proceedings in *U.S. v. Liddy*, McCord charged, had been grossly tainted by perjury and backstage political pressure. Sirica's reading of the letter in open court unleashed a frenzy in the news media and a new round of congressional and grand jury investigations. Dean, Magruder, and other midlevel officials scurried to negotiate plea bargains for themselves, exchanging their testimony for lenient sentences. Soon the grand jury handed down perjury and obstruction of justice indictments against the president's top aides: Mitchell, White House chief of staff H. R. Haldeman, and domestic adviser John Ehrlichman.

Watergate had now become a national obsession, at least among the political classes, the overriding issue in a superpower engaged in cold war struggles across the globe. Then, in televised Senate hearings that dominated the summer of 1973, came an even more stunning disclosure: Nixon had surreptitiously recorded virtually all his meetings and phone calls, from February 1971 onward, in his White House and EOB offices. This set off a desperate, yearlong legal battle for access to the tapes, which Nixon lost, resulting in disclosure of his early awareness of, and fitful participation in, the cover-up. He resigned in August 1974; a month later he was granted a pardon for all crimes he committed "or may have committed" while in office by his handpicked successor, Gerald R. Ford.

When it was all over, investigators discovered Hunt and Liddy had stage-managed an earlier break-in, targeting the psychiatrist who treated Daniel Ellsberg, leaker of the Pentagon Papers; and the original crime metastasized into a massive complex of scandals, triggering an inquisition of the Nixon administration as comprehensive as the Nuremberg trials. The Watergate Special Prosecution Force formed five separate task forces, focused on crimes as disparate as political espionage, abuse of the Internal Revenue Service, antitrust collusion, influence-peddling, and campaign finance violations, and ultimately secured convictions against more than fifty men and nineteen corporations.[8]

What was Mitchell's role in all this? History commonly records that he ordered the Watergate break-in, an unofficial verdict that cast on the shoulders of the former attorney general ultimate responsibility for the improbable chain of events that climaxed in the disgraceful end of the Nixon presidency, and the corresponding diminution in American superpower influence. But the former attorney general, who collapsed and died from a heart attack on a Georgetown street in November 1988, always steadfastly denied ordering the break-in; and no court of law ever determined who did give the order.

Instead, Mitchell was convicted on five criminal counts for his role in the cover-up: A jury of eight women and four men from the District of Columbia found that Mitchell lied under oath to the grand jury and Senate Watergate committee; ordered Magruder to destroy evidence; instructed Dean to obtain FBI case reports; directed a third aide, Robert Mardian, to engineer McCord's premature release from jail; personally authorized, and tried to rope CIA into subsidizing, the payment of "hush money" to the arrested men; and extended promises of executive clemency to them.

Mitchell's Watergate conviction, announced on New Year's Day 1975, came eight months after another federal jury, seated in New York, acquitted him and another Nixon cabinet member, former commerce secretary Maurice Stans, on influence-peddling charges. Mitchell and Stans stood accused of illegally soliciting a $200,000 campaign contribution from Robert Vesco—the "fugitive financier" who fled the country rather than face charges he looted a mutual fund of $224 million—in exchange for their quiet help in derailing a Securities and Exchange Commission inquiry into Vesco's activities. After a two-month trial, the jury found, correctly, that $200,000 was not a lot of money compared to the sums the '72 Nixon campaign routinely took in; that the SEC case against Vesco hummed right along, absent any sign of tampering by the defendants; and that Mitchell was guilty only of arranging, with a phone call here and there, a few meetings between willing government officials and polite Vesco associates.

That Mitchell should have won acquittal in the Vesco trial at the height of the Watergate frenzy, in April 1974, only to be convicted in similar proceedings in Washington less than a year later marked a curious turn of events that should have attracted the attention—but never did—of the nation's burgeoning new corps of investigative reporters. After all, a number of the same elements were present in both trials: To cite but two examples, the "Vesco trial," as *U.S. v. Mitchell-Stans* came to be called, saw the first playing of the Nixon tapes in public and the courtroom debut of John Dean, the witness whose testimony in the Watergate cover-up trial would prove critical to the convictions of Mitchell, Haldeman, and Ehrlichman. Did Mitchell's luck just run out—or were other, more sinister forces at work?

Dozens of questions clamor for answers: If John Mitchell didn't order the Watergate break-in, who did—and why? What role did CIA, and the intelligence community at large, play in Watergate? If the great scandal represented, as *Harper's* observed in November 1973, "a major modern metamorphosis . . . the poisonous afterbirth of Vietnam," then questions from the cold war period leading up to Watergate also command attention today. In the conception and execution of the Nixon-Kissinger foreign policy, Mitchell played a substantial, and purposefully unheralded, role. Was there some connection between that policy and the administration's ignominious end? Were Nixon and his men forced to pay a price for their embrace of détente with the Soviet Union and rapprochement with Red China? Why were the nation's top military commanders discovered committing espionage against Nixon and Kissinger, for thirteen months in wartime, and what did the president—and Mitchell—do about it?

No less significant are the issues raised by the administration's domestic policies. Indeed, as the very symbol of "law and order" in Nixon's America—and then again as a symbol of a different kind in Watergate—John Mitchell bore witness to the most searing political turmoil in America since the Civil War. After all, it was Mitchell who ran the Department of Justice, and the administration of justice in those years occupies the central role in all lingering controversies from that era: Was justice done in the enforcement of school desegregation and antitrust laws? In the battles against antiwar protesters and radical groups? At Kent State and Jackson State? In the cases of Daniel Ellsberg and Lt. William Calley, Jimmy Hoffa and Robert Vesco, Abe Fortas and Clement Haynsworth, John Lennon and the Berrigan Brothers, the Black Panthers and ITT?

These and other mysteries continue to haunt Americans not merely because they involve colorful figures of intrinsic interest or because their answers remain so elusive, but because the times that produced them—the "decade of shocks" that spanned the Kennedy assassination to Nixon's resignation—marked a frightening watershed in American history, an age when wars raged on earth while men walked on the moon, when media began transmitting social upheavals in real time, and when the continued existence of the republic seemed, for the first time since Reconstruction, imperiled.

For the crimes of Watergate, no one paid a higher price than John Mitchell; but it would be a mistake to believe Mitchell's incarceration, and denial of parole, were meant to punish him *solely* for the crimes of Watergate. The times—and the *Times*—demanded his ritual sacrifice. As Mitchell's brother remarked wistfully in later years: "The climate was right for putting someone like John in jail."[9]

If answering such questions definitively is a central aim of *The Strong Man*, so, too, is the resolution of a number of disputes over Mitchell's personal biography. There is, for example, no agreement on when he first met the two individuals who had the greatest impact on his life—Richard Nixon and Martha Mitchell—nor on what medals he was awarded in World War II; whether he married twice or thrice; earned $200,000 a year on Wall Street, or $2 million; or, as family lore held and the Associated Press reported in his obituary, he played professional hockey for the New York Rangers. Salvaging the truth from the ceaseless clash of claims and counterclaims surrounding Mitchell, and evoking his true personality—his mordant wit, wry fatalism, and desperate attempts to raise a daughter against staggering legal and financial odds—were no less important than corralling the elusive, though not irretrievable, facts of Watergate.

Indeed, none of those crucial questions about recent American history can be answered in isolation; all, in varying degrees, require each other's answers for their own to come into view. No one can reckon whether Mitchell "politicized" Justice, served the greater good or acted as a conscious malefactor in a criminal regime, deserved his fate in Watergate or fell prey to cruel and cynical antagonists, without understanding the man's personality, the way his mind worked. This, in turn, can only be attained through a look at his background and rise to prominence, and a thorough examination of his exercise of power and unparalleled fall from it. At the end of this process lies: truth and judgment.

Arriving there involved a personal journey that endured through two decades of research, synthesis, and writing. It began with the relevant secondary sources: the five hundred books published on Watergate, the Nixon presidency, and the convulsions of the sixties, as well as the voluminous, if necessarily imperfect, record established by the era's many fine daily-deadline journalists. Fresh interviews were conducted with 250 people, including two presidents, a vice president, two chief justices, three secretaries of state, three secretaries of defense, four attorneys general, two CIA directors, and a great many staff members of the Nixon White House and the Committee for the Re-Election of the President: individuals alternately central, peripheral, and wholly unrelated to Watergate. Also questioned were party officials and secretaries employed at Democratic National Committee headquarters in June 1972. These sessions included the only extensive interviews ever conducted with the woman whose telephone was wiretapped in the Watergate break-in and surveillance operation, and more than eight hours of interviews with the only man who monitored that wiretap.

Aggressive use of the Freedom of Information Act, pursued over several years' time, pried loose hundreds of thousands of previously undisclosed documents and tape recordings. Most of these were located at the Nixon Presidential Materials Project, the branch of the National Archives that houses the ex-president's papers and tapes and those of his staff aides. Of especial value was the long march, on microfiche, through every sheet of Haldeman's and Ehrlichman's 200,000 pages of yellow-pad notes from their meetings with President Nixon; since there was no taping system for the president's first two years in office, these notes constitute the best evidence of Nixon's thoughts and statements, on a whole range of issues, during that critical period. In Haldeman's case, the notes formed the raw material for *The Haldeman Diaries*, which proved, in several instances, less candid than the underlying scribbles.

Surprisingly, some invaluable sources of Watergate evidence—whole archives of contemporaneous documents—had never before been mined, or even requested for inspection, by the armies of earlier scholars. These included the internal files of the staff lawyers on the Watergate Special Prosecution Force (WSPF) and the sworn testimony taken by the Senate Watergate committee in closed-door executive session. The former archive revealed what the WSPF lawyers knew about Watergate and when they knew it: their reliance on, and active role in reshaping, the deeply flawed testimony of their star witnesses, Dean and Magruder. The latter collection contained more than five thousand pages of testimony from the major witnesses before the Senate Watergate committee: Dean, Magruder, McCord, Hunt. Like the WSPF records, the executive session interrogations had never been examined by any researcher and revealed witnesses consciously changing their stories, both to implicate Mitchell more deeply and to conceal their own culpability. These were major factors in the outcome of Watergate and have never been exposed; taking account of them enabled *The Strong Man* to resolve the questions that bedeviled Mitchell to his grave, including the central mystery of who authorized the break-in.

Rounding out the picture were intimate letters written by Mitchell in his own hand, from prison; his federal tax returns from the years 1950 to 1973; the complete transcripts of his two criminal trials; documents compiled during his bitter divorce from Martha Mitchell; court filings and fresh depositions generated by recent Watergate-related civil suits; and many other relevant documents. In sum, no previous study has encompassed so comprehensive a research effort, mounted over two decades' time, nor benefited from the wealth of newly declassified evidence now available.

Americans may fairly wonder after all these years, after all the hearings, articles, trials, books, documentaries, films, and plays, after the seemingly endless releases of new Nixon tapes and the "revelations" in 2005 about the identity of Deep Throat, Bob Woodward's shadowy (and highly suspect) source, whether there is, at this late date, anything *new* to say about Watergate. The answer extracted from these mountains of new evidence, and discernible as much from the source notes as from the narrative text, is both unmistakable and unassailable: Assuredly, the scandal presented in *The Strong Man* is not your father's Watergate.

At all points, the research task was made incalculably more complicated by a subject notorious for his inscrutability, one who left behind no large cache of personal or official papers and whose most memorable remark advised listeners to observe what he did rather than what he said. If taciturnity and sleights of hand served some perceived interest during Mitchell's lifetime—and the stay at Maxwell suggests the opposite—they certainly serve none now that he, and Nixon, are long gone. For only through the establishment of an accurate record of those tumultuous times, their passions cooled by the passage of almost four decades, can America hope to avoid destructive repetitions of what President Ford called "our long national nightmare," an experience no one lived more personally and fully than John N. Mitchell.

THE STRONG MAN

INTO THE FIRE

I don't think anyone ever really knew him. He lived
within himself very much.

—Robert Mitchell to the author, 1998[1]

"DO YOU REALLY want to hear about this?"

John Mitchell was, in his lawyerly way, questioning his questioner, gently needling a young reporter who came to the Department of Justice in the spring of 1970 to interview the attorney general
about, of all things, his childhood. On that sunny day in May, the
reporter found Mitchell—currently embroiled in searing controversies over the killings at Kent State, two failed Supreme Court nominees, and the potentially explosive desegregation of Southern school
systems—utterly at ease in his dark, thickly carpeted office, absently
tilting his large frame back and forth in his swivel chair, lighting and
relighting his pipe, tossing the still-burning matches into his waste-
basket.

Yes, replied the reporter from Long Island's *Newsday*, he did indeed want to know about Mitchell's childhood; the subject would in-

terest readers in Mitchell's hometown of Blue Point, New York, and there was, for all the attorney general's fame in those days, little known or written about Mitchell's formative years.

Reluctantly, his pale blue eyes becoming distant as his mind conjured the sights and sounds of coastal Long Island in the 1920s, the attorney general remembered a "normal" childhood spent, he said, "like Huck Finn," immersed in the twin pastimes of sports—"I played them all," he boasted, including baseball, hockey, golf, hunting, fishing, and sailing—and mischief. At one particular memory, Mitchell began to chuckle, softly at first, then uncontrollably, until he was "half-bent" in laughter and brought back into the moment only by a coughing fit.

"I'll tell you, there was one thing, there was one incident," Mitchell began. He described his old wooden school by the railroad tracks, at the intersection of Blue Point's Main Street and River Road, on which his family lived for a time. One night, he said, a fire burned the school clear down to the ground. "Whole damned school went," he said. Again now, Mitchell was laughing hard, and took a few moments to collect himself. "My brother and I were there," the attorney general continued. "We watched it. We were so damned glad to see that thing burn down. We watched it! We threw our books into the fire. We were so glad. We just threw our books in. My father gave us a good whack. I'll always remember that. Whew!"

The memory prompted Mitchell to tell the *Newsday* reporter another, similar anecdote from his youth, about an equally destructive fire. "You know, I burned down the house in Blue Point," Mitchell said. "It was one Fourth of July. We had sparklers and it was daylight and, you know, we were supposed to wait until dark. Well, I was a kid who didn't want to wait, so I took some of those sparklers down under the porch and—well, it burned down the house." *You didn't have anything to do with the school fire?* the reporter asked. "No," Mitchell assured him. "That was in the middle of the night. This was during the day. Of course not."[2]

With these beguiling stories, in which the stern-faced monument to law and order allowed a glimpse into a younger, more reckless self, one never permitted to emerge in his public appearances as attorney general, there was only one thing wrong: They weren't true. Mitchell's younger brother, Robert, who supposedly heaved his books into the schoolhouse fire along with Mitchell, told the first reporter ever to interview him, in 1998, that the story was complete fiction.

"Nothing happened!" Robert proclaimed. One night, he explained, he and young John Mitchell, or Jack, as his family called him, were awakened by whistles and sirens screaming past their house. "[W]e knew there was a fire somewhere, but didn't know anything about it. Next morning we went to school, and we got up there, and the school was an old frame school. They had just bought fire escapes for it, metal fire escapes. And they were laying in the yard. And we went up there, and the school—it was burnt to the ground, and the nice, new fire escapes were laying all around the edges of it, unused . . . But that's all . . . We never heard how the fire started or anything else."

It was much the same with the attorney general's sparkler story, which Robert laughingly dismissed as "another slight exaggeration." Yes, there was an Independence Day celebration at the Mitchells' home in Blue Point, where the boys, looking to escape a stiff wind, lit some sparklers under their back porch. "We went under that [porch] to try and light [the sparklers]," Robert remembered. "And I guess we— a couple of the leaves caught fire there, and we went scrambling out. And one of the adults there, I don't know who it was, took a pail of water and threw it on the leaves, and that was the end of it. The house never burned down. The porch didn't even burn down."

The falsity of the attorney general's childhood tall tales might be easily written off as inconsequential, an Irishman's love of lore, were it not for his multiple perjury convictions in Watergate, and for the recurring theme of factual dispute that accompanies all accounts, and every phase, of his life. That John Newton Mitchell was born in Detroit on September 5, 1913, the fourth of five children, the first three of whom died young, are incontestable facts.[3] Yet little else in Mitchell's early biography is so invulnerable to challenge.

Mitchell's paternal lineage is usually traced to Scotland, but exactly when his forefathers came to America varies in the telling. The attorney general's daughter, Jill Mitchell-Reed, believed her family got its start in the States with a stonecutter from Edinburgh who settled in Rutland, Vermont, before moving to Chicago and ending up in Rockport, Maine.[4] Perhaps the most reliable authority—Robert, sole surviving member of the attorney general's boyhood family— said their grandfather, James A. Mitchell, a stonecutter seeking proximity to New Hampshire's granite quarries, emigrated from Aberdeen, Scotland, in the mid-1800s to Rock*land*, Maine.[5]

After meeting and marrying Margaret Porter, an immigrant from Newfoundland "of English extraction," James A. Mitchell fathered three sons. The youngest of them, Joseph Charles, born around 1882 in Rockland, Maine, was to become the attorney general's father.[6] Skillfully exploiting his family's limited connections, Joseph, when still a young man, joined the trading stamp business owned by an uncle, Esden Porter. Itching to start his own firm, but unwilling to compete directly against his uncle, Joseph left New York for the Midwest, initially eyeing Columbus, Ohio, before settling on Detroit. There he began the People's Legal Stamp Company.[7]

But before that, on an evening in 1906 or 1907, at the East Flatbush home of an older brother, Joseph met his future wife, Margaret Agnes McMahon.[8] Margaret's family was "very well off," her granddaughter Jill Mitchell-Reed recalled.[9] Peter McMahon, Margaret's father, died in his early fifties, but left behind a considerable fortune from his stake in Peter's Chop House, a Greenwich Village steakhouse he owned.[10]

Joseph and Margaret's first two children, a boy and girl, they named after themselves—though with typical Mitchell inscrutability in the matter of names, the boy was addressed as Scranton. The couple's third child, John Newton, died at birth.[11] The name was given anew to their fourth child, the future attorney general, in 1913.

John Mitchell's mother was unusual for her time: a Hunter College graduate[12] and an indomitable presence at home. "She was quiet but her force was felt in the family, no question about that," her last child, Robert, born a little more than a year after John, remembered.[13] Countless times, her husband, Joseph, recounted for the family how he had asked Margaret, in 1907, to marry him: "I would call her up on the phone and say, 'Margaret, will you marry me?' And she said, 'Yes—who is this?'" Seventy-five years later, this line still made Robert laugh. "That's Yankee humor," he chuckled.[14]

Humor was in need in the earliest years of the twentieth century, when the Mitchell family was wracked by wild fluctuations in its financial fortunes. "[H]e was successful," Robert said of his father, "up until World War I came along." Wartime rationing of consumer goods left little need for trading stamps—goods were valuable enough without stamps as a purchasing incentive—and one day, as Robert remembered sadly, "[M]y father was without a business."[15]

By 1918, the family had moved from Detroit back to Blue Point, where Peter McMahon, Mitchell's restaurant-owning grandfather, had spent summers away from his swank Harlem apartment. Desperate for work, Joseph took a sales job with the Cudahey meatpacking firm, switching shortly thereafter to Cudahey's main competitor, Wilson. He traversed Long Island's butcher shops and groceries, peddling Wilson's meats. Though it was a big step down from owning his own business, Mitchell's "lovably stern" father had, by 1920, secured the job that would keep his family afloat throughout the Great Depression.[16]

A resort town, Blue Point came alive in the summertime, but winters were often severe. The water would freeze over and the town became, as Robert recalled, "a dead place."[17] To wring excitement from the deadness, the brothers rode ice floes down the Great South Bay, refusing to return home until wet clothing and freezing temperatures left them no alternative. As the seasons changed, they hunted ducks, rabbit, and geese with shotguns, and caught and ate snapper. An undated photograph, circa 1925, captures two skinny boys seated on a decaying wooden pier, bamboo fishing poles in hand, alone together on a deserted marshy inlet along the bay. Robert smiled rakishly at the camera; his older brother, Jack, the future attorney general, stared into the water below.[18]

The oldest and handsomest of the children, Scranton led his brothers in their outdoors exploits, and, like many an older brother, occasionally grew domineering in dealing with his siblings. Mitchell's older sister, Margaret, was a good-looking, athletic woman who inherited her mother's strong-willed nature. By the time she turned seventeen, a modeling dream led her to abandon high school for Manhattan, touching off a furious row with her father, Joseph. "I guess my father was probably too strict on her hours," Robert remembered. "And she was a little headstrong, and she just took off on her own." A persistent illness, later diagnosed as pneumonia, landed her in a Manhattan hospital. Within a few weeks, Margaret was gone, dead at twenty-three.[19] In another ten years, Scranton, too, would be gone, victim of a heart attack he suffered when, during World War II, he responded to an air raid alert in his Long Island community.

Like Richard Nixon, then, John Mitchell had, by his early thirties, experienced the agony of seeing *two* siblings die young. Whether Nixon realized this is unknown, but it is unlikely that Mitchell, as Nixon's campaign manager, somehow remained ignorant of so potent and widely disseminated an element of his candidate's personal biography as the deaths of Harold and Arthur Nixon.

As a student at the Blue Point School from 1919 to 1921, Mitchell, "smaller and slighter than most boys his age," demonstrated both native intelligence and uncommon discipline, amassing, according to one assessment, "a handsome sprinkling of As and Bs."[20] As he went further in school, he developed a winning, if somewhat withheld, personality as well. At Jamaica High School, the future attorney general launched his only campaign for elective office, a successful bid for the presidency of his senior class. A B+ student and popular athlete, Mitchell was the handpicked candidate of a group of students already running the student organization. It was Mitchell's first involvement with machine politics.[21]

Mitchell rapidly developed into a formidable athlete, excelling at several different sports. Unlike the young Richard Nixon—who persisted at football, a sport for which his diminutive frame left him ill-suited, and who accordingly absorbed "a vast amount of brutal punishment"—the young John Mitchell played to his strengths. In hockey, for example, he became adept at skating around bigger players and avoiding their brutal body checks. Ken Agnew, who practiced with Mitchell on Long Island's ponds and played with him on the Jamaica High School team, later remembered Mitchell as intensely competitive. "He had a lot of drive and incentive," Agnew told the *New York Post* in 1970. "He wanted to win. He played the game the way it should be played."[22]

The Jamaica team won the city hockey championship thirteen years in a row, and the 1927 squad, on which Mitchell played, was rewarded with a visit the following February to the White House— Mitchell's first—and an audience with President Calvin Coolidge.[23] Mitchell was so skilled that he played (for "blade sharpening money," he said, twenty-five dollars a Saturday) for the Jamaica Hawks in the Metropolitan League. Some league games were played at Madison Square Garden, giving rise to a myth—persisting even into Mitchell's Associated Press obituary—that he skated for the New York Rangers.

At golf, too, Mitchell excelled, becoming captain of his high school team and tying for New York's coveted Police School Athletic League title. When Mitchell went on to Fordham University, his captain was Malcolm Wilson—later the governor of New York—who remembered Mitchell giving golf lessons on the side for money.[24] During a joint appearance with Mitchell on *The Dick Cavett Show* in 1970, White House communications director Herb Klein told the host, "John was once a professional golfer." "Is that so?" Cavett asked. "Yes," replied Mitchell, "but that was a long time ago. You can't imagine what happens to your handicap when you're in the Justice Department. You have other handicaps," Mitchell said, to the audience's laughter.[25]

As a young man, Mitchell showed no interest in two vices that later became his trademarks: alcohol and tobacco. Tales of Mitchell's love affair with Dewar's Scotch abound in the literature of the Nixon presidency; and so ever-present in Mitchell's hands and mouth did tobacco pipes become that the Watergate conspirators, speaking in cryptic terms over the telephone, adopted "The Pipe" as their code name for Mitchell ("What a great cover name," he snapped sarcastically, six months before his death).[26]

According to his daughter, Jill Mitchell-Reed, when Mitchell first saw Elizabeth "Bette" Shine, a pretty member of the girl's basketball team, on a bicycle one day in 1936, he proclaimed to his friend Doug Giorgio: "That's the woman I'm going to marry."[27] The prophecy became a reality. The pair deferred their wedding until Mitchell earned his law degree. One photograph shows Bette—an entrancing blonde with a trim, athletic figure, sunken eyes, prominent cheekbones, and a glamorous smile, Faye Dunaway before the fact—beaming in a new fur coat; on the reverse, she recorded in pencil that Mitchell bought her the coat after passing his bar exams in 1938.

Bette was "kooky, like *I Love Lucy*," recalled Susie Morrison, Mitchell's secretary from 1963 to 1971 and a close friend of the family. Once, Bette found herself locked out of her house; an hour later, she realized the doorknob was in her pocket. "Little things like that happened on a daily basis with Bette," laughed Morrison. "She was cute, and I think down to earth . . . maybe a little flaky, but a lovable kind of flake. Not the kook Martha was . . . She wasn't harsh, brassy. She was fun, but in a more subdued way."[28]

On stationery bearing the gothic imprint of Fordham's legal fra-

ternity, Gamma Eta Gamma, Mitchell composed whimsical love letters to his future bride. "Bette darling," he wrote on May 6, 1937,
"your two letters . . . have broken the spell of inactive distemper
caused by the lack of seeing One Miss Shine and lack of work to keep
me from thinking about that One Miss Shine, the dream." Three
months later, in response to the girl's demand for more letters,
Mitchell indulged in playful, pun-ridden verse, then roguishly suggested he could more effectively demonstrate his love in person,
where he could "make gestures." "Night my love," Mitchell signed
off, withholding his name. "If you [are] thinking I'm signing this so
that you have something on me, another guess."[29]

After two years as an undergraduate at Jesuit-run Fordham University in the Bronx, Mitchell entered the school's nighttime law school
program. By day he worked as an "office boy" at the law firm of Caldwell and Raymond, founded in 1887 by "Judge" James H. Caldwell
(a title, Mitchell once quipped, recognized only in the court of public opinion). As new railroad lines were branching across America in
the second half of the nineteenth century, the firm had developed a
legal specialty refereeing disputes between the small western towns
that had floated bond issues to pay for new lines and the railroad
companies that often reneged on their bond debts.

Mitchell worked hard to make himself indispensable. Just before
he graduated from law school, Judge Caldwell handed him a thankless task. "See if you can make anything out of this mess," he told
Mitchell.[30] The "mess" was the paperwork supporting the bond program for one of the nation's earliest federal public housing initiatives.
The concept of the federal government supplying grants, low-interest
loans, and other incentives for developers to build new housing units
for low-income citizens was a product of the Great Depression, part
of President Franklin Roosevelt's effort to combat the intertwined
problems of rising unemployment and the spread of slums. A series
of bold federal initiatives—including the passage by Congress, in 1933,

of the National Industrial Recovery Act, the creation of the Public Works Administration and its Housing Division, and Congress's enactment, four years later, of the United States Housing Act, with its accompanying Housing Authority—empowered local governmental and banking institutions across the country to construct more than 370 projects, housing some 120,000 families at a cost of $540 million ($7.2 billion in current figures).[31]

The conservative Caldwell regarded the Roosevelt initiative, whose first test was planned for Syracuse, New York, as a boondoggle. "Take this damn fool New Deal idea and work it out," he dismissively told Mitchell. Soon after, a delegation from Syracuse arrived, seeking Mitchell's counsel on how to develop a pilot program to finance low-income housing; although the rest of the conservative municipal bond bar greeted the endeavor "coolly," the young lawyer from Long Island leapt at the challenge.[32]

Mitchell's interest in housing, an ingredient in what one business associate later termed his "passion for cities," likely stemmed from the fact that he had come of age during the Depression. Mitchell's father and uncles, like most Americans at the time, struggled to get by. "The brothers were either all the way up or all the way down," Jill Mitchell-Reed said. "I mean, they amassed fortunes and lost them." Jack, the older brother of the attorney general's father, had only recently alighted on Wall Street, trading stocks and bonds and making a killing—until Black Tuesday. "The Depression came along and then he went broke," Mitchell's brother Robert said, seventy years later. "[H]e lost everything. He was actually a pauper. And he had three young daughters from his second marriage and a wife to support. I know my father helped support him for several years. . . . He never really recovered." Asked if the family history offered any prologue, or analogue, to Mitchell's own fall in Watergate, Robert thought back to Black Tuesday, and mused: "[M]aybe John remembered the glory days of Uncle Jack . . ."[33]

Though susceptible to the allure of Wall Street, with its soaring potential and palpable peril, Mitchell also recognized the investment community was "pretty sour" on low-income-housing subsidies. Few financial analysts imagined the revenues generated, principally through rent payments, could ever match the sums paid out in start-up loans, a calculation that usually saddled low-income-housing bonds with exorbitantly high interest rates; after all, if the projects went south, who would repay the loans? Yet Mitchell was determined to make the concept work. The disarmingly simple idea he took back to Judge Caldwell—the tax-exempt municipal housing bond—later revolutionized public finance, and set Wall Street on fire. What if the federal housing authorities, while not legally bound to make good on loan defaults, *pledged their intention* to do so? And what if, as a good-faith measure, the agencies maintained verifiable reserves for just such a rainy day? "In other words, this was not a guarantee by the government, but they would *promise* to make annual contributions," recalled William A. Madison, a colleague and law partner of Mitchell's for nearly two decades. "It was a—sort of like a gimmick."[34]

After researching constitutions and bylaws in states where bonds were to be issued, Mitchell would draft legislation for the states' legislatures to enact, and, upon that foundation, issue his firm's legal opinion on the validity and tax-exempt nature of those bonds. Francis X. Maloney, another longtime law partner, agreed the "requisition agreements" Mitchell designed did not bind the federal government to backstop locally issued bonds, but served nevertheless to secure them, to Wall Street's satisfaction, with the force of the federal government. "[W]hen the bonds were issued," Maloney explained, "you knew damn well that they were going to get paid, and of course, Moody's and Standard and Poor's felt that way because they rated the bonds Triple-A."[35]

"They sold like hotcakes," Mitchell himself recalled, with other municipalities rushing to duplicate Syracuse's success. Even before graduating from law school, Mitchell was drawing new clients to the firm on the strength of his name. On a straight commission basis, he later remembered, he was "making more money than most partners on Wall Street"—more, in fact, than the astonished partners at Caldwell and Raymond. As Mitchell told a reporter years later, the firm soon recognized, after Judge Caldwell's death, that it "became cheaper to make me a partner."[36]

He had created a money machine—but it was more than that. Jill remembered her father working away at a card table at home on weekends. The little girl learned what municipal bonds were and did through small demonstrations by her bemused, pipe-smoking father. On drives to Manhattan, they would pass a shantytown in Manhasset, where the less fortunate—bums then, the homeless today—took shelter in crates and discarded refrigerator boxes. "No water, no nothing," Jill recalled. "And I can always remember how sad I felt for those people, particularly with the naïveté and innocence of young children: Someone should give them a home. That was my solution." One day, they drove past the same spot to find the shantytown replaced by a gleaming public housing project. "And that's how I understood what municipal bonds did when I was very, very young: They built houses so that people like that could live in houses."

> I can remember him showing them to me, and he was very proud . . . "You see, now the people have a home and everything. They cleaned it up, brought in the bulldozers, cleaned it up, and put grass on it." And it's a beautiful place still today.

On another occasion, Jill remembered asking her father what he was working on, and him peering up from the card table to say he was helping a small town acquire a fire engine. "This is not what we usually do," he chuckled, returning to his papers. With a child's naïve indignation, Jill replied that it was terrible for someone to make money if a town needed a fire engine. Her father "took his pipe out of his mouth, and said, 'We're not making money off of this one,' or something like that. And I know he was particularly proud of doing things like that." A decade later, Mitchell's stepson witnessed the same passion. "He thought as a lawyer all the time, not just when he was in

the office," said Jay Jennings. "He was in love with what he did. . . .
It wasn't just writing bonds. . . . There were beneficial public out-
comes that affected people's lives."[37]

These were good years for John Mitchell. He was in his early thirties, married to his high school sweetheart, father of a healthy baby
daughter, living in suburban Long Island with his parents close by, a
partner in a prestigious Manhattan law firm with money, as he put it,
"tumbling in." Less than a year after his admission to the bar, he was
helping to draft the federal Housing Act of 1939. Already a nationally
renowned expert in housing finance issues, Mitchell, a Scotch-Irish
kid from the South Shore, had catapulted himself in a phenomenally
short time into the top tier of the municipal bond bar, a notoriously
stodgy bastion of old boys' school attitude.

On May 4, 1942, the *Daily Bond Buyer* heralded the young man's
arrival: "Caldwell and Raymond, Esqs., of New York City, announce
the change of the firm name to Caldwell Marshall Trimble and
Mitchell. . . . Partners in the firm are Charles C. Marshall, John T.
Trimble, and John N. Mitchell." Not surprisingly, the hotshot lawyer
came to exhibit a sense of self-confidence that in some eyes "verged
on arrogance." "He is a very hard-nosed guy," said one former New
York State official who dealt frequently with Mitchell. "And like all
bond lawyers he is three steps above the archangels."[38]

MORAL
OBLIGATIONS

Through all his years in bonds, no one knew what
Mitchell's politics were or, indeed, whether he had
any. One old associate has said that in thousands of
conversations with Mitchell he couldn't recall a single mention of a political position or preference.

—New York Post, *1973*[1]

ON NOVEMBER 12, 1988, as the U.S. Navy Band played the Navy
Hymn at Arlington National Cemetery, six white horses clip-clopped
slowly forward, tugging a caisson that bore a bronze coffin, draped by
the American flag, inside of which lay the body of the former attorney general. Four days earlier, he had succumbed to a massive heart
attack. When the caisson came to rest, seven sailors fired three volleys.
A bugler played taps. Because of his naval service—but more likely in
deference to his cabinet rank, his Watergate convictions, here only, set
mercifully aside—John Mitchell was interred in storied Section 7-A,
hallowed ground just downhill from the Tomb of the Unknowns, the
final resting place for the likes of former heavyweight champion Joe
Louis; Lee Marvin, the combat veteran and tough-guy actor; and Air
Force colonel Stuart Roosa, pilot of the command ship on Apollo 14's
mission to the moon.

Delivering the eulogy was Richard A. Moore, a lifelong friend who first met Mitchell on a high school hockey rink in 1930, later served as his consigliere at Justice, then followed him to the witness chair at the Senate Watergate hearings.[2] Moore told the mourners: "You all know, of course, that [Mitchell] served in the Navy in World War II."

> But the only thing that most people know about his war record is that John F. Kennedy served under him. I don't know whether John was annoyed or pleased about that— probably a little of both; [but it was] because John never talked about it. I knew he had served in combat in the Pacific but I never knew until yesterday that he received the Navy's treasured award for gallantry in combat—the Silver Star. Nor did I know that he had been twice wounded, receiving two Purple Hearts.

Amazing tales, but—as with the childhood fires—wholly untrue. The JFK story first surfaced in a September 1968 *New York Times Magazine* article in which Richard Reeves, observing Mitchell's "intelligent, dignified . . . and unexciting" demeanor, found it "hard to believe that Mitchell commanded squadrons of PT boats during World War II." When Reeves asked about Kennedy, the most famous PT boater, Mitchell replied: "I hardly knew him. He was just one of the dozens of junior officers I had to deal with every day." The *New York Daily News* recycled these remarks two months later, followed by Milton Viorst in the *Times Magazine* the following August.[3]

In fact, there is no evidence Mitchell ever encountered, let alone commanded, Kennedy or his unit. Mitchell's squadron, "Ron" 37, was not commissioned until March 1944—seven months after the Japanese destroyer *Amagiri* had already sunk Kennedy's PT 109. According to Alyce N. Guthrie, executive director of a Memphis-based company that operates a PT boat archives and museum: "The idea that Mitchell served with Kennedy may have come from the fact there was another Mitchell who served under JFK on PT 59. From reading various clippings it looks like an error could have been made in linking the two, an error which Mitchell could have let be perpetuated."[4]

And what of the medals—the Silver Star and two Purple Hearts? Asked once by an acquaintance of what he was proudest, Mitchell cited his war injuries. "When you spill blood for America," he said, "that's the highest sacrifice you can make." Pressed on the nature of his wounds, Mitchell replied tersely: "When I go to the beach, I wear long pants." Jill Mitchell-Reed once asked her father about a scar on his leg; he said it came from a Japanese machine gun. The medals and citations are long gone; according to numerous accounts, Martha Mitchell, suffering a psychotic fit in 1974, set them on fire. Yet available Navy records show no evidence Mitchell was ever decorated at all.[5]

Ensign "J. N. Mitchell" reported for duty at the Brooklyn Navy Yard on June 14, 1944. Years later, he would tell an interviewer the navy wanted him to do legal work, but he refused, insisting on a combat role. That July, Mitchell and the crew of PT boat 536, commanded by Lieutenant Thomas R. Wardell of Phoenix, began leaving New York for frequent, twelve-hour trips to the Motor Torpedo Boat Squadron Training Camp at Melville, Rhode Island. There the men received extensive training in the firing of small arms, antiaircraft guns, mortar rounds, underwater depth charges, and torpedoes. They were also schooled in radar tracking, night navigation, and covert troop deployments.

As the second in command of PT boat 536, Mitchell was required to record and sign, in his own hand, the daily log of the vessel's operations and movements. These logs show he spent the summer and fall of 1944 navigating the shores of New Guinea and the Solomon Islands, overseeing repairs, conducting simulated attacks, and ferrying around superior officers. A monthlong stay at Tulagi Harbor reportedly included pleasantries with a man he never saw again, but who would later cause him considerable grief: E. Howard Hunt, then with the Office of Strategic Services.[6]

The day after Christmas, Ron 37 launched its first offensive operation. Allied planes bombed and strafed coastal Japanese installations along Bougainville Island for fifteen minutes; then the PT boats, stationed 200 yards offshore, spent the next eight minutes firing 37,000 rounds at the enemy. If Mitchell's logs offer the best evidence of his military service, his life was never in danger; however, he likely saw many Japanese soldiers shot and killed, and may even have killed some himself. Over ten days in February 1945, Mitchell's boat took part in several more strikes at "enemy bivouac and supply areas" in the Solomons. His commander later testified to murky theater conditions and significant enemy casualties.

After these operations, Mitchell's navy tenure was uneventful. On February 7, he was promoted from ensign to lieutenant junior-grade, two weeks before his boat arrived at Espiritu Santo in New Hebrides. There, on April 18, he was named commander of his own boat, PT 541, also part of Ron 37. The next two months saw intensive training for the expected invasion of mainland Japan. But after the atomic bomb was dropped on Hiroshima, combat in the Pacific was finished. By November, with the war over, Lieutenant Mitchell was relieved, reassigned, and sent home to New York.[7]

If much of Mitchell's war record seems exaggerated, even fabricated—as with the Kennedy myth, the unverifiable injuries and decorations, and numerous other tall tales—the personal portrait of Mitchell as a young man of thirty, developed in interviews with half a dozen World War II veterans who served with him, proves equally conflicted.

Some of the men, or their descendants, told admiring tales of a benevolent lawyer-statesman who loaned money to broke sailors on shore leave, freely shared his liquor, and casually continued advising law clients back home. Russell Addeo, a mechanic aboard PT 536, remembered a "hell of a nice fellow" who'd always "rather be with the enlisted people than the officers." Yet radioman Adam Mancino, with whom Mitchell was said once nearly to have come to blows, recalled an "aloof" elitist who "wouldn't even stick his head in the crew's quarters." The sharpest words came from Lieutenant Wardell, the one man on the boat who outranked Mitchell. "The crew hated his guts. . . . He was an arrogant son of a bitch. . . . I got along with him because I had to, but I really didn't like him. . . . Everybody thought he was a son of a bitch, that's about the short of it."

Other veterans disputed Wardell's harsh memory. Yet all except Wardell and Mancino, the most hardened in their views, seemed to agree with Addeo, the mechanic, who confessed: "I can't visualize him doing what they claim when he was attorney general. He wasn't that kind of person."[8]

While Mitchell was away at sea, Caldwell Marshall Trimble and Mitchell hit hard times. The war had largely frozen municipal bond sales, and Trimble was the only partner still working. Then, as staff attorney Bill Madison recalled, "Mitchell came back—and *voom!* The firm took off."[9] The postwar ad pages of the *Daily Bond Buyer* show Mitchell picked up right where he had left off. In 1949, the federal housing laws were overhauled, extending low-income initiatives and plunging the federal government into a new era of urban renewal. Mitchell recalled spending "a great deal of my time helping to draft those pieces of legislation and also to perfect their financial documents."[10]

By the early fifties, Mitchell "had no peer" on Wall Street. It was perhaps inevitable that he attracted the attention of the undersecretary of Housing, Education, and Welfare, a wealthy New Yorker only five years older than Mitchell named Nelson Aldrich Rockefeller. The precocious heir to the Rockefeller fortune had already served, thirteen years earlier, as a senior State Department official setting Latin American policy. In late 1952, President-elect Dwight D. Eisenhower tapped him to chair an advisory panel on government reorganization—a vehicle Rockefeller seized upon to create HEW, the very agency he now, as undersecretary, effectively ran. The future New York governor shared Mitchell's passion for cities and took note of the accomplishments of the nation's leading municipal finance lawyer.[11]

"Perhaps Nelson's greatest genius," said Roswell B. Perkins, assistant secretary at HEW, "was to identify a problem and get the best minds to work on it that he could find. He harnessed good minds probably as well as anyone in political history." With that charge, Rockefeller's aide, Frank Moore, a former lieutenant governor and state comptroller, approached the young Wall Street wizard and asked if his alchemy could be brought to bear on an intractable problem: financing school construction nationwide. Mitchell "twirled the problem around in his supple mind," then devised a plan. Once again, semi-autonomous state agencies would be created to issue bonds, build the needed facilities, lease them to local districts, and pay off the bonds with the revenues. Once the bonds were paid off, the school districts would own the schools. And once again, authorities would maintain a special "reserve fund," backing up the bonds in the event of a revenue shortage. Half the fund's money was to be contributed by the states, the other half, an estimated $150 million, by the federal government. The states themselves, though not legally obligated to make good on the bonds' default, nevertheless acknowledged a "moral obligation" to do so.[12]

Rockefeller loved it. When Eisenhower unveiled his massive education plan, vowing to bankroll $6 billion in school construction over three years, Mitchell's concept lay at its core. Yet the reaction was muted: Politicians and educators found the scheme convoluted; the teachers' unions favored outright grants. The plan never made it out of committee. Still, for Mitchell the experiment proved a boon: His salary in the years 1955 and 1956, when he worked on it, exceeded his 1954 earnings by an average of $51,000 (roughly $352,000 in current figures). He had also made an important new friend.[13]

As his practice prospered, so did Mitchell's net worth. In later years, after he became attorney general, published estimates of his private sector earnings varied wildly, some citing an annual salary of $2 million. In fact, a review of Mitchell's tax returns from 1950 through 1973 shows his best year was 1968, when, as Richard Nixon's law partner, he listed a gross income of slightly more than $495,000.[14]

When the navy interrupted Mitchell's career, he, Bette, and their two kids—Jack and Jill, born in 1941 and 1943, respectively—were living with Mitchell's parents in a large old house in St. Albans, Queens. By 1950, with Mitchell's parents deceased, he moved his family northward, to Port Washington in Long Island's Nassau County. But by all available accounts, Mitchell himself spent little time there. As his stock on Wall Street rose, he traveled more frequently. "[M]y practice took me into, I think, all of the fifty states," he testified in 1975.

Accomplished, articulate, and often alone, Mitchell appears to have looked outside his marriage for companionship. Tales told by law partners and others who knew him in these years suggested he was prone to affairs; the dangerous combination of physical estrangement and susceptibility to temptation took its toll. In later years, Mitchell's decision to separate from Bette, when he was in his early forties, would have been called a midlife crisis; at the time, he kept his feelings, characteristically, to himself, and reportedly sprung his decision on his wife with stunning suddenness. In the only published quote ever attributed to her, Bette Mitchell said, in 1973: "John just walked in one morning and asked for a divorce." However, Jill Mitchell-Reed regarded the quote with suspicion, and others close to Mitchell depicted the dissolution of his first marriage as far more complex. "I think what killed their marriage is what kills a lot of marriages," said

Susie Morrison, Mitchell's secretary from 1963 to 1971. "It's the distance. It's that John was up and coming. He was ambitious. He wasn't home, and she was lonely."

Still others, including Mitchell-Reed and longtime friends Ken and Peggy Ebbitt, confirmed Morrison's assessment. Mitchell's punishing travel schedule left Bette alone too often; nor did it help that he had gone to sea during the war and grown accustomed to a footloose existence incompatible with family life. In those years, American women were less likely to protest inequities in their marriages, and Mitchell lived, enthusiastically and without recrimination, by the norms of his day. "Maybe he watched too many John Wayne movies," Mitchell-Reed mused decades later.

Bette moved to Reno's Biltmore Ranch in November 1957. Within six weeks, she established residency in Nevada and filed a complaint charging Mitchell with extreme cruelty, a charge he denied. In granting their divorce, the court ruled for joint custody of Jack and Jill, and for the couple's house, furniture, and boat to be awarded to Bette. A published report from 1973 described the breakup as "amicable." "I said I would take care of you forever," John told Bette when they parted, "and that's what I am going to do." The terms of the divorce transformed Mitchell's moral obligation into a legal one: He agreed to pay Bette 35 percent of his gross annual income *regardless* of whether she remarried.[15]

Mitchell was single again—but hardly alone. Eleven days after his divorce from Bette, at an elopement center in Elkton, Maryland, he remarried.

History records multiple versions of how Mitchell first met Martha Elizabeth Beall, the vivacious, buxom blonde from Arkansas, five years his junior, who became his second wife. Newspapers and magazines, friends and strangers all proffered stories of the lovers' first meeting, said to have occurred at various points between 1953 and August 1957—when Martha's divorce from her first husband, Clyde

J. Jennings Jr., was granted in Dade County, Florida—and cast, alternately, as a chance dinner-party encounter, a blind date in Greenwich Village, and a night of sin in Little Rock. The truth is irretrievable.[16]

Daughter of a cotton broker and elocution teacher, Martha Mitchell was born in Pine Bluff on September 2, 1918, and raised primarily by her African American "mammy." Though dyslexic and hamstrung by a stuttering problem, Martha developed a Southern belle's charm and an aversion to silence, attributes that sometimes complemented one another but more often clashed to her disfavor. Her father, estranged from her mother, committed suicide by shooting himself in the head in 1943, when Martha was twenty-five. By then, Martha had graduated from the University of Miami, where, after transfers from two other schools, she earned, in between serial dates and sorority capers, a history degree. She taught grade school in Mobile before returning to Pine Bluff to work at an arsenal. When her commander was transferred to Washington, Martha tagged along, serving as a research analyst in the office that later became the Army Chemical Corps.

In October 1946, she married Clyde J. Jennings Jr., an army captain and businessman from Virginia. A year later the couple's only child, Jay, was born. Later, during her divorce, Martha hired a private detective to document Jennings's alleged physical abuse; instead the gumshoe testified it was Martha who was "neurotic . . . sick and all mixed up." "I was so happy to get out of that situation," Jennings recalled decades later, "I just left with nothing." At the height of Martha's notoriety in the early seventies, a reporter sought out Jennings's insights into her personality before she met John Mitchell and attracted nationwide publicity. "She would have a few drinks," Jennings recalled, "and then talk down to people. She gave a bad time to headwaiters, taxi drivers, doormen, anyone who was menial. It was an insecurity problem."[17]

After Watergate, critics of the Nixon administration depicted

Martha Mitchell as a brave lady surrounded by evil but determined to tell the truth, an ordinary woman driven insane by her husband's unholy alliance with Richard Nixon. Yet friends of John Mitchell who got to know Martha in the late 1950s and 1960s, long before her husband formed any association with Nixon, painted a much different portrait. "Everybody said, 'What in God's name did he see in her?' " recalled Bill Madison. "They despised her! She could breed instant hate! Oh God, she was awful, an awful woman."

Brent Harries, a Wall Street publishing executive who worked with Mitchell in the fifties and sixties, first met Martha when Mitchell was dating her and still married to Bette. Harries remembered with undiminished horror the time his pal brought Martha to a cocktail party at the home of Roald Morton, Harries's boss. "It was a beautifully done party," Harries remembered thirty years later. "If you wanted a drink there would be a nudge at your arm and there would be a waiter standing there with a tray."

> Martha showed up with John. John was smoking his pipe, Martha—in a bouffant hairdo that went all over the place, this mini-pleated skirt that was very gaily colored, with her high-heels, very stiletto-type heels. And it was a very refined cocktail party, very quiet; I think there was music, maybe a harpist or a violinist. All of a sudden, Martha for some reason either thought she wasn't getting enough attention, or people weren't paying enough attention to her . . . All of a sudden, she jumped up on a couch to sing or do something. . . . And John just kind of looked at her, had his pipe in his mouth and kind of smiled like, "Isn't she cute?" type of thing. I assume he was very much in love with her, and he just overlooked this kind of stuff.[18]

So what *did* Mitchell see in Martha? No love letters have surfaced, but Martha needed little coaxing to explain her side of the attraction. "John is the most intelligent man in the world," she would beam. "John stimulates me. He's soft, warm, sweet and cuddly." Mitchell, not surprisingly, never expounded on what drew the buttoned-down Wall Street bond expert to his zany Southern belle. But a story told by Thomas W. Evans Jr., one of Mitchell's law partners, shed some light on the Mitchells' relationship, notwithstanding the fact that the story recounted events from the 1968 New Hampshire primary season—more than a decade into their marriage.

"He and I shared a room at the Concord Motor Inn," Evans recalled. "When we were just about to retire for the night, I called my wife to see how everything was and the conversation took about a minute or two. John Mitchell then called Martha, and proceeded—I was right there. I mean, I was about five feet away, seated on my bed. And baby talk? The most—sweetest—I mean, it was a *very* romantic interlude. I went into the bathroom and closed the door. I could still hear it. And it went on for a long time. I'm mentioning that because John Mitchell was head over heels in love with Martha Mitchell."[19]

Only after 1960 did Mitchell's earnings place him among the nation's most elite lawyers. That year, he reunited with his old friend, Nelson Rockefeller, who two years earlier had been elected governor of New York. As Rockefeller prepared to assume office in Albany, he received a briefing from aides who estimated that in order to provide adequate housing for New York State by 1975, it would be necessary to construct 125,000 units each year—even though the previous decade had seen only 90,000 units built each year. Tasked by Rockefeller to develop ideas, an advisory committee recommended in June 1959 that he employ essentially the same concept that Mitchell had devised for HEW's doomed school-construction program five years earlier. The report suggested Rockefeller propose legislation creating a semi-autonomous state entity—aptly named the New York State Housing Finance Agency (HFA)—that could underwrite New York's unprecedented building boom.[20]

Rockefeller sent his housing chief, James Gaynor, to reenlist Mitchell, whose expertise was to prove essential both in drafting the legislation creating HFA, and in launching the nascent agency's borrowing program. Gaynor did not come away disappointed. "What I found in Mitchell," he told a reporter in 1970, "unlike too many lawyers, he was able to come up with a solution within the law . . . [A]lmost immediately he could give you an answer that turned out to be correct."[21]

Once again, Mitchell's concept—sewn into the legislation creating HFA—was to establish a capital reserve fund whose sole purpose was to secure the bonds HFA issued. The money in this fund, accumulated through rents, mortgage repayments, and other revenue generated by HFA housing projects, would always equal one year's debt service, or the total sum of the principal and interest on the agency's outstanding bond offerings. If for some reason HFA executives foresaw a shortfall in revenues endangering the fund, the agency's chairman was required by law to alert the governor, who would, in turn, during the next legislative session, notify state lawmakers. Once again, the legislature was not *legally* obligated to replenish the missing funds, but it was, as Mitchell later said, "incumbent" on the lawmakers to do so. For the state, then, it was a moral obligation, and regarded as such on Wall Street. If the legislature failed to restore the fund, the state's ability to borrow on "full faith and credit" would suffer accordingly. As it happened, HFA's projects never suffered a revenue shortfall, and New York State was never called upon to honor its moral obligation to back up HFA's bonds.[22]

In April 1960, Rockefeller signed into law the measure creating HFA, with an initial mandate for the agency to float $500 million in middle-income-housing bonds. The following year, the agency's first offering secured a high rating by Standard and Poor's, the premier investment ratings agency, and garnered an interest rate from Wall Street so favorable it was only .33 percent higher than offerings backed by the state's full faith and credit. The governor hailed Mitchell's concept in typically grandiose terms: "The greatest system ever invented!"[23]

So it seemed at the dawn of the 1960s, when municipalities across the country aimed to upgrade their prewar housing stock, medical centers, campuses, courts, and prisons to meet the standards of the space age. What made the moral obligation concept so attractive to politicians like Rockefeller was that it enabled them to issue bonds for costly state projects without having to submit those projects to skeptical voters in statewide referenda. Under Mitchell's plan, so long as the state agencies issuing bonds were not borrowing on the "full faith and credit" of the state, only pledging a "moral obligation" to make good on defaults, the states could undertake massive spending projects—*without* exceeding the debt ceilings set in state constitutions, an act that usually required a ballot initiative for approval. Asked if his invention was a creature of "political elitism," because it bypassed voters, Mitchell shot back: "That's exactly the purpose of them."[24]

Governors and mayors everywhere jumped on the bandwagon. Semi-autonomous agencies began sprouting up across the country, virtually all of them using Mitchell's technique and Mitchell himself, or his law firm, as bond counsel. New Jersey was the first state to ape New York, with large and medium-sized cities like Camden and Atlantic City pursuing major urban renewal projects; lesser venues like Neptune, Pennsauken, and Burlington County put the bonds toward items as small as voting machines. Then came Florida, where the state retained Mitchell's firm to help build a turnpike; jails and courthouses in Broward and Marion Counties; roads and bridges in Pinellas and Manatee Counties; an electricity grid in Jacksonville; an office complex in Tallahassee; water and sewer systems for Boca Raton. Forty states followed suit; the fees poured in. Mitchell traversed the country, meeting politicians and judges and making himself rich.[25]

Exposed to elected officials across America, Mitchell metamorphosed into a certain kind of political animal: a bipartisan power broker unfazed by backroom norms. Among lawyers he belonged to "that special breed of practitioner who operates best behind closed doors in city halls and statehouses across the land, clinching deals with a handshake and a wink." "He wasn't the kind of politician who goes out there and gets himself elected to office," said an intimate. "He was the kind of politician who's the kingmaker." *Business Week* reported Mitchell was on a first-name basis with as many elected officials as any full-time politician in America.[26]

Sway in financial circles eased his way in political circles, and vice versa. Asked once if he could get investment rating agencies to change their view of a bond issue with a single telephone call, Mitchell deadpanned: "It wasn't quite that easy. It was all done with pure, cold, hard logic. But frequently their consideration of matters were not sufficiently in depth to make a proper judgment and so, through a little further education . . . the ratings were improved."[27] Thus on Mitchell's word hung the fortunes of scores of mayors and governors accountable to the American people.

No politician clung more tenaciously to Mitchell's star than Rockefeller. Yet the depth of their relationship was later commonly exaggerated, both by conservatives—who distrusted Mitchell's inclination toward pragmatic compromise and feared its influence on President Nixon—and on the left, where moral-obligation bonds were seen as stealthy instruments of fascism. Even Rockefeller was not above taking a little license. The *Wall Street Journal* once reported that Nixon, shortly after being elected president, encountered Rockefeller at a social function and tried to introduce him to John Mitchell. "Don't you know?" Rockefeller asked Nixon, incredulous and condescending. "John is *my* lawyer."[28]

By the mid-1960s, Mitchell was living the good life, joined by his new wife, Martha, their baby daughter—Martha Elizabeth, or "Marty," born in 1961—and Martha's son, Jay, from her previous marriage. In 1963, Caldwell, Trimble, and Mitchell (Marshall's name had been removed from the shingle) traded up from lower Broadway to swank new digs at Chase Manhattan Plaza. The next year, the Mitchells left their ten-acre spread in Norwalk, Connecticut, for an enormous Georgian-style brick home perched along the seventeenth fairway of the Apawamis Country Club golf course in Rye, New York. With his brother, Robert, as his attorney, Mitchell purchased the Rye home for $150,000 (nearly $900,000 in current figures); when he left five years later to serve in government, Mitchell sold it for twice as much. In 1966, Mitchell achieved the honor of becoming one of only two lawyers ever to head the Municipal Bond Club, a privilege normally reserved for members of New York's banking elite. "Mitchell was a man with whom men liked to work, who inspired loyalty among his associates," an aide remembered. "Men with whom he had worked on legal matters invariably, it seemed, became his devoted friends."[29]

If personal magnetism was one key ingredient in Mitchell's success, another was his proximity to political power—or, more accurately, his indispensability to those holding power. Equally helpful was his essentially apolitical outlook. "He'd seen the system work too often not to believe in it," observed Lewis Lapham, "too many hospitals built, too many roads and schools, and if it was imperfect, at least it accomplished those things and provided the most good for the greatest number." Mitchell knew the system was bipartisan, that injecting his own politics was bad for business—an approach he also tried years later to bring to Justice. Only once was Mitchell asked point-blank—by Barbara Coleman, host of *Here's Barbara,* a local Washington TV show—to define his principles.

COLEMAN: It sounds like you believe in the philosophy of Emerson or Thoreau. What, what—what is your philosophy? What's important to you?
MITCHELL: Pragmatism.[30]

Yet Mitchell's proximity and indispensability to the powerful would prove a double-edged sword. On December 31, 1966, his law firm merged with that of a man who, like Nelson Rockefeller, also saw John Mitchell as indispensable, a man who—unlike Rockefeller—succeeded in attaining ultimate political power in America, and in whose fall from power lay the seeds of Mitchell's own consummate ruin.

THE
HEAVYWEIGHT

I used to have a very good reputation until I ran
into that fellow, Nixon.

—*John Mitchell, 1969*[1]

"MY HUSBAND'S GREATEST desire," Martha Mitchell once
lamented, after Watergate wrecked her life, "was to build the biggest
law firm in the country." That fantasy edged toward reality on New
Year's Eve 1966, when Mitchell signed—three lines below Richard
Nixon—the contract that legally merged their law firms. Nixon Mudge
Rose Guthrie Alexander and Mitchell immediately boasted 120 staff
lawyers and five floors of posh offices at 20 Broad Street, in the
shadow of the New York Stock Exchange. A Mudge Rose partner remembered the merger following an intense "wooing" of Mitchell,
with Nixon as the closer. Mitchell was thought by some to be power
hungry. "John Mitchell, personally, wanted to be close to Richard
Nixon," recalled partner Tom Evans. "That was a major motivator in
his bringing his firm into this firm."[2]

In later years, a myth arose that Mitchell, Nixon, and their wives
became close friends. At parties in the Mitchells' Rye home, went one

account, Nixon "would play organ-piano duets with Martha Mitchell, and sing a bit . . ." In fact, only once did the Nixons visit the Mitchells in Rye—at a Southern-themed party Martha threw to celebrate the merger, and at which Nixon did, indeed, play piano—and only once did the Mitchells ever socialize at the Nixons' Fifth Avenue apartment, at a law firm Christmas party. At neither event were the two couples alone with each other.[3]

"When Dick Nixon first came back here to practice law in my firm," Mitchell told a friend in 1968, "he was a beaten man." The native Californian's path to Wall Street had been rocky and jagged. Fueled by a peculiar mixture of intellectual brilliance and seething class envy, principled anti-communism and naked careerism, Nixon had vaulted to the highest stratum of American political life with a speed and polarizing effect unseen before or since. As a young lawyer, navy veteran, and congressman representing Whittier, California, in the forties, he campaigned ferociously against the putative communist sympathies of his Democratic opponents and pressed for the prosecution of Alger Hiss, a favorite son of Franklin Roosevelt's New Dealers, as a Soviet spy. The congressman skillfully used his perch on the House Committee on Un-American Activities (HUAC) and the country's emerging mass media to attain national recognition and ascend to the Senate. There Nixon cast himself as a palatable alternative to the far less disciplined, more reckless and toxic anti-communist crusader, Senator Joseph McCarthy; more quietly, the Californian intervened to ensure early civil rights bills made it onto the Senate floor.

Tapped by Dwight Eisenhower to serve as his vice presidential running mate in 1952, Nixon soon confronted unfounded ethics charges, which he rebutted with a dramatic prime-time address on nationwide television: the "Checkers" speech, so named because of its author's corny, yet canny, evocation of his daughters' beloved cocker spaniel. Simultaneously an appeal to average Americans and an oblique challenge to General Eisenhower's manliness in the political arena, the Checkers speech marked an innovative use of the new medium of television and saved Nixon's spot on the GOP ticket. As vice president over the next eight years, he traveled widely, strengthening his grasp of foreign policy and elevating the office itself. In tense encounters with Soviet premier Nikita Khrushchev and anti-American rioters in Venezuela, and then again when Eisenhower was temporarily incapacitated by a heart attack, Nixon kept his poise and drew applause, even from opponents, for his erect bearing and coolness under fire.

Yet the estrangement from Eisenhower continued (he "saw DDE alone about 6 times in the whole deal," Nixon would later tell H. R. Haldeman); and when Nixon ran for president himself, against John F. Kennedy in 1960, Eisenhower, pressed at the height of the campaign to name one major idea of Nixon's that he had adopted, snapped before concluding a news conference: "If you give me a week, I might think of one. I don't remember." As a world-class debater, experienced television performer, and better-traveled candidate, the vice president should, by all rights, have enjoyed a decided advantage in televised debates against Kennedy; but the "cool" medium favored the handsomer, more relaxed senator from Massachusetts, and served to even the playing field between them. Nixon's loss on election night was both heartbreakingly close and very likely the result of voter fraud in swing states.

Even more humiliating, Nixon lost by a decisive margin when he sought, two years later, to reestablish his political base with a run for the governorship of California. Flush with embarrassment and the one or two drinks it took for him to exhibit the effects of intoxication, Nixon capped his electoral defeat in the wee hours of the morning by angrily confronting the news media, which he had always regarded as antagonistic, with a shrill cry of self-immolation: "For sixteen years, ever since the Hiss case, you've had a lot of fun, a lot of fun. You've had an opportunity to attack me, and I think I've given as good as I've taken. . . . As I leave you, I want you to know: Just think how much you're going to be missing. You won't have Nixon to kick around anymore. Because gentlemen, this is my last press conference."

Now Nixon had come East, to New York, to lick his wounds, make money, and run what he called "the fast track." " 'Fast track' was a word [*sic*] he repeatedly used," recalled Nixon's aide and biographer, Stephen Hess. "For him, New York was the place where people worked harder, were smarter and became more successful than anyplace else. He figured he would get on that fast track himself." Nobody more epitomized this success in his eyes than John Mitchell. William Safire, a public relations consultant who had known Nixon since 1959, keenly observed Nixon's early interaction with Mitchell:

> Mitchell was a successful New York lawyer, a front-runner on what Nixon liked to call the "fastest track of all." . . . Easy to rely on, hard to get, untrammeled by past defeat and with no commitments to other candidates on the national scene, Mitchell became Nixon's most sought-after trophy. And unlike most of the men Nixon had been attracting . . . Mitchell was tough. . . . It was Mitchell whom Nixon went to for answers; he had a way of getting to the nib of a problem and then laying out alternative routes to the solution, proposing his recommendation, and then—this is where he left many politicians behind—picking up the telephone and making something happen. . . . John Mitchell was the rock upon which Nixon built his church.[4]

What Nixon prized in his new friend, perhaps above all else, was that Mitchell, while not born to the upper class, moved easily among its inhabitants, like the Rockefellers, inspiring their respect and confidence and making tons of money, yet still retained at day's end, Scotch in hand, a bemused blue-collar contempt for their pretensions. Where Nixon simmered with resentment toward the East Coast establishment, scorning and craving its approval, Mitchell exuded indifference. "I have no use for the New York line," he once told a reporter, his casual dismissal of the privileged class he had swiftly joined reflecting the confidence of a true self-made man—something Richard Nixon, with his tangled psychology and shaky finances, could never be.[5]

Nixon was in awe of Mitchell. "I've found the heavyweight!" he exclaimed to William Safire at the beginning of 1967. "Mitchell was the teacher and Nixon was the student," said one aide, who observed them together both before and after Nixon won the presidency. Despite being eight months younger than Nixon, Mitchell seemed older, more mature, more self-possessed. Even after he became president, Nixon would steal glances at the silent, pipe-puffing Mitchell during cabinet meetings, seeking some sign of approval—a nod or grunt—suggesting Nixon should continue. "Mitchell was really very much the station master of those Cabinet meetings," recalled Donald Santarelli, an aide to the attorney general. "Nixon would keep an eye on him, and if Mitchell [was] agitated, he would jiggle or puff on his pipe with some vigor. Nixon would get the signal and switch subjects, or terminate that line of conversation. If Mitchell looked serene—and that was really the only word for it—Nixon would go on."[6]

In a 1971 interview, Mitchell sized up the president's personality for columnist Frank van der Linden: "Nixon is a tough cookie. The thing that has impressed me most about him is how he handles the crises. He does not get into an uproar, but calmly goes on to the next problem, not chewing the rug or climbing the wall." Certainly, Mitchell shared Nixon's contempt for the news media. He told van der Linden: "I'm impressed, too, because [Nixon] is not side-tracked by minutiae but keeps his eye on the big target, not the TV bulletin. One thing that makes the editorial writers so damned mad is that he ignores them. They needle him, but he won't jump."[7]

Of course, White House documents and tapes later revealed almost the complete opposite of everything Mitchell said: that Nixon never put the resentments of the early sixties behind him; that he frequently flew into uproars, during and between crises; that he seldom moved breezily on to the next problem but chewed the same ones over and over again, often to no discernible resolution; that he got sidetracked by minutiae, such as the placement of end tables in the East Wing and wine selection for state dinners, every day of his presidency; and that, most acutely, far from ignoring the needles of the press, Nixon literally obsessed over them, spent hours dictating punitive memoranda in response to them, was driven quite near insane by them.[8]

Beyond putting the best public face on his boss, Mitchell was likely having a bit of sport with van der Linden, as he'd had with the *Newsday* reporter who inquired about his childhood, baldly propounding things he knew to be untrue purely for the perverse pleasure of making fools of reporters. A series of private remarks later reported publicly, some heretofore unpublished, reveal Mitchell harbored a far different view of Richard Nixon than his comments to van der Linden implied. Out of earshot, Mitchell derisively referred to Nixon as "Milhous"—the middle name Nixon loathed so much he banished even the letter *M* from his press releases and gravestone. Senator Howard Baker never forgot what Mitchell said when Baker introduced him to his wife at the 1968 Republican National Convention. "Oh, I've heard of you," Mrs. Baker said cheerfully. "You are in Mr. Nixon's law firm." "No, madam," Mitchell replied pointedly. "Mr. Nixon has joined *my* law firm."[9]

Mitchell's remarks were even more pointed shortly after he assumed control over Nixon's '68 campaign, when a group of Republican congressmen summoned Mitchell for a luncheon on Capitol Hill. *What business*, the lawmakers wanted to know, *did a bond lawyer have running Richard Nixon's campaign?* "I'm the only man," replied Mitchell, "who can say 'no' to Richard Nixon. I've made more money in the practice of law than Nixon, brought more clients into the firm, can hold my own in argument with him and, as far as I'm concerned, I can deal with him as an equal."[10]

Indeed, over the years, Mitchell occasionally voiced contempt for Nixon. Mitchell's press secretary at Justice, Jack Landau, remembered his boss "didn't think Nixon was very smart. He didn't think he had any resolve." "Nixon couldn't piss straight in the shower if I wasn't there to hold him!" Mitchell once told Landau. This feeling persisted until Mitchell's death. "I have ceased to be mystified by Nixon's actions," he told an interviewer in 1988. "Everybody always says what a complicated individual [Nixon] is. He's about as complicated as my grandson."

What, then—if not awe of intellect or will—explained Mitchell's boundless loyalty to Richard Nixon? Certainly it was not any expectation of reciprocity. Asked once if Nixon failed to return Mitchell's loyalty, Henry Kissinger paused. "I think that's a fair statement," he finally answered.

Nixon had no really close relationship with anybody. So I thought Nixon had high regard for Mitchell. And since Mitchell never asked for anything for himself, at least as far as I could ever tell, [Nixon] had less of a hold over Mitchell than over some others. And I think he respected him. Which didn't keep him from sending him over the wall at the end.

Why did Mitchell, even after the White House tapes revealed Nixon's betrayal, persist in undiminished loyalty, never turning on the disgraced ex-president to improve his own prospects before courts of appeal, the bar of history, or the publishing industry? Ultimately, the answer resides not in Mitchell's view of Nixon but in his conception of self. He had always aspired to be—and became—the lawyer's lawyer, the consummate professional. To testify against Nixon, to trade evidence, real or fabricated, in exchange for a lighter criminal sentence and a fat book deal, like many of the other Watergate conspirators, was abhorrent to Mitchell *as a lawyer*. "Why John never told it all," an intimate remarked after his death, "can only be attributed to the fact that Richard Nixon was his client. And good lawyer that he was, he protected the president to his grave."[11]

For all Nixon's talk of the New York "fast track," the practice of law bored him, just as it had two decades earlier in Whittier. The former vice president found that while ambition, doggedness, and resilience had taken him far in politics—a heartbeat away from the presidency by age thirty-nine—those attributes had done little to prepare him for the prospect of life outside the realm of campaigns and elections. In 1964, and in the midterm elections two years later, he campaigned tirelessly for Barry Goldwater and GOP congressional candidates, piling up political debts to be repaid when his own time came again. If he kept practicing law, Nixon would half jest, he'd be mentally dead in two years, physically dead in four.

Nixon knew earlier than anyone else, of course, that he would return to the game—but remained circumspect. In his memoirs, he admitted he began to "think seriously" about the White House as early as New Year's Day 1965. "I had finally come to the realization that there was no other life for me but politics and public service," Nixon wrote. "I did not reveal to my family or anyone else that this was what I had in mind. I knew that Pat and the girls would again be disappointed." Asked years later how early he learned Nixon would seek the 1968 Republican nomination, H. R. Haldeman, who was as close to Nixon as any political operative, replied "not til '67. *Late* '67, actually, for sure." It is thus doubtful that Mitchell, at the time of the merger, knew his partner would again seek public office. Surely it was clear to all that if Nixon chose to run again, he could do worse for a base of operations than a major New York law firm.[12]

Mitchell's nationwide network of political contacts had attracted Nixon's eye. Asked in December 1968 how he wound up managing the campaign, Mitchell suggested, with a smile, that he had been a reluctant bride: "It was an evolution. I got sucked in gradually. I guess somebody had to do it. I was blithely practicing law, and calling up friends around the states to get some Nixon organizations formed."[13] It was in the summer of 1967 that Nixon began to realize his imperturbable law partner could, in addition to salving psychic wounds, also fill a political void. Mitchell accompanied California GOP chairman Gaylord Parkinson on a trip to Wisconsin. Mitchell's legal contacts in the Badger State were unmatched; but from a Wall Street lawyer with no campaign experience Parkinson was unwilling to take direction. He rejected Mitchell's idea to organize the state for Nixon by delegating responsibility to a private sector group: "Parky said no and stuck with it."[14] Ignoring Parkinson's objections, by July Mitchell had organized a team of forty-two campaign professionals—including a chairman for each of Wisconsin's seventy-two counties, its ten congressional districts, and its fifteen to twenty largest cities. Nixon reconvened his own group. Given a choice between Mitchell and Parkinson, the group chose Mitchell to run the campaign, with Nixon's acquiescence.[15]

The pros were impressed. "Mitchell in his first outing," reported the *Los Angeles Times*' Jules Witcover, "managed to tie up the key Republicans in Wisconsin. In the succeeding months, he was to launch similar operations in most other states, drawing in almost always the influential and effective members of the local Republican establishment."[16]

Mitchell ran the same playbook in California. Jeb Magruder, then an obscure businessman and young Republican, recalled with admiration how Mitchell and his campaign deputy, investment banker Peter Flanigan, bypassed California's "top-heavy, fouled-up" GOP organization to set up their own precinct operation—obtaining registration rolls, renting office space, installing phone banks—then repeated the process, with similar success, in other states.[17]

To organize Western states, Mitchell reached out to someone he knew only "by reputation": Richard Gordon Kleindienst of Phoenix, then forty-four, a fiercely combative, brilliant lawyer—magna cum laude from Harvard and Harvard Law—and director of field operations in the 1964 Goldwater campaign. Kleindienst swiftly fielded a national slate of Nixon precinct captains.

Len Garment, then chief of the litigation department at Mudge Rose, suggested Nixon take the next obvious step and name Mitchell campaign manager. A Jew who played swing jazz clarinet to pay his way through Brooklyn Law School, Garment cut an odd figure among the pinstriped Wasps at 20 Broad Street, and remained an outsider in the Nixon White House, where he first worked on "liberal" issues like the arts and Native American outreach, subjects of little moment to Nixon, and again later, when, following the dismissal of John Dean, Garment took over as counsel to the president. "I remember the Mitchell moment," Garment later wrote. "It was the end of 1967, and we were in Nixon's office. Suddenly, the light bulb clicked on over my head . . ."

> I announced, "The answer to our problem is sitting twenty feet away from us, in the next office, a guy who looks, walks and sounds like a campaign manager, knows more about politics than all the other guys you've been talking about, and his name is John Mitchell." Nixon reacted by doing something he did . . . very rarely. He abruptly stood up—shot up, actually—and started pacing the room. Mitchell. But of course.[18]

Nixon told Garment to sound Mitchell out: "But do it gently." A few weeks later, Garment ran into Mitchell in the restroom at a black-tie firm dinner at the University Club. "Say, John," Garment said, "how would you feel about managing a presidential campaign?" Pipe clenched, Mitchell replied with a question of his own. "Are you out of your fucking mind, Garment?"[19] "John Mitchell turned out to be just what Nixon needed," Garment recalled in 1992. "Mitchell had status. He had national standing as a major lawyer . . . He knew all the politicians in America. . . . And he had his own money. I mean, he wasn't, this wasn't—he wasn't dependent upon this. He had all those qualities of being a smart man, kept guy, loyal man, intelligent, humorous, interested, animated by the single mission, which was to try to get Nixon elected."[20]

As Nixon and his men soon learned, Mitchell's political contacts were only one factor that made him an ideal campaign manager. A second, surely, was Nixon's deep trust in Mitchell, from which arose the candidate's unprecedented deference to someone else's political judgment. The third, a surprise, was Mitchell's managerial excellence. The same agile mind that revolutionized municipal finance now focused on getting Richard Nixon elected president.

Central to Mitchell's effectiveness was his indifference to public criticism. As campaign manager he gave not a single news conference. Working from "a bare desk in a shabby office" at 445 Park Avenue, Mitchell was dubbed by the *Washington Evening Star* the campaign's "hidden figure," a status he happily accepted. "It was a very simple precept," Mitchell said. "The candidate is the one who ought to get the publicity."[21]

With taxonomic precision, Mitchell eyed the deviants malingering about the campaign. He loathed "party hacks" and "prima donnas," freeloaders and hangers-on, publicity seekers and "damn fool advance men." "About a third of the people are in politics for the joy-popping," Mitchell said in a 1988 interview. "It's a great time to have free whiskey and women . . . [but] you have to be very careful. You don't want some guy . . . more interested in the joy-popping than he is in the hard business." Such characters he banished to "the Upper Volta entertainment committee." Last but not least came the donors he saw "coming around later looking for a *quid pro quo*."[22]

A group of pro-Nixon congressmen learned not to question Mitchell's authority. At a luncheon in a private dining room in the Capitol building, in the spring of 1968, one lawmaker challenged Mitchell's qualifications to run Nixon's campaign. "You people know Dick Nixon perhaps better than I do," Mitchell's reply began, "and you think he can't have a campaign manager. I've got news for you," he continued.

> I'm his campaign manager, and I'm running the show. . . . When I tell Dick Nixon what to do, he listens. I'm in charge. So, if you have questions about the campaign, call me. But you won't be able to reach me because I'll be busy electing a president of the United States. I'll get your message. But call *me*, don't call *him* [Nixon], because *I'm* running this campaign.

Mitchell calmly resumed eating his lunch. The congressmen sat in silence.[23]

Devising their strategy, Nixon and Mitchell recognized a paramount obstacle: the pervasive idea that Nixon, who had not won an election on his own since 1950, was a loser. The word haunted Nixon like no other, and to dispel its dark aura, he and Mitchell decided early on that the candidate simply had to run—and win—the GOP primaries. Strong victories would reestablish Nixon as a proven vote winner and defuse claims he was hiding behind a smokescreen of carefully crafted TV ads.

At first, the plan went off perfectly. By May 7, Nixon had scored victories in New Hampshire, Wisconsin, and Indiana, soundly thrashing his undeclared opponent, Nelson Rockefeller. In Nebraska, Nixon fended off a challenger from his right flank—California governor Ronald Reagan—holding him to 22 percent of the vote. After winning in Oregon, where both Rockefeller and Reagan campaigned hard, Nixon and Mitchell knew they had the nomination sewn up. "The staff did it," Nixon told the Associated Press. "Best campaign staff any candidate ever had."[24]

On April 29, Mitchell had called a staff meeting in New York to announce the addition to the campaign of two men whose services he said would ensure "the best and most effective use of Richard Nixon's time and energy."[25] These two men were to play a decisive role in the history of the nation—and in unraveling the good life Mitchell enjoyed that day.

Harry Robbins (Bob) Haldeman was new to the '68 campaign, but not to the candidate. In the vast literature chronicling the Nixon presidency, most commonly noted of Haldeman's background was his long service—twenty years—as an executive in the San Francisco, Los Angeles, and New York offices of the J. Walter Thompson advertising agency. Mistaking this management career in advertising for a creative one later enabled hostile reporters to cast Haldeman, inventor of the term "news cycle,"[26] as a leading villain in the creation of a corrupt Information Age presidency. By contrast, few have noted Haldeman's intelligence, described as "near-genius" level, his World War II service record, his directorship of California's Better Business Bureau, or his membership on the University of California board of regents and the Salvation Army board of directors. With his tanned, lantern-jawed good looks and trademark crew cut, Haldeman was the kind of hopelessly square, community-minded *uber*-citizen who made America what it was, or is popularly remembered as having been, in the fifties.[27]

Somewhere along the line, though, Haldeman's commitment to Nixon, developed as the former studied business at UCLA and the latter pursued Alger Hiss, became all-consuming. Starting as an advance man, Haldeman worked his way up to campaign tour manager in 1960, and overall manager of Nixon's ill-fated California gubernatorial bid. In '68, Haldeman returned with a clear role. He would run the candidate—Nixon's schedule, staff, travel—while Mitchell ran the campaign: relations with party and political organizations, volunteers and fund-raisers, "everything other than the candidate himself." The two generally got along fine. "I have always found Bob Haldeman to be an honest, straight-forward individual," Mitchell recalled in 1988.[28]

Of the second man he introduced that day, however, Mitchell

could scarcely say the same; indeed, he soon came to view John Ehrlichman as "a conniving little S.O.B." A native of Tacoma, Washington, John Ehrlichman enlisted in the Army Air Corps and flew twenty-six missions over Europe as a B-24 navigator in World War II. Portly and balding, a UCLA classmate of Haldeman's and fellow Christian Scientist, Ehrlichman was recruited by Haldeman to serve as an advance man for Nixon in 1960. He continued helping Nixon, both in the '62 debacle and again two years later, at the Goldwater convention. But Ehrlichman frowned on Nixon's drinking, which had fueled the self-destructive "last press conference" and an equally ugly occasion at the '64 convention, during which Nixon, according to Ehrlichman, "made some clumsy passes" at a young woman. Asked four years later to manage scheduling and credentials at the GOP convention, Ehrlichman insisted on a tête-à-tête with Nixon, in which he audaciously bartered his support for a promise that the candidate would forswear alcohol; Nixon agreed.[29]

In his 1982 memoir, *Witness to Power*, Ehrlichman recalled his first meeting with Mitchell. "His picture was all over the papers and magazines then," Ehrlichman wrote, "smoking his pipe, taciturn, aloof, a sort of Wall Street Gary Cooper."

> In his pictures he looked better than he did in person, however; the day I first met him, at the headquarters . . . he said a few cordial words to me about the convention, named some Seattle bond lawyer we both knew and in a minute sent me on my way. . . . [Later] I began to see that he wasn't as gruff and remote as he appeared. . . . [H]e was withdrawn and quiet, but hardly forbidding.

Haldeman and Ehrlichman's arrival on the scene dramatically changed the campaign's internal dynamics; one key player felt its "happy, carefree environment came to a screeching halt." Where the inner circle was previously divided between California and New York men—Nixon's past and present—the fault lines were now drawn along personal, not geographic, lines. "There was a lot of talk about the Haldeman crowd and the Mitchell crowd," Robert Mardian recalled. "Kleindienst and I, we were all the Mitchell crowd." These fault lines would persist through the Watergate cover-up trial.[30]

The electoral waters of 1968 were unusually rough. Within four months, the nation witnessed the Democratic primary insurgency of antiwar senator Eugene McCarthy of Minnesota; LBJ's stunning abdication; the entrance into the race of Robert F. Kennedy (who, as late as October 1966, had sworn against running); the assassinations of Dr. Martin Luther King and RFK; and fiery, bloody riots in dozens of American cities. It all played out against the backdrop of the war in Vietnam, and, too, the great social upheavals occurring at home: the civil rights movement; the sexual revolution; the emergence of a "generation gap" and middle-class drug culture; mind-boggling advances in science, medicine, space exploration, communications and data retrieval systems, mass-marketing. America and the world around it were changing rapidly, hurtling toward the twenty-first century through enormous leaps and scarring convulsions.

Nowhere in the United States did this change come more slowly, and exact greater human cost, than in the South, where Reconstruction-era electoral constellations had begun shifting amid the new realities of integration and two-party politics. Once solidly Democratic, the Deep South had seen Alabama, Georgia, Louisiana, South Carolina, and Mississippi depart from one hundred years' tradition by awarding their electoral votes, in 1964, to Goldwater. Mitchell and Nixon saw the South as integral to the construction of a new GOP electoral majority—a theme soon to be enshrined by a twenty-seven-year-old political analyst working for Mitchell that year, Kevin Phillips, in his political science classic, *The Emerging Republican Majority*. To capture the nomination, Nixon needed 667 convention delegates; his primary victories had locked up 112, while the Mitchell-Kleindienst delegate operation had garnered another 108 from the Rocky Mountains region. Next came the pivotal South, which required special handling.[31]

On May 31, Mitchell and Nixon flew to Georgia to meet with thirteen Southern Republican state chairmen at Atlanta's Marriott Motor Hotel. The chairmen demanded a promise: If Nixon won the White House, he had to steer patronage jobs to Southern party workers. They had long memories of Eisenhower's failure to deliver on this score. Nixon's inclination was to refuse—he knew a Democratic Congress could frustrate any patronage plan—but Mitchell nudged him to mollify the chairmen, and Nixon followed this counsel. In exchange, Nixon asked the Southerners not to commit their convention delegates to anyone else—especially Reagan—until Nixon had exhausted his prospects for victory. The Southerners agreed.

From Atlanta, Nixon headed to Key Biscayne to take stock. Ten aides accompanied him, including Mitchell, Haldeman, and Ehrlichman. "It was here finally," a reporter later observed, "that Mitchell emerged, in the phrase of one of the participants, as 'El Supremo.' " The following night, Mitchell sat out a torrential downpour in his Key Biscayne villa, puffing on his pipe. His companions included Haldeman, who quietly sipped a beer, and campaign press secretary Herb Klein, a veteran of Nixon's California days just joining the campaign. Mitchell and Haldeman dissected the Atlanta summit while Klein took Mitchell's measure. "I suspected initially," Klein wrote later, "that the real manager would be Haldeman. . . . I soon found that Mitchell was stronger and understood more of the realities of national politics than I had anticipated."[32]

On the eve of the Miami convention, rattled by Ronald Reagan's attempts to poach Southern delegates, Nixon dialed Mitchell from Montauk, Long Island, where the candidate was resting. "Is there anything I need to know before I come down there?" "No," Mitchell replied tersely, and hung up. The next day, as the convention gaveled to order, Reagan, with a showman's timing, officially declared his candidacy just as Nixon arrived. From his Hilton Plaza suite, Nixon again nervously called Mitchell, looking to assess Reagan's impact. "John, what's the count?" he asked. "I told you that you didn't need to worry, Dick," replied Mitchell. "We've got everything under control."[33]

Mitchell's confidence bespoke the breadth and depth of the delegate tracking mechanism he and Kleindienst had devised, an elaborate system of files and charts laying out delegates' names, contact information, philosophies, hobbies, friends, enemies. A ten-year veteran of GOP campaigns called Mitchell's system "the most thorough I had seen . . . aimed at taking a constant political pulse on the feelings of each delegate." Nothing less would have sufficed, for delegate preferences, especially in the South, proved more fluid than anyone anticipated. Alabama's Nixon captain, Jim Martin, worried aloud he would "get lynched when we get home" if his delegation did not cast some votes for Reagan; Congressman James Gardner, of North Carolina's delegation, declared flatly: "I'm for Ronnie." A CBS News count, conducted at 9:30 p.m. that night, found Reagan still 434 delegates shy of Nixon, but rapidly gaining steam.[34]

Something had to be done. Mitchell turned immediately to South Carolina senator Strom Thurmond. A Democrat until 1964, the sixty-six-year-old Thurmond was emerging as a pivotal figure in the transformation of Southern politics, and in these desperate hours of the '68 convention, he anointed himself chief arbiter of the greater Southern interest. Under that guise, he demanded Nixon and Mitchell reassure him, and Dixie, on two central points: school desegregation and the vice presidential nominee. On the former, Nixon reaffirmed his support of state autonomy, and his opposition to forced busing— but not his opposition to desegregation per se. This was code the South well understood. Thurmond agreed to tend his flock, shepherding delegates into Nixon's welcoming arms—*if* Nixon agreed to repeat the same reassurances to the delegates themselves the following morning. "Okay, I'll do it," Nixon said.

The next day, two Southern delegations trekked to Nixon's hotel for private meetings, at which they would judge his sincerity for themselves. The first session, which included delegates from Arkansas, Kentucky, North Carolina, South Carolina, Tennessee, and Virginia, was secretly recorded by a delegate whom the *Miami Herald* had outfitted with a tape recorder. After breaking the ice with a few quips, Nixon emphasized he would neither "forget the South" nor treat it "as a whipping boy." Forced busing of a child, he said, will "destroy that child." He could be counted on to appoint judges who would interpret the law, not make it. On open housing—which Nixon had already supported on record—he cast the issue as settled, something he embraced to "get it out of the way." Finally, on the matter of his running mate, he dismissed "cockeyed stories that Nixon has made a deal with this one or that one." While reserving the right to decide for himself, Nixon assured the delegates he would not "divide this party."[35]

Those who later claimed Mitchell and Nixon pursued a "Southern strategy" to capture the presidency, selling their souls to Strom Thurmond for Southern delegates, often cited the *Miami Herald* transcript as the receipt for the transaction; in fact, a close reading reveals Nixon gave the South nothing substantial. Even the *New York Times* acknowledged most of what Nixon said was consistent with previous public pledges. As a Georgia historian has noted, Nixon emphasized themes appealing to conservatives, but always remained "cautious enough not to make any kind of blatant regional, much less racist, appeals . . . no unreasonable commitments."[36]

While Nixon emerged from the affair unscathed, it gave him and Mitchell a foretaste of what it would be like to see their private remarks surreptitiously recorded and splashed, in transcript form, across the nation's front pages.

By Wednesday night, the balloting was finally at hand. Mitchell sat in his Hilton Plaza suite overlooking the Atlantic, fielding phone calls from across the country. He was eager for the action to begin. "I was with Mitchell before the convention opened," *Newsweek*'s Hal Bruno recalled, "and somebody called in to say, 'Governor Rhodes of Ohio is now coming out for Nixon.' And Mitchell said, 'Tell him the train left the station,' because they had been working on Rhodes for a long time, and he kept horsing around with them. And one thing you didn't do was horse around with John Mitchell—because he remembered." Nixon approached the moment with less equanimity. Minutes before roll call, he dialed Mitchell's deputy and spewed into the phone: "All right, Kleindienst, it's your ass now." Kleindienst was in no mood for it. "Fuck you, Nixon," he spat back—perhaps the only man ever to speak those words. Nixon hung up—then redialed. "You're right," he said, by way of apology.

As the balloting progressed, Nixon's anxiety melted away. His years of toiling in the Republican vineyard and Mitchell's months of meticulous preparation had finally paid off. Mitchell perched himself in a command trailer near the convention floor and coolly puffed his pipe. "John showed no emotion," an aide recalled. "[T]he delegate counting and hunting," said Hal Bruno, "they had it wired, and Mitchell was superb at this." In the end, despite defections from Ohio and Pennsylvania, Nixon secured 692 delegates, 25 more than necessary for the nomination. Among the fickle Southern delegations, Mitchell's courting of Thurmond yielded handsome dividends. Of the thirteen Southern caucus states, Reagan captured a majority in only one—ironically, Thurmond's own South Carolina. It was Wisconsin—where Mitchell first showed his managerial prowess—that put Nixon over the top.[37]

When Nixon mounted the stage to accept the nomination that he and Mitchell had worked so hard to secure, the candidate trumpeted the themes that drove him through that turbulent, bloody year. Among Nixon's promises, perhaps the most compelling rationale for his counterrevolutionary candidacy, was his vow to restore law and order. Throughout the campaign, he had promised to replace Ramsey Clark, whom Nixon cast as soft on crime and national security.

"If we are to restore order and respect for law in this country," Nixon told the delegates, "there is one place we are going to begin. We are going to have a new attorney general of the United States of America!" Mitchell, like the rest of the conventioneers, applauded.[38]

After months of Democratic Party turmoil—manifest most vividly in the skull-cracking riot outside the party's Chicago convention hall—Vice President Hubert H. Humphrey emerged as the Democratic nominee for president. A former mayor of Minneapolis and senator from Minnesota, he had long promoted civil rights and other progressive causes. As LBJ's vice president, however, Humphrey found himself outside the loop, belittled by the bully Texan who regarded him with wariness and contempt. For his '68 campaign, Humphrey adopted "The Politics of Joy" as his slogan; but the balding, ruddy-faced vice president exuded precious little of it. Struggling to exploit the advantages of incumbency while dodging responsibility for the war waged by the administration he embodied, Humphrey evoked indifference on the center-right, hatred from the Democratic left. Humphrey, in turn, viewed Nixon's rise, contemporaneous with his own, with fear and loathing. "Nixon's belief in corporations and corporate managers bordered on religion," he sneered.[39]

There was also, as befit the volatile year, a wild-card candidate: Alabama governor George Wallace. Four years earlier, the snarling segregationist had campaigned against LBJ in the Democratic primaries and captured between 30 and 43 percent of the vote in states like Indiana, Wisconsin, and Maryland. Now Wallace was running on the American Independent Party label, his overtly racist appeals ("Segregation now, segregation tomorrow, and segregation forever!" he had thundered in 1963) swathed in the rhetoric of states' rights and anti-intellectualism. With Nixon's and Humphrey's core constituencies in place—racially tolerant conservatives and GOP moderates for Nixon, blacks and mainstream liberals for Humphrey—the great battle between the two camps was to siphon a majority of those angry white voters who identified with Wallace, but who were not such bigots as to vote for him. Mitchell and Nixon did not initially agree on how best to counter the Wallace threat. Nixon wrote in 1978 that Wallace's candidacy was "depriving me of a substantial number of votes. . . . [I]f George Wallace had not run for president, I might have received the same overwhelming mandate then that Eisenhower had received in 1952."[40]

To Mitchell, the breakdown was not so simple. Painting the governor as an unelectable bigot would surely bring some Wallace voters Nixon's way; but Mitchell also thought his candidate's lead in northeastern states derived not from intrinsic strength, but from Wallace's usurpation of blue-collar workers who would ordinarily vote Democratic. "I always thought," Mitchell told an interviewer in 1969, "that when the Wallace vote in the North woke up, it would go back to its labor-oriented base in the Democratic party." Humphrey sensed this as well, warning a Detroit crowd: "George Wallace has been engaged in union-busting whenever he's had the chance . . . and any union man who votes for him is not a good union man." Luring voters to Nixon without awakening traditional union Democrats from their angry Wallace idyll became the task at hand; Strom Thurmond, who told Dixie that a vote for Wallace was a vote for Humphrey, was once again the chosen instrument.[41]

Between August and November, Thurmond's associate Harry Dent flew to New York once a week to meet with Mitchell, who personally approved the banners, ads, and country music jingles deployed in this "bootleg" operation. Dent's partner in the effort was Fred LaRue, the rangy, tight-lipped Mississippi oil and gas man who later became Mitchell's neighbor, close friend, special assistant—and Watergate accuser. "This was a very low-key, very subtle advertising campaign," LaRue recalled of the effort to undermine Wallace. "We used a lot of radio, used a lot of country and western music stars: Minnie Pearl, Roy Acuff, Connie Francis."

Thus Nixon's was a two-front war—three, if one counted the news media. Despite much talk of a "new Nixon" that year, reporters were mostly skeptical. Relman Morin of the Associated Press, a two-time Pulitzer Prize winner, was among the believers. "[Nixon's] manner had changed so greatly," Morin wrote. "He was more mature, more stable. He wore an air of easy assurance, the air of a man who could see everything proceeding exactly according to plan. This was not the harried, insecure young man in a hurry who had scowled more often than he smiled in 1960. . . . What had changed and created the 'new Nixon' came from the inside."[42]

But for many reporters, old suspicions about "Tricky Dick" lingered. Part of their problem was with the highly corporate nature of the Mitchell operation. There was, for one thing, the money: Nixon's '68 campaign was by far the most expensive in American history to that point, costing roughly $34 million (or more than $176 million in current figures). Then there was what *Newsweek* called Mitchell's "authoritarian, all-business austerity" and embrace of modern technology. "It is hard to imagine that a political campaign was ever run with such crisp, mechanical efficiency as Nixon's drive on the presidency in 1968," observed the *Times* of London. "[I]t drew liberally upon almost every usable device produced by the communications and data-processing industries, and not infrequently a certain institutional enthusiasm about all this hardware slopped right over into self-parody, as when campaign manager John Mitchell declared that it was his job to 'program the candidate.' "[43]

Mitchell's shrewdness extended beyond managerial competence, into the heart of politics itself. Having watched—undoubtedly with a mixture of horror and elation—the bloody clashes roiling Chicago, and the only slightly less chaotic scenes unfolding inside the Democratic convention hall, Mitchell "saw a chance to emphasize the differences between Nixon and Humphrey." He proposed the Republican nominee make his first general election appearance in Chicago. It was a risky move. If radicals descended on Nixon's rally, he would lose the calming, counterrevolutionary mantle he had seized in Miami, and forfeit whatever profit he derived from the turmoil in Chicago. But Mitchell's gamble paid off. On September 4, one week after Democratic demonstrators drowned out Humphrey's paean to the politics of joy, Nixon returned to the city's downtown Loop, drawing a massive crowd of 400,000 cheering, well-behaved supporters. The turnout exceeded even Mitchell's expectations.[44]

The first Gallup poll after the conventions showed Nixon leading Humphrey by a whopping sixteen percentage points. Both Mitchell and Nixon knew the race would tighten, though both probably underestimated by how much. "Anyone who's honest," Mitchell recalled in 1969, "will admit you never know what you did right or wrong in a campaign. But this one was relatively easy. The factors were clear. We just set a course and stuck by it." Some Republicans pressed Mitchell to concentrate solely on major industrial states, but he rebuffed them.[45]

Sure enough, as autumn unfolded, Nixon's lead steadily dwindled. The Harris poll showed that over September and October, George Wallace lost eight points and Humphrey picked up twelve; by October 21, Gallup showed, Humphrey had cut Nixon's early lead fully in half. On election eve, Gallup showed Nixon ahead, 42 percent to 40, with 14 for Wallace; Harris actually had Humphrey *leading* Nixon, 43 to 40 percent, with 13 percent for Wallace. To reporters, Mitchell dismissed the Harris poll as "a gratuitous concoction" that would not "con the voters."

What Mitchell really regarded as gratuitous—if not surprising—was Lyndon Johnson's announcement of a bombing halt in Vietnam, an act from which, over the campaign's final weekend, Humphrey derived a five-point bounce. "[T]his was anticipated," Mitchell remembered two decades later. "The way he did it, in conjunction with Hubert Humphrey, wasn't anticipated. That was quite distressful."[46]

In anticipation of LBJ's "October Surprise," Mitchell and Nixon had steeled themselves for months. Their secret strategy was to establish back-channel contact with South Vietnamese leaders—and with foreigners thought to hold sway over them—and privately urge Saigon not to agree to any last-minute deal at the Paris Peace Talks that could swing the election to Humphrey. Opponents of Ho Chi Minh, the Republicans argued, would fare better with Nixon in power. In fact, the South Vietnamese needed little convincing to frown on the Paris talks: They resented the inclusion of parties at the table that the South did not formally recognize, and President Johnson's attempt to "bully" the South into attending.[47]

But Nixon and his campaign manager were taking no chances. In July 1968, Bui Diem, South Vietnam's ambassador to the United States, appeared at Nixon's Fifth Avenue apartment for a closed-door strategy session, the first of many discreet contacts. Also present were Mitchell and the curious figure who would serve as the campaign's primary interlocutor with Saigon: Anna Chennault, the Chinese-born widow of a famous American aviator in World War II and a force in her own right, both as a GOP hostess and member of the China lobby. This was the influential group of expatriates who advocated the return to power of the Nationalist Chinese over Mao's ruling Communists. With her painted eyebrows, slender hips, and extravagant parties, "the Dragon Lady"—as Chennault was dubbed, after a character in the *Terry and the Pirates* comic strip—cut a unique figure in Washington, and Mitchell apparently accepted her claims to influence.

In her 1980 memoir, *The Education of Anna*, Chennault asserted a uniquely familiar relationship with Mitchell, both as a colleague who collaborated "closely" with him on the '68 and '72 campaigns and as a neighbor at the Watergate, where she watched Martha Mitchell ruin more than one dinner party with tearful, sometimes shoe-flinging outbursts. At such ugly moments, Chennault wrote, Mitchell would gently escort his wife from the room, "much as a long-suffering parent comes to soothe a troublesome child." Chennault also charged that throughout the '68 campaign, Mitchell—employing all the paranoia and techniques of the spy trade, including cryptic codes and daily changes of contact information—used her as a back channel to pass secret messages to the South Vietnamese that undercut American diplomats at Paris.[48]

Any concerns Mitchell harbored about being monitored were well founded. Declassified documents later showed U.S. intelligence agencies had begun conducting surveillance of Chennault and Bui Diem as early as April 1968. One account has suggested Mitchell's own phone was wiretapped. If it is true that, at the height of the campaign, she and Mitchell were talking at least once a day, as Chennault claimed, it is highly likely the Johnson White House learned, by one means or another, of Mitchell's and Nixon's shadowy dealings with the Dragon Lady. How else would Johnson have known, in his conference call with the presidential candidates on the night of October 31—minutes before announcing on live television the very bombing halt Mitchell and Nixon had feared all along—to issue an oblique reproach for the sotto voce intimations made "by some of our folks, even *including some of the old China lobbyists*, that a better deal might be made with a different president"?[49]

Nixon said nothing to betray guilt. But the admonition apparently spooked Mitchell. Later that night, according to *The Education of Anna*, a "nervous" Mitchell called Chennault to say: "Anna, I'm speaking on behalf of Mr. Nixon. It's very important that our Vietnamese friends understand our Republican position, and I hope you have made that clear to them." "Look, John," she snapped, "all I've done is relay messages. If you're talking about direct influence, I have to tell you it isn't wise for us to try to influence the South Vietnamese. . . . I don't think either we or the Democrats can force them to act one way or another. They have their own politics, you know." Mitchell pressed for assurances Saigon had not been swayed by Johnson's speech, then, after urging Chennault to stay in touch, dejectedly hung up. The next day, President Nguyen Van Thieu announced South Vietnam would boycott the next round of peace talks in Paris.[50]

Election Day finally came on Tuesday, November 5. Nixon and his family, Mitchell, and the campaign's senior staff ensconced themselves on the thirty-fifth floor of New York's Waldorf-Astoria Hotel to await the televised returns.

By 12:30 a.m., NBC News reported Humphrey ahead by 600,000 votes. If Nixon was to win, a few crucial states—California, Illinois, Missouri, Ohio—had to go his way. "Mitchell was confident Missouri was going to come through and I had learned to trust his confidence," Nixon later wrote. True to Mitchell's word, Missouri went for Nixon, by a margin of 20,488 votes. Anxious, fidgety, constantly revising the electoral vote count with his ubiquitous pens and yellow pads, Nixon remained closeted in his suite, separated from his wife and daughters and allowing visits only from select members of his inner circle, like Mitchell, Haldeman, and Ehrlichman.[51]

Although crucial returns in Cook County, Illinois, remained under wraps at the orders of Chicago mayor Richard Daley, one of the last great Democratic machine bosses, Nixon nevertheless concluded, around 3:00 a.m., that he had won. Mitchell, summoned to Nixon's suite along with Haldeman, concurred. Still, Daley's shenanigans "irritated" Nixon, and he ordered Mitchell to do something about it. The order betrayed Nixon's bitter memories from eight years earlier, when his heartbreakingly close loss to John F. Kennedy had turned on a margin possibly as slim as 111,000 votes nationwide, and Illinois emerged as the pivotal state in Kennedy's ledger. Nixon and his entourage always believed political skulduggery by the Daley machine in Cook County had cost him Illinois.[52]

With that in mind, Mitchell had, in the spring, authorized Operation Eagle Eye, a mission by GOP precinct captains in Chicago to prevent a repeat performance by the Daley machine. Vigilance in Chicago wards formed one element; the other was Mitchell's order for downstate Illinois forces to withhold their vote tallies until Daley had released Cook County's. "So," Len Garment later recalled, "hour after hour, John Mitchell and Richard Daley dueled, each withholding his ultimate weapon as the sun rose over a still-sleeping America."

About 8 a.m., Nixon, out of patience, told Mitchell to place a call to Mike Wallace, who was live on CBS television, and challenge Daley to release his votes. We watched the TV screen as Mike took Mitchell's call and put Mitchell's challenge to Daley.[53]

Finally, Mitchell and Haldeman convinced Nixon to get some sleep. Six a.m. came, and with 94 percent of nationwide precincts reporting, Humphrey's lead over Nixon had shrunk to 5,000 votes. Two hours later, the networks declared Nixon the winner in California and Ohio; only Daley's returns remained outstanding. Finally, at 8:30 a.m., Dwight Chapin, Nixon's young personal assistant, dark-haired and handsome, burst open the doors to the candidate's suite and excitedly blurted out the news: "ABC just declared you the winner! They've projected Illinois. You got it. You've won." Still groggy, Nixon led the rush to a television set in an adjoining room to confirm his victory. No one in Nixon's camp missed the delicious irony: Illinois, the very state that had cost him the 1960 election, now put him over the top.[54]

After a few moments savoring the dream emanating from the television set before them, Nixon put his hand on Mitchell's shoulder and looked to the future: "Well, John," Nixon said expansively, "we had better go down to Florida and get this thing"—the Nixon presidency—"planned out." Yet Mitchell, who had labored so hard to engineer the moment, could scarcely enjoy it. A tear streamed down his face, and he answered quietly: "Mr. President, I think I'd better go up to be with Martha." Nixon remembered the scene, in his memoirs, as a "moving moment" for both men. "It was the first time anyone had addressed me by the title I had just won," Nixon wrote. "It was also the first time that Mitchell had directly referred to his wife's problems, which I knew had been an immense emotional strain on him. . . . I fully understood his desire to be with her now."[55]

Martha Mitchell had never thought much of Richard Nixon. "I talked my husband into becoming a Republican [in 1966]," she rued in a 1974 television interview. "He'd always been a Democrat. And the day I talked him out of calling the president 'Tricky Dick'—I could still shoot myself!" Perhaps for this reason, Mitchell's management of the Nixon campaign had begun as a secret from his wife. "Mitchell is so unassuming," reported the *Daily News*, "that his family didn't learn he was Nixon's campaign manager until five weeks after the appointment."[56]

At first, Mitchell tried to mollify Martha with sweet talk during his campaign-related road trips. But the last few years had not been entirely happy ones for the Mitchells. Jill Mitchell-Reed remembered a Thanksgiving dinner ruined when her volatile stepmother, unhinged by Jill's brief, college-age flirtation with communism, responded by hurling pots and pans.[57] For eight years after Mitchell married Martha in 1957, her son, Jay Jennings, had lived with them. Ten years old when Mitchell became his stepfather, Jay fled to his father's home in Lynchburg, Virginia, shortly before he graduated from the Peekskill Military Academy in 1965. "When I left home, it was not under the most pleasant of circumstances," Jennings recalled in 2002.

> I had gotten into an argument [with my mother] . . . And she took a swing at me, and I put my arm up to block her swing, and she hit her forearm on my forearm and hurt herself. And then she said I had hit her and told me to go to my room, which I did. When John Mitchell came home that night—in the only violent act I've ever seen this man commit—he walked into my room, swung the door open and, without a word, hit me so hard across my face that it flung me across the room. Open hand. I'd never seen him do anything like that ever before. And I was really disappointed, because he didn't even ask me for an explanation. I'm sure he came in, my mother said I'd hit her, and he reacted to it. But

for me that was it. I called my father and I said: "I'm out of here."[58]

Adding to the strain, Martha's mother, who had also lived with her and John for several years, died in 1967. That year, Mitchell's firm merged with Nixon's, and the increasing devotion Mitchell showed his new partner left Martha lonely and embittered. As a cry for attention, she impulsively bundled up Marty, their six-year-old daughter, packed their belongings, and boarded the RMS *Queen Mary* for Europe, spending five weeks there before Mitchell flew to Scotland and persuaded her to return.

When the campaign began in earnest, Martha, already unstable, plunged into even deeper despair. She became convinced Mitchell was carrying on affairs with at least two prominent Republican women, and lashed out through her favorite weapon: the telephone. Her crazed shrieking into Herb Klein's ear in June was, for many in the Nixon orbit, a regular occurrence. With Mitchell immersed in the delegate hunt, Martha instructed an attorney to initiate divorce proceedings, only to relent after Mitchell again calmed her down. Fueling the rash behavior was a long-standing problem with alcohol. "The more distressed and abandoned Martha felt," a friend remarked of this period, "the more she sought comfort in the bottle." Finally, several weeks before Election Day, Mitchell arranged for Martha to be institutionalized at Craig House, a psychiatric facility in Beacon, New York. According to one account, it was merely "the first of many trips to the hospital alcohol would cause her to make."

Now, on Wednesday morning, November 6, 1968, moments after watching ABC News project him the winner in Illinois, Nixon came face-to-face for the first time with the Martha Mitchell problem. While he "understood" Mitchell's need to be with Martha at that moment, Nixon repeatedly intruded on their time at Craig House with telephone calls demanding Mitchell's attention to the pressing business of forming a government.[59]

Another problem that lingered beyond Election Day was Anna Chennault. Having carried Nixon's private messages to the South Vietnamese throughout the campaign, she now felt entitled to payback, or at least a measure of respect—but she got neither. Mitchell abruptly canceled her first meeting with the president-elect, then—with equal abruptness—instructed her to tell the South Vietnamese to return to the Paris talks, the better to smooth Nixon's transition into office. Chennault felt betrayed.

Nixon and Mitchell realized they could ill afford to make Chennault angry—or talkative, especially with reporters starting to sniff about. "You're going to get me in a lot of trouble," she coquettishly told one journalist. "I know so much and I can say so little." "Whatever I did during the campaign," she told another, "the Republicans, including Mr. Nixon, knew about." She wrote later that Mitchell remained "concerned even after he was confirmed" as attorney general that she would go public.[60]

Concern at the White House also reached high levels. Peter Flanigan, Mitchell's deputy during the campaign and now the White House liaison to the Business Roundtable, wrote Mitchell to say he had heard "indirectly that Anna Chenault [*sic*] is unhappy because she has not been recognized by the Administration."

> Since you had the liaison (if it can be called that) with this good lady I'd like your suggestions as to whether we should take some action to recognize her. If the answer is "yes" should this be in terms of an invitation to dinner at the White House or something more important . . . [?][61]

Flanigan was not alone in his anxiety. In previously unpublished notes, H. R. Haldeman recorded with alarm that *Boston Globe* reporter Tom Ottenad was

running intensive invest of Mrs. Chennault episode
[talking to] *people in Austin + around country*
asked to see LBJ + Tom [Corcoran, a Democratic lawyer
and friend of Chennault]—*both refused . . .*
Jan. '69 they published first stories
re Repub. efforts to sabotage [the Paris talks]
reason for renewed interest—have recently
obtained new info
Repub ldrs approved activity—have exact names
feel this is an impt. footnote on Am History
wants to see LBJ—no quotes—just info
also [LBJ aides Walt] *Rostow,* [George] *Christian,* [Arthur]
Temple, all told to avoid seeing + if so—say not <u>one</u> word
they are not playing ball w/ them at all
but someone may
could cause a problem . . .[62]

Presumably Mitchell and even Nixon himself were among the "Republican leaders" whose "exact names" were in the *Globe*'s possession—a state of affairs that indeed "could cause a problem" for the White House. Fortunately for Nixon and Mitchell, the *Globe*, for reasons unknown, dropped the story.

But the two men took their cue. They started periodically inviting Chennault to White House and Justice Department functions, and the president, according to Haldeman's unpublished notes, ordered his aides to give the Dragon Lady a "high-level title"—with the added admonition that it "can't be in government." "We have to finesse her," Nixon privately told Henry Kissinger.[63]

Amazingly, despite all the investigations, hearings, and trials that marked the collapse of the Nixon presidency, Mitchell seems never to have been questioned on the record, or under oath, about the Chennault affair. More than three decades later, its significance remained a point of sharp dispute. Richard Holbrooke, who served in 1968 on the American delegation at Paris and later became U.S. ambassador to the United Nations, charged Nixon and Mitchell with having "massively, directly, and covertly interfered in a major diplomatic negotiation."[64] Former defense secretary Robert McNamara was more direct: "It was a criminal act."

Nixon speechwriter William Safire saw nothing "criminal" in the affair, but conceded it was "was not one of American politics' finest hours." John Lehman, an aide to Kissinger on the National Security Council and later secretary of the navy, simply shrugged. "That sort of thing goes on all the time," Lehman said in 2001. "There are October Surprises and back-channels . . . [Nixon and Mitchell] knew that Johnson was rubber-hosing Thieu and the South Vietnamese government. And basically they just sent the message: 'Hang on' . . . And so it didn't seem to me that it was particularly unusual. I mean it was the way the game is always played."[65]

A source close to the affair—who demanded anonymity—strongly challenged the veracity of the prime witness. "Simply do not trust what Anna Chennault says about this incident," said the source, a senior policy adviser to Nixon and other GOP politicians in later years. "She manufactured the incident, then magnified her self-importance."

> She caused untold problems with her perpetual self-promotion and, actually, self-aggrandizement, because she was ultimately interested only in the money. I do not put it in the realm of fantasy that she was being paid by the SVs [South Vietnamese]; she had them bamboozled, believing she was an authentic and important "channel" to the campaign. John Mitchell . . . did not have the bullocks to kiss her off, a tough and persistent woman who could grind you down. . . . Anna thought of herself as a puppet master. She had no assignment, no tasks, and was an over-the-transom type that can never be suppressed in a campaign.[66]

Yet the Chennault affair continued to haunt Nixon's presidency. His infamous orders to burglarize the Brookings Institution, issued in the summer of 1971 following publication of the Pentagon Papers and never carried out, stemmed from the president's concern that the Washington think tank possessed documents related to "the bombing halt"—a euphemism for Nixon's and Mitchell's own back-channel machinations to counter it.

Later still, when Watergate raised the specter of wide-ranging congressional probes into wiretapping by the Nixon administration, the president asked Mitchell, by then out of government, to marshal evidence showing that LBJ had ordered the bugging of Nixon's own campaign plane in 1968. The plan was abandoned when former president Johnson threatened anew to expose the Dragon Lady's activities. Mitchell's fitful attempt at gathering this evidence, including calls to old chums in and out of the FBI in early 1973, was likely driven by a wish to help Nixon survive Watergate—but also by Mitchell's desire to examine the archival record for evidence of his own involvement in the Chennault affair.

At a minimum, the episode served notice on high-level Washington, as early as the spring of 1968, that Richard Nixon and John Mitchell were men to be watched carefully. And when they assumed office, as president and attorney general of the United States, respectively, few of their peers in the intelligence community—at the Pentagon and Central Intelligence Agency, especially—forgot that lesson.

Richard Nixon had finally won the presidency—but what, exactly, had John Mitchell contributed? Did he mastermind the candidate's remarkable comeback from the debacle of '62—or had Mitchell's rigidity and inexperience almost cost Nixon the election? Syndicated columnists Rowland Evans and Robert Novak faulted Mitchell for missing "a golden opportunity" to enlist blacks and liberals, a mistake that "very nearly proved fatal" to Nixon's candidacy. They even bestowed a derisive name on the Wall Streeter's supposedly divisive and overly cautious approach: "Mitchellism."[67]

By contrast, Richard Kleindienst called Mitchell the most politically astute operative he ever saw—and nothing argued more strongly in Mitchell's favor than victory itself. Republicans accounted for only 26 percent of all registered voters that year, yet Nixon carried thirty-two states (302 electoral votes) compared to Humphrey's thirteen (191) and Wallace's five (45). Mitchell's machine captured Florida, Kentucky, North and South Carolina, Tennessee, and Virginia; turnout in each, save for Kentucky, exceeded 1960 and 1964 levels. "[W]hat Mitchell accomplished in 1968 was incredible," Dwight Chapin marveled.[68]

Operating with "complete autonomy," Mitchell took few risks—and made few mistakes. He ensured his candidate stuck to the themes of Miami: honorable peace in Vietnam, law and order at home. Where Nixon considered televised debates with Humphrey, if only to redeem his ashen performance against JFK, Mitchell knew better and, as he put it, "turned off any debates." The *New York Times* reported that Mitchell "kept the staff lean and on its toes. . . . Even during the toughest moments of the campaign, Mitchell apparently never lost his self-possession or his temper." *BusinessWeek* agreed:

A key and possibly crucial difference between Nixon's 1960 and 1968 presidential campaigns was organization, and it was Mitchell who provided the administrative hand that made the Nixon machine a textbook operation. Even under the pressures of the tightening campaign, Mitchell is not recorded to have ever lost his temper, blamed anyone else for a mistake or even stalled a decision.[69]

Mitchell felt his work was done. He could now return to Wall Street and resume his bond practice, buoyed by his nationwide stature and ready to reap the benefits of his law partner's ascension to the presidency. Martha Mitchell could also resume her old, quieter life, as a mother and the lovably eccentric, perpetually inebriated housewife of a rich lawyer in Rye. It all sounded idyllic—but Richard Nixon had other plans.

LAW AND ORDER

Of all the public officials I ever met in my life, [John Mitchell] cared less about what people thought about him than anybody.

—*William D. Ruckelshaus, 1994*[1]

IN MIAMI, MITCHELL boasted he was "invulnerable" to any appeal to join the new administration. But Nixon insisted. "Even as John Mitchell was helping me develop a list of candidates for attorney general," Nixon wrote in 1978, "I decided that I would try to persuade him to accept the position himself. I wanted someone who shared my concern about permissiveness in the courts and even in many law enforcement agencies. Mitchell was tough, intelligent, and fair. Moreover, I counted him my most trusted friend and adviser and I wanted to have his advice available, not just on legal matters but on the whole range of presidential decision-making."[2]

The day after the election, Nixon asked Mitchell to take the job; but as John Ehrlichman remembered, "Martha Mitchell was in a sanatorium, drying out, and Mitchell declined Nixon's offer." "I spent a day with him, workin' on him," Nixon told David Frost in 1977. "I didn't know why he wouldn't do it. As a matter of fact, he didn't even want to come down for the election night business, and all that sort of thing. And he told me a little about Martha's problem, but only saying, you know, 'She's, she's not really up to it emotionally.' "[3]

Mitchell, who privately referred to Washington as "Disneyland East," made no secret of his reluctance to serve. "I did decline this post repeatedly—twenty-six times, I think," he told an interviewer in August 1969. "This was the last thing in the world I wanted to do. I've got all the things I've ever wanted. I'm a fat and prosperous Wall Street lawyer, which is just what I always wanted to be."[4]

Nixon sensed the real obstacle. Had she remained in Rye, Martha Mitchell could have continued on in her blissfully intoxicated way, another rich eccentric; but in the glare of the Washington spotlight, the aging belle's fragile psyche would be placed in the cruel hands of opportunistic partisans and dowdy society columnists. "[N]umber one [problem in Mitchell's mind] would be Martha Mitchell," recalled Len Garment, "who had very real psychological problems that pre-existed the presidency."

[T]hey were discernible to everyone. I mean, she was—whatever she was clinically, she manifested very profound characteristics that were, I mean, that were—that were *aberrant*. I mean, that were *uncontrollable*. . . . So [Mitchell] knew that and he knew that would present a problem, bringing her down to this heady hothouse atmosphere of Washington. Sort of like carrying an explosive substance into a very hot area.

So what convinced Mitchell his wife could survive Washington? For one thing, Nixon was unrelenting, disrupting the Mitchells' stay in Beacon with a steady stream of plaintive calls, pleading for Mitchell to change his mind. Nixon told Frost he rebuffed Mitchell's assertion that Martha was "not really up to it emotionally" by contending, against all reason, that public life might actually *help* her: "Being an amateur psychiatrist—we all are, aren't we?—I said, 'If you move her to Washington, she may be better.'" Susie Morrison, Mitchell's secretary, said Martha's psychiatrist had agreed: "It was her doctor's decision it might be good for her."

But there was another reason behind the change of heart. Mitchell simply could not turn down a direct request from the president-elect of the United States, even if it came from a man he felt could not "piss straight in the shower" without his help—or perhaps *especially* if it came from such a man. "John Mitchell, I believe, was an intense patriot. He loved his country more than God," said Brent Harries. "He was guided by ethics and morals that transcended common sense. . . . I do remember Mitchell saying, 'When the president of the United States asks you to do something, it isn't just a request.'"

Decision made, Mitchell now aimed to sell it to his wife. According to Martha, he used a lot of "sweet talk and patriotic speeches" and claimed he needed her, "with her superior insight into human nature," to help him choose the new cabinet. Flush with visions of power, Martha practically leapt out of bed. As she checked out of Craig House, she implored the hospital staff to hurry; their delays were "holding up the selection of Nixon's Cabinet." In later years, when he looked back on Martha's tragic trajectory, her ex-husband, according to an intimate, felt "very responsible for having brought her to Washington, and having gotten her into [this] kind of life . . ."[5]

Nixon got his man, but Mitchell imposed a price. Richard Kleindienst, the hard-nosed Goldwater operative who proved instrumental in Nixon's victory, had returned to Phoenix to resume his own law practice. Mitchell called him a week after the election. "Dick, the president-elect wants me to be the attorney general." "Super, John, and congratulations," Kleindienst replied, elated. "I really don't want the job," Mitchell shot back. "I'd much rather stay in New York and practice law. However, [Nixon] is adamant. To come to the point, I've just informed him I would do it if I could have you as my deputy. How about it?" Kleindienst begged off; he had kids in school and needed to make money. Within forty-eight hours, Nixon was on the line. "Dick, I need John as the attorney general. He's agreed to do it if you come back and help him." To this direct appeal from the president-elect, Kleindienst also proved helpless to resist.[6]

On December 11, 1968, Nixon introduced Mitchell and the rest of his cabinet on nationwide television. The next day, the *New York Times* quoted an unnamed source as saying Mitchell was "very pragmatic and has no hard-cut ideological viewpoint. Some would classify him as a liberal, some see him as a conservative." The *Washington Post* called Mitchell a "take-charge man" who had switched his registration from independent to Republican less than two years earlier.[7]

Mitchell granted his first interview to Lyle Denniston of the *Washington Evening Star*, which ran a scowling photograph of the attorney general-designate beneath the headline: "He's No 'Gang-Buster' Type." Denniston neatly captured the attitude and mannerisms that became hallmarks of Mitchell's strained relationship with reporters: the "frayed elegance," his "jealous worry that his privacy may be fading," and his "sometimes caustic way of putting off a question he considers to be an inanity." Thus when Denniston asked where Mitchell stood on crime and law and order, Mitchell replied tersely, "I am against crime and in favor of law and order." He also fretted: "I've somehow got to dispel the notion that I'm a tough cop and an arch-conservative."[8]

Perhaps Mitchell, following the attacks on Ramsey Clark, was trying to smooth the way for his own confirmation hearing, which came to order before the Senate Judiciary Committee on January 14. Having prevailed by the slimmest of pluralities, Richard Nixon entered office facing opposition control in both houses of Congress, the first chief executive so disadvantaged in 120 years. The Senate's advice and consent on the Mitchell nomination afforded Democrats their first theater of revenge. "[S]ome liberal Democrats on the committee who resented the Republicans' attacks on Clark intended to rough up the man who devised them," the *New Yorker* reported.[9]

The senators focused heavily on civil liberties, a response to Nixon's disparagement of Clark and accompanying vow to combat more aggressively the surge in street crime that marked the sixties. According to FBI statistics, crime between 1961 and 1969 rose nearly 150 percent, with violent crimes soaring by 130 percent, murders more than 60 percent, and robberies 180 percent. Organized crime, then a $50 billion industry ($260 billion in current figures), formed a large part of the problem; yet Clark, on philosophical grounds, had prohibited federal prosecutors from wiretapping organized crime figures. Such measures, Clark argued, were warranted only in national security cases, a stance that made him Nixon's campaign whipping boy.[10]

Taking his seat before the Judiciary Committee, Mitchell opened with the chummy collegiality of the legal fraternity, praising Clark as "an outstanding individual of great legal capacity" who had done "a fine job" as attorney general. Then Mitchell redeemed Nixon's campaign pledge, testifying that the wiretapping provisions in the Omnibus Crime Control and Safe Streets Act, passed by Congress the previous year, "should be used . . . not only in national security cases but against organized crime."

Reporters covering the two-hour session thought Mitchell had an "easy time of it," demonstrating he "isn't likely to talk his way into trouble when representing the Nixon administration on Capitol Hill." Only one senator gave Mitchell a hard time: Samuel J. Ervin, the disarmingly folksy, seventy-two-year-old North Carolina Democrat who, despite a decade of opposition to racial integration, considered himself the Senate's leading constitutional conscience. Ervin grumbled there was "something incompatible with marrying the function of the chief political adviser and chief agitator with that of prosecutor of government crimes." Mitchell told Ervin he would run the Justice Department as "the legal, and not the political, adviser of the president." The '68 campaign, he said, was "my first entry" into politics, and added: "I trust it will be my last." "I commend your answer," Ervin replied. With that, the committee voted unanimously to recommend Mitchell's confirmation to the full Senate.[11]

America in 1969 was a nation of TV-watchers: More than 90 percent of U.S. households boasted a television set, with 78 million in usage. A veteran of the Checkers speech, the 1960 debates, and the media-savvy campaign just concluded—derided in a bestselling book as "the selling of the president"—Nixon knew his war on crime had to be waged in the streets *and* on the small screen. In this he saw John Mitchell as his most potent weapon. With his stern features and no-nonsense speaking style, Mitchell could project exactly the crime-fighting image the president sought for his administration as a whole. "In the '68 campaign, 'law and order' became one word," recalled Mitchell aide Jack Hushen. "And there was no question that President Nixon was going to try to have a tough-appearing lawman running the Justice Department."[12]

Loyal soldier that he was, Mitchell gamely went along with his scripted role, willingly colluding in the creation of the false, authoritarian public image that President Nixon demanded of him. Few at the time recognized that as attorney general, Mitchell *was* playing a role, one he saw as distasteful but necessary, and that, like most actors, he occasionally bristled at his lines. Partly this reflected recognition of the role's incongruity; Mitchell was warm and genial in private, his eyes more likely to twinkle than glare. Yet his unease with Nixon's PR plan also reflected the times: Liberalism in the late 1960s dominated American culture, popular and political, and Mitchell knew he would pay a high price for challenging it. In his legal career, he had cultivated a nonpartisan image; now Mitchell was to become America's preeminent symbol of counterrevolution in the age of amnesty, acid, and abortion. Mitchell's discomfort showed when he sought to "dispel the notion that I'm a tough cop and an arch-conservative."

But the president, according to Haldeman's previously unpublished notes, held an almost romantic vision of Mitchell's "toughness" and its PR value to the administration:

> *problem is not what we do—but appearance*
> *not getting the points we shld on crime . . .*
> *shld have Mitchell do like J. Edgar [Hoover] used to—*
> *no one else in Admin. can put this on*
> *play tough SOB role—as crime fighter*
> *time to go on real crusade—not just do good*
> *put all PR effort we can into this area*
> *need to make asset of Mitchell's toughness*
> *He should do more on TV, speeches etc.*
> *VP + others shld build up Mitchell . . .*
> *as helluva crime-fighter—fair . . .*
> *don't make John likable—*
> *make him a tough crime-fighter*[13]

Mitchell stepped into character immediately. Shortly after being sworn in, his "balding forehead perspiring profusely," Mitchell held his first news conference. Here he introduced his top aides. As deputy attorney general, Dick Kleindienst would run day-to-day business at DOJ. Then came the assistant attorneys general, most of them politicians: Jerris Leonard, head of the civil rights division, was a former GOP state legislator in Wisconsin whom Mitchell had known since 1963. William Ruckelshaus, chosen to lead the civil division, had failed in his bid to unseat Indiana senator Birch Bayh. Will Wilson, a former Texas state attorney general and state Supreme Court justice, would oversee the criminal division. For antitrust, Mitchell selected Richard McLaren, a corporate lawyer from Chicago with no political background. Finally, as assistant attorney general for the office of legal counsel—a job known as "the president's lawyer's lawyer"— Mitchell, relying on Kleindienst's recommendation, selected a forty-four-year-old former Supreme Court clerk and Goldwater campaign worker named William H. Rehnquist.[14]

"We will always have crime, and you're always going to have a hell of a lot of it," Nixon conceded privately. But he also understood that the president and the attorney general needed to stand up for the uniformed cops manning the front lines—and so did Mitchell. "[O]n more than one occasion," Rehnquist recalled in 1993, Mitchell "took the side of 'law and order' against the advice not only of the usual critics outside the administration, but of other critics within it."[15]

Watergate later made it unfashionable to mention, but as attorney general, John Mitchell played an invaluable role in modernizing, strengthening, and relegitimizing American law enforcement. He was the most visible federal official in the early 1970s to look beyond the hostility to cops then in vogue and see that, with proper training and equipment, police could turn the tide against crime—and serve with honor. Picking the right battles on Capitol Hill; backing career prosecutors; donning the tough-guy mask to preach law and order in an era of radical chic: These were Mitchell's weapons.

Only in the District of Columbia did the federal government exercise jurisdiction over law enforcement; so Nixon decided to make the capital a showcase for his war on crime. Three days after taking office, he ordered Haldeman to "move . . . fast" on an anticrime initiative. "[Push] hard on law and order," the president demanded. "Announce a tripling of police." Four days later, in his first news conference, Nixon said he'd ordered Mitchell to develop an "urgent" plan to vanquish D.C. crime.[16]

Over the next two years, Mitchell responded with a broad range of reforms aimed at both the District of Columbia and federal criminal statutes. "This model anti-crime program will point the way for the entire nation," he would declare, "at a time when crime and fear of crime are forcing us, a free people, to alter the pattern of our lives."[17] Mitchell's proposals included "no-knock" drug laws, preventive detention of criminal suspects, expanded wiretapping powers, interagency strike forces against organized crime, steep budget increases for police groups. The news media painted Nixon and Mitchell in *A Clockwork Orange* tones, sinister futuristic jailers armed with nightsticks, computers, and syringes. But by latter-day standards, most of the attorney general's proposals were fairly tame and included notable civil liberties precautions; preventive detainees, for example, were only locked up on a judge's order, after a hearing. Critics on the left were apocalyptic. "There will be no storm troopers, swastikas or brown shirts," warned an alliance of the nation's largest student and radical groups. "The slogan for fascism in the United States will be 'law and order,' and that is what preventive detention laws are all about." The *New York Times* lamented the "hard line . . . straight-to-the-right dourness in criminal matters that perfectly reflects the campaign promises of the president and the public personality of the attorney general, John N. Mitchell."[18]

Mitchell defended the constitutionality of preventive detention in his first major television interview, on CBS News' *60 Minutes*. "It's long been an article of faith in the United States that a man is innocent until he's proven guilty," correspondent Mike Wallace argued. "The fellow we're talking about has not been proven guilty yet, has he?" "In the instance, no," Mitchell replied, "but the greater and better needs of society I think require the judge . . . to protect society. And if the track record is such . . . I think the judge has every conceivable right to keep that fellow in preventive detention." Elsewhere, Mitchell complained of seeing the recidivist criminal "turned loose just because his mother lives in the same city."[19]

In the end, Congress consolidated the Nixon-Mitchell proposals into several pieces of legislation: the District of Columbia Court Reform and Criminal Procedure Act, the Organized Crime Control Act, the Uniform Controlled Dangerous Substances Act. President Nixon signed them into law. "[T]hose who are fighting against crime will have the tools that they need to do the job," Nixon declared at one signing ceremony, held at the Justice Department in October 1970 as Mitchell and J. Edgar Hoover looked on, adding, "they will do the job."[20]

In pure statistical terms, Mitchell's performance as a crime fighter was undeniably impressive. In 1970, for the first time in fourteen years, fewer crimes were committed in the District of Columbia than in the year before. By the following year, Mitchell had steered twenty-seven pieces of anticrime legislation to passage by Congress; doubled the number of organized crime strike forces; and secured indictments or convictions against half the top bosses in the nation's two dozen largest organized crime syndicates.[21] Baltimore, Kansas City, Pittsburgh, Seattle, and St. Louis all saw reductions in street crime;[22] in the first three months of 1971, sixty major cities reported the same. The amount of heroin and cocaine removed from U.S. markets more than doubled, tripling in the case of marijuana.[23] And by March 1973, the FBI reported that in the previous year—Mitchell's last as attorney general—the national crime rate decreased for the first time in seventeen years.[24]

Forbes hailed him "the most effective gang-buster . . . and menacer to the drug menace who ever held the attorney general's office."[25] "In city after city," trumpeted *U.S. News & World Report*, "the grip of organized crime is being weakened." Asked once if the war on Cosa Nostra was not "an endless process in which you catch one group of operators but others move in immediately to take their places," Mitchell replied: "It used to be that way. . . . Now, with the use of electronic surveillance, we pretty well get the whole criminal organization."[26] Refusing to wiretap mobsters, as Ramsey Clark had, Mitchell likened to "fighting with one hand tied behind your back." Over time, Mitchell's views on combating organized crime gained wide acceptance; among the believers was his former Mudge Rose intern, a future U.S. attorney and New York City mayor named Rudolph Giuliani.

Indeed, it was Mitchell who proposed a new racketeering law authorizing action against legitimate businesses infiltrated by organized crime, a measure later known as the RICO (Racketeer Influenced and Corrupt Organizations) act, and employed, with devastating effect, against the New York Mafia. And it was Mitchell who narrowed the circumstances under which immunized witnesses could escape criminal prosecution—a provision later used, during Watergate, to compel testimony against the former attorney general himself.[27]

The severest charge against Attorney General Mitchell was that he systematically subordinated the mission of his department to the political fortunes of the president he served. The truth, as Nixon's secret tapes later showed, was quite different. Far from "politicizing" the Department of Justice to serve Richard Nixon's interests, Mitchell actually protected it from political interference, to a degree never popularly understood in his lifetime. "The most important feature of [Mitchell's] tenure," Richard Kleindienst wrote in 1985, "was the shield he erected between Justice and the White House staff." "Nobody ever interfered with me at the Department of Justice, and again, it goes back to Mitchell," Kleindienst reaffirmed in a 1992 interview. "Because of his stature and relationship with the president, he had insulated us from that."[28]

Those quick to discount the opinion of Kleindienst because he was Mitchell's deputy and friend must conversely honor that of the late Erwin N. Griswold. A lifelong Democrat, the silver-haired Griswold served as dean of Harvard Law School, president of the American Bar Association, and, from 1967 to 1973, as solicitor general of the United States, the official charged with arguing the federal government's cases before the U.S. Supreme Court. There are few more respected figures in the history of American jurisprudence, and his appraisal of Mitchell's stewardship at Justice reflected the feelings of many nonpartisan officials. "[Mitchell] ran a pretty good department," Griswold recalled in 1994. "And it was always square shooting as far as I was concerned. . . . I wasn't loyal to the president because I never conceived of my responsibility to be to represent the president. I conceived of my responsibility as representing the people of the United States. And I think that Mitchell rather welcomed that point of view, because on the whole it was somewhat rare in the government."[29]

Offering a similar recollection was Thomas E. Kauper, a deputy assistant attorney general in the Office of Legal Counsel, which provides opinions on the constitutionality of an administration's actions and policies. Since an adverse ruling from this office could potentially scuttle any presidential initiative, regardless of size or scope, any attorney general bent on "politicizing" the Department of Justice would necessarily seek to control the office's work product; yet here again Mitchell took a hands-off approach. "Requests for opinions did not come through Mitchell, and they were never routed back through [him] unless they were quite spectacular," Kauper recalled in 1988. "They generally were sent to the White House without the attorney general's input."[30]

One high-ranking federal official who did not share Mitchell's hands-off approach to the career officials at Justice, his recognition of the need for institutional continuity despite political and philosophical changes at the top, was Richard Nixon. "Mitchell . . . didn't want to be political," Nixon complained in August 1972. The president had already arrived, more than a year earlier, at the depressing conclusion that John Mitchell would never be as ruthless and cynical in the manipulation of the levers of Justice as Robert Kennedy had been for his brother. "Actually, when Mitchell leaves as attorney general, we're going to be better off in my view," Nixon confided to H. R. Haldeman on July 1, 1971. "John is just too damn good a lawyer, you know. He's a good, strong lawyer. It just repels him to do these horrible things, but they've got to be done."[31]

DAYS OF RAGE

There are organizations in this country that are
dedicated to the destruction of our society and our
governmental institutions. If that is the description
of a revolution, then a revolution is in process.

—John Mitchell, 1970[1]

AS A VILLAIN of the sixties counterculture and antiwar movement,
Attorney General John Mitchell attained special, almost iconic, status. Even more than the detested president he served, Mitchell represented everything against which rebellious youth were, in an age of
antiheroes, rebelling. Where Richard Nixon harbored the politician's
longing for universal approval, occasionally making awkward overtures to the young, the attorney general suffered no such longings.
Dutifully, Mitchell played his assigned role as the disciplinarian, im-
poser of law and order against radical chic, the dour authoritarian
face of Nixon's counterrevolution against hippies, pushers, and protesters.

Mitchell assumed office at a time when militant students' faith in
violence as a political instrument was reaching its apex, and when the
response from the education establishment was feeblest and most mis-
guidedly conciliatory. The Berkeley Free Speech Movement of 1964,

the seizure of Columbia University in 1968, and the steady radical-
ization of American youth in the late sixties all disgusted Mitchell.
His lawyer recalled him expressing contempt "for these kids at Columbia, who he thought had everything in the world, running around
raising hell." Mitchell's secretary said her first glimpse into his conservatism came when they watched a "mob" of students burning the
American flag on television. *"Those Goddamn bastards!"* Mitchell spat,
pounding his desk.[2]

President Nixon felt the same way. During his first month in office, he ordered his attorney general to draft new laws cracking down
on college radicals, as evidenced in H. R. Haldeman's previously unpublished notes.

> [Tell] *Mitchell . . .*
> *there will be legis. very soon for action re campus*
> *riots.*
> *need precisely drawn plan . . .*
> *have Justice draw up . . .*

As with his war on crime, Nixon believed that appearing to crack
down on campus militants mattered as much—if not more—than
the reality of whether he did so. He demanded Mitchell flex some
muscle, even if the problem proved intractable.

> *Doesn't matter if we can do anything*
> *must say something strong, though*
> *show no sympathy*
> *hit it hard . . .*
> *Is Justice doing enough + are we publicizing enuf?*
> *What they are doing in law enforcement*
> *—esp. what they are doing re: campus stuff*[3]

On cue, the attorney general announced a plan to prosecute "hard-
line militants" who crossed state lines to foment riots on college cam-

puses. "A great deal of evidence has been collected on this aspect of campus disorders," Mitchell said, calling the involvement of professional agitators "a very serious component" of the problem. In this Mitchell followed the lead of FBI director J. Edgar Hoover, who had told the Commission on the Causes and Prevention of Violence in September 1968: "Communists are in the forefront of civil rights, antiwar and student demonstrations, many of which ultimately become disorderly and erupt into violence."[4]

It was on May 1, 1969—May Day to committed socialists, Law Day to the rest of the nation, which was theoretically obliged to spend it, by decree of President Eisenhower, in solemn contemplation of the law as "the heart and sinew of our Nation"—that the new attorney general took his great public stand against campus extremism, and enshrined himself forever in the student radicals' pantheon of villainy. Speaking to the Detroit Bar Association, Mitchell declared that the time for patience with unruly demonstrators had come to an end, that "seizures of university buildings and imprisonment of university officials" were not "legitimate" acts of civil disobedience. "If there must be arrests," Mitchell warned, "arrests there shall be."

Testifying before a House subcommittee three weeks later, Mitchell—despite Nixon's orders—opposed introduction of new laws to combat the problem. Such measures, he argued, might "play into the hands of the militants"; better the existing laws should be enforced, Mitchell said, that moderate students should dissuade "the sheep from running with the wolves." Putting a sharper point on these views was Mitchell's deputy, Richard Kleindienst, who vowed "radical, revolutionary, anarchistic kids" would be "rounded up and put in a detention camp."[5]

Mitchell did more than make speeches. He created a thirty-man "campus rebellion" task force and revived the Justice Department's Internal Security Division, dormant since its McCarthy-era heyday, as a potent weapon against a new generation of subversive groups advocating violent overthrow of the government. He also took the unusual step, in March 1969, of personally announcing the indictment of eight of the nation's most prominent radicals on charges of conspiracy and incitement to riot at the 1968 Democratic convention.

The eight indicted men included a smorgasbord of leading dissenters: Abbie Hoffman and Jerry Rubin, Yippie pranksters best known for media-savvy acts of civil disobedience like "levitating" the Pentagon and showering dollar bills, confetti-style, on the floor of the New York Stock Exchange; Tom Hayden and Rennie Davis, founders of Students for a Democratic Society (SDS) and veteran antiwar organizers; David Dellinger, a fifty-four-year-old pacifist and principal of the "Mobe," or National Mobilization Committee to End the War in Vietnam; Black Panther Party founder Bobby Seale; and two academics, Lee Weiner and John Froines, widely seen as "acquittal bait" for fair-minded jurors.[6]

Mitchell's predecessor, Ramsey Clark, had ignored "intense and growing" pressure to file charges against the rioters who had made mayhem in Chicago. The new attorney general saw the case differently, and his decision to authorize the indictments, and announce them himself, earned him everlasting enmity on the left. "Mitchell used grand juries to harry and hound dissenters," wrote liberal historians Nancy Zaroulis and Gerald Sullivan. "It was the Chicago case that taught the Nixon administration how to use the grand jury process, originally designed to protect the rights of citizens, for malicious, contrary purposes."

That the Chicago Eight promptly turned their trial into an unruly circus—"Fascist pig liar!" Bobby Seale shouted at the judge, before being bound and gagged—was hardly unanticipated by Mitchell and Nixon, who reckoned they would profit politically whenever "the movement" advertised its extremism. And, fulfilling his confirmation pledge, Mitchell expanded the Justice Department's wiretapping program to include domestic subversion cases. He authorized surveillance on five members of the Chicago Eight. The disclosure was made in a June 1969 legal brief in which the Justice Department asserted the government's inherent right to wiretap, without a warrant, any group the attorney general determined a threat to "attack and subvert the government by unlawful means."[7]

Rennie Davis, chief organizer, with Tom Hayden, of the Chicago protests—and the only defendant, aside from Abbie Hoffman, to testify at the conspiracy trial—also recognized the signal being sent by the prosecution of the Chicago Eight. "I saw a shift in the attitude towards leadership in the antiwar movement," Davis recalled. "Mitchell was really the architect of it. . . . He was primal—fundamental—to the architecture of both [our] being on trial as well as the political response to us that could be expected from the Nixon administration."

Indeed, to many leading radicals, John Mitchell *was* the devil. In October 1969, Hoffman showed up outside the Justice Department wearing boxing gloves, challenging Mitchell to come out and fight. It marked the first time in postwar America—but hardly the last—that the Justice Department became the prime target of antiwar wrath in the Vietnam era. Nor was the rage limited to Mitchell's workplace. The day after convictions were handed down in the Chicago Eight case, in February 1970, a thousand angry protesters rioted outside Mitchell's residence, Watergate East, throwing rocks and bottles and screaming "Pig! Pig!" and "Burn the fucking place down!" The six hundred riot cops ringing the building unleashed two waves of tear gas, swung nightsticks "freely," cracking at least two skulls and a collarbone, and arrested more than 145 people.[8]

Under Mitchell's leadership, DOJ intensified its investigation and infiltration of militant left-wing groups. "One of the problem areas that I found when I got to the Department of Justice was the lack of intelligence in this area," Mitchell told an interviewer in August 1969. "So we are putting together more of an intelligence apparatus than has existed." This was no small feat. Twenty federal agencies collaborated on a program that one leftist historian later called "maximum surveillance, disruption, and harassment of the New Left." The U.S. Army monitored 18 million civilians; the Civil Service Commission recorded the names of 15 million suspected "subversives"; the Secret Service assembled 50,000 dossiers; the Department of Health, Education, and Welfare staffed two offices devoted to intelligence-gathering on student activists; and the Internal Revenue Service assigned seventeen men to track the finances of leading political organizations. On Capitol Hill, the House Internal Security Committee kept index cards on 754,000 alleged revolutionaries. CIA, ignoring statutory prohibitions on domestic spying, conducted surveillance on, and prepared psychological profiles of, more than three-dozen radicals. Hoover's FBI put 2,000 agents on the case.[9]

The New Left felt the heat. Unknown to the public at large until his nomination as attorney general, the stern-faced Mitchell, with his vows to crush the movement, quickly instilled in American radicals a palpable sense of dread. "Mitchell and the rest are out to destroy youth culture," proclaimed a revolutionary group in Boston. An SDS member spoke of the "darkened" climate for activists, "more menacing" than under the previous administration; the Black Panthers' David Hilliard declared America "a dictatorship headed by Attorney General Mitchell."

"Mitchell was a symbol," said Bill Ayers, a member with his wife, Bernardine Dohrn, of the infamous Weathermen. A Marxist offshoot of SDS, the Weathermen took their name from a line in Bob Dylan's 1965 alienated-youth anthem "Subterranean Homesick Blues": "You don't need a weatherman to know which way the wind blows." Initially they mounted resistance to "Amerikkkan" imperialism in armed street clashes with police. Later they assumed clandestine identities, changed their collective name to the Weather Underground, and began detonating bombs at courthouses, correctional facilities, police stations, the Capitol, the Pentagon. In Mitchell's rise to power Ayers saw "one more step in . . . a kind of impending American fascism."

In their 1974 manifesto, *Prairie Fire: The Politics of Revolutionary Anti-Imperialism*, Ayers and his comrades, by then among America's most sought-after fugitives, charged that Nixon, Mitchell, and Hoover "set into motion a plan to discredit, divide and set back the movement. . . . Infiltration and sabotage were carried out by a variety of police agencies, including the FBI, the Nixon-Mitchell team, military intelligence, and local red squads. . . . In the last period they have inflicted some serious blows which have set back the struggle."[10]

Mitchell may have authorized the government's counterinsurgency against the New Left, but the executioners of his policies often acted without his knowledge or consent. Of the FBI's Counter Intelligence Program, known internally as COINTELPRO—a covert campaign of infiltration and disruption targeting groups ranging from the Socialist Workers Party to the Weather Underground, the Black Panthers to the Ku Klux Klan—Mitchell was later found to be wholly unaware. At one point, in fact, the enormous surveillance net cast by the federal government in the late sixties and early seventies ensnared Mitchell himself: A wiretap directed at an FBI target captured the attorney general's own voice.[11]

From this great surge of police activity against radicals and antiwar activists came a series of federal indictments that solidified Mitchell's image as the era's reigning symbol of law and order. Paradoxically, the success of Mitchell's campaign would be measured not in the number of convictions secured—the prosecutor's traditional metric—but by its cumulative impact on the targeted groups. In the Chicago Seven trial, for example, none of the five riot convictions withstood appeal. The Harrisburg Eight were acquitted of conspiring to kidnap Henry Kissinger (indictments Mitchell later said he authorized to "get Hoover off the hook" after the FBI director prematurely aired the charges in public). The case of the Seattle Eight, in which members of the Seattle Liberation Front were slapped with conspiracy and riot charges after a February 1970 protest, ended in a mistrial (though six of the eight wound up serving time). The prosecutions of Daniel Ellsberg and Anthony Russo, indicted in the Pentagon Papers case, were thrown out amid revelations of government misconduct. And the trial of the Gainesville Eight, which CBS News called "the seventh major conspiracy case in which the Justice Department took on the radical antiwar movement," ended with a Pensacola jury acquitting the defendants of plotting to disrupt the 1972 Republican convention.[12]

Contemporaneous commentators initially saw this string of acquittals and overturned convictions as evidence of Mitchell's ineptitude, the inevitable result when a Wall Street bond lawyer tried to play top cop. Only after Mitchell's tenure in government, and the ebbing of the antiwar movement, was it possible to look back and discern the causal connection between the two. "I think the movement *was* set back by Nixon and Mitchell," reckoned Ayers. "But the measure of their effectiveness is not how many convictions they got. It's what they did to disrupt and dismantle."

By 1973, students were more likely to attend kung fu classes than antiwar protests. Broad social trends—the rise of individualism, the drug culture—also contributed to attitudinal changes among American youth; but it was of incalculable symbolic significance that the attorney general of the United States stood firm in the media age against the lawless, nihilistic excesses of "the movement." "Mitchell's greatest tactical success came from his handling of the high-riding radical left," *Newsweek* declared in the spring of 1973. "[Although] the Justice Department has not sustained any major convictions . . . the cost in time and money to the defendants was sufficient to defang the antiwar left nearly two years before Mr. Nixon was able to bring U.S. troops home from the Vietnam War."[13]

Each spring and fall of Mitchell's years in power witnessed record-shattering marches on Washington, unprecedented breakdowns in civil order, and bloody street clashes that included challenges and threats directed at Mitchell himself.

During his first days in office, Mitchell worried most about black militants. He discussed the Black Panthers with an FBI bodyguard, and the agent, following strict orders, typed and sent up the Bureau chain of command every word Mitchell said. These remarks invariably made their way to the desk of J. Edgar Hoover, who actively used Mitchell's security detail, previously unpublished documents show, to spy on the attorney general. Thus when Mitchell rued the popularity the Panthers enjoyed among white youths, Hoover took note, underlining the passage in his agent's report.

> The attorney general . . . commented on the objectionable content of the films shown him by the [FBI's] Domestic Intelligence Division . . . entitled "Huey Newton's Birthday" and "Off the Pig," two Black Panther films used to recruit and for propaganda purposes. [Mitchell] stated what was of particular note was the number of white girls in attendance at Black Power rallies, and the fact that one of these objectionable films has been shown at Cardoza [*sic*] High School and that both films had been shown at high schools and college campuses across the country.

A week later, Mitchell expressed apprehension to his FBI detail over the prospect of "racial demonstrations" on the first anniversary of the assassination of the Reverend Dr. Martin Luther King Jr. In this Mitchell proved prescient. FBI documents showed that "due to the racial tension in the Washington, D.C., Detroit and Chicago areas . . . the attorney general delayed his departure from the office last night." That Mitchell touched a nerve among the country's leading black revolutionaries became clear when Bobby Seale accused Mitchell of moving the country "closer and closer to open fascism" and publicly exhorted black brothers and sisters, from a San Francisco jail cell, to "bust the Nixon-Agnew-Mitchell regime in their asses and let them know the struggle is here."[14]

The Nixon administration closely monitored the New Left's internal dynamics and schisms, leading the president himself to caution Mitchell that month that "we may soon have to face up to more than dialogue." Nixon's prophecy soon came true. The Weathermen announced a return to Chicago that would "bring the war home . . . attack the beast from within as the peoples of the world attack it from without." Dubbed by organizers the Days of Rage, the plan called for thousands of armed, angry young revolutionaries to gather on the evening of October 8 in Lincoln Park—where helmeted police had routed demonstrators fourteen months earlier—then plunge into the city's streets to wreak havoc and "off the pig."

In large measure, the action was a personal challenge to Nixon's tough new attorney general, a test of his mettle. Weatherman leader Mark Rudd hoped the Days of Rage would make a "national statement" and "get the attention of those who would fight Mitchell." Another Weatherman, Susan Stern, exulted that a previous demonstration, in Seattle, had "made John Mitchell look like an idiot," and routinely excoriated him in public and private settings. "Nixon's the real conspirator—him and all the other capitalists—Rockefeller, Mitchell; they conspire against the people of the world," she told reporters. Stern also anxiously wrote her mother: "We are reliving the McCarthy era, and Mitchell and Nixon will shut up any voice that even attempts to speak up for freedom and truth. If I can't speak for such things, then I don't want to live at all."[15]

As the Days of Rage approached, the White House watched with apprehension. An aide to John Ehrlichman alerted the attorney general to the president's growing concern. "From all reports," the aide wrote, "leftist leaders are counting on serious disorders in Chicago, with resulting 'police brutality,' to polarize student opinion and increase participation in the Moratorium activities." Nixon instructed Mitchell to "work closely" with Chicago officials to "keep the [Days of Rage] from getting out of control."[16]

On the appointed night, Ayers, Dohrn, and their Weatherman comrades gathered in Lincoln Park. But the army of angry youths— "tens of thousands," the underground press had promised—stayed home. In all, "no more than a couple hundred" people showed up. "My stomach sank," Ayers wrote, years later. "I felt like running away, slipping into the darkness and disappearing, but I knew I couldn't. . . . There's no turning back now, I said to myself." The group swiftly set out for Chicago's Gold Coast, the city's wealthiest section. Whooping and hollering, the rabble flung bricks and pipes, smashing the windows of a bank and a Rolls-Royce. However, as David Dellinger disapprovingly noted, the Weathermen also vandalized "a disproportionately high percentage of . . . Volkswagens and other old and lower-priced cars . . . small shops, proletarian beer halls, and lower-middle-class housing."

More than a thousand Chicago police officers—scarred by the previous year's convention rioting and primed for a "kill or be killed" confrontation—perched along barricades. Amid the ensuing frenzy of bullets, nightsticks, and tear gas, a squad car plunged into a live crowd; "bodies were just mangled." After two hours, twenty-eight policemen lay wounded and at least six Weathermen were shot; sixty-eight were arrested and untold others fled with their injuries. Recurring clashes over the next three days led to almost 300 arrests and damage to 1,400 businesses, residences, and automobiles.[17]

Mitchell pronounced the Weathermen "psychopaths." Episodes like the Days of Rage he blamed on "Leninists and Trotskyites." Testifying in federal court in 1980, he identified the Weather Underground as "one of the radical, if not the most radical, groups" ever to operate in the United States. Mitchell recalled President Nixon expressing concern that the group was "impacting on foreign policy." Nixon's worry, Mitchell testified, was that the North Vietnamese would balk at negotiating as long as "groups like the Weather Underground were creating disturbances."

To Mitchell, the violence posed a basic question: "Who's going to run the show—the present Establishment or a new Establishment?" "They're stuck," he told an interviewer shortly after the Days of Rage. "They want to burn down buildings, but they don't have anything with which to replace them. In the theater, they'd call it a second-act problem. . . . It's all very well to break the law in the name of the higher morality," he added, "but the hard part is submitting to the penalties imposed by the law."[18]

The Weathermen had no intention of submitting to Mitchell's

penalties; instead they would escape them, by forming a clandestine nationwide network. Between October 1969 and September 1973, the Weather Underground would claim credit for twenty bombings across the country, in which no one was harmed—save three of the organization's own members, who perished in a Greenwich Village townhouse in March 1970 after one of their own creations exploded prematurely.

Death was never far from the Weather front, as the youthful residents of the doomed townhouse—and John Mitchell—came to understand. In the Weather Underground's third communiqué, dated July 26, 1970, and mailed to the editors of the *San Francisco Chronicle* and *New York Post*, the group exulted how "every move of the monster-state tightens the noose around its own neck." The group also issued a chilling warning to the attorney general: "Don't come looking for us, dog; we'll find you first."[19]

With the Days of Rage over, Nixon and Mitchell steeled themselves next for a massive march on Washington over the long weekend of November 13–16, 1969. The organizing group, the New Mobilization Committee to End the War in Vietnam, or "New Mobe," estimated more than 250,000 people would participate, a record turnout for the first major antiwar action against the administration. Peaceful and radical groups were both expected to attend. An ad hoc crisis group, including top officials from Justice and the Pentagon, concluded the potential for calamitous damage to the capital, even casualties, was "extremely high," with the disorder likely to exceed anything seen in the 1967 encircling of the Pentagon, the 1968 Democratic convention, or the Days of Rage.[20]

At the White House, a young aide named Tom Charles Huston—later infamous as the author of the Huston Plan, a broad menu of domestic spying programs made public during the Watergate hearings—circulated a series of "intelligence memos" assessing the likelihood of violence at the New Mobe march. Previously unpublished, the Huston memos show Mitchell was a primary target of the protesters. Relying on information supplied by undercover informants, Huston reported that Abbie Hoffman and Jerry Rubin were organizing a mob to "break into the Justice Department [by] breaking windows and possibly using Molotov cocktails"; then, while police raced to Justice, the group would "blow up" the Vietnamese embassy. Another informant claimed the Revolutionary Youth Movement and SDS' "Mad Dog" and "Running Dog" factions were planning "action tactics" at DOJ and the embassy.[21]

Mitchell sounded the alarm. Playing off of Spiro Agnew's recent denunciation of antiwar activists as "an effete corps of impudent snobs," the attorney general told *Meet the Press* some New Mobe leaders were "more than snobs . . . active militants" eager to "destroy . . . the institutions of our government." Marchers were to include the Weathermen, the Yippies, a lesser-known outfit called the Crazies, and the New Mobe's own steering committee, "dominated," according to one account, by members of the Communist Party USA and the Socialist Workers Party. Indeed, North Vietnam's prime minister cabled the group: "I wish your 'fall offensive' a brilliant success."[22]

When DOJ denied the New Mobe's request to march up Pennsylvania Avenue, the left lambasted Mitchell. Senator George McGovern, the liberal Democrat from South Dakota who would become the Democrats' standard-bearer in 1972, harrumphed that Pennsylvania Avenue "belongs to the people of America—not to Attorney General Mitchell." McGovern also denounced Mitchell's "inflammatory" predictions of violence. Columnist Clayton Fritchey likewise accused the attorney general of conjuring a "faceless enemy" to justify repression: "The Justice Department foresees violence. But from whom? From peace leaders like Mrs. Martin Luther King, Dr. Benjamin Spock, and the Reverend William Sloane Coffin?"[23]

During the testy negotiations that followed, a new figure from the administration held his first news conference: a handsome, blond-haired thirty-one-year-old aide to Kleindienst named John W. Dean III. To Dean, the attorney general privately exhibited a "blasé" attitude about the marchers and their demands: "What a nuisance this all is," Mitchell would say. "He'd attend the meetings at Justice," Dean recalled in 1977, "and sit there puffing away at his pipe, annoyed by the whole thing." Unlike Mitchell and Kleindienst, Dean felt the marchers' demand for Pennsylvania Avenue should be granted and admittedly worked, in tandem with another young aide, "behind the backs of our superiors" to reverse DOJ's ruling. Even so, the New Mobe was vowing to march up Pennsylvania Avenue no matter what. Kleindienst nervously asked how they could be stopped. "Concertina wire, several rolls of it," a general replied. Aghast at the vision of Coretta Scott King ensnared in barbed wire, Kleindienst called Mitchell. "This is absurd," he said. Mitchell also heard from the president. Soon after, the New Mobe's request was approved.[24]

Knowing Mitchell was a target of the demonstrators, the FBI urged him to bolster security around his office. The attorney general waved off these warnings—but acted swiftly to fortify the capital. If violence erupted on a mass scale, the decision of whether to deploy federal troops—as well as the specific units called up and the timing and duration of their deployment—would be the attorney general's to make. So stated a secret memorandum drafted by Mitchell and the Pentagon, entitled "Interdepartmental Action Plan for Civil Disturbances," and approved by Nixon the previous spring.[25]

Some 28,000 troops in the Washington area were available for deployment. The Defense Department also ordered several units outside the city's 100-mile radius to a "state of readiness." As the demonstration neared, the Pentagon moved an additional 9,000 troops, all "thoroughly trained in civil disturbance control," DOD officials said, to special posts across the city's network of military installations. Unless Mitchell called for the troops' active deployment, however, primary law enforcement responsibility during the action lay with a special 2,000-man detail of Washington's Metropolitan Police Department. Backing up the cops would be 1,500 members of the National Guard; 400 park police; 300 reserve officers on desk duty; and 2,500 self-policing "marshals" supplied by the New Mobe.[26]

Mitchell yielded no quarter. On the eve of the march, he spoke at a GOP fund-raiser in Milwaukee, striking what the *Washington Post* called "the most partisan notes of his ten months in office." The antiwar protests were part of a larger "disease of cynicism" that Mitchell attributed to the "deception" of the previous administration. LBJ had tried to solve problems through an "illusion of words," Mitchell argued, the nourishment of "impossible dreams"; as a result, "the poor and the black who had relied on Utopian promises . . . now distrust the government's ability to act on their behalf." Middle-class families who trusted Washington to manage the economy were now "caught in increasing inflation," and the young, dispirited by the dashed hopes of the sixties, felt driven to "reject the established political process and . . . turn to violence and confrontation."

That last route, Mitchell warned, was a dead end; confidence in the law and "civil tranquility" would be restored. "The foreign policy of this government cannot—and will not—be formulated in the streets of Washington," he declared.[27]

At 6:00 p.m. on Thursday, November 13, an icy rain dampening their clothes but not their spirits, the first of 45,000 Americans began the March Against Death, parading solemnly from the gates of Arlington National Cemetery to the White House four miles away. Each marcher carried a candle and a sign that bore the name of a fallen soldier or a flattened South Vietnamese village; drummers kept up a steady, funereal beat.[28]

The real action was yet to come. Along with speeches and marches, conferences on "United States Imperialism" and "The Transition to a Peacetime Economy," and orderly demonstrations by groups like the Radical Social Workers and Psychologists for a Democratic Society, the following afternoon called for a rally at the Justice Department by the Yippies, who had secured a three-hour picketing permit to protest the trial of their leader, Abbie Hoffman, and the other members of the Chicago Eight.

A large crowd—estimates ranged from one to three thousand people—converged on a park across the street from Justice. Dr. Benjamin Spock, the left-wing obstetrician prosecuted by Ramsey Clark for aiding and abetting draft resisters, condemned Attorney General Mitchell's "disgraceful" and "unconstitutional" prosecution of the "eight brave men" standing trial in Chicago. Now the Yippies swarmed toward Justice and demanded an audience with Mitchell. "We want to see the Wizard!" three hippies shouted, pounding on the bolted doors. Soon the crowd was chanting: "One, two, stop the trial! Three, four, stop the war! Five, six, kill the pigs! Seven, eight, smash the state!"

Jack Landau, Mitchell's press secretary, braved the crowd. He told Spock that Mitchell was busy preparing for Saturday's action and promised an appointment with "someone" at a later date. The crowd handed Landau a stack of petitions demanding freedom for the Chicago Eight. Fearing an explosion, New Mobe lawyer Phil Hirschkop stepped in and urged Spock to lead the crowd away. The doctor heeded the lawyer, and marched the Yippies back to the Mall, blaming their retreat on "insoluble tensions."[29]

Finally, Saturday came. The sky was sunny, the air crisp, temperatures in the low thirties: a fine day for the largest protest in the capital's history. More than a quarter of a million citizens, "nearly all of them young, white and apparently middle-class," surrounded the Washington Monument to register their peaceful opposition to the war in Vietnam. "Official estimate was 250,000," Haldeman recorded in his diary. "By our photo count, it was 325,000. Anyway, it was really huge."

After speeches by Senator McGovern and others, all "largely ignored" by the restive crowd, the New Mobe introduced the final speaker: David Dellinger, the oldest, and putative leader, of the Chicago Eight. After introducing codefendants Hoffman and Rubin, Dellinger urged the enormous crowd, after the march up Pennsylvania Avenue, to join the Yippies and Weathermen in an unsanctioned march on Justice. Richard Kleindienst later identified this moment as a "breach of faith" that all but ensured chaos. "The New Mobe leaders deliberately planned mob violence," Kleindienst maintained years later. "Dellinger delivered one of the most fiery revolutionary speeches ever given to such a large gathering . . . a call to arms against America and its institutions of government."[30]

Mrs. King led a peaceful march up Pennsylvania Avenue, joined by Senators McGovern and Eugene McCarthy of Minnesota, the antiwar Democrat who had helped drive LBJ from office, united in refrains of John Lennon's antiwar anthem, "Give Peace a Chance." Then came the march on Justice. At first, Mitchell and his aides only heard the chanting in the distance: "Free Bobby Seale!" "As long as I live," Kleindienst wrote in 1985, "I will never forget watching from John Mitchell's office as some ten thousand revolutionaries began their march down Constitution Avenue toward us."

In the front ranks, protesters carried a giant papier-mâché effigy of Mitchell's face. More chanting: "Ho! Ho! Ho Chi Minh! The NLF is gonna win!" A clutch of militants rushed toward the flagpole outside the attorney general's office, lowered the American flag, and replaced it with the Viet Cong's. White House aide Egil Krogh, assigned to Mitchell's office for the day, told Haldeman the sight of the enemy banner being hoisted above Justice and a "very strange emotional impact" on him. "Whole business is sort of unreal," agreed Haldeman. Police struggled to restore Old Glory while the protesters set a small fire.

What happened next no Weatherman could have forecast: John Mitchell himself, the object of all this fury, emerged from his fifth-floor office to watch the fracas from his balcony. In a breach of security protocol unimaginable in later times, Mitchell leaned far over the railing to point at a close-knit section of the crowd, telling an aide:

"That's the hard-core, linked arm to arm." The revolutionaries below could scarcely believe their eyes. Caleb Rossiter, a student activist from the University of Chicago, stood under the balcony that day.

> With unbridled delight at getting a chance to communicate with one of the enemy—Nixon was spending a restful afternoon in the White House watching football—we screamed "Fuck you Mitchell, fuck you Mitchell," and threw at him whatever debris we could find. He looked down calmly from the railing, which was far too high for our missiles, holding his pipe, and with great deliberation gave us the finger right back.

Suddenly, a series of pops: firecrackers exploding. D.C. police chief Jerry V. Wilson's walkie-talkie crackled with the sound of an officer asking if help was needed. Just keep your men on standby, Wilson replied. I'll tell you when we need you. The moment came sooner than he wished. "The situation was rapidly getting out of control," an eyewitness observed. One to squad, Wilson called out. Teams of riot cops swarmed in. Wilson threw the first tear gas canister himself. Mitchell would later tell his wife: "It looked like the Russian Revolution."[31]

With tear gas choking the air, the protesters scattered. "To the White House!" someone yelled, but no one listened. Hubcaps flew, fistfights broke out. Random gangs roamed downtown, smashing bank windows—but the gas was inescapable. "Within minutes," the *Evening Star* reported, "the air conditioning system inside [Justice] distributed the fumes throughout the building, including the office of Attorney General John Mitchell." Krogh reported to Haldeman: "Tear gas bad in Mitchell's office." Assistant Attorney General William Ruckelshaus found he could "hardly speak." In the lobby of the Washington Hotel, several blocks away, protesters lay strewn about, struggling to recover. Strong winds carried the toxic agent for miles, dousing innocent shoppers and even police headquarters on Indiana Avenue.[32]

Jack Landau remembered it all vividly. "[Mitchell] and I were standing out on the balcony of the attorney general's office and one of the disruptions happened right under the balcony. And the police shot in tear gas and the wind blew the wrong way and the tear gas hit us."

> And we started coughing and he started coughing very badly, and he fell forward and there's a wire along the balcony that's electrified to get the pigeons off, and he got electrocuted—not electrocuted, but shocked. He got shocked by the wire and pulled back, and started to cough very badly and he stumbled backwards into his office to his chair, which was right near the window and he looked at me and started to turn purple. He said: "If I pass out, don't let Kleindienst call in those troops!"[33]

Despite the massive numbers of protesters who rallied for the march, antiwar leaders closed out 1969 feeling frustrated. A Gallup Poll that month showed nearly 65 percent of Americans supported the president's conduct of the war. Nixon's steady troop withdrawals undercut claims he was expanding the fighting. The November action, for all its strength, had not stopped the killing in Southeast Asia; and turnout for the New Mobe's next action, in December, proved infinitesimal by comparison. As one historian noted, the winter of 1969–70 marked "a time of significant depression" for the movement. With the radicals in retreat, few—including Mitchell—foresaw that the fiery zenith of campus unrest still lay ahead, and that the spark would be lit not on the marble steps of Berkeley, or in the streets of Washington, but along a placid grassy slope in the great middle of the country.[34]

On Thursday, April 30, 1970, President Nixon announced in a prime-time televised address that he had ordered U.S. forces to commence offensive operations inside Cambodia, a limited incursion designed to "clean out" North Vietnamese and Vietcong "sanctuaries" serving as staging grounds for attacks on American troops. Nixon knew the decision would arouse strong emotions, especially on college campuses; but he, like Mitchell, was determined not to let student radicals control the foreign policy of a nuclear superpower. "We live in an age of anarchy, both abroad and at home," Nixon warned. "We see mindless attacks on all the great institutions which have been created by free civilizations in the last 500 years. Even here in the United States, great universities are being systematically destroyed."[35]

Within hours, American campuses were ablaze with anger. Stanford students rioted Days of Rage–style, smashing windows and looting shops. At the University of Maryland, an assault on the ROTC building, and the cops defending it, injured fifty. Protesters at Princeton firebombed an armory. At Ohio State, a six-hour battle between students and police, backed by the National Guard, saw one student shot, six hundred arrested. Strikes shut down classes at Columbia, Princeton, the University of Pennsylvania, the University of Virginia, Notre Dame, Brandeis—a firestorm that spread to 80 percent of the nation's colleges and universities.[36]

Nowhere was the tension greater than at Ohio's Kent State University. Reared mostly in the heartland, the student population had, over the preceding two years, grown increasingly radicalized. As a freshman later told the FBI, in previously unpublished testimony, the school by May 1970 harbored as many as a thousand "hard-core militants who would destroy the system by violent means . . . [and] many more who are sympathetic to such militants." After two days and nights of lawlessness in the streets of Kent, including the torching of an ROTC building and skirmishes with the National Guard, a rally at noon on the fourth of May drew more than a thousand demonstrators to the Kent State campus commons. The provocations— profane chants and taunts, hurled rocks and bottles—conformed to the deplorable norms of the day; but the response did not. After tear gas failed to disperse the mob, the jittery Guardsmen, armed with

World War II– and Korean War–era rifles, and not much older than the students they faced, turned suddenly and fired into the crowd, squeezing off sixty-seven shots in thirteen seconds, killing four and wounding at least nine. "My God," a woman screamed, "they're killing them!"[37]

On May 4, 1972, *Doonesbury,* the syndicated satirical comic strip, depicted Zonker Harris, a long-haired, perpetually stoned student-philosopher, leaning on a wall in a meadow and sharing his thoughts with silent protagonist Michael Doonesbury. "They say it's very pretty in Ohio this time of year," mused Zonker in the first panel. "They say it was a very pretty day exactly two years ago at Kent State," he continued in the second. The third panel was wordless. Finally Zonker added: "Have a nice day, John Mitchell."

The cartoon captured the extent to which Mitchell, 350 miles away on the fourth of May, became forever identified with the killings at Kent State. His dark association with one of the most traumatic events in American history was immortalized on August 13, 1971: the day Mitchell announced publicly that Justice would not empanel a federal grand jury to determine whether criminal charges should be brought against any of the Guardsmen. Mitchell told reporters there existed "no credible evidence of a conspiracy" by the Guardsmen and—more important—"no likelihood of successful prosecutions of individual Guardsmen." "Mitchell Drops Kent State Case" cried the front page of the *New York Times*; four days later the paper acknowledged, in an editorial titled "Justice at Kent State?" that Mitchell was "probably right" when he cited the impossibility of tying specific Guardsmen to specific deaths.[38]

Only years later did it become clear that the attorney general followed orders and not his own conscience. Previously unpublished notes and documents establish the Kent State case as perhaps the clearest example of Mitchell's curious collusion, against his own inclinations, in the villainous public role Nixon assigned him. Although

Mitchell supported the Cambodian offensive, he warned the president on April 26 it would create "political difficulty" at home. Yet the day before the killings, according to previously unpublished notes, Nixon sat in the Oval Office and pondered how to extract political mileage from the fevered sentiment he excited among the young. "Never underestimate the value of turning the student thing to our advantage—especially if they get rough," Nixon told Haldeman. "We *have* to go on the offensive against the peaceniks."[39]

When word of the shootings flickered across news wires, "grim-faced" White House aides huddled over clacking ticker-tape machines, aghast that National Guardsmen had gunned down unarmed American students on a Midwest college campus. Both Nixon and Mitchell grasped at once the moral gravity and political explosiveness of the Kent State case. Jerris Leonard, the assistant attorney general for civil rights, was among the first to see Mitchell after the news broke. "He was pretty shocked," Leonard recalled. "He couldn't believe it. . . . His immediate impression was, 'Get cracking on it, get the facts.' " The facts proved elusive. Within days, the FBI had three hundred agents working the case; but KSU had shut down and its students scattered across the country, hugely complicating the investigation.[40]

Over the next few weeks, DOJ lawyers prepared a thirty-five-page summary of the FBI's findings, and transmitted it to Mitchell on June 22. While acknowledging that the final moments preceding the shootings were "shrouded in confusion," the DOJ summary also noted that six Guardsmen had "pointedly" told the FBI their lives were *not* in danger, that "it was not a shooting situation." Multiple eyewitnesses agreed, and the summary speculated that some Guardsmen's claims of imminent, life-threatening peril were likely "fabricated subsequent to the event."

In the end, however, despite the fact that the DOJ summary discounted this evidence and held the Guardsmen at fault, the Department faced an insurmountable hurdle in prosecuting them because the FBI possessed "no ballistics evidence to prove which Guardsmen shot which student."[41]

Richard Nixon had his own ideas about what happened at Kent State, and from the first moment he worked assiduously to ensure those ideas prevailed. Haldeman informed Nixon of the tragedy: NBC News was reporting that the Guard had "gunned down" the students. Nixon processed Kent State as he did all other phenomena: through the prism of political opportunism. Haldeman's previously unpublished notes recorded the president's first reaction.

> *need to get out story of sniper*
> *can't we get something going—Mitchell* [. . .]
> *this will finish* [Ohio Governor] *Rhodes*
> *unless he turns this*

As public outrage mounted—compounded by the shooting deaths on May 14 of two black students, during a night of campus violence at Mississippi's Jackson State College—the president alternated between two modes of response. On one hand, he struggled to "find [a] more effective way to communicate in view of [the] tragedy," asking Mitchell to "brainstorm the school problem" and ordering the vice president:

> *don't say anything about students*
> [be] *non-political in every respect*
> *pitch one nation—reconciliation*
> [. . .]
> *must be conciliatory re: youth*
> *+ some way admit we're wrong in our rhetoric*
> *need to show sincerity in saying*[42]

At a hastily scheduled news conference on May 8, Nixon spoke in similar terms when asked what he thought students were trying to tell him. "They are trying to say that they want peace," Nixon replied. "They are trying to say that they want to stop the killing. They are trying to say that they want to end the draft. They are trying to say that we ought to get out of Vietnam. I agree with everything that they are trying to accomplish." He added defensively: "I did not send these men to Vietnam."

Yet at other times, Nixon hardened. He resented the harmful impact the domestic upheaval was having on his foreign policy, and came to regard *all* student dissent as an expression of radicalism. To him the episode showed the "totalitarianism of the left," and evoked in him the language of war. "Have to get out the anti-student line," he told Haldeman. "Get our offensive launched."

> *we now have the lines drawn* [. . .]
> *just as well to have the student thing out* [in the open]
> *they want to run the country* [. . .]
> *K. State showed people against students*
> *people are fed to teeth w/ rioting kids* [. . .]
> *the public is not with students*[43]

John Mitchell took a less embattled view. When thirty black students descended on his office to protest the Jackson State killings, the attorney general sat them down for a friendly chat, then personally visited the campus—overruling the objections of agents in the FBI's Jackson field office. He told a group of students from Fordham law school, his alma mater, the Kent State shootings "sickened and saddened" him. Though he blamed the unrest on "nihilists," he also pointed out that National Guard regulations called for minimal use of force.[44]

Mitchell was the first administration official to state publicly that both students and Guardsmen committed "apparent violations of federal law" at Kent State. In his preferred scenario, a federal grand jury would have been fruitlessly convened—for appearances' sake, since Mitchell, having read the DOJ summary, knew no Guardsman could be tied to a specific death—leaving authorities in Ohio to file whatever state charges they thought appropriate. Acting through Jerris Leonard, the attorney general ordered DOJ lawyers to share investigative data with Ohio prosecutors. Indeed, even before the shootings, Mitchell had ordered the FBI to investigate whether the torching of the Kent State ROTC building on May 2, an oft-forgotten prelude to the bloodshed, involved violations of "sabotage, sedition and civil rights laws."[45]

Nixon wanted no prosecutions of Guardsmen at all. Three days after the shootings, he ordered Mitchell to summarize for him the "nature and scope" of the FBI's investigation. The president also decreed that John Ehrlichman should receive copies of the Bureau's raw investigative files so the White House could monitor the probe on a daily basis. When the *Akron Beacon Journal* obtained an internal DOJ memorandum outlining the case that could be made against six of the Guardsmen, Nixon angrily called J. Edgar Hoover and ordered him to "knock down" the story. In October 1970, previously unpublished notes show, Nixon laid down the law to his attorney general.

Mitch. re Kent State—
there must be no action on K. State
no Federal grand jury—or anything else here [at the federal
  level]
Hoover swears FBI did not find guilt[46]

Mitchell acceded—for the moment. That same month, an aide informed Nixon by memorandum that Mitchell had agreed to "your request" to defer any indictments in "the Kent State situation" until after the 1970 midterm elections. Mitchell "has assured us that nothing will take place from a federal standpoint . . . until after the election," the aide wrote.[47] Behind the scenes, however, Mitchell continued pushing for a federal grand jury, a show of stubbornness that irritated Nixon. On November 18, one day after the *Washington Evening Star* carried comments by Jerris Leonard suggesting a federal grand jury was still under consideration, Ehrlichman fired off an "Eyes Only" memo to the attorney general conveying the president's displeasure.

> In your office the other afternoon I showed you the president's memorandum on this subject and it was my understanding that you understood that the president had decided that no such grand jury would be sought. Will you please ask Mr. Leonard to advise the president by letter or memorandum that he fully understands the president's instruction in this regard?[48]

More than two months after Ehrlichman's menacing memorandum, however, Mitchell continued to press his case internally, and even seized on Nixon's own remarks to try to nudge him in the right direction. "The president indicated this morning that the attorney general still feels we should have a Kent State grand jury," Haldeman reported to Ehrlichman, in a previously unpublished memo dated January 28, 1971, "but the president's feeling is very strongly against this."

> Apparently the attorney general feels that because the president mentioned his sorrow about Kent State in the TV conversation, it is now necessary to follow that up with a grand jury. The president doesn't agree and wants you to work this out with the attorney general. . . . The president's view is that this should be left where it is at this point.[49]

Nixon also talked that day with Ohio senator Robert Taft, a Republican who shared the president's aversion to further investigation, and asked Taft to contact Ehrlichman. The latter's notes from that call, also previously unpublished, read:

Kent Grand Jury—
Let's don't do it—
Stone-wall—[50]

At last, begrudgingly, Mitchell did as told. Two months later, a source at Justice passed word to a *Washington Post* reporter that no grand jury would be convened. "Only final approval by Attorney General John N. Mitchell is needed to ratify [the] decision," the *Post* reported; in fact, the decision had already been made, and by an authority higher than Mitchell. The days before Mitchell's infamous announcement of August 13 were spent biding time, waiting out a series of public events related to Kent State—the shootings' first anniversary, the publication of a bestselling exposé by novelist James Michener, the release of an independent report—so as not to appear a reaction to them.[51]

Uniquely among the dramatic events that marked his tenure as attorney general, Kent State took a toll on Mitchell. Although he began meeting regularly with student groups and could sometimes disarm them with the old Irish charm, the attorney general was neither impressed by what he saw nor able, in most cases, to soften the young in their attitudes toward him. The contempt Mitchell had long harbored for academia only deepened. Ironically, his turn of mood came just as Nixon began entertaining suspicions that his attorney general had gone soft on campus militants. "AG—turn off your campus visits—stay on right side of social issue," Haldeman recorded Nixon warning.

The president need not have worried. At a dinner hosted by the Women's National Press Club, Mitchell was overheard discussing Nixon's reading habits. "I'll tell you who's not informed," Mitchell said next, veering off topic. "It's these stupid kids."

Why, they don't know the issues. They pick the rhetoric that they want to hear right off the top of an issue and never finish reading to the bottom. Why, I talked to the kids from the Harvard Law School in my office and I was flabbergasted at how uninformed they are about what's going on inside government. And the professors are just as bad if not worse. They don't know anything. Nor do these *stupid bastards* who are ruining our educational institutions.

Mitchell closed his soliloquy with a prediction: "Listen, there is no such thing as the New Left. This country is going so far right you are not even going to recognize it." For all the controversy that greeted the attorney general's "bastards" remark, his prophecy of America's rightward political drift proved far more enduring. Few in the fall of 1970 understood, as Mitchell did, that the New Left was already dead, an illusory construct of its own members and handmaidens in the media. As Hunter S. Thompson, *Rolling Stone*'s fiendish national affairs correspondent, later conceded, only after election night 1972, and Nixon's forty-nine-state landslide, did it become "fashionable to go around calling ex-Attorney General John Mitchell a 'prophet.' "

Widespread support for the National Guard in the wake of Kent State proved that Americans were indeed "fed up to the teeth" with student rioters, as Nixon had said. The killings also served to discourage younger students from pursuing radical activism. "At Kent State, the country seemed to announce that whoever among the young felt deeply enough to continue the practices of the 1960s had to be ready to die for them," observed Milton Viorst. "Few were ready to die, and so the decade reached its end."[52]

As the fall of 1970 approached, Mitchell predicted a "much calmer" semester on American campuses. He saw coolness replacing "the emotions of last spring" as the charge of government repression "just fades into the background."[53] So it went. The New Left's last gasp came almost exactly a year after Kent State. It began with a four-day protest in Washington in mid-April 1971, staged by more than a thousand members of Vietnam Veterans Against the War (VVAW). Not since the Bonus March of 1932, when President Herbert Hoover ordered the forcible eviction of 20,000 veterans seeking back pay, had so large a group of discontented war veterans stormed the nation's capital.

Encamped on the Mall in fatigues and pup tents, the Vietnam vets were a disheveled lot, prone to public fornication and open drug and alcohol abuse. "Unemployable scum," Henry Kissinger spat. Nixon faced a delicate task: how to neutralize the veterans without appearing the ogre Herbert Hoover had. On April 19, according to previously unpublished White House tapes, Haldeman mused aloud it would "great if . . . all the hardhats could go in and bust 'em up." Haldeman's fantasy evoked a scene that erupted four days after Kent State, when construction workers on Wall Street had attacked a group of antiwar protesters, injuring seventy. "We're gonna beat the shit out of some of those veterans," Haldeman decided. Nixon recoiled. "Well, beating veterans," he demurred. "I think I'd let them go."[54]

Mitchell, as usual, chose the sanest route: He obtained a court injunction banning the veterans from camping out on the Mall. Only after they refused to budge did Mitchell argue they should be forcibly evicted; but Nixon remained haunted by the ghost of Herbert Hoover. "I don't wanna, uh, you know—like the Bonus March and all that stuff," he fretted to Mitchell and Haldeman. "You recollect poor old Hoover. . . . They never forgave him."[55] Previously unpublished tapes show the impasse touched off a furious row between the president and the attorney general. As Nixon later told Haldeman and Kissinger: "Mitchell was arguing strenuously about the law this morning, and I said, 'God damn it, forget the law.' "

NIXON: I had to raise hell with Mitchell today. He wanted to go out 'n' clean 'em out, and I said, "Not on your life. Leave 'em there. Leave 'em there."

HALDEMAN: Mitchell was gonna clean 'em out?

NIXON: Well, he's—there's a court order.

HALDEMAN: I know . . .

NIXON: I said, "Just delay it. . . . I don't want a hand laid on 'em." I said, "You can go in and hand 'em the order and say, 'Gentlemen, you're asked to leave,' and—but then just leave 'em alone. Let the sons o' bitches [stay] there." And I want them up there at the Capitol. I'd like a few scruffy people up there, grabbing congressmen when they come through [after] screwing their secretaries.[56]

Mitchell was already looking past the Vietnam vets to a far larger protest, scheduled for early May, by the People's Coalition for Peace and Justice (PCPJ). Its leader was Rennie Davis, the cerebral Chicago Seven defendant whom Spiro Agnew once crowned "the most dangerous man in America." Slight of build and bespectacled, Davis held enormous influence in revolutionary circles. The Yippies regarded him as "the most inspiring speaker in the New Left, a humanitarian evangelist on acid." A champion of Gandhian nonviolence, Davis was also capable of inciting followers to join him in "closing down that mother-fucking Pentagon," and, too, of declaring that the seventies "will be the time for burning banks." The FBI warned Mitchell that PCPJ was "heavily infiltrated" by communists and "self-avowed Marxist-Leninist revolutionaries."[57]

The high concept of the May Day protests, envisaged as "the boldest and costliest antiwar demonstration in history," lay in a slogan advertised prominently in PCPJ's tabloid, the *Quicksilver Times*: "If the government won't stop the war, the people will stop the government." The plan called for hordes of protesters to fan out across Washington on Monday morning, May 3, and, using only their bodies, obstruct the rush-hour traffic flow into the city. By choking off key bridges, traffic circles, and intersections, the demonstrators aimed to shut down the capital and—at least temporarily—the bureaucratic machinery vital to the conduct of the war. As the May Day Tribe stated explicitly in its "tactical manual," the overall goal was "to raise the social cost of the war to a level unacceptable to America's rulers . . . to create the specter of social chaos."[58]

In preparing for May Day, Mitchell drew on the lessons learned in the New Mobe insurrection of 1969. Now, as then, he heard the professions of pacifism and saw visions of violence. On April 24, after more than 200,000 antiwar protesters filed past the White House without incident, Mitchell expressed relief—but still predicted the worst for May Day. "There is nothing that I have seen today that would change that," he told reporters. This prediction proved accurate, as did another: Mitchell rightly reckoned that the very publicity Rennie Davis needed to succeed—drawing Gandhian throngs to the capital, after all, always requires advance notice—would enable police to neutralize it. "In order to get the sheep to follow these *terrorists*," Mitchell said, using a word not yet in vogue, "they have to talk about what they're planning to do."[59]

As initial projections of twenty-five hundred protesters multiplied tenfold, Mitchell became "personally involved in directing the defense of the capital." He authorized Defense Secretary Melvin Laird to deploy as many federal troops as necessary to keep the federal government open. In a classified memorandum, Mitchell said it was "quite plain" the protesters "may well be successful unless armed forces are . . . made available." Laird responded with ten thousand men. Soldiers of all kinds—police battalions, National Guardsmen, Army riot-control units, airborne paratroopers, Marines—flew into nearby bases on high alert. Five thousand District of Columbia cops were also ready. To the task of repelling the May Day protesters, whom they regarded as little better than rodents, the soldiers and Marines came thirsty for action and heavily armed: M-14 automatic rifles with fixed bayonets; heavy-machinery cranes; half a dozen Chinook helicopters; Army Jeeps with wire-mesh fronts; a fleet of V-100s, state-of-the-art armor-plated riot-control juggernauts outfitted with gun turrets and rubber wheels, and capable, the Army noted proudly, of "running over a car."[60]

Mitchell also braced for another assault on the Department of Justice. A White House official who visited DOJ in this period saw teams of uniformed infantrymen patrolling the building's acute-angled hallways with belt-fed light machine guns. "Any of the mob who managed to overwhelm the General Services Administration guards and enter the building to shut it down would be cut to pieces by machinegun fire," the official wrote. "Nobody fucked with John Mitchell."[61]

Yet once again, Mitchell was the protesters' preferred target. On the afternoon of April 30, 1971, more than two thousand demonstrators converged on Justice, an odd site for a rally whose participants identified themselves as "antiwar and anti-poverty." What really made Justice the epicenter of countercultural conflict in those years was Mitchell's preeminent power in the Nixon administration and his singular identification with the "repressive" concept of law and order. It was as if the revolutionaries recognized the full depth and range of Mitchell's influence in Nixon's America, and accordingly visited upon him the fury that, by virtue of their stated causes, they might have directed elsewhere—the Pentagon, say.

Now the anti-Mitchell mob lay sprawled across the steps of Justice, blocking all entrance. Female DOJ employees in short skirts were forced to climb, amid jeers and harassment, over the prostrate rabble. Finally a hundred cops, marching in formation, swept through the crowd with nightsticks and armored vehicles. "Come down here Mitchell, and get these police," thundered the Southern Christian Leadership Conference's Hosea Williams, a leader of the march on Selma. "They are abridging our constitutional rights!" Three hundred and seventy people were arrested.[62]

That Monday, May the third, a reporter recalled years later, dawned as "a perfect May morning, scented with spring flowers and tear gas." Before the sun rose, some 50,000 government employees, urged to commute early, were already on the job. In that sense, May Day's primary goal—preventing federal workers from reaching their desks—went unmet. The *Evening Star* reported the government's 318,000 employees showed up in "normal" numbers, with attendance at some agencies, like the Departments of Transportation and Interior—and Mitchell's DOJ—*above* normal.[63]

Scattered and leaderless, hunted by an army of angry cops, the protesters panicked and ran wild, abandoning Gandhianism for one last flash of the Days of Rage. Richard Kleindienst catalogued the lawlessness:

> They rolled boulders into streets, laid metal pipes across roadbeds, strung barbed wire and ropes across streets, set fire to trash cans, spread nails on roads, threw rocks at passing motorists, removed manhole covers, slashed at motorists with wooden poles, smashed windows, slashed tires, overturned cars, pushed parked vehicles into traffic lanes, ripped down signs and traffic markers. They stopped a fire truck trying to get to a fire. . . . They blocked police emergency vehicles, turned on fire hydrants, disabled city buses and commuters' autos, abandoned old cars on bridge approaches and in tunnels, and dumped all manner of trash into the streets. They stoned and beat policemen.[64]

"D.C. was a war zone," said one Yippie. "It was Halloween to the tenth power," agreed CBS News' Eric Sevareid. Demonstrators remembered policemen swinging their nightsticks indiscriminately, "clubbing like grotesque wind-up toys"; Nixon's silent majority saw the May Day protesters as "ugly mobs of thugs . . . murderous . . . hate-filled." Disorder spread so widely and quickly that at 6:30 a.m., Chief Wilson suspended the rule requiring his officers to fill out arrest forms. This was May Day's pivotal event. Over the next four hours, more than seven thousand citizens were dragged off the streets, thrown into police cars, paddywagons, trucks, ambulances, any kind of vehicle the cops could get their hands on, and carted off to city jails and detention centers. When those sites overflowed, the police emptied their human cargo onto a Washington Redskins practice field hemmed in with concertina wire. It was—and remains—the largest number of mass arrests in American history.[65]

At the White House and Justice, the president's men quarreled over what to do next. Haldeman's unpublished notes captured the chaos and Nixon's hourly responses.

7:30 [a.m.]—*4,000 arrested*
traffic open—city under control
running loose—arresting fast
trashing—garbage, logs, etc.
lots of film [being broadcast] *of arrests, etc.*

E[hrlichman cites] *prob*
6,000 in a pen—ugly mood . . .
surrounded by troops
knows that it's a bad situation [but]
AG feels they shld be held 'til tonite

John Ehrlichman later claimed he faulted Mitchell for treating the arrested protesters too harshly. "I was . . . concerned that the administration might seriously overplay its hand," Ehrlichman told an interviewer in 1985. "And in fact it did . . . and I moved in as quickly as I could to try and set it right. . . . [RFK Stadium] looked like a concentration camp. . . . I got on the Justice Department to do something about it." Yet the notes Haldeman took on May Day show that when Mitchell proposed releasing "non-critical" detainees after the evening rush hour, Ehrlichman—and Nixon—opposed him.

AG is running this—
we thk this bass ackwards

[to] *let them out & disrupt traffic*
would reverse policy P. & AG worked out

A mid-afternoon meeting in the attorney general's office between Mitchell and Ehrlichman failed to resolve their dispute. Confronted with the clash of opinions, Nixon backed Mitchell, as Haldeman's notes confirmed.

His own feeling is that he believes
let them out & [let them] raise a little hell today
may temper off tomorrow
doesn't want [pictures on the] evening news of 5,000 in a cage
better to have trashing etc
pic. on evening news is critical

At 10:00 a.m., Mitchell emerged, like Caesar at Gaul, to declare victory. "The city is open," he announced to newsmen, "the traffic is flowing, the government is functioning." Rennie Davis conceded defeat at his own news conference, shortly before his arrest on conspiracy charges.[66]

But the action wasn't over yet. The following afternoon, May 4, another two thousand die-hards converged on Justice. The issue was no longer the war, clearly, but John Mitchell. "Power to the people!" the youths chanted. "Off the pigs!" The cops moved in once more, this time methodically filling out arrest forms. The protesters, seemingly "broken in strength and spirit," went quietly, with outbreaks of fighting infrequent. In all, two thousand people were arrested, right under the aquiline nose of the attorney general. For as in the siege of 1969, Mitchell stepped out onto his fifth-floor balcony to survey the scene. It was his last look at the New Left, a kind of "youth culture carnival." The *Washington Evening Star* published a photograph on its front page showing Mitchell, pipe in mouth, taking it all in calmly, "looking for all the world like Stalin" to the weary protesters beneath him. Mitchell watched intently as FBI agents, squawking into walkie-talkies, closed in on John Froines, the former chemistry professor and acquitted Chicago Seven defendant, haranguing the crowd and wanted on charges similar to Davis's. "We have him! We have him!" the agents cried, as Mitchell looked on.[67]

More than 12,000 Americans, "generally young [and] white," were arrested over May Day's seventy-two hours. More than 7,000 were detained on Monday alone, and 70 percent of those individuals were released by noon the next day; by Tuesday night, the 500 still in custody were those who refused to be fingerprinted and photographed. Most of the criminal charges stemming from the action were dropped. The nation's capital stayed open, the war continued. The protesters had been soundly defeated, without a single shot fired. Little wonder the Yippies later declared the movement "lost the revolution at May Day."[68]

Mitchell wanted all of America to know who won and who lost. Speaking a week later to the California Peace Officers' Association, following a warm introduction by Governor Ronald Reagan, the attorney general urged local police to emulate the "decisive opposition to mob rule" that capital authorities had shown. It had been two years since May Day 1969, when Mitchell famously declared an end to patience with student rioters; now the "high tide" of violence as an instrument of social protest had passed. Mitchell said the May Day militants reminded him of "another group of civilians who roamed the streets of Germany in the 1920s, bullying people, shouting down those who disagreed with them, and denying other people their civil rights. They were called Hitler's Brown Shirts."

Polls showed 71 percent of Americans disapproved of the May Day action, with 76 percent regarding the mass arrests as justified. The *Washington Evening Star* editorialized that the "willfully lawless mob" had been "dealt with appropriately and effectively." The symbolism was unmistakable: The attorney general had succeeded in removing the badge of "fascist" from the forces of law and order, where it had resided since the heady days of Berkeley and Columbia, and stuck it on the protesters. The left turned purple; the sixties had been stood on their head.[69]

For his bloody victories over the movement—the Days of Rage, the New Mobe, Kent State, May Day—John Mitchell was never forgiven. When the tables turned, and the former attorney general found himself transformed, unthinkably yet unmistakably, into an American outlaw, a target of Justice hunted as vigorously as the most radical Weatherman, no one took greater pleasure than the revolutionaries Mitchell had so thoroughly vanquished.

As late as April 1973, with the "Radical Chic" of the sixties long supplanted by the self-absorption of the "Me Decade," as Tom Wolfe observed, five hundred die-hard Yippies staged one last march on the Mitchell home, no longer the Watergate but a grand apartment building on Manhattan's Fifth Avenue. "Free Martha Mitchell!" they chanted. "Fuck John!" When the Mitchells finally appeared at the window to see what all the commotion was about, the stoners cherished their last "eye-to-eyeball confrontation with Mr. Law 'n' Order." To commemorate the moment, they placed a giant marijuana joint on the Mitchells' doorstep.

Mitchell's ruin in scandal brought joy to the hippies and radicals who once dreaded him. "It took six years, but as we watched the daily Watergate soap opera, watched Mitchell shatter," wrote Yipsters Dana Beal and Steve Conliff, "the busts and beatings and bummers and burns all started to feel worthwhile. . . . Mitchell became the first attorney general ever to be sent to prison. The biggest joke of the Seventies was the persecutors turned out to be the criminals." Timothy Leary, the LSD guru imprisoned on a marijuana conviction in 1970, shared in the elation: "I watched my federal pursuers join me—the attorney general, John Mitchell."

Other radicals savored not merely the personal irony in Mitchell's incarceration, but cosmic validation of the movement itself. Rennie

Davis, the May Day impresario, felt Mitchell's going to prison represented "the inevitable outcome" of the sixties. "The attempt to suppress, close down, jail, imprison, vilify, [and] curse had its ultimate salvation in Mitchell having to face what he had to face," said Davis. "It just seemed like a completion to a long process to take a stand for this country, its democracy, its openness, its stability for democratic institutions." William Ayers, unrepentant founder of the Weather Underground, struggled to put into words the euphoria he felt upon seeing Mitchell imprisoned. "Such a wonderful—such a wonderful *vindication*," he said. "It was a feeling of tremendous justice. I mean, what could be more just than John Mitchell, the chief law officer and also the chief lawbreaker, being sent to jail?"

Mark Rudd, the SDS leader and Weatherman revolutionary who led the seizure of Columbia in 1968, regarded Mitchell as "a Wall Street Nazi" and savored his incarceration—but only briefly. "I was ecstatic!" Rudd remembered. "I was thrilled. It seemed almost as if the revolution had won—although I knew it hadn't."[70]

THE COMEDOWN

Mrs. Mitchell commented that she might need an agent to accompany her full time to protect her from the press. . . . She was advised that she could easily avoid the press by simply stating, "No comment" to their inquiries. She indicated she could not do this.

—*Assistant FBI Director J. P. Mohr, 1969*[1]

FOR THE MITCHELLS, Washington had been a mixed blessing. The attorney general had tasted all the benefits that high-level service to the nation can offer: instant access to the president of the United States; substantive, even decisive, influence over federal policy, across the broadest spectrum of issues; 'round-the-clock transportation and protection, for him and his family, by the FBI; nationwide notoriety and its attendant perks; and interaction with highly accomplished people in and out of government.

But as the most talked-about cabinet couple soon discovered, good things in Washington tend to come at a steep price. Instant access to the president, in this case, also meant constant accountability to him, and Nixon was an exceptionally needy client: consumed by politics, disdainful of leisure pursuits, personally insecure, and restless at odd hours. The constant presence of their FBI escorts was, unbeknownst to the Mitchells, a vehicle for J. Edgar Hoover to spy on them, their every word in the agents' presence transmitted directly to the devious and manipulative director. Fame brought the need for physical protection; and the Mitchells' hectic schedules cut into the time they could spend, in lieu of nannies and aides doubling as nannies, with young Marty.

November 1969 saw Mitchell's clout in the capital at its apex. Within the preceding five months, the attorney general had muscled Abe Fortas into resigning from the Supreme Court, by quietly supplying evidence of Fortas's financial improprieties to Chief Justice Earl Warren, himself soon to retire; had stage-managed the swift Senate confirmation of Warren Burger to replace the chief; and had faced down the Yippies, Mad Dogs, and Weathermen from his balcony at Justice. That fall Mitchell appeared on the cover of *Newsweek* atop the headline: "Mr. Law and Order."[2]

But what the media build up, they delight in tearing down. Five days after the New Mobe left town, the Senate rejected Nixon's next Supreme Court nominee, Clement Haynsworth, an exceptionally fine man and brilliant jurist sacrificed, by Senate Democrats, as payback for what Mitchell had done to Fortas. And in April 1970, the Senate voted down G. Harrold Carswell, the administration's second choice to fill the Fortas vacancy; a "mediocrity" with a racist past, Carswell, as even Nixon admitted (to David Frost in 1977), never deserved nomination to the nation's highest court.[3]

With these defeats, Mitchell's reputation took a beating. The headlines were grim: "Disenchantment over Mitchell Grows in Ranks of Republicans"; "Mitchell Has Not Mastered His Job, Republican Senators Now Believe." "Mitchell's days of glory are really ending; the handwriting is becoming visible on the wall," reported Evans and Novak. The *National Observer* agreed: "Except for a handful—mostly Southerners—who still see Mr. Mitchell as a political asset, congressional Republicans believe Mr. Nixon's close friend and political confidant has become an unnecessary burden both to the party and the president." *Life* magazine, in a rare editorial, demanded he resign. "In this capital," the *Washington Post* observed, "the obvious possession of great power by any man nearly always generates a counter reaction . . . a drive by other men to bring him down." Now it was Mitchell's turn: "Senators are grumbling, pundits are moving to the attack, and some of the critics believe they smell blood for the first time."[4]

Dissatisfaction with Mitchell was also acute at the White House. "P concludes principal fault is Mitchell's," Haldeman recorded in his diary. "I think probably the rejection of both Haynsworth and Carswell did hurt Mitchell with the president," agreed William Rehnquist. Most vocal in this view was the attorney general's prime antagonist in the administration, John Ehrlichman. "[Mitchell's] influence was much stronger at the beginning than it was toward the end," Ehrlichman recalled in 1992. "In fact, after the Haynsworth and Carswell debacle, I would say his influence was pretty nearly zero." Yet Ehrlichman's dire assessment was not universally shared. "I don't think that's true," responded Henry Kissinger. "I couldn't tell that." Similarly, Haldeman, who spent more time with Nixon than any other aide, recognized that the defeats of Haynsworth and Carswell, while ascribed in the president's mind principally to Mitchell, did not cause a complete loss of confidence. "I would say that Ehrlichman was more dissatisfied with Mitchell's performance as attorney general than the president was," Haldeman said.[5]

Indeed, as Haldeman's previously unpublished notes show, Nixon responded to the attacks on his embattled attorney general by ordering the White House PR apparatchiks—speechwriter Pat Buchanan, Press Secretary Ron Ziegler, and Communications Director Herb Klein—to make sure Mitchell was seen and photographed sitting next to the president in the stands at a football game, a gesture intended as the kickoff in a concerted campaign to restore the old Mitchell mystique.

Major speech for Mitchell . . .
Buchanan write it

> Z[iegler] *announce as major admin. stmt.*
> *Klein take him on as major project*
> *+ get him a new PR man at Justice*

A reporter who interviewed Mitchell in late April 1970, when the criticism was reaching its crescendo, found him absorbing it all "without anger or embarrassment . . . full of certitude about himself and the world as he knows it." But the new atmosphere in the capital, vicious and unsparing, was not without its effect. These were the days when the attorney general was most apt to puff on his pipe and remind visitors that he never really wanted the job in the first place. "I'd much rather practice law," he grumbled.[6]

Then there was Martha, who had begun to attract media attention of a kind never before accorded a cabinet wife. The first break in the dam was her interview on *CBS Morning News* shortly after the New Mobe protests. Although Martha had observed little of the sporadically violent demonstrations, she freely volunteered the attorney general's opinion of them. "My husband made the comment to me," she told Marya McLaughlin, "looking out the Justice Department it looked like the Russian revolution going on. As my husband has said many times, some of the liberals in this country, he'd like to take them and change them for the Russian Communists."[7]

What was this? the Washington press corps wondered. *A new species! The cabinet wife who blabs her husband's private thoughts!* Hordes of reporters began flocking to the Watergate East, eager to exploit the new source of snappy comment inside an administration once derided as "twelve gray-haired guys named George." Others took cheap shots from their desks. "To some of us," opined the *New York Post*'s "ladies" columnist, Harriet Van Horne, Martha's "tirade on CBS . . . sounded like an old strip of film from the white Citizens' Council of Birmingham."

Like George Wallace, Mrs. Mitchell has a ready-made constituency in this country. To rally that constituency one needs
only to articulate the meanest prejudices of the most confused, embittered people. That such people are out there—
anxious, troubled, sick of the war, of protesters, of taxes—is
part of our national shame.

Such criticism forced the attorney general, not for the last time,
into the delicate contortion of disavowing his wife's remarks without
appearing to disavow his wife. Lamely, Mitchell contended Martha
had used the term "so-called liberals"—never mind that her interview
was captured on film. "If you will transpose the word 'liberal' into
'violence-prone militant radicals,' I would be delighted to change
them for some of the academically inclined Marxist Communists,"
Mitchell continued. "I'd trade for the academic Marxists two-for-one,
because they don't necessarily advocate violence."[8]

The stampede on the Mitchells' apartment only made things
worse, for Martha seldom thought before she spoke, and the times
were volatile. "Anytime you get somebody marching in the streets,"
she told *Time*, "it's catering to revolution. . . . My family worked for
everything. We even had a deed from the King of England for property in South Carolina. Now these jerks come along and try to give it
to the Communists." She also lamented the "comedown" her husband's government service had imposed on the Mitchells. "We're not
living on the same means that we had in Rye," she complained. "I
had to sell my stock, and now we are having to dip into the till. I
think the government should give us free housing."

Taxpayers could be forgiven for believing otherwise—especially
after *Women's Wear Daily* reported that Martha needed four closets to
house her clothes: one for "afternoon and short cocktail things," another for handbags and shoes, another for fur coats. America now had
its own media-age Marie Antoinette, a *bouffant* blonde in a Southern
accent and sling-backed stilettos, perched above the Potomac in her

Watergate condo, dispensing disdain on opponents of a deeply divisive war fought mainly by boys from the lower classes.[9]

Mitchell tried to skate through the commotion by affecting an air of imperturbability. "Anything my wife does is fine with me," he would say. But official Washington was unimpressed. "Wives, all politically knowledgeable," wrote one political reporter, "were particularly affronted by the amateurishness of Mrs. Mitchell's performance."[10]

So was Richard Nixon—but for now, the president kept his peace. He expressed anger not at Martha's outspokenness but at press accounts attributing anger to him. After the *CBS Morning News* fiasco, he dictated two memoranda to Haldeman to ensure Mitchell did not think the president had been trashing the attorney general's wife. "Be sure you let John Mitchell know that I have never expressed any criticism of Mrs. Mitchell to members of the staff. When I have such criticisms, I will tell him before I tell anybody else!" Later that day, Nixon told Haldeman he had heard criticism of Mrs. Mitchell from "within the staff and among some Cabinet people." The fault lay not with Martha or CBS, Nixon said, but with the Mitchells' advisers.

What followed was a primer, Nixon's four "fundamental principles" of press relations: "a great majority" of reporters opposed his administration; even friendly reporters prized the story above all else; it was, therefore, "vital always to be on guard" with reporters; and interviewees should never tape more exchanges than the reporter will use. Nixon noted that Martha had answered *eighty-three* questions from Marya McLaughlin. Cabinet wives like Martha must grasp these rules, and "If they are not bright enough to understand it, then that's just too bad." To Martha herself, whom Nixon knew to be unstable, he sent only a gracious note betraying none of his displeasure.

> Dear Martha,
> Don't let the critics get you down—Just remember they are not after you—or John—but me—I appreciate deeply the

loyalty and courage you and John have consistently demonstrated. We'll come out on top in the end.

RN

Still, for this outburst of indiscretion, the president quietly imposed one penalty on Martha: He terminated her office privileges at
the Department of Justice building.[11]

Recognizing a cash cow when they saw one, the media began feeding the country a daily diet of Martha Mitchell. Seldom was the
product healthy for the Nixon administration. Word now surfaced
that during the Haynsworth battle she had brazenly called several
senators' wives, crudely lobbying for their husbands' votes. Betty Fulbright, wife of Democrat J. William Fulbright of Arkansas, Martha's
home state, reported that Mrs. Mitchell, threatening to campaign
against her husband, had used "vile and nasty" language. The attorney general's wife exercised none of the restraint Nixon counseled. Instead, she donned outfits so licentious her husband, walking in on
one of her interviews, wondered aloud if she was wearing her nightgown.[12]

And she failed, time after time, to hold her liquor. Once, the
Mitchells were invited to hear General Lew Walt, commander of the
Third Marine Amphibious Force and freshly returned from Saigon,
address a small group of administration officials and their wives at
dinner. Halfway through the evening, with Lew in mid-sentence,
Martha suddenly burst into tears, wailing about how sad the war was
and how the United States had no business being in Vietnam. "A
pained and embarrassed hush fell over the dinner table," an eyewitness later wrote, "broken only by the awkward sounds of another
guest who was sitting next to Martha trying to soothe her." Seconds
later, the attorney general had Martha on her feet and out the door,
"much as a long-suffering parent comes to soothe a troublesome
child." "She's had a long day," the attorney general apologized.

On another occasion, Martha ruined an evening at their neighbor's apartment by quarreling with her husband in front of their host, who never forgot the incident.

Martha suddenly threatened to throw her shoe across the room at her husband. "Just you try," was Mitchell's tired response. With one swift motion, Martha reached down, pulled one spike-heeled, sling-back shoe off her foot, and hurled it at Mitchell who, either from frequent practice or excellent reflexes, neatly ducked the flying object.

But war had been declared, and Mitchell rose from his chair, shoe in hand, hovering over his wife, and said, "It's time to go home." Martha looked down at her other shoe and began to rub it. "I don't want to go home," she said, in a flat sort of voice, but it was not a serious challenge, and after a few seconds, she got up to leave.

At another dinner party, Martha found herself seated beside Senator Charles Percy, the centrist Illinois Republican who had voted against Haynsworth and Carswell. "It's liberals like you who are selling this nation down the river to the Communists," she barked. Percy stormed off "muttering to himself all the things he would like to have said to Mrs. Mitchell." Looking on, the attorney general only smiled broadly. Ugly as it was, the Percy incident was but mere prelude to a far more damaging episode.[13]

Had Mitchell stayed in New York, practicing law, his wife's antics would have remained their private shame. But when the wife of the most powerful man in the cabinet telephoned reporters in the year 1970—late at night, drenched in whiskey, spitting venom—it made headlines. Shortly after 2:00 a.m. on April 10, less than forty-eight hours after the defeat of Carswell, Mrs. Mitchell quietly slipped out of the bed she shared with her husband, downed a few shots, and snuck into their master bath. There she picked up the lime green telephone receiver mounted on the wall, and, over the next hour, placed three rambling calls to the *Arkansas Gazette*, which recorded some of the discussion. Once again Martha directed her anger at Senator J. William Fulbright, who had voted against Carswell. "I want you to crucify Fulbright and that's it!" she ranted into the receiver. She said the senator "makes me so damn mad I can't stand it. . . . Mr. Fulbright does not represent the state. He is not representing the people of Arkansas."

A few hours later, after Martha had returned to bed, the attorney general woke up, turned on the radio, and heard the sound of his world turning upside down. An aide to Mitchell later recalled: "He was up-*set*!" Call the *Arkansas Gazette* and find out what the hell happened, Mitchell barked. In the meantime, Mitchell's phones were ringing off the hook. *What comment do you have on Mrs. Mitchell's remarks?* "I love her, that's all I have to say," Mitchell said curtly. *Do you, too, want to see Senator Fulbright crucified?* "I just laughed and laughed and laughed," Mitchell demurred, again seeking shelter behind a façade of patriarchal bemusement. Later he said he'd prefer if his wife spoke thereafter in Swahili. *Were you asleep when Mrs. Mitchell made the calls?* "I am always asleep," Mitchell cracked. Pressed still further, the attorney general finally pleaded impotence. "What else can I do, but let her speak? She has no inclination to be quiet. She's not politically motivated; she's just saying what she feels." *Are your wife's comments causing you problems at the White House?* "Nobody around here tries to throttle her," Mitchell said.[14]

This was, as Mitchell knew, wishful thinking. Richard Nixon was more than ready to throttle Martha Mitchell and had already begun plotting who, with her husband incapable or unwilling, could best handle the job. Nixon saw that the press swarmed to Martha because it could profit politically and financially from her indiscretion. Reporters and editors, in turn, knew that the free-spirited, often belligerent tone of Martha's public comments, even when offered in support of the administration, neatly undermined the buttoned-down image Nixon and his aides strove to project and the policies they aimed to advance. Haldeman's previously unpublished notes, taken the day after the Fulbright eruption, captured Nixon's mood: "We have to turn off Martha."[15]

In public, Mitchell portrayed his boss as delighted. Dining at the Rive Gauche, then Washington's most fashionable restaurant, Mitchell told friends that whenever the president wanted to say something important, he reached for the phone and asked: "Now just how would you put it, Martha?" Once the after-dinner bonhomie was over, however, Mitchell grasped the growing danger, both to the administration and his own standing within it. The day after the *Gazette* story ran, Mitchell hired Kay Woestendiek, a former "women's editor" at the *Houston Post*, as a press secretary for Martha—another dubious first for a cabinet wife—to handle the fifty interview requests piling up each day.[16]

More than four hundred letters descended daily on the Mitchells' Watergate apartment, including a fair number from Americans who urged the attorney general's wife to "shut your big fascist mouth." But Martha, unable to distinguish between good and bad publicity, relished the attention. "I think I'm going to join the Women's Liberation Movement!" she declared two days after the crucifixion controversy. The weeks that followed saw Martha recounting her old opposition to *Brown v. Board of Education* ("Are you going to be prejudiced against me because my grandparents had slaves?"); pronouncing herself "awfully sick" of the Vietnam War; and confiding her secret support for the opposition party. Appearing on *60 Minutes* in May 1970, Martha smilingly confided to CBS News correspondent Mike Wallace: "I love the Democrats."[17]

Nixon was beside himself. Haldeman's unpublished notes, scribbled the day Martha's comments about joining the women's liberation movement hit newsstands, show the president casting about for ways to stop this uncontrollable force that now appeared, suddenly yet unmistakably, a threat to his presidency. "Some concern about Mitchell, and *especially* what can be done about Martha," recorded

Haldeman in his diary. The unpublished notes on which Haldeman based this entry were even blunter. Nixon vacillated between confronting his heavyweight himself and enlisting others: Dick Kleindienst; Charles "Bebe" Rebozo, a personal friend of the president and Mitchell's; or Dick Moore, Mitchell's high school chum, now a counselor at Justice.

> *Moore—explain to MM press lady*
> *MM shld have no interviews w/ press*
> *she must realize all press are her enemies*
> *they'll all chop her. . . .*
> [Ask] *Kldst in confidence—*
> *what shld be done re MM?*
> *Bebe take on frontally?*
> *P. take M[itchell] on directly?*[18]

For Nixon, who abhorred personal confrontations and invariably swallowed his bravado in them, such an encounter with his indispensable, steely-eyed strong man was unthinkable. It would not be the last time Nixon recoiled from the necessary task of summoning Mitchell to the Oval Office and urging self-sacrifice. So, two days later, Nixon returned to the idea of an emissary: "Someone has to talk to John." Yet no one did, it seems, and the president's anger boiled over when he saw the attorney general's wife making merry with Mike Wallace—a scene, to Nixon, akin to a lion toying with a dull-witted mouse. *Had no one read his primer? Didn't anyone get it?* "Did Moore put Martha on TV?" Nixon demanded of Haldeman. "Why?" Haldeman's notes capture Nixon at a breaking point, ready to part with his consigliere if the fee for his services included his wife's indiscretions. As the president bluntly told his chief of staff: "Mitchell goes—if Martha doesn't."[19]

WATCH
WHAT WE DO

What we're dealing with is desegregation, not integration. It's desegregation. It's an entirely different concept, but it has to be right. It's the difference between governmental action and an open and free society.

—*John Mitchell, 1970*[1]

IN FEBRUARY 1968, as Nixon prepared to launch his presidential campaign, CBS newsman Mike Wallace thought it strange he had not yet met the man widely known to be running it. "Hey," Wallace asked his former CBS colleague Frank Shakespeare, then handling Nixon's press, "isn't it about time that I met John Mitchell?" A few days later, Shakespeare invited Wallace to an off-the-record lunch at New York's posh 21 Club.

As the men took their seats, Wallace mischievously asked if Nixon planned to address the same group of black publishers Hubert Humphrey recently had. Mitchell's answer startled the newsman: "I don't want Dick to go over there. You can buy those monkeys, anyway." "Frank Shakespeare turned pale and I could see him kick Mitchell under the table," Wallace wrote in 1984. "They quickly shifted to another subject." If the incident bespeaks racial bigotry in Mitchell, it is not the final word on the subject. The *New York Times* reported in the summer of 1969 that although Mitchell "still uses the word 'colored' in his conversation, he nonetheless recognizes the need to press desegregation suits in the courts."[2]

This peculiar schism in Mitchell—retention of private prejudice amid the nobler conduct of public office—mirrored precisely Nixon's own duality of thought and action, most pronounced, in the president's case, in his strange combination of anti-Semitism and support for Israel; indeed, Nixon may have been the first presidential candidate to call for the U.S. to *guarantee* Israeli military superiority. It was a duality Mitchell shared. *Newsweek's* Hal Bruno remembered Mitchell, upset once by a *New York Times* article, grumbling about the "Heb reporter" who wrote it. Another person close to Mitchell, also a Jew, remembered Mitchell referring privately to Henry Kissinger as "that kike."[3]

And yet, for reasons never stated—perhaps innate decency, or simple calculations of realpolitik—the attorney general, too, used his power to help Israel and Soviet Jews. Max Fisher, the late Jewish industrialist, philanthropist, and pro-Israel lobbyist, remembered pleading with Kissinger in 1970 to speed up American delivery of a few dozen Phantom fighter jets for which Israel had paid, but, owing to pressure from Arab states, never received. Completion of the deal would mark a decisive shift in American policy toward Israel: from neutrality to the guarantee of military supremacy Nixon had advocated as a candidate. Kissinger feigned impotence; Secretary of State William Rogers handled Middle East matters, he said. Israel needed the planes desperately, Fisher said. Who could convince the president? "Go see John Mitchell," Kissinger said.

Stunned that an attorney general would be so deeply involved in foreign policy, Fisher did as told—and got what he wanted. "Bill Rogers was a little mixed up in his perception of the Middle East," Mitchell wryly recalled years later. "I saw to it that the Phantom deal received proper consideration." Shortly thereafter, Israel's ambassador to the United States, Yitzhak Rabin—later the Jewish state's prime minister—noted the "growing . . . sympathy" for Israel within the

Nixon administration, "especially on the part of Attorney General John Mitchell."

Later in 1971, Mitchell accompanied Fisher to a Philadelphia airport to watch a group of Russian Jews clamber off a plane onto American soil. Fisher's biographer, Peter Golden, recorded the scene: "The immigrants had undergone colossal hardships to leave the Soviet Union; they had lost their jobs, been harassed by their government and charged an exorbitant tax. Mitchell had made their journey possible by clearing several obstacles through the Justice Department. Fisher watched as the Russian Jews walked toward the terminal, and a lump rose in his throat. He glanced at Mitchell. The attorney general was crying openly, not bothering to wipe the tears from his face."[4]

For America's blacks Mitchell shed no tears, but to ensure racial progress he did more than any executive branch official of the twentieth century. A generation after the Supreme Court's landmark ruling in *Brown v. Board of Education,* requiring public elementary and secondary schools to desegregate "with all deliberate speed," the schools were still the primary civil rights battleground—and still largely segregated. In January 1969, when Mitchell took office, 68 percent of Southern black children attended all-black schools; nearly 80 percent attended schools that were 80 percent or more black.

For Nixon and Mitchell, the central issue was whether to continue enforcing Title VI of the 1964 Civil Rights Act, which authorized the Department of Health, Education, and Welfare to cut off federal funds to dilatory school districts. HEW secretary Robert Finch, Nixon's old protégé and the former lieutenant governor of California under Ronald Reagan, favored the cutoffs; Mitchell, who liked Finch but privately ridiculed him as "Secretary Fink," did not. The president and attorney general regarded the cutoffs, and publicized deployments of federal marshals to Southern districts, as overly provocative acts, less likely to bring about harmonious integration than to stir Southern resentment and hasten violent clashes.[5]

Early on, Mitchell signaled that the administration, while committed to desegregation, opposed compulsory integration. Asked if he would sue to desegregate all-black schools in Harlem, Mitchell answered: "What you have in Harlem is a *de facto* situation that results from housing patterns, and we do not believe that it is practical to upset such a picture at this time." By no means was Mitchell foreswearing action in the North; indeed, a northward thrust would later become a central part of Nixon's bid to "nationalize" the race problem, and destigmatize the South.[6]

Nixon's vision was blurry from the start, however. In his first month in office, he publicly supported Finch's approach. "I believe that funds should be denied to those districts that continue to perpetuate segregation," he told reporters. But Nixon's sympathies soon swung to Mitchell, who saw litigation, not cutoffs, as the best way to bring recalcitrant Southern school districts into line with the times. Mitchell's route offered two advantages: It gave white leaders more time—to stall, in some cases, yes, but more often to grasp the inevitable, and let them sell it to the most intractable among their flock. Litigation also removed the political onus of desegregation from the Oval Office, and placed it upon the nation's courts—which protected Nixon in 1972.[7]

Within days of his endorsement for Finch, Nixon abruptly about-faced—and demanded a purge of Finch's office. That the president privately wanted Mitchell in the driver's seat ("John reign Bob in," Haldeman's notes recorded) became further evident when Finch was forced to grant sixty-day desegregation deadline extensions to five dilatory Southern school districts, including two in South Carolina, where Senator Strom Thurmond had toiled so devotedly for Nixon's election. In arguing for the extensions, Mitchell warned Nixon about the dangers of disappointing Thurmond, and his followers, so early in the president's term.[8]

Such actions fed the African American view of Mitchell, akin to the Yippies', as the devil incarnate. Roy Wilkins, executive director of the National Association for the Advancement of Colored People

(NAACP), proclaimed Mitchell the cabinet member "furthest removed from the Negro problem." Supporters of Mitchell pleaded with black friends not to prejudge him; most often, they cited his private practice work in the field of public housing. Meeting directly with black leaders for the first time in February 1969, Mitchell himself promised to avoid "haphazard" courtroom thrusts on desegregation, to "establish a pattern" that would "make a big impact."[9]

Indeed, working behind the scenes, Mitchell enforced the most progressive racial policy he could without damaging the reelection fortunes of his "client." Nixon's views on race relations were conflicted. As vice president, he had helped steer civil rights legislation, over the objections of Southern segregationists, to the Senate floor; and as late as 1966, he publicly warned GOP officials in Mississippi: "Republicans must not go prospecting for the fool's gold of racist votes." By the time he became president, however, Nixon's personal views had hardened, succumbing both to his small-town prejudices and the polarization of the times. Ninety days into his term, discussing the Great Society, Nixon told Haldeman welfare reformers "have to face the fact that the *whole* problem is really the blacks. . . . There has never in history been an adequate black nation, and they are the only race of which this is true."

Still, Nixon supported school desegregation. "Don't expect PR results," he told Haldeman in April 1969, "just do what is right." "You're not going to solve this race problem for a hundred years," he told an aide the following year. "Intermarriage and all that, assimilation, it will happen, but not in our time. Desegregation, though, that has to happen now." In the hands of a smart politician, he reckoned, the explosive issue could be resolved peacefully and justly—and without electoral sacrifice. Thus began what the White House's resident liberal intellectual, Daniel Patrick Moynihan, termed, only half in jest, Nixon's and Mitchell's "schizophrenic" behavior on desegregation: pushing quietly for biracial classrooms while publicly courting white Southerners.

The only real losers in the deal were Bob Finch and his liberal

aides at HEW. When newspapers reported that Finch planned to delay certain desegregation timetables beyond a September 1969 deadline "in a furtive and quiet manner," Nixon barked: "Bob—I want
them relaxed in a *direct forthright* manner." Seemingly everything
Finch's agency did ran countrary to the president's wishes—and Attorney General Mitchell gleefully made sure Nixon knew it. "The
president . . . was embarrassed for Finch," Ehrlichman recalled, "and
Mitchell poured gasoline on that flame."

Mitchell was "a proponent of civil rights," recalled Jerris Leonard,
DOJ's top civil rights officer, years later. "I brought a *lot* of lawsuits
into John Mitchell's office, put 'em on his desk. I never heard him say,
'Why are we favoring these niggers?' . . . Our object wasn't to try to
press the envelope. Our object was to try to get kids into desegregated
school systems, [get] black people jobs . . . [get] black people housing. . . . The liberals didn't like it, because they didn't give a damn
about whether or not we got black people into schools and got [them]
jobs. What they wanted to do was to reformulate the whole system
and turn it over to the government."[10]

In the friction between Mitchell and Finch the press found an
irresistible story line: the cabinet-level policy dispute that turns personal. The *New York Times* reported Mitchell "hard-pressed to conceal his disdain for Robert Finch."

Nixon wanted his administration to speak with one voice. A
meeting was accordingly called to bring together Mitchell, Finch, and
their top aides; tellingly, the meeting was held in Mitchell's office.
Finch's young deputy, Leon Panetta—later a nine-term Democratic
congressman and the Clinton White House's last chief of staff—
found the attorney general hardly the ogre he'd imagined. "Like all
such meetings with notorious public figures," Panetta later wrote,
"the actual character is never quite so villainous as you had pictured
him to be. Mitchell, with his pipe, was no exception. He came on
more as a fatherly figure than Machiavellian."

Finch handed Mitchell one of Panetta's statistical breakdowns. "Well, look at this," Mitchell said. "No wonder the Southerners scream about enforcement in the North. There's some justification to that criticism, isn't there?" "That's right," Finch answered, "there are few cases in the North." "Why is that?" Mitchell asked. "It seems to me that if we are after segregation, it's bad wherever it exists." Mitchell knew the administration was not about to tackle de facto housing patterns, but he deliberately invoked the North to aggravate Panetta. Mitchell's aide, Jerris Leonard, vowed to "move on some key Northern systems to help establish some needed law." The meeting was yielding exactly what Nixon had ordered in February 1969: *Find a Northern school district to hit, too.* "Good, let's do that," Mitchell replied. When Panetta tried to argue against extensions for dilatory districts, Mitchell turned the discussion to recent Supreme Court decisions, then brought the meeting to a close. Panetta realized the matter had already been decided in the Oval Office. Mitchell, the winner, had lain down no cards because he didn't need to; Finch, the loser, because he had none.[11]

The president ordered the two cabinet officers to sign a joint statement outlining administration policy. Scribbling on an early draft, Mitchell called for a "PR statement" that would contrast Nixon's "even-handed" and "equitable" enforcement with Kennedy's and Johnson's hostile, anti-Southern approach.[12] Perhaps because all of Washington knew that "Mitchell won and Finch lost," as Ehrlichman put it, Nixon worried that Finch would disown the final product. He told Haldeman:

> *When stmt goes out F*[inch] *must stand up*
> *+ support it*
> *don't give appearance we rolled him . . .*

The Mitchell-Finch compact was finally released on July 3, 1969. Southern segregationists were disappointed to see no extension of timetables beyond the 1969–70 deadlines the Johnson administration had set. The statement also shifted major enforcement responsibility from Finch's HEW to Mitchell's Justice; by that fall, a record number of children sat in desegregated classrooms.[13]

So convulsive were the sixties in American race relations that school desegregation represented only one of several fronts on which African Americans were waging their battle for equality. Nor was it the only race controversy in which Attorney General Mitchell played a decisive role. Another landmark law from the Kennedy-Johnson era, the 1965 Voting Rights Act (VRA), was set to expire in August 1970. It would be Mitchell who decided the Nixon administration's response: whether to extend the act, with or without amendment, or simply let it expire.

Letting VRA lapse was never a viable option. Its enforcement helped enfranchise an estimated 800,000 black Americans. The only advocates for letting the law expire were staunch segregationists like Senator Sam Ervin, the North Carolina Democrat who decried the original law as "repressive" and "contrary to the Constitution"—and who later presided, with great piety, over the Senate Watergate committee. That left reenactment as the only option, the only question whether to amend it or not. Once again, as analyst Michael Barone has written, Nixon "tailored his policies to left-leaning opinion leaders while crafting his rhetoric to propitiate the right-leaning 'silent majority.' "

House Judiciary Committee chairman Emanuel Celler, the feisty Brooklyn Democrat, had introduced legislation extending VRA, without amendment, until 1975. That the new administration despaired of addressing this extraordinarily sensitive issue became clear when the attorney general canceled five scheduled appearances before Celler's committee in six weeks. Southern whites lobbied Mitchell to apply VRA to all fifty states—currently, it applied only to seven, all below the Mason-Dixon Line—and warned the administration it would be breaking faith if it allowed a simple extension.

Privately, Mitchell predicted to the president and GOP leaders that the House "likely will pass a simple five-year extension of the act"; but he agreed, once more, to don the heavy mask Nixon assigned him. Thus, when Mitchell finally took the witness chair before a Judiciary subcommittee, on June 26, he stunned Celler, and even fellow Republicans, by announcing that the Nixon administration opposed the extension of VRA. "I cannot support what amounts to regional legislation," Mitchell testified. "While Congress may have had sufficient reason to pass regional legislation in the 1965 act, I do not believe that this justification exists any longer."

Under the modified extension Mitchell proposed, bans on literacy tests and state residency requirements for presidential elections would be extended nationwide, and a panel would be formed to study voting discrimination. The Nixon-Mitchell plan also authorized the attorney general to dispatch election monitors and file voter-discrimination lawsuits anywhere in America, not just in the seven Southern states covered by the original legislation. Most controversially, it shifted the burden of proof for the validity of new election laws from the states to DOJ. When Celler objected, Mitchell explained that more than 50 percent of eligible black voters in every Southern state were already registered. More voting-age blacks in the Deep South had cast ballots in 1968 than in Watts, Los Angeles; and as the attorney general noted dryly, in his coup de grace, only one-third of those in Celler's beloved Manhattan, Brooklyn, and the Bronx had done so.

Celler harrumphed that the Nixon-Mitchell plan "bristles with complications." But the chairman had a problem: His usual allies—the ACLU, the NAACP, the Leadership Conference on Civil Rights, the U.S. Commission on Civil Rights—had all endorsed Mitchell's proposal for a nationwide ban on literacy tests. Celler likened the Nixon-Mitchell bill to the suggestion that "because you have a flood in Mississippi, you have to build a dam in Idaho." In fact, the eighty-one-year-old Celler simply resented being outfoxed. As leading civil rights historian Hugh Davis Graham has noted, Mitchell, "seizing the reformer's initiative . . . cast Celler and his liberal majority on Judiciary in a conservative role as defenders of the status quo."

In the end, the extended VRA contained Mitchell's nationwide ban on literacy tests, a weakened ban on residency requirements, and, thanks to the intervention of Democratic senators Birch Bayh and Edward M. Kennedy—against Nixon's wishes—full voting rights for eighteen-year-olds. The president signed the Voting Rights Act of 1970 into law on June 22. But as he did so, Nixon announced he was instructing Attorney General Mitchell to launch a swift court challenge against the eighteen-year-old voting provision. On December 21, the U.S. Supreme Court upheld the measure's constitutionality, in the ruling of *Oregon v. Mitchell*.[14]

John Mitchell's signature statement on civil rights turned out to be one of the most memorable pronouncements on the relationship between politics and government ever uttered by an American official. On the morning of July 1, 1969, before Mitchell left for testimony on Capitol Hill, thirty African Americans, joined by one white friend, politely opened the door to Mitchell's outer office, sat down on the available chairs and couches, and—when those filled up—the floor. *We'd like to see the attorney general,* announced the group's leader, Mrs. James Hadnott of Prattville, Alabama. Mitchell's secretary told Mrs. Hadnott the attorney general was busy; Mrs. Hadnott replied that the group members were staging a sit-in to protest Mitchell's desegregation policies and, until he came to see them, they would wait patiently right where they were.

And there they sat—for the next two and a half hours, as news photographers, alerted to the commotion on Justice's fifth floor, clicked away. Finally, Jerris Leonard told the group Mitchell would see them in the Department's auditorium. At the appointed hour, Mitchell heard out the group's grievances, artfully deflating the tension and deploying, as in similar encounters with students and hippies, the old-school Irish charm. But he left the group's members with something to think about. "You will be better advised," he told them, "to watch what we do instead of what we say."[15]

This tantalizing proverb Mitchell later repeated to a group of prominent black leaders, who leaked it to the press. Nothing could have proven Mitchell more correct—that blacks and liberals would *not* pay greater attention to deeds than words—than the furor the attorney general's words created as they reverberated across the country and down through the ages. Where *Fortune* magazine wondered if Mitchell hadn't suffered an "unintentional burst of candor," the *New Yorker* scornfully hailed "the most astonishing admission of high-level duplicity in government history."[16]

Mitchell's own explanations of his famous maxim—boiled down to "watch what we do, not what we say"—changed somewhat over time. PBS' Paul Niven was the first reporter to press him on it, in a December 1969 interview.

NIVEN: When you met with a group of Negroes who had come to your office, you said on one occasion, "Judge us not by what we say but by what we do." What did you mean by that?

MITCHELL: Very simple: that our accomplishments during our administration in the enforcement of the statutes relating to civil rights would speak for themselves and that they would be recognized as such. And there was no sense carrying on large dialogues about what might have been done, or what might *be* done, that we would rather stand on the record than carry on this dialogue that might be presumptuous on our part.

By 1986, when he was last asked to explain his cryptic words, Mitchell—long removed from public life—candidly acknowledged to author Len Colodny the electoral importance of the South and his own impatience with black leaders at the time.

It was very simple. I made it to Coretta King and [Ralph] Abernathy and a lot of the rest of 'em that were screaming about the Nixon civil rights policies. We had [a] double problem, as you know. One was to keep the South happy and the second was to desegregate the schools and carry out the civil rights requirements of the statutes and the court decisions and so forth. And so that was the meaning of it.[17]

The most thoughtful meditation on Mitchell's statement came, ironically, from Daniel Moynihan, who was no fan of Mitchell's—he once wrote privately that he wished Mitchell "acted a bit more lawyer-like"—and who himself had been pilloried by liberals and the news media for suggesting, in a leaked memo to Nixon, that the whole issue of race relations in America might benefit from a bit of "benign neglect." "How much more explicit can one be?" Moynihan asked. "[Mitchell] was saying that the rhetoric of the national government would now change, would now begin to reward other groups, but that the actual conduct of the administration would not change. This is about what happened. If, however, Mitchell expected blacks to see this as an improved, or even as an acceptable, situation he was, of course, asking for disappointment."

"Few grasped," Moynihan concluded, "that Nixon was putting forth a set of administrative and legislative proposals designed fundamentally—and deliberately—to fulfill the promises of the 1960s."[18]

As children prepared to return to school in the summer of 1969, educators in thirty-three Mississippi districts faced especial anxiety. At DOJ's request, the courts had ordered twenty-nine of the districts to be completely desegregated by September 11, the other four by 1970. Mississippi senator John Stennis, the hawkish sixty-seven-year-old Democrat who chaired the Senate Armed Services Committee, lobbied Mitchell for more time, citing the prospect for "public unrest" if desegregation measures were pushed too fast. When Mitchell demurred, Stennis went to the top. He sent President Nixon a handwritten letter containing an implied, but unmistakable, threat: If the desegregation issue required his presence in his home state, Stennis would have to skip the critical vote on the antiballistic missile (ABM) system, a cornerstone in Nixon's national security strategy. Teletyped out to Nixon in San Clemente, Stennis's proposal was clear: If Nixon wanted his ABM system, the Mississippi districts had to have more time.

Mitchell, Finch, and Defense Secretary Melvin Laird all put in calls to Stennis, who was unmoved. Ultimately Nixon exalted cold war missile defense over the complaints of liberal bureaucrats, and made sure Bob Finch understood as much. Under pressure from his own aides, Finch shrugged that he would "call the attorney general and see what can be done." Once again, however, Mitchell, operating behind the scenes, emerged triumphant. Accordingly, the HEW secretary—in a humiliating public repudiation of his own aides' work—wrote to the appellate court on August 19, requesting the Mississippi schools be given until December 1 to submit new plans. The current timetables, Finch said, had been devised "under great stress in approximately three weeks," and would "produce chaos, confusion and a catastrophic educational setback to the 135,700 children, black and white alike, [in] the 222 schools of these Mississippi districts." The Fifth Circuit set a district court hearing in Jackson the following week.

Outraged civil rights groups immediately sued the government, leading to an unprecedented courtroom showdown. On Monday, August 25, Jerris Leonard, representing the federal government, conceded he was "somewhat embarrassed" at having to argue against the administration's previously submitted plans. Roy Reed, the *New York Times*' veteran civil rights reporter, marveled that "the NAACP Legal Defense and Education Fund and the Justice Department for the first time were on opposite sides of a desegregation case." Yet the Court granted Mississippi the delay. Despite all the symbolic rewards Nixon and Mitchell had accorded the white South, this marked the only time the Nixon administration actually intervened to delay school desegregation. The Senate approved the ABM system by a vote of 51 to 50.[19]

At the White House, a reporter asked Nixon whether, in light of the actions in Mississippi, the administration wasn't in "retreat" from *Brown v. Board of Education*. Nixon replied that twice as many schools were desegregated as a year earlier and cast himself as a levelheaded centrist. "There are those who want instant integration and those who want segregation forever," Nixon said. "I believe that we need to have a middle course between those two extremes."[20]

The Supreme Court demanded more. On October 26, 1969, six days after hearing oral arguments from Jerris Leonard and lawyers for the NAACP Legal Defense and Education Fund, the High Court issued its historic ruling in *Alexander v. Holmes County Board of Education*, in which the justices struck down the Fifth Circuit's decision to grant a deadline extension to the thirty-three Mississippi school districts. Calling the case "of paramount importance," Justice Hugo Black, who wrote for the unanimous Court, held public schools could no longer desegregate with "all deliberate speed"—the standard the Court had adopted in *Brown*—but must do so "immediately."

Publicly, Mitchell appeared stunned, telling an interviewer he had believed "the Court would respect the administration's wishes" for more time. *Holmes* now made "instant integration"—a position Nixon had cast as extreme—the law of the land, and ostensibly put the president and the attorney general on the spot: How could they end segregation "immediately" in the 156 dual-system school districts that remained? Some wondered whether Nixon and Mitchell would even honor the Court's decision. In fact, the decision was a gift to Nixon and Mitchell: It focused Southern resentment on the judiciary, not the executive, and allowed the president and attorney general to pose as reluctant executioners of a policy their constituency regarded as hostile. Thus Mitchell assured the nation he would "bring every available resource to bear . . . [to] enforce the mandates issued by the courts pursuant to the Supreme Court decisions."[21]

Now Mitchell had to take action. "Psychological acceptance [is] the key," Nixon told Mitchell, Finch, and Ehrlichman in early 1970, before asking: "Can we get the orders to be more reasonable?" According to Ehrlichman's previously unpublished notes, Mitchell replied: "We can hang our hat on the fact that there were 'plans' before the court in past cases." As Nixon recognized, *Holmes* rendered the Mitchell-Finch compact obsolete; a new comprehensive statement of administration policy was needed. As Haldeman's notes show, the president, to his credit, grasped at once the gravity of the "historic crisis" he faced; the need to cool, rather than inflame, the nation's passions; and the political advantage that could be won if he could, with his statement, reassure the Supreme Court that no more stringent rulings like *Holmes* were necessary.

> *can't go on fuzzing the issue*
> *need to give P. the options—not a single solution*
> *prob. is no one has sat down + done this*
> *we have just reacted—never got ahead of it [. . .]*
> *re: race—no speech before live audience . . .*
> *don't want an emotional response—shld be*
> *sound, reasoned approach—probly wld rather write than*
> *speak [. . .]*
> *this is a very historic crisis—country must not move*
> *in wrong direction—must hit it effectively*
> *in a way that will affect the Court*
> *there's only mileage in this for demagogue—for a man*
> *who <u>wants</u> to be Gov.—<u>not</u> man who has to be P.*
> *have to say in way that doesn't throw down gauntlet to*
> *Court too directly [. . .]*
> *On black issue—just want to take a position*
> *can't be on both sides—get hit both ways*[22]

A forceful act would be better than issuing a statement, Nixon thought. He ordered Mitchell to "move fast" on the development of a constitutional amendment banning compulsory busing as a desegregation tool. "We should bite the bullet and bite it soon," Nixon said. "If it's racism, so be it." Mitchell's performance on busing had actually displeased the president. The issue was coming to a head in Charlotte, North Carolina, where a federal judge had ordered an extensive program of busing, at a cost of $4 million, to combat de facto segregation in the nation's forty-third largest school system. Even Finch found the plan "unusually harsh." In a previously unpublished memorandum to the president, White House congressional liaison Bryce Harlow complained that Mitchell's Justice had argued in court in favor of busing as a valid means of attacking de jure segregation. "Perhaps you were aware of this," Harlow wrote Nixon. "I was not." Morever, Mitchell had expressed "doubt . . . that [DOJ] can make a case against the district court order" in Charlotte. "Therefore," Harlow wrote, "it appears more likely that we will get action indicating administration displeasure and concern from HEW than from Justice."[23]

Ultimately, Nixon decided—for the moment—to abandon the constitutional amendment. Instead, on March 24, 1970, he released an 8,000-word statement whose central thrust, as Evans and Novak reported, was "just as John Mitchell had planned it all the time." On one hand, the manifesto vowed the Nixon administration was "not backing away" from enforcing *Brown*, that it would "disappoint" those who "wish the clock of progress would stop or be turned back to 1953." At the same time, it ordered federal officials "not go beyond the requirements of law in attempting to impose their own judgment on the local school district," and pledged to leave de facto segregation, a product of unregulated housing patterns, in place. The statement's main purpose lay between its thousands of lines: persuading the Supreme Court the Nixon administration was addressing the issue without need for further rulings. "We should not provoke any court," the statement read, "to push a constitutional principle beyond its ultimate limit in order to compel compliance with the court's essential, but more modest, mandate."[24]

To enforce the mandate in *Holmes*—immediate desegregation— Nixon established a cabinet-level committee, chaired by Vice President Agnew, which in turn created regional panels whose members were expected to sell desegregation to the most intransigent members of their communities. As executive director of the committee, the White House named Robert Mardian, the Mitchell loyalist who had, as HEW's general counsel, kept an eye on Finch. "We accomplished in eight months [what] the Democrats couldn't do in fifteen years," Mardian later boasted. He ascribed this success to the regional panels, which included "everybody from some Ku Klux Klanners to the chairman of the NAACP in the state, to work together to get the job done. And we got it done."[25]

Less than ninety days later, Spiro Agnew, perhaps fearful that involvement in race issues could damage his presidential ambitions, asked to be relieved of the assignment. Disgusted, Nixon turned to the most pleasant surprise of his first term: George P. Shultz, the secretary of labor and vice chairman of the desegregation committee. A Princeton-educated former Marine who had taught economics at the Massachusetts Institute of Technology and served as dean of the University of Chicago business school, Shultz possessed the intellectual furniture to grapple with any complex public policy issue; what he lacked was a certain intimidating quality that could be useful with intractable bigots. For this Shultz turned to the attorney general. Years later Shultz recalled Mitchell's belief that desegregation "was going to have to proceed as a legal matter."

John Mitchell was opposed to busing. He didn't like the big busing businesses, although we had to take those cases. And, I think there's good reason to worry about all that busing. I thought that he proceeded with great integrity as far as [desegregation] was concerned. Nixon did, Mitchell did. Although they were capable of devious things, my experience with most people in politics is that they do a lot of political calculating. It's not unusual.[26]

The first of the seven regional panels to visit the White House came from Mississippi. Shultz convened the group in the Roosevelt Room, then watched in silence as the black and white members quarreled ferociously. After two hours, Shultz intervened. By prearrangement, he had the attorney general enter the room, since Mitchell was, in Shultz's words, "known in the South as a tough guy, and on the whole was regarded by whites as sympathetic to their cause."

I asked Mitchell what he planned to do about the schools. "I am attorney general, and I will enforce the law," he growled in his gruff, pipe-smoking way. He offered no judgments about whether this was good, bad or indifferent. "I will enforce the law," he repeated. With that, he left. No nonsense. Both the blacks and whites were impressed.

Shultz repeated this theater for each panel, each time with Mitchell reprising his showstopping cameo. After the attorney general's departure, Shultz would tell the groups: "This discussion has been intense and revealing, but you can see that it's not really relevant. The fact is, desegregation is going to happen, whether you like it or not. You have a great stake in seeing that this effort is managed in a reasonable way."[27]

"We had broken the back of school desegregation by September of 1970," Jerris Leonard later boasted—and the numbers bore him out. Prior to 1969, only 186,000 of 3 million African American children attended desegregated Southern schools. In the fall of 1969, after nine months of Nixon-Mitchell leadership, 600,000 Southern blacks sat in desegregated classrooms; in 1970, the number edged closer to 3 million. "In this sense," concluded civil rights historian Dean

Kotlowski, "Richard Nixon was the greatest school desegregator in American history."[28]

The man who really made it happen was John Mitchell. Without an attorney general committed to enforcing them, the Supreme Court's historic decisions would have been so much wordplay. Mitchell also championed—against resistance inside and outside the Nixon administration—the controversial Philadelphia Plan, a pioneering affirmative-action program that required all Philadelphia-area bidders on federal construction contracts worth more than $500,000 to meet minority-hiring goals. The unprecedented nature—and Republican parentage—of the Philadelphia Plan led civil rights historian Robert R. Detlefsen to conclude, in 1991, that "contrary to conventional wisdom, contemporary federal affirmative action policy owes far more to the likes of John Mitchell, George Shultz and Richard Nixon than to Lyndon Johnson, a fact that stands in sharp contrast to the typical caricatures . . . one finds in contemporary political folklore."[29]

While Nixon and Mitchell never sought, and as a matter of political expedience could never receive, public acclaim for their historic accomplishments in race relations—*watch what we do, not what we say*—Watergate all but ensured their exemplary record would go unnoted in their time. "The people who were perpetuating the Watergate scandal," charged the National Urban League's Vernon Jordan, shortly after Mitchell testified before the Senate Watergate committee, "are the same people who were the architects of the [civil rights] retrenchment, the retreat, of 'benign neglect,' and we see here some cause and effect relationship." What went unmentioned was the huge decrease in the percentage of Southern black children attending segregated schools—from 68 percent in 1968 to 8 percent in 1972—under the leadership of Nixon and Mitchell.[30]

What's more, there were still other areas of substantial progress for blacks—besides affirmative action, voting rights, and school desegregation—in which Attorney General Mitchell cut new ground. It was, for example, Mitchell's Justice that filed the first federal lawsuits charging cities with manipulation of zoning laws to discriminate on the basis of race. These lawsuits won the applause even of Roy Wilkins, the NAACP official better known for telling the press that Mitchell's racial policies made him want to vomit.[31]

Mitchell never minded the diminution of his role, by contemporaries or historians, in the rise of a more color-blind nation. The point was *not* to get credit for it; African Americans, after all, were not going to get Richard Nixon reelected in 1972. It was yet another example of Mitchell colluding in a false public image of himself for Nixon's benefit. "[Mitchell] wasn't a guy to get on a white horse and a sword in his hand and charge down the street," remarked Richard Kleindienst. "I don't think he had any animus towards blacks. I don't think he hated anybody. But I think pragmatically, from the standpoint of the Republican Party and electing a Republican president, I don't think he was very much interested in chasing black votes all over the country."[32]

ROBBING THE PRESIDENT'S DESK

If I found out that the military was spying on a president of the United States, it would worry the hell out of me.

—*W. Donald Stewart, 1974*[1]

A FEW MONTHS after Nixon was sworn in as president, Mitchell and his press secretary, Jack Landau, were traveling in upstate New York, near Vermont, where the attorney general was to give a speech. The two had just checked into their hotel rooms when the telephone rang. On the line was Secretary of State William Rogers, a longtime associate of Nixon's who had served as attorney general under President Eisenhower. Rogers gave Landau a message: "Please tell the attorney general that I do not know what's going on in the Paris peace negotiations." "I said thank you," Landau recalled, "and went to the next room and said the secretary of state would like you to know that, quote, 'I do not know what's going on in the Paris peace negotiations.' And Mitchell looked up at me with this wonderful grin and said, 'He's not *supposed* to know what's going on.' "[2]

That was the way Richard Nixon liked it. His style of governance was highly secretive, and the bold foreign policy thrusts of his presidency—withdrawal from Vietnam, détente with the Soviet Union, the opening to China—hung precariously on constantly shifting lines of wartime "back-channel" communication that the president encouraged, wherein some key players, like Mitchell, Henry Kissinger, and Kissinger's deputy, Alexander Haig, knew what was going on, but others, like the easily foiled Rogers, the wilier defense secretary Melvin Laird, and even the Joint Chiefs of Staff, did not.

Kissinger, whom Mitchell had recruited into the administration, was often at the center of the subterfuge. Nixon admired Kissinger's intellect but suffered no delusions about his loyalty. He was, after all, a Jewish intellectual who had flowered in Nixon's forbidden zone, the Ivy Leagues—Harvard, no less—and spent the '68 primary season advising Nixon's rival, Nelson Rockefeller. But Kissinger's blend of brilliance and unabashed duplicity intrigued Nixon; as the election unfolded, the Harvard professor switched allegiances without blinking an eye, passing classified information about the Paris talks, obtained through his work with the American delegation, to Mitchell.

If Nixon saw in Kissinger a kindred spirit, an equally ruthless realpolitik practitioner who understood the value of deception in the conduct of foreign policy, he also saw through Kissinger's unctuous attempts at flattery ("You do these office press conferences so damned *vell!*"). "Nixon didn't entirely trust Henry, and I can vouch for that," recalled John Ehrlichman. Once, after Kissinger finished a classified cabinet briefing, Nixon snapped: "And there goes Henry, out to call the *Washington Post*." Roiling with insecurities, Kissinger guarded his proximity to Nixon zealously. But he knew better than to try to interpose himself between the president and the man whose counsel Nixon valued most. "Mitchell, so far as I can tell, had no views on foreign policy," Kissinger said in 1995, before correcting himself: "He had no *knowledge* of foreign policy. He had good judgment, and he wanted to make sure things got done properly."[3]

Among the broad range of foreign affairs issues on which Nixon consulted his attorney general were monetary policy (Mitchell was "basically in favor" of abandoning the gold standard), nuclear arms control (he urged American negotiators to demand on-site inspections of Soviet stockpiles), German reunification (on which the pivotal strategy sessions were held in Mitchell's Watergate apartment), and an array of covert operations carried out across the globe.[4] Mitchell was privy to CIA's Project Jennifer, a top-secret plan, with the Hughes Tool Company providing cover, to raise a sunken Soviet submarine.[5] When the White House strong-armed CIA director Richard Helms, a holdover appointee long wary of Nixon, into producing the agency's records on the Cuban Missile Crisis, Mitchell was among the few men permitted to review the documents—heavily sanitized—that Helms supplied.[6] Mitchell knew, before Kissinger, Rogers, or the Joint Chiefs, about Nixon's plans for rapprochement with China.[7] The attorney general sat in on—and composed the official memorandum recording—the somber Oval Office meeting of April 28, 1970, when Nixon informed Rogers and Laird about the incursion into Cambodia.[8] And there Mitchell was again, silently puffing on his pipe, when the president, on September 15, 1970, bluntly ordered CIA to use any means necessary to thwart the inauguration of Chile's newly elected Marxist president, Salvador Allende.[9]

Mitchell sat on the National Security Council and the "40 Committee," an even more elite group that derived its name from the document that created it: National Security Decision Memorandum 40. Chaired by Kissinger, the committee's function, in theory, was to approve CIA's covert operations and monitor the intelligence branches of the armed forces. Helms later recalled Mitchell in these meetings as "sort of a shadowy figure, sometimes asking questions, sometimes being absolutely silent." Mitchell, for his part, eyed the CIA director suspiciously, regarding him as "capable but very devious," a Johnson appointee who "didn't like the Nixon administration or anything about it." The attorney general's dislike for Helms mirrored Nixon's own, and anticipated the director's—and CIA's—later intrigues in Watergate. "Dick Helms would knock off his grandmother," Mitchell would later say.[10]

Of all the foreign policy councils on which Mitchell sat, the most

time-consuming and least productive was, by far, the "little committee" that was formed to keep Henry Kissinger on an even emotional
keel. The national security adviser conducted a daily battle with Bill
Rogers, who, excluded from critical decisions, often made ill-timed
and ill-informed public pronouncements, gaffes that drove Kissinger
mad and generated more than one emotional threat of resignation. At
first, Nixon took Kissinger's side; later he realized Kissinger himself
was the problem, and asked the attorney general, El Supremo, to rein
him in.[11]

Both Kissinger and Rogers were "acting childish and unpleas-
antly," H. R. Haldeman recalled. "We brought Mitchell in frequently
as a heavyweight to try and deal with the two of them and get them
back on the track. I had to do a lot of that, but there were times when
I couldn't cope with it, and Nixon would ask Mitchell to come in on
it." But as Nixon's esteem for Kissinger waned, and Mitchell gave up
trying to mediate the ceaseless feud with Rogers, the president turned
increasingly to Kissinger's deputy, Colonel Alexander Haig, perhaps
the era's shrewdest practitioner of palace politics, for national security
advice and help in tempering Kissinger's emotionalism.[12]

A former aide to General Douglas MacArthur and Cyrus R.
Vance, secretary of the army under President Kennedy, the physically
vigorous Haig moved more easily among hawkish Democrats and
Pentagon generals than Kissinger's left-leaning staff, which Haig, with
a snicker, dubbed "the Harvard faculty." But Haig was as effusive and
insincere a flatterer of his boss as Kissinger was of Nixon, leading
Kissinger to remark once, quite in error, that Haig was the only aide
he could fully trust. Mitchell at first took little notice of Haig, but
later saw in him a "Machia-fucking-vellian . . . psychopath."[13]

In such an atmosphere it was natural—inevitable—that leaks and
internal spying would flourish. Indeed, under Nixon, unauthorized
disclosures of classified material to the news media reached a kind of
zenith, with the timeliness, depth, and scope of government secrets

splashed across front pages far exceeding anything policymakers had ever before confronted. Since these were violations of law, Attorney General Mitchell played a central role in the Nixon administration's determined effort to stanch them.

The battle was joined shortly after Nixon's hundredth day in office, with the publication in the *New York Times*, on May 9, 1969, of William Beecher's front-page story "Cambodia Raids Go Unprotested." Beecher accurately reported that B-52 bomber planes had secretly attacked North Vietnamese supply depots in Cambodia, the ostensibly neutral border country the North had long used as a base of operations. Though Beecher's report generated no public outcry—unlike the firestorm that erupted four years later, when the secret bombing of Cambodia was revealed in greater depth—the story enraged Kissinger.[14]

From Key Biscayne, Florida, where he and Nixon were staying, the national security adviser wasted no time calling FBI director J. Edgar Hoover, demanding the Bureau undertake a "major effort" to identify who was behind this "extraordinarily damaging . . . very dangerous" leak. Later that day, Hoover called Kissinger back with the prompt assessment that the Beecher story, and others he had recently published, "probably" relied on leaks from a member of Kissinger's own staff at NSC. According to Hoover, a livid Kissinger vowed to "destroy whoever did this if we can find him, no matter where he is." Hoover named several suspects, and by 6:00 p.m. that night, the home telephone of one such staff member, Morton Halperin—also staying in Key Biscayne that weekend—was placed under surveillance. Under current laws, no court order was required for the national security wiretap, only the signature of the attorney general, which Hoover sought, and got, three days later.[15]

Thus began a wiretapping program that continued for the next twenty-one months, expanding to include twelve government officials and four prominent newsmen. In May 1973, fourteen months after Mitchell resigned as attorney general, and one year after Hoover's death, the *Times*, fittingly, exposed the program, which later figured prominently at Nixon's impeachment hearings. Mitchell was questioned under oath on the subject five times: first by the FBI in May 1973; again, briefly, that July, in his appearances before the Senate Watergate committee; by staff lawyers for the Watergate Special Prosecution Force that December; and twice more in July 1974, first by investigators for the House Judiciary Committee, then by lawmakers in public session. The records of Mitchell's classified interrogations by the Watergate prosecutors and the House investigators are previously unpublished.

At first, responding to questions from two FBI agents in his New York law office on May 11, 1973—the day after his indictment in the Vesco case—Mitchell maintained that he "never saw nor approved any such requests" for wiretaps, that "none were submitted to him by the FBI." He said he received no fruits from the wiretaps and claimed to have first learned about the whole program in "the spring or summer" of 1969. How likely was it, the agents pressed, that the attorney general would be unaware of the FBI wiretapping prominent journalists as well as senior officials at the NSC, Pentagon, and State Department? Mitchell said it wouldn't have been unusual for him to have been unaware of the program "at its inception." Director Hoover, he contended, would often "circumvent the attorney general's office" on sensitive matters, and deal directly with the president. Mitchell claimed he warned either Kissinger or Alexander Haig—the wiretaps' chief consumer—that the program was "explosive," and urged a halt to the "dangerous game we were playing."[16]

These answers did not stand for long. Two days later, the acting FBI director, William Ruckelshaus, a former Mitchell aide, announced at a news conference that all of the records relating to the 1969–71 wiretaps had been retrieved from the White House safe of John Ehrlichman, where they had been relocated in the summer of 1971.[17] Ruckelshaus said the records revealed that Mitchell had personally approved the wiretaps, and had even assured Hoover, mistakenly, that no record of them existed.[18] Mitchell promptly dashed off a "personal and confidential" letter to Ruckelshaus demanding to know the basis for both assertions. "My purpose in writing," Mitchell said, was "not to generate a confrontation with the FBI . . . but to obtain factual information which, if it exists, is contrary to my best recollection."[19]

Ruckelshaus responded with a "top secret" letter in which he revealed that the FBI had discovered fifteen wiretap authorization forms signed and submitted by Hoover, each approved with Mitchell's own signature, the earliest dated May 12, 1969. One form featured Mitchell's handwritten request that the device be "installed as soon as possible," another his scribbled notation that a "higher authority"—meaning Nixon—had "requested that this be done immediately."[20] A third FBI document, captioned "Request for Electronic Surveillance by Attorney General and President," recorded Mitchell's order, in September 1969, for the placement of "immediate electronic surveillance (wiretap)" on CBS News correspondent Marvin Kalb. Mitchell further requested the transcripts be sent "only to Mr. Ehrlichman . . . and himself." That same day, Hoover sent over, and Mitchell signed, the by-now-standard authorization form for the Kalb wiretap.[21] Also unearthed was Hoover's handwritten note recording Mitchell's mistaken assurance that all of these documents had been destroyed. An angry Ruckelshaus all but accused Mitchell of lying to the FBI:

At the time you were interviewed by FBI special agents on May 11, 1973, and denied that you had seen or approved any such requests from the FBI for wiretap coverage, we had not recovered the FBI file material and, accordingly, the agents were not in a position to apprise you that direct evidence to the contrary existed.[22]

Thus by July 1973, when Mitchell testified before the Senate Watergate committee, the evidentiary picture had changed considerably. When Chief Counsel Sam Dash, a hostile interrogator, asked if Mitchell had been "aware of the leaking and those wiretaps," Mitchell answered with great caution. "I find it very hard to give you a specific answer other than the fact that, yes, I was," Mitchell testified. "To what extent, I do not know." *Didn't the taps require the attorney general's authorization?* Mitchell agreed the FBI "probably" wouldn't have operated without it. Then he mentioned that as attorney general, he had instituted a rule mandating all national security wiretaps be reauthorized every ninety days. However, pointing this out was, at best, a ruse; for while Mitchell had indeed enacted such a rule, it was, as he well knew, never observed in the case of the 1969–71 taps. As Ruckelshaus had noted, the Bureau's review found "no ninety-day continuations were apparently sought," despite the fact that some taps remained in place much longer—nearly two years, in Halperin's case.[23]

When the Watergate prosecutors interviewed him about the wiretap program, in December 1973, Mitchell, perhaps fearing indictment, abandoned the ruse and other key aspects of his earlier testimony. According to the only record of this interrogation, previously unpublished, Mitchell still maintained he did not recall signing any authorizations, especially for the tap on White House speechwriter William Safire, which Mitchell said would have "raised my eyebrows." However, Mitchell also "admitted that probably the project did not comply with the departmental regulations" requiring reauthorization every ninety days. And where Mitchell had told the FBI he was "unaware of any summaries . . . setting forth the results of these wiretaps," he now acknowledged having received directly from Hoover "a limited number of summaries . . . which were kept in his safe." Mitchell had no choice but to admit as much, as the documents showed he had explicitly ordered the data from the Kalb tap routed to Ehrlichman and himself. Finally, Mitchell renounced his claim that he first learned of the program months after its inception, saying he "knew the wiretap information was originally sent to Haig."[24]

Despite the fifteen authorization forms bearing his signature, Mitchell never acknowledged signing them to any of the investigators who interrogated him during the Watergate era. "A pipe dream," he told *Time* in February 1973. "Wiretaps on reporters were never authorized by me."[25] As late as July 1974, he told the House Judiciary

Committee he "[did] not recall specifically authorizing any wiretaps himself."[26] That same year, Richard Kleindienst said Mitchell "told me once that he had not authorized them."[27] Not until 1987, to author Len Colodny, did Mitchell finally acknowledge—haltingly, almost begrudgingly—his true role in the affair.

> **COLODNY:** It's either gonna be Kissinger, Haig or Haldeman. . . . Because those taps were only authorized by those people. Or requested. I'm sorry; you authorized all of them. They, they requested them.
>
> **MITCHELL:** Gosh, Len, I, um—they, um—after those meetings they had—I'm talking about, ah, Nixon, Kissinger, Hoover, and so forth and so on—ah, they sort of came over and, as I recall, in a bunch. And they, ah—the way it was handled was that, uh, Hoover would take and put together the back-up material, and, um, uh, send it over to my office for consideration. And I'd look at it, with the background I had, [and] *would authorize it.*[28]

In the end, Mitchell's deceptions were unnecessary. As Ruckelshaus wrote, the FBI found no basis to suggest the wiretaps were anything "other than lawful." This view was echoed by Ruckelshaus's successor, Elliot Richardson, who so advised the Senate Foreign Relations Committee, in writing, in September 1973. Even Winston Lord, one of the wiretapped NSC aides, recognized the valid concerns underpinning the surveillance. "At the time when this apparently took place," Lord told CBS News in May 1973, "there were massive leaks affecting national security, and I think the administration had a responsibility to try to stop those leaks."[29]

Early on Sunday morning, June 13, 1971, four months after the NSC wiretaps were shut off for good, the phone rang in Mitchell's Watergate apartment. Melvin Laird, the secretary of defense, was on the line. When Mel Laird wanted to talk, Mitchell took the call. A Nebraska native and World War II veteran, Laird began serving in the Wisconsin state legislature in 1946, when he was twenty-four. By 1952, he was elected to Congress, where he remained for the next sixteen years, serving on the House Appropriations Committee. Nixon chose Laird to run the Pentagon because he was popular on Capitol Hill; but if he imagined Laird would simply accept his and Kissinger's deceptions, as Rogers did, the president was disappointed. One Pentagon insider recalled Laird habitually exceeding Nixon's troop withdrawal orders in Vietnam: "Mel Laird *never* did what the President told him to do. He would frequently do just the opposite."[30]

Now, on this Sunday morning in June 1971, Laird wanted Mitchell's advice. The defense secretary was about to appear on *Face the Nation* and wanted to know what he should say if he was questioned about that morning's front-page story in the *Times*, by Neil Sheehan, headlined "Vietnam Archive: Pentagon Study Traces 3 Decades of Growing U.S. Involvement." The story described how Robert S. McNamara, secretary of defense under Presidents Kennedy and Johnson, had commissioned a massive internal study entitled "History of U.S. Decision-Making Process on Vietnam Policy," consisting of several thousand classified documents and dubbed the Pentagon Papers—which the *Times* had obtained and was now publishing in serial form. Mitchell, according to an aide, "hadn't even seen the paper yet." "Just tell them that you've referred it to the Justice Department," Mitchell advised, "and don't say anything else."[31]

Ironically, Laird was not asked about the story that morning, even though his questioners included a *Times* correspondent—a breach of corporate synergy unimaginable in later years. Sheehan's article met with like indifference at the White House. Entirely ignorant of the Pentagon Papers, Nixon skipped over the *Times* story, his concerns that morning fixed instead on obtaining the latest Vietnam casualty figures and reviewing the press coverage of his daughter Tricia's wedding. Not until Nixon asked Alexander Haig, halfway through a casual telephone conversation, "Nothing else of interest in the world today?" did anyone even discuss the matter with him. Yes, Haig said, there was something "very significant" going on: "This Goddamn *New York Times* expose of the most highly classified documents of the war." Nixon asked if the documents had been leaked out of the Pentagon. Haig explained that McNamara had commissioned the study, and that it had been compiled by "the peaceniks over there"—a snide reference to Halperin and other Kissinger aides.[32]

Several accounts of the Pentagon Papers have pointed to Nixon's next call that Sunday afternoon—one he received—as decisive in changing his outlook, from indifferent opportunism to punitive fury. The caller was Kissinger, then in California. In his memoir, *The Ends of Power*, H. R. Haldeman claimed Kissinger aggressively needled Nixon to impress upon him the seriousness of the *Times*' challenge to his authority. "It shows you're a weakling, Mr. President," Haldeman quoted Kissinger as saying. "The fact that some idiot can publish all of the diplomatic secrets of this country on his own is damaging to your image, as far as the Soviets are concerned, and it could destroy our ability to conduct foreign policy. If the other powers feel that we can't control internal leaks, they will never agree to secret negotiations."[33]

In a 1995 interview, Kissinger rejected the widely accepted notion that he incited Nixon into unwisely aggressive action in the Pentagon Papers case. The former national security adviser acknowledged only that he favored legal action to halt further publication. "I thought the government had a duty to protect its secrets," he said. "People have to remember: The Pentagon Papers did not affect Nixon at all. None of the Pentagon Papers dealt with the Nixon administration. They all [*sic*] dealt with the Johnson administration. Nothing would have been easier than to get political benefit from them and say, 'This is what we inherited, see the mess?' So neither Nixon nor I had any concern that it was any damage to us, personally. But we felt that if the government didn't protect its secrets, the whole apparatus would be in danger."[34]

The "apparatus," of course, was not merely the foreign policy process as it existed on organizational charts, but the elaborate network of secret back-channels, in and out of government, that Nixon and Kissinger used to conduct war and diplomacy. Nixon sought no injunctions or prosecutions that Sunday. The president expressed contempt for the *Times*—especially that "bastard," Sheehan, and the paper's Washington bureau chief, "that damn Jew [Max] Frankel"— but instead of ordering a swift and massive counteroffensive, Nixon mused aloud about letting some time pass: "If the statute of limitations is a year . . . we can charge them then . . . just go in and . . . subpoena all these bastards and bring the case." Indeed, when Haldeman repeated Haig's argument that immediate action would only escalate the crisis, Nixon replied: "I think he's right."

The *Times* published its second installment of the Papers on Monday morning, under the headline "Vietnam Archive: A Consensus to Bomb Developed Before '64 Election, Study Says." The accompanying documents showed the Johnson administration had secretly developed plans for full-scale aerial attacks on North Vietnam even as the White House castigated the president's GOP opponent, Barry Goldwater, for advocating the same tactic. Entering the Oval Office shortly after noon, Haig made the first mention to the president of the name of the culprit behind the massive leak. "Ellsberg," Nixon repeated. "I've never heard of him."

The son of Midwestern Jews who converted to Christian Science, Daniel Ellsberg, then forty, was a former Marine who had earned his undergraduate and doctoral degrees and returned to teach at Harvard. There he became a leading exponent of the theory of "madness" as an instrument of national security policymakers—cutting-edge stuff in the mid-fifties—and received an invitation to lecture on "the conscious political use of irrational military threats" from his more distinguished colleague, Henry Kissinger. Ellsberg completed two tours of Vietnam, as a Pentagon consultant for the RAND Corporation think tank and later as a member of the counterinsurgency team led by Major General Edward G. Lansdale in Saigon. Once a proponent of the war, Ellsberg returned to the States in 1967 harboring grave doubts about the efficacy, and morality, of continued American involvement in it. In 1969, through contacts at RAND, Ellsberg obtained a set of the Pentagon Papers and began reading the study in its entirety. He spent the next two years hardening in his opposition to the war, and in his antipathy for Kissinger. Early efforts to make the Papers public through members of Congress failed, and not until he contacted the *Times'* Sheehan, to whom he had previously leaked information, did Ellsberg find a willing partner in the largest unauthorized disclosure of classified material in American history.

Now, on the second day of Sheehan's series, the Nixon administration had zeroed in on Ellsberg as the likely culprit. Attorney General Mitchell, undisturbed by Sunday's report, heard again from Laird on Monday morning, and this time, according to Mitchell, the defense secretary advised that continued publication of the Papers would harm the national defense.[35] Mitchell decided to act. In a telephone call Monday evening, Ehrlichman told the president that Mitchell wanted approval for DOJ to send a cease-and-desist telegram to the *Times* before Tuesday's editions came out. "Hell, I wouldn't prosecute the *Times*," Nixon replied. "My view is to prosecute the Goddamn pricks that gave [the Papers] to them." Seconds later, Nixon had Mitchell on the line. "What is your advice on this *Times* thing, John?" the president asked. "You would like to do it?" Nixon assumed he and Mitchell both knew what he was talking about. "I would believe so, Mr. President," Mitchell replied. "Otherwise, we will look a little foolish in not following through on our legal obligations."

Nixon then announced that Kissinger had joined them on a separate line. Kissinger promptly conveyed to Nixon and Mitchell the view—which he attributed to former president Johnson and Walt Rostow, Kissinger's predecessor as national security adviser—that the *Times* series represented "an attack on the whole integrity of government. . . . If whole file cabinets can be stolen and then made available to the press, you can't have orderly government anymore." Mitchell agreed to initiate an "undercover investigation," but couldn't resist a dig at Kissinger. "We've got some information we've developed as to where these copies are and who . . . leaked them," Mitchell said. "And the prime suspect, according to your friend Rostow you're quoting, is a gentleman by the name of Ellsberg."

Mitchell crafted the telegram to the *Times*, and sent it off shortly after Nixon approved the gesture; final authority over its language, however, belonged to Mitchell. Addressed to *Times* publisher Arthur Ochs Sulzberger, the telegram read:

I have been advised by the Secretary of Defense that the material published in the *New York Times* on June 13, 14 1971 captioned "key texts from Pentagon's Vietnam Study" contains information relating to the national defense of the United States and bears a top secret classification.

As such, publication of this information is directly prohibited by the provisions of the Espionage Law, Title 18, United States Code, Section 793.

Moreover, further publication of information of this character will cause irreparable injury to the defense interests of the United States.

Accordingly, I respectfully request that you publish no further information of this character and advise me that you have made arrangements for the return of these documents to the Department of Defense.

Mitchell's communiqué left unspoken what consequences would befall the *Times* if it continued publishing the Papers, but the attorney general's invocation of the espionage statute left little doubt what he had in mind. The *Times'* senior management split on whether to continue with further installments. When publisher Sulzberger weighed in from London with permission to publish a third install-ment, the *Times* responded to Mitchell's telegram with a terse public statement:

> We have received the telegram from the attorney general ask-ing the *Times* to cease further publication of the Pentagon's Vietnam study. The *Times* must respectfully decline the re-quest of the attorney general, believing it is in the interest of the people of this country to be informed of the material con-tained in this series.

That night, the *Times'* Tuesday edition rolled off the presses, its front page featuring Sheehan's third installment, headlined: "Vietnam Archive: Study Tells How Johnson Secretly Opened Way to Ground Combat." But that was not the paper's lead story; that holy real es-tate, four columns across, was reserved for the headline topping Max Frankel's piece: "Mitchell Seeks to Halt Series on Vietnam but *Times* Refuses." A newspaper series documenting the duplicitous conduct of the Vietnam War by the Kennedy and Johnson administrations had now been transformed into what Mitchell would later call a "monumental lawsuit" over the scope of press freedom, pitting the Nixon administration against the world's most influential newspaper. Mitchell's central role in the legal battle over the Pentagon Papers ce-mented his image as the supreme authoritarian of modern times, the keeper of evil secrets and enforcer of unjust laws. Yet in the ensuing blur of motions, injunctions, and rulings—amidst which selections from the Papers were published by seventeen other newspapers, only three of them enjoined by the government, and in which the U.S. Supreme Court would ultimately rule in favor of continued publica-tion—Mitchell played virtually no day-to-day role. Where the attor-ney general *did* remain deeply immersed was in the investigation to determine responsibility for the leak—and in the daily assuagement of his high-strung client.

The Pentagon Papers excited Richard Nixon's passions and prejudices like no other event of his presidency. That Daniel Ellsberg, the culprit, was a creature of Harvard University and the liberal think tanks; that he had been a Kissinger protégé and a confidant of those *disloyalistas* purged from Kissinger's office, like Mort Halperin, on whose residential wiretap FBI agents had overheard Ellsberg's voice no less than fifteen times; and that Ellsberg was, by his own description, a Jew, like Halperin and Leslie Gelb, who had actually overseen the preparation of the Pentagon Papers; all this proved too much for Nixon to bear. Finally, when DOJ reported that a set of the Papers had reached the Soviet embassy, the affair served to crystallize a quarter century of Nixon's deepest beliefs and fears: namely, that there existed a vast left-wing conspiracy, in and out of government, led by Jewish intellectuals and their handmaidens in academia, the news media, and hostile think tanks, that was bent on destroying postwar America and Nixon himself.

Throughout the affair, the president alternated between strategizing how best to exploit the leak for partisan advantage, demanding Ellsberg's head, and decrying the deviousness and disloyalty of the Jews. "Can you haul in that son-of-a-bitch Ellsberg right away?" Nixon asked Mitchell three days into the *Times* series. Nailing the antiwar intellectual, who spent ten days underground before surrendering to authorities in Boston, consumed Nixon as wholly as the pursuit of Alger Hiss, the Soviet spy, had a generation earlier. "What we're up against here is an enemy worse than the Communists," Nixon told Haldeman and Kissinger on July 1. And in Nixon's mind, both cold war menaces, the communists and the antiwar left, shared a common, defining element: the Jews. Day after day, the president of the United States sat in the White House and stewed in the basest anti-Semitism: There was Frankel, "that damn Jew," and the culprit, derisively tagged "Ell*stein*," elsewhere referred to simply as "the Jew."[36]

With Mitchell, however, the president was careful to express his anti-Semitism in guarded terms, even apologetically. "You can never put, John, any [judge] who is a Jew on a civil rights case, or freedom-of-the-press kind of case, and get even a 10 percent chance [of a favorable ruling]," he told Mitchell on June 22, after an adverse ruling by a Jewish judge. "Basically, who the hell are these people that stole the papers? It's too bad. *I'm sorry.* I was hoping one of them would be a Gentile. [Laughter] . . . The three Jews—Gelb—the three suspects. All Jews." Nixon's apology for his anti-Semitism here was unique; no other example of such an expression can be heard on the Nixon tapes. And Mitchell, so far as can be ascertained from the thousands of pages of White House tape transcripts that have entered the public domain, never responded in kind—as other advisers, like Haldeman, Charles Colson, and Ron Ziegler, often did.

Indeed, it was during the Pentagon Papers crisis that Mitchell's aquiline demeanor began, for the first time, to *bother* the president. On the evening of June 19, after a federal judge granted an initial injunction against the *Times*—a historic order, the first time in American history a court had stopped a newspaper from publishing an article—Nixon called Mitchell to emphasize that while litigation was fine enough, paramount importance lay in pressing the administration's case in the court of public opinion. "Get some strong language, like 'a massive breach of security,' things of that sort . . . in the public mind," the president said. "We're not just interested in making the technical case for the lawyers. . . . Use some really high-flown adjectives." Mitchell agreed, assuring the president—with open sarcasm—that all court filings would be cleared through the White House, "so your phrase-coiners and word-makers can get a crack at it." It was Mitchell's way of saying: The attorney general would mind the law; Nixon and his junior ad men could tinker with adjectives.

But the president thought Mitchell missed the point, failed to grasp the lessons of the Hiss case. "Don't worry about [Ellsberg's] trial," Nixon ordered the attorney general on June 30. "Just get everything out. Try him in the press. Try him in the press. Everything, John, that there is on the investigation—get it out, leak it out. We want to destroy him in the press. Press. Is that clear?" The following morning, Nixon complained to Haldeman and Kissinger that Mitchell lacked the necessary ruthlessness to handle the case. "We won the Hiss case in the papers," the president explained.

> I had to leak stuff all over the place. John Mitchell doesn't understand that sort of thing. He's a good lawyer. It's hard to him. . . . But what I mean is we have to develop a new program, a program for leaking out information. We're destroying these people in the papers. . . . I know how to play this game and we're going to start playing it.[37]

The following day, Nixon's dissatisfaction reached its apex, as the president ordered Mitchell excluded from a strategy session on the Pentagon Papers—"he doesn't see it clearly"—and spoke longingly of a glorious future unburdened by his upright former law partner, campaign manager, and cabinet heavyweight. "Actually, when Mitchell leaves as attorney general," Nixon told Haldeman, "we're going to be better off in my view. . . . John is just too damn good a lawyer, you know. He's a good, strong lawyer. It just repels him to do these horrible things, but they've got to be done."[38]

Horrible things—including the burglary and ransacking of Ellsberg's psychiatrist's office—were not far off. The burglary was the work of the White House Special Investigations Unit, better known as "the Plumbers," a team of leak-plugging covert operatives assembled, on Nixon's order, following the sluggish performance in the investigation of the Pentagon Papers by J. Edgar Hoover and the FBI. As Nixon later confirmed, Mitchell opposed the Plumbers' creation; nor did he learn of their break-in at the Los Angeles office of Dr. Lewis Fielding, Ellsberg's former psychiatrist, until June 1972, some nine months after the fact.[39] Just two weeks after the break-in, Mitchell displayed his ignorance of the Plumbers' ongoing operations, but also his tolerance for "a little bit of dirty tricks," in an Oval Office strategy session with

Nixon, Haldeman, Ehrlichman, and Colson. The group was discussing Nixon's demand to "hang FDR and Truman" via swift declassification of incriminating old documents.

> EHRLICHMAN: God, there's a ton of paper in this crazy thing. . . . It's a life's work. . . . [T]o go through this stuff is nearly impossible . . .
>
> NIXON: I don't understand it. And we just don't have anybody worth a damn fighting our side of it. I have to go up to bat all the time myself.
>
> MITCHELL: Can we get somebody that could devote full time to this project that's knowledgeable?
>
> NIXON: We have that.
>
> EHRLICHMAN: We do have that, John, and we've got [Plumbers supervisors] Bud Krogh and Dave Young virtually full time on this with three other people. [. . .]
>
> MITCHELL: John Ehrlichman was talking about somebody that's on our side 100 percent, is knowledgeable about foreign affairs, could devote his whole time to this thing and has a little bit of dirty tricks to play.
>
> HALDEMAN: David Young?
>
> MITCHELL: Well, Young is off the NSC staff and knows where all the bodies are buried in that group . . .
>
> EHRLICHMAN: Well, we have a couple of fellows under Krogh—Liddy and Hunt—who know what they're doing and have been around.[40]

As mention of Liddy and Hunt portended, publication of the Pentagon Papers marked a watershed in the Nixon presidency. Leaks were now at the very top of the president's agenda. The White House adopted a "reverse of the legal burden of proof," under which, as Haldeman aide Gordon Strachan later testified, "You had to be able to establish that you were *not* the source of the leak." The summer of 1971 also brought Nixon's first wish for Mitchell's replacement at Justice. The problem was not Mitchell's intelligence, diligence, or loyalty—all beyond question—but, rather, his innate civility, his reverence for the law, his opposition to the Plumbers, and his reluctance to use raw investigative data to smear Ellsberg in the press.[41]

Nixon always assumed left-wing bureaucrats, opposed to his conduct of the Vietnam War, were to blame for the steady stream of damning, damaging leaks, and that his attorney general had become a liability in the battle to stop them. But the next major leak crisis to bedevil the administration, the most serious of all, revealed Nixon was wrong in both assumptions. It was not the liberal left that was most actively sabotaging his national security policies, but the conservative right; not lowly pencil pushers buried in the civilian bureaucracy, but the most senior uniformed commanders at the Pentagon. And when the eyes of the commander-in-chief were opened to this astonishing revelation, it was Mitchell who again emerged as the indispensable figure, the strong man of the Nixon presidency.

At 6:09 p.m. on December 21, 1971, the president summoned Mitchell for an extremely rare—and tense—evening session in the Oval Office. Also present were Haldeman and Ehrlichman. The men had gathered to discuss a crisis unique in American history—"a federal offense of the highest order," as Nixon termed it that night. Just days before, Navy Yeoman Charles Radford, a lanky young stenographer attached to the Joint Chiefs of Staff (JCS) liaison office with the NSC, had confessed to a Defense Department interrogator that, for more than a year, he had been passing thousands of top-secret NSC documents to his superiors at the Pentagon. Radford had obtained the documents by systematically rifling burn bags, interoffice envelopes, even the briefcases of Kissinger and Haig. According to the yeoman, he had given the documents to his supervisors, two admirals, who had in turn passed them to Admiral Thomas H. Moorer, chairman of the Joint Chiefs, and occasionally to Admiral Elmo Zumwalt, the chief of naval operations, among others. It was, in short, an unprecedented case of internal espionage at the highest levels—in wartime.[42]

Like so much of the internecine intrigue of the Watergate era, the military spying had its origins in the Kennedy-Johnson years. Kennedy and the Joint Chiefs developed a mutual distrust after the Cuban Missile Crisis, as documented on Kennedy's own White House tapes; and LBJ, in the early stages of the Vietnam War, made a virtual science of circumventing the chiefs. By August 1967, they bordered on mutiny: After Secretary of Defense Robert McNamara sharply undercut the chiefs in congressional testimony, they met "in complete secrecy, late into the night," to plot retaliation. JCS chairman Earle Wheeler advocated resignation en masse; the others agreed. Only with Wheeler's withdrawal, amid acute chest pains, did the plot, undisclosed until the 1980s, collapse.[43]

By decade's end, the chiefs had come to regard their NSC liaison office, with its perch inside the White House complex, as a kind of intelligence asset, a means through which the brass could monitor national security policymaking in successive, and increasingly secretive, administrations. Even before the end of the Johnson presidency, the liaison office was being used for clandestine purposes, "doing end-runs around the secretary of state and secretary of defense . . . sometimes the whole Cabinet and national security structure," Mel Laird recalled. "I don't think Clark Clifford or McNamara really realized it, but I knew what they were doing, because . . . I had a lot of friends in the military that had warned me about it."[44]

In April 1970, Nixon elevated Admiral Moorer, a fifty-eight-year-old native of Mt. Willing, Alabama, to chairman of the Joint Chiefs. High school valedictorian and Naval Academy graduate, Moorer was a cocksure aviator whose early career, in the thirties, saw him piloting fighter planes off the decks of aircraft carriers. On December 7, 1941, Lieutenant Moorer was serving with Patrol Squadron 22 at Pearl Harbor, one of the few pilots that dark day to get a plane into the air. He drew as the attack's central lesson: "Why didn't you buy more defense?" Decorated for valor in combat, Moorer swiftly ascended through the ranks, making admiral and becoming head of the Pacific Fleet by 1964. He also tended toward insubordination, criticizing his superiors in memoranda and meetings. When he publicly called Vietnam a "dirty little war," the Johnson White House rebuked him.[45]

As JCS chairman under Nixon and Kissinger, Moorer only hardened in his view of the civilian command. According to a Defense Department study, the chairman "often found his and the chiefs' advice disregarded by the president and the secretary of defense." It is true that Moorer helped Nixon and Kissinger direct the 1970 Cambodian operation, and backed their decision, in February 1971, to provide tactical support for missions in Laos. Moorer also orchestrated the mining of Haiphong Harbor in May 1972 and the subsequent "Christmas bombing" of the North. Yet Nixon and Kissinger only intermittently included Moorer and the chiefs in planning, something on which the generals and admirals, conditioned by Kennedy and Johnson, had already reckoned. Enlisted in devious end-runs around others, like Laird, the chiefs knew better than to imagine they were not also being played.[46]

And for what? Despite Nixon's reputation as a staunch anticommunist, his foreign policy as president—withdrawal from Vietnam, engagement with China, détente with the Soviets—alarmed the chiefs, as did the heavy hand of Kissinger. Admiral Zumwalt saw Kissinger as a dangerous appeaser who believed "the dynamics of history are on the side of the Soviet Union [and] that before long the USSR will be the only superpower on earth." Certain facts on the ground fueled this alarmism. Every day of the Nixon presidency, it seemed, fresh headlines heralded the Soviets' ascendancy in strategic weapons production, and Washington's attendant retreat from postwar hegemony. "American Power Margin Is Slipping" cried the *Washington Post*. "Parity" became the era's grim watchword.

Nixon, for his part, grew to despise the brass. More than once, he angrily shouted at Moorer—unusual for this commander-in-chief, who invariably shrank from personal confrontation—and expressed contempt for the chairman's slipperiness in war planning sessions. "I don't want any more of this crap about the fact that we couldn't hit this target or that one!" Nixon thundered at one point. "Goddamn it, the military, they're a bunch of greedy bastards!" he ranted in April 1971. "They want more officers' clubs and more men to shine their shoes. The sons of bitches are not interested in this country."[47]

From this long-simmering cauldron of suspicion and deceit bubbled the high-stakes espionage case that drew Mitchell, Haldeman, and Ehrlichman to the Oval Office on the chilly evening of December 21, 1971. The matter had begun a week earlier, as yet another leak investigation. Syndicated columnist Jack Anderson, a thorn in Nixon's side since the fifties, had published a series of columns detailing the deliberations of the Washington Special Action Group (WSAG), an elite crisis management group comprised of senior State, Defense, and CIA officials, and chaired by Kissinger. The group had been weighing options for U.S. action on the Asian subcontinent, where chronic tensions between India and Pakistan had erupted into full-scale war. Personally distrustful of Indira Gandhi, the Indian prime minister, the president had secretly ordered Kissinger, despite public professions of neutrality, to find ways to bolster Islamabad, which had used its good back-channel offices to foster Nixon's opening to China.[48]

Anderson had somehow obtained five top-secret White House and Defense Department memoranda, as well as minutes of the WSAG meetings of December 3–4, the day war broke out. "I am getting hell every half hour from the president that we are not being tough enough on India," the minutes quoted Kissinger as saying. "He doesn't believe we're carrying out his wishes. He wants to tilt in favor of Pakistan."[49]

Coming so soon after the Pentagon Papers, and after publication a month later, also in the *Times*, of classified data relating to the Strategic Arms Limitation Treaty (SALT) negotiations with the Soviet Union—a national security breach that convinced the president "his very ability to govern was threatened"—Anderson's columns on the Indo-Pakistani war revived Nixon's fury over the maddening problem of leaks. Investigators immediately fastened on Yeoman Radford: The young stenographer had once been stationed in New Delhi; was known to have enjoyed a casual friendship with his fellow Mormon, Anderson; and had personally handled all the documents Anderson obtained.[50]

Radford's boss at the JCS-NSC liaison office was the stately Admiral Robert O. Welander, author of a memorandum quoted in Anderson's column of December 14. After reading Anderson's piece that morning, Welander rushed to Alexander Haig to convey his suspicion that Radford was responsible for the leak; the yeoman, Welander believed, suffered from "some kind of Ellsberg syndrome." Haig, in turn, directed the nervous admiral to John Ehrlichman and the Plumbers. Within twenty-four hours, Radford was placed under virtual house arrest; by the afternoon of December 16, he found himself attached to a National Security Agency polygraph machine, answering questions from W. Donald Stewart, the Pentagon's most seasoned investigator.[51]

Stewart was a notoriously tough interrogator and "hammered away" at the frightened yeoman "a couple of times a day." The questioning turned up Radford's acquaintanceship with Anderson—years earlier the young man had shown Anderson's parents around New Delhi—but the yeoman steadfastly denied leaking to the columnist, a claim the polygraph operator cited, according to previously unpublished documents, as an example of "deception." Under Stewart's profane assault, Radford finally broke down and wept. He would go no further without permission from Welander. When contacted, the admiral instructed the yeoman to answer all questions truthfully.[52]

It was then that Radford unloaded his bombshell—what Nixon termed "a federal offense of the highest order." Working in the JCS-NSC office and serving as an aide-de-camp for Kissinger and Haig— at Haig's insistence—on sensitive trips to India, Pakistan, China, and Vietnam, Radford had stealthily obtained or copied some five thousand pages of highly classified material, including crumpled drafts, carbons, and completed memoranda, and secretly passed the documents to his bosses: Welander and his predecessor, the late Admiral Rembrandt Robinson. Welander and Robinson had in turn funneled the papers to Admiral Moorer.[53]

What started as an investigation to determine the sources for the classified data that routinely, if no less alarmingly, showed up in Anderson's columns—Don Stewart had run eleven such probes on Anderson in the past nine months—had morphed into a far more serious matter: wartime espionage against the commander-in-chief by the nation's top uniformed officers.[54] "Under the implied approval of his supervisor, the admiral," Ehrlichman told the Oval Office group on the evening of December 21, Radford "has systematically stolen documents out of Henry's briefcase, Haig's briefcase, people's desks—anyplace and everyplace in the NSC apparatus that he could get his hands on—and has duplicated them and turned them over to the Joint Chiefs, through his boss." He added, "This has been going on now for about thirteen months."

The secret tapes of Nixon's meetings and telephone conversations about the Moorer-Radford affair, as the episode later came to be known, remained classified until October 2000, when they were released by the National Archives along with some four hundred hours of other Nixon recordings. Unpublished until now, these tapes, covering late December 1971 and early January 1972, rank among the most important of the Nixon presidency, for they offer insights into how a wartime commander-in-chief coped with an unprecedented crisis in American history. They also show how instrumental Attorney General Mitchell was in shaping the president's response.[55]

In the nighttime session, his first briefing on the matter, Nixon wondered aloud whether Kissinger's deputy, Alexander Haig, a Pentagon loyalist, had known about the spying; it was Haig, after all, who had selected Radford for the overseas trips. "I don't know," Ehrlichman said. "I suspect Haig may be aware, but by back-channel basis." "Is Haig wiretapped?" Nixon asked, unmindful of the irony that it was Haig who had managed the wiretaps on Kissinger's aides two years before. "Why not?" Haldeman replied. But Nixon never ordered a wiretap on Haig—for tactical reasons. "We are going to continue to handle the Chiefs . . . through Haig," Nixon told Haldeman and Ehrlichman on December 23. "But we'll let them know what they're *supposed* to know."

Only after Ehrlichman, the Plumbers' overlord, finished recounting the facts during that first meeting did the attorney general weigh in. "Mr. President, I'd like to point out that this thing goes right into the Joint Chiefs of Staff. . . . The important thing in my way of thinking is to stop this Joint Chiefs of Staff operation, and to buck up the security over here."

> NIXON: [Welander] had to know he was getting stuff from Kissinger's and Haig's briefcases. That is wrong! Understand? I'm just saying that's wrong. Do you agree?
> MITCHELL: No question about it, that the whole concept of having this yeoman get into this affair and start to get this stuff back to the Joint Chiefs of Staff is just like coming in and robbing your desk.
> NIXON: Yes it is.

The president thirsted for revenge; prosecuting Moorer was "a possibility." The attorney general agreed Moorer deserved punishment, but warned Nixon, without elaborating, about "what this would lead to if you pursued it by way of prosecution of Moorer." The in-house deceptions and private back channels, the secret bombing of Cambodia—all this would likely become public if Nixon pressed charges against the chairman of the Joint Chiefs. Mitchell proposed his own remedy, speaking quietly but with such authority and finality that to hear the surviving recording is to wonder who was giving the orders in the Oval Office that night and who was taking them; indeed, the president followed Mitchell's prescription almost to the letter.

> **MITCHELL:** What has been done has been done. I think that the important thing is to paper this thing over.
> **NIXON:** Hmmph!
> **MITCHELL:** This way—first of all, get that liaison office the hell out of NSC and put it back at the Pentagon.
> **NIXON:** Correct.
> **MITCHELL:** Secondly, get a security officer into the NSC.
> **NIXON:** Correct. Well, what about Henry Kissinger?
> **MITCHELL:** Well, I think that whoever goes in there is going to have to ride herd not only on the rest of the [NSC] staff but on Henry. . . . With respect to the Joint Chiefs, you have to get, in my opinion, this guy Admiral Welander the hell out of there, by way of a signal. That way you can transfer him to Kokomo, or Indiana, or anywhere we want to have him, along, of course, with this yeoman. And I think the best thing to do is for me—and we'll leave Laird aside for a moment— but for me to sit down with Tom Moorer, and point out what this scene is that's been going on, and it's the end of the road. . . . This ball game's over with.

Mitchell's remedy reflected his pragmatism ("What's done is done") and his toughness. He knew someone had to take on the Joint Chiefs. This daunting task the attorney general arrogated unto himself, first because he saw robbing the president's desk as a criminal matter; second, because Mitchell had the nerve to confront Moorer and he knew Nixon, who flinched from direct confrontation, did not. "I think the strategy you suggested," Nixon meekly told Mitchell, "is the one that I would pursue." The next day, in an even softer voice, the president confessed to Haldeman: "I created this whole situation, this—this *lesion*. It's just unbelievable. Unbelievable."

"John Mitchell knew Tom Moorer and liked him," Ehrlichman recalled. "Our bad news distressed the attorney general greatly."[56] Perhaps for that reason, Mitchell, in interviews with writers and historians in later years, never fully disclosed what he knew—what the declassified tapes later *showed* he knew—about Moorer's complicity in the espionage. "Moorer was totally uninvolved and blameless," the former attorney general told a disbelieving Seymour Hersh in 1982. "I don't believe Tom Moorer was spying to this day," he repeated to author Robert Gettlin in 1985. To Len Colodny, Gettlin's coauthor on *Silent Coup: The Removal of a President*, with whom Mitchell conducted some eighty hours of recorded telephone interviews in the last three years of his life, the former attorney general initially dissembled about the conclusions he and the president had reached in December 1971.

> **COLODNY:** Did Nixon ever discuss with you what he really thought?
> **MITCHELL:** [Sigh] Um, trying to refresh my recollection. . . . Our discussions were to the point that, uh, these other characters attached to the JCS were doing all this without Moorer's concurrence or, or, uh, cooperation.[57]

Colodny did not have the December 21 tape, but, building on the work of other scholars, he amassed enough evidence to force Mitchell to change his tune. By June 1986, the former attorney general effectively abandoned the pretense of Moorer's innocence—but still stopped short of implicating his old friend by name. "It was not in the interest of the government to stir up a situation which would indicate that the military was acting contrary to the interests of the president," Mitchell said, "and you probably put your finger on it: because of the back channel aspects of it." Mitchell's companion, Mary

Gore Dean, proved far more forthcoming, telling Colodny in October 1987: "I asked John. . . . He said, 'Admiral Moorer was up to his eyeballs in it.' "[58]

Why did Mitchell muddy the historical record? Perhaps he was confident the December 21 tape would never surface, at least during his lifetime, and he still regarded the Moorer-Radford affair as an explosive subject with real national security implications. Another possibility is that Mitchell, deep in debt after his stint in prison, despaired of angering Moorer, with whom he had business dealings.[59]

Questioned by historian Stanley Kutler in February and April 1988, Mitchell said he "interviewed" Moorer at the time and "got a flat, outright statement that he knew nothing about it . . . a complete denial."[60] Not until the twenty-first century, and the release of the relevant tapes, could the truth be known. On the afternoon of December 23, 1971, Ehrlichman briefed the president on Mitchell's showdown with Moorer.

> **EHRLICHMAN:** [Mitchell] said that Moorer admits that he saw stuff, but that he operated on the assumption that his liaison man was working this all out with Henry. . . . I said, "Well, did you get a plea of guilty or a not guilty?" And [Mitchell] says, "I got a *nolo contendere.*"
> **NIXON:** [Did Mitchell] tell him about the briefcases and all that?
> **EHRLICHMAN:** Yup.
> **NIXON:** And?
> **EHRLICHMAN:** Moorer said, "Why, that's shocking." Told him, "Whoever did that should go to jail."

Next, Haldeman briefed the president on Ehrlichman's first attempt to break all of this to Henry Kissinger. Struggling to get a read on the various players, Nixon asked what Kissinger—the primary target of the spying—had said about the prospect of criminal prosecution. "What do you do on that?" Kissinger had asked. "Well,"

Ehrlichman responded, "it's in the hands of the attorney general. . . . Admiral Welander thinks that we should put the yeoman in jail; Admiral Moorer thinks we should put Welander in jail." Kissinger thought Moorer should go to jail. "John and I both laughed," Haldeman told the president. "As you go up the ladder, everybody's going to crucify the guy under him, and nobody'll take the blame himself."

The following morning, Kissinger and Haig visited Ehrlichman's office. There they heard the tape of the interrogation of Admiral Welander that Ehrlichman and the Plumbers' David Young had conducted on the afternoon of December 22. The admiral had admitted knowing about Radford, and that he himself had funneled the stolen papers to Moorer. After the tape ended, Ehrlichman later wrote, Kissinger exploded in purple rage. "[Nixon] won't fire Moorer!" he shouted. "They can spy on him and spy on me and betray us and he won't fire them! . . . I assure you," Kissinger intoned before stalking out, "all this tolerance will lead to very serious consequences for this administration!"[61]

Kissinger was never more prescient. Though unnoticed at the time, Ehrlichman's interrogation of Admiral Welander also confirmed Nixon's early suspicions about the role in the affair played by Alexander Haig. "I think you have to talk to Al Haig on this," the admiral told his questioners. "It's been a two-way street." At another point Welander stated flatly: "Al Haig has cut me in on what [the White House has] been thinking about . . . and given me a copy of game plans and so on."[62]

Mitchell harbored few illusions about Haig, whom he came to consider "a power grabber . . . pleased to abandon Nixon to maintain his power base in Washington and the military." Shown the transcript of the Ehrlichman-Welander interrogation many years later, the former attorney general declared that had Nixon seen it, he would never have appointed Haig to succeed Haldeman as chief of staff. Had that happened, of course, historians would never have had to grapple, as they have, with like questions about Haig's conduct—and loyalties— in the latter stages of Watergate: the disclosure of Nixon's taping system, the origins and discovery of the eighteen-and-a-half-minute gap, the pardon. Asked if the failure to move on Haig in December 1971 marked "one of those crucial turning points that could have saved the Nixon presidency," Mitchell answered affirmatively: "It would have taken and put Haig in a different light and probably . . . got [him] the hell out of there."[63]

Thus by the time he died, Mitchell realized his burial of the Moorer-Radford scandal—undertaken to spare the nation a court-martial involving the Joint Chiefs of Staff, and to give Nixon a "whip hand" over them—effectively sealed the president's own fate. By allowing men he distrusted, and who distrusted him, to remain in place in the White House and at the Pentagon, Nixon ensured that the culture of secrecy and paranoia that infused his first term persisted until the Watergate scandal aborted his presidency.

As Nixon's knowledge of the Moorer-Radford affair deepened, he faced the unpleasant task of addressing it with those involved. He chose the least confrontational manner—telephone calls—with the Christmas holiday as his pretext. The recipients of these phone calls got different messages, delivered with varying doses of subtlety. First came Haig, shortly after 5:00 p.m. on Christmas Eve, 1971. After lathering up the colonel with gossipy talk about Kissinger—Nixon was a master at playing the two off each other—the president got down to business, directing his words as much to Moorer as to Haig.

> NIXON: Incidentally, on the Moorer thing. That's just—you just couldn't even dream of having Moorer out of that thing. I mean, he's part of a system. And the damn thing, I'm sure, started before he was there.
> HAIG: That's right.
> NIXON: I think—I think it goes back over years, and it probably went further than he ever expected it was gonna go. That's my guess.

HAIG: That's what I think, sir—

NIXON: And I—we gotta remember that, basically, he's our ally, in terms of what we believe in. And the worst thing we can do now is to hurt the military. I—I tried to get [that] through Henry's head. But—but that's what, that's the line we're playing on today.

HAIG: Sure.

NIXON: Don't you agree?

HAIG: Absolutely.

NIXON: We [have] just got to do that. And in June [when Moorer's term as chairman was to expire], of course, we can take a look—but not now. . . . After all, Moorer's a good man, and he's with us. This thing, of course, is pretty bad! It's, uh—understand: not the, not sending the information over [to the Pentagon], but goin' through briefcases, that goes too far!

Of Haig's self-incriminating display of familiarity with the spying operation—"that's right" he said, when Nixon suggested the wrong-doing predated Moorer—the president took no note. Instead, phoning Haig two days later, Nixon further assuaged the guilty, retracting his implied threat about Moorer's reappointment. If Moorer "thinks maybe now he's blown it," Nixon wanted to Haig to know, "he hasn't."[64]

Minutes after hanging up with Haig on Christmas Eve, Nixon had Mitchell on the line. His mind fixed on Yeoman Radford, and, too, on the federal prisoner whose sentence Nixon had just commuted—former Teamsters boss Jimmy Hoffa—the president offered Mitchell, destined within six years' time to become the highest-ranking U.S. official ever to be incarcerated, some eerily prophetic words.

NIXON: I'll tell you, being in prison isn't, isn't all that, uh, that it's cracked up to be. You have some lonely days.

MITCHELL: I would certainly believe it . . .

NIXON: Incidentally, on our other subject [Moorer-Radford], I think we are better advised—I mean to—we've really just got to keep the lid on it . . . keep it under as close control as we can. But I, uh—we cannot move to do anything to discredit the uniform. That's what I'm convinced of.

On Christmas Day, Nixon rang the party he trusted least: Mel Laird. Mitchell had already spoken to the defense secretary, and heard his smug reminders about how he had warned Kissinger, early on, about the JCS treachery under President Johnson. After holiday greetings, the president clumsily transitioned to the Moorer-Radford affair ("Oh, incidentally, on that, er, matter that you're familiar with . . .") and spun a tale that acknowledged the case's severity yet preserved the fiction of Moorer's remove from it.

NIXON: I've given the orders around to everybody, that we not allow this thing to hurt the military. You know, we, we know it's wrong—

LAIRD: I know.

NIXON: —but we must cut it. So we gotta clean it up, but we gotta stand by Moorer and these fellows, because they are good guys. They just—they just got trapped in a system that was bad.

Ironically, Laird, who played no role in the spying, received the only presidential rebuke in the affair. On the tape, Nixon's tone is sharp and reproachful.

NIXON: As you pointed out to Mitchell, apparently, eh, you knew about this *years* ago. This has been goin' on for *years!* And they—

LAIRD: Yeah.

NIXON: —and it's just surprising they had it now, and I just think it's the way the system works.

LAIRD: Well—

NIXON: But now that it's done, we'll, uh—

LAIRD: . . . I'm just gonna stay out of it now, and just shut it off.

NIXON: Absolutely. Leave it. Stay out of it, and let Mitchell do whatever has to be done.

The next day, Nixon rang Admiral Moorer. Mitchell, of course, had already done the tough work of confronting the chairman, freeing Nixon to stay above the fray and discuss only the previous night's (aborted) air raids over Vietnam. The commander-in-chief's tone was inquisitive and deferential, a layman eager to learn from the expert ("Can you do that?" he asked after Moorer said his pilots would rely on instrument readings to launch attacks during bad weather). Moorer, in turn, played the dutiful subordinate, wishing the boss Merry Christmas, repeatedly and artlessly touting his dedication: "I know what your objectives are. . . . We're keeping the Situation Room fully up to date. . . . I just want to show you I'm watching it . . . I assure you."

Finally, on New Year's Day, the president interrupted his preparations for a prime-time interview with Dan Rather to reach out to the one man out of whom Nixon, all along, had insisted he did not want to hear a peep: Kissinger. In the mercurial former professor, the Moorer-Radford affair was just the kind of thing to bring on another bout of neurotic insecurity and resignation talk. As it happened, they ignored the passing crisis, focusing instead on Nixon's plan to end the draft and Laird's opposition to it. Suddenly Kissinger had an idea. "Let me talk to Moorer," he proposed. "He owes us one." "He sure does," Nixon replied.

The two had come full circle. Less than two weeks after learning of the Joint Chiefs' spying—a "lesion" Nixon admitting having created with his and Kissinger's incessant back-channel plotting—the president had blithely resumed scheming with his national security adviser, whom he had ten days earlier described as "not a good security risk," to use the Joint Chiefs as a back channel to circumvent the secretary of defense.

Save for his rejection of Mitchell's proposal to wiretap Jack Anderson, the president had followed all of the attorney general's recommendations during the crisis: The liaison office was abolished; Radford and Welander were banished to remote posts; Moorer was confronted but retained as chairman; Laird was held at bay; a security officer was installed at NSC; and Kissinger was dissuaded from raising holy hell.

In later years, John Ehrlichman would argue that Mitchell's performance as attorney general, especially his fumbles in the Supreme Court nomination battles of 1969–70, progressively diminished the president's esteem for his former law partner. "[Nixon] had very high confidence in [Mitchell] to begin with and that eroded over time," said Ehrlichman, "until by 1973 it was down below zero."[65]

Yet the Moorer-Radford tapes show that as 1972 dawned, some sixty days before Mitchell left the government for good, the president's admiration for his attorney general had rebounded completely from its nadir—which was not the back-to-back rejection of Nixon's Supreme Court nominees, but Mitchell's insufficiently ruthless response to the Pentagon Papers. Six months earlier, Nixon had mused how much "better off" he would be after Mitchell was gone. Now the president marveled anew at Mitchell's singular indispensability.

"Boy, you couldn't have a better man than Mitchell over to talk to Moorer," the president waxed to Haldeman on December 23. "He's the only one in the Cabinet who even approaches as much respect as [Treasury Secretary John] Connally. Connally, as you know, is strong, tough; but Mitchell is even more steely than Connally."

"He is," Haldeman agreed, "and he's a little more serious. . . .

Mitchell scares ya. I mean, to people who don't know him—I didn't really realize it, but people are really afraid of John Mitchell."

"That's right. 'Cause he looks at them with those steely eyes, and he doesn't—he puffs on his pipe . . ."

"And he is—he is a tough cop!"

CLOUD OF
SUSPICION

If everybody had just gone in and told the truth.
But maybe they didn't know what the truth was.

—*Richard Nixon, 1972*[1]

FROM THE MOMENT they met in 1967, John Ehrlichman resented John Mitchell. The undistinguished zoning lawyer from Seattle had known Nixon longer, worked more menial jobs for him; but the renowned Wall Street bond expert had gone straight to the top, enjoying the more privileged relationship with the candidate.

In the White House, Ehrlichman worked tirelessly to expand his portfolio. At first he supervised the seedy investigations of Nixon's private gumshoe, Anthony Ulasewicz, and acted as a neutral paper-pusher in policy battles embroiling more senior men; by 1970, he exercised near-total control over U.S. domestic policy. In widening his turf, Ehrlichman seized on the president's periodic disappointments with the attorney general, seeing them as mandates to annex Mitchell's areas of influence. Ehrlichman always denied this, saying his actions reflected only the president's deepening dissatisfaction with Mitchell; but the patterns were pronounced.

One of Ehrlichman's tactics was to cultivate Mitchell's own aides. William Rehnquist recalled Ehrlichman asking him, in 1969, to draft an opinion on a desegregation statute without telling Mitchell. "I felt, 'Gee, that's an odd thing to do. Here's the guy I work for, John Mitchell, and I'm supposed to not tell him what I'm doing?' " Rehnquist recalled in 1993. "I felt there was antipathy [there]."

At other times, Ehrlichman's instigations reached across departmental lines. Frank Carlucci, later President Reagan's defense secretary, remembered chairing his first meeting, in 1970, as deputy director of the Office of Management and Budget. "Ehrlichman called me aside and said, 'The president doesn't think John Mitchell's managing worth a damn! His place is a mess! You're to go over and tell him to shape up!' That was my very first assignment," Carlucci recalled in 2001. "I screwed up my courage and went over and tried to tell John Mitchell in a very nice way that he was—that he needed to take a more—a deeper interest in the management of his department. And I can still see him just puffing on his pipe. He didn't blow up. He just sort of looked at me and said goodbye." Such crude manipulations Mitchell generally dismissed as "typical Ehrlichman," the annoying but ultimately irrelevant agitations of a "smart ass" Mitchell regarded as "full of shit."

Still another Ehrlichman tactic was to develop elaborate critiques of Mitchell's policy performance and present them to Nixon, who invariably instructed Ehrlichman to right things as he saw fit. In no area of federal policy was Ehrlichman's *lebensraum* campaign more determined than that of antitrust law. "From the administration's earliest days," John Dean wrote, "Ehrlichman viewed antitrust policy as a weak link in Mitchell's ties to the president, a subject the conniving domestic policy czar could, with the right approach to the president, successfully wrest from Mitchell's control." Like any agency chief, Mitchell resisted such encroachments; as the *Washington Evening Star* noted, Mitchell "succeeded more than any other Cabinet officer in warding off White House intrusion upon his preserves." But in the case of antitrust, Ehrlichman's poaching would have catastrophic repercussions: the biggest Washington scandal since Teapot Dome.[2]

At the time Mitchell selected him to head DOJ's antitrust division, Richard W. McLaren was a respected Chicago lawyer and former officer of the American Bar Association. McLaren's lucrative practice defending corporate clients against antitrust charges initially raised questions about whether, as the government's chief trustbuster, he would vigorously press such cases.

The business climate of the late sixties offered genuine cause for alarm. Under Presidents Kennedy and Johnson, the United States experienced the greatest merger mania in its history, with almost 10,000 formerly independent firms absorbed into other companies. Over 1966–67, corporate acquisitions rose by 26 percent, a surge the Federal Trade Commission termed "the sharpest increase in merger activity in modern industrial history." By 1968, 200 corporations controlled more than 60 percent of America's manufacturing assets and total annual profits.[3]

McLaren swiftly signaled his intention to arrest these trends. In early 1969, the new assistant attorney general vowed to "go after big company mergers" and cozy reciprocal deals between parent and subsidiary companies that "freeze out the little guy." In this McLaren clearly enjoyed the confidence of his boss. Mitchell promised the *Wall Street Journal*: "The public is going to be protected. That's the purpose of the antitrust laws, or at least that should be their purpose." By August, DOJ had challenged six high-profile mergers in court, and the trend continued.[4]

Nixon was not impressed. The president's dissatisfaction surfaced as early as March 1969, after *Barron's* editorialized that conglomerates had become "corporate scapegoats." "The real villains happen to be the U.S. trustbusters," the magazine charged. Upon reading this, Nixon wrote to Mitchell, in previously unpublished notes: "John—This is right! I agree." Underlining the word "trustbusters," Nixon ordered:

"Keep a very close watch on them. They tend, at times, to be anti-business professionals." "It was a constant battle," Mitchell later told the Watergate prosecutors. "There were always complaints about McLaren not carrying out administration policy, basically from Ehrlichman, but also from Stans, Connally, Flanigan. . . . Everybody in Washington bitched about McLaren. I was McLaren's strongest defender."[5]

Indeed, McLaren kept up his jihad against conglomerate mergers over the next three years—and Mitchell consistently backed him. Even the *New York Times*, never effusive in its enthusiasm for the administration, acknowledged McLaren had proved "rather aggressive" in his stewardship of the Antitrust Division; and the minions of consumer advocate Ralph Nader, even more hostile, conceded McLaren "has been fully supported by Mitchell in this campaign."[6]

None of this was lost on Nixon, who, in a March 1972 conversation with Charles Colson, captured by the White House taping system and transcribed by the Watergate prosecutors, lamented Mitchell's strong support for McLaren.

> NIXON: [Treasury Secretary John] Connally was very, very strong, as you may recall . . . against this whole antitrust policy.
> COLSON: Oh, hell everybody—yeah, the whole administration was.
> NIXON: Except for Justice.
> COLSON: Except for McLaren.
> NIXON: Mitchell, McLaren. . . . Mitchell was on the other side. To his credit, he defended McLaren.[7]

Ehrlichman eagerly stoked the fires of Nixon's discontent, writing to him in early 1971: "Your strong views on how the administration should conduct antitrust enforcement are not being translated into action. . . . You should authorize us to require all government-wide antitrust policy work to be coordinated through one White House office." Nixon agreed. Ehrlichman's notes captured Nixon's mood that fall.

> *McLaren threatening resignation—he should go* [. . .]
> *Mitchell problem . . . anti-trust*

What Ehrlichman really needed to gain control of the policy was a perfect example of the "Mitchell problem," a crystalline case in which the Antitrust Division could be seen unmistakably exceeding its charter. In fact, that case was there all along, weaving its way through the courts since 1969, ever fraught with the potential to explode, which it finally did on Mitchell's last day as attorney general.[8]

"You read a book from beginning to end," Hal Geneen once said. "You run a business the opposite way. You start with the end, and then you do everything you must to reach it." Born in Bournemouth, England, in 1910, the baptized son of a converted Russian Jewish father and Roman Catholic Italian mother, Harold Sydney Geneen moved to the United States with his family when he was one year old. He parlayed his New York University accounting degree into a series of corporate positions, including an executive stint at Raytheon, where he was acclaimed as a management genius. In 1959, he became president of International Telephone & Telegraph (ITT).

Over the next decade, Geneen, a stalwart Republican, elevated corporate mergers to an art from, steering ITT through takeovers, uncontested and hostile, of 110 domestic and foreign companies, with another 61 to follow in his eleventh year at the helm. This rapacious gobbling of other companies—in rather disparate fields—enabled ITT to maintain an annual growth rate of 11 to 12 percent. By 1969, ITT was the nation's largest pure conglomerate, with sales and assets totaling almost $8.5 billion—roughly $50 billion in current figures.[9]

That year, the Nixon administration inherited—but actively prosecuted—lawsuits against three separate ITT mergers: with the Canteen Corporation, a leading vending machine company with operations in forty-three states worth over $322 million; the Hartford Fire Insurance Company, the nation's fourth-largest property-casualty insurance company, with consolidated assets worth almost $2 billion; and the Grinnell Corporation, a leading manufacturer and seller of sprinkler and burglar-alarm systems, with sales and assets of nearly $525 million (all in 1968–69 figures).[10]

Geneen trained his indefatigable energies on one all-important goal: getting the Nixon administration to rescind its opposition to those three mergers. Retaining Hartford Fire, whose annual premiums exceeded $1 billion, was especially critical to ITT preserving its annual growth rate. DOJ had already sent one positive signal: Since Mitchell's former law firm had represented an ITT subsidiary, the attorney general recused himself from the case when, in April 1969, McLaren sought approval for an injunction to halt the Canteen merger. In Kleindienst's hands, this request was denied.[11]

Encouraged, Geneen launched a multiheaded lobbying offensive, with himself in the lead. He was determined to start at the top—but was rebuffed in his attempt, in June 1969, to meet directly with Nixon; such a session, the White House concluded, would be "inappropriate." Geneen kept at it until the following summer, when he, along with forty-five other prominent executives, dined with Nixon aboard the presidential yacht, *Sequoia*. According to one account, Nixon and Geenen talked privately for ten minutes—though no relief for ITT emanated from whatever discussion they had.[12]

Less than three weeks later, on August 4, 1970, Geneen propelled himself into Ehrlichman's office. For the occasion, the ITT president brought along William R. Merriam, the company's top man in Washington, and Edward ("Ned") Gerrity, ITT's New York–based public relations chief. Geneen sensed Ehrlichman's growing power in the White House and took the lead role in presenting ITT's case to Ehr-

188 | The Strong Man

lichman, who needed little persuading to believe the worst about Mitchell and McLaren. When McLaren got wind of Geneen's visit, and demanded to know what was discussed, Ehrlichman instructed an aide to tell the antitrust chief "nothing of significance . . . needed to be passed along." For good measure, the aide pointedly told McLaren their respective bosses had already discussed the meeting, and sneered: "Perhaps the attorney general could give you more specific guidance."[13]

Geneen was on a roll, but Mitchell—at least temporarily—stopped it. On the same day as his tête-à-tête with Ehrlichman, the ITT president sat down with the attorney general, this time with no aides present. Questioned later why he agreed to such a meeting when the government's cases against ITT were pending and he had recused himself from them, Mitchell told the Senate that he had, in communications between the two men's secretaries, imposed on Geneen the "express condition that the pending ITT litigation would not be discussed." Geneen had agreed, Mitchell testified, adding: "The pending ITT litigation was not discussed at this meeting."

During their half hour together, Geneen told Mitchell he thought the Antitrust Division was attacking ITT on the basis of its size, not its market effect, an approach he took as DOJ policy. Mitchell later insisted the exchange was "entirely theoretical" in nature, that he "completely rebuffed" Geneen's arguments about DOJ policy, and made "no change in it" after their conversation. Jack Anderson, the ubiquitous muckraker, later heaped scorn on this claim: "Just a little philosophical discussion between two theoreticians who happened to get together for an academic exercise." Yet Mitchell owed Geneen no favors; so far, the business tycoon had contributed to neither Nixon's '68 nor '72 campaigns.[14]

Here the ITT lobbying machine kicked into third gear. Ned Gerrity, who had served in the same unit as Vice President Agnew during World War II, asserted in a letter to his old comrade on August 7— three days after Geneen's meetings with Ehrlichman and Mitchell— that Mitchell had promised the ITT president he would "talk with

McLaren and get back to Hal." Apprised of this, Mitchell laughed and called its contents "preposterous." A more serious problem was brewing that very day in the Oval Office, where, according to previously unpublished notes, Ehrlichman raised the "ITT problem" with Nixon in a meeting that also included Haldeman and Assistant to the President Donald Rumsfeld.[15]

In truth, ITT held a decisive advantage in the forum that, for all Geneen's lobbying across the executive branch, really mattered most: the judiciary. Federal district and appellate courts almost invariably dismissed antitrust cases, and few prominent lawyers besides Mitchell believed that McLaren's novel extension of Section 7 of the Clayton Act to cover conglomerate mergers would prevail at trial. Now, on September 15, 1970, the government's case against ITT's acquisition of Grinnell opened in federal district court in Connecticut. Two days later, Ehrlichman sent Mitchell an infamous memorandum, its condescension matched only by its futility.

> I was disappointed to learn that the ITT case had gone to trial with apparently no further effort on the part of Mr. McLaren to settle this case with ITT on the basis of our understanding that "largeness" was not really an issue in the case. . . . I think we are in a rather awkward position with ITT in view of the assurances that both you and I must have given Gineen [sic] on this subject. . . . I would appreciate your reexamining our position in the case in view of these conversations. Gineen [sic] is, of course, entitled to assume the administration meant what it said to him.

Key was Ehrlichman's reference to "assurances that both you and I *must have* given" Geneen: The domestic policy czar knew about his own promises to the ITT president, but was left to assume Mitchell "must have" done likewise—an assumption that proved wrong. As the court proceedings in Connecticut made clear, Mitchell had articulated Justice's position, Ehrlichman Nixon's. Therein lay the trouble.[16]

On December 31, the federal district court in Connecticut decided the *Grinnell* case in ITT's favor. Chief Judge William H. Timbers expressed incredulity at the government's "paucity of evidence" that the merger would lead to reciprocal dealings by ITT subsidiaries, and "emphatically declined" McLaren's expansive reading of the Clayton Act as an "invitation to . . . judicial legislation."[17]

McLaren announced he would appeal the government's loss in *Grinnell* to the Supreme Court. He had until March 31, 1971, to file the necessary paperwork. Ten days before that deadline, Erwin N. Griswold, the white-haired, universally respected Johnson-era holdover who served as solicitor general of the United States, and thus argued the federal government's cases before the Supreme Court, sought and received a routine thirty-day extension. Now McLaren and his team had until April 20 to appeal the *Grinnell* decision.

As that date approached, the Geneen machine cranked up again. John Ryan, an ITT director and McLean neighbor of Kleindienst's, complained to the deputy attorney general about the litigation, "in an almost belligerent manner," during a party at Ryan's home. He asked if a company man could visit Kleindienst at his office to discuss the litigation's damaging economic impact on ITT. Kleindienst agreed, and soon found diminutive ITT director Felix G. Rohatyn, perhaps the era's premier investment banker, sitting across from him at the Justice Department, pitching him and McLaren on the disastrous effects a government victory would have not only on ITT's multinational fortunes but on America's larger balance of payments.

On Monday, April 19, the day before the *Grinnell* appeal papers were due in court, John Ehrlichman called Kleindienst and informed him bluntly: "Dick, the president has instructed me to order you to drop the appeal before the Supreme Court in the *Grinnell* case." Not one to take Ehrlichman's intrusions lightly, Kleindienst struggled to maintain his composure. He had approved the appeal personally, he told Ehrlichman. If Nixon wanted to discuss the matter, fine; but for the president's own sake, dropping the appeal was inadvisable. "Oh, we'll see about that!" Ehrlichman snapped, and hung up.[18]

An hour later, Ehrlichman marched into the Oval Office. He launched into a discussion of the "antitrust thing" by observing that although Nixon was to meet with his attorney general the following day, "by then it might be too late, in a sense, [for] the ITT case, where God knows we have made your position as clear as we could to Mr. What's-His-Name over there." "McLaren," Nixon said; the president knew Mr. What's-His-Name's name all too well. Ehrlichman breezily explained the background: how Mitchell had cited a conflict of interest early on and assigned Kleindienst to monitor McLaren's work on the ITT cases, which the White House aide—conveniently ignoring the relevant facts and case law—described as "an attack on conglomerates, on a theory which specifically had been contemplated by the Johnson administration and laid aside as too anti-business."[19]

Too anti-business? That was all Nixon needed to hear. "Kleindienst is in this?" the president asked. Then he reached for his phone. "Dick Kleindienst," he barked at a White House operator. While she tracked down the deputy, Ehrlichman explained the looming appeals deadline. "They're not going to file [the papers]," the president vowed. "Well," Ehrlichman purred with satisfaction, "I thought that was your position." A few minutes later, the deputy attorney general was on the line. "Hi, Dick, how are you?" the president asked. Then Nixon—who normally avoided personal confrontations—got down to brass tacks with uncharacteristic speed and bluntness.

The ensuing tirade, among the most infamous on the Nixon tapes, marks the moment when two years of simmering friction between the Nixon White House and Mitchell's Justice finally boiled over. "I'm going to talk to John [Mitchell] tomorrow about my general attitude on antitrust," Nixon began, "and in the meantime, I know that he has left with you the IT-and-T thing because apparently he says he had something to do with them once."

NIXON: Well, I have, I have nothing to do with them. And I want something clearly understood, and if it is not understood, McLaren's ass is to be out within one hour. The IT and T thing—stay the hell out of it. Is that clear? That's an order.

KLEINDIENST: Well, you mean the order is to—

NIXON: The order is to leave the Goddamned thing alone. Now, I've said this, Dick, a number of times, and you fellows apparently don't get the me—the message over there. I do not want McLaren to run around prosecuting people, raising hell about conglomerates, stirring things up at this point. Now you keep him the hell out of that. Is that clear?

KLEINDIENST: Well, Mr. President—

NIXON: Or either he resigns. I'd rather have him out anyway. I don't like the son-of-a-bitch.

KLEINDIENST: The, the question then is—

NIXON: The question is, I know, Dick, that the jurisdiction—I know all the legal things, Dick, you don't have to spell out the legal—

KLEINDIENST: [Inaudible]—appeal filed.

NIXON: That's right.

KLEINDIENST: That brief has to be filed tomorrow.

NIXON: That's right. Don't file the brief.

KLEINDIENST: Your order is not to file a brief?

NIXON: Your—*my order is to drop the Goddamned thing, you son-of-a-bitch! Don't you understand the English language?* Is that clear?

KLEINDIENST: [Laughs] Yeah, I understand that.

NIXON: Okay.[20]

Ten minutes later, Haldeman scribbled notes that, previously unpublished, captured Nixon's determination to bring the Antitrust Division to heel.

must smoke disloyals out of the woodwork [. . .]
ie anti-trust—P. won't stand for it
P. now into ITT case—shldn't have to be[21]

Kleindiest's first move was to call Mitchell. Susie Morrison told Kleindienst the attorney general was in the middle of a meeting and couldn't be disturbed. Kleindienst threatened to interrupt the meeting unless Mitchell immediately took the private elevator connecting their offices. Minutes later, for the first and only time in their three years of government service together, Mitchell walked into his deputy's office. "I told him, 'John, if I've got to follow this directive, I've got to resign,' " Kleindienst recalled in 1992. McLaren and Griswold, he warned, would also resign. "That fucking Ehrlichman is putting Nixon up to this," Kleindienst spat. "Just take it easy," Mitchell replied. At his suggestion, Kleindienst agreed to call McLaren and Griswold into his office and ask them, without explaining why, to seek a second filing extension on the *Grinnell* appeal. That would give Mitchell time to work on the president.[22]

The next day, Justice John Harlan granted Griswold's request.[23] Mitchell kept a scheduled appointment with Nixon on April 21. The attorney general's mission was a delicate one: to persuade the president to revoke his order to Kleindienst, allowing the *Grinnell* appeal to proceed to the Supreme Court, while enabling Nixon to feel as though his forceful assertion of executive authority hadn't been in vain. "I would like to get some time to talk to you, Mr. President, about this antitrust business," Mitchell began, "because this is political dynamite." When Nixon brought up McLaren, the attorney general wisely steered them to the area he knew the president prized most: politics.

MITCHELL: I'm talking about the whole picture of this ITT—what can develop out of this Senate investigation [by the Antitrust and Monopoly Subcommittee] and so forth, if you don't need it. You don't need it for these bastards up there to burden us with it. I don't know who's been giving you the information, but it's a bad political mistake. I'm not talking about the merits of it, either.

NIXON: John, the problem we've got is this: that we've got is that—I don't give a damn about the merits either. But we have a situation—and Connally has spoken to me about it—but where the business community, for, for—believes that we're a hell of a lot rougher on them in the antitrust than our predecessors were.

MITCHELL: All right. Now let me—

NIXON: And they don't think you are, they think McLaren is.

MITCHELL: Well, there, there are reasons for it.

NIXON: Because he leads you to believe this.

MITCHELL: And it wasn't McLaren, you know, that started all this. It was your Council of Economic Advisers and [Federal Reserve Chairman] Arthur Burns, and it was done in order to help cool this economy and the stock market, and I could go on a lot of other things. And the things that they're accusing McLaren of are just—made out of whole cloth. It's just not true. There are antitrust cases here, but what I want to talk about is the political aspects of it. . . . You just can't stop this thing while up at the Supreme Court because you will have Griswold quit, you will have a Senate investigation. . . . There are other ways of working this out.

NIXON: Okay. You—

MITCHELL: But I'm—I want to ta—I want to—

NIXON: Well, go ahead, you could—yeah, I understand that. If that's the problem politically, go ahead.

Here was one of Mitchell's finest hours as a public servant. Within minutes, he had talked Nixon down from the ledge on the *Grinnell* appeal, taken a shot at Ehrlichman ("I don't know who's been giving you the information, but it's a bad political mistake"), and defended his own man ("the things that they're accusing McLaren of are just made out of whole cloth"). At Justice the next day, Mitchell called his deputy aside. "By the way," the attorney general bemusedly told Kleindienst, "your friend at the White House says that you can handle your fucking antitrust cases any way you want."[24]

Ten days later, on the first of May, John and Martha Mitchell attended the 1971 Kentucky Derby as personal guests of Republican governor Louie Nunn. After the race, the Mitchells and scores of other guests repaired to the governor's Beaux Arts mansion in Frankfort for a lavish buffet dinner. Also on hand was an ITT lobbyist, a regular at Governor Nunn's Derby bashes, named Dita Davis Beard.

An irrepressible character in her mid-fifties, twice divorced with five children, the gray-haired Beard had been a hard-drinking, chain-smoking, foul-mouthed fixture on the Washington political scene since 1961, when she joined ITT's new capital offices. It was Beard who "put ITT on the political map," plying congressmen with corporate catnip: rides to and from their districts on ITT planes, free limousines and booze, ghostwritten floor speeches. With her nerve and verve, Beard transcended the era's limitations on women. And she had one other thing going for her: a mutual admiration society with Geneen, whom she, uniquely among the corporation's top executives, freely called "Hal." The ITT president adored his lady lobbyist, admiring her pluck, fattening her expense account, and invited her to deal directly with him—an arrangement resented by her boss, Bill Merriam.[25]

From their mutual friend, Governor Nunn, Beard knew in advance that Mitchell would be attending the Kentucky Derby dinner. She and Mitchell had never met. When she first approached him, Mitchell listened politely as Beard complained about DOJ's pursuit of ITT; he patiently explained that he had disqualified himself from the litigation and therefore "could not and would not" discuss it with her. Mitchell later estimated the exchange took all of "two minutes at the most, possibly three." But Dita Beard wasn't done. Minutes later, as the Mitchells and Governor Nunn filed through the buffet line, "Mrs. Beard again approached me," Mitchell later testified, "with the same harangue. . . ."

> I repeated my desire not to discuss the subject matter and advised her that I did not appreciate her pressing the subject. We went . . . to the dinner table and sat down, and while we were eating our dinner it is my recollection Mrs. Beard approached us again. . . . I lost my sweet disposition. . . . I said in no uncertain terms that I didn't appreciate her pressing me on the subject and said, in effect, "Shove off."

Governor Nunn, present for the entirety of Mitchell's exchanges with Beard, later confirmed his version. That night, Beard collapsed to the floor, apparently in a drunken stupor, and was removed from the mansion after being revived by Nunn's aides.[26]

Mitchell would hear more from Dita Beard—but for now, he still had to contend with John Ehrlichman. The White House aide was still seething over Mitchell's success in convincing the president to reverse his blunt orders on the *Grinnell* appeal. Ehrlichman wrote Mitchell on May 5, a time when both men were consumed by the May Day riots, demanding a three-way meeting with McLaren, at which they might discuss "the present status of the ITT cases, in order that we can achieve the agreed-upon ends discussed by the president with you."[27]

Mitchell simply ignored Ehrlichman's provocations, a luxury the attorney general could afford because of his own unique standing with the president. Settlement negotiations between Justice and the conglomerate were hurtling forward, anyway: Felix Rohatyn, the Lazard Frères investment banker and ITT director, had been briefing Kleindienst and McLaren on the adverse consequences that divestiture of the Hartford Fire Company would impose on ITT—and on the country. Kleindienst later remembered he was "quite taken by" Rohatyn, not least because the banker conceded at once, as a legal matter, that "McLaren was right and ITT was wrong."

> Anybody else who ever came in to talk to me about IT-and-T, they'd say, "You're wrong, Goddamn it!" . . . [Rohatyn] came up for the first time with the approach of what kind of effect this would have on ITT, and *ergo* the economy. . . . I said to him, "This is the first time anybody has ever mentioned that, and I would like to have you go down and meet with Mr. McLaren." And thereafter, Mr. McLaren conducted those meetings. You know, he kept me informed on what the progress of them was, until that final day when they came up with that settlement.[28]

Critics later made much of Rohatyn's mysteriously persuasive effect on McLaren. Why was the antitrust chief suddenly willing to countenance ITT's retention of Hartford, a company the conglomerate had gone ahead and acquired despite repeated warnings by DOJ? As McLaren himself told Kleindienst in June 1971: "ITT's management consummated the Hartford acquisition knowing it violated our antitrust policy; knowing we intended to sue; and in effect representing to the court that [it] need not issue a preliminary injunction [barring the merger in advance] because ITT would hold Hartford separate and thus minimize any divestiture problem if violation were found."

Yet in the same memorandum McLaren conceded Rohatyn's arguments that forcing divestiture of Hartford now would "cripple ITT financially and seriously injure its 250,000 stockholders," leading to the loss of "well over $1 billion" in stock value and a likely "ripple effect" across Wall Street and the economy. McLaren "reluctantly" concluded that the government must "weigh the need for divestiture in this case—including its deterrent effect, as well as the elimination of anti-competitive effects . . . against the damage which divestiture would occasion." The government, moreover, had already lost two of its three ITT cases—*Grinnell* and *Canteen*—at trial.[29]

McLaren always maintained that he alone had decided to settle the ITT cases, and that the final deal—while allowing the conglomerate to keep Hartford Fire—represented a triumph for the government. Senator Philip Hart, the Michigan Democrat whose subcommittee probes of antitrust policy Mitchell had pointedly warned Nixon to avoid, later claimed the final settlement was "not substantially different" from terms the antitrust chief had rejected back in November 1970. Yet this was demonstrably false: Where ITT's 1970 settlement proposal had offered to divest the company of Canteen, the industrial piping division of Grinnell, the domestic operations of Levitt and Sons (a huge home construction company ITT owned), and other assets, the final consent decree—signed on July 31, 1971, and approved by the federal district court on September 24, thus spelling the end of the ITT cases—forced the conglomerate to sell off Canteen, Grinnell's fire protection division, Levitt's domestic *and* foreign operations, 46 percent of Hajoca Corporation (a plumbing company that provided synergy with other ITT assets), and all foreign and domestic operations of the Avis Rent A Car Company.

In addition, ITT agreed to a ten-year injunction forbidding the conglomerate from acquiring any insurance companies, as well as any company worth more than $100 million, or any company that posted $25 million in revenues while cornering 15 percent of a given market. Neither these ten-year restrictions nor the divestiture of Avis or Hajoca was contemplated in the 1970 proposal. All told, the final consent decree imposed divestiture of some $937 million in 1971 sales, 56 percent more than what ITT proposed in 1970; and divestiture of some $792 million in forsworn assets, 58 percent more than what ITT proposed in 1970. Indeed, ITT's stock dropped 14 percent in the first two days after the settlement was announced. "We didn't halt prosecution—they caved in," McLaren declared. Solicitor General Griswold, a figure of unquestioned integrity, said later: "We got 100 percent of what we asked for."[30]

Mitchell welcomed the end; the ITT cases had generated endless irritation inside the administration. But he also reveled, quietly, in his demonstrated power to ward off White House intrusions on his turf. He hailed the Antitrust Division for negotiating "the largest divestiture of any corporation in the history of U.S. business," and likened ITT's acquiescence to "the defendant pleading guilty." The end of the three-year *todeskampf* between the Department of Justice and ITT was, to Mitchell, "a confirmation of the antitrust policy of the administration . . . not a denial of it or an abrogation of it."[31]

Now the attorney general looked ahead—to the coming election year and the massive, and unwelcome, task awaiting him: managing Nixon's reelection campaign. A million things demanded Mitchell's attention, from staffing the skeletal Committee for the Re-Election of the President (CRP) to staging the GOP convention. After some difficulty, San Diego, Nixon's "lucky city," had mustered the funding to bid on, and win, the privilege of hosting the convention.

Key to that had been a sub-rosa pledge of at least $100,000 from San Diego's Sheraton Hotel, a subsidiary of ITT. Did Mitchell know about that? Who could recall, amid the welter of people and paper that crossed the attorney general's desk every day? And what difference did it make? Beyond such tedium lay the nirvana Mitchell craved: return to New York and the private practice of law. Surely the intricacies and propriety of the ITT settlement, and whatever relation they bore to the convention's financing—then questioned only by a handful of shrill partisans—would fade from the newspapers, and Mitchell could get on with his life.

An exchange of handwritten letters on February 15, 1972, marked the end of Mitchell's three-year tenure as attorney general, a brief but uniquely turbulent period that had witnessed the Days of Rage, Kent State, and May Day; the Black Panthers and the Pentagon Papers;

major struggles over school desegregation and the reform of the criminal justice system; contentious Supreme Court nominations and antitrust battles; and not least of all, the daily conduct of the Vietnam War and the treachery of the Moorer-Radford affair.

"It has been a great"—"distinct," Mitchell's handwritten draft had said—"privilege to serve in your Cabinet and administration, and for this opportunity and experience I am most appreciative. Respectfully submitted, John Mitchell." On White House stationery, the president penned his "Dear John" reply, including an oblique allusion—Nixon couldn't help himself—to the disparity in their private finances.

> In my 25 years in public life I have found there are very few indispensable men.
>
> In the campaign of 1968 and in our first three years you have been one of those rare men.
>
> My only regret is that you are also the indispensable man to run the campaign of 1972.
>
> But fortunately we will still be working together in the same cause.
>
> I can't pay you what you are worth. But if just plain "thank you" will do—you have that a thousand fold—(and Martha too!)
>
> RN[32]

All that remained was the matter of Mitchell's successor. Less than a year after he had assaulted Kleindienst over the phone—*You son-of-a-bitch, don't you understand the English language?*—Nixon formally nominated him as the nation's sixty-eighth attorney general; nine days later, after a perfunctory hearing, the Senate Judiciary Committee voted unanimously to recommend confirmation.[33]

Lanky, long-haired, sharp-witted, twenty-seven-year-old Brit Hume was already an experienced reporter when he started working, in autumn 1970, as a "legman" for Jack Anderson, the columnist whose knack for obtaining highly classified memoranda had just won him a Pulitzer Prize. Full of "brash bravado," Hume knew news when he saw it, and on Tuesday, February 22, 1972, it dropped into his lap like a gift from the heavens.[34]

"This is a good one," said Opal Ginn, Anderson's secretary, as she handed Hume a two-page typed document. Beyond noting the ITT stationery, the reporter was initially too busy to examine the item; later, he returned to it and realized at once that it was "the single most incriminating piece of paper I had ever seen." Dated June 25, 1971, and marked "Personal and Confidential," it was an original ITT memo from "D. D. Beard" to "W. R. Merriam," captioned "San Diego Convention." It read, in full:

> I just had a long talk with EJG. I'm so sorry that we got that call from the White House. I thought you and I agreed very thoroughly that under no circumstances would anyone in this office discuss with anyone our participation in the Convention including me. Other than permitting John Mitchell, Reinecke, Bob Haldeman and Nixon (besides Wilson, of course) no one has known from whom that 400 thousand committment [*sic*] had come. You can't imagine how many queries I've had from "friends" about this situation and I have in each and every case denied knowledge of any kind. It would be wise for all of us here to continue to do that, regardless of from whom any questions come; White House or whoever. John Mitchell has certainly kept it on the higher level only, we should be able to do the same.
>
> I was afraid the discussion about the three hundred/four hundred thousand committment [*sic*] would come up soon. If you remember, I suggested we all stay out of that, other

than the fact that I told you I had heard Hal up the original amount.

Now I understand from Ned that both he and you are upset about the decision to make it four hundred thousand in <u>services</u>. Believe me, this is not what Hal said. Just after I talked with Ned, Wilson called me, to report on his meeting with Hal. Hal at no time told Wilson that our donation would be in services ONLY. In fact, quite the contrary. There would be very little cash involved, but certainly some. I am convinced, because of several conversations with Louie re Mitchell, that our noble committment [sic] has gone a long way toward our negotiations on the mergers eventually coming out as Hal wants them. Certainly the President has told Mitchell to see that things are worked out fairly. It is still only McLaren's mickey-mouse we are suffering.

We all know Hal and his big mouth! But this is one time he cannot tell you and Ned one thing and Wilson (and me) another!

I hope, dear Bill, that all of this can be reconciled—between Hal and Wilson—if all of us in this office remain totally ignorant of any committment [sic] ITT has made to anyone. If it gets too much publicity, you can believe our negotiations with Justice will wind up shot down. Mitchell is definitely helping us, but cannot let it be known. Please destroy this, huh?[35]

The import of the document, dated a month before the government announced its surprise settlement in the ITT cases, was both seismic and unmistakable: Mitchell was "helping" to fix the antitrust suits against ITT in exchange for the company's "noble committment" to help finance the 1972 Republican convention. Several of the names mentioned, like "EJG," "Ned," "Hal," "Louie," and "Wilson," Hume did not recognize; but he certainly knew those of Nixon,

Mitchell, McLaren, Haldeman, and Ed Reinecke, California's lieutenant governor under Ronald Reagan.

The reporter's first stop was his own source: Opal Ginn. "It sounds like Dita Beard," she snapped; now Hume knew the first name—and gender—of the memo's author. Ginn said Beard was ITT's capital lobbyist and had met her once, finding the encounter unpleasant. Hume quickly ascertained that the memo's intended recipient was ITT's Washington vice president, Bill Merriam; that "EJG" and "Ned" were the same person—Edward J. ("Ned") Gerrity, ITT's public relations man in New York; that "Hal" was Harold Geneen; that "Louie" was Kentucky governor Louie Nunn; and that "Wilson" was Congressman Bob Wilson, the Republican who represented San Diego.

Hume's next task was to get Beard to authenticate the memo. This he did the next day, with a mixture of guile and boyish charm, during an interview of Beard at the company's Washington offices attended by two ITT public relations men. According to Hume, he showed Beard the original memo without asking if it was genuine; Beard responded by saying the penciled initial beside her name was indeed "my own little 'D.' " After leaving to check her files, Beard, according to Hume, returned, announced she could find no trace of the document in her office, and asked: "All right, what do you want to know about it?" This Hume took as confirmation of the document's authenticity.

Next he contacted Richard McLaren, and read him the memo over the phone. Now a federal judge in Chicago—his departure and relocation so swift they raised eyebrows[36]—the former trustbuster chuckled at the memo's reference to ITT suffering "McLaren's mickeymouse," then said: "Mitchell had absolutely nothing to do with the negotiation and settlement of that case. I never discussed it with him. It was completely my operation. I made the decision as to what was the proper basis for a settlement."

By Thursday, February 24, Beard was requesting to see Hume again. They arranged for the reporter to visit her Arlington home at ten o'clock that night. Hume arrived to find Beard dressed in the same dingy clothes she'd worn two days earlier, joined by her teenage son, Bull, her secretary, and an ITT colleague. "The atmosphere was tense and gloomy," Hume later recalled, "as if there had been a death in the family." He and Beard repaired to her kitchen to talk privately; her bleary eyes and slurred speech betrayed tears and drink. Over the next two hours, the lobbyist nursed a highball and chain-smoked Chesterfields as she "veered erratically from one subject to another," alternately cocky and pathetic, weepy and profane. Thinking a notebook would inhibit his high-strung subject, Hume took no notes, but typed up a recap when he got home.

"Of course I wrote it," Hume quoted Beard saying of the memo. She said it was meant to "put some sense into the head of that stupid shit, Merriam," whom she depicted as unequal to the political sophistication his lofty position demanded. The PR villains at ITT wanted Beard to tell Hume she had made the whole thing up—"but that would be a lie," she said, "and I wouldn't lie like that." As well, after Hume's visit to the ITT office, Beard said, a team of security men from New York had descended on her files and started indiscriminately shredding documents, including her personal papers.

She claimed Mitchell had been informed of ITT's role in the convention financing by Ed Reinecke, the lieutenant governor from California, during one of Reinecke's swings through Washington—but insisted the convention pledge was unrelated to the antitrust settlement. According to Hume's memo for the record, Reinecke had confided to Beard that when he apprised Mitchell about the existence of a $400,000 pledge to ensure San Diego hosted the convention, Mitchell had asked: "From whom?" "From Dita Beard," Reinecke had supposedly answered. "Humph," Mitchell reportedly replied.

The hour grew late. At last the reporter zeroed in on his target: *Did John Mitchell fix the ITT cases?* The question prompted Beard to pour forth, in between bursts of uncontrollable crying, her own version—actually, the *first* of her versions—of the Kentucky Derby encounter, which Hume recorded in his memorandum.

She said that as they were going in to get in the buffet line, Mitchell took her arm and took her aside. It was just the three of them then, she said, Mitchell, herself, and Gov. Nunn. She said that Mitchell proceeded to give her a scathing, hour-long scolding in the bluntest language for putting the pressure on the Justice Department [to approve] the mergers via Capitol Hill and other means instead of coming to see him. She said Mitchell said he had been told she was the "politician" in the company and he had heard much about her long before coming to Washington. She said he kenw [sic] about all the speeches she had written and gotten delivered by friendly members of Congress. She said Mitchell knew all about her, even asked about son Bull's grades. . . . She said Mitchell told her he had gotten a call from Nixon saying "lay-off ITT." Later she changed this to something, [sic] like Nixon saying "make a reasonable settlement." she [sic] said Mitchell told her he was sympathetic but that his great problem was McLaren, whom she described as a "shit." She said she did what she could to fight back, but she was overwhelmed by Mitchell's diatribe. She blessed Louie Nunn for staying at her side during the whole thing. Finally, she said she asked him, "Well, do you want to work something out," or words to that effect. She said he replied in the affirmative. She said he said, "What do you want," meaning what companies did ITT wish to retain in the merger case settlement. She said she told him they had to have the Hartford Insurance Company "because of the economy." And she added that they also wanted "part of Grinnell." She said she couldn't remember what else she asked for, but it was exactly what the company got in the settlement.

She said the agreement was reached, actually, as they went through the buffet line and then sat down to eat. She said that Harold Geneen knew nothing of the fix with Mitchell and that he still does not. I pressed her repeatedly on this, saying I found it hard to believe but she stuck to it all the way. She said this was the only meeting or conversation she has ever had with JM. She said that their discussion had nothing whatever to do with the convention negotiations and later said that her conversation with Reinecke about Mitchell's reaction to the proposed San Diego location came after the Kentucky session.[37]

There was much here for a skeptical reporter to question, starting with Beard's claim that she withheld from Harold Geneen any word of the fantastic lobbying coup she had supposedly scored—on a buffet line—in Kentucky. In fact, almost every element in Beard's story about her encounter with Mitchell was, prima facie, preposterous.

But that had no bearing on the news value of the memo Hume had in hand. As he continued researching it, the reporter got Felix Rohatyn, who denounced the memo as "absolute bullshit," to disclose his meetings with Kleindienst and McLaren. Those sessions appeared to contradict what Kleindienst had stated in a letter to Democratic Party chairman Lawrence F. O'Brien. In December 1971, O'Brien had written Mitchell questioning whether there was "a connection between ITT's sudden largesse to the Republican Party and the nearly simultaneous out-of-court settlement of one of the biggest merger cases in corporate history, to ITT's benefit." Replying to O'Brien, Kleindienst had asserted: "The settlement between the Department of Justice and ITT was handled and negotiated *exclusively* by Assistant Attorney General Richard W. McLaren." Now Hume had Rohatyn, an ITT director, casting Kleindienst as a party to the settlement talks. It was time to go to print.[38]

Hume's article appeared, under Jack Anderson's Washington Merry-Go-Round byline, on February 29, 1972—Mitchell's last day as attorney general. The headline in the *Washington Post*, one of seven hundred papers that carried Anderson's column, read: "Secret Memo

Bares Mitchell-ITT Move." "We now have evidence," the column began,

> that the settlement of the Nixon administration's biggest antitrust case was privately arranged between Attorney General John Mitchell and the top lobbyist for the company involved. We have this on the word of the lobbyist herself, crusty, capable Dita Beard of the International Telephone and Telegraph Co. She acknowledged the secret deal after we obtained a highly incriminating memo, written by her, from ITT's files.
>
> The memo, which was intended to be destroyed after it was read, not only indicates that the antitrust case had been fixed but that the fix was a payoff for ITT's pledge of up to $400,000 for the upcoming Republican convention in San Diego. Confronted with the memo, Mrs. Beard acknowledged its authenticity. . . . She said she met with Mitchell at the governor's mansion in Kentucky during a dinner reception given by Republican Gov. Louie Nunn last May after the Kentucky Derby.[39]

Waking up on his final day in office, Mitchell likely chuckled at the Anderson column. The account of his Kentucky Derby encounter with Dita Beard was so fanciful as to merit little concern. Alerted to the column's content the day before it ran, the attorney general's press secretary, Jack Hushen, had rushed out a press release in which Mitchell summarized his own version of the Derby encounter, then added a final flourish: "With respect to allegations that the president discussed the matter with me, there would be no occasion for him to do so and he did not."[40]

This was, of course, disingenuous at best, a blatant lie at worst: Mitchell and Nixon had indeed discussed the ITT case. Whether Mitchell believed his discussion with the president, in which he persuaded Nixon to reverse his order to Kleindienst to drop the litigation, was divorced from the merits of the case—technically true—was immaterial to the broad denial contained in Mitchell's statement. As Nixon had told Haldeman: *P. now into ITT case—shldn't have to be.* Mitchell would have stood on surer ground had he limited his denial to the specifics of Beard's tale: Nixon had never instructed Mitchell to "lay-off ITT" or "make a reasonable settlement." But Mitchell had no idea the Oval Office was bugged, and no reason to believe the matter would gain any traction. The next two columns by Anderson and Hume, and the "ripple effect" they caused, quickly disabused Mitchell of that notion.

"Kleindienst Accused in ITT Case" screamed the headline over Anderson's column of March 1. It charged the attorney general-designate, still awaiting a full Senate vote, had told "an outright lie" in his letter to Larry O'Brien. "We have now learned that Kleindienst himself held roughly a half-dozen secret meetings on the ITT case with a director of the company before the settlement was reached," wrote Anderson and Hume. Their implication of Kleindienst was based solely on Hume's interview with Rohatyn; the leaked ITT memo, after all, hadn't even mentioned Kleindienst. "Kleindienst's duplicity is further evidence that the administration has much to hide in the ITT affair," Anderson thundered, "which looks more suspicious the more we investigate it."[41]

The final installment in Anderson's troika of ITT columns, published March 3, charged Mitchell and the conglomerate were "trying to lie their way out of a scandal over the suspicious, sudden settlement of a landmark antitrust suit against ITT." The columnist seized on Hushen's press release, which featured Mitchell saying he had "no knowledge of anyone from the [Republican National] committee or elsewhere dealing with International Telephone and Telegraph." "This is false," Anderson charged.

> In mid-May last year, California Lt. Gov. Ed Reinecke and an aide, Edgar Gillenwaters, met with Mitchell in his Washington office to discuss efforts to hold the convention in San Diego. We could not reach Reinecke, but Gillenwaters told

us he and Reinecke personally informed Mitchell that ITT had offered to put up as much as $400,000 to support a GOP convention in San Diego. "He liked the idea of [having the convention in] San Diego," Gillenwaters said of Mitchell. "He didn't need any persuading. He said, 'If you can do it, more power to you.' "[42]

In fact, this was false: Reinecke and Gillenwaters had *not* met with Mitchell in May 1971. Having confirmed as much through his office logs—which recorded meetings with the California duo on April 26 and September 17, 1971[43]—Mitchell might have expected to extinguish the matter with the cooperation of Reinecke, his fellow Republican. But the lieutenant governor, then a leading candidate to succeed Reagan, was busy giving interviews to seemingly every reporter who called to follow up on the Anderson column, expertly sticking his foot, with every question and answer, in Mitchell's mouth. To the *Washington Star*'s Bob Walters, who asked if it was true that he and Gillenwaters had informed Mitchell of the ITT pledge, contrary to Mitchell's denials, Reinecke blithely answered: "Yes, we discussed it. That was part of the package we were offering to the party." The Californian unthinkingly described the attorney general as "my input to the political arm of the administration," and told Walters he had the impression Mitchell already knew of ITT's pledge from Congressman Wilson. "It was widely known then that it was [Mitchell] who was making the political decisions," Reinecke foolishly added to a reporter the following day.[44]

Without checking his own records or consulting Mitchell, one of the most powerful and respected figures in their party, Reinecke had blindly gone on record with a version of events that was both wrong, at least as to the dates involved, and highly damaging to men whose fortunes bore significantly on Reinecke's own. From Mitchell's point of view, it was difficult to tell which of Reinecke's implications was worse: that contrary to his own denials, Mitchell knew about ITT's convention pledge while the antitrust cases were being settled, or that he was, while serving as the nation's chief law enforcement officer, "making the political decisions."

Before the day was out, according to later testimony, Reinecke received a call from Assistant Attorney General Robert Mardian in Washington. Shortly thereafter, the lieutenant governor commenced one of the most pronounced about-faces in American history, beginning with a written statement "clarifying" his earlier remarks. "After checking and verifying our records," Reinecke said of himself and Gillenwaters, "we learned that our meeting with . . . Mitchell was on April 26, 1971. At this time we did not discuss the Republican convention because the idea had not developed at that date. . . . [W]e never discussed or thought of any connection between the Sheraton Hotel and ITT." His earlier statements had been in error, Reinecke said, because he had been "trying to recall the purpose and dates of several trips to Washington at a time when I was out of town and did not have access to my files or records."[45]

In fact, even had Reinecke and Gillenwaters drowned Mitchell in details about the ITT pledge in their April 26 meeting, it would not have left the attorney general "pleased" or "delighted," as Reinecke at one point claimed. Previously unpublished documents show that Mitchell—a full two months *after* the April 26 meeting—was urging Haldeman to "slow down" on preparations for San Diego as the host city "until the president has had an opportunity to give serious thought to San Diego." Surely Mitchell would not have egged Reinecke on if Nixon had not yet settled on San Diego.[46]

Reinecke's witless responses to the swirling charges would have occasioned little long-term concern but for the equally unwise intervention, at this juncture, of Kleindienst. Incensed by Anderson's allegations, the attorney general designate demanded the Senate Judiciary Committee reopen its hearings into his nomination, a move that was, Kleindienst admitted years later, "rather impetuous." "I did not want to live the rest of my life under a cloud of suspicion," he said. He tracked Mitchell down at the White House and told him the plan. Mitchell counseled against it. *What did he need that for? Who cared what Jack Anderson wrote?* Kleindienst was adamant. "John, if the record isn't made straight at once, this matter will make the Teapot Dome scandal look like a tea party."[47]

What had, until Kleindienst's display of haste, been a Washington hullabaloo, of scant interest to the electorate, was now far graver: a congressional hearing, a legal matter, the wood from which perjury indictments are carved. It was also an election year, with a Democratic Congress eager to embarrass the Republican president seeking reelection. The nightmare Mitchell had warned Nixon about—"you will have a Senate investigation . . . these bastards up there [will] burden us with it"—was now upon them.

Presided over by Judiciary Committee chairman James O. Eastland, a conservative Mississippi Democrat and regular ally of Mitchell's, the Kleindienst nomination hearings became the longest in American history, running twenty-two days and consuming 1,751 pages in testimony and exhibits. The committee heard sworn testimony from Mitchell, Kleindienst, and McLaren; Reinecke and Gillenwaters; Louie Nunn, Jack Anderson, and Brit Hume; Harold Geneen and a half dozen other ITT officials, and—under the most unusual circumstances—Dita Beard.

Democrats used the hearings to exhume the ITT settlement and assail the administration's antitrust policy. The Nixon White House, under siege as never before, threw its full array of resources into the fight: lawyers, PR men, congressional arm twisters—even covert operatives. Indeed, the administration's working group on the ITT controversy fielded a roster of future Watergate veterans: John Dean, Charles Colson, Robert Mardian, Richard Moore, E. Howard Hunt. The last, a former CIA officer hired by the White House to declassify sensitive documents and conduct covert operations, like the Ellsberg break-in, played a singular role in debriefing the affair's central witness.

Distraught and teetering on the verge of mental collapse, Beard followed the orders of ITT executives and fled the capital. She boarded a United Airlines flight for Denver on March 2, just before the third Anderson column. An hour before touchdown, she told a stewardess she felt faint. The flight attendant returned with an ammonia inhaler, whereupon Beard, according to the plane's passenger illness report, "started turning gray and blue around the mouth." Within hours of landing, Beard checked into the Rocky Mountain Osteopathic Hospital, where a doctor retained by the Judiciary Committee later determined she was suffering from "coronary artery disease with angina pectoris."

Under orders from Colson aide Wally Johnson, Hunt flew to Denver to interview the elusive witness. Sporting an arresting wig and fake credentials acquired, like all his other tools of the trade, from old comrades at CIA, Hunt appeared at Beard's bedside one night around 11:00 p.m. Initially "very suspicious" of Hunt, the sedated patient agreed to talk with him on her daughter's assurances. Beard told Hunt she had fled the "hostile environment" of Washington because she felt there was "nobody she could trust." On the prime question— *was the memo implicating Mitchell authentic or not?*—the stricken lobbyist yielded little of value. "She was quite sure that she had not written it," Hunt later told the Senate Watergate committee, in previously unpublished testimony; but he also added that she "left it up in the air" and was responding "under heavy sedation."[48]

With the aid of David Fleming, Beard's ITT-paid attorney, and Robert F. Bennett, a shadowy power broker and CIA operative in Washington (later U.S. senator from Utah), a sworn statement was drawn up and issued in Beard's name. In it she called the original memo a "forgery" and a "hoax." "I did not prepare it and could not have," Beard swore, "since to my knowledge, the assertions in it regarding the antitrust cases and former Attorney General Mitchell are untrue." Beard also sharply challenged Brit Hume's account of their talk in her kitchen on the night of February 24. "Who in their right mind would write something like this?" she claimed she told Hume. "This isn't mine." "I don't care what you say," she quoted Hume as replying, "I'm going to prove a connection between San Diego and the settlement, and I'm going to use you to prove it." She remembered discussing the Kentucky Derby encounter, but added: "I had had several drinks. I was suffering intense chest pains at that time . . . I can in no way recall what I said to Mr. Hume."

It was much the same when a select panel of the Judiciary Committee, led by Senator Edward M. Kennedy, arrived in Beard's hospital room to interrogate her. She had the full complement of dramatic-testimony-from-her-hospital-bed accoutrements, including nervous doctors and lawyers, a closely watched electrocardiogram, and tubes protruding from her nostrils. Midway through Kennedy's questioning about the memo, the witness suffered a seizure; her deposition was over.

Six days later, however, Beard felt well enough to repair to a nearby apartment to chat with Mike Wallace for *60 Minutes*. Beard stuck with her revised account of the Derby incident, which now matched Mitchell's version—unwavering from the start—wherein the irrepressible lobbyist unwisely pressed her luck with the notoriously stony attorney general. "I'll never cease to be ashamed of that," she blushed to Wallace, "and I don't know why in the world I did it. It was really more in fun than anything." She also confirmed Nunn's recollection that she had been drinking heavily that day: "When you start out on Bloody Marys and then mint juleps all afternoon . . ."[49]

Inside the White House, the ITT scandal now loomed as the preeminent threat to the president's reelection. At first, Nixon nervously rescheduled a news conference because, as Haldeman noted, "there's no way he can adequately handle the ITT question." By the time he was ready to face reporters, on March 24, the president had devised a suitable, and clever, response. "ITT became the great conglomerate that it was," Nixon said, "in the two previous administrations primarily, in the Kennedy administration and in the Johnson administration. It grew and it grew and it grew, and nothing was done to stop it. In this administration we moved on ITT. . . . We required the greatest divestiture in the history of the antitrust law." He added: "If we wanted to do a favor for ITT, we could just continue to do what the two previous administrations had done, and that is nothing, let ITT continue to grow. But we moved on it and moved effectively."[50]

In the pitched combat of the ITT hearings, Mitchell played a unique dual role: He offered strategic advice, as in the days of Haynsworth and Carswell, on how best to bring the hearings to a swift, successful end, even as he prepared to testify before them. With Mitchell's chosen successor on the line, old divisions resurfaced between the White House and Justice, between Haldeman, Ehrlichman, and Colson on the one hand, and Mitchell, Kleindienst, and Mardian on the other. The former group derided the nominee as "a damn fool," and urged Nixon to withdraw the nomination, thereby ending the hearings and stanching the flow of administration blood. Mitchell, who later rued at his Watergate trial how the Kleindienst hearings were "made into a public circus," stuck by his old deputy and "weighed in very heavily" to persuade Nixon to do likewise.[51]

Once again, the president followed Mitchell's counsel—despite profound misgivings, voiced in an angry, and previously unpublished, session with Haldeman. "I really think that we're gonna have to really rub John Mitchell's nose in this," the president said. The conversation ended with Nixon wishing Kleindienst would recognize the inevitability of defeat, maybe "as a result of some prodding by me." But the nominee, recalling the lashing he had taken from Nixon on ITT a year earlier, was not about to do this president any favors.[52]

Finally, on March 14, 1972, Mitchell took his turn at the Senate witness table. As he raised his right hand to be sworn in, the former attorney general still appeared, at least to Anderson, the epitome of arrogant officialdom, "wearing his petulant air of affronted dignity and annoyance with the inconveniences of the democratic process." Over two days of questioning, Mitchell wearily described his support for McLaren's antitrust enforcement; defended the ITT settlement; recounted his meetings with Geneen and Rohatyn; gave his version of the Kentucky Derby incident; and dismissed the substance of the Beard-Merriam memo. "As far as I can see, there are no grounds for suspicion in this case," Mitchell declared. "I think it is a house of cards that has been built up." There were rough patches, however, owing chiefly to Mitchell's overly broad denials that he had known *nothing* of the ITT-Sheraton convention pledge; had *never* discussed the ITT case with Nixon; and had, as attorney general, made *no* political decisions. *Newsweek* reported the witness "cool but testy"; Washington doyenne Mary McGrory was struck by Mitchell's "wintry face and chilling humor," attributes that combined, she wrote, to "unnerve" the trained lawyers on the Judiciary Committee and make the witness seem "as approachable as a medieval Cardinal."[53]

Committee Democrats bore down on the two meetings with Reinecke and Gillenwaters, in April and September 1971. Mitchell conceded that Reinecke "might have talked about the possibility of locating the Republican convention in the state of California" during the April visit; but this stopped short of admitting Reinecke had specifically mentioned ITT's involvement. Likewise Mitchell reasoned that Reinecke "wouldn't be discussing [the convention] with me in September because I understand the decision had already been made," but again allowed as how Reinecke "may have" touched on the subject. When Senator John V. Tunney, the California Democrat, asked explicitly if Reinecke had mentioned ITT's financial pledge, Mitchell replied: "It is quite possible Lieutenant Governor Reinecke mentioned the convention in San Diego and Sheraton Hotel or something else but it would have made no impression upon me whatsoever, I not having that interest in it."[54]

In many respects, Mitchell was right to denounce the ITT scandal as a house of cards. There was no solid evidence he knew about ITT's convention pledge at the time of the antitrust settlement with the conglomerate, nor any evidence—beyond the wild buffet-line tales of Dita Beard—to suggest Mitchell intervened to dictate the outcome of the settlement negotiations. Yet the former attorney general undeniably perjured himself at the Kleindienst confirmation hearings. When Senator Tunney asked Mitchell, "Did Mr. Reinecke ever discuss, to your knowledge, in May or April, the ITT offer to bring the Republican convention to San Diego?" Mitchell replied, "No, senator." He then thought to add: "As far as I can tell, Mr. Reinecke must have had me mixed up with somebody else because he didn't meet me in May, and I have also read in the paper he has retracted that statement since then about that meeting in May."[55]

The second part of Mitchell's answer framed the issue solely in terms of his *meetings* with Reinecke, but he had answered, with a flat negative, a question that was *not* so limited. Tunney had asked not whether Reinecke had *met with* Mitchell to discuss the ITT pledge in April or May, but whether Reinecke had *discussed* the subject with Mitchell during that time. Neither Tunney nor any other member of the Judiciary Committee ever thought to ask Mitchell whether he and Reinecke had *spoken by telephone* during the relevant time frames—but they had.

When Reinecke appeared before the panel, more than a month after Mitchell, the last senator to question him was Republican Hiram Fong of Hawaii, who, like Tunney with Mitchell, queried the witness about information exchanged on the ITT pledge, and without limiting his question to face-to-face meetings.

> **FONG:** So the only time you discussed the convention with Mr. Mitchell was in September after the ITT case had already been settled?
> **REINECKE:** That is correct, Senator.

Reinecke also told Senator Kennedy he had "no way of knowing" whether Mitchell knew of the ITT pledge by September.[56] Later, when the ITT case consumed the energies of a whole division of the Watergate Special Prosecution Force, investigators obtained Mitchell's office records and found he had in fact spoken to Reinecke on the phone three times between April and September 1971, all before San Diego won the convention rights and the ITT cases were settled.[57] When the special prosecutors confronted Reinecke with this evidence, in July 1973, Reinecke acknowledged he had misled the Judiciary Committee: "I realize [I] was not describing the entire situation, but relied on the first law of the courtroom. . . . Answer questions only and do not volunteer." Reinecke pleaded that he was tired during his Senate testimony—which occurred after one day's notice, a red-eye flight from California and four hours of White House coaching, and with no counsel present—and responded to Kennedy and Fong as he did because "every substantive question regarding Mitchell referred to meetings and not to other communications by letter, telegram or phone."[58]

The prosecutors were unmoved, and Reinecke struck a deal—or so he thought—to testify against Mitchell in exchange for being left alone; immunity was never formally conferred. Accordingly, on February 4, 1974, Reinecke told a federal grand jury that the purpose of his telephone conversations with Mitchell in the spring of 1971 was "to bring [Mitchell] up to date on details . . . about the progress of the convention, particularly the financial commitments." He reported Mitchell's reaction was "encouraging, tolerant and fatherly," but added the attorney general "was like most of those fellows in the White House. They all say the same thing, which is very little."[59]

Two months later, with Reinecke a leading candidate in California's Republican gubernatorial primary, a Washington grand jury indicted him on two counts of perjury before the Judiciary Committee. Reinecke maintained his innocence, stayed in—and lost—the gubernatorial primary, and was subsequently convicted on both counts. The following year, his conviction was overturned because the Senate had failed to follow proper procedure in establishing a quorum.[60] Though Mitchell was not called as a witness, the New York Times noted that the charges in Reinecke's prosecution implicitly "raise[d] questions" about Mitchell's own testimony before the Judiciary Committee.[61]

Yet his dealings with Reinecke were not the only subject on which Mitchell lied at the ITT hearings. The second was his interaction with Nixon. Unlike Haldeman and a handful of White House and Secret Service aides, Mitchell was kept in the dark about the existence of Nixon's secret taping system, and thus never imagined evidence would surface to challenge his assertion, to Republican Senator Roman Hruska of Nebraska, that "with respect to ITT or any other litigation, no, I have never talked to the president about it."[62]

Questioned by Watergate prosecutors after they obtained the tape of Mitchell's April 21, 1971, meeting with Nixon, the former attorney general said he had "forgotten completely about the Kleindienst-Nixon incident and did not discuss it with anyone."[63] The ITT task force later decided not to indict Mitchell for this instance of perjury because the incriminating evidence against him was, in fact, exculpatory: The tape showed Mitchell honorably upholding the law, by intervening to persuade Nixon to preserve, not scuttle, the antitrust case.[64]

Mitchell also lied at the hearings, finally, to preserve the fiction that as attorney general he had kept himself strictly divorced from political matters. Everyone who followed politics in those days knew, as Reinecke mindlessly told newsmen, that Mitchell was Nixon's preeminent political adviser and would eventually resign from Justice to spearhead the president's reelection drive. Later, stacks of memoranda would emerge, typed on DOJ and CRP letterheads, showing Mitchell's involvement, throughout the calendar year 1971, in countless (though not all) decisions relating to Nixon's reelection. But Mitchell felt he could never admit as much before the Judiciary Committee, any more than Robert F. Kennedy could ever have confessed publicly that he minded his brother's political fortunes while running the Justice Department.

Betraying no grasp of this irony, Senator Kennedy sought energetically to pin Mitchell down on the point. "Do you remember what party responsibilities you had prior to March first?" Kennedy asked, citing the date of Mitchell's resignation as attorney general. "Party responsibilities?" Mitchell asked. "Yes, Republican Party," Kennedy said. "I do not have and did not have any responsibilities, and I have no party responsibilities now," Mitchell answered. *No reelection campaign responsibilities?* Kennedy pressed. "Not as yet," Mitchell said. "I hope to. I am going to make the application to the chairman of the committee if I ever get through with these hearings." The committee room erupted in laughter, and minutes later Mitchell was gone.[65]

Seen in historical perspective, the ITT scandal was a dry run for Watergate, which erupted soon afterward and eventually subsumed the ITT case under its massive investigative aegis. The Age of Scandal was now upon Nixon and his men—and the country. The president, for one, glimpsed the bleak future. "At the present time," he told his aides during the ITT hearings, "you just gotta figure that they're gonna be investigating us in all things."[66]

When it was all over, the central premise of the ITT scandal— that John Mitchell fixed the antitrust cases in exchange for the conglomerate's financial support for San Diego's bid for the 1972 Republican convention—remained unproved, if not outright refuted. Even the *Washington Post*, which published Jack Anderson's columns and hardly saw eye to eye with Nixon and Mitchell on antitrust policy, or much else, conceded—in late July 1974, less than three weeks before Nixon's resignation—that the "connection" between ITT's convention pledge and the disposition of the antitrust suits "has never been made convincingly."[67]

Consequently, Mitchell's perjury at the ITT hearings was either unnecessary or calculatedly protective of the president, who had far more to conceal. A similar pattern would emerge in Mitchell's behavior in Watergate. The irony is that while the episode revealed Mitchell's willingness to break the law as a private citizen—he was no longer a public official when he testified falsely before the Judiciary Committee—it also confirmed his integrity as an attorney general, in which capacity he repelled countless attempts over a three-year span by White House figures, from the president on down, to tamper with the ordinary processes of the Justice Department, most specifically in the enforcement of antitrust policy.

In denying he had ever talked with Nixon about the ITT case, Mitchell's lie concealed his secret honor in the conduct of public office, and Nixon's corresponding iniquity. This trade-off left Mitchell the poorer—as had his willing collusion, throughout his tenure as attorney general, in the false, sternly authoritarian public image Nixon assigned him—but Mitchell never seemed to mind; instead he seemed to regard it as a reasonable price to pay in the service of some greater good. Asked once about his role in the ITT scandal, he replied, "It would take me about an hour to explain it."[68]

PETTY THIEF

John Mitchell is not a terribly responsive man,
sometimes.

—*John Dean, 1974*[1]

ON FRIDAY NIGHT, March 12, 1971, Mitchell stood on a receiving line in New Jersey, honoring a debt to the man beside him: Harry Sears, the retiring Republican majority leader of the New Jersey State Senate, in whose honor the evening's $100-a-head testimonial dinner, at the Chanticler Restaurant in suburban Milburn, was being held. Sears's political muscle had helped deliver eighteen of New Jersey's contested delegates at the '68 convention; he was Mitchell's man in the Garden State. In 1970, at his party's request, Sears had run in the GOP gubernatorial primary; lacking in money and name recognition, however, he finished third in a field of five and plunged $50,000 into debt. Mitchell's appearance at the Chanticler was meant to help pay off that debt.

As the reception line snaked along, the sight of one face caused Sears to stop the procession. It belonged to his most generous financial contributor, a wealthy young businessman from Boonton, tall with slick black hair and a pencil mustache, a bulbous nose, and puffy little eyes. "John, I would like you to meet my friend Bob Vesco and his wife, Pat," Sears said to Mitchell. "This is the friend I have been telling you about."

Mitchell and the man exchanged brief pleasantries. Later, during the dinner, Vesco offered hellos to Sears and Martha Mitchell, seated together, then slipped round their table and spoke briefly—for "less than a minute"—with Mitchell and Sears's wife Emma. Asked later if he remembered meeting Vesco on this occasion, Mitchell said no. All he recalled was that the man reminded him, in appearance, of his long-deceased brother, Scranton. Vesco, however, was determined to make a more lasting impression.[2]

Born to first-generation Americans in Detroit in 1935, Robert Lee Vesco always wanted to get rich quick. A voracious reader and fast learner, he dropped out of a technical high school to lay brick and repair cars. Married at seventeen, soon a father of three, Vesco held middle-management jobs in the automobile industry and juggled other odd pursuits: small-time gambling, bingo parlors, a highway bar called the Powder Mill Inn. A relentless exaggerator and name-dropper with "an uncanny ability to find people who were weak," Vesco managed to acquire controlling interests in some failing machine parts companies, which, in 1965, he consolidated and incorporated as International Controls Corporation (ICC); within a year, he achieved his childhood dream of becoming, at least on paper, a millionaire, and by 1970, he oversaw thirteen subsidiaries and five thousand employees.[3]

But one goal remained elusive: respect. So Vesco went international. The aggressive financier—who drew the attention of federal regulators as early as 1968—naturally gravitated to the largely unregulated world of offshore mutual funds, then an inviting source of practically unlimited, nontaxable risk capital. With characteristic grandiosity, Vesco set his sights on Investors Overseas Services (IOS), the Geneva-based mutual fund empire that dominated offshore finance in those years. Undermined by legal woes and a "chaotic management structure," IOS was ripe for takeover. The company's battle with the Securities and Exchange Commission (SEC) hardly helped. SEC staff lawyers had been demanding access to IOS client lists, both in America and overseas. IOS refused, citing Swiss secrecy laws. By 1967, a shaky truce—or "consent order," as the lawyers called it—was forged: The feds would leave IOS alone as long as the company did no business in the United States. Eyeing IOS's internal chaos and enormous assets from afar, Vesco worried little about the technicalities of the consent order. He insinuated himself into the IOS hierarchy, and, through a complex series of transactions cloaking his ownership, purchased 6.6 million of the company's shares. In February 1971, IOS's board of directors elected Vesco its chairman.[4]

On March 18, six days after Vesco shook Mitchell's hand at the Chanticler restaurant, the SEC launched an investigation of ICC, Vesco's mothership company. At issue—initially—was whether Vesco's takeover of IOS violated the 1967 consent order. SEC subpoenas began piling up, demanding thousands of internal ICC documents. A profane man with a "short fuse," Vesco grew enraged, cursing the government's "witch hunt." Against his lawyers' advice, he impulsively countersued the SEC, its chairman, William J. Casey, and Attorney General Mitchell.[5]

To the garrulous nouveau riche entrepreneur from New Jersey, an audience with the SEC chairman, remote and patrician, became a kind of holy grail: If he could just meet Casey personally, Vesco thought, he could talk his way out of SEC's crosshairs. He made several approaches to Casey through various routes, but each time the wily Office of Strategic Services (OSS) veteran, later CIA director under President Reagan, rebuffed him. So Vesco turned to Harry Sears, whose failed gubernatorial campaign Vesco had lavishly supported, and whose chumminess with John Mitchell had been on vivid display at the Chanticler two months earlier. On May 16, Vesco wrote a personal letter to Casey and asked Sears to steer it to Mitchell for forwarding. Sears in turn penned a "Dear John" letter.

> Bob's concern is that the suit may be viewed out of context by the administration. Basically he is trying to get past the [SEC] staff level to the chairman and apparently has been unable to do so to date. . . . Bob is a good friend, otherwise I would not trouble you with this information, which, as I said, is for the sole purpose of insuring that there can be no misunderstanding with regard to his motives and purposes.

Sears's note drew only a boilerplate response, drafted a month later by Mitchell's secretary, Susie Morrison. A week later, a group backed by the Rockefeller family expressed interest in acquiring IOS. Sears again wrote to Mitchell, alerting him to the potential deal. "I have no way of knowing whether your conversation with Bill Casey may have encouraged this," Sears wrote. Mitchell later testified he did not recall seeing any of Sears's letters, and never talked to Casey about the Vesco case at that time. Asked why Sears would have invoked "your conversation with Casey" if Mitchell had not, in fact, had such a conversation and recounted it to Sears, Mitchell pleaded ignorance and suggested Sears was only trying to mollify his demanding patron.[6]

On November 30, 1971, in between calls with Henry Kissinger, the House and Senate minority leaders, the secretary of state, and the president's personal secretary, Attorney General Mitchell took his first affirmative step on Vesco's behalf. It started with a return call to Sears. Normally understated, Sears sounded agitated: Vesco was in a Swiss jail cell, being held without bail on charges filed by a disgruntled IOS stockholder. What's more, Sears fretted, "Nobody had been able to get through to the United States Embassy." "Are you positive Vesco cannot get bail under any circumstances?" Sears recalled Mitchell asking. Yes, Sears replied. Mitchell then offered to contact the U.S. ambassador to Switzerland, Shelby Davis, a friend for thirty years. But the ambassador was out of town. So Mitchell spoke with Richard Vine, deputy chief of mission at the embassy in Bern. A career Foreign Service officer who had met Mitchell in passing, Vine later testified he told Mitchell that Vesco's jailing was "warranted in Swiss law" and would probably be resolved the following day. Mitchell asked a few questions, Vine recalled, and asked to be kept apprised of developments.[7]

Mitchell called Sears back. According to Sears, Mitchell reported that he had managed "to get some word through to the Embassy and he hoped that it would be of some assistance." Recounting this call to the grand jury, however, Mitchell said nothing about being "of some assistance." Instead, he told the grand jurors he simply "called Mr. Sears back and told him they were working—looking into the subject matter." Mitchell added at trial: "I didn't do anything in the Swiss matter except make a phone call." That was untrue. W. Mark Felt, the number-two man at the FBI—later revealed as Bob Woodward's infamous Watergate source, Deep Throat—testified Mitchell summoned him to the attorney general's office, and there asked Felt to ascertain the facts surrounding Vesco's jailing. Confronted with Felt's testimony, Mitchell conceded: "I must have completely forgotten about the occasion of my meeting with Agent Felt [sic]." As Vine predicted, Vesco was released the next day, after posting $125,000 bail. Upon his return to the United States, he presented Sears with a check for $10,000. When Sears protested that his call to Mitchell had been a favor, Vesco insisted Sears keep the check: "It may seem like a lot of money to you, but it's small change to me."[8]

Buoyed by Mitchell's show of concern during the Swiss jailing incident, Vesco revived his campaign to get the attorney general to rein in the SEC. "See if you can get John Mitchell to give you some help . . . with the commission," Vesco again ordered Sears, who by January 1972 had joined the payroll, serving on the boards of ICC and the Vesco-controlled Bahamas Commonwealth Bank. Sears tried gently to discourage further exploitation of the Mitchell connection. "Bob, we didn't do too much good last year," he pleaded. But Vesco continued to see Mitchell as a route to Casey, and harbored, too, a weird fascination with Mitchell himself. "On occasion," a biographer noted, Vesco "impressed visitors by asking them to step outside a moment so he could take a confidential call from John N. Mitchell." There were no such calls.[9]

Sears's first move was to visit the White House, and the ubiquitous John Ehrlichman. Where Mitchell was slow to act, Ehrlichman was eager—even though previously unpublished notes show he was informed of Mitchell's call to the Swiss embassy and warned not to provide similar assistance. "[D]on't help," read Ehrlichman's notes, "SEC investi[gati]ng." Undaunted, Ehrlichman followed up Sears's visit by firing off a memo to the attorney general, requesting calls be placed to several embassies on Vesco's behalf. This Mitchell did not understand—perhaps because the request came from the reviled Ehrlichman—so the attorney general reportedly called Sears at home and asked for a briefing at their next meeting, set for January 12.[10]

Sears cut to the chase. The SEC probe was murdering Vesco and ICC. Creditors were growing "disturbed" by the negative publicity, and Vesco was "deathly afraid" the SEC lawyers would recommend formal charges against him. Sears asked "if it would be at all possible to try and get some assistance in terms of . . . an opportunity for . . . ICC and Vesco . . . to sit down with either the chairman or the commission." Mitchell remained reserved. According to Sears, the attorney general "listened and puffed and nodded," then allowed as how Vesco and ICC appeared to deserve some kind of help. "I would at least discuss it with Bill Casey," Sears quoted Mitchell as saying. Sears later claimed that before leaving, he gave Mitchell two documents: a memo to the attorney general from Sears, explaining Ehrlichman's requests; and a memo from Vesco's corporate lawyer, detailing SEC attempts to keep Vesco behind bars in Switzerland. Sears testified Mitchell "did scan" the documents; Mitchell claimed he never saw them until trial.[11]

Casey later testified it was in December 1971 or January 1972 that Mitchell first discussed the Vesco case with him. The SEC chairman hardly felt as though the attorney general was attempting to put in a fix; to the contrary, he remembered Mitchell "merely bringing the situation to my attention." Yet one small divergence in their recollections later prompted a perjury charge against Mitchell: whether he mentioned to the chairman, as Casey claimed, that the SEC staff had tried to keep Vesco in jail in Switzerland.[12]

Unwisely, Mitchell plunged deeper into Vesco's netherworld. The financier was eyeing Intra Bank in Beirut, into which the U.S. government had deposited foreign aid funds. On January 19, Mitchell again summoned Mark Felt, this time to ask if the FBI had a man in Beirut. Felt assured Mitchell the Bureau did indeed have a legal attaché—code for spy—at the U.S. embassy there. As Felt later testified, "[Mitchell] said that he would like to send a message to the ambassador but through the FBI communications channel because he didn't want to go through the State Department channel. . . . He had requested that a message be sent relating to the ambassador to the effect that Mr. Vesco was highly regarded by the attorney general and by the administration and that any cooperation they could give to him would be appreciated. So a cablegram to this effect was sent."

According to published reports, Mitchell also personally telephoned Theodore A. Korontjis, the FBI legal attaché in Beirut, and instructed him to approach Ambassador William B. Buffum directly on Vesco's behalf. To establish contact with Korontjis, Mitchell used the FBI's communications system, again bypassing State. Ambassador Buffum reportedly "did not take kindly" to Mitchell's methods. Incensed, the ambassador cabled Washington to ask why Vesco deserved special treatment, only to hear back that he didn't. Queried by the State Department, Mitchell said Korontjis must have misunderstood him or exceeded his instructions.

The Beirut episode, like the Swiss jailing incident, came to haunt Mitchell. "The genesis of this," he later testified, "was a request from somebody over at the White House—I believe it was John

Ehrlichman—that such a representation be made in connection with whatever Mr. Vesco's activities were in Lebanon, which had, I gather, been hampered somewhat by the Swiss jailing incident." Asked on cross-examination if he had tried to open doors for Vesco abroad, Mitchell testified it was "more to establish a fact or clear a misimpression than . . . to open a door." Yet Mitchell's claim that his overtures to Ambassador Buffum came solely at Ehrlichman's instigation contradicted Mitchell's corresponding claim never to have received the memo in which Ehrlichman requested such overtures; no one caught the discrepancy.[13]

"Are you sure Bob Vesco is everything you represent him to be?" So a newly skeptical Mitchell greeted Harry Sears in the attorney general's office on the morning of February 11, 1972. Sears's reply was notably ambivalent: "Bob Vesco is my friend and I am his advocate. . . . I have to take this position until somebody proves I am wrong."[14]

Like all of Sears's meetings with Mitchell in this period, the February 11 session later provoked sharp clashes of memory—and criminal charges against the former attorney general. Most important among these disputes was Sears's claim to have informed Mitchell on this occasion that Vesco wished to contribute to the president's 1972 reelection campaign; in typical style, the ICC chairman "wanted to be among the top contributors" to the Committee for the Re-Election of the President (CRP). "I told [Mitchell that Vesco] was talking about giving very substantial amounts," Sears testified. Mitchell supposedly asked what Vesco had given in '68; Sears didn't know. Mitchell then supposedly said this was a matter for Maurice Stans, the former secretary of commerce now managing CRP's finance committee, to handle.[15]

Owlish and bespectacled, a big-game hunter and enjoyer of the finer things, the sixty-two-year-old Stans stood imperiously astride the nexus of politics and finance. As head of CRP's Finance Committee, he was, by March 1972, well on his way toward raising $60 million for Nixon's reelection drive, a then unheard-of sum for a political campaign and equivalent to roughly $256 million in current figures. Prior to joining Nixon's cabinet—where Stans developed courteous, but never especially close, relations with his Watergate neighbor, Mitchell—Stans had served as President Eisenhower's budget director. In between his government stints, Stans earned millions as a senior partner in a powerhouse New York investment banking firm, and was elected, in 1960, to the Accountants' Hall of Fame.[16]

On March 8, 1972, Vesco himself and ICC president Laurence Richardson arrived at CRP, located at 1701 Pennsylvania Avenue, across the street from the White House, to meet with Stans and Daniel Hofgren, a CRP fund-raiser. Vesco, according to Richardson's testimony, began by saying he had contributed generously to Nixon in '68 and wanted to do better in '72. "But I have a problem," Vesco said. "My company and I are under investigation by the SEC. . . . It's completely without merit and amounts to a personal vendetta and harassment." He concluded: "I want to find a way to bring the case to a conference and a settlement." Stans, according to Richardson, replied: "Well, I can't help you with this, but let's see if we can get you an appointment with John Mitchell today while you are here."

Richardson recalled that Stans picked up the phone, but failed to make the appointment with Mitchell. "How much you got in mind to give?" Stans asked. "I want to be in the front row," Vesco answered, his *arriviste* ambitions laid bare; he proposed $500,000 in two installments. Stans asked if Vesco understood the new election law. "I'm not sure I do," Vesco replied. After April 7, Stans explained, all contributions of the size Vesco had in mind had to be publicly reported, along with the donor's name; thus Vesco might want to make the first payment of $250,000 before April 6. Vesco agreed.

As he and Richardson left, Vesco bragged how "clever" he had been in broaching the SEC problem; he had not asked directly for a quid pro quo for his contribution, but made plain his desires. In fact, it was the white-haired Stans who'd played the snickering Vesco for a fool. "Stans was a true professional," wrote Vesco's biographer. "He knew exactly where to draw that line while giving Vesco the come-on. Vesco . . . did in fact think he was buying influence. Although Stans did not offer any discouragement, he knew how not to transgress the boundaries of criminal liability."[17]

That same night, Daniel Hofgren strolled the corridors of the Washington Hilton, wading among two thousand tuxedoed guests at a fund-raiser for GOP candidates. At one point, Hofgren spotted a familiar face: John Mitchell, whose resignation as attorney general had taken effect a week earlier. "I recall going up to him and saying, 'Did you see Mr. Vesco?'" Hofgren later testified. "And [Mitchell] turned around and said, 'You stay away from that,' and that was the sum and substance of my conversation." Asked what happened next, Hofgren replied: "When John Mitchell says, 'You stay away from it,' I stay away from it." Mitchell, of course, remembered no such conversation—and once again, it earned him a perjury charge.[18]

If the Watergate era was defined by the corrupting influence of cash in the American political system, the moment when Richardson and Sears showed up at the well-appointed offices of Maurice Stans, on April 10, 1972, was paradigmatic—even if, as a jury later found, no crimes occurred. Assembled were three upright, business-suited members of "the greatest generation," one carrying a briefcase stuffed with $200,000 in hundred-dollar bills. The meeting, like the briefcase, bulged with connotations: No one suffered any delusions the cash was being given anonymously, past the date required by the new law, because Robert Vesco believed in détente or wage and price controls.

Ever the hustler, Vesco had had trouble rounding up the cash. In the end, he required a loan from the Bahamian bank he controlled. At ICC offices on April 7, he had scowled at Richardson: "One more thing. I have got a message for Stans that I want you to give him." "What's the message?" "Tell Stans to get that fuckin' SEC off my back," Vesco said. "Well, I will give him the message," Richardson replied, "but not in those words." "Be damned sure you give him the message," Vesco persisted.[19]

Now, the following Monday, Richardson placed the briefcase atop Stans's desk, angled it toward him, and opened it just enough for the former commerce secretary to see the Ben Franklins stacked inside. "Mr. Stans, here is your currency," Richardson said. "Do you want to count it?" Stans said that wouldn't be necessary. Richardson closed the briefcase, set it aside, and sat down. According to Sears, seated on a couch across the room, Richardson then uncorked the genie. "Mr. Vesco wants me to deliver you a message," Sears quoted Richardson as saying. "He'd like to get some help." "Tell him that's not my bailiwick," Stans supposedly replied. "That's John Mitchell's department." "Now, wait a minute," Sears interjected, bolting from the couch. "What we brought here today is a political contribution. There's nothing else involved. Larry, I think perhaps we better leave." Richardson took the hint. When the two were alone, Sears was spitting mad. "Larry, what the hell is that all about?" "Well," Richardson replied, "I really think Bob would have wanted me to deliver the message stronger."[20]

That afternoon Sears went to see Mitchell, now officially campaign manager. According to Sears, the meeting dwelt on two main topics: Vesco's cash contribution, delivered in the bulging briefcase to Maurice Stans in the same building hours earlier; and Vesco's continuing desire for an audience with William Casey. Mitchell denied learning about the briefcase, but agreed the question of an audience with Casey had again arisen. "The situation is worse, if anything, as far as the SEC staff attitude," Sears pleaded. Having shared a drink with Casey at his own Watergate apartment four days earlier, Mitchell knew this was so; the agency's staff believed Vesco guilty of crimes. Rather than tell Sears that himself, Mitchell picked up the phone and asked his secretary to get Casey on the line. "Harry Sears is here," Mitchell told him. "He would like very much to sit down with you for a few minutes." Casey was free at four o'clock; Sears finally had his elusive audience with the SEC chairman.[21]

To federal prosecutors, Mitchell's brief call to Casey formed the heart of the crime, epitomized the discreet, businesslike abuse of power they aimed to punish. By all accounts, however, Mitchell, in requesting the meeting for Sears, made no mention of Vesco's contribution. This exculpatory fact the prosecutors stood on its head: They made it the first obstruction of justice count in Mitchell's indictment, arguing he had to keep Casey ignorant of the contribution, so as to enlist his aid in quashing the SEC probe.

At 4:30 p.m., Sears entered Casey's office to find the SEC chairman and his youthful general counsel, Brad Cook, the resident expert on ICC. Sears laid out Vesco's position: The SEC's endless subpoenas had far exceeded the original scope of the investigation; the "high emotional feelings and abrasions" between the SEC's lawyers and Vesco's own were certain to produce an adverse ruling that Sears did not want to see rubber-stamped by Casey and the other four commissioners. "Well, Mr. Sears, I can assure you of one thing," Casey replied. "We don't rubber stamp staff recommendations down here. We consider them very carefully."

Cook conceded that "fights" and "confrontations" had broken out during Vesco's depositions. "But there is something that you should know," Cook continued, "and that is that there is a very good possibility that there is no way that this case can be settled without an injunctive order. A report recommending suit . . . is a very likely eventuality here. . . . There is also a possibility in this case that Vesco may be subject to a perjury charge. . . . Vesco lied when he was here on deposition, and if Vesco lied, we have to consider the possibility of a criminal referral."

Sears cannot have been taken entirely by surprise; by his own account, Mitchell had given him an internal memo Cook had written that said all the same things, a full sixty days earlier (another charge Mitchell denied). Still, the New Jersey politician seemed unnerved by Cook's blunt talk of perjury and criminal referrals. Sears offered to be of help in getting the SEC whatever documents it needed, then looked imploringly to Casey: Did he have the chairman's assurance Vesco would be permitted another opportunity to plead his case before the filing of any suits or referrals? "Mr. Sears," Casey repeated icily, "we don't rubber stamp anything." The audience was over.[22]

At CRP headquarters, meanwhile, Maurice Stans called in Hugh Sloan, the CRP treasurer, a young, handsome former White House aide, and gave him a white bank bag containing $200,000 in cash. Stans ordered Sloan to count it, then store it in a safe. According to Sloan, he asked his boss who the donor was. Appearing before the grand jury, Sloan testified that Stans replied: "For the time being, list it under John Mitchell's name." Yet a year later, testifying as a government witness at the Mitchell-Stans trial, Sloan claimed that Stans, in his reply, attributed this order to Mitchell himself, and specified the entry should not use Mitchell's full name. "John Mitchell wants it listed under the initials 'JM' for the time being," Sloan quoted Stans as saying.[23]

In his ledger, Sloan listed Vesco's contribution and the initials "JM." To the prosecutors, Mitchell's initials represented incontrovertible evidence of corruption. Another witness testified the use of the initials "was based on a telephone conversation [Stans] had with John Mitchell." But Stans himself, testifying before the grand jury in March 1973, said he only told Sloan to "put [down] Mitchell because it came through his end: Sears." Mitchell testified that he first discovered his initials appeared alongside the entry for the Vesco contribution in February or March 1973. When he found out, Mitchell testified, he growled at Stans: "What the hell did you ever do that for?" He continued: "Mr. Stans said he didn't know. . . . He did not have a rationale for it."[24]

Small wonder that Mitchell, asked on the stand if he considered

Stans a close friend, replied, "I *believe* so"; or that the *New York Times*, observing the interaction between the defendants at their historic trial, reported: "The two men seldom speak."[25]

Vesco and Sears paid another grim visit to Brad Cook in May 1972. If it would end the SEC's probe, Vesco said, he was willing to commence, in the parlance of the era, the "deVescoization" of ICC. Cook sternly replied that any settlement would have to include an acknowledgment of wrongdoing by Vesco, and an injunction against further violations of federal securities laws. At this, the volatile financier blew his stack. "Your investigation has been going on for a year," he fumed, "and you have nothing!" When Cook alluded to perjury, Vesco grew angrier: "There is nothing to that! There is no way I'm going to settle the case in a way that will leave open a perjury charge." Finally, when Cook mentioned criminal referral, Vesco became defiant: "No way, baby!"[26]

Now knowing the feds considered him a criminal, Vesco soon found himself, for the first and last time, in John Mitchell's office, where Sears "reintroduced" the two men. "John, this is Bob Vesco," Sears said. "You met him at my dinner." After some pleasantries, Vesco retreated to a couch along the perimeter of Mitchell's office, while the former attorney general spent the next fifteen minutes talking politics with Sears. For all his wealth and grandiose aspirations, his infatuation with Mitchell and hunger for status and respect, Vesco, in this setting, was a zero—reduced to looking on from afar, sitting mute while his elders, masters of electoral realpolitik, conversed on a level beyond his ken.

From Vesco's perspective, the meeting was a bust: Sears didn't even broach the SEC issue with Mitchell! But the financier had other cards to play. He put Nixon's knockabout nephew, Donald Nixon Jr., on the payroll. And he called in a favor from an overseas friend. Since 1969, Vesco had quietly been funneling money to Costa Rica, where his investments, mostly in government bonds, would eventually total an estimated $60 million. Of that money, $2.15 million landed in the accounts of San Cristobal, S.A., a holding company controlled by the country's aging president, José Figueres Ferrer, aka "Don Pepe." A vain little tyrant—he stood five-three, got a hair transplant and facelift in his mid-seventies, and once smacked a protester who called him *un hijo de puta*, or "son of a bitch," saying, "I'll teach you respect"—Figueres was only too happy to help his rich *gringo* patron when Vesco asked.[27]

Thus on July 22, 1972, President Figueres wrote to "Your Excellency Richard M. Nixon" saying he was reaching out "in the spirit of good relations which exist between our two countries." Figueres said Vesco's largesse "may provide the ingredient that has been lacking in our plans to create . . . a show piece of democratic development." Then came the pitch, president to president.

> Mr. Vesco has had difficulties with the Securities and Exchange Commission, because of his past association with the I.O.S. Ltd. *Mr. John Mitchell, your former attorney general, is familiar with the matters.* I am concerned that any adverse publicity emanating from the S.E.C. against Mr. Vesco might jeopardize the development of my country. . . . If we are apprised in time, we may take precautions to counter the adverse effects.

Figueres had not asked Nixon to do anything more than provide advance notice in the event the SEC moved against Vesco; but the implication was plain: If the SEC took down Vesco, Costa Rica's fledgling democracy might crumble too, leaving only Latin American communists to benefit! Figueres had also dropped Mitchell's name, insinuating that Nixon's most trusted confidant supported the Vesco cause. Yet the letter never reached the Oval Office. Vesco later told Sears that proud "Don Pepe" received only a "cryptic, unsatisfactory" response from "some low-level White House staff." Vesco's stab at international diplomacy had failed.[28]

That month, SEC lawyers concluded Vesco and his corporate cronies were guilty of "looting" ICC's companies on a massive scale: Assets had been shifted, shell companies created, controlling interests, supposedly relinquished, secretly maintained. Where SEC lawyers focused originally on the takeover of IOS and the veracity of Vesco's sworn statements, they now saw larceny on an unprecedented scale, with investors across the globe losing their savings so Vesco could jet around in his Boeing 707, *The Silver Phyllis*, outfitted with the world's only airborne sauna and discotheque.[29]

On September 29, 1972, the SEC summoned Vesco for an October 11 appearance. Vesco immediately suspected the feds were wise to his contribution to CRP, or at least to the unexplained movement of $250,000 in cash. Sensing the end was near, Vesco flew into a rage: "Those bastards would like nothing more than to nail me and the president to the wall together," he ranted. "There's no way that I'm going to testify. . . . It's going to be blown up like the ITT affair. Nixon may survive some of the other things but this would be the crusher."

Since suasion and $200,000 in cash hadn't got him anywhere, the furious financier turned to blackmail. Perhaps the very thing that most imperiled him could prove his salvation. He told Sears: "Get hold of Mitchell and those guys and tell them that they will have that thing quashed or I'll blow the lid off the whole thing." Sears left the room "angry" but, still indebted to Vesco, agreed to see what he could do.[30]

That fall, Mitchell spoke frequently with Sears, but as always, their recollections differed sharply. Sears claimed he told Mitchell that if Vesco were forced to testify in the closing days of the campaign, it would have a "devastating" effect on Nixon's electoral fortunes. Mitchell supposedly agreed, asking: "Why would the SEC be interested in where the money went? Their investigation is about where Vesco is getting his money from." Sears said he and Mitchell pondered how to delay Vesco's testimony until after the election. Mitchell swore he had "no recollection of ever discussing a subpoena to Robert

Vesco during that time frame at all." Had Sears asked him to "quash" or "postpone" the subpoena? No, Mitchell said.[31]

As it happened, Vesco's subpoena was adjourned, but not past Election Day. So informed by Sears, the former attorney general—who already knew from friends in government how dire Vesco's situation was—mumbled vaguely that he hoped it would all work out. When Sears said Vesco would likely plead the Fifth, Mitchell supposedly wondered whether another adjournment could be secured. "Do you think that is possible?" Sears recalled asking. "Well, I would certainly hope so," he quoted Mitchell as saying, "if they have any concern for the president of the United States."[32]

On October 18, Vesco, on the advice of his high-priced counsel, Arthur Liman, pleaded the Fifth Amendment at his SEC deposition. "I hope the hell I make them happy," Vesco said of Nixon and Mitchell, adding his refusal to testify should be considered "an additional contribution" to the campaign. Within forty-eight hours, Sears notified a "relieved" Mitchell. "Please tell Bob that I am grateful," Sears recalled Mitchell saying. But other ICC employees were also scheduled to testify. Sears said he again called Mitchell, and pleaded: "What, if anything, do you think can be done?" Mitchell, according to Sears, replied, "Well, don't tell Vesco, but this time I will go through the White House. I am going to talk to John Dean."

The action Mitchell supposedly took next—calling the White House counsel and asking him to contact Bill Casey, with the goal of getting the ICC subpoenas postponed until after Election Day—later formed obstruction of justice Counts One and Four in Mitchell's indictment. And Mitchell's answers before the grand jury to questions about the ICC subpoenas formed three of the five perjury counts he later faced in the affair. Count Seven charged Mitchell with lying to the grand jury when he claimed he and Sears had never discussed Vesco's subpoena or blackmail threat. Count Eight charged Mitchell with lying when he told the grand jury he never plotted with Sears about how to delay or prevent the other four ICC employees from testifying. While Mitchell acknowledged he had "a number of conversations" with Sears about the employees' impending depositions, he claimed these talks were limited to Sears telling him the employees had retained private counsel. The same count alleged Mitchell lied when he was asked if he spoke to John Dean about the ICC subpoenas, and he flatly told the grand jury: "I didn't talk to John Dean about any subpoenas." Count Nine charged Mitchell also lied to the grand jury when he denied having asked Dean to contact Casey.[33]

On November 2, 1972, five days before Election Day, Laurence Richardson and three other ICC employees pleaded the Fifth to all questions posed by SEC lawyers. Sears claimed he apprised Mitchell of this and the former attorney general replied: "Well, I'm sure relieved." Remembering the same conversation, Mitchell said his only response was: "That's fine."[34]

Three weeks later, the SEC filed a formal complaint in U.S. District Court, Southern District of New York, charging Vesco and twenty-one associates with diverting more than $224 million from four offshore mutual funds into two Bahamas and Luxembourg banks controlled by Vesco. Calculated imprecision in the complaint's wording fed a myth that Vesco had simply absconded with the massive sums, equivalent to $9.5 billion in current figures. However, as Vesco biographer Arthur Herzog later noted, the complaint never said the proceeds from the $224 million in securities that were indisputably sold were "stolen"; instead the complaint used words like "diverted" or "spirited." "The SEC counted the same figures again and again in reaching the total," said one lawyer representing IOS shareholders. Since precise figures in Vesco's case were always hard to come by, it was somewhat fitting that by 1984, a dedicated band of lawyers, accountants, and bankruptcy trustees had "recovered" $500 million in assets supposedly misappropriated by Vesco—more than double the amount the SEC originally charged him with "diverting," but still $100 million shy of what he was believed to have stashed away at that point.[35]

Early 1973 saw all the protagonists—except Mitchell—scurrying for cover. Vesco struggled to persuade the ICC board to pay his legal fees. Sears sat for two days of sworn questioning by SEC lawyers. A federal grand jury in New York began probing Vesco's cash contribution, which CRP returned after its disclosure in a lawsuit filed by Common Cause, the liberal public advocacy group. Laurence Richardson, locked in a "dogfight" with Vesco for control of the ICC board, made the first of seventy-nine appearances before the U.S. attorney's office and grand jury. Of Vesco, Mitchell had finally had his fill, exclaiming to Sears: "The bastard is nothing but a petty thief!"[36]

In late February, Mitchell got a call from his successor, Attorney General Richard Kleindienst. A criminal investigation into Vesco's dealings was under way, Kleindienst explained; would Mitchell take a telephone call from Whitney North Seymour Jr., U.S. attorney for the Southern District of New York? Of course, Mitchell answered. Shortly thereafter, Seymour asked if the former attorney general would consent to being questioned "informally" by two of Seymour's assistants. Of course, Mitchell said.

The following day, on February 27, 1973, Assistant U.S. Attorney John Wing and an aide, David Brodsky, arrived in Mitchell's New York office. Brodsky said later he thought Mitchell's demeanor was "nervous." However, Mitchell was not so nervous as to deny the prosecutors full access to his logs and diaries for the years 1971–72. After a quick check with Kleindienst, to confirm there was no impropriety in turning over internal documents generated by an attorney general, Mitchell handed the records over.

On March 6, Harry Sears made the first of his ten grand jury appearances in New York. With the handwriting plainly visible on the wall, Vesco fled the country. The world now had its first "fugitive financier."[37]

Mitchell, too, was a hunted man. Almost in parallel to the Vesco affair, the Watergate scandal, a wholly separate, though equally Byzantine, set of events, involving a few of the same players—Dean, Ehrlichman, Stans—had gestated and begun to explode. By March 1973, as Mitchell limped along Wall Street, he more likely worried about Watergate, and the collapse of the Nixon presidency, than about the travels and travails of Robert Vesco.

That was soon to change. On March 20, Assistant U.S. Attorney James Rayhill called Mitchell's office, saying there were some matters the grand jury wanted Mitchell to help resolve. Rayhill arranged for the attorney general to be picked up by a government limousine outside his Broad Street office. When Mitchell got in the car, he found Rayhill seated beside him, offering pleasantries about the weather. Soon they arrived at the federal courthouse in Foley Square, where Mitchell was driven through the judges' private entrance, taken up to the grand jury via the judges' private elevator. Rayhill's matter-of-fact tone and extraordinary deference had the desired effect of lulling his target into complacency. As Mitchell's lawyer John Sprizzo later noted at trial, "It is very unusual to chauffeur a man who is under suspicion to a grand jury on two occasions without alerting him on two occasions that he is under suspicion."[38]

Seated before the grand jurors, the former attorney general was read his rights and questioned on a wide range of subjects relating to Vesco, Sears, Casey, and the SEC. That night, according to John Dean, Mitchell told him the prosecutors had given him "a hell of a grilling." "Those little bastards in the Southern District were all over me," Dean quoted Mitchell as saying. According to Dean, Mitchell urged him to call Kleindienst and find out what the hell was going on. The next day, Dean raised the case in the Oval Office, during the counsel's infamous "cancer on the presidency" meeting with Nixon.

> DEAN: We have a runaway grand jury up in the Southern District. They are after Mitchell and Stans on some sort of bribe or influence peddling with Vesco. They are also going to try to drag Ehrlichman into that. Apparently Ehrlichman had some meetings with Vesco. Also, Don Nixon, Jr. [the president's nephew] came in to see John [Ehrlichman] a couple of times about the problem.

NIXON: [. . .] Ehrlichman never did anything for Vesco?
DEAN: No one at the White House has done anything for
Vesco.[39]

In ensuing months, drowning in scandal, Nixon marveled that
the Vesco case occasioned any controversy at all. "Vesco didn't make
any money," he cried. "We're prosecuting him!" "Vesco is a crook,"
the president would say. "I never met the man."[40]

On April 24, Rayhill again picked Mitchell up outside 20 Broad
Street. This time, reporters and cameramen surrounded the judges'
entrance, so Rayhill dropped Mitchell off at a nearby subway stop
connected to the courthouse, then met him inside the courthouse
basement. But there was no avoiding the news media, which had
been tipped off. Reporters and photographers battered Mitchell upon
his arrival. Responding to shouted questions, the former attorney
general depicted himself as largely ignorant of Vesco and his money.
"There was a contribution made," Mitchell acknowledged. "You'll have
to ask Mr. Stans about that. I'm not familiar with the transactions—"
Did you know about it at the time? "I learned about it afterwards."
Three and a half hours later, through with the grand jury, Mitchell
was in no mood to entertain more questions. He told reporters only
that he "testified fully and frankly and fearlessly."[41]

Curious about the increasing frequency—and tension—of
Mitchell's after-hours meetings with lawyers, Martha Mitchell began
asking her husband what was going on. "Stans is in trouble" was all he
would say. Then one day, Mitchell reportedly asked his wife: "Do you
have dresses to wear to my trial?" Martha stared in disbelief, bolted
from the room, and, as she put it, "cried and cried and cried." She later
recalled her husband's deteriorating state over that spring and summer:

> He wouldn't go out. He ate at his desk. He let his hair grow
> and wouldn't shave. He wanted *me* to cut his hair. Finally, I

got a non-English-speaking barber to come in. John didn't want to see anyone. He wouldn't give me my phone calls. He'd say I was out. And if I answered, he'd listen. He was drinking and taking tranquilizers. There were nights our daughter, Marty, and I, and the maid, had to drag him to bed.[42]

Up to the morning it happened, Mitchell dismissed as "ridiculous" the mounting newspaper accounts saying he would soon be indicted. On May 10, he proceeded with a planned appearance before investigators for the Senate Watergate committee, traveling to Washington for the interview. Not until he reached the office of his attorney William Hundley did Mitchell learn he had been indicted by the Vesco grand jury in New York. "He appeared to be sick," said an associate present at the time. He "immediately went into the bathroom . . . then emerged pale and haggard."[43]

The forty-six-page indictment charged Mitchell, Stans, Vesco, and Sears with attempting to quash the SEC probe into Vesco's affairs, then lying to the grand jury about it. If convicted, Mitchell and Stans faced possible prison terms of fifty years and fines of $75,000 each. Leaving for Washington that day, Mitchell silently fought his way through hordes of reporters and camera crews clustered outside his apartment building and disappeared into his limousine. After his session with the Senate investigators, he told reporters the indictment was one of the most "irresponsible" things he'd ever seen. "There's no wrongdoing on my part or on the part of any of those people that I know of, and I'm sure that in an appropriate judicial proceeding, I'll be vindicated."

Eleven days later, Mitchell showed up for arraignment. The former head of the Municipal Bond Club and sixty-seventh attorney general of the United States was fingerprinted, had his mug shot taken, and entered a formal plea. He stood before Judge John Cannella and said, without emotion: "I am prepared, Your Honor, to plead 'not guilty.'" Do you so plead? Cannella asked. "I so plead." After Stans repeated the process, prosecutor John Wing asked Cannella to set bail at $1,000 for each defendant. "That's ludicrous!" Cannella cried. "These men had to be investigated by the FBI before they held their government jobs." He released both without bail. As his limousine screeched away, Mitchell was asked the inevitable, lamentable question: "How do you feel?" "I've been better," he replied.[44]

Heralded as a "trial of the century," the Mitchell-Stans case has since been forgotten. Although it marked the first and only trial of two former cabinet members; the first time the Nixon tapes were played in public; the first time that John Dean, the president's chief accuser in Watergate, testified in open court and faced rigorous cross-examination; and the first prosecution of senior Nixon administration officials, not a single comprehensive account of the Mitchell-Stans trial has been written since the spring of 1974, when its every twist made headline news. To some extent, *U.S. v. Mitchell-Stans* was simply overshadowed by its Washington cousin, *U.S. v. Mitchell*, the Watergate cover-up trial, held six months later. Mostly, however, the Mitchell-Stans trial vanished from memory because its verdict did not fit the story line of the times: All the president's men were supposed to be guilty of all things.

After months of delay, the trial began shortly after 9:00 a.m. on February 19, 1974, when Mitchell's black Chrysler Imperial pulled up at Foley Square. He ambled up the courthouse steps, swarmed by reporters. Stans and his retinue followed several steps behind, unrecognized and unmolested. Breaking free of the media crush at the courthouse door, Mitchell and his attorneys took the elevator up to Room 905, a small, oak-paneled courtroom. At 11:57 a.m., a court marshal pounded the door and all rose as Judge Lee Gagliardi entered.[45]

Mitchell took his seat, a green leather armchair, and rested his chin in his hand. He watched as Stans's attorney, John Diuguid, introduced a motion to dismiss the charges based on pretrial publicity.

244 | The Strong Man

The Watergate case was unrelated in substance, but the media's saturation coverage of it could potentially be turned to Mitchell's and Stans's advantage. Diuguid submitted a five-inch stack of clippings and broadcast transcripts, along with curio items like "The Watergate Coloring Book," and drew especial attention to a February 14 *New York Daily News* article headlined: "Watergate Staff Claim Solid Case Against Mitchell." "Now, under the circumstances," Diuguid said, "it is hard to know how any literate person in New York could be impartial as he approaches this trial."[46]

The judge did not agree, and he told them so: The only way to determine whether a fair jury could be impaneled, he ruled, was to try. Thus began the trial's decisive phase, completed even before the first scrap of evidence was in: jury selection. Concerned about the pretrial atmosphere, Gagliardi ordered an unusually large pool of 1,500 prospective jurors. Of these, 196 were examined, producing a voir dire record that ran 2,000 pages. Prospective jurors were questioned about the hardships of sequestration, their knowledge of Watergate, and their media consumption habits.

Gagliardi also allotted the defense twenty-three peremptory challenges against undesirable jurors, the government eleven. Prosecutors left two of their challenges unused, while lawyers for Mitchell and Stans exercised all of theirs. This was pivotal. Later studies of the jury's composition at each stage of selection showed Mitchell's and Stans's lawyers were far more adept at winnowing the panel down to an advantageous profile. Where 45 percent of the original panel had some college education, only 8 percent of the final jury did. Likewise, the percentage of Republicans on the final jury jumped from 15 to 25 percent, while the percentage of jurors "well informed" about Watergate decreased from 32 percent to a mere 8 percent.[47]

Once the jury was seated, thirty-six-year-old Jim Rayhill, his certificate of appointment as a federal prosecutor signed by Attorney General Mitchell, began delivering the government's opening statement. "This case," Rayhill said, "is about a contribution of $200,000 in cash, a briefcase full of $100 bills, to buy the political influence of John Mitchell and Maurice Stans. It is a case about fraud, about deception and about deliberate lies under oath. It is about the concealment by Mitchell and Stans of the $200,000 cash contribution by Robert Vesco, a man under investigation. It is about the illegal attempts by Mitchell, Stans, [and] a lawyer by the name of Harry Sears to help Robert Vesco by influencing, or even stopping, a federal investigation of Vesco and his companies."[48]

Rayhill described how Mitchell had contacted William Casey on Sears's behalf, and supposedly used John Dean to try to delay or quash the SEC's subpoenas against Vesco and his employees. The prosecutor depicted Mitchell and Stans as supremely smooth operators, past masters in the dark arts of influence peddling. "The means used by these defendants in committing these crimes were neither crass nor crude," said Rayhill. "Everything was underplayed." The defendants then lied about it all before the grand jury, Rayhill argued. "The perjury charges . . . are the heart of this indictment, for . . . if their acts were perfectly innocent, there would have been no reason to lie about them in the grand jury."[49]

Then the prosecutor crossed the line:

> As you sit through this case listening to the testimony and observing how the witnesses behave, consider how essential it is that a jury be given truthful testimony under oath . . . and as you listen to the witnesses testifying before you, *put yourself in the place of the grand jurors who investigated this case, citizens like yourselves.*

At that, Walter Bonner, Stans's lead attorney, leapt to his feet. "I object to this," Bonner shouted. "Sustained," Gagliardi replied. "I have indicated to the jury what an indictment is, that it is nothing more than an accusation." He turned to the jurors themselves: "That is the only weight and credit to be given to the indictment in this case. The defendants have denied the charge. Now proceed." Rayhill completed his opening statement a few minutes later, and Gagliardi sent the jury out for lunch.

"I move for a mistrial," Bonner declared, "because it was stated by Mr. Rayhill . . . that because people just like this petit jury had indicted these two men, that they should draw a natural inference from that fact that these men were guilty." Mitchell's attorney Peter Fleming joined in Bonner's motion. The judge deferred a ruling, but added: "I'm very seriously considering a mistrial," and recessed for ninety minutes.

After lunch, the jury still absent, Gagliardi told the lawyers: "I am gravely concerned over the apparent excess on the part of the prosecutor in bringing into his opening statement . . . references to the grand jury and its functions and bringing to it his personal conclusions, as though he were a witness in the matter." Then he brought the jurors back in, instructed them anew that an indictment did not confer guilt, and adjourned for the day.

The prosecution's case had barely begun—and was now in serious trouble. Yet the following Monday, Gagliardi chose to continue the trial, finding the reference by Rayhill "brief and ambiguous." Moreover, the jurors had been instructed five separate times on the difference between their role and that of the grand jury.[50]

Where Rayhill stumbled, Peter Fleming was brilliant. Six-foot-six, rakish gray hair flopped over his collar, the heavy-lidded, chain-smoking Fleming, educated at Princeton and Yale, looked like Robert Mitchum and sounded like Gregory Peck. He had spent twelve years as a federal prosecutor and reportedly "never lost a case." His ring savvy, theatrical flair, and comic touch (asked once how long his cross-examination would take, Fleming replied, "It depends on how quickly he cracks, Your Honor") made him one of New York's most sought-after defense lawyers.[51]

In his opening statement, Fleming earned every cent of the

$300,000 Mitchell paid him that year (nearly $1.2 million in current figures). He recounted Mitchell's service in World War II, his self-made success on Wall Street and reluctance to become attorney general. "Mr. Mitchell didn't want that eminence, didn't want that lofty position," Fleming told the jurors, "but took it for his friend and for his president." Fleming also heaped doubt on the coming parade of government witnesses—Sears, Richardson, Dean—saying each was buying leniency with his testimony.

Then Fleming executed his masterstroke, a bit of rhetorical genius that cleverly, and decisively, recast the charges against his client. "That's a big number," Fleming acknowledged of the $200,000 in cash Rayhill had repeatedly mentioned; but where his own client was concerned, Fleming said, "it didn't go to him . . . in four years of public service John Mitchell never got a red cent himself." Moreover, Vesco's money represented only a tiny fraction of the $60 million Stans and company had raised—less than one-third of 1 percent of all of the money contributed to reelect the president:

> It is as if, in an election costing $100,000, Vesco had contributed $300. It is as if, in an election costing $100, Vesco had contributed, I think, thirty-three cents. So we just ask you to think of $200,000, which didn't go to him but went into a campaign fund . . . whether, in essence, John Mitchell would sell his life for thirty-three cents.[52]

The prosecutors' problems continued with their first witness. Harry Sears spent seven days on the stand, recounting his wretched existence as Vesco's emissary to Mitchell. But which side benefited more from Sears's testimony was often difficult to discern. Again and again, CBS News correspondent Robert Schakne reported, Sears "found it hard to recollect some important events; and on cross-examination, he seemed delighted to defend his old friend, John Mitchell."[53]

"And so it went for the prosecution—one step forward and another backward," *Time* reported. William Casey reprised his drinks at Mitchell's Watergate apartment, the fateful call he received from Mitchell on April 10, 1972, his own meetings with Sears. Like Sears, however, William Casey proved a thorny government witness. Where prosecutor Wing wanted to prove that Mitchell had improperly passed to Sears one of Casey's internal memos, Casey steadfastly maintained the memo in question always remained in his, or his trusted assistant's, hands.[54]

Central to the case against Mitchell was the charge that he had sought to delay or quash subpoenas against Vesco and his ICC employees, and that to enlist Casey's assistance in this effort, Mitchell had used John Dean as his agent. Consequently, the prosecutors realized that where Casey's testimony had failed to establish Mitchell's criminal intent, Dean had to hit the mark. They had little to fear on that score; unlike their previous witnesses, Dean's motive to testify against Mitchell was unquestionable, almost palpable. For where Sears enjoyed immunity from prosecution, and Casey was never charged with wrongdoing, Dean was awaiting sentencing in the Watergate case, and—as the youthful former White House counsel openly admitted during cross-examination—he hoped his testimony at the Mitchell-Stans trial would earn him a lenient sentence. The stage was set, then, for the government's star witness to take the stand.

Mitchell savored what happened next for the rest of his life. "Peter Fleming got Dean on the witness stand and destroyed him," Mitchell exulted to an interviewer in August 1988, ninety days before his death. "Absolutely *destroyed* him."[55]

Indeed, after the Mitchell-Stans jurors rendered their verdict, a determined effort was made to minimize Dean's importance to the outcome, and for obvious reasons: Those most heavily invested in his success as a witness in the Watergate case—Dean himself, the prosecutors, the media—could ill afford for Richard Nixon's chief accuser to be branded unbelievable in a trial as important and high-profile as

Mitchell-Stans. Dean grumbled after the verdict that he didn't know anything about the case and couldn't understand why anyone considered him its star witness. Wing tried to reassure Dean, only thirty-five, that the unsophisticated jury was the problem, not his poor performance under Fleming's withering cross; the jurors, Wing said, were used to policemen and judges receiving cash under the table, and were probably impressed that Mitchell and Stans had never taken Vesco's money for their own use.[56]

"Dean was definitely not the central witness," Wing recalled; Rayhill remembered Dean's role as "small." However, in the days leading up to Dean's testimony, Wing and Rayhill sang a different tune. So crucial was Dean to their case that they delayed opening the trial because of uncertainty over whether Dean would be permitted to testify about his taped conversations with Nixon. The prosecutors even told Judge Gagliardi: "We cannot risk trying this case without Mr. Dean's testimony."[57]

First the prosecutors had Dean recap his brief government career: his time as minority counsel to the House Judiciary Committee in the 1960s, his service under Mitchell at Justice, and his transfer, in July 1970, to the White House. Then they led him through his phone calls and meetings with Mitchell in the summer and fall of 1972, building their case that Mitchell used Dean as his instrument to block the SEC's subpoenas. To buttress that notion, Rayhill asked the witness if he was known as "Mitchell's man in the White House." "Yes, I was," Dean answered, pliant.[58]

Then it was Fleming's turn. His performance later became—literally—a model used in legal textbooks. To cross-examine Dean, excerpts from his tape-recorded conversations with Nixon were read aloud—the first time contents of the Nixon tapes were made public (the White House's edited transcripts were released a month later, and are still circulating in paperback form). Given the widespread—and erroneous—belief that the tapes completely vindicated Dean's memory and testimony in the Watergate case, it is ironic that the tapes were first used to discredit him.[59]

Excerpts from Dean's taped meetings with Nixon also undermined the prosecution's central thrusts. *Wasn't that Dean himself telling the president no one had done anything for Vesco?* The disparities led even Judge Gagliardi to question, outside the jury's presence, whether "something in those tapes may be inconsistent with something that [Dean] said on the stand." Fleming also skillfully exploited the changes in Dean's testimony, not only from grand jury to trial, but from day to day within the trial. To attack Dean's character, Fleming posed a series of razor's-edge questions—most of them stricken by Gagliardi—reprising allegations about Dean's unethical conduct in private legal practice and embezzlement of campaign funds, his ownership of a Mercedes-Benz, and negotiations to write a book.[60]

The circumlocutory, evasive, often nonresponsive answers that had served Dean so well at the Senate Watergate hearings the previous summer found no quarter with Fleming. At one point the defense lawyer asked Dean if he had previously testified that a certain telephone call had taken place on December 8, 1972. "I did use that date, yes," Dean answered. "Not 'use that date,' " Fleming shot back. "You answered that that *was* the date." "Yes, that's correct," Dean agreed. So accustomed had Dean grown to answering questions as he saw fit that Judge Gagliardi was forced—repeatedly—to admonish him, a distinction unique to Dean among the trial's fifty-nine witnesses: "Mr. Dean, I don't want to reprimand you again, sir."[61]

The jurors took note. Interviewed after the trial, foreman Sybil Kucharski said the jury found Dean "often unbelievable," in contrast with those "credible men," Mitchell and Stans. "We didn't feel that they had any reason to lie or to perjure themselves," she said. "John Dean we didn't feel the same way about." Even a dispirited John Wing acknowledged after the trial "these twelve people didn't believe [Dean] beyond a reasonable doubt as to some things he said about facts in this case."[62]

By the time the government rested, few thought Wing and Rayhill had established Mitchell's guilt beyond reasonable doubt. "Every prosecution witness who takes the stand somehow turns into a defense witness," reported *Newsday*'s Joe Treen. Winning the case now depended on the prosecutors' ability to rattle defense witnesses—primary among them, Mitchell himself. To the reporters who crowded him each night, Fleming kept coy about whether his client would testify in his own defense. "It's a surprise," he would say. Years later, he acknowledged otherwise: "[Mitchell] was going to testify and we always knew he was going to testify." Fleming was a strong believer in defendants taking the stand. "That's all a jury wants to hear, is a defendant's testimony," he said.[63]

Getting the client to cooperate was another matter. It was as if Mitchell's original slowness to acknowledge his peril was followed by a stubborn refusal to prepare for his testimony in any normal sense; his confidence in his own legal acumen, the foundation of his life for four decades, never buckled. Two days before Mitchell was to testify, Fleming tried to go over the areas they would address on direct examination. "I ask him about four questions," Fleming recalled, "and he says, 'Ah, I'm tired of this.' So I say, 'Fuck it, we'll do it tomorrow.' He comes down Tuesday. I ask three questions and he says, 'Forget it. I'll just testify.' " Fleming couldn't believe Mitchell's insouciance. "*Fuck* you!" he spat. "We've been breaking our ass for you for ten weeks with this trial, and you can't even let us ask you questions to prepare?" "Oh, get out of here," Mitchell replied. Stymied by his own client, Fleming drew up on yellow legal paper a two-and-a-half-page outline of topics he planned to cover on direct examination, and had it delivered to Mitchell the night before he was to take the stand. The next morning, Fleming picked Mitchell up and headed for Foley Square. Inside the car, Mitchell handed back the outline and said simply: "Let's go."[64]

Shortly after 2:00 p.m. on April 10, 1974, Mitchell took the stand, the first attorney general in such straits in a half century. Fleming began by having Mitchell recap his life story, especially his reluctance to join the Nixon administration. "There were [*sic*] a series of re-approaches," Mitchell cracked, "and finally, after the twenty-fifth or twenty-sixth—I forget how many there were—I relented and accepted his appointment." Fleming also emphasized Mitchell's financial sacrifice, contrasting the attorney general's salary—initially $42,500—with what Mitchell had earned the year prior to his appointment ("somewheres in excess of $300,000").[65]

Soon it was the prosecution's turn. "Mr. Mitchell," Wing began, "how did it come about that Vesco's $200,000 cash contribution was listed under your initials on April 10?" "I have no idea, Mr. Wing," Mitchell replied. *When did you first learn of it?* About the time Stans testified before the grand jury in 1973, Mitchell answered. *Was it about that time or precisely that day?* "In my recollection," Mitchell said, "it was precisely that day, but Mr. Stans told me that he had advised me a few weeks in advance of that; if he did, it made no impression on me. But it certainly came home to me after he had testified up here in March of '73 before the grand jury, and we had lunch and he told me about it." In this first confrontation, the prosecutor flailed. Wing repeatedly asked if Mitchell was sure of his version of events, and Mitchell held fast; when Wing revisited Mitchell's grand jury testimony on the matter, it matched what he was saying now.

When Wing next rolled out Mitchell's grand jury testimony, it was designed to show Mitchell was either mistaken or lying when he claimed, at trial, that he had never reviewed his logs prior to his grand jury appearance, to check when he had met with Sears. "I have looked at my diaries," Wing quoted Mitchell as saying in his first grand jury appearance, "with respect to the meetings I had with Sears . . ." "Now is that a fact, Mr. Mitchell," asked Wing, "that you *did* review your logs, looking for meetings with Mr. Sears during the—" Mitchell cut him off. "Mr. Wing, you have mixed up the diaries with the logs. That [grand jury testimony] refers to the diaries, which are personal appointments." Now the old Wall Street legend was schooling the younger lawyer. *You weren't referring to your logs at that time?* Wing asked. "I said 'diaries,' " Mitchell replied tartly.[66]

Since Mitchell's grand jury appearances consumed hundreds of pages, it was inevitable that discrepancies would arise between his testimony in that forum and at trial. But Wing never got Mitchell anywhere close to admitting he was party to corruption.

> **WING:** It never occurred to you that Mr. Vesco was looking for anything as a result of giving a sum of money in that amount, is that correct, Mr. Mitchell?
>
> **MITCHELL:** It never occurred to me in any form, shape or manner, because if Mr. Vesco in my opinion thought he was going to get a favor, he would have been looking for something more than a meeting with the chairman of the Securities and Exchange Commission, just a meeting.
>
> **WING:** [. . .] Do you think, Mr. Mitchell, that Casey's treatment of this particular case would be somewhat affected by the fact that you were the one calling up asking for him to meet with Sears?
>
> **MITCHELL:** No, Mr. Wing, I wouldn't flatter myself to that extent.[67]

Nothing shook Mitchell from his account of the Swiss jailing incident, nor elicited from him, on the Beirut bank episode, anything more than an acknowledgment of forgetfulness where the meetings with Mark Felt were concerned—acknowledgments Fleming had already wisely elicited on direct examination. Nor did Wing budge Mitchell on the contents of his meetings with Harry Sears, or on whether Mitchell had ever given Sears, or received from him, any documents. Similarly, Mitchell held fast in his denials that he discussed Vesco with Dan Hofgren, or did anything to delay or quash the SEC's subpoenas.

Frustrating Wing's task was Mitchell's masterful facility, honed over a lifetime of practice, with the peculiar language of the law—and, too, his instinct for knowing when to abandon it. To one repetitive thrust he exasperatedly replied: "Mr. Wing, I have answered that three different ways. I will try it again." At another point, when Wing referred to his interview of Mitchell in the latter's law office in February 1973, Mitchell corrected his questioner: "Mr. Wing, I think you took very bad notes at that meeting." Asked if he was "responsible in part" for Casey's nomination as SEC chairman, Mitchell turned Socratic: "When you say 'in part,' would you describe it for me, or would you like me to describe my part in connection with it?"[68]

Among those who came away from Mitchell's testimony with newfound respect for him were his tormentors, the prosecutors. "I was impressed with Mitchell, the way he dealt with the case," Wing recalled. Rayhill agreed, calling Mitchell "a stand-up guy" and a "very strong human being." Rayhill said he came to believe Mitchell genuinely "did not feel he had done anything wrong . . . in connection with the Vesco investigation . . . that he thought he was doing what an average American would do."[69]

For Fleming's summation, Mitchell angled himself toward the jurors, one hand cupping his chin, the other draped over his chair. In a five-hour closing argument, Fleming derided the government's case as "a joke," "a dream," "a creation," "a fairy tale," "an Easter egg hunt," "Christmastime," "*Alice in Wonderland*," "*Wizard of Oz*," "Mulligan stew," "mush," and "chicken hash."

Fleming choked back tears extolling his client and assailing Mitchell's accusers. "Had Harry Sears not sought the golden calf of Robert Vesco," he said, "none of us would be here." The prosecutors "bought [Sears's] testimony. He's bought and paid for. You measure it. . . . Is [John] Dean Saint Paul on the road to Damascus, who is struck by the lightning of God and becomes a Christian? Or is John Dean struck by the letter of [Watergate burglar] James McCord to

Judge Sirica?" He said the case boiled down to one simple question: *Who do you believe?*[70]

Fleming's emotionalism, coupled with that of Stans's lawyer, Walter Bonner, who alternately preached, shouted, pleaded, and cried in asking the jurors to give Stans back his good name, contrasted starkly with the coolly reasoned approach John Wing adopted. "This isn't a 'fix' case," he said, using Fleming's preferred word. "It is a case of men *trying* to use their political power to influence the officials in the SEC. . . . These men don't call a fix a fix—it would be *gauche*. They call a fix a 'request for help.' "

> John Mitchell took the stand and deliberately lied to you to get out of this. . . . Ladies and gentlemen, John Mitchell has no right to lie under oath any more than you or I or anyone else has, and if you find that John Mitchell lied under oath and if he gets away with it, what man in the country shall have respect for law?[71]

Stans remembered himself and Mitchell reacting differently to Wing's summation. "John Mitchell was a tower of strength," Stans recalled in 1992. "There were times when my confidence would flag because of the manner in which the prosecutor was demonstrating bravado. . . . It bothered me particularly when I heard Wing give his closing address to the jury. Mitchell had to firm me up, [saying] 'Maurice, this is just part of the show they're putting on. It's not going to affect the jury in any way. Just relax and we'll see.' He was confident of acquittal. . . . I took a lot of consolation from being in with him rather than being alone, I'll tell you."[72]

The nine men and three women on the jury deliberated for twenty-eight hours over three days. Inside the jury room, foreman Sybil Kucharski later told the *New York Times*, it was her "impression" that the jury was initially inclined to vote eight-to-four for conviction. But no formal vote was taken. In fact, in the first voice vote, on the indictment's first count—a conspiracy charge against Mitchell—the jury split evenly, five for conviction, five for acquittal, and two undecided. "We were off in little groups and screaming and yelling," Kucharski said. "Some of us were emotional."[73]

With the jurors embroiled in screaming matches, the panel's wealthiest and best-educated member, investment banker Andrew Choa, a late substitute for an ailing juror, encouraged them to skip ahead to the perjury counts, and to consider the witnesses' credibility. "The overall perception of Mitchell by the jury was that he was a man of integrity," Choa recalled two decades later. Soon, the jurors were asking for copies of the indictment and documentary evidence presented at trial. They asked Gagliardi to reread portions of the election laws and his instructions about what constituted conspiracy and perjury. Later—showing they were again proceeding meticulously through the indictment—the jurors asked for the testimony of Mitchell and Hofgren, and that of Sears on his efforts to enlist Mitchell in quashing the SEC subpoena against Vesco.[74]

Finally, at 12:50 on Sunday, April 28, jury foreman Kucharski sent Judge Gagliardi a note saying the verdict was in. "How do you find the defendant Mitchell on Count One?" asked Court Clerk James E. Matarese. "Not guilty," Kucharski announced, provoking gasps in the courtroom. The process was repeated fourteen more times. Stans collapsed in nervous exhaustion and tears. Fleming bolted up and began to cry. Mitchell, "seemingly the coolest man in the courtroom," told Fleming to "take it easy, you worked hard."[75]

Holding court at an impromptu press conference, Mitchell lauded the jurors as "a cross-section of America" embodying the genius of the nation's legal system. "If there is a place you can get justice, it is from the American people," Mitchell waxed. "That's why I have great faith in America, and why I love the American people." Suddenly, a long-haired youth started shouting: "It is the fascist ruling class like you—" before marshals dragged him from the room. "It's all right," quipped an unfazed Mitchell. "He wasn't on the jury." *Do you think the verdict will affect your Watergate trial?* "You are off bounds with your question," Mitchell growled. *Had the Nixon administration been exonerated by the verdict?* "I don't believe the Nixon administration was involved." *Do you know if President Nixon has been informed of the verdicts?* a female reporter asked. "Honey," Mitchell smiled, "I guess you never covered the White House."[76]

That evening, Suite 555 of the Essex House erupted in laughter, liquor, and song. "Within an hour, I'll have my first drink," Mitchell joked, downing his second Dewar's. Soon he was launching into "When Irish Eyes Are Smiling." Someone turned on the local news, which led with the verdict and interviews with the jurors. The room fell silent. "Great people," Mitchell shook his head. "Real Americans. Honest people."

A reporter asked if Nixon had telephoned Mitchell to congratulate him. "I wouldn't tell you that one way or the other," Mitchell snapped. As revelers began filing out, a doctor, unknown to Mitchell, shook his hand. "If you ever need a psychiatrist," the man said, "I'd be glad to help." "If I ever need a psychiatrist," Mitchell shot back, "I'll plead guilty first."[77]

GEMSTONE

Mitchell's an honest man. He just wasn't tending the shop—he had problems with his wife—these jackass kids and other fools around did this thing, and John should have stepped up to it. That's what happened, in my opinion.

—*Richard Nixon, 1973*[1]

MITCHELL STOOD AT the brink of ruin. From the Vesco scandal he had escaped with his freedom—but not for long. His indictment in the Watergate case was handed down the very day the jury was selected in the Vesco trial. Unable to practice law, his fortune drained, Mitchell now faced war on a second front, a *todeskampf* against the unlimited resources of the Watergate Special Prosecution Force and the news media.

Vilified from coast to coast, his name and image demonized on every newsstand and broadcast outlet, the former attorney general was now a professional defendant, the highest-ranking in American history. Rumors abounded that regardless of the outcome in the Watergate trial, Mitchell would also be indicted in the ITT scandal and the milk fund case (an investigation into whether the Nixon administration illegally exchanged milk price supports for large campaign contributions from dairy lobbyists). Who could withstand such an onslaught? "One of these days," Peter Fleming told Judge Gagliardi, "we are going to find that we reach a due process point where, by the sheer proliferation of charges, a government can force a man either to admit a guilt which he does not feel or to bankrupt himself. . . . The economics of this thing are overwhelming."[2]

How had it come to this? How had the nation's top law enforcement official become Public Enemy Number One? Mitchell's woes originated in the fact that his confederates, in and out of government, were too often beneath him. If Mitchell grasped this, he likely regarded it as part of the devil's pact he made when, at Nixon's insistence, he left Wall Street for the grimier councils of government. Indeed, the attorney general was surrounded by men who would never have made it into his office at Mudge Rose.

If there was one single moment where Mitchell could have changed the course of his life, intervened to avert his rendezvous with ignominy, it was shortly after eleven on the morning of January 27, 1972, and the arrival in his office at the Department of Justice of three men: John Wesley Dean III, Jeb Stuart Magruder, and George Gordon Liddy.

Trim and mustachioed, self-assured to the point of cockiness, Gordon Liddy was general counsel to the Committee for the Re-Election of the President—CRP to insiders, CREEP to detractors. He cut an odd figure. A graduate, like Mitchell, of Fordham and its law school, and an ardent anticommunist, Liddy joined the army in 1957 and later served for five years as an FBI agent. By the mid-1960s, he was an assistant district attorney in Dutchess County, New York, where he led a celebrated raid on Timothy Leary's LSD-drenched compound. He also pulled odd stunts, like firing a live pistol in a courtroom to impress a jury, and lost a bid for Congress. In 1969, GOP connections landed him a job in the Treasury Department. Two years later, he sought a transfer to the White House, but met resistance. For reasons never explained—perhaps the Fordham connection—Mitchell went to bat for him. At the White House, Liddy's curious persona again set him apart. He harbored a weird fascination with Germany, and the Third Reich in particular, peppering his speech with Nazi-specific terms like *Einsatzgruppen* and arranging a White House screening of *Triumph of the Will*, the landmark Nazi propaganda film. "Adolf Hitler incarnate!" a colleague muttered.[3]

In September 1971, along with E. Howard Hunt, Liddy conceived and supervised the break-in at the Los Angeles office of Daniel Ellsberg's psychiatrist. By year's end, however, the Nixon White House was shifting focus from Ellsberg to the task of reelecting the president, and to attendant fears that antiwar radicals would disrupt the Republican convention. Liddy wanted to be near the action. Bud Krogh, an aide to John Ehrlichman, arranged a meeting between Liddy and John Dean.

Callow and slight of build, his "ferretlike" face framed by light blond hair that hung shaggily over his suit collar, Dean was hardly Liddy's kind of man. But the youthful lawyer had an intriguing proposal: How did Liddy feel about coming over to CRP as general counsel and running a "first-class intelligence operation"? According to Liddy, he told Dean such an operation, supporting professional clandestine missions of an offensive and defensive nature, would cost a hell of a lot of money, and Dean shot back: "How's a half a million for openers?" Liddy, impressed, told Dean that was "just about right"—for openers—but that when all was said and done, the figure would likely double. "No problem," Dean replied.[4]

After Ehrlichman sanctioned Liddy's transfer to CRP, Dean arranged for Liddy to meet his new boss: Jeb Magruder, CRP's campaign director until Mitchell could leave Justice and assume the reins. Young, slender, and handsome, his jet-black hair and sad brown eyes offset by smartly patterned shirts and ties, Magruder was a protégé of H. R. Haldeman, who had installed Magruder at CRP over Mitchell's objections. Born on Staten Island, Magruder came from a financially comfortable family. Foundering at Williams College, he volunteered for the army and served as a guard along the Korean demilitarized

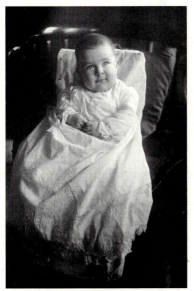

Born in Detroit on September 5, 1913, the future attorney general moved with his family to Long Island when he was five years old. He excelled at many sports, especially golf and ice hockey, and industriously sold fishing bait and muskrat hides. At Jamaica High School, from which he graduated in 1930, Mitchell was a B+ student and president of his senior class—his only bid for elective office.

"There were three sons," held a Mitchell family saying, "and they were guns." Top: From left, James Robert Mitchell, John N. "Jack" Mitchell, Joseph "Scranton" Mitchell, and their parents, Joseph C. Mitchell and Margaret Agnes McMahon (partially obscured), circa 1930. Both Scranton and an older sister, Margaret, not pictured here, died young. Bottom: Mitchell, his girlfriend Elizabeth "Bette" Shine, and an unidentified classmate on June 15, 1938, the day Mitchell graduated from Fordham University's School of Law.

With his parents and Bette on
wedding day, October 12, 1940.
ily lore held that the moment
chell first saw Bette he vowed
arry her. In a love letter dated
6, 1937, Mitchell reassured her:
will certainly be the favorite
ghter-in-law as well as the favorite
-in-law." Bottom: With daughter
nd son Jack, circa 1950.

Top: U.S. Navy lieutenant Mitchell in the South Pacific, circa 1944. Bottom: Mitchell, second from right, steering a PT boat on the high seas. Mitchell served honorably and was buried at Arlington National Cemetery, but neither official military records nor a privately owned PT boat museum could verify claims that he earned two Purple Hearts and the Silver Star, that he commanded the young John F. Kennedy, or that he rescued Colonel "Pappy" Boyington at sea. FBI director J. Edgar Hoover was later said to have discreetly informed the attorney general that the Bureau knew about these exaggerations.

Top: Flush with success on Wall Street and living in upscale Rye, New York, Mitchell entertains an unidentified lady friend as Bette enjoys a cigarette, circa 1953. "I think what killed their marriage is what kills a lot of marriages," a family friend said of John and Bette. John was up and coming. He was ambitious. He wasn't home, and she was lonely." Bottom: With daughter Jill and second wife Martha Elizabeth Beall, circa 1960. Mitchell married Martha at an elopement center in Elkton, Maryland, on December 19, 1957—eleven days after his divorce from Bette was finalized.

Top: President Nixon watches as Chief Justice Earl Warren swears in Attorney General Mitchell January 22, 1969. Martha Mitchell holds the Bible. Bottom: Mitchell and his Justice Department team. Top row, from left: Assistant Attorneys General William Ruckelshaus, Will Wilson, Sr., Johnnie M. Walters, Richard McLaren, William Rehnquist, Jerris Leonard, and J. Walter Yeagle. Seated from left: Assistant Attorney General Leo Pellerzi, Deputy Attorney General Richard Kleindienst, Mitchell, Solicitor General Erwin Griswold, and Assistant Attorney General Shiro Kashiwa.

"Nixon had no really close relationship with anybody," Henry Kissinger told the author; but Mitchell was the closest thing to a friend Nixon had in government. Top: The president watches as Mitchell introduces him to Justice Department employees on January 30, 1969. Bottom: The two attend the Los Angeles Rams–Kansas City Chiefs football game on August 23, 1969.

Top: Standing in the Rose Garden at the White House on June 20, 1970, the attorney general addresses winners of an essay contest about the perils of drug abuse as wife Martha and daughter Marty look on. Bottom: Donald Rumsfeld, then the director of the Office of Economic Opportunity, busts up HEW secretary Robert Finch (left), Martha Mitchell, and the attorney general, during a black-tie party in the Mitchells' Watergate duplex, January 29, 1970.

zone. By 1963, he had attended IBM training school and earned a master's in business administration from the University of Chicago. A romance with politics formed in 1962, with impressive Chicago ward work for a first-time congressional candidate named Donald Rumsfeld. After a stint in the Goldwater campaign, Magruder managed Southern California for Nixon in '68. The following year, Haldeman brought him to Washington to streamline the White House's sprawling communications apparatus. Magruder later wrote that he tried to get along with everyone he met, as a matter of instinct; his eagerness to please made him vulnerable to pressure.[5]

Liddy disliked Magruder even more than he did Dean. Magruder admitted he knew nothing about intelligence and balked at Liddy's salary and title demands. "I knew that I had to resist him from the onset," Liddy wrote later, "in what I knew would be a prolonged conflict." The dispute over job terms required a decision from Mitchell. Accordingly, on November 24, 1971, John Dean escorted Liddy into the attorney general's office for the first meeting between the two men. Mitchell wasted few words: Liddy could have the title and salary he wanted. To Liddy's surprise, there was no discussion of intelligence, which, from his talks with Dean, Liddy understood to be his primary function. "I didn't spend a hell of a lot of time with Liddy," Mitchell recalled. "[I] left the matter to Dean."[6]

After the meeting, Dean instructed Liddy to prepare a proposal for a comprehensive campaign intelligence plan that could be presented to Mitchell. Excited, Liddy shared the good news with his old partner in crime, E. Howard Hunt, and took up residence at CRP in December 1971.

It was to John Dean's everlasting regret, and the nation's, that at his own moment of decision, he didn't take Mitchell's advice. When Dean came to the attorney general in July 1970 and said he had been offered the job of counsel to the president, Mitchell, in between puffs on his pipe, advised him not to take it. Dean was better off staying at

Justice, Mitchell argued, where the young man had a bright future; but Dean, ambitious and status conscious, ignored this wise counsel and opted for the White House job.[7]

Now, at 11:00 a.m. on January 27, 1972, Dean once again found himself seated in one of the faded red leather chairs in the attorney general's office, alongside Magruder and Liddy. The lawyer–cum–covert operator was finally going to present his master plan for a "first-class" campaign intelligence operation to Mitchell. Liddy strode into the attorney general's office carrying an easel and, under his arm in a brown paper wrapper, a set of large, professionally printed charts. Mitchell lit his pipe and began gently rocking in his big black chair. After preliminary talk about campaign finance laws, Liddy summarized his qualifications for the covert mission at hand, the many experts he had consulted, and the tight security precautions surrounding the entire operation. Next, he distributed sheets of paper with dollar figures on them.

Then came the charts. There were half a dozen, all multicolored and prepared—in Liddy's first breach of security—by Howard Hunt's friends at CIA. Each chart was three feet tall and four feet long, "artistically composed," as Mitchell later recalled, and bore the name of a precious stone or mineral. Each stone or mineral, in turn, comprised a component in the overall plan, which Liddy code-named Gemstone.[8]

First came Operation Diamond, aimed at neutralizing the unruly hordes of antiwar radicals expected to disrupt the '72 convention. Liddy explained that the most effective riot-control techniques ever developed originated with the Texas Rangers, who, despite vastly inferior numbers, penetrated a given mob, "beat the hell out of" its leaders, then easily dispersed the stunned remainder. Indulging his fondness for all things Germanic, Liddy proposed a similar program for the '72 convention, under which, as he put it, "special action groups"—a mordant reference to the Nazi *Einsatzgruppen* units that liquidated 1.5 million Jews—would kidnap and drug antiwar leaders and remove them to Mexico until the convention ended.

Liddy paused to extol the caliber of his agents, "professional

killers who have accounted between them for twenty-two dead .
far," Liddy said, "including two hanged from a beam in a garage."
Mitchell gazed unblinkingly, puffed on his pipe, and posed his first
interjection. "And where did you find men like that?" "I understand
they're members of organized crime," Liddy said. "And how much
will *their* services cost?" Mitchell asked. Liddy pointed to a hefty figure on the chart: "Like top professionals everywhere, sir, they don't
come cheap." "Well," Mitchell said dryly, returning to his pipe, "let's
not contribute any more than we have to to the coffers of organized
crime."[9]

Liddy sensed his pitch was not going over well. What's more, he
was getting no help from his *confreres*, Magruder and Dean, who
stared motionless at Mitchell "like two rabbits in front of a cobra." In
slow succession, the charts came off the easel, Liddy explaining how
each component fit into his overall plan. Ruby entailed the placement
of spies in the Democratic contenders' campaigns. Coal called for the
covert funneling of cash to Shirley Chisholm, a black female con-
gresswoman whose quest for the Democratic nomination stood to divide the party along racial and gender lines. Emerald outlined how
Liddy could intercept airborne and wireless communications from
the planes and buses of opposing candidates by using a "chase plane"
outfitted with state-of-the-art electronics gear. Quartz, an explication
of how the Soviet embassy intercepted telephone signals using mi-
crowave systems, proved nearly incomprehensible. Crystal envisioned
the rental in Miami, where both parties were holding their conventions, of a luxury houseboat, from which Liddy's men would monitor wiretaps and bugs. The bedroom of the houseboat, wired for
sound, would also serve the purposes of Sapphire, wherein sophisticated call girls would seduce and debrief Democratic politicos.
"Mitchell listened to that impassively, as did Dean," Liddy later recalled. "Magruder, however, wore a look of eager interest."

On it went. Opal's points I through IV set aside funds for four illegal break-ins, in which the aforementioned wiretaps and bugs would
be installed. As targets, Liddy specified the Washington campaign

headquarters of Senators Edmund Muskie and George McGovern; the Democratic Party's convention headquarters in Miami; and one target to be chosen by Mitchell, who kept silent when Liddy paused for suggestions. Next came Topaz, the illicit photography of documents; followed by Garnet, the clandestine recruitment of unappealing hippies to endorse opposition candidates; and Turquoise, a plot for Hunt's Cuban mercenaries to sabotage the air-conditioning system at the Democrats' convention. Two final charts, Brick and Gemstone, broke down the costs by mission and projected dates of expenditure.

When Liddy was finished, the room was silent. All power emanated from Mitchell, and it was to him the other three looked for direction. The attorney general was dumbfounded. "Mr. Liddy put on his performance," he later testified, "and everybody just sat there with their mouths open." What to say? Calmly, Mitchell repacked and re-lit his pipe, puffed a bit, then delivered one of his classic understatements: "Gordon, that's not quite what I had in mind." Contrary to later claims, Mitchell's primary basis for objection to Liddy's proposal was not its cost, but its criminality. As Magruder told the Senate Watergate committee, in previously unpublished testimony, Mitchell "indicated that [Liddy's plan] was not acceptable both in its scope and its budget." The attorney general, according to Magruder, stated "the type of activity discussed here" was "way out of line." Likewise, Dean told the Senate that Mitchell had furtively winked at him, indicating Liddy's proposal was "out of the question."

Liddy was furious. Why the hell had he gone to all this trouble? He had operatives standing by, awaiting orders, on the basis of a million-dollar budget that—supposedly—had already been approved! As Liddy restacked the charts, preparing to retreat, red-faced and blood boiling, from Mitchell's office, the attorney general piped up. "And Gordon?" he said. "Yes, sir?" "Burn those charts; do it personally."[10]

One week later, on February 4, 1972, at 4:00 p.m., the same cast of characters reassembled in the attorney general's office. Dean arrived late, slipping into the room to find Mitchell, Magruder, and Liddy poring over sheets of paper that Liddy, having burned his charts, as ordered, distributed instead.

The revised Gemstone, Magruder later testified, was "less spectacular and therefore more acceptable." Liddy had "eliminated most of the activities, particularly the kind of reprehensible activity . . . The call girl thing was out, the kidnapping was out. That just didn't go over with Mr. Mitchell." What remained, Magruder said, was "primarily oriented to the wiretapping and photographing of documents."[11]

Contrary to Dean's later assertions that he joined the February 4 meeting "very late," he did not miss the bulk of it. Mitchell testified Dean arrived "shortly" after the session started; Magruder recalled Dean being present for "most" of it. When the counsel came in, Liddy had just finished explaining which precious stones and minerals he had chucked; his discussion of what remained *in* the plan Dean heard in full. Dean's later testimony on what he heard became crucial, in view of Mitchell's and Magruder's sharply divergent recollections, and Liddy's decision to withhold his account, the most reliable of all, until the publication of his autobiography, *Will*, in 1980.[12]

In testimony before the Senate Watergate committee in June 1973, Magruder asserted that he, Mitchell, and Dean "discussed possible targets" for wiretapping during this second meeting with Liddy. The first name that arose, Magruder claimed, was that of Lawrence F. O'Brien, chairman of the Democratic National Committee (DNC), a longtime Democratic operative and intimate of the Kennedys. Magruder said he shared with the others a rumor that the DNC was accepting kickbacks from convention vendors. This supposedly led to a discussion of Liddy and his men placing wiretaps inside the headquarters of the Democratic presidential nominee; inside Miami's Fontainebleau Hotel, where O'Brien was to stay during the convention; and inside DNC headquarters at the Watergate complex, where

O'Brien kept his Washington office. Magruder testified that O'Brien made an especially attractive target because he was "very effective in his attacks . . . relating to the ITT case. At this time, that was the hot issue."[13]

Magruder's testimony was demonstrably false. Although Larry O'Brien did effectively exploit the "hot issue" of ITT, that scandal did not erupt until Jack Anderson first broke the explosive antitrust allegations in his column on February 29, 1972—twenty-five days after the February 4 meeting. Equally false was Magruder's claim that Mitchell, at the February 4 session, ordered Liddy to explore the feasibility of cracking the safe of a Las Vegas newspaper editor—a subject only Magruder, in vacillating testimony, remembered arising. Incredibly, in its final report, the Senate Watergate committee failed even to mention Mitchell's denial that any targets were discussed.[14]

John Dean, granted immunity by the Senate Watergate committee, evidently struggled with his testimony on this question of whether specific targets were discussed. "When I got there," Dean said in executive session testimony before the Senate, previously unpublished, "they were talking about the same sort of thing [as in the first meeting], but [with] more specific focus into the electronic surveillance area; and that is the first time I heard about Mr. Larry O'Brien and the Fontainebleau Hotel." Several days later, testifying on live television, Dean changed his story, saying he could not recall "for certain" whether targets were discussed during the first or second meeting in Mitchell's office. Thus on the one hand, Dean testified that when he entered the February 4 session, the talk had turned to "electronic surveillance" of O'Brien and the Fontainebleau; yet when committee Democrats sought to nail down that O'Brien and the Fontainebleau were discussed as "targets," Dean grew vague, saying there "may have been something as to potential targets." Later he returned to certainty, saying flatly of targets: "None were named." By the fall of 1974, when he spent nine days on the stand in *U.S. v. Mitchell*, Dean had apparently overcome the internal conflicts he exhibited before the Senate. Recounting the February 4 meeting in response to questions from chief Watergate prosecutor James F. Neal, Dean said that within a "few moments" of his entrance into the attorney general's office, the others began "talking about targets, possible targets of electronic surveillance."[15]

Dean always maintained that he abruptly terminated the February 4 meeting because he wanted to spare the attorney general further discomfort. In his 1976 memoir, *Blind Ambition*, Dean recalled how he cleared his throat and announced to the assembled that he didn't think this kind of conversation should take place in the office of the attorney general, a pronouncement that had the effect of clearing the room. Yet both Mitchell and Magruder recalled that it was the objections of Mitchell, not Dean, that brought the meeting to a halt, and that Dean had simply chimed in.[16]

Finally, there was Gordon Liddy's account, which unflinching devotion to the soldier's code of honor kept him from sharing with investigators during the endless hearings and trials of the seventies, at the personal cost of serving Watergate's longest prison sentence: four years. Liddy's recollection of the February 4 meeting did not always accord with Mitchell's; but on the major points in dispute, he supported Mitchell. It was the attorney general, Liddy recalled, who effectively ended the meeting, saying he would think about Liddy's proposals and get back to him. Only then, according to Liddy, did Dean offer his famous objection, spoken not to the room at large, as Dean claimed, but to Mitchell directly, and not as a matter of moral propriety, but one of plausible deniability: "Sir, I don't think a decision of this kind should come from the attorney general's office. I think he should get it from somewhere else—completely unofficial channels." Most crucially, Liddy's memoir made no mention of wiretap or burglary targets having been discussed during the February 4 meeting. "The Watergate was never, ever, *ever* mentioned at any of those meetings," Liddy stated emphatically.[17]

Had Liddy forsaken the code of *omertà*, the testimony of Dean and Magruder against Mitchell would have crumbled. As it was, the tales told by Mitchell's two chief accusers brimmed with internal illogic and frequently contradicted one another; but in the fevered climate of Watergate, none of that seemed to matter. On one overarching point, however, the four men present at the creation of the great scandal all agreed: Gordon Liddy left the attorney general's office on February 4, 1972, without approval of his intelligence plan, and without any orders to wiretap DNC headquarters at the Watergate.

Persistence was one of Gordon Liddy's strong points; patience was not. In the weeks that followed the February 4 meeting, he relentlessly hounded Magruder to secure approval of Gemstone from John Mitchell. The attorney general had announced his resignation on February 15, 1972, and left Justice for CRP on March 1. To keep their chops sharp in the meantime, Liddy and Hunt performed an odd assortment of investigative jobs, including an examination of Jack Anderson's finances and a review of the best options for murdering the columnist, none of which panned out. Hunt also flew to Denver to conduct his bizarre interview of Dita Beard, the ITT witness.

Anxious to move forward on his master plan, Liddy began looking to others in the Nixon orbit who might help him get Gemstone up and running. In this he knew John Dean would be of limited value. After the February 4 meeting, the White House counsel had airily told Liddy they should never again discuss such subjects, and Liddy had said he understood. In the months that followed, however, Dean asked Liddy, in writing, to develop "more info" on the Democratic convention kickback scheme; intervened with Magruder when the latter moved, unsuccessfully, to get Liddy fired ("Jeb, you don't want to let your personal feelings get in the way of an important operation," Dean said); and worked with the covert operator, newly released tapes suggest, well into the 1972 primary season.[18]

If Dean was careful to keep his support for Liddy on the down low, no such qualms afflicted Charles Colson. The special counsel to the president was a rising star in the Nixon White House—much to

Mitchell's consternation. A former Marine Corps captain and lawyer, Colson possessed a sharp mind and even sharper instincts for the jugular. He read *Six Crises*, President Nixon's 1962 memoir, fourteen times, and said famously he would walk over his own grandmother to reelect Richard Nixon. In the White House, Colson earned a reputation as an "evil genius," Nixon's "hatchet man," a canny and ruthless political operator whose official function was to build grassroots, union, and special interest support, but whose duties soon grew to include a wide range of sub rosa, and sometimes illegal, projects. More than any other individual, Colson was the moving force behind the White House "enemies list." He brought Howard Hunt on board, supervising his efforts to dredge up derogatory information about Daniel Ellsberg and forge State Department cables implicating President Kennedy in the assassination of Ngo Dinh Diem, the first president of South Vietnam. It was Colson whom Haldeman cited when he told the president, in a taped Oval Office conversation in May 1971, of arrangements having been made for Teamster "murderers" to maim antiwar protesters. All of this appalled the attorney general. Asked once to identify Colson's constituency, Mitchell snapped: "The president's worst instincts." When Haldeman contended that Colson wouldn't have taken part in a dirty trick against Ted Kennedy, Mitchell laughed derisively and said: "Colson did nothing *but* that kind of thing." To Len Garment, Mitchell most bluntly expressed his view: "That fucking Colson is going to kill us all."[19]

Liddy didn't see Colson that way. He knew from Hunt that Colson had a taste for the covert, and suspected the former marine might make a better rabbi than either Dean, who feared overt association with Liddy, or Magruder, who feared Liddy himself. Accordingly, on March 8, 1972, his beloved Gemstone having languished for more than a month without gaining Mitchell's approval, Liddy, escorted by Hunt, paid a visit to Colson's office. It was late in the afternoon, and Hunt, happy to let Liddy cultivate his own relationship with Colson, sat on a couch at the far end of the office, smoking his pipe and reading a magazine. "We are now over at the [reelection] committee working," Liddy told Colson, "and we are anxious to get started, but can't find anyone who can make a decision or give us a green light."[20]

Liddy did not spell out the specifics of Gemstone; there was no need. Colson knew exactly what kind of program Liddy and Hunt had in mind. Now, with Liddy before him, Colson decided to take action himself. He picked up the phone, called Magruder, and laid into the younger, more timid man. "Jeb, these guys are in my office and they have got some plan they want to present, and it is time to fish or cut bait," Colson recalled telling Magruder. "What's the matter with you guys over there? You can never decide anything." Magruder remembered the call slightly differently, telling the Senate: "Colson called me one evening and asked, in a sense, would we get off the stick and get the budget approved for Mr. Liddy's plans, that we needed information, *particularly on Mr. O'Brien*."[21]

Yet Colson's importuning did not prompt Magruder to approve Gemstone himself; that was a greater risk than the CRP deputy was willing to accept. As he later told the Senate Watergate committee, "I certainly was aware of the legality, or illegality" of Liddy's plan. But Colson's urgings did have an effect: They prodded Magruder to make one last stab at getting Gemstone approved by John Mitchell.[22]

The former attorney general was worn out. The month of March 1972, his first in the private sector in three years, should have been consumed with congratulatory parties and overdue calls to old chums in New York. Instead, Mitchell spent it grappling with the ITT scandal, a labyrinth of antitrust meetings and memoranda. His testimony at the Kleindienst confirmation hearings had been a testy, nerve-racking affair, fraught with the perils of perjury. Worst of all, he had to contend with Martha Mitchell, whom, unlike his other problems, he had no prospect of controlling.

So as March came to a close, Mitchell took his high-strung wife and their ten-year-old daughter to Key Biscayne, Florida, where they stayed in a villa known as the Florida House, owned by the president's close friend, Charles "Bebe" Rebozo, and located just a few doors down from where the president himself vacationed. The relaxed climate there offered Mitchell some peace and quiet, a chance to catch up on the many aspects of the reelection campaign that awaited his decision. At 4:00 p.m. on March 30, he sat down to review twenty-nine decision memos compiled by Magruder and the third man present for their meeting, Fred Cheney LaRue.

Bald, sinewy, steely-eyed, and tight-lipped, the forty-four-year-old LaRue had cut his teeth enlarging his Mississippi family's formidable oil and gas fortune; however, his life was touched by tragedy when he killed his own father in a hunting accident. LaRue rebounded and entered politics, working the South for Goldwater; four years later, Mitchell deputized him to lure white voters away from George Wallace's segregationist flock. Impressed with LaRue's savvy and discretion—attributes Mitchell prized above all others—the attorney general brought the taciturn millionaire to Washington, and installed him in the White House for the token salary of a dollar a year. "My official title was special consultant to the president," LaRue recalled years later. "I basically reported to no one." In meetings, he said nothing; but others around the table recognized that he was, as Ehrlichman put it, "Mitchell's eyes and ears." When Mitchell sent a photograph of himself to LaRue, it was inscribed: "To the best friend the president and I ever had."[23]

Now, in Key Biscayne, LaRue sat alongside Magruder as Mitchell methodically disposed of the matters put to him, the minutia of direct mail and advertising campaigns, slogans and state chairmen. Finally, Magruder brought up an old subject: Gemstone. Of what happened next, all three men later offered sharply conflicting accounts—Magruder alone, in the years that followed, contradicted his own version of events multiple times on multiple points—with devastating consequences for the Nixon presidency and the nation.

The first forum in which Magruder gave sworn testimony about the Key Biscayne meeting was the grand jury in Washington, D.C., where he appeared on May 2, 1973. There, Magruder was careful to avoid directly attributing the final order for the Watergate break-in to any one individual. "I think *we all agreed* that there was [*sic*] potentially problems" with the Gemstone operation, Magruder testified. "But basically *we* did agree to fund the projects, because *we* felt that there were enough individuals that were interested in this information and *we* thought that there could possibly be some use put to this information by *ourselves* as well as [by] other individuals in the White House."[24]

Unpublished until now is Magruder's executive session testimony before the Senate Watergate committee, conducted behind closed doors on June 12, 1973, declassified in 2002, and obtained through the Freedom of Information Act. There Magruder testified: "The method by which I worked with Mr. Mitchell, he would take the copies that were in his files and he would mark them in whatever form. He usually wrote little notes on them, checked off what he was interested in. We went through that process. *He indicated verbal approval, gave me back the sheets, and that was it.*"

Not content to hear that Mitchell offered only "verbal" approval of Gemstone, the Senate Watergate committee's Democratic counsel, Sam Dash—a liberal critic of the Nixon White House who had once sued Mitchell to block his anticrime initiatives—moved quickly in this private session to prompt the witness, with a leading statement, to say Mitchell's order was in writing. Magruder, seeking leniency, took his cue.

> DASH: There was a notation that Mr. Mitchell made.
> MAGRUDER: My recollection is that I gave him the papers and he jotted some things down on the papers, but I can't recall what that was, exactly. Just simply some comment about the thing, gave it back to me. I just can't recall what he noted on these papers. It was some input he wanted to make.

With further help from Dash, Magruder managed admirably, by the time he testified in public session—two days later—to refresh his memory. He went from recalling nothing about Mitchell's jottings to remembering that they "indicated the project was approved," and, too, the "targets" Liddy was to wiretap, "specifically Mr. O'Brien's office."[25]

Finally there was LaRue. From his first sworn testimony to interviews he gave three decades later, LaRue never wavered in testifying that Magruder left Key Biscayne *without* approval of Gemstone. Appearing before the grand jury in April 1973, LaRue recalled that at the end of the lengthy meeting, Magruder gave Mitchell the last of the twenty-nine decision memos, Mitchell read it over, and asked LaRue: "What do you think?" "I don't think it's worth the risk," LaRue quoted himself replying. Then Mitchell, after a few seconds of silence, declared: "Well, we don't have to do anything on this now." "That was the end of the meeting," LaRue testified. His story remained the same before the Senate, the House, and the jury in *U.S. v. Mitchell*.[26]

LaRue's testimony obviously posed severe problems for Magruder, who had depicted Mitchell not as withholding decision at Key Biscayne, but as actively approving Gemstone, marking up the document and handing it back. According to a previously unpublished memorandum by a staff lawyer on the Watergate Special Prosecution Force (WSPF), just six days after LaRue testified on nationwide television in July 1973, Magruder, his memory suddenly "triggered," appeared at the WSPF offices to amend his story of the Key Biscayne session, and advanced, for the first time, the dubious claim that Mitchell gave the order when LaRue was on the phone or out of the room. "Basically," LaRue replied, "the guy that's lying is Magruder."[27]

Mitchell was never formally charged with ordering the Watergate break-in. However, the notion that he did order it, LaRue's testimony be damned, persisted, a cloud that loomed larger over Mitchell's legacy than any of the criminal acts for which he was actually tried.

In July 1973, Mitchell spent three days testifying before the Senate Watergate committee, the first of many forums where he publicly denied, unwaveringly and under oath, authorizing the break-in. Indeed, the constantly mutating story of Magruder, and the constancy of Mitchell's, in forum after forum, provided one of the most striking contrasts in the whole affair. To the Senate, the former attorney general noted that the Gemstone plan was the last item submitted for his review on that day in Key Biscayne, leading him to wonder aloud "whether somebody thought they were going to sneak it through, or there would be less resistance" at the end of a long session on other matters. When Magruder handed him the document, Mitchell told the Ervin committee, his reaction was very simple: "This again? We don't need this. I'm tired of hearing it. Out. Let's not discuss it any further. . . . It was just as clear as that." The former attorney general said his rejection was so swift the matter received "practically no discussion."[28]

Mitchell held to this story at all points: the Senate hearings, the House impeachment hearings, *U.S. v. Mitchell.* A previously unpublished House staff memo recorded Mitchell's claim that he told Magruder to "take the plan and 'shove it.' " Asked at his trial if he, Magruder, and LaRue had discussed the pros and cons of Liddy's modified plan, Mitchell told the jurors: "I am not sure we ever got that far"—though he did acknowledge he understood the plan "proposed a crime."[29]

Mitchell grew no less adamant with age. "I turned down Magruder in Key Biscayne," he told an interviewer less than two months before his death. "I turned that down out of hand." Asked if he was forceful enough in rejecting Magruder's Gemstone pitch at Key Biscayne, Mitchell replied: "Under the setting and the circumstances, what was said was vehement enough to [convey] 'Get the hell out of here and don't bring any of that nonsense around me.' . . . The conclusion I've come to in my own mind [is] that these things were under way and they were going to go ahead regardless."[30]

Closing out a week in the Florida sunshine with his wife and daughter, Mitchell had no idea he would spend the rest of his life entangled in *Rashomon*-like clashes of memory over meetings and phone calls with a cast of younger men he'd treated like sons, with criminal charges in the offing. In his next meeting with President Nixon, in the Oval Office on April 4, 1972, Mitchell said nothing about having approved a covert break-in and wiretapping operation against the chairman of the Democratic Party. Instead the former attorney general spoke fondly of Key Biscayne, a period of rest, relaxation, and only a little business. "We had some of the people down from the committee," Mitchell told Nixon, "where we could spend a couple of days, you know, with quiet."[31]

DNC

Watergate is probably unique among major political scandals—no one got hurt except the perpetrators.

—*Raymond K. Price Jr., 1977*[1]

THE SENATE WATERGATE committee's final report devoted only four of its 1,250 pages to the break-in. It did not say who ordered the Watergate operation. Similarly, the House Judiciary Committee's final report recoiled, at least initially, from hard judgment about the events of Key Biscayne: "*They* considered the proposal for electronic surveillance, and, according to Magruder, approved its revised budget." Elsewhere, however—even after acknowledging Fred LaRue's exculpatory testimony—the House report stated flatly the break-in was "approved in advance by Mitchell . . . [and] implemented under Mitchell's direction."[2]

Historians largely agreed. "Most investigators have been unwilling to accept [Mitchell's] disclaimers," wrote J. Anthony Lukas in his 1976 landmark *Nightmare*, the first major study of Watergate. "Because of the events that followed, they largely accept Magruder's version of the [Key Biscayne] meeting." Several biographers of Nixon hewed the same line, and as late as 2004, the *New York Times* repeated the falsehood in—of all places—LaRue's obituary.[3]

If Mitchell did not give the order, who did? Conspirators ascribed various motives to the skulduggery when they testified before the major investigative bodies, one of which—the House impeachment committee—never even mentioned in its 755-page final report the name of R. Spencer Oliver Jr. The executive director of the Association of State Democratic Chairmen was the one DNC employee whose telephone was actually monitored during the three-week life span of the Watergate surveillance operation. The other wiretap "victim" was Chairman O'Brien, on whose secretary's phone Watergate burglar James McCord placed a defective wiretap, which sat, inoperative and undisturbed, for the duration of the Watergate operation. This led Earl Silbert, the original lead prosecutor in Watergate, to tell the Senate he and his staff concluded one possible motive for the DNC mission was "blackmail . . . to compromise Oliver and others."[4]

Blackmail? R. Spencer Oliver Jr.? Why on earth would John Mitchell—trusted adviser to the president of the United States on the highest affairs of state—have bothered to order the bugging of an obscure DNC apparatchik? The answer, of course, was that Mitchell never did; the machinations that led to the famous arrests of June 17, 1972, transpired unbeknownst to him. Burning curiosity about who ordered the break-in gripped Mitchell to his grave. Only after his death was the mystery solved.

A few hours after the Key Biscayne meeting ended, Magruder instructed his administrative assistant, Robert Reisner, to give Gordon Liddy the long-awaited word: *Go.* Of this development Magruder also made sure to keep his own patron, H. R. Haldeman, well informed. On the day after the Florida House session, Gordon Strachan, a young lawyer who had joined Haldeman's staff in August 1970, following a two-year stint with the Nixon-Mitchell law firm in New York, informed Haldeman in writing: "Magruder reports that

1701 now has a sophisticated political intelligence-gathering system with a budget of 300 [thousand]." Haldeman was scheduled to sit down with Mitchell to discuss a wide variety of political matters on April 4, 1972. For this event, Strachan, following custom, prepared a "talking paper" to guide Haldeman through likely areas of discussion. The paper's second item concerned intelligence. "Gordon Liddy's intelligence proposal ($300) has been approved," wrote Strachan. "Now you may want to cover with Mitchell . . . who should be charged with the responsibility of translating the intelligence into an appropriate political response."[5]

Most intriguing about these communications between Strachan and Haldeman was that Strachan twice specified $300,000 as the price tag for Liddy's intelligence operation—even though, by all accounts, the final plan submitted for review carried a budget of only $250,000. Here was the first hint that something was amiss in the story of Mitchell approving Gemstone at Key Biscayne. For his part, Strachan insisted he accurately recorded the figure Magruder cited to him. He told the Senate that when Magruder called to say Gordon Liddy's plan had been approved, it was simply "assumed" that it was Mitchell's approval Magruder was conveying.

For the Democrats on the Senate Watergate committee, Strachan's assumption wasn't good enough. "A $300,000 expenditure could only be approved by Mitchell, is that so?" asked Wayne H. Bishop, the committee's chief field investigator, during Strachan's July 1973 testimony in executive session, previously unpublished. "Well," Strachan answered, "that is a very different question."

> Magruder made expenditures of substantial amounts of money without Mitchell's knowledge. . . . He spent $100,000 on a Republican National Committee film that Mitchell didn't know anything about. And when I told Haldeman and gave him a copy of the script, Haldeman called up Mitchell, and I was on the phone when he was talking; Mitchell went through the roof. . . . Another time, Magruder told me that he and

LaRue decided to increase the direct mail budget from $4.5 million to $5.5 million without Mitchell's approval.

Thus Magruder, when it suited him, acted behind Mitchell's back. As Strachan also told the Senate, Magruder "would frequently inform me that a matter had been decided by someone when it had not in fact been decided by that individual."[6]

Some historians later cited Strachan's April 4 "talking paper" as evidence of Mitchell's ultimate complicity in the Gemstone operation. This was misguided. For one thing, the talking paper was worded, like Strachan's memo of the previous day, in vague passive tense ("Liddy's intelligence operation proposal . . . *has been* approved"), without any explicit assertion of Mitchell's authorization. Second, and more important, the document made no reference to wiretapping or any other illegal activity.

As it happened, during their meeting on April 4, neither Mitchell nor Haldeman raised the subject of Liddy or his intelligence program. "My meetings with Mitchell very rarely, if ever, followed the agenda," Haldeman later testified.[7]

Gordon Liddy also assumed, when he got Magruder's message to move forward on Gemstone, that Mitchell was behind the order. Now that he had his "go" order, Liddy confidently came calling on Hugh Sloan, CRP's treasurer, demanding a first cash installment of $83,000 on the promised $250,000.

Sloan was taken aback by the numbers involved and refused to disburse the money before checking with his own boss, CRP finance committee chairman Maurice Stans, who in turn promised to check with Mitchell, the campaign manager. Stans tracked Mitchell down and mentioned Liddy's request for a "substantial" sum. "What is it all about?" According to Stans, Mitchell replied: "I don't know. . . . Magruder is in charge of the campaign and he directs the spending." Stans was incredulous. "Do you mean, John, that if Magruder tells Sloan to pay these amounts or any amounts to Gordon Liddy that he should do so?" "That is right," Mitchell answered.

To Mitchell, the matter was routine; by that point Magruder had authorized millions in campaign expenditures. Still, the concern exhibited by Stans, a peer in rank and age, evidently made an impression on Mitchell, who, according to previously unpublished testimony, soon cornered Magruder on the issue. "Does Liddy need that much right away?" Magruder recalled Mitchell asking. "Yes, he does," Magruder replied. The fact that Mitchell pressed Magruder like this showed the former attorney general was surprised by the amounts Liddy was demanding—a surprise Mitchell never would have exhibited if, just seven days earlier, he had signed off on a $250,000 wiretapping operation to be run by Liddy.[8]

A few weeks later, near the end of April, Liddy recalled, he was summoned to Magruder's office, where the CRP deputy asked a curious question. "Gordon, do you think you could get into the Watergate?" It marked the first time anyone had mentioned the Watergate complex to Liddy. Yes, he answered, the Watergate was a high-security building, but it could be done. "How about putting a bug in O'Brien's office?" Magruder continued. This was even more curious, for by that point it was a matter of public record that the DNC chairman was spending most of his time in Miami, preparing for the convention. "For that, it's a bit late," Liddy replied. "Okay, so he's in and out," Magruder countered. "We want to know whatever's said in his office, just as if it was here, what goes on in this office." Liddy agreed to do the job. "The phones, too," Magruder added. "And while you're in there, photograph whatever you can find."[9]

To line up trustworthy operatives, Liddy relied on Howard Hunt, the acerbic and tweedy career CIA officer and author, under various pseudonyms, of more than forty pulp spy novels. Hunt turned to Bernard Barker, an old comrade from the Bay of Pigs days. Across Miami's Cuban exile community, Barker maintained a small network of soldiers of fortune, fanatical anti-Castro *machismos*, Bay of Pigs veterans with old—and, in at least one case, ongoing—ties to CIA.[10]

Liddy felt fortunate to have a man like Hunt at his side. Obligingly, CIA supplied Hunt with all kinds of assistance: the multicolor Gemstone charts, fake identification documents, disguise items, even the camera used when Liddy and Hunt executed the messy, but as-yet-untraced, break-in at the office of Daniel Ellsberg's psychiatrist (a camera from which only CIA, a dismayed Liddy found, could extract the film). But there were aspects of Gemstone that required expertise beyond even Hunt's wide swath of covert experience; for example, neither man knew the first thing about modern electronics equipment, the miniaturized radio-frequency transmitters, receivers, transceivers, and other hi-tech gear essential to a professional surveillance operation. For help in this area, Liddy spent the early months of 1972 picking the brain of the one character in the Watergate saga even stranger than himself: James W. McCord Jr.

Balding, soft-spoken, demure to the point of shyness, the Texas-born McCord had become CRP's chief of security in January 1972, following an extraordinary—and still murky—career in clandestine service. An FBI agent who specialized in counterespionage missions, McCord crossed over to CIA in 1951 and spent much of his time with CIA working for the Security Research Staff, a shadowy branch of the agency's larger Office of Security. An air force colonel recalled in 1973: "McCord was just not somebody's little wiretapper or debugging man. . . . He's a pro, he's a master. Allen Dulles introduced him to me . . . and said: 'This man is the best man we have.' " A former CRP employee close to McCord during Watergate said: "I could actually sense a *fear* of Richard Nixon with Jim McCord. . . . [He felt] Richard Nixon wasn't a team player, wasn't an American, wasn't, you know, 'one of us.' "[11]

When McCord joined the Nixon reelection campaign, CRP was preparing to assume responsibility for the expensive round-the-clock security that John and Martha Mitchell had, for three years, received from the FBI. But by February 1972, two months before Liddy in-

...ᴗd him to join the Watergate mission, McCord confided to FBI colleagues that he intended to move beyond his security role, the dreary stuff of camera installations and guard schedules. McCord's true aims were recorded in a previously unpublished internal FBI memorandum: "He reiterated that he believes his position will be one of intelligence and that ultimately he will become more and more involved in Mr. Mitchell's political activities and less involved in personal security."

This memo offers the earliest glimpse into what investigators later termed McCord's "secret agenda" at CRP. The wireman's goal was to infiltrate Mitchell's political circle and shift into an "intelligence" function. Clearly, the chief beneficiary of McCord's "security" work was not to be Mitchell and CRP, but CIA. Liddy offered McCord an extra $2,000 in salary each month, plus $2,000 per surreptitious entry, to join the mission. Hardly surprised by Liddy's offer—McCord later said Liddy's repeated inquiries about electronics gear had made it "clearer and clearer" he was plotting a surveillance project—the new security chief readily accepted.[12]

Never did Liddy imagine, as he planned the Watergate break-in, that he had surrounded himself with men of such dubious loyalty. Faced with mounting evidence that officials in the White House and CRP had set up their own covert operations unit, with Liddy the central player, CIA acted as any intelligence organization would. After all, permitting Liddy's little unit to operate unchecked, targeting anything and anybody in Washington, utterly beyond the watch or influence of the nation's premier spy agency, would have violated every known principle of bureaucratic behavior, and the spy game especially. The Plumbers, quite simply, had to be monitored, infiltrated—neutralized.[13]

Howard Hunt and James McCord insinuated themselves into the Nixon White House and CRP, respectively, at crucial times: Hunt, shortly before the creation of the Plumbers, McCord, shortly after the Ellsberg break-in, the Plumbers' first illegal break-in. There is persuasive evidence the two men, despite their disclaimers, first met each other long before Liddy supposedly introduced them in 1972. En-rique "Harry" Ruiz-Williams, a Cuban Bay of Pigs veteran, recalled meeting "dozens" of times with Hunt and McCord—together—in the years immediately after the failed invasion of Cuba. And in pre-viously unpublished testimony before the Senate Watergate com-mittee, Felipe DeDiego, one of the Cubans who raided Ellsberg's psychiatrist's office, told investigators he instantly recognized McCord as the same man who a decade earlier, in Florida, had helped organize "an infiltration group . . . of Cubans working for the CIA."[14]

Finally, the CIA had one of Barker's men—Eugenio Martinez, another Bay of Pigs veteran—on the payroll at the time of the DNC break-in. Martinez's mission was, in part, to keep the Agency abreast of the Plumbers' plans. Hunt admitted to the Senate, in previously unpublished testimony, that he had "learned . . . from Martinez at one point . . . that his case officer had been made aware that I was in the Miami area and had asked him for a report of my activities." Of this Hunt professed to be unconcerned: "It was never made explicit to Mr. Martinez that I was no longer with the agency. I never said that I was or wasn't. It was just not a matter of discussion. I was at the White House, obviously in a senior capacity of some sort, and I had been able to obtain CIA items of issue for the Fielding operation and so forth. And all of this certainly would suggest strongly to anyone on a clandestine relationship with me that I had some sort of authorized official relationship to the intelligence community in the United States government."[15]

That Langley received Gemstone updates from Eugenio Mar-tinez, independent of Hunt and McCord, was further confirmed in a previously unpublished memo dictated by CIA director Richard Helms on December 4, 1973. As the country braced for the coming impeachment battle, Helms learned that Alexander Haig, by then White House chief of staff, was trying to get an influential senator to allege that CIA "knew about the Watergate burglary thirty min-utes before it occurred." Mere mention of the agency's foreknowledge of the break-in alarmed Helms, who fretted privately: "It is still not clear to me whether [Haig] would have been basing his allegation on *information from Martinez* or just what."[16]

The role of CIA in the collapse of the Nixon presidency was a subject of intense controversy during the Watergate era, and a mystery that bedeviled Mitchell to his grave. It reminded him of the spying conducted against the administration by the Joint Chiefs of Staff. "I'm sure the CIA knew more about Watergate than it's ever come out," he told an interviewer in 1987; by the time he died, the former attorney general had concluded "the CIA was behind the whole thing."[17]

With the Plumbers now firmly in CIA's grip, Gordon Liddy unaware that control of Gemstone had been silently, effortlessly wrested from him, only one position on his DNC crew remained unfilled. It was the operation's most important job: the wiretap monitor. Liddy asked McCord, the electronics expert, to find someone to man the headphones and log the results. This was Liddy's biggest mistake, for it ceded to McCord complete control over the Watergate operation: It would be McCord's man listening in on the intercepted conversations and furnishing the fruits directly to McCord, who would in turn heavily edit the data before submitting it to his superiors at CRP. Liddy, in short, never saw the raw intelligence produced by his own covert project.

McCord's next move was explicable only as the product of a secret agenda. He chose for the DNC mission an undistinguished former FBI agent with barely two years in the Bureau, a lackluster career after leaving it, and zero experience in wiretapping. This was Alfred C. Baldwin III, a portly and affable thirty-five-year-old lawyer (West Hartford Law School class of '63) and former instructor of police science (New Haven College). When McCord first contacted him, at home on the night of May 1, Baldwin was unemployed. Seducing his prey with talk of campaign "security work" and an annual salary of up to $20,000—"I wasn't sure somebody wasn't playing a joke on me," an astounded Baldwin later recalled—McCord had Baldwin fly to Washington that night.[18]

Over breakfast the next day, Baldwin learned his first duty would be serving as a bodyguard for Martha Mitchell, who was spending the spring barnstorming the country for the Nixon-Agnew ticket, its most popular and bankable surrogate. However, to accompany her on such trips—indeed, to deal with Martha Mitchell at all—was universally regarded by CPR staff as the campaign's most thankless task. McCord minimized the unpleasantness to Baldwin, and less than twenty-four hours after their first conversation, Baldwin was driven to the Mitchells' Watergate apartment, where he met Mrs. Mitchell and her personal assistant. By 4:00 p.m. the whole entourage was at Union Station—flying terrorized Martha—boarding Amtrak's Broadway Limited to Chicago.[19]

Al Baldwin's tour of duty with Martha proved brief and unpleasant, in large part because of his additional assignment as the procurer of Mrs. Mitchell's liquor, the most incendiary ingredient in an already highly flammable personality. "There were several occasions where I had to actually take, say, a cup of what would be Scotch to her, in the guise [of] it being coffee," Baldwin confessed. "A couple of times I thought it was unusual, because it was early . . . ten-thirty, eleven o'clock [in the morning], during a speech." Martha, for her part, disliked Baldwin, thought him devious and "gauche." The hapless aide was forced to sign a statement swearing he had not talked about Martha behind her back.

When the entourage arrived back at the Watergate, Baldwin helped unload Mrs. Mitchell's luggage, then politely excused himself to wait for a ride back to CRP. Then word came: *Mr. Mitchell wants to see you.* Ushered into the Mitchells' study, Baldwin found the former attorney general relaxing in a sweater and slacks, smoking his pipe. But instead of reprimanding him, as the unsophisticated former FBI man feared, Mitchell thanked him. "I've got good reports . . . about your work," Mitchell said, "and I want to welcome you to the team." Baldwin left stunned but relieved. What he hadn't taken into account was that nobody knew better than John Mitchell how difficult Martha Mitchell could be.[20]

On May 11, at McCord's direction, Baldwin moved his belongings into Room 419 at the Howard Johnson's Motor Lodge, located directly across the street from the Watergate office complex. Over the next two weeks, Baldwin mingled in antiwar crowds and posed as a tourist in the Capitol offices of several members of Congress—Kennedy, Muskie, Jacob Javits, Bella Abzug, Chisholm, Ed Koch—selected by McCord. Then, on the afternoon of May 25, Baldwin opened the door to Room 419 to find, to his astonishment, James McCord positively awash in electronic equipment: portable shortwave radios, debugging devices, tape recorders, a Samsonite suitcase concealing a radio-frequency receiver.

"We've got this operation," McCord announced. According to an account Baldwin gave, in presence of counsel and previously unpublished, McCord said "bugs had been installed on two phones across the way and that their job was now to monitor these phones." This account is significant, for it confirms that McCord installed listening devices in the DNC at least three days *before* he and the Cubans made their first successful entry into the Watergate, following three failed attempts, over May 26–27. This means McCord deceived his confederates throughout the operation, pursuing a secret agenda.[21]

McCord demonstrated how to use the equipment by tuning in an actual conversation for Baldwin to monitor. Shortly after the Watergate arrests, Baldwin told the FBI this initial chatter had featured "a man talking with a woman and discussing their marital problem." In March 1973, Baldwin told the Senate Watergate committee the man with the "marital problem" was Spencer Oliver. This set the tone for the highly personal conversations Baldwin was to monitor over the next three weeks, until the arrests of June 17 abruptly terminated his mission. In October 1972, Baldwin told the *Los Angeles Times* that many of the conversations he logged in May and June involved DNC staffers besides Oliver, who traveled frequently, and that the contents were often "explicitly intimate." "We can talk," the DNC secretaries would say. "I'm on Spencer Oliver's phone."[22]

Since January 1973, a gag order imposed by the Court of Appeals for the District of Columbia has prevented the Watergate wiretap monitor from disclosing exactly what he overheard; but as the years reeled by, bits and pieces of the illegally intercepted conversations seeped out from other sources, and Baldwin himself, during an extraordinary seven-hour interview at his home in East Haven, Connecticut, in the summer of 1995, and in sworn testimony he subsequently gave in civil litigation, opened up considerably. By describing the contents of the conversations intercepted at the DNC, Baldwin helped solve the mystery of who ordered the wiretapping in the first place.[23]

"I don't know who Mr. Spencer Oliver is," John Mitchell testified in September 1972. And why should he have? The former attorney general operated on a political plane miles above that of Oliver and, and as far as Mitchell was concerned, he had rejected Liddy's bugging plans three times.

To the Senate, Mitchell stated flatly he had "never seen or talked to" Liddy after February 4, 1972, the day of the second Gemstone meeting—with one exception. On June 15, 1972, Mitchell told the committee, he met with Liddy and others to review a letter Liddy had sent the *Washington Post*, defending CRP against arcane allegations involving the Corrupt Practices Act. "I looked at the letter and gave it [my] approval and that was the end of it," Mitchell testified. "That was the only conversation I had with Mr. Liddy."[24]

Mitchell's story was false in two minor respects. First, he had indeed seen and spoken to Liddy between February and June: once, at a May 8 briefing on Vietnam at the White House, at which Liddy advocated the targeting of civilian population centers in North Vietnam and Mitchell rebuked him for offering "amateur military advice."

However, that encounter had occurred as part of a large gathering and was wholly unrelated to Liddy's Gemstone intrigues. The other minor problem with Mitchell's testimony was that the *Washington Post* letter was not his sole topic of discussion with Liddy on June 15.

According to Liddy's memoir, he did indeed visit Mitchell in his office on that day to discuss "nonintelligence matters." Because his interaction with Mitchell was so rare, and despite the fact that "intelligence wasn't on the agenda," Liddy brought with him a bulging, unmarked manila envelope containing a "thick sheaf" of material generated by the Oliver wiretap. Believing all along that Mitchell was the intended consumer of this data—the man who'd ordered the DNC operation—Liddy placed the envelope on a corner of Mitchell's desk and said: "That's for you, general." To Liddy's chagrin, the former attorney general scarcely acknowledged Liddy's presence, just nodded and puffed on his pipe while reading other papers, and made no move at all to retrieve the envelope. "Indeed," Liddy later recalled, "the entire time I was in his office, he never touched it." When Mitchell *did* finally pay attention to Liddy on this occasion, it was, again, to chastise him: this time for plotting to have hippies urinate in a Miami hotel room soon to be occupied by Senator McGovern—and thereafter by Mitchell himself.

In his version of the June 15 meeting, Mitchell omitted his rebuke of Liddy over the never-executed McGovern prank, and made no mention of the bulging envelope, of whose existence Liddy thought the former attorney general totally oblivious. In all other respects, Liddy's story confirmed Mitchell's: They had not met, per se, between February 4 and June 15, and only then on "nonintelligence matters"; most importantly, Liddy's account offered no evidence that Mitchell ever touched, let alone consumed, the fruits of the Watergate operation, the wiretap data from the Oliver telephone.[25]

Jeb Magruder, however, testifying in exchange for leniency, told a very different story—or several of them, as was his habit. According to Magruder, in early June he received from Liddy two "worthless" packages of wiretap data. "The telephone calls told us a great deal more than we needed to know about the social lives of various members of the Democratic committee staff," Magruder wrote in 1974, "but nothing of political interest." After showing the logs to a disgusted Gordon Strachan ("This idiot is just wasting our time and money!"), Magruder claimed he brought the wiretap fruits directly to Mitchell, who angrily summoned Liddy for still another censuring, this time over the quality of the DNC wiretap data. It was after Mitchell's reprimand, Magruder claimed, that Liddy vowed to send his men back into the Watergate to correct the problem. If such a meeting had occurred, it would have been of historic significance: the catalyst for the final, fateful Watergate break-in of June 17.[26]

Yet Magruder's story was full of holes. For starters, Magruder told the grand jury his standard procedure was to withhold from Mitchell all material that held zero "interest" or "value." Why, then, would Magruder have shoved the "worthless" DNC data under Mitchell's nose? It was a question for which, at Mitchell's trial, Magruder had no good answer. Second, Magruder had trouble supplying accurate details about this fateful meeting. He could never fix the date. In one early version, he claimed Mitchell delivered his rebuke to Liddy over the phone; elsewhere it was face-to-face, in Mitchell's law office. Then there was the supposed substance. "Mitchell chewed out Liddy for the quality of the intelligence," Magruder told the Watergate prosecutors in April 1973; later he remembered Mitchell having addressed Liddy in a "rather understated way."[27]

Despite their many internal contradictions, Magruder's multiple accounts all featured one common element: They all implicated Mitchell as the trigger man for the catastrophic events of June 17. The one major problem with all of these stories was that the evidence and testimony undermined them. Asked at the Senate hearings to respond, Mitchell coined one of the scandal's most memorable phrases.

DASH: But do you recall Mr. Magruder testifying that he had taken these documents [the wiretap logs] and shown them to you?

MITCHELL: I recall it very vividly, because it happens to be a palpable, damnable lie.

Mitchell said his secretary kept "very accurate" office logs, which reflected no record of any such session. Of course, the Senate, and later the Watergate prosecutors, also knew Magruder's own calendar also showed no record of the meeting.[28]

Also available to the prosecutors was the testimony of a number of individuals who spoke to Gordon Liddy immediately after the arrests of June 17, all of whom recalled him specifying that it was Magruder—not Mitchell—who precipitated the final entry into the Watergate. Robert Mardian, the CRP lawyer who formally debriefed Liddy on June 21, reported to the Senate that Liddy "made the entry at the insistence of Mr. Magruder." Fred LaRue, present for that debriefing, likewise told the Senate that Liddy felt "pressure from Magruder to improve the surveillance."[29]

What was not available to Watergate investigators in the 1970s was Liddy's testimony; not until he published *Will* in 1980 did his account emerge, and it demolished Magruder's multiple versions. Liddy recalled no discussions with Mitchell at all about the quality of the DNC wiretap data. In fact, it was Magruder who admonished Liddy about the DNC data, who fretted over its cost, who urged the wiretaps be upgraded. "On Friday, June 9," Liddy reported in *Will*, "Magruder called me in again . . . [and] said that the content of the logs to date was hardly worth the effort, risk, and expense we had gone to." Three days later, Magruder impatiently ordered Liddy back into the Watergate: "Take all the men, all the cameras you need."[30]

It was, then, this sharply worded order from Magruder—and not any prodding from Mitchell—that sparked the final Watergate break-in. That Magruder gave the order on June 12—the one specific date he used when attributing the directive to Mitchell—was more than a coincidence. Liddy's belated account begged the question of why the "agitated" Magruder issued this order when he did—and on whose authority. What had happened prior to June 12 to make Magruder push Liddy so hard—*take all the men, all the cameras you need*—to go back into the Watergate?

On June 9, three days before Magruder's order to Liddy, John Dean summoned two federal prosecutors to his White House office to brief him on their investigation into what had been dubbed, in that morning's *Washington Evening Star*, a Capitol Hill call-girl ring. At one point in the meeting he asked to keep portions of the evidence in the case, a request the prosecutors, though awed by their surroundings, properly refused.[31]

The prostitution rings servicing Washington in the freewheeling early 1970s tended to share key players; this was certainly true of the outfit described in the *Evening Star* story and the Columbia Plaza call-girl ring, so dubbed because its personnel operated, as police records confirmed, out of the fashionable apartment complex of that name, two blocks southeast of the Watergate. There was, in turn, a connection between Columbia Plaza and DNC. One of the federal prosecutors summoned to Dean's office that day subsequently testified he had developed evidence that "employees at the DNC . . . were assisting in getting the Democrats connected with the prostitutes at the Columbia Plaza," but that his investigation was "shut down" in the summer of 1972 by the district's U.S. attorney, who felt "the DNC should not be pursued, that it was a political time bomb."[32] Al Baldwin testified years later that eight of ten people—laypeople, not attorneys or law enforcement officers—if exposed to the same chatter he overheard at the DNC, "would have said, 'That's a call-girl ring. This is a prostitution ring.' " He told an interviewer in 1995 he had monitored "a lot of conversations of a sexual nature"; asked to elaborate, he grew terse, saying only they were "in line with [people making] arrangements and things."[33] As Earl Silbert suggested, the conversations monitored on Spencer Oliver's telephone could conceivably be used as "blackmail . . . to compromise Oliver and others."

Such racy activity was the only thing that made the DNC, with

...rman O'Brien in Miami, worth bugging at all.[34] In the 1990s it was alleged in lengthy civil depositions—conducted, ironically, at Dean's own instigation—that Dean's wife, Maureen, had her own ties to Columbia Plaza.[35]

Dean always denied ordering the break-in. "I wasn't even aware of the Watergate until after it happened," he reaffirmed in 1999. Yet Dean's knowledge of the players and their complex interconnections, documented in the civil litigation he initiated to try to suppress the "call-girl theory" of Watergate, arguably makes him the final answer to the three-decades-old question of who ordered the Watergate operation, who among the president's men pressured Jeb Magruder to send Liddy and his team back into the DNC.[36]

Though he later professed not to have "a disposition or a like for this type of activity," it was Dean who acknowledged in *Blind Ambition* that he saw intelligence as his way "upward" in the Nixon White House, the means by which to make himself "more valued by the policy-makers"; Dean who intervened on Liddy's behalf, and devised new assignments for him; Dean who requested that White House gumshoe Jack Caulfield place Senator Kennedy under twenty-four-hour surveillance; Dean who ordered Caulfield to probe Senator Muskie's connections to the sugar lobby; Dean who directed Caulfield to investigate Senator McGovern's fund-raising sources; Dean who dispatched Caulfield to New York to identify the clients of Xaviera Hollander's "Happy Hooker" call-girl ring; and Dean who reportedly asked Anthony Ulasewicz, Caulfield's sidekick, to case the Watergate complex prior to the DNC mission. Kenneth Tapman, a long-haired Department of Interior employee who had sat alongside Dean in negotiations with antiwar groups, remembered Dean once inviting him to lunch at the White House and asking if he "was interested in spying, basically, on anti-Republican groups prior to the 1972 convention."[37]

Dean knew enough about the peculiar goings-on at the DNC to inform H. R. Haldeman, on September 12, 1972, as the Democrats' civil suit against CRP was entering discovery, that depositions probing "the sexual activities of employees of the DNC . . . should cause considerable problems for those being deposed." Similarly, in all the countless meetings and tapes, only Dean raised with President Nixon, three days later, the notion that the Democrats "were hiding something" that might be exposed, in the aforementioned depositions, by "getting into the sex life of some of the members of the DNC."[38]

Magruder would have done anything Dean told him to do. Too timid to approve a venture like the Watergate operation on his own, Magruder let it be known at the White House that Gemstone could move forward if someone "countermanded" Mitchell's opposition to the project. Though Magruder's credibility has been shattered by the sheer multiplicity of the tales he has told about, and at, each stage of the scandal, he has, over the years, occasionally told the truth about Dean. The first time was when the Watergate cover-up started unraveling, and it began to dawn on Magruder that he was either going to be thrown to the wolves or could surrender to the prosecutors. In late March 1973, recently declassified tapes show, Magruder passed word to his former superiors at the White House that he was prepared to bring Dean down with him.

> **HALDEMAN:** [Magruder] has now clarified his memory and figures that he's got to—he's now got to—if they're going to haul everybody up, he's got to clean himself up, too.
> **NIXON:** Right.
> **HALDEMAN:** And that what really happened on the Watergate was that all this planning was going on and Dean set it up and was involved in getting the planning worked out. . . . Magruder has chosen to say he believes [this] to be the actual fact now, and he told these two lawyers this. And Dean said: "Don't discount Magruder as a witness; he's a hell of a convincing guy."[39]

Five years later, in a little-noticed book about his Christian rebirth entitled *From Power to Peace*, Magruder again hinted at Dean's centrality, listing him as the "initial" planner of Watergate. And in an interview in February 1990, Magruder was asked: "If you thought it through now, what would you say . . . to a direct question, 'Who told you to go back in?' " "I'd say probably John Dean," he answered. Six months later, he went even further. "Mitchell didn't do anything," he said. "All Mitchell did was just what I did, [which] was acquiesce to the pressure from the White House. We [at CRP] didn't do anything; we weren't the initiators. Hell, the first plan that we got had been initiated by Dean. . . . The target never came from Mitchell."[40]

Questioned under oath about these statements in a deposition in August 1995, Magruder claimed he had been quoted out of context and withdrew his allegations against Dean. "I don't recall John Dean talking to me about Gemstone after the second meeting with Mitchell, Dean, and Liddy," Magruder testified, reprising the story he had told the Senate. Yet elsewhere Magruder's deposition unmistakably implicated Dean as a prime mover in the DNC operation.

QUESTION: Is it true that John Dean was one of the people in the White House that was pushing for the Gemstone plan?
MAGRUDER: Yes.
QUESTION: [. . .] Is it, in fact, truthful that you and John Dean had prior knowledge of the Watergate break-in?
MAGRUDER: Yes.[41]

To his death, Mitchell remained puzzled by Magruder's lies. "Why in the hell would he be protecting Dean?" Mitchell would ask. "In order to protect himself?" The answer was simple and lay, as Mitchell should have understood, in the way successful criminal prosecutions tend to unfold. In April 1973, as the Watergate cover-up crumbled and Nixon's men jockeyed to secure the shortest possible prison sentences, Dean, always a step ahead of his White House peers, beat Magruder to the U.S. attorney's office by two weeks. When Magruder showed up to see Earl Silbert, ready to trade testimony for leniency, the witness learned he would have to deliver bigger fish than

John Dean to whet the prosecutors' appetites. "One thing I did tell Silbert early on, when I decided to cooperate, was that Dean was as involved as I was," Magruder recalled in 1990. "I made it clear to Silbert that Dean was in from the beginning, but Silbert didn't care about that . . . 'cause Dean was already in their pocket."[42]

If, on the other hand, Magruder could implicate higher-ranking officials—like the former attorney general of the United States—then the Watergate prosecutors would listen.

Mitchell knew he had been set up. In later years, his mind reeled at the singular confluence of amazing characters that produced Watergate—Dean, Magruder, Liddy, Helms, Hunt, McCord, Martinez—and reckoned himself and the president, neither of whom enjoyed foreknowledge of the Watergate break-in, victims in the affair. "The more I got into this," Mitchell said in June 1987, "the more I see how these sons of bitches have not only done Nixon in but they've done *me* in."[43]

On June 16, 1972, following a morning meeting with the vice president, Mitchell met up with his wife and child, and with Magruder and Mardian they boarded a Gulfstream II bound for Los Angeles. They checked into the Beverly Hills Hotel, where the Mitchell party occupied an entire wing. It was going to be a memorable weekend, capped by a star-studded Saturday night party at the Bel Air home of MCA president Taft Schreiber.

The next morning, Mitchell woke early, enjoyed breakfast with his family in their suite, and proceeded to his first meeting of the day: a session in a nearby room with Mardian and Thomas C. Reed, a Republican committeeman from California (later President Reagan's secretary of the air force). The meeting, Mitchell later testified, was called to discuss the sorry state of the GOP in Texas, "where they were having the usual donnybrook among factions in the party." At one point—the timing of which later became crucial—there was a knock on the door. Mitchell went to answer it, and found Fred LaRue standing before him. LaRue had sobering news and suggested they speak privately.

Mitchell excused himself from Reed's company and followed his most trusted aide into an adjoining room. There LaRue broke the news to Mitchell that five men, including CRP's security chief, James McCord, had been arrested overnight inside the headquarters of the Democratic National Committee at the Watergate complex and were now in jail. LaRue never forgot Mitchell's astonished reply: "That is incredible."[44]

THE NEEDLE

I was all over this thing like a wet blanket. I was everywhere—everywhere they look they are going to find Dean.

—*John Dean, 1973*[1]

THE NIGHT BEFORE, Mitchell had retired "several hours earlier" than Martha, who turned in "drunk" around 2:00 a.m. She, not surprisingly, remained in bed while the former attorney general and their daughter, Marty, awoke after seven and ate breakfast in their suite.

Downstairs, at the Beverly Hills Hotel's chic Polo Lounge, Jeb Magruder was beginning breakfast with his wife, Gail, the LaRues, and others, when a waiter informed Magruder he had a telephone call. It was Gordon Liddy from Washington. At first, Liddy insisted Magruder call back on a "secure" phone from the air force base in nearby El Segundo. Impatient with Liddy's "cloak-and-dagger games," Magruder refused. Then Liddy told him about McCord's arrest. Magruder, reeling with shock, left the table abruptly and headed for a pay phone.[2]

What happened next—indeed, everything that happened over

the next eleven months—was later disputed by the participants. This was Watergate: an endless clash of memories over the substance of meetings and telephone calls featuring a revolving cast of self-interested men, most of them lawyers. Only with the passage of time, the accumulation of testimony and memoirs, the release of declassified documents and tapes, and the interviewing and reinterviewing of the scandal's players, could a true picture be drawn of the Watergate cover-up, which commenced immediately. That Mitchell played a role is indisputable; however, it is equally true that the former attorney general was, in simplest terms, framed, a casualty of a wicked alliance between coconspirators eager to tell lies and prosecutors eager to believe them.

Magruder's account of the Watergate cover-up came in kaleidoscopic form, contradicted, as usual, by his own testimony and that of others. First he told prosecutors he received Liddy's shocking call not at breakfast, but earlier, in his hotel room, and that he immediately convened a meeting of Mitchell, LaRue, and Mardian and "told them the problem." Mitchell then supposedly ordered Bob Mardian to call Powell Moore, a CRP spokesman back in Washington, with the instruction that Moore was to find Attorney General Kleindienst, golfing at Burning Tree Golf and Country Club in Bethesda, and beg him to spring McCord from jail. The next day Magruder changed his story: Mitchell had ordered Mardian to get in touch not with Powell Moore, but with Gordon Liddy, to have *him* find Kleindienst.[3]

In his 1974 memoir, *An American Life*, Magruder sought refuge in vagueness and passive tense:

> *We all agreed* that McCord was the heart of the problem. "If we could just get him out of jail before they find out who he is," *someone* suggested, "then maybe he could just disappear." *I don't recall who made what specific suggestions during this talk. . . . Someone* recalled that McCord had once worked for

the CIA.... *One of us* suggested that Mitchell call Dick Kleindienst, his successor as attorney general, and see if he could help us get McCord out of jail. "No, that wouldn't be appropriate," Mitchell said. "It would be better if Bob called him."[4]

If this actually occurred—Mitchell ordering his aides to enlist the attorney general in a scheme to obstruct a criminal investigation—the Beverly Hills Hotel was itself the scene of a crime. Indeed, the discussions that took place between Mitchell and his men in Los Angeles on the morning of June 17 were later depicted by prosecutors as the inception of the Watergate cover-up, with Mitchell's alleged order cited as the first "overt act" in his indictment, a charge of conspiracy to obstruct justice on which the former attorney general was convicted and incarcerated.

Magruder's house of cards began crumbling during his turn on the witness stand at *U.S. v. Mitchell*. Until then he had never been subjected to rigorous cross-examination; in impeaching Magruder's testimony, the Democrats on the Senate and House Watergate committees lacked interest, the Republicans, sufficient skill. Neither was wanting in Plato Cacheris, Mitchell's defense lawyer at his criminal trial. There Magruder was reduced to claiming that the Kleindienst idea had come from—Liddy himself! Special prosecutor Jill Volner gently corrected the witness, asking casually what happened "after *Mr. Mitchell suggested* that Mr. Mardian call Liddy to call Mr. Kleindienst."[5]

Once again, Fred LaRue emerged a crucial witness. Though it changed somewhat over time, his account posed acute problems for the prosecutors' case against Mitchell. LaRue recalled Magruder leaving the group's breakfast table to take Liddy's call shortly after 9:00 a.m., returning soon afterward, and confiding the news. "Last night was the night they were going to go back into the Democratic National Committee," a shaken Magruder whispered. After ten to fifteen minutes, LaRue testified, Magruder left the table again in search of a pay phone. When he returned, LaRue recalled, Magruder made no show of calmly finishing breakfast, as he claimed; rather Magruder promptly told LaRue what he knew, then watched as the Mississippian stalked off to see Mitchell. LaRue told the grand jury:

> LaRUE: I went upstairs and got Mr. Mitchell over into another room. I think we used the security man's room and I informed Mr. Mitchell of this.
> QUESTION: What did he say?
> LaRUE: Mr. Mitchell said, "That is just incredible." As I recall, he asked me some details and I had no idea, I had no knowledge of any details. . . . Governor Reagan was in the lobby waiting for Mr. Mitchell . . . so we had no time for discussion.

Three months later, LaRue appeared before the Senate. Here he remembered that Mitchell had indeed, as Magruder claimed, gathered his men before the motorcade rolled, and had indeed issued an order for one of them to contact Kleindienst—but not for the evil purposes Magruder asserted. "Mr. Mitchell asked that someone call Mr. Liddy and have him contact Mr. Kleindienst," LaRue told the Senate, "and have Mr. Kleindienst get in touch with [D.C. Police] Chief [Jerry] Wilson and see what details we could find out about this situation."[6]

Where LaRue rebutted Magruder's tale on points of fact, Bob Mardian exposed its prima facie absurdity. Mardian was participating in Mitchell's meeting with Tom Reed when LaRue interrupted them. Mardian denied making any calls that morning, either from Mitchell's suite or from nearby pay phones. The most implausible element in Magruder's tale, where Mardian was concerned, was its central thrust: the idea that the former assistant attorney general for internal security would have taken part in the scheme Magruder described, a preposterous four-bank shot that employed unnecessary intermediaries and held out the fantastical hope that McCord could be prematurely sprung from jail—on a Saturday.[7]

Mitchell's story also changed somewhat, but held firm on the essential point: He always denied ordering anyone to do anything to get McCord sprung. As a former attorney general, thoroughly familiar with the internal workings of the criminal justice system, Mitchell understood, as he told an interviewer shortly before his death, that "the concept of going to Kleindienst to get people out of jail is ridiculous." Mitchell first testified about Burning Tree in September 1972, in a deposition for the $1 million civil suit that the Democrats, three days after the arrests, filed against McCord and CRP. The former attorney general said he first learned of the Watergate break-in "sometime during the early afternoon, California time . . . twelve or one o'clock, possibly later." Asked what actions he took, Mitchell testified: "I asked the people that were with me to inquire into it. . . . I did not call, myself." Mitchell was later asked if it occurred to him that the arrests bore some connection to the presentations Liddy had made in his office. "Yes, it was one of the first things that crossed my mind," he said.[8]

In fact, Liddy had already embarked on his frantic drive out to Burning Tree, Powell Moore in tow, before Mitchell, in California, even learned of the arrests. Liddy's memoir eliminated all doubt about who ordered him out to Burning Tree and why: It was not Mitchell but Magruder himself. Liddy recounted how he had used the White House Situation Room that morning to place a "secure" call to Magruder at the Polo Lounge. A "short while" later Magruder called Liddy back from a pay phone. "Why did you use McCord?" Magruder cried. Liddy struggled to keep Magruder focused on the most urgent matter: preparing a statement for Mitchell's use at an afternoon press conference. Contrary to Magruder's testimony at *U.S. v. Mitchell*, Liddy never raised the idea of getting hold of Kleindienst. Liddy returned to 1701 and immediately reassured Powell Moore, the spokesman on duty that morning, that the CRP leadership in California was aware of the arrests and at work on a statement for Mitchell. Then Magruder called again. "I was set for another bout of sniveling," Liddy wrote, "but it never came; instead he had a message for me from Mitchell. I was to find Dick Kleindienst, the attorney general, and ask him to get McCord out of jail immediately. 'Tell him "John sent you" and it's a "personal request from John." He'll understand.'"

Liddy immediately grasped the futility of Magruder's plan but felt bound to carry it out. "An order from John Mitchell," he wrote, "was not to be disobeyed." It was precisely the combination Magruder was banking on: the force of the Mitchell name and Liddy's Germanophilic reverence for orders. It was Liddy, as directed by Magruder, who placed a call to locate the attorney general, and who was told by Kleindienst's wife, Marnie, where the attorney general was. Liddy grabbed Moore and raced for Bethesda.[9]

By all accounts, Liddy's excursion to Burning Tree proved as disastrous as his raid on the DNC. He found the attorney general seated at lunch and, using hand gestures, beckoned Kleindienst from his table. Kleindienst had met Liddy only once before, three years earlier, and held him in low regard. Kleindienst excused himself and strode to the archway where Liddy and Moore stood. "I'm carrying a personal message from John Mitchell," Liddy said; "could we speak privately?" The three retreated to an empty locker room. Though the men recalled different language, all agreed on the outcome.

"What's this about John?" Kleindienst began. Liddy started to inform him of the arrests, but Kleindienst already knew about them. Liddy then said the arrested men had been working under his direction. "Jesus Christ!" Kleindienst exclaimed. Liddy announced he was relaying a message from Mitchell, but Kleindienst shrewdly interrupted. "Did you receive it from Mitchell directly?" No, Liddy acknowledged; it came through Magruder. "I don't know how you can do this," Liddy began, "but I'm supposed to tell you that it's a 'personal request from John.' Anyway, he wants you to get McCord out of jail right away—before it's found out who he really is."

Liddy tried to make clear he understood the preposterousness of Magruder's request, asking rhetorically what would happen to Kleindienst if word of such intervention got out. "Me? Fuck what happens to me!" Kleindienst exploded. "What happens to the president if I try a fool thing like that? It's the Goddamndest thing I ever heard of! Jesus Christ! That's what everybody ought to be thinking of—the president! What the fuck did you people think you were doing in there?" Liddy started to explain, but Kleindienst cut him off. "God, this is terrible," he said. "I can't imagine John Mitchell asking me to do a thing like that. . . . You tell whoever it was that John Mitchell knows me well enough to call me himself." Kleindienst curtly dismissed Liddy, then called a senior DOJ official and ordered him to treat the Watergate case like any other.[10]

Chatting with Governor Reagan as their limousine sped across Los Angeles, Mitchell had no idea Liddy had visited Burning Tree, nor any clue a criminal conspiracy, falsely invoking his own name, was under way. In fact, Mitchell did not learn about Burning Tree until the following day, when an informant reported him "amazed." Seated next to Reagan that morning, all the former attorney general knew was that he faced a press conference in less than two hours' time and needed a statement in case reporters asked about the arrests. As it happened, no reporters asked Mitchell about Watergate. That night, the Mitchells, the Magruders, and the other CRP couples attended the party at the Schreiber estate. Vicki Carr sang as the CRP crowd mingled at poolside with Jimmy Stewart, Jack Benny, Zsa Zsa Gabor, John Wayne, and Clint Eastwood. The sublime evening was the last peace Mitchell ever knew.[11]

Before boarding the Gulfstream II that carried them back to Washington on Monday, June 19, Mitchell and Fred LaRue—the only man besides the former attorney general who could pacify Martha Mitchell when she was on the warpath—resolved to keep her in the dark as long as possible about the Watergate arrests. The plan called for Martha to remain at the plush Newporter Inn at Newport Beach while Mitchell headed back to the capital. "I think you need a rest," he told her. Fatigued from her cross-country train treks in behalf of Nixon-Agnew, she agreed to stay for a while. That Sunday, Marty and two other young girls, daughters of an FBI agent who formerly guarded the Mitchells, went to Disneyland; that evening, there was another swank party, this one attended by the president's brothers, Edward and Donald Nixon.[12]

It wasn't until Monday morning, when her husband had already left for Washington, that Martha finally read about the arrests in the *Los Angeles Times*. "Jesus Christ!" she said later. "I jumped out of bed like a sheet of lightning." For all her lunacy, Martha reacted to the news that ultimately destroyed her life with remarkably clear vision. First she wondered whether McCord, the man responsible for "debugging" the Mitchells' Watergate apartment, was a double agent. Then she saw the future. "This could land my husband in jail," she said. A previously unpublished FBI report recounted the eyewitness testimony of Steve King, the ex–FBI agent guarding Martha for CRP:

> Mrs. Mitchell then began drinking straight gin (no ice) from the wet bar on the first floor of the villa. Typical of her comments at this time was the statement, "Those bastards left me out here without telling me anything."

Phone calls, usually a comfort, brought Martha only more dissatisfaction; her husband, Magruder—all of them were giving her the runaround. Restless and agitated, she reached for her Salem Longs and a pack of matches. When she struck the sulfur, however, the entire book exploded, "severely" burning her right hand. A doctor was summoned to the Mitchells' villa, gave her an injection to ease the pain, and prescribed Phenaphen to get her through the next few days.[13]

While her husband grappled with the embryonic scandal back home, Martha prowled her villa, bitter at being deceived. On Wednesday, young Marty, accompanied by a personal aide to the Mitchells, Lea Jablonsky, returned to Disneyland. Steve King was supposed to pick the girls up, but he contacted the FBI agent who had done so three days earlier and asked him to repeat the favor, since "something very serious had come up at the room and he could not leave under any circumstances." The previously unpublished FBI report containing the agent's account is the saddest document of the Watergate era.

When we arrived at the Newporter Inn, I told [Jablonsky] that I would help her carry some of the numerous packages that they had purchased at Disneyland to the villa. When the three of us got within approximately fifty feet of the villa we heard a loud woman's voice. MARTY MITCHELL then said, "Oh, oh, mother has been drinking again."

When we got to the door of the villa, it was locked. [Jablonsky] knocked and [King] answered the door. We walked into the vestibule of the villa, at which time I noted Mrs. MITCHELL standing in the living room of the villa, screaming at [King]. When she saw me she stated, "[Redacted] you FBI fellows never treated me like a prisoner or kept me locked up like this son of a bitch. This son of a bitch won't let me leave here." [Redacted] then went over to Mrs. MITCHELL and attempted to calm her. I told Mrs. MITCHELL that everything would be all right and departed the villa.

[King] followed me outside and then advised me [that] at some time in the afternoon Mrs. MITCHELL had gotten hold of one or two bottles of whiskey in her upstairs bedroom, without his knowledge. After she had consumed quite a bit of it he heard her making telephone calls. Acting upon orders from Mr. MITCHELL not to let her use the telephone when she was drunk, he tried to get her to hang up the telephone by talking to her through the locked door. However, when she would not hang up the telephone, he forced the door open and pulled the plug of the telephone from the wall . . .

When I arrived at the Newporter Inn, [King] met me outside the villa and stated that when Mrs. MITCHELL had awakened that morning she seemed quite calm but suddenly for some reason she started ranting and raving again and insisted that she be allowed to go to the main section of the Newporter Inn and make a telephone call. [King] stated that when he would not let her out of the front door, she attempted to force her way. She swung at [him] and when he ducked, she hit the front door glass with her hand and arm, broke it, and began to bleed quite profusely.

Once again, a doctor was summoned. King and others forcibly restrained Martha while the physician, brandishing a needle, removed her pants and administered sedatives. The shots only further inflamed the hysterical woman. King, only thirty-one, finally called John Mitchell, who in turn dialed a man he knew only casually: Herb Kalmbach, the president's chief fund-raiser, based in Newport Beach. Kalmbach took Martha to the hospital, where her hand received six stitches. In the meantime, Mitchell arranged for longtime personal friends Ken and Peggy Ebbitt, of Bronxville, New York, to fly cross-country and bring Martha back to New York on a red-eye flight. "She needed psychiatric care," Ken recalled.[14]

Installed in the Westchester Country Club until Mitchell could fly up from Washington to reclaim her, Martha again took to the telephone, announcing to UPI's Helen Thomas: "I'm not going to stand for all those dirty things that go on." Finally, on Monday, June 26, the former attorney general appeared at the Westchester Country Club. According to Winzola McLendon, Martha's gossip*frau* and ersatz Boswell, Mitchell "broke down and cried" when he saw his wife's injuries. On the morning of the twenty-eighth, he eased her into a private limousine (though an official with the Federal Aviation Administration sighted Mrs. Mitchell boarding a helicopter in White Plains). The media feasted on the cross-continental tragedy of "the nation's most talked-about marriage." "John Smuggles Martha Out of Sight," shouted the *Daily News*.[15]

In retrospect, these awful days immediately following the Watergate arrests marked the beginning of the end for Martha Mitchell, a long, irrevocable slide into mental and physical anguish and alienation from her family and the world at large. Yet as the great scandal unfolded, a number of writers, some with personal or financial interests at stake, conspired to depict this tragic episode as somehow emblematic of the Nixon administration's latent fascism, the former attorney general's disturbed and drunken wife as a brave "political prisoner" beaten into silence to stop her from disclosing all the "dirty things" she knew. Lecturing at the University of Delaware in 1974, Shana Alexander claimed Martha was "the only one in Washington" who had consistently told the truth: "Everybody else was lying, and if ever a heroine was unsung, it's Martha Mitchell." Helen Thomas gushed that Martha "seemed to speak for a broad spectrum of women in the country—and some men too—in a way that no other female public figure has in recent times," and lauded Mrs. Mitchell's "patriotism" for "bucking the most powerful people in the country even though she was afraid." In fact, when Martha was finally given her chance to speak truth to power, to expose, under oath and on the record, all the "dirty" business she had been forced to witness in the years when it had been her terrible misfortune to be Mrs. John N. Mitchell, she rambled inconclusively for seventy-three pages of deposition testimony before emerging, amid a swarm of reporters and cameramen, to say meekly: "I've never really known anything about the Watergate case."[16]

The sad, unappealing truth was that Martha Mitchell was a sick, mean, and ignorant woman, roiling with vanity and insecurity, demeaning to people she considered beneath her, and prone—as if all that weren't enough—to violent bursts of alcoholism. Sally Quinn, wife of *Washington Post* executive editor Ben Bradlee and coanchor of the *CBS Morning News*, recalled how the more responsible reporters "began to get a little afraid" of Martha's outbursts. "We sort of stepped back and said, 'Wait a minute; this doesn't sound right to us,'" Quinn said, on-air. Helen Thomas suffered no such compunctions. A White House aide, spotting her, once taunted: "Why don't you get some class, Helen, and hang up on Martha Mitchell?" Nixon personally followed Thomas's reporting—with disgust. "For her to print another story on that poor sick Martha," he fumed. "She knows Martha's sick. . . . God almighty, I'd just say that's unconscionable." This dichotomy between friends and users, reporters with integrity and cynical exploiters of an ill person, emerged clearly even to a child—Martha's own. Thomas reported that during one of her calls with Martha, young Marty Mitchell could be heard "screaming" in the background: "Don't talk to her, she's no friend."[17]

Jeb Magruder's first move after returning to Washington was to set up a strategy session immediately after Mitchell, Mardian, and LaRue got back from Los Angeles. For good measure, Magruder requested the presence of John Dean, who, himself returning from an unusual trip to Manila, had arrived at his office to find a secretary's note requesting his presence at Mitchell's Watergate apartment at six that evening.[18]

By the time the June 19 evening meeting commenced, bringing together Mitchell, Magruder, Dean, LaRue, and Mardian, their options were fast evaporating. The FBI had already uncovered McCord's true name and CRP affiliation, and linked the Cubans to Howard Hunt, who was still on the White House payroll. Gordon Liddy remained, for the moment, under the authorities' radar, but the prospect of containing the scandal, the CRP men's only hope, was rapidly diminishing. Dispensing scotch and sarcasm that night, the jet-lagged Mitchell knew far less about the state of play than some of his visitors. Dean, for example, concealed the fact that a few hours earlier, he had met privately with Liddy and, as Liddy recalled, assured him: "Everyone'll be taken care of."[19]

Magruder later told prosecutors the evening session had chiefly been a discussion "about alternatives." But he also claimed the talk turned to the subject of destroying documents. Notes taken by the prosecutors, previously unpublished, read: "Jeb said he better get rid of stuff and they concurred." Later that night, Magruder took his Gemstone documents—Liddy's proposals, the wiretap synopses prepared by Baldwin and heavily edited by McCord, the spurious photos of Democratic documents (purportedly taken near O'Brien's file cabinets but set against a shag rug found only in the Howard Johnson's motel)—and burned them in his home. He later wrote of sitting cross-legged before his fireplace, chuckling one last time over the "graphic details" that the wiretaps had captured about the personal lives of DNC staff members.[20]

In his testimony before the Senate Watergate committee, Magruder shifted blame for the document destruction from himself (*Jeb said he better get rid of stuff and they concurred*) to the room at large: "It was agreed generally, and *I can't get specific as to who said what at this meeting exactly,* but get rid of the files." Magruder's story changed still more dramatically when he retold it in *An American Life.* Now he suddenly remembered the scene with precision, how Dean had arrived a few minutes before himself, and the men, drinking freely, grew dour and self-pitying. Before leaving for a tennis date with Vice President Agnew, Magruder wrote, he asked Mitchell what should be done with the Gemstone file; Mitchell supposedly replied by saying maybe Magruder "ought to have a little fire" at his house that night.

The idea that he should "get rid of stuff" had been Magruder's own, in his early talks with prosecutors; it became a "general" consensus when the witness testified before the Senate; and then, in Magruder's book, the idea had become Mitchell's.[21]

On the witness stand at *U.S. v. Mitchell,* Magruder stuck with this story, adding only the detail that he reported back to Mitchell the following morning that the deed had been done. Under cross-examination by Plato Cacheris, however, Magruder was forced to admit that the first time he recalled Mitchell ending the June 19 meeting with the "little fire" suggestion was in December 1973, during an office interview with WSPF prosecutor Jill Volner. In all previous forums, the witness agreed—his confession to federal prosecutors in April 1973, his grand jury appearance in May 1973, and his Senate testimony in June 1973—Magruder had *never once* mentioned Mitchell ordering the destruction of documents. Moreover, Magruder admitted he had already made plans to destroy all incriminating documents—with the ubiquitous Gordon Strachan—on the morning of June 19, some seven hours before the meeting in Mitchell's apartment.[22]

The indictment in *U.S. v. Mitchell* listed the order to destroy the Gemstone documents as the fifth "overt act" in the Watergate cover-up conspiracy, the third ascribed to Mitchell. The former attorney general, of course, always denied the charge: "There was no suggestion by me or anybody else at that time that Mr. Magruder would actually, in June, start a fire in his fireplace." Most other witnesses agreed. Even John Dean, who was present for the entirety of Magruder's visit to the Mitchell apartment and whose own testimony would, in time, create equal trouble for the former attorney general, never heard the damning order that Magruder attributed to Mitchell. Nor did Mardian.

But on this point, LaRue, for once, supported Magruder's version of events, and Mitchell was accordingly convicted of ordering the destruction of evidence. The decision to testify against Mitchell was not one LaRue arrived at lightly; the strain of betrayal, of bearing false witness, pained him like none of Mitchell's other protégés. "LaRue broke down and cried like a baby yesterday," Assistant Attorney General Henry Petersen reported to Nixon on April 17, 1973, as the tapes rolled, after LaRue's first appearance before the grand jury. "He was not so bad on admitting the obstruction of justice and subornation. Resigned, said he'd probably plead . . . but when it came to testifying about John Mitchell he just broke down and started to cry. It is a terrible thing."[23]

The day after that session at Mitchell's Watergate apartment, Fred LaRue and Bob Mardian finally did what Dean had been smart enough to do a day earlier: Pick Gordon Liddy's brain.[24] The setting was LaRue's apartment at Watergate West. "My recollection is pretty vivid," Mardian later testified. "The first thing [Liddy] asked Mr. LaRue was whether or not he had a radio." Liddy cranked up the volume and motioned Mardian to sit beside the radio. "It is not that I don't trust you," Liddy apologized over the din, "but this conversation cannot be recorded." Next Liddy insisted Mardian agree they were covered by attorney-client privilege. Mardian agreed, but asserted a right to report everything to Mitchell, manager of the campaign that employed Mardian as counsel; Liddy consented.

Now Liddy unfurled his astounding story for the first time, telling the wide-eyed LaRue and Mardian all about his partnership with Howard Hunt: the hiring of the Cubans, with their CIA and Bay of Pigs backgrounds; the earlier break-in at the office of Ellsberg's psychiatrist; Hunt's bedside visit to Dita Beard, the ITT witness; and the three-week wiretapping operation at DNC. Since the arrests, Liddy said, he had shredded his files and believed the burglars themselves would keep mum; he also volunteered, as he had to Dean, to be told "what corner to stand on and he was ready to be assassinated." That evening, LaRue and Mardian briefed Mitchell on the wild contents of their debriefing of Liddy. Asked Mitchell's reaction, Mardian testified the former attorney general "appeared to be as sincerely shocked as I was when I got this information."[25]

Here Mitchell approached a great fork in his life's road. He knew now, for the first time, the full range of the Plumbers' activities in the Nixon White House, the dark portfolio of cloak-and-dagger ventures he later pointedly dubbed "the White House horrors." And it was here the former attorney general, absorbing this information, made his fateful decision to withhold what he knew from his client, the president of the United States. "To this day, I believe that I was right in not involving the president," Mitchell told the Senate, calling the horrors "a great deal more damaging" than Watergate.

> Watergate was already out. Watergate was the issue. It was the subject of a suit by the Democratic National Committee. It was constantly in the newspapers. The White House horror stories were not out. They were not under discussion. And these were the things that would have more impact upon the election, in my opinion, than the Watergate matter.

Duly informed, Nixon would have "lowered the boom" on the guilty, a move Mitchell argued would have cost the '72 election. "I still believe that the most important thing to this country was the reelection of Richard Nixon," Mitchell testified, "and I was not about to countenance anything that would stand in the way of that reelection."[26]

Nixon, of course, knew far more about the Plumbers than Mitchell did. Nixon was also privately willing, as his tapes later made painfully clear, to entertain dark thoughts about his dear friend, Mitchell, and his role in Watergate. As his White House burned, Nixon returned frequently, both in his mind and aloud, to The Question—*Did Mitchell do it?*—and came, over time, to believe the worst. Nixon's first known recorded conversation about Watergate was a late afternoon talk with Haldeman on June 20, 1972.

> NIXON: Have you gotten any further word on that Mitchell operation?
> HALDEMAN: No, I don't think he did [know].
> NIXON: I think he was surprised.[27]

That night, Nixon and Mitchell held their only known talk about the substance of Watergate. Their brief telephone call, initiated by the president, was not taped; but into his beloved DictaBelt machine Nixon later recorded his recollection of the exchange. The president said he "tried to cheer [Mitchell] up a bit"; he thought the former attorney general sounded "completely tired and worn out." Mitchell said he was "terribly chagrined that the activities of anybody attached to his committee should have been handled in such a manner" and expressed regret he had "not policed all the people more effectively in his own organization." There was no talk of complicity: Nixon couldn't bring himself to ask, and Mitchell wrongly presumed his innocence was assumed.[28]

Three days later, on June 23, 1972, unbeknownst to Mitchell, the president, seated at his Oval Office desk, enthusiastically approved a proposal—spelled out by Haldeman but conceived by John Dean, along with the false claim that Mitchell "concurred" in it—calling for the White House to apply pressure to the CIA to compel the spy agency to block the FBI's Watergate investigation on national security grounds. "All right, fine, I understand it all," Nixon sighed after giving the order. "We won't second-guess Mitchell and the rest." Prosecutors later dubbed the tape of this damning conversation the "smoking gun"; its disclosure, in August 1974, triggered Nixon's resignation three days later.[29]

On Saturday, June 24, 1972, one week after the arrests, Mitchell arrived at his law office to find "a hell of a knock-down drag-out donnybrook" under way between Jeb Magruder and Hugh Sloan. At issue was the exact sum Sloan had disbursed to Gordon Liddy prior to June 17. Magruder wanted a figure he could feed the grand jury; Sloan wasn't talking. "When the going gets tough," Mitchell famously sneered, "the tough get going." Mitchell later claimed he was not suborning perjury, only consoling Sloan, who seemed "pretty low."[30]

Mardian wandered in and clapped Sloan on the back. Then, after Sloan and Magruder skulked out, Dean entered; later LaRue joined them. According to the special prosecutors, the first of several plans to raise "hush money" for the burglars was conceived at this meeting, with Mitchell and Mardian supposedly instructing Dean to petition the Central Intelligence Agency to provide the arrested men with "covert funds." Of this, too, the seventh "overt act" in his indictment, Mitchell was convicted. On the hush-money charges, Mitchell's chief accuser was not Magruder but the far smarter Dean, who cleverly portrayed himself to the prosecutors, the press, and the public as a mere messenger between two sets of amoral masters: Haldeman and Ehrlichman at the White House, and Mitchell, Mardian, and LaRue at CRP. In time the prosecutors, at least, saw through Dean's ruse— but still built their case on his deeply flawed testimony.

The first time the idea of payments to the burglars had been broached with Mitchell was on June 21, when Mardian and LaRue briefed the former attorney general on their interrogation of Liddy. Mitchell had immediately rejected the idea of CRP providing any funds, Mardian said. Now, three days later, in Mitchell's law office, Dean testified, Mitchell "suggested that the CIA might be of assistance because these people were obviously CIA operatives, or had been at some point in time, [and] might compromise the CIA."

Both Mardian and Mitchell denied this. Dean, moreover, needed no nudging to view CIA as a potential savior. It had been Dean's idea the day before, as captured on the "smoking gun" tape, to try to get CIA to run interference with the FBI, a bold gambit that Dean also knew had failed. If the Agency was unwilling to force an end to the FBI probe by applying political pressure from the top down, perhaps Langley would be more comfortable resolving the matter from the bottom up, silencing the burglars with untraceable cash? It was a logical progression of thought, but one for which Dean, naturally, never took credit, instead casting Mitchell and Mardian as its authors.[31]

That week the calculating White House counsel met three times with a top CIA official to request covert cash, to no avail. All three times, the Agency's deputy director, taken aback at how the young lawyer "kept pressing" the issue, turned him down cold. "He was almost pleadingly asking me for some theory, for something that would help him out in this," the official, Vernon Walters, later told the House Armed Services Committee. Dean left "looking glum." A House intelligence subcommittee that investigated the Dean-Walters meetings later concluded it was "not clear . . . whether other top White House aides were aware of Dean's activities."[32]

Hush money remained a viable option; the cash just had to come from a source other than CIA. In his Senate and House testimony, Dean suggested that the Agency's rebuffs had sent him scurrying back to Mitchell for a new plan of action, and that Mitchell obliged during a meeting in the former attorney general's law office on Wednesday, June 28, with Mardian and LaRue also present. Dean's executive session testimony before the Senate, previously unpublished, quoted Mitchell as saying: "I think we are going to have to get Kalmbach involved in this."[33]

Herb Kalmbach was one of the greatest fund-raisers in American history. In Nixon's '68 campaign, he reportedly raised $6 million (more than $30 million in current figures). After turning down an offer to serve as undersecretary of commerce, Kalmbach returned to Newport Beach, California, where, on the strength of his White House connections, he quietly fattened his private law practice. But he never completely left Washington, and its underside, behind. Using leftover campaign funds, Kalmbach served in 1969–70 as the paymaster for Anthony Ulasewicz, a former NYPD detective whom Ehrlichman and Dean had assigned various unsavory chores, including a probe of Senator Edward Kennedy's sex life. Mitchell's dealings with Kalmbach were rare. They had met in '68, but seen each other only seldom thereafter; it was only coincidence, born of geography and dire necessity, that the former attorney general had dialed Kalmbach when Martha Mitchell, crying and bleeding at the Newporter Inn, required immediate assistance.[34]

During the June 28 meeting, according to Dean, Mitchell again saw Kalmbach as his savior. Dean testified that Mitchell instructed him to enlist the fund-raising genius on behalf of the Watergate burglars. The Kalmbach gambit was the third scheme for obstructing the FBI probe that Dean attributed to his former mentor. When Dean appeared before the full Senate committee, nine days after his executive session, he introduced a number of new elements to strengthen his charge about Mitchell and Kalmbach. "After some discussion which I cannot recall with any specificity at this time," Dean said, pressing an uncharacteristic claim of forgetfulness, Mitchell "asked me to get the approval of Haldeman and Ehrlichman to use Mr. Herbert Kalmbach to raise the necessary money." Then the witness recalled, for the first time, that Mitchell's damning instruction went unheard by the other men present, Mardian and LaRue:

> Before I departed the meeting, I remembered [*sic*] that Mr. Mitchell, in an aside for my ears only, told me that the White House, in particular Ehrlichman, should be very interested and anxious to accommodate the needs of these men.[35]

A master manipulator, Dean made sure Haldeman and Ehrlichman believed the Kalmbach gambit was the brainchild of a very desperate John Mitchell. Ehrlichman recalled Dean telling him that Mitchell "felt very strongly" the arrested men needed competent attorneys, and that Dean added: "I am going to see if we can get Herb Kalmbach wound up to raise some attorneys' fees for John Mitchell, who says we really have got to do it. . . . If [Kalmbach] checks with you, back me up on this."[36]

That night, at Dean's request, Kalmbach caught a red-eye flight to Washington. The next day Dean steered the older man away from a prearranged meeting at the Hay-Adams Hotel into outdoor Lafayette Park, in the shadow of the White House, and instructed him to gesture broadly as they talked—in case they were being watched. "We would like to have you raise funds for the legal defense of these defendants and for the support of their families," Dean announced. He never explained who "we" were. Further instructions, Dean said, would come from himself and Fred LaRue. Kalmbach asked why a public defense fund couldn't be established; not enough time, Dean said.[37]

That was all Kalmbach, hungry for "tough and dangerous" assignments, needed to hear. Over the next three months—taking his orders from Dean and LaRue, and employing the stealthy services of Tony Ulasewicz, who devised a system of phone contacts, code names, and blind drops at airports—Kalmbach steered some $220,000 to the burglars' lawyers and Mrs. Howard Hunt. A month into the intrigue, however, Kalmbach grew queasy; he wondered if Dean actually had the authority to order such a dicey operation. The master fund-raiser demanded a meeting with John Ehrlichman, and got it July 26. Pressing for assurance his was a "proper" assignment, Kalmbach later recalled that Ehrlichman looked him straight in the eye and said: "Herb, John Dean does have the authority, it is proper, and you are to go forward." But Kalmbach was not reassured for long; by mid-September 1972, he dropped out for good. Dean would have to find a new source for the burglars' hush money.[38]

It didn't take the special prosecutors long to spot the holes in Dean's story of how Kalmbach got roped into the cover-up. For starters, Dean claimed that Mitchell proposed the idea during a meeting in his law office on June 28; but the former attorney general was out of town that day and totally incommunicado, consumed by the Martha Mitchell nightmare then reaching its dénouement at the Westchester Country Club.

"I never tried to get Mr. Kalmbach into raising money," Mitchell testified at his trial, a position he reasserted in 1988: "I didn't have anything to do with Kalmbach. . . . Why would I fish Kalmbach out of all of the people that were around Stans raising money?" Conversely, Mitchell suggested, it would have been quite natural for Dean—who admitted he "often" worked with Kalmbach in Nixon's first term—to look to him for fund-raising assistance. Mitchell's claim of estrangement from the hush-money business was no last-minute confection manufactured for a jury's consumption. Kalmbach himself confirmed as much. In April 1988—in the only interviews he ever gave—Kalmbach told author Len Colodny: "I never met with John Mitchell at all. Mitchell never asked me to raise money."[39]

Mitchell's absence from Washington during the week of June 26 created serious problems for the WSPF prosecutors, even beyond the question—important as it was—of who enlisted Kalmbach. For example, Dean had also claimed, in testimony before the grand jury, to have "kept Mitchell informed" about the three meetings with General Walters of CIA; yet Dean's logs showed no calls to or from Mitchell, in New York or anywhere else, on any of the days on which Dean met with Walters. These discrepancies between Dean's testimony and the evidence embodied in Mitchell's logs were material and glaring. The special prosecutors couldn't just throw Dean on the stand and expect the defense lawyers at *U.S. v. Mitchell* to ignore them; they had to be ironed out—eliminated. In a previously unpublished draft memorandum prepared in July 1974, WSPF lawyer George Frampton—the same man who helped Magruder rework his testimony—summarized the difficulty he faced with Dean.[40]

> Dean's Senate and grand jury testimony leaves the impression (which is explicit in the Senate) that his approach to Mitchell about using Kalmbach came only *after* it became clear CIA would not cooperate. However, Mitchell's logs and schedule suggest that the two possibilities—use of Kalmbach and use of CIA—were probably discussed at the same time, and that *Dean exercised somewhat more discretion himself to forge ahead with getting Kalmbach into the picture than he has admitted.* . . . Our case will probably have to be based on the *theory* that Mitchell asked Dean on Saturday, June 24, to explore both the CIA and Kalmbach possibilities; or that Mitchell's logs are incomplete.[41]

The Frampton memo is a "smoking gun" in its own right: irrefutable evidence of what the Watergate special prosecutors knew, and when they knew it, about their star witness, Dean, and his false testimony against the prosecution's prime target, Mitchell. The changes to Dean's story that emerged during his testimony at *U.S. v. Mitchell* reflected the prosecutors' handiwork. Now Mitchell's muttered remark about Haldeman and Ehrlichman having a special interest in the payment of hush money, the "aside" meant solely for Dean's ears, came not on June 28, as Dean originally asserted, but on Saturday, June 24, in the meeting at which Mitchell and Mardian had supposedly encouraged Dean to try the CIA route. In this latest iteration, Mitchell's "aside" was aimed at getting Haldeman and Ehrlichman to consider *both* the Kalmbach *and* CIA options. To disguise this testimonial sleight of hand, Dean now remembered, for the first time, that when he brought Mitchell's idea to Ehrlichman—*mere messenger!*—the latter had instructed Dean to "hold on it with Kalmbach" and "explore [further] with CIA."

While prepared to discard previous testimony, amend dates, and change the substance of alleged conversations with his colleagues, Dean was unwilling to abandon his twin claims to have "kept Mitchell informed" about the trio of meetings with Walters and to have received from Mitchell the final order to set Kalmbach in motion. To acknowledge that he kept Mitchell in the dark about the Walters meetings, or that he enjoyed no communication with Mitchell prior to Kalmbach's red-eye flight, would have amounted to a public concession by Dean of that which the Frampton memo, privately, made plain: that the witness exercised "more discretion" in the hush money business "than he has admitted."

Thus Dean clung to the fiction that he visited Mitchell's office on June 28 and spoke with him, even though the former attorney general was in transit from Westchester. *How was that possible?* The conversation, Dean explained at *U.S. v. Mitchell*, was conducted via telephone, with Dean seated in Mitchell's office and Mitchell at some unspecified location, on the other end of the call. "That happened from time to time," Dean said with a straight face. "We had meetings in his office when he wasn't there." It was in this imaginary call that Dean "reported" to Mitchell the unhelpful response of General Walters, then asked, in language theretofore unrecalled: "Should we go back and try the Kalmbach angle?" Yes, Mitchell supposedly replied, telling Dean to contact Kalmbach, Haldeman, and Ehrlichman, and make it happen.[42]

Unfortunately for the former attorney general, and for history, Dean's deceptions at *U.S. v. Mitchell* fooled only those who mattered most: the judge, the jury, and the news media. The defense knew better and so did the WSPF lawyers. The Frampton memo, for example, noted "significant discrepancies between Dean's anticipated trial testimony [and] that of other Government witnesses or evidence." Another internal WSPF memorandum, prepared in February 1974 and also previously unpublished, demolished the myth, promulgated by Senator Ervin, among others, that Dean's testimony before the Senate Watergate committee was "corroborated in all significant respects by the taped recordings" of President Nixon. The WSPF memo bore the title: "Material Discrepancies Between the Senate Select Committee Testimony of John Dean and the Tapes of Dean's Meetings with the President."[43]

Dean was a problem the WSPF lawyers inherited. The original prosecutors, led by Assistant U.S. Attorney Earl Silbert, concluded, according to previously unpublished internal memoranda, that Dean not only stood "at the center of the criminality" in Watergate, but had withheld crucial evidence in his plea-bargaining sessions, engaging in "a gradual escalation as to who is culpable." Initially, Dean's attorney boasted his client could "deliver Mitchell" and "deliver Magruder"; two weeks later, when Magruder began cooperating with prosecutors, offering up himself, Mitchell, *and* Dean, the latter began implicating Haldeman and Ehrlichman—and, eventually, the president. Silbert and his team smarted when they discovered that Dean had "withheld the incriminating role he played with regard to Walters" and neglected to inform them about Kalmbach. Dean's lawyer later claimed the omissions were "inadvertent."[44]

The president, meanwhile, wrestled with doubts about the complicity of his old friend, and whether his old friend's batty wife could ever be kept quiet. Perched in his "hideaway" quarters in the Old Executive Office Building on June 26—the day Dean held the first of his secret meetings with General Walters—Nixon plotted with Haldeman about how to ease the campaign manager out of the campaign. Media coverage of Mrs. Mitchell's meltdown in California was "blowing now . . . getting pretty big," Nixon fretted. "Well, yeah," Haldeman replied, "this stuff about throwing her on the bed and sticking a needle in her behind . . ." The chief of staff assured his boss they were "nowhere near" such a point, but it was possible—*possible*—Martha's situation could raise "potential problems on the other thing, Watergate."

"You could use this as a basis for Mitchell pulling out," Haldeman proposed. At this early stage, however, Nixon, secure in the power and trappings of the presidency, viewed so naked a sacrifice of his former law partner as unfathomable, and loftily rejected it out of hand: "I can't do that. I won't do that to him. I'd rather, shit, lose the election. I really would." This sentiment did not last long. Two days later, the same men returned to the same subject in the same room. "I think," said Haldeman, "lurking way down behind there is the question of [Mitchell's] involvement in the Watergate caper." If Mitchell left CRP, it might be a good move, the chief of staff reckoned. Nixon added his own touch: "And we would leak out the fact that [Martha's] not well."

Still, the nagging Question—*Did Mitchell do it?*—lingered. The next day, June 29, brought more rumination. Nixon clung to the idea that Mitchell had approved Liddy's operation without knowing specifically about the DNC wiretapping: "I think John said, 'Well, we're trying to get the information . . . don't tell me anything about it.' You know, that's the way you do it, thinking probably they were going to do it the way you always do, planting a person on the other side, which everybody does." Unlike Nixon, Haldeman was still talking daily with Mitchell, and brought from their discussions the welcome news that he was not opposed to resigning from the campaign. "If this thing escalates," Haldeman quoted Mitchell as saying, "I think it would be very good if I'm out of the place and you could say, 'Well, there's a whole new team over there.' "

Yet Haldeman remained convinced Mitchell's resignation would be useless without an accompanying mea culpa: "The thing that bothers me is that it's a time bomb." Aghast at Haldeman's (prescient) nightmarish vision—an endless stream of investigative discovery and media disclosure—Nixon concluded at last that Mitchell had to go. Haldeman assured him the story would prove a net plus for the White House. "It'll hang totally on Martha," he stressed. The president gave the final order: "Call the press." Ever attentive to protocol, Haldeman suggested Mitchell receive a private audience with the president, if only for appearance's sake. "Do it," Nixon ordered.[45]

Mitchell, for his part, was willing to go, but for the ill-starred adventure at the Watergate, he had no intention of shouldering the blame. He was, to be sure, "terribly chagrined" over the incident, as he told Nixon on June 20—but *guilty*? No. Meeting with Haldeman on June 29, the day after the Mitchells returned from Westchester, the former attorney general acknowledged his wife was unable to cope with the strain of Watergate and expressed fear she might "harm herself." "He feels she's suicidal as well as a little cracked, plus drinking very heavily, and that there's nothing he can do to cure it," Haldeman recorded in his diary. Mitchell's desire to resign was thus cast in purely personal terms.[46]

When he arrived at the Executive Office Building the next day for lunch with the president and Haldeman, it was not Mitchell but the others who repeatedly linked his resignation to Watergate. In so doing, Nixon and Haldeman tried—subtly, gingerly—to probe the strong man, to see whether some admission of culpability might be forth-coming. Haldeman, the former advertising executive, spoke of how "surprised" the public would be to see the gruff John Mitchell "tak-ing this route," heeding the demands of his eccentric but lovable wife. Nixon joined in the lathering, adding that if Mitchell waited to resign "it will be tied right to Watergate." Here, however, Nixon realized he had gone too far; in Mitchell's departure, the president wanted his friend to believe personal considerations, not politics, were para-mount. He needed to throw a bone in that direction. "I just want it to be handled in a way that Martha's not hurt," Nixon said. "Yeah, okay," Mitchell grunted; as usual, he understood the most and said the least.[47]

In his testimony before the Senate Watergate committee, Halde-man remembered Mitchell arriving "reluctantly" at the decision to re-sign, and worrying that it might appear as though he were using Martha to deflect attention from Watergate. In fact, as the tape of the meeting shows, it was Nixon and Haldeman who expressed concerns about Watergate, not Mitchell. Testifying before the Senate a month before Haldeman—but without his knowledge that the luncheon had been recorded—Mitchell depicted Nixon as the reluctant one. "The president asked me to—urged me to stay on," Mitchell testified. "I said I could not under the circumstances. . . . Finally . . . [Nixon] re-luctantly consented to the fact that I was going to leave, and we dis-cussed a successor."

By July 1974, when Mitchell testified at the House impeachment hearings, the tape of the luncheon had surfaced. Asked about the divergence between his Senate testimony, which maintained Water-gate was never discussed, and the tape, which prominently featured Haldeman's warning about "more stuff . . . surfacing on the Water-gate," Mitchell pleaded ignorance. "I don't remember that being said at all," he testified, "and I was surprised when you gentlemen showed it to me." Conscious of a possible perjury charge, he pleaded for com-mittee members to place the remarks about Watergate in their "total context," pitifully invoking Martha Mitchell's mental problems.

Most of the discussion at the luncheon, Mitchell argued, was focused on who would succeed him at CRP. "It had nothing whatsoever to do with the Watergate," he said, "and I am surprised the word is even in here." At *U.S. v. Mitchell*, the former attorney general clung to his story, testifying his exit from CRP stemmed from "purely personal" considerations; asked if he resigned for any other reason, he replied: "None whatsoever." No charges were filed against Mitchell in connection with his testimony about the luncheon, but the scare he received, amid all his other legal woes, offered the starkest reminder of the supreme discourtesy his friend, the president, had shown in recording all their conversations and never telling him.[48]

p: Antiwar demonstrators
.sh with police outside
e Justice Department
ring the May Day riots,
ay 4, 1971. Bottom:
itchell and his aides
serve the day's chaos from
s office balcony. Protesters
emed to sense Mitchell's
iquely powerful place in
e Nixon cabinet, and
cordingly trained their
tiwar fury more on the
stice Department than
e Pentagon during the
xon years.

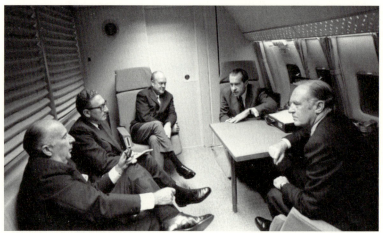

Top: Riding aboard Air Force One en route from Washington to Florida on November 9, 1969, Mitchell holds court as national security adviser Henry Kissinger, Defense Secretary Melvin Laird, Nixon, and Secretary of State William Rogers listen. Mitchell played a pivotal, though deliberately unheralded, role in the formation of Nixon's foreign policy. "Henry had his ideas," Mitchell later said of Kissinger, "but what could he do? He had no feel for politics." Bottom: Nixon makes a point to Chief of Naval Operations Admiral Thomas Moorer aboard the U.S.S. *Saratoga* in the Atlantic Ocean on May 17, 1969. Later, as chairman of the Joint Chiefs of Staff, Moorer received classified documents illegally obtained by a yeoman who served on Kissinger's National Security Council staff. John Ehrlichman, seen here peering over Nixon's shoulder, led the investigation into the JCS spying case, but it was Mitchell who was sent to confront the admiral. "Boy," Nixon said at the time, "you couldn't have a better man than Mitchell over to talk to Moorer."

Top: Vice President Agnew, Nixon, and Mitchell receive California governor Ronald Reagan in the Oval Office on January 23, 1971. "Have to have Mitchell handle . . . contact with Reagan," Nixon had decreed. As the preeminent symbol of law and order in the age of "radical chic," Mitchell's voice was equally, if not more, prominent than Reagan's in the advocacy of conservatism during the Nixon era. Bottom: John Ehrlichman and H. R. Haldeman aboard Air Force One on April 27, 1973, three days before Watergate forced both men out of the White House. "I have always found Bob Haldeman to be an honest, straightforward individual," Mitchell said in 1988; Ehrlichman he considered "a conniving little S.O.B."

Top: White House aides applaud the president in the Roosevelt Room on Election Day, 197
From left, Nixon, press secretary Ron Ziegler, Haldeman, Kissinger, Rose Mary Woods, Her
Stein, John Dean, Harry Dent, Arthur Flemming, Charles Colson, William Safire (partially
obscured), and Peter Flanigan. Bottom: Nixon visits the headquarters of the Committee for
the Re-Election of the President at 1701 Pennsylvania Avenue on September 18, 1972. Fror
left, Clark MacGregor, Fred LaRue (with pipe), Jon Foust, Paul Wagner, Robert Marik, Nixc
and Jeb Magruder. This is the first published photograph showing Nixon with either LaRue
or Magruder, who recently had gotten "roaring drunk" together to celebrate the confinemen
of the original Watergate indictments to the five arrested burglars, G. Gordon Liddy, and
E. Howard Hunt.

Top: Surrounded by reporters and photographers, and trailed by his attorney, Plato Cacheris, Mitchell is led into the Senate Watergate hearings on July 10, 1973, by the same uniformed policemen who once cheered his law-and-order gospel. Such chaotic scenes, at courthouses and federal prison, grew more common for Mitchell as he became, like Sherman McCoy in *The Bonfire of the Vanities*, a "professional defendant." Bottom: Attorney William Hundley leans in as Mitchell, who was rarely photographed in his eyeglasses, prepares his testimony that day. CBS News correspondent Lesley Stahl and UPI reporter Helen Thomas hover nearby.

Top: Suite 555 at the Essex House on Central Park South roars with
Scotch and song on the evening of April 28, 1974, as Mitchell celebrates
his acquittal in the so-called Vesco trial. From left are Mitchell defense
attorney John Sprizzo; the former attorney general; Walter Bonner,
an attorney for Maurice Stans; and an unidentified reveler. Bottom:
Ex-president Nixon welcomes Mitchell and his daughter Marty, then
eighteen, to San Clemente for a party on September 2, 1979, thrown
in honor of Mitchell's release from prison. With guests assembled
poolside, Nixon praised Mitchell for his "character, loyalty, and guts."

Top: Mitchell watches as his companion Mary Gore Dean opens Christmas gifts at Marwood, the Gore family estate in Maryland, in December 1985. "You just dream after you have lost your husband, as I did," Mrs. Dean told the author, "that someone this wonderful could come into your life." Bottom: Mary's daughter Deborah Gore Dean, who referred to Mitchell as "Daddy," attends a function with him, circa 1985. In Deborah Dean's federal indictment in the HUD scandal, Mitchell would be listed, posthumously, as unindicted co-conspirator number one; the special counsel in the case publicly blamed Mitchell for having denied him a seat on the Supreme Court.

Top: Attorney General William French Smith welcomes Mitchell back to the
Department of Justice for the unveiling of his official portrait, by artist Gloria
Schumann, on January 7, 1985. Rose Woods was among the two dozen people
on hand for the private ceremony. Bottom: From left, Richard A. Moore, Nixon,
Mitchell, and Vice President George H. W. Bush at a party, circa 1986. Nixon's
inscription, dated February 14, 1987, reads: "To John Mitchell, who helped all
three of us in our political careers. From Dick Nixon."

OFF THE RESERVATION

DAVID FROST: Which in general is easier to do as attorney general: hide [a mistake] or change it?
MITCHELL: Well, over the long haul it's probably easier to change it. In the short haul it's probably easier to hide it.

—The David Frost Show, *1971*[1]

IT ALL WENT exactly as Haldeman planned. The newspapers improbably cast Mitchell as a modern-day Duke of Windsor—an incurable romantic who surrendered political power for the woman he loved. Suggestions that Watergate prompted Mitchell's abdication were muted. "Investigation today turned up no evidence that any pressure had been applied to Mr. Mitchell to resign," reported the *New York Times*; the *Washington Post* quoted a CRP spokesman who insisted Mitchell had "absolutely no knowledge" of the break-in, and resigned solely "for the reason stated."[2]

In the Oval Office, the president sighed with relief, marveling to Haldeman how "the Mitchell thing couldn't have come at a better time from our standpoint." *Our standpoint*: That Mitchell's interests diverged from his own the president now assumed as fact. Nixon also believed, wrongly, that Mitchell planned to accept full blame for Watergate. "He goes in and he takes responsibility for it. He understands that, doesn't he?" "He mentioned that himself," Haldeman replied, equally erroneously.

Even more amazing, they still expected Mitchell, in addition to confessing, to obstruct the ongoing FBI investigation. "I want [Mitchell] to call Kleindienst and [Acting FBI Director L. Patrick] Gray in," Haldeman fantasized, "and say: 'Look, this happened. I used to sit on the National Security Council. . . . Your people are investigating stuff that must not be investigated. That's the signal you've gotten from the CIA. For Christ's sake, smarten up. Smarten up and turn this off. Go ahead and toss your cards to the grand jury on the open-and-shut case [of the arrested men], and let it go at that.' "[3]

Throughout the summer of 1972, as a trickle of minor disclosures kept Watergate in the news, Mitchell repeatedly denied his resignation from CRP had had anything to do with the "caper" that was growing, slowly but surely, into a scandal. Seated next to Mrs. Mitchell on an Amtrak Metroliner to New York, joined by a reporter, Mitchell smiled at the mere suggestion and jabbed his pipe in Martha's direction. "She spent a million dollars last year, and now I have to earn it!"[4]

The means to that end was a return to the old Nixon-Mitchell law firm, which, after the ascension of two partners to the presidency and attorney generalship, had been renamed Mudge Rose Guthrie Alexander, and had cultivated, in legal and governmental circles, a reputation the *Times* described as "*the* firm to see." But of the fourteen new partners hired during Mitchell's stint in government, eleven were in their thirties, the rest in their forties; they were far less likely than lawyers who had been with the firm prior to 1969 to applaud the administration's conduct of the Vietnam War, and they proved, upon Mitchell's return, less than welcoming. When he returned full-time, under an agreement that his name would rejoin the firm's shingle effective January 2, 1973, the short lapse between the Watergate arrests and Mitchell's sudden return to the full-time practice of law—

and, too, the ugliness of the Martha Mitchell incident in Newport Beach—lent an uneasy air to Mitchell's homecoming.[5]

And, as Haldeman predicted, Mitchell's departure did nothing to slow the Watergate investigation. On July 5, 1972, two FBI agents appeared at the Mudge Rose offices to interrogate the former attorney general. After several parries—including a few answers at slight variance with his later testimony—Mitchell joked he hoped the interview would end soon "so that we could get some work done." But the session didn't end without a serious misstep. Asked what he knew about the origins of the break-in, Mitchell replied he had "no knowledge . . . other than what he has read in newspaper accounts" of the incident—a remark that later formed the basis of Count Three in his indictment.[6]

The agents' questions showed the FBI was on to Gordon Liddy. There Nixon's men hoped, in vain, the investigation would rest; the moment authorities ascended up the next rung of the CRP ladder, to Jeb Magruder, spelled real trouble, for it was Magruder who represented, as an observer later described him, "the key link between the political figures such as Haldeman and Mitchell and the operational types, notably G. Gordon Liddy and E. Howard Hunt." Within a month of the arrests, John Dean had privately begun clamoring for Magruder to be served up to the U.S. attorney. "Dean feels that [the authorities] are going to move on Magruder and that the only thing we can do is have him take the rap that they'll hit him with," Haldeman recorded in his diary July 18.[7]

Around this time, Magruder later claimed, he approached Mitchell and offered to "take the heat"—tell the prosecutors the whole thing had been his idea—but Mitchell supposedly rejected the idea. Magruder recognized that if investigators ascended any higher than Liddy, they would scarcely pause to dwell on Magruder before moving to Mitchell himself—a development that would leave the scandal at the doorstep of the president himself. The same day the FBI quizzed Mitchell, Magruder made his first appearance before the grand jury.

"Don't volunteer," the former attorney general counseled Magruder. The session proved brief and harmless: Neither the prosecutors nor the grand jurors had a firm grasp of the case, and they excused the witness after a short series of questions about CRP's organizational structure. The picture changed considerably by mid-August, when Earl Silbert officially informed Magruder he was a "target" of the investigation, and summoned him for a second grand jury appearance on August 16.[8]

On August 14 Mitchell returned to the Oval Office for the first time since the Watergate arrests, attending a meeting with the president, Haldeman, and Mitchell's successor at CRP, former congressman Clark MacGregor. Nixon shrewdly reckoned that if the imminent indictments in the burglary and wiretapping of the DNC did not extend beyond the five arrested men to "others like Magruder, Sloan and so forth," the scandal would live on. "There will be immediately an outcry for: 'What are the facts with regard to the others? What are they covering up?' " "I think we have to be very careful to know what the facts are going to be and what's going to come out of that grand jury," Mitchell advised. This was not what Nixon had in mind at all. He proposed "to say Mitchell has hired this high-powered firm of investigators. . . . These grand jury proceedings take a long time. We want to know what the facts are." *A Mitchell Report!* This would ensure they "cut the losses on the damn thing," as Nixon put it.[9]

Given his recurring doubts about Mitchell's culpability, the president's proposal for a Mitchell Report served only one purpose: To set Mitchell up to take ultimate blame in the likely event his "report" was contradicted by the grand jury. To agree to this idea Mitchell was far too smart; and he cannot have left this meeting—his last in the Oval Office—under any delusion that his friend, the president, still had his best interests at heart.

At 4:30 that afternoon, Mitchell welcomed Magruder into his office at Mudge Rose. Two weeks earlier, when Mitchell had resigned from CRP, the younger man was moved to tears, and volunteered to leave, too. Now Magruder had a story to share: the false one he had been concocting for the grand jury. He later wrote that the basic ingredients of the cover story were cooked up in a series of meetings in Mitchell's law office in the month following the arrests. Magruder's descriptions of these meetings—unlike his accounts of most other points in the Watergate saga—rang true, for they comported with what the Nixon tapes later showed about the cover-up sessions in the Oval Office and elsewhere. In all cases, the conspirators maintained a refined, outwardly cool posture, speaking in vague, distinctly bureaucratic, even corporate, terms, unable to admit, even to each other, that they were engaged in a criminal conspiracy.[10]

Now, Magruder sat in Mitchell's office for a half hour and rehearsed his false story about Sloan giving Liddy $250,000 for convention security expenses. Though no reference to this meeting appeared in Mitchell's indictment, the prosecutors cross-examined him harshly on it, and the quiet encouragement he gave Magruder during his recitation of planned perjury bespoke Mitchell's complicity in the cover-up. In his Senate testimony, Mitchell effectively admitted guilt on this count.

> **SENATOR ERVIN:** You were also informed by Magruder that he, Magruder, was prepared to commit perjury when he went before the grand jury in August [1972] rather than to reveal what he knew about these matters?
> **MITCHELL:** That was correct, sir.
> **ERVIN:** Now did you agree that that was the proper course of action to take?
> **MITCHELL:** It was a very expedient one, senator. At that time in the campaign, so close to the election, we certainly were not volunteering any information.[11]

Mitchell still sought to protect himself against future indictment, distinguishing between knowledge of perjury and subornation of it:

"Magruder would seek an audience to review his story that he was going to tell, rather than somebody was trying to induce him to do so."

But why did Mitchell participate in the cover-up at all, even to this limited extent, if he did not order the break-in? Answering this question is central to understanding Mitchell's conduct in Watergate, and his ultimate fate. Mitchell's paramount concern in the affair, aside from Nixon's reelection, was that the three meetings at which the Gemstone plan was presented to him *should never be disclosed*—even though he had rejected Liddy's plans all three times. Who, after all, would believe that the attorney general who had publicly clamored for expanded wiretapping powers would have privately rejected the bugging of Democratic headquarters?

In preparing his perjury, Magruder received even greater assistance from John Dean. On August 15, one day before Magruder's return to the grand jury, the White House counsel spiritedly cross-examined the CRP deputy for two hours, probing for weaknesses in his cover story.

Of all the president's men, Dean enjoyed by far the most thorough knowledge of where the authorities stood in their investigation. "I was totally aware of what the Bureau was doing at all times," he once boasted. "I was totally aware of what the grand jury was doing." *How?* Preying on the misguided solicitousness of L. Patrick Gray III, the acting FBI director, Dean between June 30 and October 12 obtained eighty-three FBI investigation reports, along with two thick folders containing Bureau teletypes, raw interview summaries, known as "302s," and other documents compiled by the Washington Field Office.

Here again, Dean cast himself as merely carrying out Mitchell's orders; accordingly, as the twelfth overt act in the *U.S. v. Mitchell* indictment, the WSPF prosecutors accused Mitchell of having "advised" Dean, at some unspecified point in "mid-July" 1972, to obtain the FBI reports. Once again, Mitchell denied the charge, but was convicted. Yet this allegation, too, was based on constantly shifting testimony that the special prosecutors' own records showed they had good reason to disbelieve. In his executive session testimony before the Senate, previously unpublished, Dean claimed it was Mardian who was "pushing so hard to see the 302s," and that Mitchell merely "agreed" with him. Eleven days later, in public session, Dean claimed the idea came "initially . . . from Mr. Mitchell." Finally, under cross-examination at *U.S. v. Mitchell*, the witness was forced to admit that when he had appeared before the grand jury, in November 1973, he had not only cited Mardian as the instigator, but—Gordon Liddy! Testimony by other witnesses—Kleindienst, Gray, and Petersen before the Senate, Liddy in his memoir—showed Dean asked senior DOJ officials for access to the FBI records as early as June 19.

In fact, Dean needed no prodding from others to recognize the value of the FBI reports in his successful effort to monitor the Bureau's investigation. Among the exhibits Dean himself turned over to the WSPF prosecutors—previously unpublished and never made available to defense counsel at *U.S. v. Mitchell*—was a memorandum he had written back in September 1970 to then deputy attorney general Kleindienst. The White House counsel had inquired about news reports suggesting the FBI was investigating Bebe Rebozo, the president's friend. "We ought to have as much information concerning this situation as possible," Dean wrote, before concluding: "Could you discreetly obtain the FBI report connected with the investigation for my review? A little precautionary work often avoids getting caught flat-footed."

Dean's fleetness of foot served Magruder well. In his second appearance before the grand jury, on August 16, the prosecutors swallowed his cover story—but warily. The next day, Dean, after consulting with Assistant Attorney General Petersen, phoned Magruder with the good news: He had survived the interrogation "by the skin of his teeth" and would not be indicted. Magruder celebrated by repairing with Fred LaRue to Billy Martin's, a legendary Georgetown pub, where the two got "roaring drunk."[12]

On September 14, nine days after enduring a harrowing deposition at the hands of the era's premier trial lawyer, Edward Bennett Williams—the power broker who represented both the Democratic Party *and* the *Washington Post*—it was Mitchell's turn to appear before the grand jury. There to greet him was Earl Silbert, the assistant U.S. attorney whose certificate of office bore Mitchell's signature. Though the proceedings were theoretically to be held in strictest secrecy, leaks were commonplace; Mitchell was reported to have denied any prior knowledge of Gordon Liddy's covert activities. One exchange became public in 1974—when it formed the basis of a perjury charge.

> QUESTION: Was there any program, to your knowledge, at the committee, or any effort made to organize a covert or clandestine operation, basically, you know, illegal in nature, to get information or to gather intelligence about the activities of any of the Democratic candidates for public office or any activities of the Democratic Party?
>
> MITCHELL: Certainly not, because if there had been, I would have shut it off as being entirely non-productive at that particular time of the campaign.
>
> QUESTION: Did you have any knowledge, direct or indirect, of Mr. Liddy's activities with respect to any intelligence-gathering effort with respect to the activities of the Democratic candidates or its party?
>
> MITCHELL: None whatsoever, because I didn't know there was anything going on of that nature, if there was. So I wouldn't anticipate having heard anything about his activities in connection with it.

Technically, Mitchell's answers here—calculated to prevent disclosure of the Gemstone meetings—were true. After he rejected Liddy's plan for the third time, at Key Biscayne, his dealings with Liddy were extremely limited. The Gemstone pitches had, of course, contemplated illegal plans to gather intelligence about the Democrats; but having turned those schemes down, Mitchell had no knowledge such a "program" or "effort" was thereafter undertaken. In Mitchell's eyes, the pitch for the project should not be mistaken for the actual project. At his trial two years later, Mitchell used this very line of defense.

Likewise, Mitchell's answer to the second question was predicated on the view that since he had not bothered, after Key Biscayne, to keep abreast of Liddy's activities, covert or otherwise, he could truthfully swear he had no "knowledge" of the intelligence-gathering "effort" Liddy thereafter mounted. To conclude Mitchell lied in these answers required believing either that he actually did approve Liddy's plans—a claim belied by the testimony of Fred LaRue—or that notwithstanding his rejection of those plans, Mitchell still reviewed the fruits of the DNC surveillance, a proposition that defied logic: Who would calmly digest data from a wiretap he quashed? But the jury in *U.S. v. Mitchell* entertained no such fine distinctions when it convicted the former attorney general of perjury.[13]

For the moment, however, the dam held. "Mitchell's public image was cold and severe," Silbert recalled in 1992. "But in front of the grand jury he was warm and charming, and seemed to be very cooperative." The day after his appearance, the grand jury, as expected, handed down indictments against Liddy, Hunt, and the five burglars. At the White House and CRP, there was elation that the criminal charges were confined to the operational figures. That evening, Nixon welcomed John Dean into the Oval Office for the first of their infamous recorded meetings about Watergate. Nixon sneered he had never used the power of the Justice Department against his enemies, "all those who tried to do us in," during the last three years—Mitchell's tenure as attorney general—but "things are going to change now." "What an exciting prospect," Dean replied.

The vengeful jubilation was interrupted by a phone call from the very man who had prevented Nixon from using the power of Justice against his enemies: John Mitchell. "Are you still alive?" Nixon joked into the receiver. He tried to buck up his old law partner, telling Mitchell not to let Watergate keep him from "concentrating on the big game." This was one of those side issues, Nixon said, where a month later everyone would wonder what all the shooting was about. "Get a good night's sleep," the president ordered, adding, "And don't bug anybody without asking me, okay?"[14]

Restful nights were not in Mitchell's future. Shortly before midnight on September 28, he was jolted out of a sound sleep in Room 710 of the Essex House, on New York's Central Park South, by the shrill clanging of the telephone. Groggily he picked up the receiver to hear a young man identify himself as Carl Bernstein, reporter for the *Washington Post.* After apologizing for calling so late, Bernstein announced that the *Post's* morning edition, due to hit newsstands in a few hours, would be carrying a story alleging Mitchell had maintained an illegal slush fund used to spy on Nixon's political opponents. "JEEEEEEESUS!" Mitchell gasped, periodically repeating his astonished blasphemy as Bernstein read aloud the story's opening paragraphs.

> John N. Mitchell, while serving as U.S. attorney general, personally controlled a secret Republican fund that was used to gather information about the Democrats, according to sources involved in the Watergate investigation.
>
> Beginning in the spring of 1971, almost a year before he left the Justice Department to become President Nixon's campaign manager on March 1, Mitchell personally approved withdrawals from the fund, several reliable sources have told the *Washington Post.*
>
> Those sources have provided almost identical, detailed accounts of Mitchell's role as comptroller of the secret intelligence fund and its fluctuating $350,000–$700,000 balance.

Mitchell unleashed a torrent of venom on his cheeky young interlocutor. "All that crap, you're putting it in the paper? It's all been denied." Then Mitchell blasted the *Post*'s imperious, socially prominent publisher. "Katie Graham's gonna get her tit caught in a big, fat wringer if that's published. Good Christ! That's the most sickening thing I ever heard." Bernstein kept pressing, in the manner of the reluctant, yet dutiful messenger—"I'd like to ask you a few questions about the specifics"—which only made Mitchell angrier. "Call my law office in the morning," he snapped before hanging up.

Adding to the insult of Bernstein's late-night intrusion was the fact that the *Post*'s story was dead wrong. Clearly the Republicans maintained a fund to bankroll the activities of Ulasewicz and Donald Segretti, head of CRP's "dirty tricks" campaign; and it was also true that Mitchell, while serving as attorney general in 1971, had acted as a de facto campaign manager for the nascent reelection operation, authorizing large expenditures and making executive decisions about the location of the '72 convention, state chairmen for the Nixon-Agnew ticket, and the like. But Mitchell never knew about, let alone "controlled," any secret fund used to finance "intelligence operations" against the Democrats.

Mitchell's scrape with Bernstein underscored the disturbing reality that, notwithstanding the limited scope of the indictments, the Watergate story was beginning to spiral out of control. A Harris poll released October 19 found more than 60 percent of voters dismissing Watergate as "mostly politics" and disbelieving charges Nixon was involved. But as Election Day drew nearer, the three television networks began joining the *Post* and the *Times* in heavy coverage of the story, specifically of the charges swirling around Mitchell. Despite the mounting turmoil, Nixon swept to reelection by one of the largest landslides in American history, capturing over 60 percent of 78 million votes cast and the electoral votes of every state save Massachusetts.[15]

Shortly after election night, E. Howard Hunt placed an angry call to his old patron at the White House, Chuck Colson. "The reason I called you," Hunt said, was because "commitments that were made to all of us at the onset have not been kept, and there's a great deal of unease and concern on the part of the seven defendants. . . . What we've been getting has been coming in very minor dribs and drabs. . . . This is a long haul and the stakes are very, very high. . . . This thing must not break apart for foolish reasons."

In anticipation of their trial on burglary, wiretapping, and other charges in January 1973, the indicted men had set November 25 as a deadline for the "liquidation" of all outstanding debts. They understood the hesitancy to pay up before the election, but that was over, and the men now expected the customs of the spy game to be observed: In the event of capture, the operatives, their families, and their lawyers would stay silent—provided they were all taken care of. "We think that now is the time when a move should be made," Hunt said, "and surely the cheapest commodity available is money."[16]

Colson took the cue. He brought a DictaBelt recording of his talk with Hunt to the office of John Dean, who made his own tape of the conversation and arranged for a transcription. On the morning of November 15, Dean rode in a government limousine to Camp David, where he found Haldeman and Ehrlichman inside the president's empty office at Laurel Lodge. After playing the Colson-Hunt tape, Dean mentioned he was flying to New York that day to meet with Mitchell. "My instructions from this meeting," Dean later testified, "were to tell Mitchell to take care of all these problems."

In that afternoon's meeting at the Metropolitan Club, on Manhattan's Upper East Side, Mitchell came face-to-face with the enormity of the problems confronting him. Joining Dean was Maury Stans, there to discuss legal and financial issues stemming from the closure of CRP, and, too, the burgeoning scandal arising from the committee's unhappy dalliance with Robert Vesco. Only after Stans finished his unpleasant business and left did Dean begin recounting the latest

Watergate troubles. Surely, Mitchell at this moment saw the future: indictment in both the Vesco *and* Watergate cases.

Dean bade the older man into a private room inside the Metropolitan Club. From a bulky Sony recorder came the scratchy sounds of Hunt, whom Mitchell did not know, and Colson, whom Mitchell knew and loathed, talking in circumlocutory fashion about the indicted men's money problems. At one point, when Hunt asserted that Mitchell had already committed perjury, Mitchell interjected: "I wonder what in the hell Hunt is talking about." Minutes later, he disgustedly told Dean to hit the stop button and stalked out. Dean told the Senate he received "no instruction or really any indication at all at that time from Mitchell" about what to do next.

This was not the first time Mitchell had been asked to resolve the burglars' financial problems; that had come back in June, shortly after the arrests, when Mitchell, still campaign manager, had "turned down and turned down cold" a request that CRP pay their bail. The Metropolitan Club meeting marked the first time the problem had reappeared at Mitchell's doorstep, in the person of John Dean, following the indictments and Nixon's reelection. Henceforth the scandal would consist of these periodic demands for cash, and accompanying pleas for executive clemency, pressed most forcefully at critical junctures in the legal process: the eve of the burglars' trial, their sentencing. And it would invariably be to Mitchell, widely and mistakenly regarded as the final authority behind the whole project, that these demands, sooner or later, were delivered.[17]

From the beginning, immediately after the Watergate arrests, the effort to funnel hush money to the burglars and their attorneys had been led by John Dean. It was Dean who practically begged General Walters to assume the burden at CIA; Dean who summoned Herb Kalmbach from the West Coast and set the fund-raising genius in motion; Dean who supervised the payments that were actually made, through Kalmbach, LaRue, and Ulasewicz. It was in Dean's EOB office, in September 1972, that Kalmbach announced his withdrawal from the money business and set fire to his written ledger of receipts and expenditures. It was Dean who pushed Kalmbach the hardest to reconsider, "the one that talked to me most often about this, to continue in this program," as Kalmbach testified. "I had the feeling that Mr. Dean was the primary person directing it." And it was Dean who, after the election, worked hardest to find a way to meet the defendants' fresh demands, playing the tape of Hunt's hair-raising talk with Colson for Haldeman, Ehrlichman, and Mitchell, hoping one of these big men would handle the task that Dean, just thirty-four years old, could not: rounding up the money.[18]

But to Dean's surprise and dismay, no one lifted a finger to help. Smart and resourceful, the fresh-faced White House counsel—whose "ringmaster" role in the cover-up appears, in retrospect, to have owed far more to his complicity in the break-in than to any sense of "blind ambition"—worked overtime in the fall of 1972 to ensure that the burglars, Liddy, and Hunt would remain, in the parlance of the day, on the reservation. Since at least the beginning of 1971, Dean had known there were "large sums of cash" floating around the White House, leftover monies from the last two election cycles. As with the Kalmbach and CIA gambits, Dean later disclaimed authorship of the idea to use this White House fund, estimated at $350,000, to meet the burglars' demands; instead, he attributed it to—*who else?*—John Mitchell.

In his executive-session testimony before the Senate, previously unpublished, Dean was decidedly vague in describing how and when Mitchell first instructed him to access the fund. "Well, the long and short of it," Dean testified, "was that Mitchell finally called me and said, could I speak with Haldeman about getting some of that money, the $350,000 that was there, and we'll pay you back." In public session, Dean claimed Mitchell, just two weeks after rebuffing Dean at the Metropolitan Club, suddenly saw the wisdom of buying the defendants' silence and contacted him spontaneously. "To the best of my recollection," Dean testified, "it was the first week of December that Mitchell called me and said that we would have to use some of the $350,000 fund to take care of the demands being made by Hunt and the others for money."

At the House impeachment hearings, Dean slid the date of this call back to some unspecified time prior to November 28. Then, at *U.S. v. Mitchell*, the witness remembered for the first time that Mitchell's call had actually come on Thanksgiving Day, which Dean spent at his parents' home in Greenville, Pennsylvania. "The call caused some excitement in the house," Dean testified, "and I took it in the back bedroom." Presumably these small but vivid details—the holiday setting, the Dean family's excitement, the back bedroom—imbued the story, in the eyes of the jury and as Dean plainly hoped, with the aura of truth; no one ever posed the obverse question, which was why, if these details made the event so memorable, Dean had theretofore failed, in several forums, to mention them. Dean then claimed he raced back to Washington, reluctantly and at Mitchell's urging, to see Haldeman and Ehrlichman, time and date again unspecified; but when asked, during friendly direct examination, what the duo said, Dean testified lamely: "I frankly don't recall what they told me."

In *Blind Ambition*, published in 1976, Dean finally perfected his story, fusing into the single call to Greenville both Mitchell's plea for the use of the White House fund and his suggestion that Dean return to Washington, events previously held separately. Also for the first time, Dean cast Mitchell's call as a specific response to another event: the receipt, earlier that week, of a fresh list of money demands that Hunt's lawyer had sent to CRP attorney Kenneth Parkinson. In no previous account had Dean linked Parkinson's name, or this list of demands, to Mitchell's call(s); now, in his memoir, Dean had Mitchell inquiring what action had been taken on Parkinson's "little list." Here Dean made a telling mistake, the most glaring of many discrepancies in his multiple accounts of the episode. *Blind Ambition* recounted Mitchell's call coming on Thanksgiving Day, which fell that year on

November 23; but Parkinson did not transmit the list of new demands until December 1. Thus it would have been impossible for Mitchell to contact Dean about a list unknown to both men for another eight days.

Mitchell, of course, flatly denied these allegations about the White House fund. "I had no control over the money and there would be no reason why I should call Dean or anybody else," Mitchell told the Senate, "and I did not so call Dean." Apparently, the WSPF prosecutors recognized the problems in Dean's story, for they chose to list in the *U.S. v. Mitchell* indictment, as overt acts in the cover-up conspiracy, Dean's playing of the Colson-Hunt tape for Mitchell at the Metropolitan Club (uncontested by Mitchell); Parkinson's transmittal of the list of demands to Dean on December 1; and Haldeman's authorization, in "early December," for the use of the $350,000. Yet in chronicling the origins of this last, and most historically significant, hush-money scheme—one that ultimately ensnared the president himself, and led to impeachment charges against him—the indictment in *U.S. v. Mitchell* made no mention whatsoever of John Mitchell.[19]

On the foggy afternoon of December 8, 1972, United Airlines Flight 553, bound from Washington, D.C., to Midway Airport, was cruising for landing at 4,000 feet when suddenly the plane's nose shifted skyward; seconds later, it plowed into a neighborhood in southwest Chicago, slicing off roofs as she careened forward, obliterating four homes before bursting into flames. Forty-five passengers died, among them Mrs. Dorothy Hunt, wife of Howard Hunt and—unknown at the time—the recipient of several deliveries of Watergate hush money. Chicago police discovered Mrs. Hunt's intact purse, which contained more than $10,000 in cash, almost all in hundred-dollar bills.[20]

A father of four, Hunt was devastated. "I was very seriously considering doing away with myself," he later confided to investigators, in previously unpublished testimony. Soon Hunt informed his Watergate codefendants he could not withstand the strain of their trial, set to begin January 8, and that he intended to plead guilty. Urging the Cubans to follow suit, Hunt warned Bernard Barker, according to previously unpublished WSPF files, that "accusations about prostitutes would come out at trial." To his old White House chums, by whom he felt abandoned—*Colson hadn't even attended Dorothy's funeral*—Hunt was now adamant that his financial needs had to be met, and fast; and that he was owed not just money but the promise of rehabilitation, to be achieved through a timely conferral of executive clemency. By March, the ex-spy was in a venomous state: "John Dean is a son of a bitch, and I want somebody to know about that before it is too late and I am in prison! . . . I am very bitter towards John Dean."[21]

Worse, Hunt was not the only Watergate defendant rattling his cage. James McCord, the inscrutable master spook who had sabotaged the June 17 break-in and deceived his fellow burglars about it, was dismayed they were now considering a "CIA defense." Under this strategy, the Cubans would plead not guilty and argue that they always believed they were carrying out an Agency mission. So fierce was McCord's determination to protect Langley that he began seeing treachery everywhere, including on his own defense team. He quarreled with his lawyers' plan to subpoena Richard Helms, and wondered why they (rightly) dismissed as hearsay McCord's attempts to implicate Mitchell. "Mitchell really didn't talk to you about it, did he?" McCord quoted his lawyers as saying, typical of their "negative-type approach." "They can go to hell," he fumed. Soon McCord was firing off threatening notes, including one to Jack Caulfield, Dean's aide, vowing that if Helms was fired, and the onus for Watergate laid at CIA's door, "every tree in the forest will fall. It will be a scorched desert."[22]

Caulfield dutifully notified Dean. The strain of marshaling hush money was bad enough; but the kind of dissatisfaction McCord was expressing couldn't be mollified with simple cash. Something else was needed: executive clemency. Up to then, all of Dean's dealings on the issue of clemency had concerned Howard Hunt and had been limited to discussions with Colson and Ehrlichman. However, in sworn testimony before the Senate, previously unpublished, Dean claimed he was prompted to action in McCord's case by a telephone call, out of the blue, from John Mitchell.

> McCord was off the reservation and they were having all kinds of problems with him, his lawyer was quite upset with him. He was not cooperating and playing ball as the others were. So . . . Mitchell called me and said he thought I should talk to [McCord] about it, and take his pulse, or make him a similar offer. I think there had been pulse-taking sessions— I'd have to check my notes on that.

Dean's testimony on this allegation in the ensuing forums followed the familiar pattern: Dates slid, a single call became multiple calls, face-to-face discussion became a phone conversation, and Mitchell's complicity deepened in each retelling. Asked if he took part in the extension of clemency offers to the Watergate defendants— whether he bore guilty knowledge of what Colson was promising Hunt, and acted, through Dean and Caulfield, to tender similar promises to McCord—Mitchell dismissed Dean's story as "a complete fabrication." "I was out of town in Florida when [Dean] started the McCord dialogue," Mitchell told the Senate, brandishing his office logs and adding "there would be no reason in the world for me to direct Mr. Dean to do anything vis-à-vis Caulfield or McCord or anybody else." This was true: On the matter Mitchell considered his greatest vulnerability—the three Gemstone meetings—Hunt and McCord could offer only hearsay testimony. Whether they talked or kept silent thus mattered little to Mitchell.

Once again, the WSPF prosecutors appear to have recognized the problems posed by their central witness and his chameleonic testimony; for in listing this charge in the *U.S. v. Mitchell* indictment, the conspiracy's thirty-third overt act, the best the prosecutors could say was that Mitchell did the evil deed, by phone, sometime "in or about early January 1973."[23]

"The crux of the problem that you always had," Dean was once asked, "was raising the money to support [the defendants], pay their legal fees and, as you testified, to keep them quiet; is that correct?" "Yes," Dean answered.

The money! The money! It was the bane of Dean's existence across the latter half of 1972 and the first quarter of 1973. By the end of January, Nixon had been sworn in for a second term as president; Hunt and the Cubans had, as promised, pleaded guilty; and McCord and Liddy had stood trial and been convicted. When Earl Silbert put Alfred Baldwin on the stand, a lawyer representing Spencer Oliver and other DNC employees had interrupted the proceedings and demanded, successfully, that Baldwin be prohibited from disclosing the racy contents of the conversations that he, as the operation's wiretap monitor, had overheard. The secrets of the DNC—and the Columbia Plaza—would remain undisclosed, for now.

To further ensure as much, Dean that month also performed what he later called the "concrete and sweaty act" of shredding three notebooks, including an "operational diary" of the Gemstone project, seized from Hunt's EOB safe. This detail Dean withheld from the Senate and, initially, from the WSPF prosecutors; he disclosed it only after his plea deal was completed. In a recent interview, Hunt termed Dean's destruction of the notebooks an act of "self-preservation," aimed at suppressing "notations that were incriminatory to him." Of Dean's presence at the creation of Gemstone, there is no better indication than his destruction of this evidence, and the lengths he went to conceal it.[24]

Only one overarching problem remained: *the money!* Despite the brush-off he had gotten from Mitchell at the Metropolitan Club in

November, Dean still saw the former attorney general as the most likely of the Big Three—Haldeman, Ehrlichman, and Mitchell—to act on the defendants' demands. Dean also remembered the solid performance of Herb Kalmbach in raising and dispensing hush money the previous summer. Therein Dean apparently saw his, and the cover-up's, salvation: If he could get Mitchell and Kalmbach in a room together, perhaps Kalmbach could be persuaded to return to the game.

On January 19, Dean encountered Mitchell and Kalmbach at a trustees meeting for the Nixon Foundation at Blair House, the official residence for foreign dignitaries, located across from the White House on Pennsylvania Avenue. Afterward, Dean told the Senate, he repaired with Mitchell, Kalmbach, and Fred LaRue to Mitchell's law office at 1701. (At *U.S. v. Mitchell,* Dean changed LaRue's status at this meeting, from attendee to discussion topic.) Within a few minutes, Dean claimed, Mitchell asked Kalmbach to resume his role in the hush-money enterprise. Dean remembered Kalmbach refusing, then demurring in response to a second request, made either by Mitchell or Dean himself, for a list of potential contributors, and leaving shortly thereafter.

Neither LaRue nor Mitchell recalled the meeting at all. Kalmbach recalled it—but not as Dean described it. The *über*-fund-raiser remembered Dean approaching him as the trustees' meeting broke up, and telling him John Mitchell wanted to see him right away. Through "misty-like rain," Kalmbach recalled, he and Dean—not Dean and Mitchell, as Dean claimed—ran the half block to 1701 and headed straight into the office of the former attorney general. There they found Mitchell and LaRue. According to Kalmbach, it was Dean who "led the conversation."

> Mr. Dean stated that they were interested in my raising additional funds for these defendants. And the minute that came up, suddenly I knew, of course, what the reason was for this

meeting. And I, of course, had made up my mind the prior August that I would not raise additional funds, and so I was just in the position of excusing myself as gracefully as possible from the meeting. . . . [I] said that I would not do anything further.

Dean was "the one that talked to me most often about this, to continue in this [hush-money] program," Kalmbach told the Senate Watergate committee; and as he told the House, it was Dean, not Mitchell, who asked him to reenter the game that drizzly day in January 1973. As for Mitchell's role, Kalmbach made explicitly clear—in the only interview he ever gave after Watergate, to author Len Colodny, in April 1988—that there was none. "Mitchell never asked me to raise money," Kalmbach said.

For his part, the former attorney general claimed he first learned of the payments to the Watergate defendants in September 1972, and that he neither aided nor impeded the scheme. He told House investigators, according to previously unpublished documents, that he thought the disbursements were solely for legal fees, and that he "knew that the payments were in cash, but he did not know of the covert manner" in which they were being made.

Since Fred LaRue worked so closely with Dean in the hush-money enterprise—deciding sums, arranging drop-offs—prosecutors hoped the Mississippian, after copping his plea, would testify that Mitchell was the driving force behind it. But LaRue's residual affection for Mitchell, on such vivid display when LaRue broke down and wept before the grand jury, apparently prevented him from further implicating his old friend. LaRue came close, previously unpublished documents show, wavered back and forth—but never pulled the trigger.

Thus after explicitly telling the Senate Watergate committee he never briefed Mitchell on his own machinations with Dean and Kalmbach, LaRue told federal prosecutors he "discussed with Mitchell these money disbursements—discussed where $ would come from." LaRue told the prosecutors "either Dean or Mitchell caused [him] to contact Kalmbach," but added Dean "appeared to be directing" the effort. The farthest LaRue went was to claim he presented a "cash disbursement summary sheet" to Mitchell in July 1972. "Mitchell said you ought to get rid of it + he destroyed it," the prosecutors' notes read. Yet in recounting to Senate investigators how he entered the hush-money scheme, LaRue spoke only of Dean, not of Mitchell, and made no mention of the incriminating summary sheet Mitchell had supposedly ordered him to destroy. LaRue also told Senate investigators he "[could] not remember whether he was getting his instructions from Mitchell or from Dean," but that, in any case, he "[did] not recall Dean seeking approval from higher-ups" in the operation. Elsewhere LaRue said that as early as June 28, 1972, he and Mitchell discussed "commitments" to the Watergate defendants; but LaRue also claimed he "did not raise the subject with Mitchell because he had the impression that this fund-raising area was Dean's responsibility and that there was consequently no need to tell Mitchell."

With House impeachment investigators in April 1974, LaRue continued his strange Mississippi two-step, claiming Mitchell "was aware of how much money was going out" but that Dean "made the final decisions." Later that year, at *U.S. v. Mitchell*, LaRue returned Mitchell to an authorial role, claiming the former attorney general "asked me to work with Mr. Dean on . . . meeting these commitments." LaRue reaffirmed he "did discuss . . . the payment of monies with Mr. Mitchell," then swore his and Mitchell's talks covered "only the vaguest generalities." Finally, LaRue told prosecutors that Dean and Mitchell had jointly dispatched him in January 1973 to solicit rich Republican donors, without betraying his true purpose, in an effort to replenish the depleted $350,000 White House fund. This was aborted when the donors, including Cincinnati businessman Carl Lindner, demanded to know the reason for their largesse. Even here, however, LaRue told the House he undertook this mission "after discussions with Dean."[25]

Until now, President Nixon had mostly been a spectator at the Watergate drama, the recipient, in his White House aerie, of news good and bad, a largely passive actor alternately baffled and intrigued, enraged and delighted as developments warranted. Outside of the "smoking gun" meeting, when Nixon acquiesced in Haldeman's proposal to get CIA involved on national security grounds—a step taken under the mistaken belief, propagated by Dean, that the proposal had the endorsement of John Mitchell—Nixon had had little role in the daily machinations of the cover-up. He had also indicated his ex post facto approval when Haldeman informed him, thirty-nine days later, that Hunt, "at considerable cost," had been made "happy"—"They have to be paid," Nixon had agreed—but even here, the president's role had been passive, and not irrefutably discernible as a witting obstruction of justice.

In the days surrounding his second inauguration, however, Nixon watched the situation deteriorate rapidly. On January 14 and 15, the *New York Times* ran a pair of articles by Seymour Hersh, far more worrisome than anything Woodward and Bernstein had published, headlined "4 Watergate Defendants Reported Still Being Paid" and "Pressures to Plead Guilty Alleged in Watergate Case." On February 7, the Senate created a select committee to probe Watergate. Nixon's thoughts on The Question ran toward the uncharitable. "I mean, let's face it," he snapped to Haldeman and Ehrlichman on December 11. "We all know who the hell should have handled this. Goddamnit, it was Mitchell, and he wasn't handling it."

NIXON: I would dump him; it would kill him financially. John Mitchell has a serious problem with his wife. He was unable to watch the campaign and as a result, underlings did things without his knowledge.

EHRLICHMAN: [. . .] The minute you dump on Mitchell indirectly by saying he didn't have a chance to watch the un-

derlings, the underlings are going to produce their diaries and show Mitchell was in eighteen meetings where this was discussed, ratified, approved, authorized, financed.
NIXON: Was he?
EHRLICHMAN: I gather so.
NIXON: Well, Mitchell, then, did it.[26]

Aides who had struggled to navigate the scandal's choppy waters now began washing up at the Oval Office, looking for a lifeline they thought only the president of the United States could throw them. The requests—framed always in the indirect bureaucratic fashion of government men managing a problem, not as desperate cries for help in a capsizing criminal conspiracy—started with pleas for executive clemency and hush money, and climaxed in demands that the president perform swiftly the unpleasant chore the coconspirators all believed, in shared delusion, would instantly and tidily dispose of the matter: Sacrifice John Mitchell. It was Nixon's response, grudging at first, ultimately enthusiastic, that sealed Mitchell's fate.

Contrary to received wisdom, Nixon's tapes did not reveal him "a manipulative, master politician overseeing every detail" (*Washington Post*), "the key figure in the cover-up conspiracy" (*Time*) who "knew virtually everything about Watergate and the imposition of a cover-up, from the beginning" (historian Stanley Kutler). Yes, the tapes showed Nixon *became* a party to the cover-up, inarguably by February 1973; this much Nixon himself confessed to David Frost. "I will admit . . . I was not prosecuting the case."

I will admit that during that period, rather than acting in my role as the chief law enforcement officer in the land . . . I did not meet that responsibility . . . in some cases going right to the edge of the law in trying to advise Ehrlichman and Haldeman and all the rest as to how best to present their cases, because I thought they were legally innocent, that I came to the edge. And under the circumstances, I would have to say that a reasonable person could call that a cover-up.

Worse than belying Nixon's Quaker morality, the tapes demolished his carefully cultivated image as a competent chief executive, a steel-trap mind harnessed to the demanding business of presidential decision-making in the atomic age. From his first days as president, Nixon's aides were privately shocked by how he wasted "countless hours" on "rambling and rumination." The president's management style, Ehrlichman recalled in 1982, "would involve his chewing on a subject for a while and then leaving it and going off to other things and then coming back to it unannounced. Very often it was hard to pick up his train of thought. . . . This could go on over a period of days."[27]

In Watergate Nixon "didn't know what the truth was," Ehrlichman told a symposium audience. "He didn't know what he had said, didn't know what he had done, and the fact was whatever he was saying was truth at that particular moment." The tapes unmasked Nixon not as the take-charge boss of a criminal conspiracy but rather as an aging and confused politician lost in a welter of detail, unable to distinguish his Magruders from his Strachans, uncertain who knew what and when, what each player had told the grand jury, whose testimony was direct, whose hearsay. Charles Colson told the House that Nixon seemed "genuinely confused by all of the conflicting accounts." Alexander Butterfield, the aide who saw Nixon more frequently than any other save Haldeman and who publicly disclosed the existence of the taping system, acknowledged that the transcripts betrayed in the president "a seeming incoherence of speaking style." "One of the things that did strike me when I read the transcripts," agreed Magruder, "was that really, how much—or how little—information [Nixon, Haldeman, and Ehrlichman] really did have."

No one benefited more from the president's estrangement from the facts of Watergate than his chief accuser, John Dean—and no one, besides Nixon himself, suffered more from this disadvantage than John Mitchell, the highest-ranking administration official imprisoned on the strength of Dean's testimony. Dean was keenly aware of his mental superiority over the president. In *Blind Ambition*, Dean wrote that Nixon was lucid and logical only sporadically, and was mostly rambling, forgetful, and disorganized, unable to remember what Dean told him from day to day. In a 1989 interview, Dean recalled much the same of Mitchell: "He wasn't sharp. . . . He didn't remember a lot of details. . . . I had to—used to prepare Mitchell to testify, to go up on the Hill. And he wasn't very good. He wasn't a very good witness. He couldn't hold facts. He couldn't hold information."[28]

Dean ended Nixon's and Mitchell's careers, producing in the president both everlasting fury and regret ("Oh, the incredible treachery of that son-of-a-bitch!"), and exposing the limitations of the mental machines that had propelled the older men, respectively, from Whittier and Blue Point to the White House and Wall Street. Dean was younger, smarter, quicker, more tightly wired into the bureaucracy, and better versed in the origins, players, and events of Watergate. Against this backdrop commenced Nixon's infamous series of meetings and phone calls with Dean—some twenty in all, between February 27 and April 17—that marked the endgame in the Watergate cover-up and changed the course of American history.

The first White House aide to approach Nixon that winter was Colson, who laid the groundwork in a chat with Haldeman. "This Watergate thing is not going to go away," Colson warned, "and it seems to me that John Mitchell must have been responsible for this. And if he was, we damn well better bring him in and make him take the responsibility." In Nixon's office February 13, Colson sought assurances the president would take a "hard nose" stand against the Ervin committee interrogating White House aides. "If they want Haldeman, Ehrlichman, me," Colson said, "we have to limit the areas that they're gonna go into." And whoever ordered the break-in, Colson argued in a clear reference to Mitchell, should say so and spare the president further grief. "If it's gonna come out in the hearings, for God sakes, let it out," he cried.

> COLSON: At least get rid of it now, take our losses.
> NIXON: Well, who the hell do you think did this? Mitchell? He can't do it; he'll perjure himself so he won't admit it. Now that's the problem.

Next came Dean. The tapes show Dean ran circles around the president, used his superior comprehension of the scandal to shape the topics discussed, options considered, and courses pursued. Asked during the impeachment hearings by Democratic congressman John Conyers if he ever withheld information from Nixon during Watergate, Dean replied: "I didn't walk in every time and volunteer everything that might be on my mind." Chief among Dean's deceptions was his implication of Mitchell. In his talks with Nixon, Dean was careful never to say explicitly that the former attorney general approved the break-in; but the counsel made his suspicions clear enough. "Mitchell probably puffed on his pipe and said, 'Go ahead,' and never really reflected on what it was all about," Dean told Nixon on March 21. Where the hush money was concerned, Dean cast Mitchell as the scheme's father, himself as a *mere messenger*:

> Arrangements were made through Mitchell, initiating it. And I was present in discussions where [it was agreed] these guys had to be taken care of.

Dean later cast the March 21 morning session, the infamous "cancer on the presidency" meeting, as his bid to end the cover-up. Yet the conversation appears, in retrospect, more an attempt to draw Nixon into the plot, precisely because Mitchell had proved so immovable. "How much money do you need?" Nixon finally asked.

Dean, citing a figure that had appeared nowhere else, estimated the defendants would cost a million dollars over the next two years. "We could get that," Nixon replied. "You could get it in cash. I know where it could be gotten." But, he added, "the question is who the hell would handle it? Any ideas on that?" "Well," Dean shot back, "I think that is something Mitchell ought to be charged with. And get some pros to help him."[29]

Dean had laid out three scenarios for Nixon that day: continuing the payments and thereby maintaining the cover-up; limited disclosure, with complicit aides appearing before a reconvened grand jury, under whatever immunity could be negotiated; and self-immolation, with all parties left to fend for themselves. Nixon recognized that all three scenarios converged, that "in the end, we are going to be bled to death, and it's all going to come out anyway." *What to do?* The immediate answer was for Dean to regroup the Big Three—Mitchell, Haldeman, and Ehrlichman—and figure something out. Mitchell should come down from New York. "Mitchell has to be there because he is seriously involved and we're trying to keep him with us," Nixon said; but the president increasingly saw his old consigliere as a toxic figure: "I think I need to stay away from the Mitchell subject at this point, do you agree?"

Dean neglected to tell Nixon that as they spoke, the hush-money gears were busily grinding away. Shortly before Dean stepped foot into the Oval Office that morning, he had contacted Fred LaRue and informed him of Hunt's latest demand: $120,000. When LaRue sought direction, Dean declared he was out of the money business; LaRue would have to decide for himself. LaRue refused to make any deliveries on his own authority. Dean's answer was predictable: Talk to Mitchell. Asked why none of this arose during his exhaustive "cancer" briefing, Dean said he was "just sort of following along."

Mitchell's response to Hunt's demand for $120,000 gave rise to numerous "overt acts" in the *U.S. v. Mitchell* indictment. These alleged acts of conspiracy included a phone call Mitchell received in New York from Haldeman, right after the "cancer" meeting, the last half of which Haldeman had attended, and Fred LaRue's phone conversation with Mitchell later that day, held at the urging of Dean, wherein Mitchell supposedly "authorized" LaRue to pay Hunt $75,000 in cash.

Neither charge had merit. Haldeman's call to Mitchell made no mention of hush money; it was, instead, classically Haldemanian, brisk and businesslike, merely to inform Mitchell the president wanted to see him in Washington. Then there was Mitchell's "order" to pay Hunt. The WSPF prosecutors tried to prove Mitchell initiated the fateful discussion, but neither phone company toll records nor Mitchell's logs showed him placing any calls to LaRue on March 21. LaRue's testimony shifted, but both men agreed he did seek Mitchell's advice. Mitchell said he asked what the money was for and whether previous payments had been made. "Legal fees," he quoted LaRue saying, and yes, there had been previous payments. "If I were in your position," Mitchell remembered saying, "I would pay the money." John Doar, chief counsel to the House Judiciary Committee, later rebuked him: "You did tell [LaRue] that it was all right and make that payment?" "No," Mitchell replied firmly. "As I testified before, Mr. Doar, he asked me what I would do *if I were he*, and I said under the circumstances I would make the payment."[30]

Once more, Mitchell had skated past the onrushing danger, which on this occasion had materialized in the person of Fred LaRue—*the best friend the president and I ever had*. Such was the poisonous pinstriped atmosphere of Watergate: Peril appeared most often in the form of smiling friends, colleagues—even the president of the United States, whom Mitchell, the next morning, flew to Washington to see, in their final meeting.

THE BIG ENCHILADA

This is the time for strong men.

—*Richard Nixon, 1973*[1]

IT WAS A MARK of their estrangement that Nixon, before seeing Mitchell, felt the need to confer with Haldeman, Ehrlichman, and Dean. The group gathered in Nixon's Executive Office Building (EOB) office on the afternoon of March 21, 1973. Dean continued to deceive: When Nixon asked what should be done about Howard Hunt's demand for $120,000—evidence the president never definitively authorized the payments in the morning's "cancer" meeting—Dean responded: "Mitchell and LaRue are now aware of it, so they know how [Hunt] is feeling." *What were Mitchell and LaRue planning to do?* "Well, I have not talked with either of them," Dean said. That was a lie: It was from Dean that Fred LaRue had learned of Hunt's latest demand in the first place.

Before they arrived in Nixon's office, Dean had cornered Haldeman and warned that "if the cover-up was to proceed, we would have to draw the wagons in a circle around the White House." "The best tactic to deal with the entire matter," he told Haldeman, "would be to get Mr. Mitchell to step forward, because if [the prosecutors] got Mr. Mitchell . . . that would solve everybody's problem. . . . They would have a big fish." In Nixon's presence, Ehrlichman piled on, arguing Mitchell should "step out." Nixon fidgeted. Mitchell's sacrifice made him uneasy. The tape ends with him abruptly fleeing his own office: "I don't have any time. I am sorry. I have to leave."[2]

At eleven the next morning, Mitchell arrived at Haldeman's West Wing office. Already present were Ehrlichman and Dean. What transpired next spawned the tenth and final "overt act" attributed to Mitchell in his indictment. Once again, accounts differed sharply on the crucial point: whether Mitchell, as the special prosecutors alleged, "assured Ehrlichman that E. Howard Hunt, Jr., was not a 'problem' any longer."

Mitchell, of course, denied reassuring anyone. "I would not know whether Hunt's problems have been taken care of or not," he told the Senate. Asked at the impeachment hearings if the March 22 meeting touched at all on Hunt's demand, Mitchell replied "none whatsoever," adding, with certain logic: "I didn't know whether LaRue had followed through on his conversation with me or not, so I would not have any basis to make that statement [that Hunt was no longer a problem]."

The most damning testimony about Mitchell's role in the March 22 meeting came, as usual, from Dean. Speaking with Haldeman four days later, as recorded in *The Haldeman Diaries*, Dean claimed that "in the meeting . . . Mitchell said there was no problem on this matter, and that's all we knew about it." More remarkable than Haldeman's entry, however, was the *absence* of one on March 22—the day on which Mitchell supposedly said, in Haldeman's presence, that Hunt was no longer a problem. Dean also recounted the March 22 meeting for Nixon on April 16, 1973:

Ehrlichman said at that time, "Well, is the problem with Hunt straightened out?" He said it to me, and I said, "Well, ask the man who may know: Mitchell." Mitchell said, "I think that problem is solved."

Ehrlichman remembered it differently. "It was *Mr. Dean* saying just, 'Is that matter taken care of?' without reference to Hunt or anybody," Ehrlichman told the Senate. Mitchell responded, Ehrlichman said, by "sort of grunting and saying, 'Maybe' or 'I guess so' or something very vague." Nor did Haldeman remember the former attorney general offering the "assurances" alleged by the WSPF: "Mitchell . . . turned to Dean and said, 'Let me raise another point. Have you taken care of the other problem—the Hunt problem?' Something like that. . . . Dean kind of looked a little flustered and said, 'Well, well, no. I don't know where that is,' or something. And Mitchell said, 'Well, I guess it's taken care of.' And so we *assumed* from that that Mitchell *had* taken care of it."

Three of four attendees at the meeting thus agreed: Mitchell never "assured" Ehrlichman that Hunt was no longer a problem. Only Dean seemed to hear the words escape Mitchell's lips. No matter; on this charge, too, the jury in *U.S. v. Mitchell* convicted the former attorney general.[3]

Still later on the afternoon of March 22, the same cast trudged into Nixon's EOB office. It marked the last time Mitchell saw Nixon during his presidency and the *only* time these five central players—Nixon, Mitchell, Haldeman, Ehrlichman, and Dean—met face-to-face. It must have been a nerve-wracking experience for Dean; at any moment talk could have turned to the question of who authorized the break-in, and after Mitchell's denial, heads would have turned Dean's way. Yet the anticipated Armageddon never happened. Instead, after strained pleasantries, the session swiftly degenerated into the kind of aimless, purposeless colloquy Nixon favored. Amazingly, those issues most desperately in need of resolution—responsibility for the break-in, the status of the hush money, the likelihood they would all soon be indicted—the participants never got around to discussing. The closest they came was when Mitchell made passing reference to impeachment, the first person to do so in Nixon's presence.

The former attorney general advised Nixon to rescind his claim of executive privilege against the Ervin committee, with three conditions. First, the White House could not, on separation-of-powers grounds, allow Dean, the president's lawyer, to appear before the committee; other White House aides could only be interrogated in executive session; and only about Watergate, without senators straying into areas like "Henry Kissinger, foreign affairs."

Soon the president cleared the room except for Mitchell. Alone with his old friend for the last time, the president harkened back to the Eisenhower days, sneering at Ike's decision to force the resignation of his chief of staff, Sherman Adams, when it surfaced that Adams had accepted gifts from a businessman under investigation. "What happened with Adams," Nixon began, "I don't want it to happen with Watergate. . . . I think [Adams] made a mistake, but he shouldn't have been sacked. . . . And, uh, for that reason, I am perfectly willing to—I don't give a shit what happens. I want you all to stonewall it, let them plead the Fifth Amendment, cover up or anything else, if it'll save it—save the plan. That's the whole point."

Investigators later cited these remarks as irrefutable evidence of both men's complicity in the Watergate cover-up. Largely ignored was the absence of any response by Mitchell and Nixon's next words, which were prompted by the rectitude he saw, and resented, in his old law partner. "On the other hand, uh, uh, I would prefer, as I said to you, that you do it the other way. And I would particularly prefer to do it the other way if it's going to come out that way, anyway."

Mitchell began to respond ("Well—") but Nixon continued his lament. It would be unfair to fire men like Haldeman and Dean. "Eisenhower—that's all he ever cared about. Christ, 'Be sure he was clean.' Both in the [Checkers] thing and the Adams thing. But I don't look at it that way. And I just—that's the thing I am really concerned with. We're going to protect our people if we can."[4]

Eighteen hours later the roof caved in, and all that remained of the life Mitchell had worked since 1938 to build—honor and distinction in the legal fraternity, solid standing in the Establishment—was destroyed forever. On Friday, March 23, spectators who had queued up to observe the sentencing of the Watergate defendants watched Judge John J. Sirica take the bench and announce he would first deal with a "preliminary matter." McCord had written Sirica a letter on March 19 that the judge, citing an appearance of impropriety, had initially refused to accept. Now "Maximum John" read the letter aloud. "In the interest of justice," McCord had written, "and in the interest of restoring faith in the criminal justice system . . . I will state the following . . ."

1. There was political pressure applied to the defendants to plead guilty and remain silent.
2. Perjury occurred during the trial in matters highly material to . . . the government's case.
3. Others involved in the Watergate operation were not identified during the trial.

Saying he had "never done this before" in fifteen years on the bench, Sirica deferred sentencing McCord until they could meet in chambers, in the presence of counsel and a stenographer. Next the judge sentenced the other defendants, with a severity that validated his nickname but was also, he announced, "provisional," contingent on the men's willingness to testify more candidly before the grand jury and Senate. Liddy, the stoic, convicted of conspiracy, burglary, and eavesdropping, received a sentence of six to twenty years; Barker, Martinez, Sturgis, and Gonzalez, each of whom had pleaded guilty to the same charges as Liddy, got the maximum, forty years each; and

Hunt, the career spy who made an impassioned plea for mercy ("Four children without a mother; I ask that they not lose their father, as well") received Sirica's unique brand of it: thirty-five years.

The reverberations from McCord's letter proved, as the *Times* noted, "explosive . . . immediate and dramatic." Earl Silbert announced the grand jury would be reconvened the following Monday. McCord, free on bond and sporting a new lawyer, appeared that Friday at the Dirksen Building offices of Sam Dash, the Georgetown University professor named chief counsel to the Ervin committee, and Fred Thompson, the Tennessee lawyer appointed minority counsel.

Previously unpublished documents show that McCord gave Dash a rather muddled account of the origins and execution of the Watergate operation, hampered both by the inherent limitations of McCord's testimony—mostly hearsay derived from Liddy, and even then severely garbled in the retelling—and, too, by McCord's dishonesty. He omitted the fact that he had begun wiretapping Spencer Oliver's DNC telephone a full three days before Liddy's men gained first entry; that he had directed Baldwin to focus "primarily" on sex talk; that he had censored and withheld the wiretap data from Liddy; and so on. What McCord did tell Dash was sometimes preposterous. "Liddy got Mitchell to change [the target] from O'Brien's apartment to O'Brien's office at the DNC," McCord charged, adding Liddy "also got permission from Mitchell to delay the project." In no other account of Watergate was O'Brien's apartment mentioned as a target, nor had Liddy secured Mitchell's sanction for delay; rather Liddy had chafed at Mitchell's *slowness* to approve the project.

The news media feasted like never before. Mitchell had told reporters he didn't have "the faintest idea what McCord intends to reveal," but his blissful ignorance would not last long. On March 26, the *Times* led with a story headlined: "McCord Reported to Link Mitchell to Bugging Plot." Similar stories ran in the *Washington Post* and *Los Angeles Times*. Roiled by the commotion, Martha Mitchell dialed the *New York Times* office and declared, with characteristic delicacy, that somebody was trying to make John Mitchell "the goat" in

Watergate. "I fear for my husband," she said. "I'm really scared. I have a definite reason. I can't tell you why. But they're not going to pin anything on him. I won't let them, and I don't give a damn who gets hurt. I can name names."

Struggling to keep his alcoholic wife in check, the former attorney general missed an appointment with the president. "You saw the paper, so you know why I didn't come by yesterday," he told Haldeman on March 28. No, Haldeman said, he hadn't seen the paper; what was Mitchell talking about? "Martha told me she called the *Times*," Mitchell said. "Good Lord, what did she say?" "Just what you'd expect someone full of whiskey to say," Mitchell snapped.[5]

In fact, Martha had anticipated the scandal's next phase, wherein each of Mitchell's former protégés, certain *he* was being made the scapegoat, sought reassurance from his former mentor. The first to arrive at Mitchell's door—always a step ahead—was Dean, who was mulling fleeing the country. "Mitchell could arrange it," he fantasized. "He, too, might consider going to some country where we'd be safe from prosecution." When Dean asked if he was "being set up," Mitchell, surely knowing better, assured him the White House would never do that to him.[6]

Next was Magruder, who visited Mitchell in New York on March 27. Fearing for his future, Magruder foraged for assurances that if he went to prison he would receive family and legal support, executive clemency, employment assistance. Mitchell supposedly advised him to "continue to hold with the cover story . . . and the conditions would be met." "I can't accept [assurances] from you," Magruder replied, calling into question his purpose in visiting Mitchell in the first place, "because you are here in New York." If similar promises could be extracted from Haldeman—the preeminent symbol, outside of the president himself, of White House power—Magruder would "feel better." The two agreed to meet with Haldeman at the White House the next day.[7]

Seated in Haldeman's office on the morning of March 28,

Mitchell later recalled, Magruder returned to "this perjury question." The trio embarked on what Mitchell described as "a quick run-through" of the improvisations Mitchell, Dean, and Magruder had spun back in September 1972, shortly before Magruder's third appearance before the grand jury, when they needed to come up with an explanation for the two pencil entries in Magruder's desk diary recording the Liddy presentations in the attorney general's office. It was, in short, Mitchell's recurring nightmare, triggered anew by McCord's defection: how to explain the Gemstone meetings. Haldeman icily told Magruder he had better iron out the differing stories with Dean and Mitchell directly.

The ensuing showdown took place that afternoon, in a vacated West Wing office. Mitchell, Magruder, and Dean—the three Gemstone veterans—approached this session, their last together, warily; Magruder, who had borne the heaviest burden of perjury at the grand jury and break-in trial, was wariest of all. He trusted Mitchell, but not Dean, who had begun sending signals he was not going to stick with the story all three had agreed upon when Magruder's diary was subpoenaed. Mitchell and Dean, meanwhile, had also spoken the day before, and the message the former attorney general sternly delivered to the younger man boiled down to: *Stiffen up.* According to Haldeman, who recounted Dean's side of the discussion to the president, Mitchell also warned Dean that if his recollection of the Gemstone meetings differed from Mitchell's, Dean would have "a problem because you won't be believed."

Magruder sought common ground. "I said to Mr. Dean that . . . he had to be able to agree there was only one meeting [in Mitchell's office], because that was [our] agreement. . . . Mr. Mitchell indicated, I think, his willingness to work on that problem with me; but Mr. Dean said that he hoped he would not have to testify. And I said, 'Fine, if you don't have to testify, there is no problem. But,' I said, 'what happens if you *do* testify?' [Dean] said, 'I can't give you any assurances as to what I would do.'" Now Magruder became desperate.

"If you go back and say, 'Actually we discussed intelligence,' I am two feet in the grave!" Mitchell, according to Magruder, tried to play "conciliator," saying he was sure Dean would step up when the time came. Magruder left the meeting scarcely reassured—and "furious" at Dean.

Dean, for his part, recalled Magruder nervously clasping his hands, Mitchell gripping his pipe, gaze averted, face "long and gray." "I was very evasive with them," Dean testified. "They were getting the message that I wasn't going to perjure myself. . . . I liked Jeb as a friend, and I wanted to let him down very easily. He had a problem with my testimony, as did Mitchell, and I wasn't going to budge an inch." Then Dean recalled that the former attorney general, responding to Dean's speculation about ultimate culpability in Watergate, suddenly and surprisingly *admitted* having ordered the break-in, under the mistaken belief that the men Liddy selected for the mission would have no connections to the campaign committee. When this passage from *Blind Ambition* was read to him one week before he died, in November 1988, Mitchell reacted incredulously. "Ridiculous," he spat, interrupting the reading. "This conversation's ridiculous." At the part where he admitted guilt, Mitchell clucked: "Oh, jeez." And when the passage was over: "Pardon me while I go out and throw up."

Dean's story carried great significance: the one and only time John Mitchell admitted authorizing the Watergate break-in. *But was it true?* The story first surfaced in Dean's executive session testimony before the Senate. Here, however, Dean made no mention of Mitchell having asked for Dean's hypothesis. Nine days later, in public session, Dean for the first time identified the fateful exchange as having come during the March 28 showdown, "at the end." Once again, Dean made no mention of Mitchell soliciting any hypotheses. At the House impeachment hearings, none of this—the March 28 showdown, the great Mitchell admission—came up at all. At *U.S. v. Mitchell*, Dean told a story largely in accord with the version he gave in *Blind Ambition*. Each retelling was liable to differ in its account of what Mitchell actually said: whether he thought the DNC operation would be "one or two times" removed from CRP, "three or four times." As usual, no investigator showed any interest in Dean's discrepancies.

At no time, however, did Dean claim that Mitchell made his momentous admission when Jeb Magruder was out of the room; indeed, Dean's accounts invariably implied that Magruder was present when Mitchell incriminated himself. Why, then, did Magruder not readily recall it? As Mitchell's sole accuser in the Key Biscayne conflict, surely Magruder had compelling incentive to remember Mitchell confessing his ultimate responsibility for the DNC operation in front of a corroborating witness like Dean.

Yet Magruder never mentioned any such confession by Mitchell to the Senate, in either executive or public session, nor in his book, *An American Life*—all forums in which Magruder recounted the March 28 showdown at length. Not until his testimony at *U.S. v. Mitchell*, offered, like Dean's, in exchange for leniency, did Magruder suddenly recall this unforgettable moment Dean claimed they both witnessed, and even then Magruder's recollection clashed with Dean's. The sharp conflicts in the three men's recollections, characteristic of their doomed entanglement, created, at a minimum, reasonable doubt that Mitchell ever said anything of the kind.[8]

However, even if Mitchell did not volunteer the mea culpa ascribed to him, his mere presence at the March 28 meeting, and in similar discussions around this time, belied his culpability in the scandal. He was party to these discussions because he feared disclosure of the Gemstone meetings—a prospect made inevitable by McCord's rupture—and he wanted to learn, before the grand jury did, what the other attendees of those meetings would testify had happened in them. Mitchell never ordered the Watergate operation, never even heard a proposal targeting that site, but he'd sat at the pinnacle of American law enforcement and twice listened to Gordon Liddy propose similar crimes and never ordered Liddy arrested or fired. Never mind that Mitchell rejected Liddy's plans; it was the same calculus, about the terrible appearance of it all, that had first thrust Mitchell into the cover-up, when Magruder faced the grand jury.

The cannibalism unleashed by the McCord letter did not go unnoticed, or unfelt, by Richard Nixon. On March 27, the president had listened as Haldeman related the view, fast gaining adherents, that "Mitchell could cut this whole thing off, if he would just step forward. . . . Mitchell did sign off on it. And if that's what it is, the empire will crack . . . all the people getting whacked around in order to keep the thing from focusing on John Mitchell, when inevitably it is going to end up that way, anyway." As usual, Nixon was wracked by indecision and unsure how, or whether, to approach his old friend. He couldn't answer The Question: *Did Mitchell do it?* "What I can't understand," he told Haldeman, "is how Mitchell would ever approve [the break-in]. Magruder I can understand. . . . He is not a very bright fellow. . . . Mitchell knows enough not to do something like that."

Yet minutes later the president could be heard agreeing "the only way" forward was for him to call Mitchell onto the Oval Office carpet and demand he sacrifice himself to the national interest—a scene Nixon immediately began rehearsing. "You've got to tell us what the score is, John. You have to face up to where we are." Within seconds, though, Nixon began backing off; who was he to advise Mitchell to waive his rights?

> NIXON: Well, what is Mitchell's option, though? . . . Does Mitchell come in and say, "My memory was faulty, I lied"?
> EHRLICHMAN: No, he can't say that. He says—ah.
> NIXON: "That without intending to, I may have been responsible for this, and I regret it very much but I did not realize what they were up to. They were—we were talking about apples and oranges." That's what I think he would say. Don't you agree?
> HALDMAN: I think so. He authorized apples and they bought oranges. Yeah.

NIXON: Mitchell, you see, is never going to go in and admit perjury. I mean, he may say he forgot about Hunt, Liddy and all the rest, but he is never going to do that.

HALDEMAN: [The prosecutors] won't give him that convenience. . . . He is as high up as they've got.

EHRLICHMAN: He is the big enchilada.

That day, and serially over the next two weeks, Nixon, Haldeman, and Ehrlichman threw out names of men who might get Mitchell to walk the plank—upright New York lawyer types—only to reject them all. Ehrlichman thought Nixon himself should do it; the president thought Ehrlichman should. In the wake of John Dean's disclosure to his confederates in early April that he had retained criminal counsel, and even darker intimations that he was actively cooperating with the prosecutors, Nixon had already deputized Ehrlichman, amateur sleuth in the Plumbers' heyday, to undertake his own probe of the scandal; by Nixon's lights, Ehrlichman was now the resident Watergate expert. "I don't think there's anybody that can talk to Mitchell except somebody that knows this case," Nixon pleaded with Ehrlichman on Saturday, April 14. Nixon then rehearsed another scenario. "The president has asked me to see you," Ehrlichman was to say, before urging Mitchell to run to the prosecutors and declare: "I assume the responsibility. Nobody in the White House is involved, et cetera and so on. We did try to help these defendants afterwards, yes."

Ehrlichman, long contemptuous of Mitchell and desperate to preserve his power in this season of upheaval, warmed to his task. Fancying himself not only a detective but a dramatist, he precociously acted out the lines he alone could deliver to the fearsome former attorney general. "The jig is up," he would say, "and the president strongly feels that the only way that this thing can wind up being even a little net plus for the administration and for the presidency . . . is for you to go in and voluntarily make a statement, a statement that basically says, 'I am both morally and legally responsible.' "

Only Haldeman, whom Mitchell always regarded as "a different kettle of fish from Ehrlichman," interrupted the rehearsals, equal parts spite and delusion, with a kind word for the former attorney general. "I don't think Mitchell did order the Watergate bugging and I don't think he was specifically aware of the Watergate bugging at the time it was instituted," Haldeman declared. "I honestly don't." The others blithely ignored this and continued fine-tuning the script. Nixon feared Mitchell, if confronted, would "take the offensive," lay the whole thing off on the White House. For this contingency Ehrlichman prepared fresh dialogue. "Look, John, we're past the point where we can be concerned about whether people in the White House are involved," he would say. "The thing is not going to go away, John, and by your sitting up there in New York pretending that it is, is just making it worse."

Nixon had some final rewrites in mind, playing up the agony the affair was visiting on the president and explaining why Nixon himself wasn't confronting his old law partner. "I think you've got to say that this is the toughest decision he's made"—Nixon here was indulging his fondness for third-person references to himself—"tougher than Cambodia and May 8 and December 18 put together." These were the dates of Nixon's most momentous war decisions: the mining of Haiphong Harbor and the launching of the Christmas Bombing of 1972, respectively. "He just can't bring himself to talk to you about it," Nixon wanted Ehrlichman to say. "Just can't do it. And he directed that I talk to you." The script was approved.

A final matter remained. Ehrlichman thought he should create a "record" of his talk with Mitchell. "Maybe I ought to get my office geared up so that I can do that," he said. Like Nixon, Ehrlichman was an inveterate surreptitious taper of his office conversations; previous victims included everyone from Richard Helms and Pat Gray to John *and* Martha Mitchell. Though his first impulse was to endorse Ehrlichman's suggestion ("Do you have a way to gear it up? Well, go gear it!"), Nixon suddenly remembered who the intended victim was and had second thoughts. Finally, he gave his blessing to the electronic entrapment of his strong man—on one condition: The president didn't want his nose rubbed in the dirty business. "I don't want to hear the record," he ordered. "Don't have me hear the record."

After nearly three hours, the group adjourned with Ehrlichman primed, in cloak-and-dagger vernacular, to smoke Mitchell out. Haldeman placed the call; the former attorney general began making his way to Washington. A "damn painful" business it was, Nixon thought. "Mitchell's case is a killer," he rasped.[9]

A GREAT TRIAL

They didn't want their little witness [Dean] tarnished. . . . Why the hell that committee didn't drag the CIA people up there and put 'em over the coals to find out [their role], I'll never know. . . . They all got their picture on television and then they forgot about these things.

—*John Mitchell, 1988*[1]

BY EARLY APRIL 1973 the Watergate grand jury was back in business, summoning James McCord for a repeat performance of the hearsay account he had given the Ervin committee. The Senate panel was set to begin televised hearings the following month. These twin probes, by the prosecutors and Congress, finally made the cover-up impracticable and spelled the effective end of the Nixon presidency. For those at the center, the scandal was a media-age maelstrom from which there was no hope of escape. "They dragged hundreds of people—contributors, workers in the campaign, members of the administration, friends of Nixon—into a great big Roman amphitheater," Maurice Stans recalled, "and they each had to individually fight their way out to prove they were entitled to get out."

Soon the men who regarded Mitchell as a "father figure" queued up to inform him, each in turn, of their cooperation with the prosecutors—in effect, to pay their last respects. First in line, as usual, was

Dean, who met Mitchell for the last time on April 10 at Mitchell's law office. Twenty days away from being fired by Nixon on national television, Dean was already bargaining for immunity with the grand jury and Senate. Before seeing Mitchell, Dean contacted his lawyer, Charles N. Shaffer, who conferred with the prosecutors. Shaffer's advice was to feel Mitchell out—but not, under any circumstances, to discuss any planned testimony with him. Then Shaffer relayed an indecent proposal from the boys at Justice: How did Dean feel about wearing a hidden microphone and surreptitiously recording his meeting with Mitchell? Dean exploded in anger. "You can tell those guys to go fuck themselves! Jesus Christ, Charlie. It's hard enough for me to turn on Mitchell. I'll be damned if I'm going to set him up like some Mafia informant."

The ensuing meeting Dean recounted twice: in a memorandum to the file two days later and, in lengthier form, in his 1976 memoir. As usual, Dean's two accounts contained significant discrepancies; but on balance he claimed Mitchell gently exhorted him not to testify, to consider the implications for Nixon's presidency and invoke one, or all, of the applicable privileges: executive, attorney-client, Fifth Amendment. Dean politely demurred. Those courses could bring contempt charges, and Dean said he preferred eating bean soup in the Senate basement to a cell in the D.C. jail. When Dean mused aloud about fleeing the country, Mitchell said he might join him; when Dean said he would take his wife, Mo, Mitchell expressed uncertainty about bringing Martha.

But the circumstances were too pressing for small talk. Mitchell abruptly asked if it was true that Dean had promised Gordon Liddy a million-dollar budget for his intelligence plans. Dean sloughed off the question and recalled—in his memo of the meeting, but not in his book—that he responded by turning the tables and accusing Mitchell of having issued the illegal orders to enlist Herb Kalmbach and use the White House fund to pay the Watergate defendants' hush money.

Within an hour the conversation had run its course. Dean urged Mitchell to retain counsel—the first person to so advise the former attorney general, who supposedly replied that if charges came, he would just "stonewall it." As a final plea, Mitchell asked Dean to keep him informed of what happened in the grand jury room; Dean demurred, citing Rule 6-E, the grand jury secrecy rule. They wished each other luck; Mitchell said he'd need it. The next time they saw each other, Dean was taking the oath at *U.S. v. Mitchell*.[2]

Four days later, a black government limousine pulled up the White House driveway and disgorged Mitchell and his ever-loyal secretary, Susie Morrison. Nervously eyeing their arrival from his office window was H. R. Haldeman, who at that precise moment happened to be on the phone with Jeb Magruder. The CRP deputy was announcing, in a "broken voice," his decision to begin cooperating, that very day, with the Watergate prosecutors. "I'm going to plead guilty and go to jail," Magruder sighed. "I've got no defense now. They've got witnesses on top of witnesses on top of witnesses . . . and I can't do it for John anymore"—a reference to Mitchell. Haldeman, having caught the bug, was secretly taping the call.

HALDEMAN: Does [Mitchell] know this?
MAGRUDER: I, I want to talk to him but I wanted to wait till I had made the firm decision rather than—
HALDEMAN: Yeah.
MAGRUDER: —hassling with him about whether I should or I shouldn't. As you know, up until yesterday, he's asked me to hold—
HALDEMAN: Huh.
MAGRUDER: —and I can't hold. . . . I mean, I've held long enough. . . . I really think, Bob, you should realize that, you know, the whole thing is going to go. . . . They're *all* going to go. I mean there isn't anybody now that is going to hold. Except Mitchell, I think.

Nimbly working the phones, Haldeman arranged for Mitchell, who had been summoned for a meeting with the president, to be diverted to Ehrlichman's office. Here was Mitchell's first clue something sinister was afoot. The second came when Ehrlichman opened his door. After bare pleasantries, Mitchell later testified, his host made an unusual request. "Most of the times when I met with John Ehrlichman, we sat on a sofa or chairs around the coffee table in one corner of the office and sort of relaxed," Mitchell said. "This particular time I was invited to sit in front of Mr. Ehrlichman's desk. After the meeting was over and I was reflecting upon it, it occurred to me that was an unusual procedure, and it might very well have been for the purpose of recording it." Indeed: While Mitchell and Morrison waited outside, Ehrlichman hid the recorder in his wastepaper basket.

The House Judiciary Committee transcript of the two men's tête-à-tête, in which Ehrlichman had vowed to tell Mitchell "you are as guilty as hell" and "the jig is up," later showed that for all his Oval Office bravado, the White House aide completely wilted, like many before him, in the presence of the Big Enchilada. Ehrlichman began by saying the president was "troubled" that some individuals might think they were best serving him by keeping silent. "Now, obviously, you're in a situation of jeopardy, and other people are, too," Ehrlichman said. "Jeb Magruder has decided to make a clean breast of things and to take a guilty plea, so that pretty well starts to work from the middle in all directions. . . . In addition, it's coming unstuck in a number of other areas—"

"I'd like to know about it," Mitchell interrupted. Ehrlichman explained that the prosecutors were now focused on post–June 17 activities, "the obstruction of justice aspect." Howard Hunt's recent cooperation with the grand jury had begun creating difficulties for Paul O'Brien, the CRP lawyer who had served as a conduit for some of Hunt's money demands. Mere mention of Hunt and O'Brien was intended to scare Mitchell, whom Ehrlichman believed culpable in the hush-money payments. "They will make a very wide-ranging case of the aftermath business." On what basis? Mitchell asked. Obstruction of justice and conspiracy, Ehrlichman replied.

> **MITCHELL:** In what way did they obstruct justice?
> **EHRLICHMAN:** In inducing the defendants to withhold testimony, is their theory for corrupt [inaudible]—
> **MITCHELL:** Is, is that factually true?
> **EHRLICHMAN:** I don't—I, I can't say that it is, from anything that I've been able to find. I have, I have not been able to find any direct, efficient actor who made that assertion.

Here Ehrlichman retreated, stammering in demurral after Mitchell effectively dared him to make a direct charge of complicity in the payment of hush money. Since Ehrlichman had bullied Mitchell with mentions of Magruder, O'Brien, and Hunt, Mitchell returned the favor with a thrust at Ehrlichman's own soft spot. The reason hush money was paid at all, the former attorney general suggested, was "to keep the lid on all the other things that were going on over here that would have been worse, I think, than the Watergate business." Here Mitchell made two incisions with one thrust: He obliquely raised the Ellsberg break-in and other Plumbers activities Ehrlichman had overseen ("all the other things that were going on"), while emphasizing they were White House, not CRP, operations ("going on over here"). Ehrlichman dialed back to the prosecutors and their focus on the hush money; Mitchell again steered the talk back to the liabilities of Ehrlichman and Haldeman, mentioning the White House fund of $350,000.

So far, the most accurate forecast of the conversation had come from Nixon, who rightly feared Mitchell would "take the offensive." Ehrlichman gamely returned to the question of what Mitchell should do next, suggesting along the way that Mitchell's guilt in the affair was paramount. "You're the captain of your own boat on this," Ehrlichman said. "But the president wanted you to [know] that he is extraordinarily troubled by the situation in which you find yourself, and, and therefore, everybody finds themselves." What did Brother Dick have in mind? Mitchell asked. The president had few options, Ehrlichman replied darkly.

Mitchell responded with two suggestions of his own. First, Nixon should "take care of his house in an appropriate way" (translation: fire you, Haldeman, Dean, and everyone else who's in this thing up to his eyeballs) and also take care "not to impinge on anybody's rights"—a warning that Mitchell had no intention of taking the rap. Mitchell also brought up Dean's meetings with Nixon in February and March, which he said had "unfortunately" created "a scenario . . . around the president" as to "when this knowledge was available." Here Mitchell raised the ugliest specter of all: criminal prosecution of the president himself.

Unaware he was being taped, Mitchell then offered his frankest and fullest explanation of the origins of Watergate, worth quoting at length.

> **MITCHELL:** There is no way that I'm going to do anything except staying where I am, because I'm too far, uh, far out. The fact of the matter is that I got euchred into this thing, when I say, by not paying attention to what these bastards were doing. And well, you know how far back this goes— this, the whole genesis of this thing was over here, as you're perfectly well aware.
> **EHRLICHMAN:** No, I didn't know that.
> **MITCHELL:** And Gordon—well, Gordon Liddy and John Dean—well, it, it goes back, I think, even further than that. But I've never been able to put the pieces together. Bob Haldeman and I were talking about this Sandwedge operation.
> **EHRLICHMAN:** I do—I remember the name.
> **MITCHELL:** Yeah, and it turned out that that was to be an entirely different operation, of course. And then it turned out that we just couldn't get enough [inaudible] players. Caulfield

couldn't do it. . . . The next order of events for the sequence was when Dean and Magruder and Liddy show up in my office with this presentation about a million-dollar intelligence operation, which we, of course, laughed at.

EHRLICHMAN: Yeah.

MITCHELL: We threw him the hell out of there. And of course, Jeb blames John Dean on that. One of the problems that—

EHRLICHMAN: Blames him for what? Turning down?

MITCHELL: No, for authorizing Liddy to prepare the—

EHRLICHMAN: Oh, oh, I see.

MITCHELL:—the million-dollar [plan]. One of the problems is, is to what if Jeb goes public. Good God, he's got a, an imagination which is incredible.

EHRLICHMAN: He's got twenty different stories.

MITCHELL: I know. Well, that was the last time I ever saw Liddy or ever talked to him until—what?—the fifteenth of June [1972], when [CRP spokesman] Van Shumway dragged him into my office with a letter to the *Washington Post* to sign about a campaign finance file. So I have had no contact with Liddy. I've never seen Hunt. And as far as Jeb and all of the dirty tricks department, I never knew a goddamn thing about it.

EHRLICHMAN: Uh-huh.

MITCHELL: So as far as my having made all these public statements [denying foreknowledge of the break-in], I'm just going to go ahead with it.

EHRLICHMAN: Just go ahead, and just, just let them come to you, in effect.

MITCHELL: Oh, yeah.

EHRLICHMAN: Yeah.

MITCHELL: Yeah, I'm going to have to do that. There is no other course. . . . I really don't have a guilty conscience. I didn't authorize these bastards.

Convinced the former attorney general had ordered the break-in, Ehrlichman needed time to regroup from Mitchell's forceful denials. Late in the match and behind on points, Ehrlichman pressed his boldest thrust yet. "They say that they've got you made here," he said, in the style of Jimmy Cagney. "You mean the U.S. attorney's office?" Mitchell asked. Yes, Ehrlichman said. Did they say how? Mitchell asked. "No. And this was before anybody knew that Magruder was going to go in." "I just don't believe it," Mitchell replied. Finally, as much for Nixon's ears, he reaffirmed: "There's certainly no possibility that I would ever turn around and say, 'Yes, I was part and parcel of this.' "

With that, Ehrlichman asked his secretary to book their guests return flights to New York ("American Airlines, first class," Mitchell snapped). But Mitchell wasn't done. He wanted updates on the grand jury: "I would like to be kept advised, within propriety, as to what the hell is going on down here." Ehrlichman mumbled about the poor intelligence flow. When Mitchell inquired again about the case being built against him, Ehrlichman replied: "The way the story is supposed to go, Magruder brought you a memorandum that said on it, 'We are now ready to go with this operation. We will need such and such amount of money. Here are the targets that are possible. Please pick the targets that you want.' " Are you serious? Mitchell asked. "Yes, sir. And, that you," Ehrlichman continued, "by some designation, circles or checks or something, picked the targets and authorized the operation." "That's about as far from the truth as it's possible to get," Mitchell replied.

Ehrlichman asked if Mitchell still wished to see the man in whose name he had been summoned to Washington in the first place. "He'd be happy to see you," lied Ehrlichman. "No," Mitchell shrugged. "I don't want to embarrass him." Ehrlichman then urged Mitchell, as Dean had, to retain a criminal lawyer. Before leaving, Mitchell pressed once more for some scrap of information about the extent of his jeopardy: Who were the damaging witnesses on the post–June 17 period? Ehrlichman mentioned Dean and O'Brien.

MITCHELL: Now what do they say is my involvement in it, other than knowing about it?

EHRLICHMAN: Not much. Just that. Knowing and acquiescing, and, uh, calling on Dean for help. And uh, uh, that's about it.

MITCHELL: How did I call on him for help?

EHRLICHMAN: Just saying, uh, "Can you, can you get those fellows over there to help us raise some money," and, uh, uh, not for what, or anything of that kind. I've not found anybody, as I said before, who could be identified as an actor in the process of inducing anybody to perjury or silence, or anything of that kind.

"Is anybody debriefing these witnesses after the grand jury?" Mitchell asked. No, Ehrlichman said; that would be "a violation of some section or another." "Sure in hell was done before the election, I assure you of that," Mitchell snapped.[3]

As Ehrlichman and Mitchell fenced to their bloody draw, the president sat in the Oval Office, getting an update from Haldeman on his depressing chat with Magruder. The news that Magruder was soon to testify against Mitchell, Dean, and Strachan dealt the White House a crushing blow. "Mike Wallace will get [Magruder] on '60 Minutes,' " Ehrlichman had warned, "and he will come across as the All-American Boy who was . . . serving his president, his attorney general, and they misled him."

Now Ehrlichman returned from his tête-à-tête with Mitchell. "All finished?" the president asked airily, as if inquiring about the disposal of an insect. "Yes, sir," Ehrlichman answered: "[Mitchell] is an innocent man in his heart and in his mind, and he does not intend to move off that position." "Give us a little chapter and verse," Nixon clamored, eager to know, after so many hours of rehearsal, how the play had gone. Ehrlichman complied, unreliably: The tapes invariably captured individuals recalling Watergate conversations far differently than they actually transpired. He emphasized how Mitchell, as Nixon had predicted, "lobbed mud balls at the White House at every opportunity," and portrayed his own timidity as a virtue. "I tried to play him with kid gloves. . . . I never asked him to tell me anything. He just told me all this stuff." Ehrlichman then reported on a subject he and Mitchell had *not* covered: the subornation of perjury in September 1972, after Magruder's desk diary was subpoenaed.

EHRLICHMAN: [Mitchell] says Dean talked Magruder into saying the wrong things at the grand jury, and so Magruder's got a problem.
NIXON: My God. . . . Mitchell was there when Dean talked him into saying the wrong things?
EHRLICHMAN: That's what he says. That is what Mitchell says.
NIXON: What does Dean say about it?
EHRLICHMAN: Dean says it was Mitchell and Magruder. It must have been the quietest meeting in history. Everybody's version is that the other two guys talked.

Nixon grew angry at his old friend. "Throwing off on the White House won't help him one damn bit. . . . The White House wasn't running the campaign committee." They talked about Mitchell's trembling hands, the likelihood of his conviction at trial. Haldeman said Dean was going to depict himself as "merely a messenger, a conduit, an agent" in the cover-up. "Boy, Mitchell sure doesn't agree with that," said Ehrlichman.

"I guess we're not surprised at Mitchell are we?" Nixon asked. No, Haldeman said. "What he is saying is partly true. I don't think he did put [the break-in] together." Though he had predicted as much, it still bothered Nixon that Mitchell's defense would pit him against the

White House: "He shouldn't throw the burden over here." Nixon conceded Mitchell was right all along about Charles Colson, the special counsel who had brought Howard Hunt into the White House. Above all, it bothered the president that John N. Mitchell, the strong man, symbol of law and order in the age of radical chic, now stood poised to enter the criminal justice system—as a *defendant*. "This damn case!"[4]

Two days later, Mitchell got a call from Magruder. The younger man announced what both already knew—that he was copping a plea—and bade Mitchell goodbye. Magruder wrote in his memoir that the talk was brief and difficult, but not unpleasant; he tried to convey his "great affection" for Mitchell, even as he made clear his intention to testify in ways sure to result in Mitchell's incarceration. According to previously unpublished testimony, Magruder began the talk with the simple, almost childlike admission: "I talked." "If you are going the other way," Mitchell supposedly replied, "I am going to have to hold, because there is no other choice for me. . . . You and I will be at loggerheads, do you understand?" "I understand," Magruder said. The next, and last, time the two men saw each other was when Magruder took the oath at *U.S. v. Mitchell.*[5]

Fred LaRue was not far behind. The most loyal of Mitchell's lieutenants still had dinner with Mitchell every night ("I don't think I've ever eaten that much Chinese food in my life") but worried about his condition. Who wouldn't crack under the strain of Watergate and Vesco, or the even crueler agonies of Martha Mitchell? "LaRue said he thinks Mitchell is on the verge of breaking, by which he means suicide," Haldeman recorded in his diary. Mitchell was said to be drinking heavily. "It became a problem in the latter stages of Watergate," LaRue recalled. "I put him to bed a few times." The cover-up was unraveling rapidly. On April 16 LaRue surrendered to the U.S. attorney's office; within seventy-two hours, Mitchell was subpoenaed by the grand jury and Seymour Hersh reported in the *New York Times* that prior witnesses had lodged "serious allegations" against Mitchell, with new indictments expected "within the week."[6]

At last, Mitchell retained a lawyer: forty-seven-year-old William G. Hundley Jr., an old-school Irishman from Brooklyn and former federal prosecutor described as "a pioneer of the government's assault on organized crime." As had been his practice with Peter Fleming in the Vesco case, Mitchell barely discussed with Hundley the origins or trajectory of Watergate; in this case, the silence owed both to the swiftness with which events were moving and Mitchell's demeanor. He supplied his lawyer only a rough outline of the Gemstone meetings, and reaffirmed his distance from the hush-money scheme. "He didn't particularly like to talk about the case," Hundley recalled. "He was very fatalistic about what was going to happen. I didn't get a story telling me how innocent he was or anything like that."[7]

April 20, 1973, was the day of reckoning. Assistant U.S. Attorney Seymour Glanzer, who was to examine Mitchell in the grand jury room, was reputed to be "fire-eating," "a bludgeon," "a very bad operator." He swiftly warned Mitchell he was a potential target, then went straight for the jugular: the Gemstone meetings.

> **GLANZER:** I am asking you whether or not you had an obligation to come down to the grand jury and inform them what you knew about the January-February meetings?
> **MITCHELL:** I did not.
> **GLANZER:** You felt you had no obligation?
> **MITCHELL:** I had no obligation.
> **GLANZER:** You had no obligation to advance the interest of justice?
> **MITCHELL:** I had no obligation to come down and inform the grand jury voluntarily of anything.

Glanzer turned to the date of June 20, 1972, three days after the Watergate arrests, when LaRue and Mardian shared with Mitchell the contents of their debriefing of Liddy.

GLANZER: Mr. Mardian did not report to you that Mr. Liddy had confessed to him?

MITCHELL: Not to my recollection, Mr. Glanzer.

GLANZER: That would be something you remembered, if it happened, wouldn't it?

MITCHELL: Yes, I would.

GLANZER: . . . Were you told by either Mr. LaRue or anybody else at the Committee [to Re-Elect the President] prior to June 28, 1972, that Mr. Liddy had told them that he was involved in the Watergate break-in?

MITCHELL: I have no such recollection.

Glanzer's grilling went on for three hours. "And when he came out," reported CBS News' Daniel Schorr, Mitchell "was no longer smiling, but grim." Indeed, Glanzer had scored a direct hit. His exchange with Mitchell about the briefing he got from LaRue and Mardian later formed the basis for a perjury charge, Count Five in the *U.S. v. Mitchell* indictment, on which the former attorney general was convicted and incarcerated.[8]

The scandal was also taking its toll on the Mitchells as a couple. When a family friend called one morning, indignant about a White House plot to "lay it all on Mitchell," Martha, eavesdropping on a separate line, started screaming: "I told you! That Goddamned son-of-a-bitch president!" On the night of May 6, Mrs. Mitchell dialed her old partner in crime, UPI's Helen Thomas, and declared: "Mr. President should resign immediately. I think he let the country down. It's going to take a hell of a lot to get him out. . . . He's been compromised."

It marked the first demand by a prominent figure for Nixon to resign; others soon followed suit. But the atmosphere that Martha's remarks helped create scarcely improved her husband's chances of finding an unbiased jury of his peers. Realizing as much, his patience drained, Mitchell finally turned the tables, picking up an extension during one of his wife's calls to Thomas. "Martha's late night telephone calls have been good fun and games in the past," he growled. "However, this is a serious issue. I'm surprised and disappointed that United Press International would take advantage of a personal phone call made under the stress of the current situation and treat it as a sensational public statement. . . . Any thought of the president resigning is ridiculous."

Speculation swirled, too, about Mitchell's condition. "He was never out of control, or unconscious, or staggering, or weak," said a lawyer who represented Mitchell at the time. "But he was a steady drinker. . . . He would be steadily drinking Scotch every night." *Time* magazine called him the Prisoner of Fifth Avenue.

> If he is depressed, Mitchell reportedly does not talk about it to friends, though they find him looking grayer and older. He has assured them that he has an adequate amount of money for his defense and his family's needs, though he is no millionaire. But not even his friends can say what happens when they are not around and John and Martha alone must confront his besmirched reputation and his shattered career.

What else could the old boy do, but kick back in his Manhattan duplex, put away another bottle of Dewar's, and take notes in front of the television set? Like the rest of the country, Mitchell sat glued to the Senate hearings, which had begun May 17 and, like every newspaper and magazine in America, showcased a daily thrashing of his once-good name. *Watergate! Vesco! ITT! The milk lobby! The Kissinger wiretaps! The Ellsberg break-in! Jimmy Hoffa and the Teamsters cash! Howard Hughes and the Vegas casinos! FBI black bag jobs! CIA assassination plots!* There was, it seemed, no scandal of the era, the "decade of shocks" from 1963 to 1974, in which Mitchell's name did not figure.

And the news media, drunk with power and waist deep at what

Kissinger called the "orgy of recrimination," seldom took care to distinguish leaks from plants, hearsay from eyewitness testimony, fact from fiction. When Mitchell was formally charged in the Vesco case, on May 10, *Newsweek* gleefully enlarged his unsmiling face so readers could see the pores on his nose, and slapped a single word across his bald head: Indicted. *Time*, with equal gaiety, declared: The Inquest Begins.[9]

For the 80 million Americans who watched the televised hearings of the Senate Select Committee on Presidential Campaign Activities, and the millions more who tuned in on radio, 1973 was the Summer of Watergate. The hearings proved, to Nixon's fatal detriment, enormously popular; his approval rating fell, according to the Harris Poll, from 57 percent at the hearings' start to 32 percent at their end. By early August, three-quarters of Americans believed Nixon either planned the break-in, knew about it in advance, or helped cover it up.

The wily Southerner banging the gavel, jowly seventy-six-year-old committee chairman Sam J. Ervin Jr. of North Carolina, was, in Nixon's eyes, a "sharp, resourceful, and intensely partisan political animal." Challenging Nixon gave Ervin a populist persona that belied his retrograde Southern Democrat record: He had opposed the Equal Rights Amendment, Medicare, and consumer legislation; supported the Vietnam War and the draft; and lobbied in behalf of the infamous segregationist manifesto, the Declaration of Constitutional Principles, which encouraged Southern states to defy the Supreme Court's landmark ruling in *Brown v. Board of Education*. Blinded by hatred of Nixon and Mitchell, the national press corps was eager to forget all that and was led, as in much else, by Walter Cronkite, the era's most trusted anchorman, who fawned over Ervin as "this Renaissance man of Washington." Mitchell thought him "a little senile."

Ervin's selection of Sam Dash as majority counsel underscored the intense partisanship that animated the work of the committee. A wiretapping expert, former Philadelphia district attorney, and George-town University law professor, the balding, diminutive Dash, with his Buddy Holly eyeglasses and benign Jewish mien, was actually an imperious, intellectually incurious ("I think we all know what happened on the early morning of June 17," he once dismissively cut off a witness), and fiercely partisan character. As a cross-examiner, he was both unpardonably sloppy, given to multiple, ponderous, often unintelligible queries—Tom Wolfe, watching the hearings, bemusedly hailed the dawn of "a semiliterate variety of solecism known as Dashism"—and anything but impartial, a rabbit-puncher known to use unfaithful paraphrases of prior testimony to frame his follow-ups. The year before, in *Samuel Dash v. John N. Mitchell et al.*, he had sued, in vain, to block the enactment of the Nixon administration's anticrime proposals, and endorsed George McGovern for president.

And the committee Republicans, his natural allies—what could Mitchell expect from them? Howard Baker Jr., a Tennessee lawyer first elected to the Senate in 1966, was the committee's ranking GOP member. Handsome and lively, Baker was thrust into a singularly thankless position, torn between his inclination, as a party man, to defend the president and his instincts, as a smart politician, to ride the televised wave of the fin de siècle, which demanded the president's head. His famous question—"What did the president know, and when did he know it?"—signaled the decision he reached. As minority counsel, Baker chose his thirty-year-old protégé, Fred Thompson. An assistant U.S. attorney whose experience was in bootlegging and bank robbery cases, Thompson offered little promise of protection for the pro-administration witnesses. "Oh, shit," Nixon moaned, upon hearing Thompson's name. "Dash is too smart for that kid."[10]

At ten o'clock on Tuesday morning, July 10, 1973, Mitchell, dressed in Wall Street suit and tie, strode into the hallowed Senate Caucus Room and took the oath, his right hand raised limply before the battalion of photographers. By this point, Mitchell stood formally indicted in the Vesco case and informally accused, on television, of numerous crimes in Watergate: approving the DNC wiretaps; reviewing logs of the illegally intercepted conversations and sending Liddy back into Democratic headquarters; launching the cover-up by ordering McCord sprung from jail; urging Magruder to destroy the Gemstone logs and commit perjury; and instructing Dean in a broad array of black arts, from obtaining FBI reports to paying hush money and extending offers of executive clemency. Of all these alleged acts, Mitchell was in fact guilty of only one: the subornation of Magruder's perjury. To keep the original Gemstone meetings a secret, he had taken extraordinary pains—and still failed.

How the former attorney general proposed to scale the awesome edifice of allegation erected around him became a subject of consuming media interest. A two-week delay in the testimony, occasioned by the visit of Soviet premier Leonid Brezhnev and July Fourth recess, only heightened the anticipation. *Time* reported Mitchell had spent the last month riveted to his TV set, "analyzing every word of testimony, closely watching for weaknesses on the part of each witness and planning to shape an air-tight position." The *London Observer* merely had him "sequestered in his New York apartment and drinking heavily." "He's become somewhat of a mystery man, an unknown force," remarked CBS News' Lesley Stahl. "Sources say not even the White House knows what he will testify to when he takes the stand."

Also of great interest to the press was Martha, whose sanity and marriage were coming unglued in the cruelest, most painfully public way. Every day brought more outlandish behavior. On the evening of June 19, Mrs. Mitchell repeatedly stormed downstairs to rebuke the press camped outside her building, growing more bellicose with each encounter. At ten o'clock she flung a doorman's cap at Associated Press reporter Judy Yablonsky, then cursed and slapped Yablonsky twice. "You are a part of the Communists, every one of you!" she raved at the assembled. "If you dare come on this side of the street I'll call Governor Rockefeller!" The awfulness ended only when little Marty Mitchell, arriving home in a chauffeured car at 10:50 p.m., took her mother by the hand and led her inside. What transpired behind closed doors was equally discouraging. "Martha and John now were communicating only when one of them hurled insults or accusations at the other," Martha's biographer wrote of this period.[11]

The morning after her assault on the press, Martha packed her things and piled into the car with Marty, personal assistant Sandy Hobbs, and the Mitchells' Hungarian chauffeur, Zolton Komadi. The group's first stop was an overnight stay in Hershey, Pennsylvania. "[Martha] spent the whole night drinking out of bottles that she smuggled on, because we didn't know she had packed them," Hobbs recalled in 1992. "She got mad at the driver, Zolton, fired him. She fired people when she got mad at them. So I drove Zolton to the airport, put him on a plane, and I drove the rest of the way." Their next destination was Greenwood, Mississippi, and the antebellum mansion belonging to longtime friends Alleta and Charlie Saunders. There they stayed during Mitchell's three-day stint in the witness chair at the Senate hearings.

At first, Martha took to her new surroundings, relaxing at poolside, finding refuge in the soft breeze and gentle sounds of her native South. Then her husband appeared on television—swearing to tell the truth, the whole truth, and nothing but the truth, so help him God—and Martha fell to pieces. "She started drinking Bloody Marys," her biographer reported, and "as far as is known, she didn't draw a sober breath during the rest of the Mississippi visit." "You're a God-damn liar!" she shouted at her husband's televised image. "Tell the truth!" Convinced Mitchell was inexplicably covering up for Nixon, Martha even dialed Fred Thompson and instructed him to "get John so mad . . . he will blurt it all out." She fought with Marty. She threatened to commit suicide. *Was Mrs. Mitchell in the South?* a reporter asked the former attorney general as he arrived on Capitol Hill. "With that accent," he quipped, "she'll always be in the South." *Were you afraid she'd upstage you?* "This is one occasion where you don't mind being upstaged."[12]

Mitchell waived his opening statement and awaited Dash's on-slaught. The chief counsel started with a brief recap of Mitchell's years in government, stressing the Nixon administration's efforts to combat leaks; the idea was to tie Mitchell first to covert projects in general, then to Liddy, specifically. "During 1971," asked Dash, "were you aware of an intelligence operation that had been set up in the White House under Mr. Ehrlichman and Mr. Krogh which has become known as the Plumbers operation?" No, Mitchell answered; not until after the Watergate arrests had he learned of it. Dash moved to Mitchell's Achilles' heel: the Gemstone meetings. After the witness described the "complete horror story" of Liddy's first presentation, Dash asked why Mitchell hadn't thrown Liddy out of his office. "In hindsight," Mitchell said, "I should have thrown him out of the window." Dash's retort—"Since you did neither"—brought the house down.

Mitchell recounted how he rejected the Gemstone plan for the third time at Key Biscayne. "Then how do you explain, Mr. Mitchell, Mr. Magruder's sworn testimony that you, however reluctantly, approved the quarter-million-dollar Liddy plan at Key Biscayne?" Here Mitchell schooled the professor in the art of cross-examination: "Mr. Dash, I can't explain anybody's testimony up here except my own." It was the first of many times Mitchell used Dash's ill-conceived questions against him.

But Dash did not close his first round of questioning, a full morning's worth, empty-handed. He extracted two key admissions: that Mitchell knew Magruder was going to commit perjury at the grand jury in September 1972 and that Mitchell knew about the Watergate cover-up and "White House horrors" but alerted neither the president nor the prosecutors for fear of jeopardizing Nixon's reelection. Dash also elicited from Mitchell one of two responses that later formed the basis for perjury charges—and convictions—against the former attorney general. The prized moment came during Dash's questioning about the meeting in Mitchell's Watergate apartment on the evening of June 19, 1972, when he supposedly ordered Magruder to burn the Gemstone logs. "I had not heard of the Gemstone files as of that meeting," Mitchell testified, "and as of that date, I had not heard that anybody there at that particular meeting knew of the wiretapping aspects of that, or had any connection with it." Though true—as Liddy could have attested—these words later resurfaced as Count Six in the *U.S. v. Mitchell* indictment.[13]

Fred Thompson used his questioning mostly to summarize the conflicts between Mitchell's testimony and that of his accusers, Magruder and Dean. No, Mitchell said, he had never ordered Dean to enlist Herb Kalmbach or CIA in paying hush money, and no, he had never urged Dean to drain the $350,000 White House fund for like purposes. Then Thompson challenged Mitchell's rationale for doing nothing to stop the cover-up. The key was the briefing Mitchell had gotten from Mardian and LaRue on June 20, 1972, in which, for the first time, Mitchell had learned about the "White House horrors."

> **THOMPSON:** As I understand your testimony this morning, the knowledge you got from that debriefing was really the reason why you, in effect, stood by while Magruder was preparing a story which, according to what you knew . . . was going to be a false story, to present to the grand jury.
>
> **MITCHELL:** Along, Mr. Thompson, with some of the other stories that Mr. Dean later brought forward . . . the Diem papers and the suspected extra-curricular wiretapping, and a few of the others.
>
> **THOMPSON:** Okay. That caused you to take that position with regard to Magruder. And also, I assume that those factors were the reasons why you, in effect, acquiesced, anyway, in the payments to the [defendants'] families of support money and lawyers' fees and that sort of thing, which I am sure you realize could have been pretty embarrassing, to say the least, if not illegal, at that time. Would that be correct so far as your motivations are concerned?

MITCHELL: That is a correct summary of my motivation and rationale for the actions that I did take.[14]

Mitchell's first day of testimony was coming to a close—but more brushes with perjury lay ahead. Herman Talmadge of Georgia, a hawkish Democrat who had been his state's governor and served sixteen years in the Senate, asked if, prior to resigning as attorney general, Mitchell had played an active supervisory role in the Nixon reelection campaign. "What I did," said Mitchell, "was succumb to the president's request to keep an eye on what was going on over there," adding that he had held "frequent" meetings with campaign officials on "matters of policy." *So you did play an active supervisory role?* The word "supervisory" bothered Mitchell; he preferred "consulting." *And it never moved beyond consulting?* No, Mitchell said with a wink—although he sometimes volunteered his opinions "forcefully and strongly."

Now Talmadge, a lawyer with four decades' experience, moved in on his prey. He brandished the transcript of Mitchell's testimony before the Senate Judiciary Committee on March 14, 1972—the Kleindienst-ITT hearings—and wondered if Mitchell remembered what he'd said then, to Senator Kennedy, about his role in the reelection campaign while at Justice. Mitchell read aloud his year-old exchange with Kennedy.

KENNEDY: Do you remember what party responsibilities you had prior to March 1 [1972]?
MITCHELL: Party responsibilities?
KENNEDY: Yes. Republican Party.
MITCHELL: I do not have and did not have any responsibilities. I have no party responsibilities now, senator.

"If I can read the English language correctly," Talmadge said mockingly, "one or the other of your statements is in error." Trapped by a lawyer whose skills equaled his own, Mitchell resorted to semantics. "Senator Kennedy . . . referred to the Republican Party," he explained, "and that was the context in which I took it." Again, Talmadge drew laughter from the crowd: " 'No re-election campaign responsibilities?' I ask you who was running? Mr. Nixon? And is he a Republican?"

> **MITCHELL:** There is no illegality about any presidential appointee engaging in the carrying out of political functions.
> **TALMADGE:** I am not arguing that point, Mr. Mitchell. . . . If I can read the English language in two places, they are the opposite of each other. You state that they aren't. If I understand English, and I learned it in a small country school, in Telfair County—
> **MITCHELL:** So did I, senator, a very small one.
> **TALMADGE:** We both studied the same English, I assume. [Laughter]
> **MITCHELL:** That is why I am surprised you don't agree with my interpretation. [Laughter]

Despite the laughter, and Mitchell's success in getting the last word, Talmadge had given the former attorney general a serious scare. To hammer home his point, the senator introduced into the record two memoranda Jeb Magruder had sent the attorney general, dated December 1971 and January 1972, requesting decisions, respectively, on funding for the RNC and a $45,000 phone bank for the Florida primary. Talmadge marveled at the witness's agility. "You are a good lawyer, Mr. Mitchell," he said—then added, "testifying under oath to a lie is commonly referred to as perjury, is it not?"

The senator wasn't finished. He ran scattershot through Watergate, from Burning Tree to Howard Hunt's final payment, and closed with an angry peroration on the duties of government men. "If they see anything going wrong involving their superior that needs immediate corrective action, they report it instantly," he said. "When you found out all these crimes and conspiracies and cover-ups were being committed, why on earth didn't you walk into the president's office and tell him the truth?" It wasn't a question of telling him the truth, Mitchell replied; it was a question of shielding him from it. "Knowing Richard Nixon, the president, as I do, he would just lower the boom on all of this matter and it would come back to hurt him, and it would affect him in his re-election." The next exchange offered the definitive statement of Mitchell's worldview.

> **TALMADGE:** Am I to understand from your response that you placed the expediency of the next election above your responsibilities as an intimate to advise the president of the peril that surrounded him? . . .
> **MITCHELL:** Senator, I think you have put it exactly correct. In my mind, the re-election of Richard Nixon, compared with what was available on the other side, was so much more important that I put it in just that context.

Mitchell had spent five hours in the witness chair. He was ordered to return the following day to face off against Chairman Ervin.[15]

The North Carolinian began by reminding Mitchell of his exchange with Talmadge, in which Mitchell had argued it was no crime for a presidential adviser to carry out political functions. Wasn't it "rather inexpedient," Ervin asked, for the nation's chief law enforcement officer to have been engaged in political activities? Mitchell agreed it was. Then Ervin dusted off the transcript of Mitchell's 1969 confirmation hearing, at which, in response to Ervin's own questions, the nominee had promised: "Henceforward my duties and functions will be related to the Justice Department, and as the legal and not the political adviser of the president." "I am very sorry that you didn't carry out the purpose you announced on that occasion," Ervin declared. "Mr. Chairman, that would have been my fondest wish," replied Mitchell. "Unfortunately, it is very, very difficult to turn down a request by the president of the United States."

"Wouldn't the evidence justify the inference," Ervin asked, "that you did not communicate your disapproval in such an emphatic enough manner [as] to prevent the bugging and the break-in?" It was a question that undermined Ervin's claim to impartiality and, too, his cherished reputation as the Senate's leading expert on the Constitution. Not only was he ignoring, as an investigator, the exculpatory testimony of Fred LaRue; he was also pressing the dubious legal argument, on the basis of an "inference," that individuals should be held accountable even for crimes they refused to sanction! Mitchell did his best to wade through the muddle, explaining patiently that he had asked Liddy only to devise a counterdemonstration plan, nothing more; but Ervin wouldn't hear it.

The remainder of Ervin's questioning was aimed not at eliciting new information, but at forcing the witness to perform, as the villain, in a ponderous morality play. Accordingly he dragged Mitchell through a rehash of things he'd already admitted he had known about, or learned, but never raised with Nixon: the White House horrors; Hunt's and Liddy's roles in Watergate; Magruder's perjury; the efforts—by others—to silence the defendants with cash. Had Nixon ever asked Mitchell to tell everything he knew about Watergate? No, Mitchell answered, not after their brief chat on the evening of June 20, 1972, in which Mitchell had apologized for not keeping a tighter rein on his men. "Well, if the cat hadn't any more curiosity than that, it would still be enjoying its nine lives," Ervin said to the room's delight, "all of them!" "Well, I hope the president enjoys eight more," Mitchell shot back.

Of the panel's three Republicans, Senator Lowell Weicker of Connecticut emerged as the most opportunistic, transparently hostile to Mitchell and Nixon. After a few preliminaries, he focused on Liddy's Gemstone pitches, especially the first and most fantastical, presented in Mitchell's Justice Department office on January 27, 1972:

WEICKER: The life of every American is, or to a great degree, his liberty, protection of all his rights, sits in the hands of the attorney general of the United States. And do you mean to tell me that you sat there through that meeting and, in fact, actually had the same man come back into your office for a second meeting without in any way alerting appropriate authorities, in this particular case, the president of the United States?

MITCHELL: That is exactly what happened, senator. And as I say, in hindsight, it was a grievous error.

WEICKER: . . . Well, the fact is, forget, for one minute, politics; let's just talk about your position as attorney general of the United States. I find it inconceivable . . . the mentality that you didn't go ahead and have the fellow [Liddy] arrested for even suggesting this to the attorney general of the United States.

MITCHELL: Senator, I doubt if you can get people arrested for suggesting such things, but as I said—

Here Weicker, a graduate of University of Virginia Law School, foolishly cut off the witness, the more accomplished lawyer, to challenge him on statutory interpretation.

WEICKER: For suggesting illegal acts to the attorney general of the United States? I think that probably is grounds for arrest.

MITCHELL: Do you really, senator?

WEICKER: I do, I do.

MITCHELL: I would have some doubts. I don't know what part of Title XVIII [of the U.S. Code] would cover that . . .

Bested on the law, Weicker engaged in theatrics, incredulously asking why Mitchell, speaking with Nixon a few hours after Liddy's first pitch, made no mention of "what had transpired in the office of the attorney general that morning." "I do not know how often you get to talk to the president of the United States," Mitchell jabbed back, "but he is the one that normally initiates the conversation and the subject matters that are discussed." "This is fantasy, this is incredible!" Weicker thundered. "You have the option of talking to the president hours after this idiot is in your office and you say nothing!" By the end of Weicker's questioning, Mitchell's air of unruffled calm appeared to have gotten under the senator's skin. After Mitchell explained why it wouldn't have been unusual for Nixon to keep to himself the contents of his March 21 "cancer on the presidency" meeting with Dean, Weicker, like Dash before him, resorted to rudeness, setting himself up for a classic Mitchell one-liner.

> **WEICKER:** Is this your definition, by the way, this kind of testimony, of—what is the expression—"stonewalling"?
> **MITCHELL:** I don't know that term. Is that a Yankee term from Connecticut?

At last it was Mitchell who brought the house down. Still, Weicker elicited one response from Mitchell that later formed a perjury charge: when Mitchell denied ordering the destruction of the Gemstone documents in his apartment on the evening of June 19, 1972. Weicker also scored with his closing question. He asked if Mitchell, as an officer of the court, felt he had done "the right thing" withholding from the authorities his ex post facto knowledge of the Ellsberg break-in. "I think, in retrospect, [coming forward] probably would have been the right thing to do," Mitchell conceded.

Another day in the witness chair, five hours long, had come to an end. As Ervin banged the gavel, Mitchell turned to Bill Hundley and murmured, in one of his patented stage whispers: "This is a great trial they're conducting up here, isn't it?"[16]

As agonizing as the Senate Watergate hearings were for Mitchell— and he had to endure a third day of often vicious questioning from

Dash—his testimony was a crucible for the nation, too. The spectacle of Mr. Law and Order parting the veil on the cynical realities of postwar American politics, dryly acknowledging he had run Nixon's reelection while still attorney general, and had purposely withheld, shortly after leaving that office, his knowledge of break-ins, forgeries, and other crimes, all committed in the name of national security— this, to many, was shocking stuff in 1973, and hard to stomach.

Though Mitchell had been one of the nation's most famous figures over the preceding five years, his three days of televised testimony marked his most extensive and sustained exposure to his countrymen, and stirred deep divisions over the truth and meaning of his words. Gallup and Harris polls showed John Dean won more favorable reviews than Mitchell (or Haldeman and Ehrlichman, who testified in August), and that Dean was more likely, despite his pervasive deception of the panel, to be seen as "truthful." At the same time, a focus group of "ordinary" Americans, conducted by the Massachusetts Institute of Technology with citizens in Dayton, Des Moines, and like locales, found Mitchell came across genially, "more of a Godfather than The Godfather."

Major newspapers split in their reactions, though on balance they took a dim view of Mitchell's performance. Most predictably reproachful were the *New York Times* and the *Washington Post*. The former expressed skepticism Mitchell would ever have disclosed the White House horrors, even with Nixon safely reelected; the latter likened his reasoning for remaining silent to the infamous remark by an army major in Vietnam: "We had to destroy the village to save it." Appraising Mitchell's testimony, the *Post* editorial board was "astounded by its arrogance . . . easy amorality and obtuseness."

Beyond the bastions of the Eastern Establishment, the response to Mitchell proved slightly more balanced. The *Los Angeles Times* withheld judgment on Mitchell's professions of innocence and the conflicts between his testimony, Dean's, and Magruder's, but its editors also found it amazing the president never picked up the phone and asked Mitchell what the hell was going on: "It is a portrayal of splendid isolation that strains belief." The *Arkansas Democrat* found Mitchell's denials "strain rational thinking and his recantations have a hollow ring. . . . Mitchell may not be that man [who approved the break-in]. But he is also not the indecisive, uninformed pushover he made himself appear to be in his testimony." The *Nashville Tennesseean* acknowledged that Mitchell "stuck to his story," but took note of how his hands began "shaking perceptibly whenever he lifted them from the witness table." The editors also harkened back to a statement Mitchell had made in 1971, after the May Day riots, in which he denounced antiwar protesters who believed "their cause is so right they can commit any wrong."

The *Richmond News Leader* assailed the Ervin committee for turning its investigation into "a political hanging party." "John Mitchell was the first witness who did not bow before the committee with the goodie-two-shoes deference of the teacher's pet," the paper editorialized. "He was sardonic, categorical. He countered countless 'do-you-mean-to-tell-me' questions with unperturbed responses that yes, that was precisely what he meant to tell them. And he was plausible." Yet in this same imperturbability, liberal novelist Mary McCarthy, writing in the *London Observer*, saw "nothing human." "The weariness and boredom of [Mitchell's] voice suggested that this was all ridiculous, preposterous, but also that he could not take the trouble to work up a lie that somebody might conceivably believe," McCarthy wrote. "He seemed rancorously determined to insult the intelligence of the committee, the press, the TV audience—everybody, the world at large." Even theologians weighed in. A Baptist minister, sermonizing on "the moral dilemma of Watergate," admonished Mitchell for violating the "spiritual law which forbids men to do evil even when they think good will come of it."

Mitchell's top-dollar lawyers had advised him not to testify at all, that to appear on Capitol Hill for televised hearings, what Eric Sevareid hailed as "the biggest Washington spectacular since those

McCarthy days," would only damage the former attorney general's chances for a fair trial. But they respected the way he took his punishment. "Mitchell knew this was a big political show," recalled Plato Cacheris. "He did not take it personally. . . . He recognized this was part of the game that was going on."[17]

BLEED FOR ME

Haven't I talked enough today? These people are
tired of listening to me.

—*Martha Mitchell, 1974*[1]

ONE EVENING IN the spring of 1995, former senator Russell Long,
the Louisiana Democrat and longtime chairman of the Senate Finance Committee, led a visitor on a tour of his fourteen-room duplex
in the Watergate apartment complex. A retired widower in sweater
and slacks, the senator had lived in the apartment since 1973, when
he purchased it from John and Martha Mitchell. The visitor followed
Long from the apartment's private elevator up through two spacious
floors and, finally, into a large master bedroom.

From there Long strode, with a sudden surge of enthusiasm, into
an adjoining bathroom, and proclaimed: "There it is!" Confused, the
visitor asked, "There *what* is?" "The telephone!" Long pointed at the
tiled wall opposite the commode, where there sat, mounted at hip
level, a faded lime-green Princess telephone, an early-seventies relic
whose circular dialing mechanism lay inside the curved, detachable
receiver.

"That's the original phone, the one Martha used to use, late at night. She and John would go to sleep right over there," Long said, pointing out to the bedroom, "then she'd get up late at night, have a few pops, and use this phone to call Helen Thomas, or whoever. Poor Mitchell wouldn't know a thing about it," he concluded, chuckling softly. "He'd wake up the next morning, open up the front page of the newspaper, and see what the hell his wife had had to say in the middle of the night!"[2]

It was no way to live. The attorney general strove to project an image of bemused indifference to his wife's antics, but the reality was that Martha Mitchell wrought havoc on their already stressful lives, and contributed mightily—as Richard Nixon always maintained—to her husband's spectacular downfall. The trouble began long before Watergate, before Martha's problems became evident to the reporters who quoted her, or to the public that alternately adored and despised her. What began as a refreshing novelty—an outspoken woman, in an age of docile domesticity, upstaging her tight-lipped, singularly powerful husband—quickly degenerated into rank commercial exploitation and, finally, into tragedy.

Compounding the difficulty was a tendency among the media, born in some quarters of genuine admiration, elsewhere of greed, to glorify Martha Mitchell, to cast her as a brave and lonely heroine—the sassy "defender of America," as Martha herself once listed her occupation. *Newsweek* crowned her "the most liberated woman in the world," notwithstanding Martha's own declaration, seven months earlier, that she wondered how feminists "have any respect for themselves." The *New York Daily News* welcomed the presence of Washington's "spirited, sexy strawberry blonde," while the *New York Post* championed her as "the essence of exquisite Southern charm."[3]

To be an American in the year 1970 was to find the image—and sound—of Martha Mitchell virtually inescapable; a single thirty-day period brought more than 5,000 newspaper items about her. She graced the covers of *Time, Look,* and *Life,* and beamed her dimpled smile from the *Today* show, *60 Minutes*, and every national and local network in the country.

Perhaps it was mildly amusing, amid the era's disquieting upheavals, when a woman of Martha's prominence traveled to the Manned Spacecraft Center in Houston to witness the opening of the first box of rocks retrieved from the lunar surface by the Apollo 14 astronauts—and she said the things looked like dirty potatoes. And maybe, in some small way, it enlivened the national discourse when the attorney general's wife chided a senator at a social function ("It's liberals like you who are selling this country down the river to the communists"), or demanded the mayor of New York City, John V. Lindsay, leave the Republican Party, or taunted him during an interview with Barbara Walters on the *Today* show, schoolyard style, by deliberately mispronouncing his name ("Lindsley . . . Lindsley . . . When I don't like somebody, I usually have a nickname for them"). And perhaps some found it refreshing when Mrs. Mitchell told reporters we should "extinguish the Supreme Court," on the well-reasoned grounds that "it's absolutely asinine for those nine old men to rule against the people."[4]

This last blast crystallized the problem with Martha Mitchell as a public figure. The catalyst for her remarks was *Swann v. Charlotte-Mecklenburg*, a landmark decision upholding the constitutionality of court-ordered busing as a means of school desegregation. Whether one agreed with the ruling or not, the gravity of the underlying problems warranted, for the benefit of the nation—or at least her husband, tasked with enforcing the ruling—the calmest possible environment in which to proceed. Yet at a time when integration was a burning issue, and the government was still committed to a "war on poverty," Martha mindlessly inflamed racial and class tensions.

In a widely publicized interview, she admitted having harbored racist views of blacks "in the last ten to twenty years," and brazenly challenged a reporter: "Are you going to be prejudiced against me because my grandparents had slaves?" "I can't get over saying 'colored,' " she said on another occasion. "I said it all my life. All the Negroes seem to resent it and I don't know why." Nor was Mrs. Mitchell's insensitivity limited to African Americans. "I grew up with [Jews]," she crowed to *Women's Wear Daily*. "Many of them are my best friends." She cited her sorority sisters, the president of the Pine Bluff Country Club, and "a lot of big people in business," members of "the Jewish race."[5]

Ill-advised as these remarks were, none of them caused John Mitchell as much trouble as her comments on Vietnam, which veered, with characteristic volatility, between clumsy advocacy and stinging criticism of the Nixon administration's policies. "War, war, war," she moaned in April 1970, "I'm getting awfully sick of it. It just turns my stomach." Yet a month later she welcomed the incursion into Cambodia as "100 percent wonderful"; by July she was urging friends to send their draft-age sons to Canada.

The discomfort reached its climax 30,000 feet above ground, aboard Air Force One, as the president and select guests flew cross-country from San Clemente to Washington, D.C., in September 1970. Unaccompanied by her husband, or some other sane person, Martha wandered back to the press cabin of the plane "looking for action." Helen Thomas opened with some harmless questions about mini-skirts. "Oh, Helen," Martha sneered, "why don't you ask me something important?" "Okay," Thomas replied, "what do you think of the Vietnam War?" "It stinks, and if it weren't for Fulbright we'd be out of it," Martha shot back, renewing her attacks on the Democratic senator she had earlier demanded be "crucified" for his vote on a judicial nominee. She kept on talking, saying national disunity over the war made her so mad she couldn't see straight. By now Secretary of State William Rogers had showed up, gingerly trying to rein her in: "Martha, why don't you stick to the Justice Department and I'll take care of foreign affairs?"

Thomas and her colleagues scribbled away, the fun just begun, when the attorney general finally strode in, no doubt alerted to the disaster movie unfolding in the back cabin, starring his wife and the

White House press corps. Would you like to know what your wife just said? Thomas asked, all coquettish. "Heavens no," Mitchell said, "I might jump out of the window." When the plane touched down, the reporters all rushed to file; the next day's *Washington Post* exulted: "Martha: 'The War Stinks.' "[6]

Part of Martha's problem with the war stemmed from the fact that her son was fighting it. In March 1971, she received a mud-stained letter from Jay Jennings mailed from Vietnam. It disturbed her terribly. Within hours of reading it, she unburdened herself to two ambassadors' wives—total strangers—at a dinner party. "I just seem to have more trouble than anyone else I know," she groaned within earshot of a *Post* reporter, unmindful of the far greater sacrifices many Americans were then bearing. "I wonder if Senator Fulbright could have had my son sent there just to get even with me for the things I have said about him. I'm going to find out!"[7]

What Martha failed to mention was that she'd never bothered to contact her son, a cadet at the Virginia Military Institute at the time the Mitchells moved to Washington, in two years: no letters, no phone calls, no visits.

Two weeks after the letter arrived, Martha rose before seven, casually walked over to her television set, pulled the button that turned it on, and flipped the dial to the *CBS Morning News*. "Martha Mitchell, the attorney general's wife," anchor John Hart began, "said a couple of weeks ago she got a letter from her son in Vietnam. He was in the fighting near the Laotian border, she said, and hadn't had a bath for ten days. . . . [Reporter] Ed Rabel visited her son at Lang Vei." Martha watched in astonishment, as her son—no longer a cadet, but Lieutenant Clyde Jay Jennings, commander of the Second Armored Cavalry Platoon, "A" Troop, First Squadron, First Cavalry, Americal Division—appeared before her very eyes. His superior officer, Sergeant Bob Barbour of Raleigh, said Jennings was doing "a real good job" for the unit. Finally, Rabel interviewed Jay himself. Do you hear much from your mother? Yes, Jay said, adding she was "a little on the shocked side" to learn he was in combat. The other soldiers had no idea who his mother was and that was fine with him; despite prodding from Rabel, the son steered clear of controversy as assiduously as his mother courted it.

> RABEL: Your mother's been critical of the Vietnamization process. Do you share her views on that?
> JENNINGS: I really don't feel I'm in a position to have a view on that. . . . In my current occupation, I just—I have to be apolitical. If I tried to impress these views on any of these men—and I'm sure they share different views than myself—it would tend to alienate people. And in a situation like this, you've got to work together.

Martha's prayers had been answered: Jay was alive and in seemingly good spirits. But hadn't the man on the television said Jay's unit was "attacked often" by the enemy? Martha resolved at once to use her proximity to power to get her son out of Vietnam. She turned—where else?—to the telephone, ringing the White House, and asking, of all people, for John Ehrlichman, her husband's most determined antagonist. Undoubtedly astonished to hear from her, Ehrlichman surreptitiously recorded the call, which, as the previously unpublished transcript shows, got off to a bad start.

> EHRLICHMAN: Hi, Martha, how are you?
> MRS. MITCHELL: Well, I'm not very good.
> EHRLICHMAN: What's the matter?
> MRS. MITCHELL: Well, my old son's over in Vietnam.
> EHRLICHMAN: Your son?
> MRS. MITCHELL: Yes.
> EHRLICHMAN: Oh, I read about that . . . Has he got a problem?
> MRS. MITCHELL: Well, no—
> EHRLICHMAN: Other than just being there, huh?
> MRS. MITCHELL: I have a problem.

EHRLICHMAN: What is your problem?
MRS. MITCHELL: My problem is his being there.

The conversation already strained, Ehrlichman sought a way out. His solution was to treat the attorney general's wife like a crackpot constituent. "How can I help you?" he asked. Martha sensed his impatience: "Well, I don't guess you can help me if you don't want to help me." "I want to help you," Ehrlichman countered, "but I don't know *how* to help you." After a few more, similarly desultory, exchanges, Ehrlichman cut things short with a suggestion that Martha contact Defense Secretary Mel Laird (whom the White House distrusted; "He runs that little empire over there," said Ehrlichman, "and doesn't talk to anybody"). "I've already talked to him," Martha snapped. The call ended with her curtly thanking Ehrlichman for his help, and Ehrlichman replying, curtly and aptly: "Not at all."[8]

"I got a lot of calls from Martha," Ehrlichman recalled in 1992. "She was unhinged. She was just not—not normal."

EHRLICHMAN: You'd be at dinner, eight or nine, ten people at dinner, at a table. She demanded that everybody at that table give her undivided attention. You couldn't conduct a separate conversation down at the other end of the table. She'd say, "You people down there, be quiet, I want to say something." And she was, you know, very insecure, very demanding and, and very unbalanced.
ROSEN: How do you think Mitchell dealt with that strain?
EHRLICHMAN: By withdrawing. . . . When she would pull something like that, he would be like a turtle going back into his shell.[9]

Such instances were numerous and legendary. Brent Harries, one of Mitchell's Wall Street chums, recalled Mrs. Mitchell leaping onto furniture at upscale private parties in the early sixties—long before Mitchell went into politics—and her husband just standing there, chuckling, helpless. Anna Chennault remembered hosting a party at her Watergate apartment that ended with Martha madly flinging one of her stiletto heels across the room at her husband. Most unforgettable, however, was the portrait drawn by Maxine Cheshire of the *Washington Post*.

> Martha's drinking problem, now well known, should have been publicly disclosed a lot earlier than it was. One *Post* reporter covered a small dinner party—one of the first the Mitchells attended when they came to town—where Martha became so drunk that she passed out and fell face down in her soup bowl. John Mitchell almost let her drown before he pulled her up. The reporter, a Republican, was outraged when a *Post* editor would not allow the incident to appear in her story the next day.

Cheshire was a frequent visitor to the Mitchells' Watergate home and therefore learned much earlier than the rest of the Washington press corps the sad truth blanketing the lives of the women John Mitchell cared for most: Martha and Marty. "One time," Cheshire wrote, "my knock was answered by the black chauffeur-bodyguard, and standing behind him was Martha, with an almost empty glass in her hand. Though it was early afternoon, she was obviously very drunk. I asked her a question, and she started to tell me that she was leaving Washington. Then she handed the glass to the chauffeur, and, placing her hand on her behind, she began a little dance, singing something about 'Goodbye to Washington,' wiggling with her fingers as she waved her posterior. At that, the chauffeur closed the door in my face."

> I returned a few days later, again in mid-afternoon, and this time my knock was answered by a large black woman in a

white uniform, who appeared to be a nurse. As I stood in the hall, eleven-year-old Marty came down the apartment's stairs. She was in pajamas and looked as if she had not been outside in the sun for months. As the woman turned toward the child, I heard the clink of metal and noticed a large key ring attached to her belt. "I want to go in my mommy's room," said Marty. "Would you open the door so I can see my mommy?" The woman shook her head. "I've told you over and over. You can't see your mother until she wakes up."

Again the door was shut in my face, but not before I saw the look of anguish on the child's face. The curtains were tightly drawn, and the interior of the apartment was in deep shadows. Whether the nurse had locked Martha in her bedroom or Martha had locked herself in, I did not know. But I later learned that one of the main items of regular "housekeeping" in the apartment was to repair or replace Martha's bedroom door. She would often lock herself in, and when threats were ineffectual, John Mitchell instructed the chauffeur to kick the door down. I didn't like to dwell on what this was doing to Marty.[10]

Why did Mitchell marry Martha in the first place? The chronology suggests their relationship began as an extramarital affair; presumably, then, the initial attraction, for Mitchell, lay in adultery's usual draws: sex, excitement, illicit adventure. A source close to Mitchell confirmed, many years later, what the FBI had learned during its background check on him in 1968: that Martha was pregnant when they married. The two made an odd couple—he in pinstripes, pipe, and wingtips; she in bouffant wigs, costume jewelry, and stilettos—and recalled Katharine Hepburn's famous commentary on Astaire and Rogers: "He gave her class, she gave him sex appeal."

Mitchell's staid exterior and resemblance to Alfred Hitchcock made it difficult to conceive of him in sexual terms at all, let alone as an edgy character. But a few saw past the Wall Street façade. Among them—working backward, in deduction, from the presence of Martha—was William F. Buckley Jr., the conservative commentator who knew the attorney general well enough to have introduced him, in 1968, to Henry Kissinger. "A bond dealer!" Buckley began his eulogy for Mitchell in *National Review*. "It was part of the grander design that John Mitchell should have had that profession, and that face. He looked like the Anonymous Man, clerking his time away until the Social Security payments began. And all the while, in private life and in public, he was a picaresque figure. Anyone married to Martha Mitchell had to be, in hidden life, one true gay blade."

Since tales of Martha's erratic behavior date back to the early sixties, Mitchell must have recognized early on in their marriage the severity of his second wife's mental and emotional problems; it was this recognition that gave him pause before he finally capitulated to Nixon's pleas to serve in government. He stayed with her, most likely, because they had a child together and he wanted to avoid visiting upon Marty the same dislocation that afflicted his children from his first marriage. His divorce from Bette Shine had also been expensive. Finally, there was some evidence, after his death, that he carried on another affair—at least one—after marrying Martha.

A family member once said Mitchell was intellectually brilliant, "but not when it came to women." Still others saw Mitchell's consuming devotion to work as the central problem in his relationships. "Martha was very family-oriented," Mitchell's brother, Robert, recalled in 1998. "John was always busy with his success. . . . I think the only problem with Martha was that as [John] got more and more, you know, successful . . . she was apparently left alone a lot and I guess she took to alcohol, that's all. And she had the weakness, and she became an alcoholic. But Martha wasn't always that way."[11]

Watergate was the final strain that pushed Martha over the edge. The bloody altercation in Newport Beach and the escalating shrillness of her calls to reporters in the spring of 1973 signaled the encroaching darkness that was to cloud her remaining days. Erratic, even dangerous behavior Mitchell, in private practice, was able to police—like the time when his wife, like some malevolent cartoon character, sprang from a concealed position in their apartment and, without provocation, smashed a chair over the head of one of Mitchell's law partners, or the occasion, far more chilling, when she got hold of a gun and trained it menacingly on Marty.

Now, however, indicted and struggling to stay out of prison, Mitchell could no longer manage his wife's madness. With the twin terrors of the Watergate scandals and Martha Mitchell, no man, no matter how strong, could cope; a change had to be made.

On September 11, 1973, with Marty safely ensconced at boarding school in Connecticut, Mitchell finally walked out on Martha, taking whatever he could carry, including an alarm clock, to the Essex House on Central Park South. Eight months later, on May 10, 1974, Martha initiated formal divorce proceedings, accusing Mitchell in court papers of "cruel and inhuman treatment and abandonment." Mrs. Mitchell—she kept the name—also sought legal advantage by reminding the court of her ex-husband's "leadership" role in "the Watergate break-in and cover-up."[12]

In his legal papers, Mitchell argued Martha had "disregarded her duties and obligations as a wife" and behaved "in such a manner as to justify" his leaving her. In a private letter he railed at "that sick [expletive] that has caused so many problems for Marty and me." Throughout the summer of 1973, he told the court, his efforts to prepare for the Vesco trial were hampered by Martha's "unstable condition, [her] refusal to sleep during the night, and harassment during the day." Worse, her "frequently . . . excessive alcohol intake" left her "unfit" to care for Marty, in whom she "instilled fear . . . subjecting her to harassment both at school and while visiting friends, and upon occasion, to physical abuse."[13]

In the annals of divorce, the dissolution of the Mitchell marriage, and the competing child-custody and property claims it engendered, surely rank among the longest, nastiest, costliest, and most painfully public of the media age. The drama played out in New York State Supreme Court, on local and national television, in the newspapers, and occasionally—as when Martha set fire to her ex-husband's most cherished items and dumped the rest in their foyer—violently. Coupled with the two criminal trials and multiple investigations he faced, the character assassination raining down on him from every newsstand and anchor desk in the nation, Mitchell's divorce represented still another front in his seemingly boundless struggle for survival.[14]

Despite her later claims to have been shocked at Mitchell's departure, Martha appears to have anticipated his move and taken preemptive action to blunt its impact. The previous July, the Mitchells had hired Soll Connelly and Marshall, a Park Avenue law firm, to assist in transferring ownership of their Fifth Avenue co-op to Martha, a move likely triggered by Mitchell's indictment in the Vesco matter two months earlier. But with the sting of the Newport Beach needle still fresh in memory, their marriage obviously failing, Martha, according to previously unpublished documents, secretly contacted Soll Connelly and requested "the advice of a firm other than Mr. Mitchell's law firm, so she could be sure her interests were protected." She knew the end was near.

Five days after Mitchell stole away in the night, Martha told Helen Thomas he had left on advice of counsel. "He walked out, yes," Martha confirmed. "But I've been trying to get him out. If you've got a man twenty-four hours a day, I couldn't stand it. He was watching the football games. I'm so glad he's out of here. Anyone who sits here and never goes out, and never accepts invitations."[15]

Soon, however, Martha realized she was entirely ignorant of the family finances and unable to perform even the most elemental administrative tasks necessary to maintain her (costly) existence. "For seventeen years of her marriage to the defendant," her lawyers later argued, "she was accustomed to a certain style of living and the security that went with it." Her security, the lawyers frankly acknowledged, derived from "having had the luxury of people taking care of her personal needs and financial needs all of those years." When

Mitchell left, he "took with him all the security that the plaintiff may have had, and the plaintiff was left on her own without being aware or knowing which way to turn to take care of *any* personal matters."[16]

But Mitchell, according to court papers, testified that he left behind

> not only my clothing and various photographs, but all of my personal effects . . . books, papers, records . . . two to four file cabinets of personal materials . . . twelve binders of newspaper clippings and documents . . . voluminous papers relating to the hearings before the Senate Select Committee on Watergate, and the trial in the Southern District of New York, *United States v. Vesco, et al* [*sic*] . . . many bound and looseleaf volumes containing complete records of various trials and hearings which were important to me . . . testimony before various congressional committees, private papers within the Justice Department, extensive personal correspondence accumulated during the years of private practice and with the government . . . speech materials . . . bank statements . . . various valuable pieces of jewelry . . . autographed pictures from several former presidents of the United States; various gifts bearing the presidential seal; [and] golf clubs.

Few of these items, including Mitchell's official papers and correspondence from his years as attorney general, were ever recovered.[17]

Mitchell's legal bills, meantime, were going through the roof. The lopsided terms of divorce in the 1970s, in which men were invariably held liable for all fees and debts their ex-wives incurred—combined with Martha's particular talent for spending—quickly laid waste to the fortune Mitchell's innovations on Wall Street had earned him. It was now clear that, as one of Martha's lawyers noted, "both parties are obviously going to have to cut back in their means of living." Mitchell offered to provide Martha with "a gracious and comfortable existence" amounting to $350 a week, which was in addition to his assumption of responsibility for "all [her] household and personal costs . . . charge accounts, credit cards, travel, entertainment and medical expenses." In their first year of separation, he paid her $51,500, about $215,000 in current figures.[18]

But by the time his Watergate trial commenced, in October 1974, Mitchell's patience, and bank account, had run out. He told the court Martha had "abused" his "largesse," that due to "changed circumstances" and "severe debt obligation," his "continuing ability to sustain [her] payments is now at an end." Far from exercising the "expected self-imposed limitation" on her spending, Martha was burning Mitchell's money faster than ever. Her monthly phone bills averaged $400 ($1,700 in current dollars), her dry-cleaning tab up to $600 ($2,500 today). On one occasion she stuck him with the bill for an Amtrak seat, along with the cost of three surrounding, unoccupied seats, to "insure her privacy." She also demanded Mitchell absorb the cost of her personal secretary, a luxury she never enjoyed during their marriage.[19]

Though it pained him to bare such matters in public documents, Mitchell was forced to provide the court with detailed accountings of his rapidly diminishing finances. His income of $5,281 per week, he explained, consisted of weekly payments of $5,000 from Mudge Rose—an arrangement "based solely on an informal agreement, subject to termination at any time," he warned—and $281 from accrued interest on municipal bonds. Mitchell then detailed his *weekly* expenditures: $630 for payments on an unsecured joint loan of $112,000; another $530 for insurance premiums; $500 for a Chase Manhattan Bank loan; $480 for carrying charges on the Fifth Avenue co-op, now occupied solely by Martha; $275 for interest on loans he took out against his insurance policies, worth a total of $257,000; and some $200 on various other charges. Then there was poor little Marty, whose tuition and board ran $3,600 a year, not counting clothing and medical needs. Finally, and not least of all, Mitchell had to bankroll his four-and-a-half-room dwelling at the Essex House; his own living expenses; a car and driver who performed "general household duties" for him; and all his and Martha's taxes.

Additional details emerged, however, in pleadings by Mitchell's attorney, Marvin Segal. While acknowledging Mitchell's "total assets" were "appreciable," Segal cautioned they were "encumbered" and did "not actually represent a financial picture . . . as generous as [Martha] claims." Segal maintained that "any negative result in the District of Columbia," where *U.S. v. Mitchell* was under way, would devastate the former attorney general's "viability as a wage earner." Already, he had shelled out $90,000 for lawyers' fees (almost $380,000 in current figures), an exigency that had necessitated "further borrowing."[20]

Mitchell's continuing alimony payments to his first wife, two decades after their divorce and notwithstanding Bette's remarriage, filled Martha with rage, and formed the basis of still another of her legal challenges. "It is a rather peculiar situation," her lawyers argued, "where the defendant [Mitchell] will be paying . . . more alimony to his first wife who has remarried than to his present wife who is totally without funds." Segal shot back that Martha seemed to have forgotten that the unusually steep alimony payments imposed under the terms of Mitchell's first divorce "[had to] be accepted in order that the marriage to [Martha] could be undertaken." Segal pleaded for the court to recognize the "almost certain eventuality" that Mitchell would go broke and to help the former attorney general avert "financial disaster" by forcing Martha to sell the Fifth Avenue property. Instead, on December 4, 1974, New York State Supreme Court Judge Manuel A. Gomez ruled Mitchell had to pay Martha a whopping $1,000 a week, retroactive to November 1.[21]

Despite the increasingly hostile tone the proceedings had acquired by the end of 1974, Mitchell calculated it would still be financially advantageous for him and Martha to file a joint tax return for the preceding year. Ironically, 1973 had shaped up as one of the most lucrative years of Mitchell's legal career: Despite his indictment in the Vesco case in May, and his grilling before the Senate Watergate committee in July, Mitchell racked up $302,000 in fees, working mostly out of his old Broad Street office.

Without advising Mitchell, however, Martha had already filed her own tax return, attaching to her 1040 form a pitiable note she scrawled on yellow legal paper:

> I may have other income which is taxable. I do not know the amount of this income. My husband has always prepared our joint income tax returns.

After being persuaded they could save $25,000 by filing jointly, Martha finally relented. The former attorney general signed their joint return and sent it off to the IRS on August 12, 1974, four days after Richard Nixon resigned the presidency. For Mitchell, these were unbearably dark days; indeed, the Internal Revenue Service soon informed him he was being audited.[22]

While her father stood trial in Washington, Marty Mitchell commuted between boarding school in Connecticut and the Essex House, where they spent weekends together. Only in "sporadic instances" was Marty looked after by others, Mitchell argued in court, and in such cases the supervisory figures were "old family friends" or "parents of contemporaries." The child herself, he said, had "repeatedly expressed the desire to be with [him], and specifically not be under the aegis of [Martha Mitchell]." On the few occasions where she saw her mother in those days, Marty rebuked her for causing Mitchell so many problems: "It's your fault that Daddy's in trouble."[23]

Certainly the most sensational charge in the saga of the Mitchells' divorce was Martha's claim of physical abuse at her ex-husband's hands. In court papers she charged that Mitchell, on or about November 1, 1972, "punched [her] with a clenched fist in the mouth, causing great physical discomfort, pain and disfigurement." Winzola McLendon recounted the incident in her 1979 biography, *Martha*.

"Soon after dinner on November 1, my telephone rang. It was Martha."

"Winnie, come help me," she screamed. "Please help me!" "Where are you?" "The Watergate! Hurry!" I heard her shout at someone, "Yes! I called Winnie and she's coming over!" The phone went dead.

My husband, Navy Captain John Benjamin McLendon, drove me to the Mitchells' apartment. I went up alone and John Mitchell answered the door. He looked terribly annoyed. With his uncombed hair and flush face, his white dress shirt opened at the neck and the tail partly out, he also looked like he'd been in a brawl. The shirt was wet, too. But I couldn't tell if it were from perspiration or if something had been thrown at him.

I asked, "Where's Martha?" He answered by calling to her, "Your *friend* is here." Martha, her face tear-stained and blotched, walked down the stairs, wearing slacks and a rumpled sleeveless overblouse that didn't hide large red marks on her arms. "Well, I'll leave 'you two girls' alone," John Mitchell said, sarcastically, before stomping up the steps. Martha said, "Thank you, Winnie, for coming," and started to cry. Only then did I see that one of her front teeth was out.

"I wanted to get her out of there," McLendon wrote, but Martha said no: "Just stay with me until I know he's sound asleep." Asked why she stayed with Mitchell if he beat her, Martha replied, "I have to." Mitchell hadn't exactly punched her tooth out, she explained: "The tooth isn't *out*. It's the cap he knocked off. All of my teeth are capped. John Mitchell didn't like my teeth from the day he met me. He made me have them capped."

With Martha's consent, McLendon summoned her husband, the navy captain, and the three talked for four hours, calming Martha down. During this time Martha placed several unanswered calls to an unidentified friend "in suburban New York" (possibly Ken or Peggy Ebbitt in Bronxville) and confided she was "scared to death" Mitchell was going to institutionalize her. By midnight she was feeling "all right," rejecting pleas she stay at the McLendons', or that they stay with her; in fact Martha "insisted we go," McLendon recalled.[24]

Absent any basis to challenge McLendon's account, the scene she found at the Mitchell apartment that night bespoke a physical confrontation that occurred shortly before her arrival. If history offers any guide, however, Martha most likely lunged at her husband and hurt herself in the process. She was prone to physical outbursts: the altercation with her son; the smashing of the chair over John Alexander's head; her unfortunate swing at Steve King; a brazen smack to Marty's face, right in front of the nuns at the child's Sacred Heart school; and the occasion outside the Mitchells' New York building, in June 1973, when she cursed and struck a female reporter three times.

Finally, there was Martha's reply to a reporter's question, in September 1973, about whether Mitchell tried to force her into psychiatric care. She called that "a goddamned lie" and added: "I never had a fight with him." This was ten months after the alleged incident.[25]

Martha made her last public appearance at a party at the Museum of Modern Art in September 1975. There she encountered a record producer and playfully asked why he hadn't invited her to record. "I didn't know you sang," he responded. With that she launched into a rendition of "What Are You Doing the Rest of Your Life?" "She was good," the producer marveled, "right on pitch."[26]

The rest of Martha's life was given over to acute pain of body and soul. "Martha Mitchell Has Blood Disease," the *Times* reported three weeks later; she had been undergoing tests for a month in Northern Virginia Doctor's Hospital. She was suffering from multiple myeloma, a rare and extremely painful form of cancer, diagnosed in less than 8,000 cases a year and cause unknown, in which the patient's bone marrow produces excessive numbers of white blood cells, creating multiple tumors in the marrow. The *Times* reported the disease was "uniformly fatal"; the *New York Post* said Martha's case was discovered at a "fairly advanced" stage. She had already suffered two cracked ribs and two fractured vertebrae.[27]

The following month, she entered New York's Memorial Sloan-Kettering Cancer Center for treatment and remained there for seven months, with Mitchell reportedly paying the bills. Though Martha's few remaining friends cursed him for choosing to "ignore" her in these dark final days, the fact was she barred him from visiting and forbade her doctors from updating him. Peter Fleming, Mitchell's attorney in the Vesco trial, recalled him calling "with emotion in his voice" and asking Fleming to find out what he could about Martha's condition: "It was evident . . . that he cared about her."[28]

When she returned to her ghostly home at 1030 Fifth Avenue, in April 1976, Martha was reported "thin, weak and fighting for her life." Her only regular visitor was her son, Jay Jennings. "Mom seems in relatively good spirits," he told the *Times*, "but she seems to have withdrawn a bit to fight this by herself." She had barely arrived home when she fell and fractured her arm.[29]

With her condition rapidly declining, Martha's lawyers filed what they called a "dire emergency motion" demanding Mitchell cough up $36,000 in back alimony payments. To the affidavit Martha attached a sheaf of her outstanding bills. On the Fifth Avenue property, she owed nearly $10,000 in rent; Con Edison was threatening to shut off her electricity; and her local supermarket, Gristedes, was discontinuing food deliveries. "Unless I receive some substantial payment from the defendant," she pleaded, "I do not know how I will survive." Mitchell, while not wishing to "exacerbate" Martha's problems, pleaded hardship, and responded with an equally pathetic filing. "I have no regular income and my expenses are financed with borrowed funds."

In contrast to [Martha's] assertions, my financial condition necessitates a basic and simple lifestyle. Not only am I living on borrowed funds, but I am also supporting [Marty], age fourteen, who, at her own insistence, has been living with me on weekends and holidays from the school she attends in Connecticut.[30]

On May 20, the New York State Supreme Court ruled in Martha's favor, ordering Mitchell to pay in full the $36,000 she demanded. Five days later, absent any indication he would comply, she signed papers authorizing attorneys to raid her safety deposit box and sell the engagement ring with which Mitchell had proposed to her in 1957; the proceeds were to be divided among two live-in nurses who had never been paid.[31]

The cancer, meanwhile, had consumed Martha's bones and spread to her adrenals, kidneys, and lymph nodes; she was hemorrhaging around the adrenals and heart; and stomach ulcers had provoked internal bleeding. She was taken, on a stretcher, unconscious, to Sloan-Kettering, where, after contracting pneumonia, she died alone before dawn on May 31, 1976. She was fifty-seven.[32]

John Mitchell took control of the arrangements for the funeral, which was held in Martha's native Pine Bluff. Reporters and photographers were relegated to the fringes, and there was no visitation; hundreds of local residents who came to pay their last respects to the deceased, once "the most quoted, vilified, idolized and satirized woman in the country," were kept, on Mitchell's orders, outside locked doors. Still, zoom lenses captured Mitchell, bookended by Marty and Jay Jennings, strolling somberly past the carnation-covered casket.

No decent person could look upon Martha's final days and fail to feel sympathy for her. She died in precisely the way she most feared to live: penniless and alone. There was some evidence she finally recognized how badly she had behaved for so many years. "Martha had a striking change of personality," McLendon reported. Doctors who'd once found her among the most difficult of patients now pronounced her the most reasonable. "I must have been cuckoo before," she said upon awakening from one of her surgeries.

There had been moments of clarity before. Once, at the height of her fame, in 1970, a perceived snub from Pat Nixon's social secretary sent Martha into one of her rages—then came the tears. "It's just unbelievable," she cried to the *Washington Post*'s Dorothy McCardle. "Somebody should get down and bleed for me. I try so hard."[33]

HANDS OF
THE GODS

God, they're going to indict a former attorney general of the United States. . . . What the hell more do they want? You know what they want. They want blood.

—*Richard Nixon, 1973*[1]

ON THE CLOUDY afternoon of October 10, 1973, Spiro T. Agnew, twice elected vice president of the United States, pleaded no contest in a Baltimore federal court to having failed to report $29,500 in taxable income for the year 1967. While governor of Maryland—and as vice president, right up through the preceding January—Agnew had been taking cash payments from local engineering firms in exchange for state contracts, a scheme that netted him roughly $100,000. The judge sentenced Agnew to three years' probation and a $10,000 fine. At that exact moment, by prior arrangement, Agnew's terse letter of resignation was hand-delivered to Secretary of State Kissinger. "I hereby resign the Office of Vice President of the United States," the letter read, "effective immediately."[2]

The vice president's stunning fall pained Mitchell. He had been instrumental in Agnew's selection in 1968, and was decisive, four years later, in persuading Nixon to keep him on the GOP ticket. As late as the mid-1980s, Mitchell continued to do business with the disgraced, reclusive figure he affectionately called Ted, and to ask others about him: "Don't you think he's a pretty decent guy?"[3] Even closer to home, however, the spectacle in Baltimore likely gave Mitchell a glimpse of his own future: Here was the vice president of the United States being treated like *a common criminal! Taken on a perp walk!* Could Nixon's former attorney general expect any better?

It was, perhaps, with such visions in mind that Mitchell, in the summer of 1973, unbeknownst to the press or public, began negotiating a deal of his own. "Mr. Mitchell wants to discuss a plea bargain and cooperation," his attorney, Hundley, declared at the outset of a secret conversation with WSPF prosecutor James Neal. Astonished and excited, Neal figured Mitchell had finally decided to testify against Nixon. While the existence of Nixon's tapes had been publicly disclosed, no one outside the White House had heard them yet, and prosecutors worried they might refute the testimony of their star witness, John Dean. A plea from Mitchell would make any case against Nixon easier to prove.

A formal meeting was set for Mitchell's suite at the Woodley Park hotel in Washington that August. Neal, a gruff former marine, arrived to find Mitchell calmly sucking on his pipe. They talked for hours, bantering and fencing, comfortable enough to address each other as John and Jim. Neal pointedly reminded Mitchell how Nixon, Haldeman, and Ehrlichman had jockeyed to make him the fall guy in Watergate: That much had become clear at the Senate hearings. "Well," Mitchell replied after a few puffs of smoke, "you don't know everything, Jim."

"Mitchell made it abundantly clear," said Hundley, that "Nixon was the greatest president that ever lived and [that he] knew nothing about him and would never, never *ever* say anything bad about Nixon because there was never anything bad to be said about him." Mitchell added: "I would never, ever testify against Haldeman or Ehrlichman." He knew all about their treachery, but believed implicating Nixon's top aides was as bad as turning on the president himself. How about

Chuck Colson? Neal asked. Now he had struck a nerve. "I would love to give *him* up," Mitchell replied. Neal began quizzing Mitchell on specific meetings. Then it suddenly dawned on him: "This man is not prepared to cooperate."

> Mitchell had come there with the idea that he would accept responsibility for everything, and he would enter a plea to whatever we wanted provided we would give up the pursuit of—he didn't care about Haldeman or Ehrlichman so much—but we'd give up the pursuit of the president. . . . We said, "Well, thank you very much. That's not what we are interested in."

"One thing John Mitchell would never be is a fink," Hundley later said. "He didn't have a fink bone in his body." The next time Mitchell saw Neal was in Judge Sirica's courtroom, at the start of *U.S. v. Mitchell.*

Like most of Mitchell's enemies, Neal secretly liked him. In August 1978 he wrote to the Parole Commission to urge Mitchell's early release from prison (it was denied). "I was convinced," Neal wrote, "that his offenses emanated not from an evil soul but from a misguided and foolish loyalty to the president of the United States."

Mitchell sparred with Neal at trial, but never took it personally. After the verdict came back, he autographed Neal's copy of *All the President's Men*: "To one of the nicest guys I know unfortunately cast in the wrong spot at the wrong time."[4]

On March 1, 1974—one day after the jury was selected in the Vesco trial—Leon Jaworski, the Houston lawyer appointed special prosecutor after Nixon's rancorous dismissal of Archibald Cox in the "Saturday Night Massacre" four months earlier, stood in Sirica's wood-paneled Washington courtroom and announced that the foreman of the grand jury had some material "to be delivered to y'all." It was a bulging black briefcase containing a fifty-page indictment. *U.S. v. Mitchell* had finally arrived. "It was a heart-rending moment," Jaworski later wrote. "I had always liked John Mitchell."

That the case bore the name of the former attorney general offered fitting tribute to Mitchell's special place in the mind and heart of Richard Nixon. Those formally charged included six former White House or CRP officials—Mitchell, Haldeman, Ehrlichman, Colson, Strachan, and Mardian—and one other man, Ken Parkinson, the outside counsel retained by CRP after the Democrats filed their civil suit. Mitchell faced six counts of conspiracy, obstruction of justice, false declarations to the FBI and the grand jury, and perjury before the Senate Watergate committee. Of those charged, he was the only former cabinet member; he faced, if convicted on all counts, the harshest possible punishment: thirty years in prison and $42,000 in fines (nearly $175,000 in current figures). "We're going to fight this all the way," Hundley told reporters, "and expect to be vindicated in the courts." Use of the plural—*courts*—hinted at a fact Hundley confirmed only years later: that Mitchell's legal strategy conceded conviction at trial and rested entirely on hopes Judge Sirica would make reversible errors.

Eight days later, a "heavy" phalanx of Metropolitan Police Department officers, the kind of uniformed cops who had cheered Mitchell on when he preached the law-and-order gospel, surrounded him on his walk of shame into the courthouse, where he was soon to enter his plea to a second round of criminal charges and be booked, fingerprinted, and photographed for his mug shot. Roughly 250 protesters came to celebrate. "Rot in jail!" they shouted. *"Sieg Heil!"*[5]

Mitchell's problems had reached their peak: He was on trial in New York, indicted in Washington, estranged from his wife, responsible for their thirteen-year-old daughter, deep in debt, vilified the world over. Private letters from this time, previously unpublished, captured both Mitchell's sadness and his determination to preserve—more for the morale of his few remaining friends, it seemed, than for himself—the old veneer of equanimity. Writing in 1973 to his former secretary, Susie Morrison, Mitchell fawned over "the little pigtailed pixie in the picture you sent" and flirted mischievously.

> As for me and my problems, it's all your fault. If you had not turned me down when I first propositioned you, I would have had entirely different interests and not gone on to the current situation. . . .
>
> As for the future there is just no way to tell where it is all going to end in this climate. I guess we will just have to wait and see how it comes out. In the meantime, it sure as hell ain't fun.

A year later Mitchell wrote again to Morrison, also embroiled in a bitter divorce:

> Your limbo situation is just like mine. All she [Martha] wants to do is cause grief on all sides and will not come to a decision. I do hope I can dispose of the matter soon. . . .
>
> I'm sure you have been following the Watergate matter in the papers and know it is still up in the air. I really appreciate your offer of help but am not sure you would be safe there with me considering all the circumstances. . . .
>
> Love ya,
JNM[6]

Following his acquittal in the Vesco case, in April 1974, Mitchell faced still another obstacle before he could stand trial in Watergate: an appearance before the House Judiciary Committee weighing Nixon's impeachment. James D. St. Clair, the president's criminal lawyer, had demanded Mitchell's appearance. For the weary witness the impeachment panel offered at best a tedious replay of the Ervin hearings, at worst another perjury trap.

On July 5, 1974, after nearly three hours of private questioning by House investigators, Mitchell insisted he would testify publicly only if compelled by legislative subpoena. The committee voted to issue the subpoena. Accordingly the former attorney general appeared before lawmakers in Room 2141 of the Rayburn House Office Building four days later, exactly a year after his showdown with the Senate. Arriving early, he found few members in attendance. Mitchell looked around, one representative recalled, "smiled that thin-lipped smile, and said, 'I guess I'm not playing to a full House.' "

A major event for Mitchell in the interval between his Senate and House appearances was his discovery, along with the rest of the country, of Nixon's taping system. Surely Mitchell shared the angry astonishment that other intimates of Nixon's, kept in the dark about the surreptitious recording, later described; but Mitchell's sense of betrayal must have been exceptional. Not only was he Nixon's closest friend in government—or the closest Nixon came to *having* one—but the edited transcripts disseminated by the White House, published widely in May 1974, painted a wretched portrait of Nixon scheming with his minions, Haldeman, Ehrlichman, and Dean, to make Mitchell the fall guy.

"You were named as the big enchilada," representative Wayne Owens declared, with vacuous glee. Congressman Charles Rangel, the gravelly-voiced Harlem Democrat, sought a "better understanding" of the Nixon-Mitchell relationship, particularly as illuminated in the tapes of April 14, 1973: the day Mitchell's entrapment became priority number one at the White House. "Why is it that in these transcripts it seems as though the president is very anxious for you to plead guilty . . . that you should be served as an *hors d'oeuvre*, to stay away from the main dish?" Rangel asked. "It just seems as though the loyalty that you have expressed . . . the president and his other people have not expressed that same deep feeling about your involvement, or lack of it. Could you help us out on why this might be?" Mitchell suggested Nixon was "operating on a lot of misinformation," but added: "I am going to have some interesting reading."

After more than a day in the House dock, Mitchell departed through one of the long corridors of the Rayburn Building. "Walking with his lawyers, he simply ignored the press," one representative observed. "To me it was a terrible shame to see him, a former attorney general of the United States . . . walking silently down halls where he had once been greeted with high praise and admiration."[7]

Nothing is known about what reaction Mitchell had, if any, to the eerie sight, on August 9, 1974, of Richard Nixon smiling as he boarded Marine One, the first president of the United States to resign, leaving the White House in disgrace with the specter of criminal prosecution hovering over him. Mitchell issued no public comment—save for one small reference, almost an aside, buried in a legal motion his attorneys filed with Judge Sirica on August 12. Seeking a postponement of the cover-up trial, due to pretrial publicity, Mitchell, through his lawyers, argued Nixon's "*forced* resignation" had unfairly lent credence to the belief that the ex-president "and his close associates, i.e., Mitchell, were criminal conspirators in Watergate."

Most historians have ignored *U.S. v. Mitchell*, dismissing it as an anticlimactic coda to the far more urgent and dramatic story of Nixon's resignation and pardon. Only in the early 1990s did a handful of scholars begin to notice the changes, subtle and astonishing, that the chief accusers of Nixon and Mitchell wove into their stories in the different forums. Even then, no extensive account of *U.S. v. Mitchell*, a kind of Nuremberg trial for the Vietnam/Watergate era, has ever been published.

Not surprisingly, little attention was paid to the flurry of legal motions the former attorney general filed in late 1974: to dismiss his indictment; to disqualify Judge Sirica for bias; to relocate the trial to a different venue; to sever Mitchell's case from the others'; to challenge the admissibility of Nixon's tapes; to correct errors in the tape transcripts; and, most notably, to halt the trial so Nixon's deposition could be taken—all denied by Sirica. Unseen outside the confines of federal district court, the Mitchell motions revealed the tenacity with which the former attorney general fought, in vain, for his freedom.

Most curious was Mitchell's use of the phrase "*forced* resignation." In implying Nixon's wounds were other than self-inflicted, the motion suggested, at least on the surface of things, that the former attorney general remained unwaveringly loyal to his old law partner. Yet elsewhere Mitchell's court filings betrayed a surprising willingness to trade on the widely presumed guilt of the ex-president for whatever legal advantage it might bring. "By accepting the pardon," Mitchell's defense team argued on September 12, four days after President Ford granted it, "Richard Nixon has unavoidably implied that he had engaged in certain illegal acts." Mitchell even cited the statement Nixon issued in accepting the pardon.

I was wrong in not acting more decisively and more forthrightly in dealing with Watergate, particularly when it reached the stage of judicial proceedings. . . . I know many fair-minded people believe that my motivations and actions in the Watergate affair were intentionally self-serving and illegal. I now understand how my own mistakes and misjudgments have contributed to that belief and seemed to support it.

On December 4, with the trial under way, Mitchell escalated his attacks on Nixon—muted, since they were buried in legal briefs, but attacks nonetheless—to their highest pitch. The former attorney general requested that Sirica adjourn the proceedings for a month, until January 6, 1975. That was the date by which a court-appointed panel of physicians had predicted the ex-president, bedridden from a nearly fatal case of phlebitis, would be well enough to withstand deposition. First the December 4 motion recited a lengthy list of events on which Nixon's testimony would be relevant to the defense: the "smoking gun" and "cancer on the presidency" meetings, among others. Then came the assault, the closest John Mitchell ever came to testifying against Richard Nixon.

> Since the Government has contended, *and the evidence now shows*, that Mr. Nixon was intimately involved in the allegedly illegal activities that form the basis of the charges against the defendants, and since Mr. Nixon, a named co-conspirator, is possessed with a great deal of information material to this case . . . his testimony must be published to the jury in order to prevent a failure of justice. . . . The evidence shows that, rather than participating in a conspiracy with Mr. Mitchell, *Mr. Nixon may have participated in a conspiracy which carefully excluded Mr. Mitchell's membership, and which was designed to have an extremely adverse effect on Mr. Mitchell's well-being.* Mr. Nixon's testimony is, therefore, essential to support Mr. Mitchell's contention that he was a victim or object of the conspiracy and not a member of it.

Here, then, at last, was—*Mitchell's revenge!* Here was evidence Mitchell understood the White House tapes' central revelation, which was not legal in nature, but personal: that Nixon turned on Mitchell so easily, so cruelly set up his old law partner and campaign manager, the man he considered most responsible for his election to the presidency. "Why don't you just gear it up?" Nixon had responded, excited when Ehrlichman offered to wire his office for the tête-à-tête with Mitchell. "Do you have a way to gear it up? Well, go gear it!" Here, in the December 4 motion, was the clearest sign that Mitchell recognized Nixon's centrality in the White House effort to frame him, that although the ex-president was badly misinformed by aides, he was also undeniably capable, under the right circumstances, of destroying the man who had made him.[8]

On October 1, 1974, Sirica banged his gavel to open the trial. Over the preceding two months, he had, with metronomic regularity, shot down every defense motion he saw. "The publicity has already died down," Sirica said on August 19, rejecting calls for a delay or change in venue. The firestorm that erupted twenty days later, with Nixon's pardon, did nothing to change his mind. To a plea for more time to study Nixon's tapes—to which even the WSPF prosecutors agreed—Sirica snapped: "I'm not impressed. I don't think it's going to take too long to listen to those tapes." On that issue, however, Sirica eventually yielded, bowing to a unanimous appellate court and giving the defendants another month to prepare.

By the time it started, the trial, expected to last through Christmas, was reduced to five defendants. That June, Charles Colson pleaded guilty to one count of plotting to defame Daniel Ellsberg and his lawyers; as part of the deal, Colson was to testify in *Mitchell* and related proceedings. More curiously, the case of Gordon Strachan was severed from the others'—at the government's request. The special prosecutors concluded that the former Haldeman aide had lied to the grand jury and to the Ervin committee, among other crimes, but that his unusual immunity deal, negotiated with the original prosecutors, made his conviction unlikely. The WSPF had other good reasons to leave Strachan alone. "Strachan's testimony so far seems on balance to be more damaging than helpful in proving charges against target defendants Mitchell and Haldeman," wrote WSPF lawyer Gerald Goldman, in a previously unpublished memorandum, in September 1973. "Strachan significantly discredits Magruder's trustworthiness or the fundamental question of whether Mitchell in fact gave his approval at Key Biscayne." The Goldman memo is another "smoking gun": irrefutable evidence the WSPF *knew* Magruder's testimony against Mitchell on the authorization of the break-in was false, but went ahead and used it anyway.[9]

Richard Ben-Veniste delivered the government's opening statement. After noting that the indictment in the case did not charge anyone with planning or participating in the Watergate break-in, he proceeded to give an account of the operation's origins that squarely blamed Mitchell for its authorization. Recapping the three Gemstone meetings, Ben-Veniste said Mitchell had "reject[ed]" Liddy's plan the first time, "deferred" consideration the second time ("still too much money," Ben-Veniste said), and "okayed" it the third time, in Key Biscayne, "after some discussion."

From this Mitchell could easily tell how the rest of the play would unfold. To make its case, the government would blithely ignore inconvenient testimony from its own witnesses, such as Magruder, who said Mitchell's opposition to the second Liddy plan was based not on cost, but on the stated view that the plan was "still too broad in scope"; or LaRue, whose unwavering testimony about Key Biscayne exonerated Mitchell of having "okayed" the Gemstone plan there. As for the doomed June 17 break-in, that came about, Ben-Veniste said, because Mitchell had been unhappy with the results of the DNC wiretaps and therefore "another entry would have to be made." Of the cross-continental scheming that sent Liddy racing out to Burning Tree, Ben-Veniste, keenly aware of the timeline problems, reverted to vagueness and passive tense, saying only that the discussions "resulted in Liddy being dispatched."

When he came to the destruction of evidence, Ben-Veniste told a flat-out lie. This concerned the materials in Howard Hunt's safe, which John Dean and his deputy, Fred Fielding, had cleaned out two days after the arrests. "So some material went directly to the [FBI] director," Ben-Veniste said, "and *the rest of it* went to the FBI agents." This assertion was, as the prosecutor knew, flatly untrue: It omitted the three notebooks Hunt had kept, chronicling Gemstone's crablike progress, and which Dean—only after completing his plea deal—had belatedly admitted destroying.

On it went: the evening session at Mitchell's apartment, the "smoking gun" meeting, the appeals to CIA, the subornation of perjury, the payments of hush money and offers of executive clemency. At all points Ben-Veniste's skewed version of history implicated the former attorney general above all others: It was Mitchell who hatched the plan to have CIA block the FBI investigation; Mitchell who told Dean to enlist Kalmbach and to get Haldeman's and Ehrlichman's approval; Mitchell who told Dean to utilize the White House fund; Mitchell who told LaRue to pay the final $75,000 to Hunt. Summing up, Ben-Veniste vowed the government would prove beyond reasonable doubt not only that Mitchell had committed all these crimes, but that he was driven by a powerful motive to do so: his desire to "suppress the fact that he was aware of, and indeed authorized, Liddy's Gemstone plan."

Bill Hundley waived his opening statement. On the trial's second day, Mardian's lawyer, David Bress, unloaded on Jeb Magruder, "the confessed perjurer." The defense strategies of Mardian and Mitchell both required exposing the falsity of Magruder's testimony on Burning Tree: the repeated changes in his story as to what time he learned about the arrests, and his claim that Mardian, acting on Mitchell's orders, had called Liddy and dispatched him to find Attorney General Kleindienst. With Liddy silent in prison, his memoir six years away from publication, the truth of the matter—that it was neither Mitchell nor Mardian who gave Liddy his orders that morning, but Magruder himself—could only be established by impeaching Magruder's credibility and timeline of events. Bress told the jury it was "not physically possible" for Mardian to have made the call to Liddy, because by the time Mitchell and his entourage in California first heard about the break-in, Liddy "had already been to see" Kleindienst at Burning Tree.

Finally, on the fourth day, with opening statements concluded, Hundley moved anew for a separate trial. The other defendants were clearly mounting defenses "legally antagonistic" to Mitchell, who was bound to "catch a lot of fall-out" along the way, Hundley said. A separate trial would also better enable Mitchell to "meet head-on" the charge that he authorized the Watergate operation and "establish who did it." Sirica's consideration consisted of two brusque words: "Motion denied."

The trial moved to the government's case, and the calling of the WSPF's first witness: John Dean. As the thirty-six-year-old former

White House counsel strode to the stand, ready to bear false witness against the man he once counted a mentor, he saw in Mitchell's face no emotion or expression whatsoever; it was as if the two had never met.[10]

By 1970, the year before seniority made him the District of Columbia's chief judge, John Sirica was reportedly the most reversed federal judge in Washington. That dubious achievement, along with his sloppy, biased conduct of *U.S. v. Liddy*, the original Watergate break-in trial, fueled Mitchell's hopes for securing an acquittal on appeal.

At the outset of the *Liddy* trial, Sirica ordered sealed a portion of the record showing he had, through staggering incompetence, allowed on the jury a man who barely spoke English. The juror was dismissed only when marshals learned he had improperly communicated with his wife. Things only went downhill from there. Civil liberties advocates—hardly sympathetic to Gordon Liddy—winced when the judge, seeing the defendant conferring with his lawyer, Peter Maroulis, snapped that he was glad to see Maroulis "getting some good advice from [your] client, the former attorney." Liddy had not yet been convicted, let alone disbarred.

Sirica's conduct of *U.S. v. Mitchell* was no better. He approved the seating of a juror who had a close friend on the WSPF staff. Another juror, Marjorie Milbourn, told the judge that while the defendants may be innocent on legal grounds, "in moral terms, [their actions] might not have been everything that is acceptable." Asked if she could still render a fair verdict, Milbourn conceded she could not "guarantee it." Over defense objections, Sirica seated her on the jury; after the trial began, she wrote an admiring note to Leon Jaworski. A third juror admitted he had "probably" expressed an opinion about the guilt of the defendants, and that it varied from moment to moment.

"I can't keep track of everything going on," Sirica complained during the trial. Indeed: At various points, he forgot to excuse a witness; forgot key dates in the case's chronology; permitted forms of cross-examination he later barred, without ever admitting error; proposed, unfathomably, that a witness be cross-examined outside the presence of the jury, then withdrew the idea; admitted he "maybe" allowed the prosecution to pose leading questions to a witness on redirect examination, a flagrant violation of courtroom procedure; admitted he "may" have improperly allowed the prosecution to make a closing argument to the jury during the questioning of a witness; admitted he "probably" gave the prosecution "too much latitude" in questioning a witness; admitted he couldn't always discern the speakers on the Nixon tapes, the trial's most important evidence; mocked Nixon from the bench; and shrugged "when you have a situation like we have, that has been highly publicized, you just can't have a perfect trial."

Most egregiously, Sirica bent the hearsay rules, even by the lax standards of conspiracy cases, to allow John Dean to relate to the jury what had been told him by individuals who were neither defendants in the case nor unindicted coconspirators. Sirica accepted the government's novel contention that Dean's discussions with these individuals, normally inadmissible in a court of law, were admissible in this case because the discussions had allegedly been "set in motion" by one of the defendants, Ehrlichman. David Bress, the former U.S. attorney representing Mardian, reeled from the implications. "I've just heard a new theory of exception to the hearsay rule," he sneered. "The set-in-motion theory. I've never seen it in any law books. There is no law to support it. It is a violation of the hearsay rule." Once again, Sirica disposed of the matter in two words: *Let's proceed*.

The worst was still to come. On the trial's eighteenth day, the seventh of Dean's testimony, Ehrlichman's defense attorney, William Frates, was completing his cross-examination. An accomplished verbal fencer with uncommon gifts for evasion, deflection, and filibuster, the "boyish-faced" witness had held up well under the onslaught, remaining "calm and unruffled," an observer reported, bloodied more on "his character rather than his credibility." He had help, of course:

Unlike in the Vesco trial, where Judge Gagliardi had refused to let Dean get away with dodging questions, Sirica had freely allowed the witness to indulge his penchant for circumlocution and even offered the jury a generous endorsement of his candor ("He has told what he knows").

Now, however, with the jury and witness excused for lunch, Sirica abruptly interrupted a dialogue with Frates, over a line of inquiry the lawyer was seeking permission to pursue with Dean, and began to attack the lead defendant. "Maybe I shouldn't say what is in my mind," Sirica said, in a fit of restraint he quickly overcame. "I will tell you what was in my mind."

It is too bad that Mr. Mitchell didn't say, "Throw them out of here, get them out fast," and you wouldn't even be in this courtroom today. It is too bad it didn't happen that way. Anyway, it is not for me to say what should have been done. The jury hasn't heard that and no harm can be done.

From the lips of the purportedly neutral umpire presiding over his trial, a defendant could scarcely imagine hearing a more prejudicial remark. Convinced he had just witnessed the crystalline example of reversible error he had been counting on Sirica to make all along, Hundley shrewdly said nothing; only after lunch did Mitchell's lawyer rise to make "an objection in the record" to this shocking lapse in judicial propriety. Sirica seemed to anticipate the moment, immediately setting forth his defense for any appellate court to see. "Yes," he said wearily, "it was out of the presence of the jury."[11]

From lead prosecutor Jim Neal, at least, Mitchell knew better than to expect impartiality, and Neal's grueling daylong cross-examination of the former attorney general lived up to all expectations. Looking back on the trial almost two decades later, Neal recalled Mitchell as "a thoroughly delightful man." The two even had their photograph taken together during the trial, posing alongside a Tennessee ham; at bottom Mitchell inscribed: "Which one is the ham?" "I got along very well with John Mitchell," Neal said. "He understood what my job was and, in a sense, he understood what his role was. . . . He knew that he was going to prison and he took it with grace and stoicism."

By the time the former attorney general took the witness stand, on November 26, 1974, the first of the five defendants to do so, twenty-six Nixon tape recordings had been played for the jury. The tapes' introduction into evidence was unprecedented in the annals of criminal law, for they raised thorny questions of foundation (were these the actual tapes or copies, and who would so vouch?); chain of custody (the WSPF had previously complained that tape logs were kept haphazardly by the Secret Service men responsible for them, including on scraps of brown paper bags); and basic constitutional fairness (Sirica had barred all efforts to secure testimony from Nixon, a key participant in the discussions; moreover, there was no way for defense counsel to cross-examine a tape recording, even though the tapes "spoke" to the jury as dramatically as any live witness).

Not until the trial's sixth day, and its seventh tape, did the jury hear Mitchell's voice; characteristically, it was the first heard to address Nixon as "Mr. President." Bill Hundley worried about the unswerving deference Mitchell showed Nixon. The former attorney general had "insisted" on testifying—it had helped in the Vesco trial—but he was otherwise loath to discuss the case with his lawyer. As he had done in the Vesco case, Mitchell left the small matter of conferral with counsel for the morning of his appearance in the witness box. "Do you have any last-minute advice, coach?" Mitchell asked. "I said two things to him," Hundley recalled.

"Number one, don't try to take on every government witness. And number two, and this is more important, I know you love Nixon, but when you're up there just defend yourself. I'm not asking you to say anything bad about Nixon, just leave him out of it." His testimony on direct was okay. Then it was Jim Neal's turn. . . . Within ten minutes of cross-examination he had Mitchell eulogizing Nixon. The D.C. jury was ready to leap out of the box and strangle Mitchell. After we finished I was slouched in the back of his limo and Mitchell said, "What's the matter with you, coach?" "You know what's the matter. Within ten minutes, Neal had you eulogizing Nixon." He said to me, "What difference does it make?" I laughed and said, "You're probably right."

"He was just saying, in essence: 'There ain't no way we're going to win this trial; I might as well go down with my colors flying,'" Hundley said, years later, laughing.

Mitchell's defense began with a cogent and impassioned statement by Hundley, in which he portrayed his client as the innocent victim of a White House conspiracy, led by Nixon, to make the former attorney general the fall guy in Watergate. Hundley conceded that his client had kept to himself what he knew about the White House horrors, but argued that that was not a crime. Mitchell, he said, had made "a conscious decision that he would not run to the police . . . [but] he did not perjure himself. He did not obstruct justice."

At the close of the day's testimony, Sirica dismissed the jury a few minutes early and, "with obvious skepticism," went to work on Mitchell himself, declaring: "I have not yet, frankly, gotten satisfactory answers." When Hundley objected to his client being interrogated outside the jury's presence, the judge turned to Mitchell himself for support, as if they were uniquely accomplished brethren in the legal fraternity. "I think Mr. Mitchell will be the first one to agree with me, as a former attorney general, that every federal judge has the right, or any judge, if he has anything in his mind that has not been developed, or he has a question, as long as it doesn't interfere with the defendant's defense in the case—" "There is no question, Your honor," Mitchell interjected agreeably, having little choice but to join Sirica in opposition to his own lawyer.

Although he framed his queries poorly, what Sirica searched for, in a half hour of questioning, was Mitchell's explanation to a single question: Why had men like Fred LaRue kept coming back to the former attorney general, looking for money for the Watergate burglars, if CRP had no responsibility for the break-in and Mitchell himself had already rejected making any payments on those grounds? "I just can't see there was any other obligation for [Dean and LaRue] to pay anything," Sirica said. "I would like to be enlightened on that subject." "I can't enlighten you, Your Honor," Mitchell replied. "I didn't start it. I didn't make the decision." As for LaRue, Mitchell surmised he was simply "asking me for my advice as a friend." Then, he gave a hint that there were better witnesses for Sirica to quiz: "Dean . . . had directed these operations during a long period of time—"

Neal leapt to his feet, "arms chopping the air," angrily pointing at Mitchell. "Your Honor, there was testimony today that he started [the hush-money scheme]." The accusation drew Mitchell's sharpest words of the trial. "Mr. Neal, that is about the third cheap shot you have had at me and I resent it. That was not the testimony. . . . You know very well that Mr. Kalmbach never mentioned me at all in connection with . . . the origin of this particular plan."

On cross-examination, Neal pummeled the witness for sitting through the Gemstone pitches by Liddy, "a one-man crime wave," and for failing to order his arrest. *You were the highest law enforcement officer in the country?* Neal asked. "Yes sir, that is correct," Mitchell replied, poker-faced. *Hadn't Liddy's first presentation included plans to kidnap radical leaders to Mexico?* Mitchell questioned whether the court should "place the legal definition of kidnapping on it," suggesting instead it was a matter of "segregating out radical leaders and keeping them from [their] activities." *Was it contemplated these radical leaders would agree to this segregation?* Neal asked with undisguised sarcasm. "I wouldn't presume so," Mitchell answered. *And hadn't Liddy proposed to use prostitutes to compromise Democrats?* "I don't have a specific recollection of it," Mitchell testified, "because we didn't get into those details. . . ." *Hadn't Mitchell based his rejection of Liddy's plan on cost, not constitutionality?* "That is not a fact," Mitchell testified.

Then Neal moved to Count Three of the indictment, which charged Mitchell with lying to FBI agents when he claimed, in July 1972, that he had no knowledge of the Watergate break-in other than what he read in newspapers. "What I said was the materials that I had information of had been in the newspapers," Mitchell testified. *Did you hear the FBI agents testify that you did make that statement to them?* Neal asked. Yes, Mitchell said, he had heard one of the agents so testify. *And he is not telling the truth?* "In my opinion, no." Mitchell then asked for a chance to explain the circumstances surrounding the FBI interview. "If you feel some urge to explain the circumstances, Mr. Mitchell, please do," Neal snapped. "I have an urge, Mr. Neal," Mitchell shot back, "to get to the truth." The former attorney general recalled how the two FBI agents were "scared to death" when they came to his office. "They asked a couple of questions," Mitchell said, "and we discussed what my knowledge was, and what had been in the paper, and they left." Neal oozed disdain: *Your urge to get to the truth, as you expressed it, didn't cause you to tell these agents about the three meetings when the Liddy plan was discussed, did it?* "I did not volunteer it for obvious reasons," Mitchell replied. Asked what those were, he stated firmly: "The re-election of the president of the United States."

On December 19, Neal began his closing argument, a four-hour affair replete with Shakespearean recitals from the tapes and laughter-provoking sarcasm. Here was the official history of the scandal, "the first real telling of the Watergate story from start to finish," in which John Mitchell naturally played the central, and most culpable, role. While noting the case was not about who authorized the break-in, Neal still charged Mitchell with having done so at Key Biscayne. When it came to the hush money, Neal relied on a form of guilt by hierarchical association. "Dean, Hunt, and LaRue all admitted this money was hush money," the prosecutor said. "These people don't have the capacity to understand [the larger picture] that a Mitchell,

Haldeman, or Ehrlichman have. If they knew it was hush money, so did Mitchell, Haldeman, and Ehrlichman."

A week later, on December 30, after the conclusion of closing arguments and Neal's rebuttal—as well as two and a half hours of instruction from Judge Sirica, who reminded them "neither the pardon of President Nixon nor any other cases or extraneous matters" should affect them—the jurors were sent to deliberate. Most of the defense lawyers objected to another element in Sirica's jury instruction: his concluding statement to the jury that its duty was "to ascertain what the truth is." This reflected the inflated vision of the court, and of himself, that had long pervaded Sirica's work on Watergate; the job of the jury, the defense pointed out, was not to ascertain the truth of Watergate but merely to decide the guilt or innocence of the defendants based on the evidence and testimony presented. It was no use; Sirica overruled them. At that point, when the case went to the jury, Ken Parkinson placed his hands on the shoulders of his fifteen-year-old son, Tony, and said: "It's in the hands of the gods now, son."[12]

On New Year's Day 1975, as a dewy rain fell in Washington, Judge Sirica received word at 4:25 p.m. that the jury had reached a verdict. Marshals entered the small waiting room off the court where Mitchell had been watching a football game and hustled him and the other defendants and their lawyers into the courtroom. Next came the press and the seven spectators who would witness the historic event, followed, at last, by Neal and Henry Ruth, the special prosecutor who had succeeded Jaworski. Finally Sirica took the bench and summoned the jury. Slowly shuffling in, the jurors averted their eyes. They had taken fifteen hours and five minutes, over three days, to decide the fate of Nixon's elite.

Have the jurors reached a verdict? asked Court Clerk James Capitanio. "Yes, they have," said foreman John Hoffar, his voice quavering. He produced a manila envelope and handed it to a marshal, who gave it to Capitanio, who turned it over to Sirica. "Absolute silence" blanketed the courtroom while the judge reviewed the contents. Then he returned the envelope to Capitanio and ordered him to read the verdicts aloud. Mitchell and the others rose at their adjoining tables, the scraping of their chairs the courtroom's only sound.

For the Watergate cover-up defendants, the moment of reckoning had finally come, and it had to be a surreal one, most especially for Mitchell. Haldeman, Ehrlichman, Mardian, and Parkinson were, to be sure, men of prominence and power, upright Christians for whom the present circumstance represented a reversal of fortune simply too fantastical to fathom. This was certainly true for Mitchell as well, but among the men now standing before judge and jury, only he had enjoyed unparalleled standing before the bar, both in the private practice of law and as the nation's chief law enforcement officer.

Now Clerk Capitanio began reading: *As to defendant Mitchell, Count One: Guilty. As to Count Two: Guilty.* . . . It continued on like that, five times in all for Mitchell, and likewise on all counts for the others—except for Parkinson, at whose acquittal the courtroom let out an audible gasp. Mitchell's face flushed, and he exhaled loudly. Then he turned to his crestfallen lawyer, Bill Hundley, and said: "Don't take it so hard." Next Mitchell reached over to shake the hand of the jubilant Parkinson—whose entire strategy had rested on vilification of Mitchell—and whispered, with a smile: "Congratulations. Good, Ken."

Haldeman's face stiffened. His daughter, Susan, a law student who had attended every day of the proceedings, burst into tears. Ehrlichman sat impassively while his wife draped her arms around him. Mardian took it hardest. He slumped forward, head in hands, shoulders atremble. "He appeared stunned and unable to move," the *Times* reported. Mitchell walked over and said quietly: "Come on, Robert," but to no avail. Even his wife's touch failed to budge Mardian from his paralysis. After he finally stood up and trudged back to his hotel room, dogged the entire way by an unfeeling reporter, Mardian exploded in rage, lashing out at the reporter with a torrent of four-letter words not even heard on the Nixon tapes. It fell to Mitchell to calm his former aide and send the reporter away.

"Mitchell was the trial's mystery man," said CBS News' Fred Graham that night, "puffing his pipe, cracking occasional jokes, refusing to attack Richard Nixon—even after the tapes proved that Mr. Nixon betrayed him—and saying little else. Tonight, after the verdict, his style hadn't changed much." Asked if he had any reaction, Mitchell kept walking and, smiling faintly, mocked his questioners: "Can't you guesstimate? Do I have to tell you?" *Do you plan to appeal?* "You'd better believe it." *Are there strong grounds for an appeal?* "I have about fifty." *What are you going to do now? Are you going to take a vacation?* "I'm going to the moon, I think. That's the best place." With that, the convicted men scattered: Haldeman back to Los Angeles, Ehrlichman to Seattle, Mardian to Arizona, and Mitchell to parts unknown. The media missed his departure, likely to New York. In their absence, official Washington returned to the drearier business of budgets and arms control, stagflation and the Middle East. After a few days, there was, for the first time in years, no more talk of Watergate.

CBS News' John Hart delivered the most insightful postmortem. "Haldeman, the public relations man, is not in the habit of self-examination; he will simply examine his greatest ad campaign over and over, looking for reasons why it failed," Hart said. "John Ehrlichman will never understand why a pious man may have to spend many of his declining years in prison. John Mitchell will understand; it was a big game for him, played by rules he understood, and he lost it."[13]

MAXWELL

Only our concept of time makes it possible for us
to speak of the Day of Judgment by that name; in
reality it is a summary court in perpetual session.

—*Franz Kafka, 1920*[1]

SHORTLY AFTER THE verdicts in *U.S. v. Mitchell* were handed
down, the *New York Times* carried a brief item buried on page 32, beneath a small, inconspicuous headline: "Magruder Says Prisoners
Might Try to Kill Mitchell." This dark premonition came within days
after Magruder and two other Watergate felons—John Dean and
Herb Kalmbach—won early release from prison. In rewarding the
men for their cooperation at trial, Judge Sirica commuted their sentences to time served: For Magruder that meant seven months; for
Kalmbach, six; Dean, only four. "I think there is no question that . . .
as far as many convicts are concerned, he is the one that put them
away," Magruder said of Mitchell; he added some inmates "might feel
very comfortable in becoming famous by eliminating the ex–attorney
general."

Such fears, along with the desire to clear his name and resume the
practice of law, gave Mitchell ample incentive to pursue the appeals

process to overturn his conviction. But it was a process in which the former attorney general never placed much faith. The first measure of the mercy Mitchell was to receive, now that he belonged to the criminal justice system he once headed, was to come with his sentencing by Sirica. Asked if the clemency given Dean, Magruder, and Kalmbach was a sign the cover-up convicts would receive like leniency, Sirica said no. "I don't think it has any bearing," he snapped.

On February 21, 1975, a large crowd of spectators gathered for the sentencing, many of them camping out the night before to ensure their admission. At 9:29 a.m., Sirica took the bench. He asked the convicted men and their lawyers to rise and form a line before him. Once again, the sound of scraping chairs filled the room. Then the judge began reading a short statement explaining how he had arrived at the sentences he was imposing—before pausing in recognition of his breach of protocol: "The defendants and their counsel will first be given the opportunity to make any statements they wish for the record." The convicts returned to their seats.

Each of the lawyers said a few words. Ehrlichman's attorney asked that his client be permitted, in lieu of prison, to perform legal work for a tribe of Pueblo Indians in New Mexico, leading Mitchell to stage-whisper to Hundley: "If they offer us Indians, turn 'em down!" Sirica, not amused, returned to his prepared statement. The judge professed to have spent "many days" giving "careful and serious thought" to the question of "proper" sentences for the men. Now it was time for the grim business at hand. *Mr. Mitchell, would you mind stepping in front of the lectern?* The former attorney general rose and approached the bench, alone. "In Criminal Case Number 74-110," Sirica read, "the Court sentences the defendant John N. Mitchell on each of Counts One and Two to be incarcerated for a period of not less than twenty months and not more than five years."

Sirica droned on about Counts Four, Five, and Six, sentencing the defendant to "not less than ten months and not more than three years" on each charge, terms to be served concurrently with each other, but *consecutive* to those for Counts One and Two—meaning a minimum punishment of two and a half years. "Just one further thing," Sirica said. "The Court recommends to the director of the Bureau of Prisons that he study this case"—meaning Mitchell's— "from the standpoint of a suitable place of confinement in a federal institution." Clearly Sirica shared in the fears about Mitchell's fate behind bars.

The rest of the "brief, somber, and tense proceeding," fifty minutes in all, must have been a blur for Mitchell. Haldeman got the same sentence, and so did Ehrlichman. Each of the Big Three now faced a maximum of eight years in prison. Mardian got ten months to three years. Afterward, Mitchell was the only one of the four to comment. On the elevator ride down, he cracked to reporters: "It could have been a hell of a lot worse. They could have sentenced me to spend the rest of my life with Martha."[2]

A few months earlier, a fifty-five-year-old widow named Mary Gore Dean was relaxing at Marwood, her family's lush estate in Potomac, Maryland, reading a newspaper article about Watergate. The article reminded her of how long it had been since she had laid eyes on John Mitchell: fifteen years, at least, sometime before the summer of 1958, when her husband, Gordon E. Dean, the former chairman of the Atomic Energy Commission, died in an airplane crash off Nantucket. The Deans adored Mitchell. The late Gordon Dean—in between his stints as a reporter, professor, Nuremberg prosecutor, senior vice president at General Dynamics, and head of the AEC—had worked at Lehman Brothers and retained Mitchell for a bond deal in Florida. Now, her eyes fixed on the newspaper, Mrs. Dean grew increasingly disturbed by the "character assassination" to which she saw Mitchell being subjected. Impulsively, she reached for the phone. "I just told him that . . . my husband would certainly want me to be his friend if he needed a friend right now," she recalled in 1992. "And of course, he said he did, so that was it."

From that phone call blossomed the long-dormant friendship

that would see Mitchell through the worst, and last, of his days. In press accounts, Mary Gore Dean was usually described as Mitchell's "companion," but this failed to describe the depth of the bond the two established and the extraordinary support she provided him. Mrs. Dean was, a friend observed in 1977, "the light of John's life." She gave Mitchell a home, a large and comfortable town house in Georgetown that he kept till the day he died and, equally important, the sense of having a large family in Washington, where, at this point, Mitchell had only his teenage daughter, Marty.

Mrs. Dean's three children, toddlers at the time of their father's plane crash, came to view Mitchell as a kind of second father—so much so that Debbie, the youngest child, eventually started calling Mitchell "Daddy." Mary's son, Gordon, once told her: "You know, Mother, the two things that have happened to me in my life that have meant the most to me is the birth of [my] little boy and the time when John came into my life." Mrs. Dean recalled Mitchell in similar terms—more of a savior to her than vice versa. "You just dream after you have lost your husband, as I did . . . that someone this wonderful could come into your life and be a substitute father," she said. "It was absolutely wonderful how he brought so much happiness and light into our family."

Whether Mitchell's relationship with Mary was solely platonic was always difficult to discern. Both were of advanced age and intensely private people. To the *Washington Post* in 1975, Mrs. Dean "denied any 'romance' is involved in her friendship with Mitchell." Bill Hundley recalled that every time he and his wife lunched with the couple, Hundley's wife would whisper: "Are they married?" "I don't know," Hundley would say. "Why didn't you ask?" Mrs. Hundley would persist. "Well, if you knew John," Hundley laughed, "you just *don't*."[3]

Baruch Korff, a retired Orthodox rabbi from New England and die-hard Nixon supporter, also struck up a friendship with the Presbyterian former attorney general. "As he struggled to come to grips with his fall," the rabbi later wrote of Mitchell, "his attitude was more disbelief than self-pity." *A man destroyed by his own explosive devices!* Mitchell would mutter. These conversations with Rabbi Korff, undisclosed until 1995, were significant, for they made clear that Mitchell understood the machinations that produced his conviction, the acts of patricide at the heart of Watergate. *Men I treated like my own children conspired against me*, he marveled of Dean and Magruder. "They wrote their own scenario, interpreting every nod, downwards, upwards, sideways. I was their scapegoat."

Over coffee one day, the rabbi, a scholar of the Talmud but not of Watergate, audaciously suggested Mitchell was equally guilty, but Mitchell held fast. "Aren't you also on tape?" Korff asked. "Nothing incriminating," Mitchell replied. "I usually met with the president in his living quarters or talked to him on a secure line." Meaning what? the rabbi pressed. "Nothing that you don't already know," Mitchell shot back, adding: *My mistake was in men, not in law.*

Remedying that mistake proved impossible. Mitchell spent the years 1975–77 struggling unsuccessfully to stave off disbarment in various jurisdictions and the prison sentence imposed by Judge Sirica. The first body to move against the former attorney general was the U.S. Supreme Court, the venerated institution that Mitchell—with his primacy over the judicial selection process during Nixon's first term, which saw the placement of four justices on the High Court—had reshaped for a generation to come. In March 1975, less than a month after the verdicts came down in the cover-up trial, the Court suspended Mitchell from practicing within its marbled halls. The lower federal were courts not far behind. But perhaps the moment of greatest shame for the man once hailed as "the lawyer's lawyer," worse even than incarceration, which at least conjured some romanticized notions of manliness, was his disbarment in New York State, where Mitchell had been a member of the bar since 1939.

On August 1, Hundley and Cacheris filed a 151-page brief seeking to overturn the former attorney general's convictions in *U.S. v. Mitchell*. The "fifty" grounds for appeal Mitchell had confidently cited immediately after the verdict had boiled down, finally, to two: Sirica's sloppiness during voir dire, which allegedly ensured the jurors were drawn "from a poisoned well," and the judge's refusal to adjourn the trial so Nixon's testimony could be taken. The latter point proved particularly timely. A month earlier, members of the Watergate grand jury had traveled to San Clemente to grill Nixon, in secrecy and under oath, for eleven hours over two days. Even so, lawyers for the WSPF argued there was "no concrete showing" that Nixon's testimony would have helped the convicted men, and they accordingly had no right to review the transcript of the ex-president's sessions with the grand jury (unpublished to this day).

The clashing briefs set the stage for a mini-reunion of the combatants in *U.S. v. Mitchell*. On January 6, 1976, all the old defense lawyers—joined only by Mardian, widely regarded as having the best chance to overturn his conviction—gathered in the U.S. Court of Appeals for the District of Columbia to argue their case. "We did not get a fair trial," began Haldeman's lawyer, John Wilson. Decrying the massive pretrial publicity, Wilson called Watergate "the greatest, the largest, the most virulent publicity situation that ever existed in America from the beginning of time." Hundley attacked the "totally inadequate" jury selection; William Frates denounced Judge Sirica for declaring off-limits the testimony of Nixon, cast here as "the producer, the director, the main character of what this trial was all about."

On October 12, 1976, the Court of Appeals announced its ruling: Mardian's conviction was overturned, the others' upheld. The judges found Sirica erred in not severing Mardian's case when his lawyer, David Bress, stricken with cancer, withdrew from the trial. Two days later, Mardian got a congratulatory phone call from a previously silent figure: Richard Nixon. Stricken with phlebitis and averse to any attempts to compel his testimony, the ex-president had managed to avoid appearing, as either witness or defendant, at *Mitchell*. Mardian's memorandum of their talk, handwritten that day and previously unpublished, offered unparalleled insight into Nixon's private thoughts about the scandal that drove him into exile, and his state of mind there.

For a half hour, Nixon railed at "what a miscarriage of justice" the cover-up trial had been; wondered how Paul O'Brien, the CRP counsel who had relayed some of the hush-money demands, had escaped prosecution; and lamented the Court of Appeals' validation of the guilty verdicts against the other men. "He said he talked to John Mitchell regularly," Mardian wrote. "Mitchell has to appeal but 'they' (presumably Haldeman and Mitchell) doubt there is a chance that the Supreme Court will grant *cert* [hear the case]." Then Nixon returned to the original crime, the Watergate break-in, mystified by its origins and purpose. On The Question—*Did Mitchell do it?*—the ex-president had apparently had a change of heart.

> [Nixon said he was] *sure that the decision was*
> *one that Haldeman, Ehrlichman*
> *and JNM were too smart*
> *to make.*

Nixon suggested the hostile political climate in Washington in the summer of 1972 had made it impossible to contemplate full disclosure to the FBI. "With a fair media or one that was favorable," the ex-president claimed, "Mitchell would have exposed the whole rotten mess before the election and ridden it out."

> *they* [the media] *just couldn't stand his* [Nixon's]
> *landslide victory and*
> *when he proved them wrong*
> *by bringing an end to the*
> *war in Viet Nam they were*

beside themselves—If it hadn't
been Watergate they'd have
gotten to him for something else.

Finally, his conscience obviously weighing heavily, Nixon asked if he "did wrong" in not pardoning all his aides. The notion was not new. Previously unpublished notes taken by John Ehrlichman show that, contrary to all published accounts of Watergate, the president toyed with the idea of a blanket pardon less than a month after the arrests. As Nixon envisioned it, clemency would also have gone to any protesters convicted of disrupting the '72 conventions. Ehrlichman's notes of July 8, 1972, read:

Can't appear to cover-up
Not a whiff of it . . .
Concern re what
Hunt might do—[absent] immunity . . .
WGF [Watergate]
Disruptions at both conventions—
If P. [is] endangered, [it is] a Fed statute viol[ation]—
Some felonies
Book & charge
Then day after elect'n, a
Genl pardon—& order
Prosecutions ended—Except: use of viol[ence]—bomb
Inflicting injury
A basis for pardon on both sides . . .
cut our losses—Blur the negatives
Q. of tone & timing of a statement or message

But Nixon, for reasons unknown, never pursued that course—an appealing one, in retrospect, since the pardon power of the chief executive has since been shown to be absolute, beyond legal challenge—

and now, four years later, Mardian could only offer the older man false solace. "I told him I didn't think he had many options and that pardoning everyone arbitrarily wasn't one of them."[4]

That Mitchell resumed his friendship with Nixon bespoke an extraordinary capacity for forgiveness. Nixon, after all, had surreptitiously taped his old friend and law partner—*for years*—and encouraged others to do so; repeatedly bad-mouthed him on those tapes; and spent several weeks in the spring of 1973 scheming to make him take the rap for a crime in which Mitchell bore no responsibility. Whether the two ever discussed all that unpleasantness—and whether Nixon ever properly apologized to Mitchell—is unknown. The opportunities were there. Mitchell and Marty spent a week with the Nixons in San Clemente in the summer of 1976. "They were close," said Mary Dean. "I know [Nixon] would call if it was [Mitchell's] birthday or if something happened that he thought John would be interested in. . . . [Mitchell] might say to me, you know, 'Dick called me today.' "

When Nixon spoke privately of Mitchell, it was with a mixture of pity and lingering admiration. During the 1976 election, for example, the ex-president urged the Ford campaign to draw on Mitchell's formidable network of political contacts, especially in New Jersey and Missouri. "He knows more about those two states than anybody around," Nixon said. "He can be useful behind the scenes—but it's got to be covert." If anyone dared to bring up Watergate, Nixon would express sympathy for his old friend. "I really feel compassion for John Mitchell," the ex-president told his military aide.

Among those who did show compassion was the man Mitchell had kept waiting when he first learned about the Watergate arrests: Ronald Reagan. After President Ford bested the former California governor in the 1976 GOP primary, Mitchell sent Reagan a note congratulating him on a spirited campaign. "How nice of you to write,"

Reagan began his handwritten "Dear John" reply, dated August 27 and previously unpublished. "Nancy and I are both more grateful than we can say."

> Naturally, we were disappointed—not because of any great hunger for the place or position but there were a few things we thought we could do. Now I'll first have to talk about them + hope they get done.
>
> Nancy sends her best + we both hope our paths will cross again one day.
>
> Sincerely,
> Ron

Mitchell needed more than good wishes, however. Talking to Mardian around this time about their staggering attorneys' fees, the former attorney general "said he was broke and probably could never recover." In his memorandum of their talk, also previously unpublished, Mardian captured Mitchell's defiant resignation to his fate.

> *His attitude is "Screw it—do*
> *what you can and take it*
> *a day at a time."*

On April 21, 1977, National Public Radio reported that the U.S. Supreme Court had decided one week earlier, at the biweekly conference attended only by the justices, not to hear the appeals of Mitchell, Haldeman, and Ehrlichman. The vote was five to three. Citing "sources" at the Court, NPR reporter Nina Totenberg said Justices Harry Blackmun and Lewis Powell had sided with Chief Justice Warren Burger in agreeing to review the case; all three owed their seats on the Court to Mitchell. A fourth in like debt, William Rehnquist, plucked from Arizona to be Mitchell's assistant attorney general before his elevation to the Court, had recused himself, citing his "friendship" with Mitchell. The Court's liberal bloc—Justices William Brennan, Thurgood Marshall, Potter Stewart, Byron White, and John Paul Stevens—voted to decline certiorari.

The NPR leak was a source of "considerable embarrassment" to the justices and a wild card in Mitchell's appeal. Some speculated the Totenberg story could work in Mitchell's favor, forcing the upending of his verdict because disclosure of the justices' private deliberations could be seen as prejudicing his appeal. But the Court declined Mitchell's request to file a memorandum for the record about the NPR report and then announced, without explanation on May 23, that it was indeed rejecting the appeals of Mitchell, Haldeman, and Ehrlichman. "Today's action ends for all practical purposes the long legal fighting over the cover-up," the *Times* declared. The nation girded for the sight of its former top law enforcement official entering prison.

On June 6, Mitchell, looking "thinner but dour as ever," returned to Sirica's courtroom for the first time since the day the verdicts came down. Haldeman joined him. Neither man spoke, and their lawyers made no pleas. Both were fingerprinted and photographed. Afterward, Haldeman addressed the assembled reporters with manly resolve. "More than four years ago I started on a legal process I thought was proper," he said. "I knew it was going to be difficult. I believed it was right. I still think that was the right decision. I'm prepared now to accept the results."

Mitchell, jostled by camera crews, proved less affable. "I hope nobody gets killed out of this," he snapped. As he struggled to navigate the sea of microphones, he barked: "I'm going to get through here first, and if anyone puts one of those things near me, I'm going to knock it down his throat."[5]

Early predictions called for Mitchell to join Gordon Liddy in the prison camp at Allenwood, Pennsylvania, a manageable three-hour drive from Mitchell's Manhattan apartment and the Long Island home of his daughter, Jill Mitchell-Reed. Jeb Magruder had also done time there. But in an unkind stab, Mitchell was instead assigned to the prison camp at Maxwell Federal Air Force Base in Montgomery, Alabama, the former home of Charles Colson and Fred LaRue, a brutal sixteen-hour drive from New York.

The selection of Maxwell reflected government concerns about a violent attack on the nation's highest-profile prison inmate. Norman Carlson, director of the Federal Bureau of Prisons, was reportedly "very concerned" about Mitchell's safety. "People were trying to get him," Carlson recalled. "Maxwell Air Force Base camp was selected at that time because that's where we felt the least possible harm would occur. . . . The inmate population was essentially non-violent, nonthreatening. There were no predatory offenders incarcerated there and as a result of the size and the fact that it was located on an Air Force base, we felt that it was the most appropriate and safest place in which he could serve his time."

That the prison contained no gates, no guns, no guard towers or bloodhounds, and that its lush, twenty-five-acre landscape was dotted by pine trees and bounded by the Alabama River and an enormous golf course—unavailable to the inmates—inevitably made for snide allusions to "the Maxwell Country Club." During spare time prisoners could avail themselves of tennis, badminton, and shuffleboard courts, a softball diamond, and an indoor recreation center boasting a color TV set and weekly movie screenings (perhaps in tribute, *The Godfather* was shown a few days after Mitchell's arrival).

Yet the amenities and pretty scenery were deceptive. Colson felt "a pervasive feeling of despair" hung over the place and an Associated Press reporter who scoped it out found "even a brief visit leaves no doubt that it is a prison where personal freedom is limited." Warden R. W. Grunska assured reporters Mitchell would feel the sting of confinement: "He can't go where he wants when he wants. We tell him when to get up, when to eat, when to go to bed. This is no country club."

Nor was there any doubt how extremely out of place Mitchell

would feel among his new neighbors. The average age of the nearly three hundred inmates was twenty-eight; nearly 20 percent of them were drug offenders. Others were doing time for bank robbery, auto theft, grand larceny, illegal gambling, tax evasion, forgery—even bootlegging. Discreetly suggesting that the Central Intelligence Agency be importuned to provide covert bail funds, and lying at nationally televised Senate hearings, were not the kinds of crimes to which the other inmates at Maxwell could easily relate.

With "uncertain anxiety" the men anticipated Mitchell's arrival. Nobody knew exactly what to expect, either from the mysterious celebrity in question or the authorities charged with his well-being. Rumors flew. One suggested "Big John," as the cons immediately dubbed him, would remain under constant watch of a two-man guard. Another had undercover marshals infiltrating the camp weeks in advance, ready to neutralize any perceived threat to the former attorney general.

Feeding the rumor mill was the unexpected set of improvements prison officials made around the grounds immediately prior to Mitchell's appearance: new air-conditioning units, hasty roof repairs, paint jobs. "I'll bet they treat him like a king," groused one con. "He is a cop and cops look after their own," clucked another. A third vowed action. *All I gotta say is they better keep a pretty close eye on that son-of-a-bitch. First chance I get and I'll stick a shiv in his belly. That mother is the reason I'm here, him and his Goddamn wiretap laws.*

Mitchell spent his last days of freedom the same way millions of other Americans did: wallowing in Watergate. The occasion was David Frost's televised interview with Richard Nixon, a nationally consuming spectacle for which the ex-president received a widely resented fee of $600,000. Broadcast in three installments in May 1977, the Frost sessions—the closest thing to a sustained cross-examination of Nixon in public—dealt first with Watergate, then with foreign policy, and then finally, in the third episode, with topics ranging from Spiro Agnew to Chile to the pardon Nixon received from President Ford. While there were some moments of candor—Nixon arguing "when the president does it, it is not illegal," and acknowledging "a reasonable person" could conclude he had taken part in a cover-up—the old fighter for the most part stubbornly resisted any admission of guilt. "I didn't believe we were covering any criminal activities," Nixon maintained. "I didn't believe that John Mitchell was involved."

This last claim was one Mitchell, having reviewed the tapes of April 1973, was uniquely equipped to rebut. He believed the whole idea of the Frost interviews a "mistake" on Nixon's part. "In his opinion," Mardian wrote after talking with Mitchell, "Nixon really had not thought the matter out when he agreed to do the shows; that he could have done it with a better format and a more sympathetic questioner. He thought Nixon was brilliant in the second interview and that the third show was 'blah.' He felt that the first show put him in a very bad light." Publicly, however, Mitchell said nothing.

Mitchell's primary fear in those days was not incarceration. Running into a reporter from the Nixon days, the former attorney general joked matter-of-factly about his date with "the slammer." He confidently told a friend: *I can face jail.* Prison was not the problem; the trouble was Marty. "The only thing he worries about is his daughter," a friend said. The question of who would look after the girl on weekends and holidays, and in summertime, when she returned from boarding school in Connecticut, was uppermost in Mitchell's mind. He settled on a rotating group that included Ken and Peggy Ebbitt, Mitchell's friends in Bronxville ("We practically raised the girl," Ken later remarked); Sandy Hobbs; and Jill Mitchell-Reed.

For Marty, only sixteen, the vilification and incarceration of her father, so soon after the ugly decline and death of her mother, made for one of the seventies' most traumatic individual experiences. "Her father was the strong person in the family that she went to when her mother was difficult and was drinking," Hobbs recalled. "So here she was, losing the strong person in her family. It was a horrible situation." "Her father was the love of her life," Mary Dean said. "She loved him more than anything in the world. I never saw a daughter and father closer."

Reporters who went looking for Mitchell at this time found he had "virtually disappeared." He was spending all his remaining free time with Marty, holed up in his East Fifty-second Street apartment building. Even there he found no refuge from the censuring eyes of the outside world: A neighbor in the building boasted to a reporter about letting the elevator door slam in Mitchell's face. "If it had been anybody else, I would have held it," the neighbor said. "It was just my way of saying, 'Screw you, John Mitchell.' " Upstairs, Mitchell and Marty whiled away the remaining hours cooking, reading, watching TV together. His last Sunday with the girl was June 19, Father's Day.

A group of old Nixon *loyalistas*, led by Pat Buchanan, tried to throw a farewell party, but the Old Stone Face wouldn't have it. All expressions of sympathy he rejected. *I don't want any of that hearts-and-flowers stuff,* he would say. *What does it lead to?* The day before he was due in Montgomery, Mitchell's most improbable sympathizer, Rabbi Korff, called once more. Was there anything he could do? No, Mitchell said, your prayers, that's all. "My call is not perfunctory," Korff insisted. "I know, and I appreciate it more than I can say," Mitchell said. "You are a great friend, and I value your friendship, but there is nothing anyone can do."

"They got what they wanted," Mitchell said of his arch nemeses, the WSPF lawyers. "But I am not down. I'll live through it. There's nothing I did that I wouldn't do again with a clear conscience." Now the rabbi quoted from Scripture: *They that hate thee will be clothed in shame.* Mitchell merely repeated what he had told the holy man once before: *My mistake was in men, not law.*[6]

Clad in a dark green pinstripe suit, briefcase bulging with notes for a planned memoir, surrounded by reporters and camera crews, the former attorney general strode onto Maxwell's grounds at precisely 11:25 a.m. on Wednesday, June 22, 1977. *Ah, we got you now, we got you now, Big John!* the inmates jeered. *Got you now. You'll be here for a while. You ain't nothin' but another convict with a number now!*

The jubilation extended beyond the prison grounds. Outlaws the world over, from radical Mark Rudd to mobster Meyer Lansky, exulted in the spectacular downfall of Mr. Law and Order. Mitchell ignored the commotion, pausing only to offer a steadying hand to a cameraman stampeded by his colleagues. "Watch it son, don't hurt yourself." Then, with that slight smile: "Good morning, gentlemen." *Anything to say today, Mr. Mitchell?* "Yes, indeed. It's nice to be back in Alabama. It's a nice day in Alabama."

Despite the surrealism of the moment and the unprecedented shame it carried for him, the certitude that he now "personified Watergate more than anyone except Nixon himself," Mitchell was walking tall. "The big man seemed as glacially composed as ever," *Time* observed. "He never complained," said Plato Cacheris, who accompanied his client on the walk. "I think he took it better than I did."

First Mitchell made the acquintance of the warden. "I indicated to him that he'll be treated like any other inmate here," Grunska said. Then came the ritual known to all convicts as R&D: receiving and discharge. It was at this point that Mitchell officially traded in his identity for an impersonal assigned number: 24171-157. Four times the former attorney general was fingerprinted. ("In case we make a mistake; they smudge sometimes," the guard said; *was he being sarcastic?*); then Mitchell was photographed a *dozen* times ("Different copies for different offices; I'm told you know all about it," the guard said—*unmistakable impertinence!*).

Next, 24171-157's belongings were confiscated and his measurements taken. The cash he was carrying was credited toward his account at the commissary, where he could purchase his beloved pipe tobacco, snack items, and popular jailhouse reading material like *Playboy* and *Penthouse*. His watch and ring were shipped home; when the same was proposed for his suit, Mitchell raised his first objection. "Just hang it up in the closet. I think I'll be needing it very soon." He didn't say why. He was permitted to keep his shoes. Then he was issued bed linens and the clothes he was expected to wear for the duration of his stay: four pairs of white boxers, four white T-shirts, four pairs of white socks, one pair of dark socks—for weekends and "off" hours—four light brown collared shirts, four pairs of dark brown khaki pants, and one pair of steel-tipped shoes.

For his first meal as an imprisoned felon, Mitchell was taken to lunch by one of the "hacks," as guards were informally known. Plodding through the cafeteria "chow line," Mitchell patiently waited his turn like everyone else. The cuisine reflected the Southern surroundings: grits, biscuits, collard greens, cornbread, Southern fried chicken, and other items that, the *New York Times* gleefully noted, "a Wall Street lawyer might find unfamiliar."

Suddenly Mitchell came face-to-face with a snarling con named Bobby Lawson, a convicted bookmaker doling out vegetables across the counter. Prison authorities had repeatedly assured Mitchell's lawyers none of Maxwell's inmates could claim any grudge against the former attorney general. Yet back in May 1974, when the Supreme Court had invalidated 494 wiretap cases, the requisite forms having been improperly signed years earlier by Mitchell's executive assistant, the case of Bobby Lawson was, remarkably, one of *four* in which Mitchell remembered signing the forms himself; thus while many other convicts had seen their convictions overturned, Lawson had not. "Welcome to Maxwell, Mr. Mitchell," Lawson now sneered. "You put enough of us here." Mitchell looked Lawson straight in the eye without budging. *You son-of-a-bitch, I didn't put anybody here*, he snapped. Mitchell let his eyes linger an extra second before moving down the chow line. He had survived his first test of manhood on the inside.

At 5:00 a.m. the following morning, a loudspeaker woke the inmates with a crisp, irritatingly cheerful "Good morning!" Mitchell rose from the steel-frame bottom bunk to which, in deference to his age and in violation of seniority rules, he had been assigned. He left his six-by-seven-foot cubicle and headed for the bathroom, where he showered, shaved, and brushed his teeth in the company of the forty-five other convicts with whom he now shared Maxwell's F Barracks. Like all new arrivals, the former attorney general was initially thrown in with a group of "unassigned" workers whose job was to report to the camp's shuffleboard court every day at noon, be counted, and await further instructions. Their orders usually included such menial tasks as hoeing the rose garden, picking up cigarette butts, and emptying wastebaskets. When, on his third day at Maxwell, he quickened his step but still arrived late for this assembly, the hack in charge relished the moment. *I don't care if your name is John Mitchell! You ain't gonna be late for my counts! You* understand *that? If you're late again, you'll get an hour's extra duty for each minute you're late!*

In time, Mitchell was assigned to toil in the prison's education department, devising new programs for the inmates, doing a little teaching, and clerking in the prison library. It did not take the other inmates long to figure the former Wall Street innovator could prove useful as a source of free legal advice; he became a popular man. Even Bobby Lawson lightened up. Mitchell wound up drafting the bookmaker's appeal. When a federal judge rejected it, Mitchell took the rebuff personally. "I appointed that man to the bench!" he marveled. "I didn't realize I'd appointed a bunch of idiots as judges!" But a chow-line friendship was now cemented. "How's the soup today, Bobby?" Mitchell would ask. "It's just like your Filipino cook used to make for you at the Justice Department," Lawson would say, smiling.

After a few weeks, Mitchell began corresponding with old friends, taking pains, as always, to minimize his troubles. To his former secretary, Susie Morrison, whom he regarded almost like a daughter, the former attorney general described his time at Maxwell as "just plain dullsville." "I do a lot of legal work for the inmates and have had a few successes," he joked, "but by and large I could accomplish more on the outside."

One inmate thought Mitchell in the early going appeared "pale, apprehensive, and perhaps a little afraid," but most prisoners treated the "celebrity criminal" with an uncharacteristic deference that bordered on reverence. Some maintained a studied aloofness, but others rushed to solicit Mitchell's friendship; few wanted to reenter civilian life unable to boast of having known Big John in the joint.

Even the prison administrators seemed in awe of him. It was not lost on the inmates that while they were invariably summoned over the PA system with a curt barking of their surname and a command to report to a given place, the first time Mitchell's presence was required, the overhead speakers emitted words never before heard at Maxwell: "Attention on the compound! *Mister* Mitchell, *please* come up to the control room."

Before long, the former Nixon consigliere acquired his own crew, a group dubbed "Mitchell's Boys." They included a recidivist criminal serving time for transporting stolen merchandise across state lines, named Gene Franklin—he and Mitchell became inseparable—and Maurice "Blackie" Malaway, a con roughly the same age as Mitchell. In the evenings, work assignments completed, the trio would haul lawn chairs out onto the Green, a meadow on the banks of the Alabama, to hold court. Some nights, pipe in hand, Mitchell would regale his boys with tales of the high and mighty characters he had known on the outside.

Gazing on the state capitol one night, Mitchell recalled Governor Wallace's fondness for booze, and mused: "I'll bet old 'Bourbon George' is up on the seventh floor and drunk as a skunk by this time." *The tapes?* They should have been destroyed. *Haldeman and Ehrlichman?* Only grunts and pipe smoke. But for the two men he considered the most despicable in the Nixon White House—Colson and Dean—Mitchell had a few choice words, all right. "The classic stool pigeon," he said of Dean. "All he had to do was keep his mouth shut. He knew what it was all about." And Colson? "If it weren't for him, Watergate would never have happened," Mitchell said. "A born-again Christian? Ha! I'd take my chances with the lions!"

That Nixon frequently telephoned Mitchell while he was in prison—three times a week, according to one report—was attested to by several sources. "I would go to see him in jail . . . in connection with parole," Hundley recalled years later, "and the camp superintendent would say to me, 'Don't go in now. He's talking to Nixon and he wouldn't want you to hear him.' Of course, I'd go in and say:

'That's great. Here you are in the slammer and he's out there in San Clemente!' " "Ah, Bill," Mitchell would shrug, "don't be like that."[7]

Three months into his sentence, Mitchell made his first bid for mercy. In court papers filed in September 1977, William Hundley disclosed his client was suffering from heart problems brought on by hypertension and from a rare and severe case of degenerative arthritis in his right hip. The condition had grown "extremely painful," Hundley wrote, with Mitchell's "mobility . . . severely impaired." Though he sought no specific sentence reduction, Hundley said Watergate had had a "traumatic and devastating" effect on Mitchell's family— particularly for Marty, who was "of sensitive years." Mitchell's finances also lay in ruins. He owed nearly $500,000 in legal fees and personal loans, Hundley said, and would remain in debt the rest of his life. "The result produced by these circumstances constitutes the severest fine," Hundley wrote.

The petition also explicitly refuted remarks Nixon had made to David Frost, in which the ex-president alleged that had it not been for Martha's "mental and emotional problem that nobody knew about . . . there'd have been no Watergate." Nixon had it backward, Hundley argued: "[Watergate] was the apparent proximate cause of the increasing mental conflicts of defendant's wife." The only other reference to Watergate was—for the first time—an expression of remorse. "Counsel is authorized by Mr. Mitchell to advise the court that he is truly sorry for and regrets those actions of his that resulted in his conviction," Hundley wrote.

After reviewing Mitchell's motion—and one filed by Haldeman, who responded to the Frost interview by angrily accusing Nixon of admitting his "guilt" only after ensuring "his pockets are lined with $600,000"—Judge Sirica was unmoved. The record, he said, was insufficient for the granting of mercy. Instead he scheduled a hearing and took the unusual step of dispatching Herbert Vogt, deputy chief of probation for the District of Columbia, to visit the Big Three—

Mitchell, Haldeman, and Ehrlichman—in their respective cells, armed with a piece of equipment sure to stir fear and loathing in all Watergate convicts: a tape recorder. If the men wanted Sirica's mercy, they would have to make their own statements of contrition, and the judge was determined they should be captured on tape, a fitting—or perhaps mocking—counterpoint to the incriminating recordings that had figured so prominently at *U.S. v. Mitchell.*

Ehrlichman took the exercise most seriously. Imprisoned at the Swift Trail Camp in Arizona, he spoke to Vogt for twenty minutes in a highly confessional, quasi-psychoanalytical tone, ruing how he had "abdicated my moral judgments and turned them over to someone else. And if I had any advice for my kids, it would be to never, ever defer your moral judgments to anybody—your parents, your wife, anybody. That's something that's very personal. And it's what a man has to hang on to." Haldeman, working as a chemist in the sewage treatment facility at Lompoc Federal Prison and reported by his lawyer to be suffering "indignity, horror, fear, shame, disgust and all the other overwhelming emotions that assail a thinking man who is required to enter prison," also spoke at length into Vogt's portable cassette recorder. Uniquely, the former chief of staff, struggling to convey how "very real" his remorse was, invoked religion. "I am sorry for what I've done, for what I've been responsible for, for what's been the result of the damage to many, many people, and, I think, to the whole governmental system," Haldeman said. "I recognize my responsibility to atone."

Mitchell, as ever, proved the most laconic. He was the only defendant to acknowledge the presence of the man operating the tape recorder—slyly calling attention to the coercive element in the proceedings—and his statement of contrition was, by far, the most lawyerlike. "Mr. Vogt," Mitchell began, "in the moving papers that my counsel filed with the courts, in support of the motion for reduction of sentence that you referred to, my counsel stated that he was authorized by me to advise the court that I was truly sorry for and regretted those actions of mine that resulted in my conviction before

the court, and I wish to confirm to you and to the court my authorization to my counsel to include that statement in the motion
papers."

Keeping safe distance from remorse, Mitchell merely confirmed
he had authorized Hundley to express regret on his behalf; moreover,
the sorrow extended only to those actions that *resulted in conviction*—
not to his actions, period. Now he fairly drowned in legalisms. "My
reflections have convinced me that the convictions resulting from my
actions—which I have reviewed and which I now, of course, find that
they have been reviewed and affirmed by the appropriate lower
courts, and I know that our judicial process has run its course and I,
of course, accept that outcome."

The question now was: Would Sirica buy it? The answer came on
October 4, 1977, in a two-and-a-half-hour hearing held in the same
courtroom where the judge had presided over *U.S. v. Mitchell*. Now
semiretired and recently recovered from a heart attack, Sirica ordered
the new Watergate tapes played in full. For the better part of an hour,
the air was thick with the eerie voices of Haldeman, Ehrlichman, and
Mitchell; Nixon, once again, was absent. Afterward, Hundley pleaded
that Mitchell was "severely crippled" by the arthritis in his hip.
Haldeman's lawyer, John Wilson, reprised old arguments about the
"legal unfairness" of Nixon's pardon. "There does seem to be an element of unfairness," Sirica allowed. "But Mr. Nixon paid a great
penalty as the first president to be forced to resign in disgrace."

After recess, the judge returned to the bench, ready at last to show
some compassion to Nixon's top aides—but only of a modified, limited kind. Having given "careful consideration of all the facts and circumstances," Sirica said, he was reducing the sentences of the Big
Three to one to four years each, making Mitchell and Haldeman eligible for parole in July 1978—still a full eight months away. Ehrlichman, who had reported to prison earlier, would regain his freedom
sooner.

Nine days later, Mitchell, unreceptive to Sirica's brand of mercy,
appealed to President Carter for immediate release. "I am in pain and

am taking drugs," Mitchell said in a signed petition. X-rays had shown advanced deterioration of bone and cartilage in his right hip; the only solution was an operation to replace the diseased bones with aluminum or plastic substitutes. "I want the operation as soon as possible," Mitchell wrote. "Without in any way reflecting on the Federal Bureau of Prisons, I do not want this delicate surgery performed within the prison system." In a separate letter to Attorney General Griffin Bell, Hundley said his client was taking excessive amounts of Valium. "I am concerned," Hundley wrote, "that the constant pain, the need for surgery and the continued incarceration, coupled with all his other problems, could be too much even for a strong man like John Mitchell."

Carter rejected the petition. But Bell liked Mitchell and was aghast his predecessor had gotten "more than a bank robber" for his sentence. A former judge, Bell granted Mitchell an "unusually long" medical furlough of two weeks, twice the normal length, so that the former attorney general could have tests on his hip conducted in a private hospital in the nation's capital. In January 1978, Dr. Joseph Palumbo, a former Washington Redskins team physician, announced that while evaluating Mitchell's hip, he discovered the patient was also suffering from a "large abdominal aortic aneurysm"—a ballooned blood vessel in his stomach—requiring immediate surgery at Georgetown University Hospital. Bell extended Mitchell's furlough through the end of the month.

The surgery took three hours, after which hospital officials emerged to say the patient was "doing well." "I was outside in the waiting room with Mary Dean," Jill Mitchell-Reed recalled with a shudder. "[The procedure] was much longer than they expected. They went in and they found another little thing . . . and they took a lot of blood."

In an extraordinary act of grace, Bell granted Mitchell five consecutive monthlong furloughs, unprecedented in the history of the Bureau of Prisons. This allowed Mitchell to recuperate from his aneurysm operation and to undergo another surgery, on his hip, on April 10, outside the prison system, to which he would return that May.[8]

On July 5, 1978, three parole examiners visited Maxwell to interview the former attorney general and determine whether, if granted early release, he would pose any further danger to the community. When the results of the interview were typed up, the regional commissioner, based in Atlanta, recommended the prisoner's release on August 16; but the U.S. Parole Commission, based in Washington, overruled him and ordered Mitchell held another six months, until January 19, 1979. By way of explanation, the commission noted Mitchell's role in Watergate had been one "of high severity."

That summer Jerris Leonard, Mitchell's former DOJ aide, flew to Maxwell to help his old boss appeal the commission's decision. "The jail time he spent never bothered him a bit," Leonard said, "except for the fact that, number one, he knew he wasn't guilty. And when Carter did to him what he did; that's the only time." *How the hell can these guys do this to me?* Leonard remembered Mitchell exclaiming.

Mitchell's appeal assailed the commission's "bias and vindictiveness" and attacked its ruling as "arbitrary, capricious, and unfair." The former attorney general had "paid dearly for his errors," his lawyers argued, and he deserved immediate release. Joining Mitchell's legal team for the effort was Charles Morgan Jr., a former executive of the American Civil Liberties Union and one of the prime early movers in the drive to impeach Nixon. (Morgan, ironically, had also successfully intervened in the original Watergate break-in trial to suppress the racy contents of the DNC wiretaps.) But unfortunately for Mitchell, his appeal was heard by U.S. District Court Judge Frank M. Johnson Jr. Back in 1971, Mitchell had squelched Johnson's Supreme Court candidacy. Years later, Johnson had not forgotten the episode. He quickly rejected Mitchell's appeal, calling his sentence consistent with Ehrlichman's.

Mitchell spent his sixty-fifth birthday, September 5, working in the Maxwell library. The final months of his sentence ticked by, a day at a time. He received "thousands" of letters from people wishing him well, and, from the government, a sixth and final furlough, this one standard, to visit family after Christmas.

Two longtime Wall Street pals, Roald Morton and Brent Harries, started the John Mitchell Defense Fund to defray their friend's exorbitant legal expenses. A solicitation letter went out to 150 people; Harries later estimated he raised about $200,000. Contributors came from Mitchell's Old Guard: friends from "the Street" and the legal fraternity. "I'd tell John that so-and-so sent in a check and here's his address, and I assume he'd put together a nice note," Harries recalled. One of Mitchell's nice notes went to Francis X. "Joe" Maloney, a partner at Mudge Rose, the law firm that once, but no longer, bore the names Nixon and Mitchell. "Brent has told me of the very large contribution you have made to the 'Save Mitchell Foundation,'" Mitchell wrote to Maloney. "I only hope that things are so good at the firm that it did not hurt to [sic] much. Needless to say, I am most appreciative."

> Jimmy and Griffen [sic] have finally decided to cancel my reservation at this country club and my membership expires next Friday. I can't wait to turn in my suit. My training here has put me in great shape and I'm looking forward to tackling that cold, cruel world.

At dawn on the morning of January 19, 1979, as Mitchell emerged from Maxwell, the last of the Watergate convicts to regain his freedom, the same convicts who had greeted him with jeers when he first arrived now cheered him. *Give 'em hell, Mitchell!* In recognition of his "free legal advice and good friendship," the inmates had even thrown Big John a going-away party. CBS News' Fred Graham found the ex-convict "caustic as ever" in his final turn on the national stage. First, he thanked his well-wishers: "It's just wonderful to have the feeling that you get from those letters." Then the former attorney general extended his congratulations to the news media, swarming him for the last time, and offered them a word of advice, one of his sharpest one-liners ever: "From henceforth, don't call me. I'll call you."[9]

GHOST

My father would not be an easy person to understand, to reach his guts and soul.

—*Jill Mitchell-Reed, 2003*[1]

CLOUDS FILLED THE nighttime sky over San Clemente. It was Labor Day weekend, 1979, and Richard Nixon, slowly emerging from
his exile at Casa Pacifica, had decided to throw a party. The ostensi-
ble occasion was the sixty-sixth birthday of his former law partner,
campaign manager, attorney general, and consigliere—"the last loyalist," as he privately referred to Mitchell—but the real occasion, of
course, was Mitchell's release from prison.

The Nixons had encouraged Mitchell to invite his own special
guests. "Have you ever gone three thousand miles for a cocktail party?"
he asked Brent Harries. No, Harries said. "Well you're going to. . . .
The president's going to have a cocktail party for me in San Clemente."
To Mitchell, that's what Nixon forever remained: *the president*.

Some 250 people, including many old White House faces, savored the outdoor Mexican buffet. Nixon, in unusually high spirits,
stood in a receiving line for more than an hour, shaking hands and

bantering with the arriving guests, bounded by Pat Nixon on his left and by Mitchell on his right. When Harries and his wife appeared, Mitchell introduced them for the first time to Mary Dean, who threw her arms around Harries and exclaimed: "I want to thank you so much for what you've done for John."

Finally, the whole group was summoned poolside: Nixon wanted to say a few words. He spoke of the history they had made, and thanked everyone for all they had done for him. No one, of course, with the exception of Pat Nixon, had done more for the ex-president than the guest of honor, and so, with a rare gaze directly into Mitchell's eyes, the ex-president raised his glass and offered a toast. "John Mitchell has friends," Nixon said. "And he stands by them."

The poignancy of the moment was not lost on the crowd. They had all read the transcripts of Nixon's tapes, which captured in stark detail the president's yearlong vacillation on The Question—*Did Mitchell do it?*—and the dark conclusion Nixon had reached. All the guests knew that Nixon's heartless betrayal of Mitchell was preserved for posterity on thousands of magnetic spools, tucked away in temperature-controlled vaults at the National Archieves. The fact was that when push came to shove, Nixon had *not* stood by his most doggedly loyal friend, and the toast that evening was Nixon's tacit way of acknowledging as much—of pleading guilty—before their assembled intimates.

After that, Nixon never again spoke publicly of Mitchell in any depth: not in any of the foreign policy books he published to rehabilitate his image, nor in the "intensely personal" set of reflections he published in 1990, two years after Mitchell's death, entitled *In the Arena: A Memoir of Victory, Defeat, and Renewal.* The book's first mention of Mitchell—one of three, all fleeting—noted only that news of Mitchell's conviction on New Year's Day 1975 had interrupted the Rose Bowl. "I could no longer even take refuge in my favorite avocation," Nixon wrote, "watching sports on television."[2]

———

"I think I have to stay away from the Mitchell subject at this point," Nixon told an aide on March 21, 1973—and, for the most part, in public, he did. The most notable exception was on the evening of September 8, 1977—Mitchell, if he was watching, would have been seated in the inmates' recreation room at Maxwell—when David Frost returned to the airwaves, after a three-month hiatus, with more of Nixon's thoughts: on China, the Supreme Court, the daily *Götterdämmerung* with Kissinger.

"Well," the host announced near the end, "we've covered a lot of ground in this program, and there's time now only for a postscript—which is not inappropriate, because Richard Nixon himself volunteered what follows, almost as a postscript to our discussions. It's a remarkable story he obviously wanted to tell about John and Martha Mitchell. But we found it personally revealing about Richard Nixon himself. Perhaps you will, too."

"Let me tell you about John Mitchell," he began. "You mind one—just a second? It's never been told before. And I haven't *asked* John whether I can tell it. But . . . he is too—I suppose *decent* a man to ever tell it. You see, John's problem was not Watergate. It was Martha. And it's one of the personal tragedies of our time."

Over the next several minutes, Nixon disclosed on nationwide television how Mitchell, in the closing weeks of the '68 campaign, had had to have Martha institutionalized; how he himself had pleaded with Mitchell to become attorney general, suggesting life in Washington might somehow make Martha "better"; how she had initially thrived, making her celebrated calls to Helen Thomas, becoming "a good thing to yuk-yuk-yuk about"; and how Martha had come totally unglued during Watergate, as in Newport Beach, when, as Nixon put it, she "busted her hand through a window."

"This sets the stage for why I feel [the way I do] about John," Nixon went on.

> I asked Bebe about it, Bebe Rebozo. John and Martha used
> to go down and stay with him on their vacations. And Bebe

said, "You know, I talked to John about Martha." This was, incidentally, during the campaign, shortly before the election. She was acting up a bit then. This was after he left the committee. And he said, "John"—and they'd had a couple of drinks, and John was talking a little freely to him. And he said, "John, why don't you put her away, like you did in '68?" Bebe said tears came into John's eyes and he says, "Well, because I love her." Well, you can't fault a guy like that. Sure, great stone face—but he loved her. He knew she was emotionally disturbed. He knew it wasn't just the booze. Sometimes she could be this way with no drinks, and sometimes be perfect with a lot of drinks.

And so I'll never forget . . . it was toward the end of the campaign, September, October. Hadn't heard from John. Called to say, "John, how's the campaign going?" He sounded very depressed. He said, "Oh, the campaign's going great." And I thought, God, maybe he's depressed about Watergate or something. No. Then I could hear, from the phone, somebody come into the room. He said, "Mr. President, would you mind saying hello to my girl?" I said, "Sure." I thought he meant Marty. That's his daughter, a sweet, lovely girl. He adores her. I said, "Sure." Martha came on the phone. Her voice—you know, she could be just as charming—wonderful when she talked. She says, "Mr. President, I just want you to know that there are only three men in the world that I love. I love John, I love Bebe, and I love you." And the next night, she was on the phone at midnight, raisin' hell about *everything*.

Okay. We come to the Watergate period . . . to the period when the axe is gonna fall on John. *And I must say, I made some statements then.* Dean came in and said, "Draw the wagons up around the White House, Mitchell is the guy," and Haldeman and Ehrlichman wanted to put it on Mitchell, and all the rest. And I said, "Well, it must look that way to me.

Indict him, and it'll be a hell of a tough couple of weeks," and all that sort of thing, but, "That's the way we have to go." This was in April.

Here Frost posed his only interjection, to remind Nixon of the term he had used to characterize Mitchell at the time: *hors d'oeuvres.* "I knew they'd want more," Nixon protested. "Somebody said it was an *hors d'oeuvre,* I said, 'Oh, no. They won't stop at Mitchell. They'll want more.' Just as I told Ray Price when Haldeman and Ehrlichman went. He says, 'You know, when Haldeman and Ehrlichman leave'—this is April 29th [1973]—he said, 'that'll be enough for them.' I said, 'No, Ray. You know writing, but you don't know politics. They're just gonna raise the ante.' But I understood. I didn't like it.

"I knew that [Mitchell] was strong," Nixon continued.

He never lets his emotions show. Except he does have a quiver in his hand at times; it's better now, I understand. But I just didn't know what was going to *break* the man! Or her! I didn't know how bad the situation was. *I've talked too long about it.* But just let me just summarize it by saying: I am convinced that if it hadn't been for Martha—and God rest her soul, because she in her heart was, was a good person. She just had a mental and emotional problem nobody knew about. If it hadn't been for Martha, there'd have been no Watergate. Because John wasn't mindin' that store. He was practically *out of his mind* about Martha in the spring of 1972! He was letting Magruder and all these boys, these *kids,* these *nuts* run this thing! The point of the matter is that if John had been watchin' that store, Watergate would never have happened.

Here Nixon paused to regroup. "Now am I saying here, at this late juncture, that Watergate is—should be blamed on Martha Mitchell? Of course not. It might have happened anyway. Other things might have brought it on. Who knows? I do say this: *I'm trying to explain my feeling of compassion for my friend John Mitchell.* John Mitchell is a smart man. He's too smart to ever get involved in a stupid, jackass thing like Watergate! And John Mitchell also knew, he was smart enough to know, of the dangers of cover-ups and that sort of thing. But on the other hand, John Mitchell could only think of that poor Martha, and that lovely child Marty.

"And so," Nixon concluded, "that's the human side of this story, which I don't—I know that you, in the press, you can't be interested in that. You can only be interested in 'Who shot John?' Well, go ahead."[3]

Uniquely among the Watergate convicts, Mitchell returned to Washington. He moved back into Mary Dean's Georgetown town house, but never recovered the life he enjoyed before the great scandal. The Wall Street wizard who once commanded the respect of the Rockefellers was now a disbarred ex-convict, his opportunities limited, the hands extended in partnership few and mostly uninspiring.

"He had lost his confidence," observed Jack Brennan, a former military aide to Nixon who befriended Mitchell around this time. "He didn't say it, but I knew. I could tell that he was always afraid people would reject him." A former Marine Corps colonel who had shepherded Nixon through his last days in the White House, then became the ex-president's first chief of staff in San Clemente, Brennan one day introduced Mitchell to an old friend and business partner, James M. Tully, at Mary Dean's town house. A Korean War veteran and former NYPD cop, Tully had refashioned himself into an international businessman, using his military pension to launch a series of companies that mostly went nowhere. On March 29, 1979, he incorporated his latest creation, the consulting firm Global Research International—"We just picked it out of the air," Tully said of the name—and set up shop five blocks from Mitchell's Georgetown home at Thirtieth and N Streets. One day Tully invited his new friend to visit Global Research, and Mitchell accepted. "Take a seat," Tully said. Mitchell began swiveling comfortably in the chair. "How do you like it?" "I like it," Mitchell said. "Well, it's your office," Tully said.

While Brennan's intent was "never to utilize Nixon for any of his activities," he knew bringing the Big Enchilada on board would suffice, in the eyes of the world, as the next best thing. As Brennan acknowledged: "The fact that John Mitchell was [Nixon's] closest ally did not hurt us at all overseas." "How would you like to be our partner?" Tully asked Mitchell. "I never thought it would be any other way," he replied. A handshake sealed the deal.

Mitchell began showing up at Global every day, walking the four blocks. He remained with the firm until his death, not merely because he "hit it off" with the two former military men who started it, but more likely for the more depressing reason that, as one intimate put it, he received "no better offers." The trio compartmentalized its work, each man pursuing his own deals, involving the others only as needed, pooling and dividing proceeds in the few instances when their efforts produced results. "Of all the activities that we undertook, very few of them were successful," Tully said years later. "There were some big numbers in terms of dollars earned; whether they were collected or not was another matter."

Global Research's core activity was the nebulous realm of overseas consulting: representing foreign firms seeking a foothold in America and American firms looking to do business abroad. At other times, Global acted as a middleman, playing matchmaker to different companies and, occasionally, to governments. A bizarre cast of foreigners paraded past Mitchell's nose and pipe, pitching Byzantine money transfers, oil deals, rice deals. Former Kentucky governor Louie Nunn, a key witness in the ITT scandal a decade earlier, lured Mitchell into a time-consuming, and ultimately fruitless, bid to standardize interstate billing for cellular phone calls. "Oh, we had everything proposed to us," Tully said. "I mean anything you can think of, we had, short of white slavery and murder."

Though in time his work would require extensive overseas travel—

London, Paris, Rio de Janeiro, the Caymans—Mitchell at first acted as a faux senior partner, the heavyweight whose mere presence, it was hoped, would compel reluctant brides to the altar and scare fakers away. Key to success was dispelling the "fear of rejection" Brennan still sensed in the older man. Since one of Global's most bankable clients was Hess & Eisenhardt, world-renowned maker of armored cars (including the limousine carrying President Kennedy when he was assassinated), Mitchell thought to contact old colleagues at the State Department, thinking they could be persuaded to retain the firm. But he wouldn't make the call. "I knew all these guys just loved Mitchell," Brennan said.

> And I would, for a long time, try to get Mitchell to call and make an appointment, and he wouldn't. He would just make excuses. And it occurred to me that he was afraid that they would say no, that they didn't want to see him. . . . And of course [we] called the State Department and they couldn't *wait* to see him! They were just delighted to see him!

Late in 1983, Brennan stumbled on what seemed like a fabulous deal: brokering the sale of $181 million in hospital, prison, and military uniforms to Iraq, which was then engaged, under the leadership of Saddam Hussein, in a long-running war against Iran. Since the seizure of the American embassy four years earlier, the United States had severed diplomatic relations with Tehran and was now beginning to tilt toward Iraq in the conflict. Brennan said he received "encouragement" from individuals "very high in our government" to go forward. So did Mitchell. "John spoke directly to [CIA director William] Casey," recalled Deborah Gore Dean, "and Bill Casey . . . suggested other areas where John may be helpful to Iraq."

As Brennan soon found, the manufacture of uniforms is a labor-intensive business, and American companies, with their stringent union requirements, found it difficult to compete with overseas firms.

So Brennan outsourced the job to Romania. But he had Mitchell do something Brennan later wished he'd done himself: ask Nixon for a letter of introduction to Romanian dictator Nicolae Ceauşescu. Nixon complied on May 3, 1984, writing Ceauşescu: "I can assure you that Colonel Brennan and former attorney general John Mitchell will be responsible and constructive." More than two years later, after the Romanians had partnered with a Saudi firm, Pan East International, to produce the uniforms, Nixon again wrote to Ceauşescu: "My good friend John Mitchell told me recently that the contract between the [Romanian] Ministry of Light Industries and Pan East International was completed, and I wanted to let you know how highly Mr. Mitchell spoke of the diligence of the Romanian workers."

Global's commerce with the Iraqi regime proceeded on other fronts. On a trip to Baghdad, Brennan had been instructed by Saddam's men to deal through Sarkis Soghanalian, a three-hundred-pound ethnic Armenian, born in Syria and raised in Lebanon, who now lived in Miami and was renowned as "the Cold War's largest arms merchant." Soghanalian, whose clients included Muammar Qaddafi and CIA, helped Global broker the sale of twenty-six helicopters from Hughes Aircraft and the McDonnell Douglas Corporation, a $27.4 million deal from which Mitchell and Brennan stood to reap a $584,000 commission. The only problem, in both the uniform and helicopter deals, was that Soghanalian never sent Global its fees, worth $3.54 million.

"These arms dealers are having a hell of a big impact on us," Mitchell grumbled to a friend. He wrote Soghanalian in August 1985 complaining about the "long, dry spell in our dealings" and demanding "your remittance at the earliest date." The collection effort went nowhere. In fact, Global's partnership with Soghanalian ended in the most rancorous way. "They would sell their mothers if they could," the arms dealer spat. Global sought recourse in the courts, but saw only Pyrrhic victories. When Mitchell was later found to have died intestate, his survivors quarreling with each other in probate court, it was the set of judgments against Soghanalian, ordering him to pay Brennan and the Mitchell estate $3.54 million in outstanding fees, that pitted Marty Mitchell against her half sister, Jill Mitchell-Reed, and other members of the Mitchell family. The money never materialized.[4]

"Everybody in this town loves me," Mitchell joked a few months before his death. But he had returned to Washington a ghostly figure from another era. Former chief justice Warren Burger—who owed his robes to Mitchell—once espied his old patron being treated like a leper at a National Geographic Society party. "John Mitchell was off in a corner, I think with his daughter," Burger recalled. "Nobody was going near him and talking to him. And my wife and I said, 'Let's go over and talk to him.' We went over and shook hands with him and engaged him in conversation for a little while, and that broke the ice and a lot of other people did, too." Other times the pariah was not so fortunate. An Associated Press reporter never forgot the lonely sight of Mitchell walking the streets of Georgetown, "a gray man plodding along in his gray way."

Mitchell's financial troubles could have been eased considerably, even eliminated, had he availed himself of the obvious option, so appealing to his fellow Watergate convicts: writing a book. In fact, he had quietly contracted to do just that, with Simon & Schuster, on July 21, 1975. Mitchell's Untitled Memoir of the Nixon Years, as the publishing agreement hailed it, was to run 100,000 words and be delivered no later than April 1, 1976; in return, Mitchell received an immediate signing bonus of $50,000, with another $100,000 due before publication.

Mitchell reportedly arrived at Maxwell with a satchel full of notes for the project. In his letters from prison, he solicited stories and materials from former associates, and mused about publishing more than one book. Years later, Jill Mitchell-Reed claimed to have found her father's incomplete handwritten manuscript, but she declined repeated requests to see it.

Others suggested the project never got very far. John Ehrlichman, a full-time author after Watergate, told an interviewer the day after Mitchell died that Simon & Schuster had hired veteran reporter Nick Thimmesch, one of the few reporters Mitchell actually liked, "to write Mitchell's book for him," but Thimmesch supposedly grew "totally frustrated" because "Mitchell didn't cotton to him and wouldn't talk to him." Bill Hundley, who represented Mitchell in his book deal, never saw page 1 from his client. "[The publishers] were very unhappy because he wouldn't write about Watergate and he wouldn't write about Martha," Hundley said. "I think they always thought they could persuade him, but they couldn't." "He thought everybody had already had enough trouble," said Mary Dean, "and he didn't want to add on to any of it."

In the end, executives at Simon & Schuster never saw page 1 of Mitchell's manuscript either, and in February 1981, the publisher filed suit in New York State Supreme Court. Mitchell was forced to cough up an immediate $7,500, and to sign a repayment schedule mandating annual payments of $10,000 for the next six years. Thereafter, he had until 1991 to pay off the accrued interest. Ultimately, he repaid only $40,000, roughly 60 percent of his debt. Simon & Schuster sued his estate and settled, in November 1992, for a $10,000 payout. Thus ended the saga of John Mitchell's Untitled Memoir of the Nixon Years.[5]

The toll Watergate took on Mitchell's family was his "deepest sorrow," Jill Mitchell-Reed recalled—and the full extent of the damage may never be known. "John, I think more than anything in the world, was sorry about the way his own family turned out," recalled another intimate. "He really felt that he was responsible. And although everybody in the world tried to tell him, 'You know, John,

only so much of this can be your fault,' he just always felt that without him, everybody would have been happy."

[His children] fell apart. And he blamed himself. Now everything that went wrong from then on [was], "Well, gee, if you
hadn't gone to jail, my marriage wouldn't have broken up,"
and "If you hadn't gone to jail, I'd be able to get a job." And
it went a little bit too far.

Some have even suggested Mitchell's disgrace played a hidden
role in the decline of his son, Jack, who, having battled alcoholism
and left a series of good jobs, finally developed a malignant brain tu-
mor. He battled bravely but died, in 1985, at the age of forty-four.
Mitchell was devastated. He adored his son's wife, Jacqueline, and
their three children. "I could have sworn my father would die the day
he rode from Riverhead to New York in the ambulance with [Jack],"
Jill recalled. "It touched my father deeply, quite deeply. He was white
when he went in and shaking when he came out. I thought that I
would lose both of them that day." "The only things that he ever
really was unhappy about," Mary Dean said, "was that if any of this
[the Watergate scandals] affected his children."

MRS. DEAN: It was the low point of his life when he lost
his son.
ROSEN: How did he deal with it?
MRS. DEAN: By remaining even more quiet. I think he didn't
want to make it too bad for those that were around him, but
he couldn't hide what was happening to him.

With his brother, James, with whom Mitchell had frolicked in
the sands of Patchogue a half century earlier, the former attorney general maintained virtually no relationship at all. The last time he saw
his brother Robert was at a post-prison release party thrown by the

Wall Street firm of Standard and Poor's in 1979, almost a decade before Mitchell died. This obvious estrangement the brother, also a lawyer, attributed both to Mitchell's innate inwardness and "a psychological reaction" on his own part. Robert never once took his older brother aside and asked what the hell had happened in Watergate, never sought even feigned reassurance he was not the irredeemably evil character that *Time* and *Newsweek* had made him out to be. "I never really had the opportunity," Mitchell's brother said, "and I don't think he would have talked about it, anyway."

Asked what it was like to watch his brother go down the way he did, one of the most vilified Americans of the twentieth century, Robert said: "Very unpleasant. You try—to try and defend him, and yet not agreeing in my heart with him. Just, just put yourself in that position. What would you do? I mean, you have your loyalty to your brother and you have your loyalty to your own principles." *What did your brother do that clashed with your principles?* The eighty-three-year-old retired lawyer paused before answering, in a quiet voice. "Well, I don't want to think about that, if you don't mind, yeah?"[6]

Mitchell went to his grave knowing he was going to cause still more pain to those he loved. For among his ventures at Global Research was a set of deals that came to haunt Deborah Gore Dean, Mary's attractive and outgoing daughter, who had come to regard Mitchell as a father.

After earning her bachelor's degree in political science from Georgetown University and tending bar at family-owned restaurants, Debbie secured a job, with Mitchell's help, at the Department of Energy; from there, using his name as a reference, she went to the Department of Housing and Urban Development (HUD), as an assistant to Secretary Samuel R. Pierce Jr., the Reagan cabinet's sole African American. A disinterested administrator, Pierce delegated ever greater authority to the twenty-nine-year-old Dean, and in June 1984 appointed her executive assistant. She stepped right into the vacuum

Pierce created. "It's common knowledge on the Hill," a representative remarked, "if you wanted to get something done in the secretary's office you talked to Deborah Dean."

Among the many projects Dean oversaw was HUD's Section 8 Moderate Rehabilitation Program. Established in 1978, Mod Rehab, as insiders called it, was essentially a giveaway program, a multimillion-dollar bonanza under which developers of low-income housing projects received rent subsidies and tax credits for approved renovations to their housing stock. Developers eager to obtain federal funding happily paid hefty fees to GOP consultants who promised direct access to HUD officials and an inside track on Mod Rehab contracts.

In early 1983, Mitchell's old friend Louie Nunn, the former governor of Kentucky, wrote the former attorney general requesting assistance on behalf of one of his clients, a Florida real estate developer named Aristides "Art" Martinez. The regional HUD office in Jacksonville had denied Martinez's request for loan increases to help refurbish Marbilt, one of the developer's low-income housing complexes; could Mitchell help? Though no record of it survives, Mitchell evidently contacted Debbie Dean. Documents show they communicated about Marbilt as early as February 1983. The following month she wrote Mitchell a "Dear Dad" letter in which she noted that the relevant HUD office had "tried as best it could to be lenient," but otherwise refused to get involved in the matter. "As you know," she wrote, "I stand behind the decision of the carreer [sic] people in Headquarters." Four months later, in October 1983, when the department reversed itself and approved Marbilt's loan increases, she sent Mitchell a copy of an internal HUD document announcing the decision and scrawled on it: "Daddy. F.Y.I." In July 1984, Nunn sent Mitchell a check for $8,613.94.

Impressed with Nunn's effectiveness, Martinez retained the former governor again, in early 1984, this time to help obtain Mod Rehab funding for 293 units in the developer's Arama project. Nunn's fee was set at $225,000 for legal fees and $150,000 in consulting fees; on the consulting contract, Nunn scribbled his intention to pay half to Mitchell. That July, Debbie Dean sent Nunn a letter—care of Global Research—informing him that the Arama request would be approved. A year later, Nunn made good on his scribbled promise and sent Mitchell a check for $75,000.

The timing of the Arama deal coincided with another on which Mitchell had been working—not with Nunn but with Richard D. Shelby, a former Reagan White House aide and regional director of the 1984 Reagan-Bush campaign. In May 1985, Shelby, also a consultant, contacted Mitchell—wholly ignorant, he later claimed, of Mitchell's relationship to Debbie Dean—to discuss the Park Towers Apartments in Miami. The Park Towers' developer, Martin Fine, had retained a local consulting firm, EMF & Associates, which had in turn subcontracted with Shelby in a quest to secure Mod Rehab funding for the complex's 143 units.

Amid a number of one-on-one meetings Shelby held with Mitchell and Dean, the three met together once, in September 1985, to discuss the project. Shelby later testified he intentionally withheld from Dean the fact that Mitchell stood to share in Shelby's fee if the deal came off; as far as Shelby knew, Dean never learned that fact until after she left HUD. Two months after the three-way meeting, the Park Towers got its Mod Rehab contract, a project worth $14 million. It took another seven months for the legal details to be worked out, but that came with a waiver which exempted the Park Towers from regulations prohibiting it from receiving the approved funds. On January 4, 1987, Shelby sent Mitchell a check for $40,000.

Art Martinez, meanwhile, must have been hard-pressed to believe his good fortune. Things had worked out so swimmingly at Marbilt and Arama, he decided to hire Louie Nunn once more. This time Martinez paid the former governor $200,000 to help obtain Mod Rehab funding for a development called South Florida I, also in Dade County. For unknown reasons—perhaps because Mitchell feared leaving his fingerprints on too many HUD deals—Nunn this time worked through Jack Brennan. The next month, in May 1986, Martinez sent letters to Nunn and Brennan audaciously requesting that they not only secure the Mod Rehab contracts, but with them an explicit declaration from HUD that the funding was set aside for 219 units.

Three weeks later, Brennan met with Debbie Dean and turned over some paperwork on South Florida I. Three months after that, HUD once again authorized Mod Rehab funding for the Metro-Dade Public Housing Authority—for precisely 219 units. Four days after the agency formally approved Martinez's proposal to refurbish the 219 apartments, in December 1986, Nunn sent Brennan a check for $109,000. That Brennan's involvement was an act of subterfuge, concealing Mitchell's role, was suggested by separate deposits into the men's personal bank accounts within the next forty-one days: $60,000 for Mitchell, $50,000 for Brennan.

All this—the intrigues surrounding Marbilt, Arama, Park Towers, and South Florida I—would likely have remained known only to a small circle of developers, consultants, and bureaucrats, denizens of HUD's obscure nether regions, had Debbie Dean not sought the position of Assistant Secretary for Community Planning and Development, a post requiring Senate confirmation. That led to hearings, and hearings led to investigations.

Spearheading the fight against Dean's nomination was Senator William Proxmire, a Wisconsin Democrat who, as chairman of the Senate Banking, Housing and Urban Affairs Committee, had cultivated a reputation as a leading penny-pincher on behalf of the American taxpayer. In colloquies with Proxmire, Dean had airily dismissed suggestions that developers lobbied her as something that would have been "a tremendous waste of time" on their part, and she declared: "I have never given or approved or pushed or coerced anyone to help any developer." In the end, the Senate withheld confirmation and Dean was denied the promotion, but the damage to her life and career was to prove far worse.

Spurred by the Proxmire hearings, HUD's inspector general launched a probe of the Mod Rehab program. Released in April 1989, the Office of the Inspector General (OIG) report documented a five-year pattern wherein hundreds of millions of dollars in Mod Rehab funds were allocated "on an informal, undocumented, and discretionary basis." A follow-up probe by a House subcommittee found "rampant abuse, favoritism, and mismanagement." From there, the Justice Department took over, and the affair acquired the one appurtenance that, in the post-Watergate era, conferred major status on medium-sized scandals: a special prosecutor.

Mitchell's death likely spared him another go-round with the special counsel, but Dean was not so fortunate, and in her thirteen-count federal indictment, issued in July 1992, the man she called "Daddy" appeared as "Unindicted Co-conspirator One." Nunn and Shelby, who cooperated with the prosecutors, were listed as numbers two and three. The indictment charged Dean with conspiracy to defraud the government, acceptance of illegal bribes (in dealings unrelated to Mitchell), and lying to Congress in her statements to Proxmire.

In a lengthy interview conducted four months before she was indicted, Dean seemed strangely at a loss in knowing what to believe—or how to feel—about John Mitchell. "What his role was, precisely, is in doubt," she said. Her one certainty was that Mitchell never divulged to her his financial stake in Mod Rehab funding decisions. "I did not know that John Mitchell had any involvement himself until after he was dead," she said, adding that he only sought two favors during her tenure at HUD. The first was a routine call seeking information; the second was a request that she write the July 5, 1984, letter to Nunn telling him the Arama project had been approved for funding.

When the OIG report was released, eight months after Mitchell's death, Dean was "flabbergasted" to see his name listed as one of the consultants who profited from the Mod Rehab contracting process. "I thought people were lying about John to get me," she said. Angrily, she telephoned the inspector general's office and took "strong exception" to the inclusion of Mitchell's name. "I want to see a copy of the check that Louie Nunn supposedly wrote to John Mitchell!" she demanded. When the agent said he couldn't produce it, she threatened to hold a press conference, exposing the OIG report as a smear of Mitchell, and hung up. Next she dialed Jack Brennan. "I am furious!" she cried. "I will not allow them to slam John like this!" "And Jack said, 'Whoa, little Debbie [laughs], whoa!' He said, 'You may not want to do that. Because John did have some dealings with HUD; they just weren't with you.' And I said, 'What?!' And he said, 'Well, how much detail do you want me to go into?' And at that point I decided that what I did not know was my defense."

Dean's case, described by the *New York Times* as "an illustration of the ways of power in Washington," took five weeks to try. If convicted, she faced up to sixty-two years in prison and fines totaling $3.2 million. She spent six days on the stand, trying to persuade the jury that despite her closeness to Mitchell, her powerful position at HUD, and the consulting fees he earned from the agency's decisions, the two never discussed the projects in which he had a financial interest—the very convergence of events that, a year and a half earlier, she had conceded to an interviewer would not "sound believable." Prosecutor Robert O'Neill hammered her mercilessly, waving the "Daddy" notes in her face and denouncing her to the jury. "Her six days of testimony is worth nothing," O'Neill said. "You can throw it out the window into a garbage pail for what it's worth."

The jury convicted Dean on all counts. Yet her legal odyssey had only just begun. At sentencing, in February 1994, she stopped short of acknowledging guilt, but, in a letter read aloud in open court by Judge Thomas F. Hogan, she said she "mourn[ed] the fact that this case has cast dishonor on myself, my family, and a department whose mission I heartily admire." As for "Daddy," she said, "I should not have entertained any inquiries from John N. Mitchell on any HUD matter." Judge Hogan sentenced her to twenty-one months in prison and fined her $5,000—only slightly more than what she was convicted of accepting in illegal gratuities. The special prosecutor denounced the sentence as "far too lenient."

Two years later, the U.S. Court of Appeals threw out five of Dean's convictions while affirming the other seven (one count had already been dismissed). Unbowed, Dean appealed her convictions to the Supreme Court, where she also lost. To pay her legal bills, which exceeded $750,000, she went into the antiques business, at first selling off pieces handed down by her mother. But she never served time. Instead, she spent six months under house arrest in 2002, during which time she was permitted to report to her Georgetown shop and make buying trips to New York.

Mitchell died before the OIG report was released, before his name surfaced publicly in the HUD scandal, and before the Justice Department commenced the longest-running independent counsel's investigation in American history. He never had a chance to defend himself, against charges real ("Unindicted Co-conspirator One") or imagined ("knowingly profited from poverty," cried the *Washington Post*'s Haynes Johnson). And there was good reason to believe that "the weight of the malice" that reduced Debbie Dean to tears was really directed, all along, at the former attorney general, for the special prosecutor in the case was Judge Arlin M. Adams, a patrician Philadelphia lawyer appointed to the Third Circuit Court of Appeals by President Nixon in October 1969.

Adams had clashed with Mitchell at the 1968 Republican convention, when the Pennsylvania politico defected to Rockefeller's camp, a betrayal that earned him a tongue-lashing from Mitchell he never forgot. In addition, Adams blamed Attorney General Mitchell for blocking his ascension to the Supreme Court. In 1990—while he was serving as independent counsel in the HUD probe and Deborah Gore Dean was under investigation, soon to be indicted—Adams told *USA Today* he "might have been a Supreme Court justice . . . if I hadn't offended John Mitchell." Naturally, Adams denied any animosity toward either Mitchell or Dean, but seldom has there been a more glaring case of a prosecutor harboring a conflict of interest.

The woman Mitchell considered his daughter carried the burden of that conflict, residue from the Nixon years, well into the twenty-first century, but this was not entirely unanticipated. "Mere mention of John's name . . . just starts all sorts of things happening," she realized after she saw Mitchell cited in the OIG report. "There are just certain names that people react to, and John has one of those names. And it really frightened me."[7]

EPILOGUE

*Everyone assumes I know the whole Mitchell story,
but no one knows the whole Mitchell story.*

—*William Hundley, 1985*[1]

DOGGED BY HEALTH problems in his final years—including a mild stroke he suffered overseas, and concealed from intimates—Mitchell still followed politics, but from above the fray. He watched the Iran-Contra scandal unfold with a sense of déjà vu, bemused both by Len Garment's reemergence as the lawyer representing former national security adviser Robert McFarlane ("a pretty heady little character" with "a hell of an ego") and by the star turn of Oliver North's bombshell secretary, Fawn Hall ("the current Mata Hari"). He worried President Reagan was verging "pretty close" to a replay of Nixon's fate.

As a former campaign manager, Mitchell took special delight in the 1988 presidential election. He recoiled when Vice President Bush chose Dan Quayle, an inarticulate, largely unknown senator from Indiana, as his running mate, and savored the moment when Bush's Democratic opponent, Michael Dukakis, looking to burnish his military credentials, donned an oversized helmet and clambered incongruously atop a tank. "I swear you couldn't tell him from Mickey Mouse!" Mitchell chuckled.

Shortly before 5:00 p.m. on November 9, 1988, with Bush's electoral triumph not yet twenty-four hours old, Mitchell was walking home from his meager Global Research office in Georgetown when he suddenly collapsed on the sidewalk outside 2812 N Street. He had been through a lot in his seventy-five years, including the unnerving sight, just four days earlier, of federal agents grilling Debbie Dean about activities he had deliberately concealed from her.

As he plodded along N Street, a nine-year-old skateboarder rolled past him, taking note of the man's "nice suit" and bald head. Then the youngster heard "an audible thump" over his shoulder, and wheeled around to see the older man's body splayed across the sidewalk, his head resting on the root of a tree. Panicked, the child ran to his house and called for an ambulance. Two passersby immediately recognized the stricken man and attempted to rouse him. "Come on, Mr. Mitchell!" they shouted. One man started performing CPR.

Paramedics briefly restored Mitchell's heartbeat and blood pressure, but he stopped breathing during the three-minute ambulance ride to George Washington University Hospital and never recovered. The strong man had succumbed to a massive heart attack and was pronounced dead at 6:27 p.m.

The networks all carried the news instantly. (ABC News' Peter Jennings committed the very first biographical error, erroneously describing Mitchell as "attorney general during the Watergate scandal"; in fact, he'd left office almost four months before the famous arrests.) In a surprisingly compassionate editorial, the *New York Times* mourned the death of this "complex, taciturn man" who, though "bright, charming and not personally ambitious," had "sadly . . . made himself a monument to unquestioning loyalty and corrosive suspicion." Early editions of the *Washington Post* carried a paragraph in Lawrence Meyer's obituary that read:

He was the ultimate Nixon loyalist. Unlike some of his co-defendants, Mitchell wrote no memoir, no kiss-and-tell insider report, no novelized version of his time in Washington. He lived according to his own code and to the end of his Watergate ordeal, *he was a stand-up guy*.

Later editions omitted the heretical words of praise. For comment, the *Post* turned, of all people, to Jeb Magruder, who sent Mitchell to prison with false testimony, but now remembered him "a mentor, almost like a father," and Bob Woodward, another tormentor who wrongly surmised "what few secrets of the Nixon administration that may still remain went with him."

The funeral service, held at St. Alban's Episcopal Church in Washington, was a bittersweet reunion of aging White House and Justice Department colleagues. Haldeman, Ehrlichman, and Kissinger stayed away, as did William Rehnquist. But Dick Kleindienst, Bob Mardian, and Fred LaRue were there, along with Bill Safire, Len Garment, Rose Woods, Ron Ziegler, Dwight Chapin, Jerris Leonard, and Don Santarelli. Last but not least, seen escorting Mary Gore Dean to her seat in the front pew, was the man Mitchell still referred to as "the president." Now seventy-five and basking in the glow of a surprisingly successful rehabilitation campaign—"He's Back!" *Newsweek* trumpeted on a 1986 cover—the ex-president had no words for the mourners or press, kind or otherwise, about his most loyal friend. Mingling inside the vestibule at St. Alban's, he could only be heard to say, in his oddly disembodied way: "He was a friend of ours."

Dick Moore, a friend since their hockey days in 1930, delivered the eulogy. "He was the strongest man I ever knew," Moore said. "It has been said that you can judge a man by the friends he makes—and keeps. By that test John Mitchell was a giant. He made good friends in every phase of his life, in his every field of endeavor . . . indeed, in every one of the fifty states. . . . It is no exaggeration to say that every friend John Mitchell made throughout his lifetime was still his friend the day he died."

It is hard to imagine a more significant testimonial but it is easy to understand. After all, those of us who really knew John Mitchell knew that what he went through was the most unfair, cruel treatment of a public figure in the life of this cynical city. But the restraint, the grace, the courage with which John Mitchell faced his ordeal made the bond of friendship—and love—even stronger.

Moore said he had tried to think of the phrase that best described his departed friend, and finally found it in—of all places—the *Washington Post*. It was the very phrase the paper's editors had cut from their late editions. "John Mitchell was a stand-up guy," Moore said. "To Mary and to John's family, I say this: You will find lasting comfort in the sure knowledge that this stand-up guy loved you."[2]

Was there something in the way Attorney General Mitchell exercised power that foreordained his fall? Or was Mitchell's disgrace the result of a fundamental flaw in the man's character, an inescapable consequence that would have obtained had he never held high office at all? Or was he simply a victim of others' malfeasance?

Such questions inevitably resurrect old debates, timeless and irresoluble, about the relative impact of historical forces and great men; but those interested in Mitchell's case—and all who consider America a nation of laws should consider his the ultimate cautionary tale—must keep uppermost in mind the vilified figure's own enduring words: "You will be better advised to watch what we do instead of what we say."

One of the central ironies of the Watergate era—a recognizable product, with its IBM management ethos, omniscient, voice-activated recording machines, and televised dénouement, of the Information Age—was John Mitchell's collusion in a public image so starkly at odds with his real personality. Eulogizing the former attorney general in the *New York Times*, William Safire noted the "abyss" between man and persona. "Dour, stern, taciturn, forbidding on the outside, and warm, loyal, staunch, steadfast on the inside," Safire wrote. "Few public men have so deliberately cultivated the widespread misconceptions of themselves." This schism persisted through Watergate, the seismic scandal in which Mitchell, the advocate of expanded wiretapping powers who bore no responsibility for the bugging in question, was falsely cast as its most culpable figure.

His conviction was heralded as a solemn reminder of the supremacy of law and "the price of arrogance," as the *New York Times* put it in 1975. Yet Mitchell, according to those who knew and worked with him, never wielded power in arrogant fashion. Unlike Bobby Kennedy, Mitchell chose the attorney general's small cubbyhole office in the Department of Justice, not the grand ceremonial room, as his working quarters. He communicated his thoughts orally and committed little to paper not because he feared self-incrimination, but because Mitchell, unlike Nixon, eschewed self-aggrandizement and knew the best way to achieve results was through the cultivation of people, not of ideas through memoranda.

"The John Mitchell I know is far different from the man the public perceives," John Dean remarked in 1977. "I don't look upon Mitchell as being the sinister force. . . . I saw him more as a restraining influence on Nixon and some of the people in the Nixon White House." Indeed, stories of Mitchell abusing his personal power— using it spitefully or punitively, throwing his weight around, demeaning subordinates—were rare, and invariably involved upstart junior types envious of Mitchell's power and determined to usurp it for themselves.

Mitchell used his power to advance the greater good, which he happened to see as indistinguishable from the fortunes of Richard Nixon. One Friday afternoon in October 1970, the attorney general was hosting a luncheon at the Department of Justice, seated at the head of a long table, when an aide brought a note that made him scowl. "Who gave her a visa?" he growled. The State Department, the aide said. The woman in question was Mrs. Nguyen Cao Ky, wife of South Vietnam's vice president, then en route to an antiwar rally on the National Mall. Support for "the Movement" from so prominent a citizen of the very country the United States was spilling blood and treasure to defend was simply unacceptable. "Where is she now?" Mitchell asked. *Over the Atlantic.* "Can we have the plane land in Boston?" Mitchell asked. *What reason could the pilots give for the diversion?* "I don't know," Mitchell blurted out, "quarantine, epidemic, anything! I don't care!" The next morning, local news radio reported a commercial airliner carrying the wife of South Vietnam's vice president had developed engine trouble and turned back for an emergency landing. Mrs. Ky never made it to the rally.

On those occasions when he saw Nixon's dark impulses threatening the national interest, Mitchell, to his everlasting credit, repeatedly intervened on behalf of the republic. He did nothing, for example, when the president, as captured in previously unpublished notes, issued this order a few months before the midterm elections of 1970:

Mitchell—no prosecutions whatever re Mafia or any Italians until Nov.

Mitchell was one of the few men, perhaps the only one, who had the standing and guts to tell the president he was wrong. This happened in the ITT case, when Nixon ordered the Justice Department to drop its appeal of a court decision favorable to the conglomerate and demanded the immediate firing of Richard McLaren, the intractable chief of the antitrust division. It happened again in the Moorer-Radford affair, when Nixon, more justifiably, wanted to prosecute the chairman of the Joint Chiefs of Staff, the nation's top uniformed military commander, for espionage; it was Mitchell who dissuaded the president from this course of action, which would have done incalculable damage to the nation and its armed forces. Mitchell's appeals on such occasions may have been couched in the language of raw political calculus, not on the basis of good governance, but Mitchell knew his man and served the greater good with the approach most likely to steer Nixon on the responsible path.

ITT and Moorer-Radford might have been Mitchell's finest hours as a public servant were it not for an even earlier episode in which the attorney general once again intervened to save Nixon, and the country, from Nixon. This was in the summer of 1970, when the interagency discord between the FBI and CIA had reached its nadir, and J. Edgar Hoover, the aged and crotchety FBI director, had imposed a total freeze on cooperation between the two agencies. The enthusiasm Hoover had previously shown for illegal entries and wiretaps, dating back to 1938, had suddenly been replaced by overriding caution and an insistence on written approval for such missions from either President Nixon or Attorney General Mitchell.

Among those irritated by Hoover's newfound priggishness was a twenty-eight-year-old White House aide named Tom Charles Huston. Imperious, abrasive, staunchly conservative, and mousy—an unsmiling executive-branch version of Woody Allen—Huston had monitored the activities of Yippie and SDS leaders in the fall of 1969, sending intelligence reports up the White House chain that encouraged aggressive action against violent student factions. Now, in the supercharged period following the killings at Kent State, with campus strikes spreading across the country, Huston reckoned the time had come to act decisively. Working in secret with William C. Sullivan, the devious assistant FBI director in charge of the Bureau's intelligence division, and with like-minded representatives from CIA, the National Security Agency, the Defense Intelligence Agency, and other offices, Huston devised a set of recommendations for the president that would effectively overturn Hoover's recent restrictions on domestic covert operations. The resultant document, later dubbed the Huston Plan, was sent in memorandum form to H. R. Haldeman in July 1970—over the footnoted objections of Hoover, who was kept in the dark about the formation and conclusions of Huston's interagency group until the last possible moment.

Perhaps the most infamous government document of the postwar era, Huston's Domestic Intelligence Gathering Plan advocated the wholesale removal of "operational restraints" on internal intelligence collection. It called for expanded surveillance powers for NSA; "intensification" of FBI break-ins and bugging missions; increases in the number of persons whose mail could be opened surreptitiously; wider infiltration of campus groups; greater use of undercover military agents on domestic soil; and major budget increases for such operations. Huston warned his plan was both "clearly illegal" and "highly risky," but could produce, if properly implemented, "the type of intelligence which cannot be obtained in any other fashion."

Nixon never approved the plan in writing, but verbally instructed Haldeman to do so, which the chief of staff did in a July 14, 1970, memorandum to Huston, captioned "Domestic Intelligence Review." "The recommendations you have proposed as a result of the review have been approved by the president," Haldeman wrote. But, Haldeman added, the president did not want to implement the plan in the way Huston suggested: a joint session with the heads of the intelligence agencies—and Hoover—in which Nixon would lay down the law and leave no doubt the Huston Plan had the backing of the highest authority. Instead, Haldeman wrote, Nixon "would prefer that the thing simply be put into motion on the basis of this approval."

Even at an advanced age, his faculties in evident decline, Hoover was a force to be reckoned with, a supremely canny bureaucrat who knew there was only one man who could get Nixon to rescind his approval of the Huston Plan. Accordingly, he and his deputy, Cartha DeLoach, brought the toxic document to Attorney General Mitchell and protested its implementation as both illegal and unwise. "I quite agreed with them," Mitchell testified at the Watergate cover-up trial, adding the plan "was not something we in the Justice Department would certainly want to participate in. . . . It had, I think, to put it mildly, some illegal activities involved. . . . I called Mr. Haldeman and the president and objected to it."

CIA director Richard Helms, who had attended the meetings

that led to the new recommendations, agreed that Mitchell "derailed" the Huston Plan with the opposition he expressed to Nixon. "The president was strongly in favor of it, was constantly stating that the FBI was not giving sufficient support to these matters, and that this was something that ought to be done," Helms recalled. "But once Mitchell got to him, that was pretty much the end of it."

The time would come again when Mitchell would be presented with a proposal from some gung ho junior aide for an illegal and unwise domestic intelligence project—and Mitchell would do unto Gemstone as he had done unto the Huston Plan. The only difference was that in the later episode, the "little IBM salesmen," as Susie Morrison derisively referred to Dean, Magruder, and the other Haldeman protégés scurrying through the White House, wouldn't take Mitchell's rejection as the final word.[3]

Attorney General Mitchell often referred to himself as "the president's lawyer" and spoke of President Nixon as his "client." This led many, friend and critic alike, to say Mitchell's "great defect . . . what ultimately brought him down" was a failure to recognize the responsibilities of high office. This in turn gave rise to the frequent charge, long before Watergate, that Mitchell "politicized" the Department of Justice. Yet many career employees at Justice attested otherwise: that Mitchell seldom interfered with the day-to-day running of the department, a claim borne out by Mitchell's actions—or inaction—in critical moments, like the ITT case and Nixon's order to lay off the Mafia. One political scientist at the time recognized the spuriousness of the politicization charge. "Mitchell seems not to have cared much what the people thought of him one way or the other," wrote Professor William F. Mullen, of Washington State University, in 1976. "In this sense he was what some critics want an 'independent' attorney general to be—oblivious to his own political career."

Indeed, Mitchell's achievements at Justice were momentous. With his political vision and force of personality, he presided over the non-violent desegregation of the Southern elementary school system and, too, over a subtle—but significant and necessary—shift in public attitudes toward law and order at the close of the sixties. Chief Justice Rehnquist, interviewed in 1993, considered this one of his old boss's signature accomplishments. "I think the Mitchell Justice Department restored the idea that it's the courts who decide what should happen to people who are charged with crimes. . . . I think he felt that very strongly. I think that was very much different from the Justice Department philosophy that existed in the preceding administration."

The crimes of John Mitchell fell into three categories. First, there were at least three he got away with. Of these the first was his illegal intervention in the 1968 Paris peace talks: when Nixon and Mitchell, with the aid of Anna Chennault, violated the laws of international diplomacy, directly contacting South Vietnamese officials to urge them not to be swayed by Lyndon Johnson's last-minute bombing halt. The second unpunished crime was Mitchell's false testimony before the Senate Judiciary Committee during the Kleindienst confirmation hearings, when Mitchell, to protect the president, concealed his own heroic role in the ITT case. The third was the set of false statements Mitchell gave, equally unnecessarily, to FBI agents investigating the 1969–71 Kissinger wiretaps, installations later termed legal by the Justice Department.

There was only one crime Mitchell committed and for which he was caught. This was his subornation of Jeb Magruder's perjury about the incriminating desk diary before the Watergate grand jury in September 1972. It was included as one of the overt acts in *U.S. v. Mitchell*, and the former attorney general served nineteen months in prison for his convictions in that case.

Finally, there were multiple "crimes" for which, largely on the strength of perjured testimony, Mitchell was prosecuted, but which he never committed. These included all his other convictions in *Mitchell* and the charges filed against him, and of which he was fully acquitted, in *U.S. v. Mitchell-Stans*, the Vesco case. This complicated box score was, perhaps, what Mitchell had in mind when, as legend has it, a woman once approached him on the street and said, "Oh, Mr. Mitchell, I'm so sorry," and he replied: "No more than I deserved, my dear."

"I don't think that John Mitchell would have ever said that he was an innocent man that went to jail," Debbie Dean said. "I believe he was very honest about what he did do, and what he did not do. . . . I don't think that John would have wanted to [be] absolutely, totally vindicated, as though he were somehow an innocent lamb that [was] set up. . . . I mean, he did something that he considered to be honorable, but that he knew in the end was not right. And he admitted that."

Yet it must also be kept in mind that *none* of the crimes Mitchell committed, and none of those for which he was wrongly prosecuted, occurred while he was entrusted with public office. His involvement in the Anna Chennault intrigues came while he was a private lawyer running the 1968 campaign; the rest of it—the Kleindienst hearings, the FBI's investigation of the Kissinger wiretaps, and Watergate—all came after Mitchell had resigned as attorney general.

Thus if Mitchell's case is a parable of power, its acquisition, uses, and abuses, the key to the story lay in the Chennault affair, which was the means Nixon and Mitchell used to acquire power. *Those who plow iniquity and sow trouble reap the same.* Top officials in the intelligence community, where the suspicious movements of Mrs. Chennault and her friends in the Nixon campaign were detected early on, determined even before Nixon and his strong man assumed office that the two did not feel bound by the (loose) norms under which that community acted; they would have to be watched, and, when the opportunity presented itself, neutralized. Thus the enlistment of Yeoman Radford as a thief of Nixon's and Kissinger's documents—selectively leaked by generals and admirals unsympathetic to the administration's foreign policy—and the deployment of Messrs. Hunt and McCord as spies, respectively, inside the Nixon White House and Mitchell's Committee for the Re-election of the President. These are best seen as institutional responses to the intrigues of 1968, products of the warped political atmosphere created by the protracted war in Vietnam.

More broadly, Mitchell's friends and family members pondered the related question: What was his great mistake in life? Why did so brilliant and accomplished a lawyer, such a warm and witty drinking companion, wind up so disgraced? The answers tended to split along a clear fault line. There were those who believed Mitchell's great mistake was marrying Martha Mitchell and those who believed it was allying himself with Richard Nixon. Perhaps the two best-known proponents for each case were, of course, Martha and Nixon themselves, each of whom blamed the other for the downfall of the man they both considered the bedrock of their lives. Of course, the answer was that both were to blame, that it was the twin pressures of Martha and Nixon that brought the strong man down.

But what did Mitchell himself think? The best evidence on that question came from Mitchell's former press secretary, Jack Landau, who considered his boss a widely misunderstood, underappreciated figure. "He was not just a flinty-eyed, one-dimensional conservative who got caught in a crime and went to jail," Landau said in 1993. "He really was an actor in American political life." Accordingly, Landau wanted to do something nice for Mitchell when he got out of prison; so he took the old man to lunch. On that occasion Landau asked point-blank: "If you had it to do all over again, what would you do differently?"

Mitchell paused for a moment. His mind reeled, and finally alighted on an incident he used to recount to his children. The year was 1960, and Mitchell was enjoying the good life in Rye, New York, with his eccentric but still sociable second wife, the former Martha Beall Jennings. He was seated in his law office at Caldwell, Trimble, and Mitchell when a secretary said he had a visitor, a man named Bobby Kennedy. Mitchell was busy at the moment and finished what he was doing while keeping the younger man waiting. Kennedy didn't like that. When Mitchell finally saw him, Kennedy said he understood Mitchell was an important man, with contacts in nearly all fifty states. *How did he feel about helping to run his brother Jack's presidential campaign?* Mitchell demurred. Kennedy was undeterred. He started waving around documents, suggesting it would be in Mitchell's interests—and those of his clients—if he reconsidered. With that, Mitchell threw the younger man out of his office.

Now, two decades later, disgraced, disbarred, an ex-convict fresh out of prison, Mitchell remembered that occasion, and began, finally, to respond to Jack Landau's question. The answer showed, unmistakably, which Mitchell thought had been the great mistake of his life: marrying Martha or allying with Nixon. "If I had it all over to do," Mitchell said with a smile, "I'd run Jack Kennedy's campaign."[4]

ACKNOWLEDGMENTS

Work on *The Strong Man* began in the fall of 1991 with a grant from the Historical Research Foundation and its Council of Elders: the late, great William F. Buckley, Jr., Van Galbraith, and Dino Pionzio. Bill Buckley also arranged for me to publish my first article, in *National Review*. Steve Hess, my professor at Johns Hopkins, was an early source of encouragement; so too was my mentor and friend, Dan Rather, and, in a previous life, before he became a cultural phenomenon, John Hodgman.

Jill Mitchell-Reed exhibited extraordinary faith to overcome her skepticism about her father's biographer, and to share with me her memories, photographs, laughs, and tears. The attorney general's brother, Robert, and Robert's son, Joseph, also provided invaluable assistance. The same is true for the Gore Dean family: Mary, Deborah, and Gordon.

Eva Zelnick was of singular help in transcribing interview tapes, performing data entry, and organizing my materials. When Eva fell ill, her mother, Pam, and sister, Marni, took up the slack. Likewise Bob Zelnick, a veteran of the Nixon-Frost interviews, offered wise counsel. Tyler Evans worked tirelessly on my tapes; Teri Schultz and David Karol also did valuable transcription work. Tim Goldsmith unearthed some of the most important documents referenced in this book. Mark Corallo walked me through the attorney general's office suite, and the late Russell Long gave me a tour of his—formerly the Mitchells'—Watergate duplex. Steve Giermek got my computer going and gave me doses of fun when I needed it. Michelle and Dave Feller-Kopman gave me everything I could ask for on my early research trips to Washington. Jeff Spector twice made his apartment ours. Barbara and Lynn Poole are my adoptive capital parents.

At the National Archives' Nixon Presidential Materials Project, I am indebted to James Hastings, Joan Howard, Scott Parham, Fred Grabowski, and the late Carlos Narvaez. Dick McNeill supplied videotapes of Mitchell's Senate testimony; Mark Fischer tracked down documents on short notice; and Steve Greene navigated the maze of tapes and photographs. Rick Moss provided life-saving late-innings relief at Archives II. Archivists David Paynter and Elizabeth Lockwood steered me through the Freedom of Information Act process to thousands of important documents in the office of the Watergate Special Prosecution Force, and the Library of Congress's Ed Schamel helped me obtain five thousand pages of executive-session testimony taken by the Senate Watergate committee. Dan Rather and his assistants, Amy Bennett, Sakura Komiyama, and William V. Madison, secured access to the CBS News library, where Cryder Bankes and Sam Register were unfailingly courteous. And Faye Haskins of the D.C. Public Library's Washingtoniana Division helped me locate several photographs reproduced herein.

Among the daily-deadline reporters and historians of the Nixon era, Len Colodny and his wife, Sandy, opened their archives, home, and hearts to my wife and me. Jim Hougan and his late wife, Carolyn, shared their papers, time, and thoughts. Robert Gettlin, William A. Gordon, Stanley Kutler, and Tom Wells all supplied transcripts of their interviews with relevant figures. James Grady, Seymour Hersh, Joan Hoff, and Dan Moldea gave excellent advice. Herb Parmet steered me to some very useful documents. Anthony Summers and Robbyn Swan allowed me inside their world. Bob Woodward shared his views at various points.

Mark Feldstein shared his massive ITT file; Manuel Miranda helped me obtain Mitchell's ITT testimony. Benton Becker, Steve Freeland, Kerry Hook, and John Williams illuminated the proceedings in *Dean v. St. Martin's Press, et al.* and *Wells v. Liddy.* William C. Herman opened his vault of *Mitchell v. Mitchell* records. Joe Treen cheerfully burglarized his ex-wife's basement to retrieve the *U.S. v. Mitchell-Stans* trial transcript. Joe Goren "borrowed" numerous books from a certain library a quarter century ago, for my benefit. Steve King, Francis X. Maloney, and the late Susie Morrison all provided handwritten letters from Mitchell; John Bonham lent me his original World War II photographs; and the late William Rehnquist allowed me to reproduce his original photograph of Mitchell's Department of Justice team. I am especially grateful to all of the interviewees listed in the source notes.

Almost everyone at Fox News over the last decade has helped me in some way, but I owe special thanks to Roger Ailes, Bob Armfield, Erin Atkiss, Fred Barnes, the late Chet Collier, Mitch Davis, Laurie Dhue, Nina Donaghy, Jim Eldridge, Major Garrett, Brian and Sir Mark Haefeli, Kim and Brit Hume, Greg Kelly, Megyn Kelly, Brian Kilmeade, Bill Kristol, Ken LaCorte, Kevin Magee, Windsor Mann, Judge Andrew Napolitano, Jamie Nelson, Jacqueline Pham, Corbett Riner, Lee Ross, Andy Ryan, H. Andrew Schwartz, Greta Van Susteren, Brian Wilson, and Maya Zumwalt. Deepest thanks of all go to Neil Cavuto.

Thanks also to Richard V. Allen, Kathy Arberg, James Bailey, Ted Barreaux, Perry Beckerman, Robert Caro, Tom Casey, Paul Ciolino, Camila Dos Santos, Marty Edelman, Rich Eisen, Ken Emerson, Stef Farrand, Deborah Feyerick, Andrew Fisher, Ken Fisher, Philip Glass, Paul Golin, the late Michael Kelly, Heath Kern, Terry Lenzner, George Marlin, Adam Mazmanian, Susan Molinari, Charles Pinck, Robert Rinaldi, Melissa Russo, Jim Rutenberg, Dr. Saud A. Sadiq and his staff, Jon Schiumo, Jonathan Schwartz, David Shipley, Jack Singlaub, Jon Talmadge, and Julie Ziegler. One accumulates many debts over seventeen years, so my apologies to anyone I have forgotten.

Patricia Hass introduced me to my unbeatable literary agents, Lynn Chu and Glenn Hartley. At Doubleday, editor in chief Bill Thomas, executive editor Adam Bellow, and editorial assistant Dan Feder all showed extraordinary understanding, patience, and skill. Peter Collier helped chop down the 500,000-word behemoth. Without these literary professionals, this book would not exist; however, any errors contained herein are, of course, solely my responsibility.

Any good thing I've ever done reflects the love and selflessness of my parents, Regina and Mike Rosen, to whom this book is dedicated. My big-hearted older brother, Eric Rosen, has given me more than I could ever begin to thank him for, including my fascination with the sixties; thanks, too, to Eric's wife, Dalene, and their children, Charles and Hannah. My in-laws, Lorraine and Joseph Durkin, along with Ryan Durkin, Jen Barron, and Quinn Durkin, have supported me in innumerable ways.

My long-suffering wife, Sara Durkin, has learned more than she ever needed to know about John and Martha, Haldeman and Ehrlichman, and she has, in return, taught me everything I know about Vern Yip, Stuart Weitzman, and—far more important—life, love, courage, and grace. Someday when we're dreaming, Aaron will understand it all.

James Rosen
Washington, D.C.
February 2008

NOTES

ABBREVIATIONS

AOP Stanley I. Kutler, *Abuse of Power: The New Nixon Tapes* (Free Press, 1997).

BLAT Baldwin *Los Angeles Times* interview. Interview of Alfred C. Baldwin III conducted by Jack Nelson, October 3, 1972.

CCT Church Committee testimony; testimony of John N. Mitchell, October 24, 1975, reprinted at *Hearings Before the Select Committee to Study Governmental Operations With Respect to Intelligence Activities of the United States Senate, Ninety-fourth Congress, First Session,* Volume 4: *Mail Opening* (U.S. Government Printing Office, 1976).

CCTF Campaign Contributions Task Force of the WSPF.

CI Colodny interview; interviews by Leonard Colodny, conducted 1985–1991, and introduced as evidence in *Maureen K. Dean and John W. Dean v. St. Martin's Press, Inc., et al.,* Civil Action No. 91–1807 (1992). CI interviews are with John Mitchell unless otherwise indicated in brackets.

CRP Committee for the Re-Election of the President.

DOJ Department of Justice.

DVS *Maureen K. Dean and John W. Dean v. St. Martin's Press, Inc., et al.,* Civil Action No. 91–1807 (1992).

DVSCM *Dean v. St. Martin's* Colodny Motion. Declaration of Leonard Colodny in Support of Motion for Par-tial Summary Judgment, [filed] December 16, 1996.

FBIM FBI files on John and Martha Mitchell, obtained by the author through the Freedom of Information Act.

FG Federal Government; NARA document classification code.

HHBP Howard H. Baker Jr. Papers; Special Collections, University of Tennessee, Knoxville.

HJC House Judiciary Committee volumes; *Hearings Before the Committee on the Judiciary, House of Representatives, Ninety-third Congress, Second Session* (U.S. Government Printing Office, 1974).

HJCFR *Impeachment of Richard M. Nixon, President of the United States: The Final Report of the Committee on the Judiciary of the House of Representatives* (Bantam, 1975).

HJCW House Judiciary Committee witness testimony volumes; *Hearings Before the Committee on the Judiciary, Testimony of Witnesses, House of Representatives, Ninety-third Congress, Second Session* (U.S. Government Printing Office, 1974).

HN Haldeman Notes; yellow-pad notes of H. R. Haldeman, 1969–1973, basis for *The Haldeman Diaries.*

HW Handwriting; annotations by President Nixon on papers in his office files (POF), available at the Nixon Presidential Materials Project, National Archives.

JDD John Dean deposition; sworn testimony of John W. Dean in *Maureen K. Dean and John W. Dean v. St. Martin's Press, et al.*, C.A. No. 92–1807.

JDE John D. Ehrlichman; used in citing documents obtained through NARA.

J-L Judicial and Legal; official organizational grouping for documents obtained through NARA.

JMRC Jill Mitchell-Reed Collection; assorted documents once belonging to John Mitchell now in the possession of his daughter and provided to the author.

KCH Kleindienst Confirmation Hearings. *Hearings Before the Committee on the Judiciary, United States Senate, Ninety-second Congress, Second Session, on Nomination of Richard G. Kleindienst, of Arizona, To Be Attorney General* (U.S. Government Printing Office, 1972).

KI Kutler interview; transcripts of interviews with John Mitchell by Stanley Kutler, conducted in 1988, made available to the author.

MACT Moreland Act commission testimony; testimony of John N. Mitchell before the New York State Moreland Act Commission on the Urban Development Corporation and Other State Financing Agencies, October 15, 1975.

MFC Mark Feldstein Collection; documents compiled by author Mark Feldstein in connection with his work on a biography of Jack Anderson and provided to the author.

MPP Mitchell Probate Papers; *In Re: Mitchell, John N.*, Superior Court of the District of Columbia, Probate Division, Adm. No. 0908–89, [filed] 2/8/90, [dismissed] 11/3/92.

NARA National Archives and Records Administration.

NARD Nelson A. Rockefeller documents; letters from Rockefeller to Mitchell contained in Rockefeller Family Archive, Record Group 15, Nelson A. Rockefeller, Gubernatorial Series 16, Fifty-fifth Street, Subseries 3,

Correspondence Files, Box 15, Folder 226, NAR Letters to John Mitchell, 1970–1972; Rockefeller Archive Center, New York.

NARR Nelson A. Rockefeller records; Letters from Rockefeller and his aides to Mitchell contained in Rockefeller Family Archive, Record Group 15, Nelson A. Rockefeller, Gubernatorial Office Records (microfilm); Name File, Reel 213, Rockefeller Archive Center, New York.

NT Nixon tapes; author's transcript from White House tapes available at the Nixon Presidential Materials Project, National Archives.

POF President's Office Files; available at the Nixon Presidential Materials Project, National Archives.

RG Record Group of the National Archives and Records Administration.

RI Reichley interview; interviews of John Mitchell and other Nixon administration figures by A. James Reichley, conducted 1969–78, available at the Gerald R. Ford Library, Ann Arbor, MI.

SECF Securities and Exchange Commission Files; documents in SEC's Robert Vesco case file obtained by the author through the Freedom of Information Act.

SJC Senate Judiciary Committee.

SSC Senate Watergate committee volumes; *Hearings Before the Senate Select Committee on Presidential Campaign Activities, Ninety-third Congress, First Session* (U.S. Government Printing Office, 1973).

SSCEX Senate Select Committee executive session. Sworn testimony in executive session before the Senate Watergate committee, obtained by the author using the Freedom of Information Act.

SSCFR Senate Select Committee's final report. *Final Report of the Senate Select Committee on Presidential Campaign Activities* (U.S. Government Printing Office, 1974).

SMOF Staff Member and Office Files, available at the Nixon Presidential Materials Project, National Archives.

THD H. R. Haldeman, *The Haldeman Diaries: Inside the Nixon White House* (Putnam, 1994).

TPOP Seymour M. Hersh, *The Price of Power: Kissinger in the Nixon White House* (Summit, 1983).

UMS Trial transcript of *U.S. v. John Mitchell and Maurice Stans* (73 CR 439).

UVL Trial transcript of *U.S. v. George Gordon Liddy, et al.* (CR 1827–72).

UVM Trial transcript of *U.S. v. John N. Mitchell, et al.* (CR 74-110).

WCHC William C. Herman collection; several hundred pages of documents, including tax returns for John Mitchell and/or his law firm from 1950 to 1973, made available to the author by a New York attorney who represented Martha Mitchell during divorce proceedings against her husband.

WGTF Watergate Task Force of the WSPF.

WHCA White House Communications Agency.

WHCF White House Central Files, available at the Nixon Presidential Materials Project, National Archives.

WHSF White House Special Files, available at the Nixon Presidential Materials Project, National Archives.

WHT *White House Transcripts: The Full Text of the Submission of Recorded Presidential Conversations to the Committee on the Judiciary of the House of Representatives by President Richard Nixon*, Gerald Gold, ed. (Bantam Books, 1973).

WI Wells interviews; transcripts of interviews by Tom Wells, conducted 1985–87, made available to the author.

WSPF Watergate Special Prosecution Force; documents from WSPF files obtained by the author through the Freedom of Information Act.

WVL I *Ida Maxwell Wells v. G. Gordon Liddy (I)*, Civil Case JFM-97-946, U.S. District Court for the District of

Maryland, Northern Division, January 2001.

WVL II *Ida Maxwell Wells v. G. Gordon Liddy (II)*, Civil Case JFM-97-946, U.S. District Court for the District of Maryland, Northern Division, 2002.

Note: Where abbreviations in footnotes are followed by roman and arabic numerals, the roman numerals refer to a volume number, the arabic numerals to page numbers within that volume. Thus "SSC, II: 579–81" refers the reader to pages 579 through 581 in the second volume of the *Hearings Before the Senate Select Committee on Presidential Campaign Activities* (the Senate Watergate, or Ervin, committee).

PROLOGUE

1. John Lukacs, *The Hitler of History* (Vintage Books, 1998), p. 1.

2. Michael Dunne, "John Mitchell Jets to Ala. & Becomes Con 24171–157," *New York Daily News*, June 23, 1977; "John Mitchell Is Jeered as He Enters Prison," *Washington Post*, June 22, 1977.

3. Fred Emery, *Watergate: The Corruption of American Politics and the Fall of Richard Nixon* (Touchstone, 1994). Emery claimed (p. 487) Mitchell's offer to plead guilty in exchange for the prosecutors' abandonment of Nixon was first disclosed in a 1994 BBC documentary on which Emery worked. In fact, Mitchell's bold proposition was first reported sixteen years earlier; see Ronald J. Ostrow, "Mitchell Offered to Take Coverup Blame to Protect Nixon, Former Prosecutor Says," *Los Angeles Times*, August 11, 1978.

4. William S. White, "John Mitchell: Dividing the Men from the Boys," *Washington Post*, July 14, 1973; Nicholas von Hoffman, "Keeping the Code of Omerta," *Washington Post*, July 16, 1973; Robert Sam Anson, *Exile: The*

Unquiet Oblivion of Richard Nixon (Touchstone, 1985), p. 214.

5. Mary McCarthy, *Mask of State: Watergate Portraits* (Harvest, 1975), pp. 53–67; Whitney North Seymour Jr., *United States Attorney: An Inside View of "Justice" in America Under the Nixon Administration* (W. Morrow, 1975), p. 73; Stanley I. Kutler, "Covering Up the Cover-up," *Times Literary Supplement,* July 19, 1991; Mark Rudd, interview with author, May 12, 2004; John Osborne, *The Second Year of the Nixon Watch* (Liveright, 1971), p. 11; "Quiet Voice: Business Suit," *The Nation,* April 20, 1970; Peter Goldman, "Mr. Law-and-Order," *Newsweek,* September 8, 1969 (Bickel); Richard Harris, *Justice: The Crisis of Law, Order and Freedom in America* (Avon, 1970), cover (Wicker) and p. 203 (signal). Osborne later had a change of heart, writing in December 1974 that Mitchell "in some respects . . . was a better-than-average attorney general"; see Osborne, *The Last Nixon Watch* (New Republic Book Company, 1975), p. 8.

6. Brenton Harries, interview with author, November 3, 1994; Robert Odle, interview with author, April 17, 1993; Kenneth W. Thompson, ed., *The Nixon Presidency: Twenty-Two Intimate Perspectives of Richard M. Nixon* (University Press of America, 1987), p. 295 (Raoul-Duval); Martin L. Gross, "Conversation with an Author: John Dean," *Book Digest,* March 1977; Statements of Senate Judiciary Committee Members on the Nomination of Erwin N. Griswold to be Solicitor General of the United States, Wednesday, October 11, 1967, cited in WH memo for John Ehrlichman from John Dean, Subject: Suggestions of Items to be Covered at 2:30 p.m. Meeting Re Kleindienst Confirmation Hearings, March 8, 1972, WHSF—SMOF, JDE Subject File, Antitrust, Box 15, NARA (Kennedy); Erwin N. Griswold, *Ould Fields, New Corne: The Personal Mem-oirs of a Twentieth Century Lawyer* (West Publishing, 1992), pp. 270–72, 315; Cornell W. Clayton, *The Politics of Justice: The Attorney General and the Making of Legal Policy* (Sharpe, 1992), pp. 100, 138 (partisan instrument); Nancy V. Baker, *Conflicting Loyalties: Law and Politics in the Attorney General's Office, 1789–1990* (University Press of Kansas, 1992), p. 122 (rule of law). Clayton wrote: "After the Justice Department's involvement in the initial [Watergate] cover-up was made public, Attorney General Mitchell and his successor, Richard Kleindienst, were forced to resign." In fact, Mitchell left office voluntarily on March 1, 1972, almost four months before the cover-up began.

7. "Mitchell, Last Watergate Prisoner, Is Freed on Parole," *New York Times,* January 20, 1979; Christopher Booker, *The Seventies: Portrait of a Decade* (Penguin, 1980), p. 79. Books on Martha Mitchell include Amram Duchovny, *On With the Wind: The Sayings of Martha Mitchell* (Ballantine, 1971); Charles Ashman and Sheldon Engelmayer, *Martha: The Mouth That Roared* (Berkley Medallion, 1973); and Winzola McLendon, *Martha* (Random House, 1979). She was also the subject of Minnie Pearl's full-length comedy LP, *My Husband Doesn't Know I'm Making This Call* (Sunflower Records, 1971) and an off-Broadway play; and her childhood home in Pine Bluff, Arkansas, was made into a museum. In 1996, Martin Scorsese reportedly contracted to serve as executive director of a film about Martha.

8. Lester A. Sobel, ed., *Post-Watergate Morality* (Facts on File, 1978), p. 17.

9. J. Robert Mitchell, interview with author, February 26, 1998.

INTO THE FIRE

1. J. Robert Mitchell, interview, February 26, 1998.
2. Kenneth Gross, "John and Martha: Growing Up American," *Newsday*, May 23, 1970.
3. Record of Birth, John Newton Mitchell, State of Michigan, Department of State—Division of Vital Statistics, Registered no. 12273, September 5, 1913; "Biography of Attorney General John Newton Mitchell," [undated] DOJ press release; and J. Robert Mitchell, interview with author, August 8, 1998.
4. Jill Mitchell-Reed, interview with author, May 5, 1992.
5. J. Robert Mitchell, interview with author, February 9, 1998.
6. Ibid., February 26, 1998. Though unsure of his father's date of birth, Robert said the date of death was January 18, 1948, at approximately sixty-six years of age; this would place the date of birth of the attorney general's father around 1882.
7. Ibid., February 9, 1998. The *New York Post* incorrectly reported Mitchell's father "had been in the trading stamp business with his *brother*"; see Rita Delfiner and William H. Rudy, "The John Mitchell Story: From Jamaica to Wall Street," *New York Post*, August 4, 1970 (emphasis added).
8. J. Robert Mitchell, interview, February 26, 1998.
9. Mitchell-Reed, interview, May 5, 1992.
10. J. Robert Mitchell, interview, February 9, 1998. Jill Mitchell-Reed claimed McMahon was somehow involved in Tammany Hall, but no authoritative accounts of the corrupt political machine that ruled New York City in the 1860s and 1870s mention his name, and her uncle Robert dismissed the notion as "hot air."
11. Mitchell-Reed, interview, May 5, 1992; and J. Robert Mitchell, interview, August 8, 1998.
12. Ann Mitchell, "A Personal View of the Attorney General of the United States John N. Mitchell," [undated; c. 1970]. The only known attempt at a Mitchell family history, this informal essay was written by Robert's daughter, Ann, as a school project; although it contains some inaccuracies, it is still a valuable source of information on the Mitchells' lineage and on the attorney general's early life. Ann died in 1986; see letter to the author from Joseph C. Mitchell, August 25, 1994.
13. J. Robert Mitchell, interview, February 9, 1998.
14. Ibid. Though Joseph and Margaret Mitchell's date of marriage is lost to history, the conventions of the era make it likely they wed before conceiving their first child, Joseph Charles ("Scranton"). Robert recalls Scranton was five years older than himself, and born on the Fourth of July; this places Scranton's birth date as July 4, 1909. Thus Joseph and Margaret likely wed sometime in 1908.
15. Ibid.
16. Ibid., February 26, 1998.
17. Ibid., February 9, 1998.
18. This photograph appeared on the front page of the *Long Island Advance* on July 19, 1973. Though no credit was given, the photograph was probably taken by a member of the neighboring Slechta family, which contributed two other contemporaneous photographs to the same edition.
19. Ibid.
20. Mitchell, "A Personal View"; Robert B. Martin, "Att'y. Gen. John Mitchell Lived in Brookhaven Tn.," *Long Island Advance*, July 19, 1973.
21. J. Robert Mitchell, interview, February 26, 1998.
22. Fawn M. Brodie, *Richard Nixon: The Shaping of His Character* (Harvard University Press, 1983), p. 45 (brutal); Delfiner and Rudy, "The John Mitchell Story" (drive).
23. Daily Calendar of the President's En-

gagements, Saturday, February 11, 1928, in Papers of Irwin H. Hoover, chief usher at the White House, Library of Congress.

24. Malcolm Wilson, interview with author, May 12, 1993.

25. A partial transcript of Mitchell's appearance on *The Dick Cavett Show* on September 10, 1970, along with Klein, HEW secretary Robert Finch, and Leonard Garment, appears in John J. Makay and William R. Brown, eds., *The Rhetorical Dialogue: Contemporary Concepts and Cases* (Wm. C. Brown, 1972), pp. 37–57.

26. CI, May 21, 1988.

27. Jill Mitchell-Reed, interview with author, November 22, 2003.

28. Susie Morrison, interview with author, January 16, 1992.

29. Letter to Bette Shine "M.D." from [John Mitchell], "Sunday" [postmarked August 12, 1937]; JMRC. Mitchell joked his letter would be "more damaging than a written proposal of marriage to a chorus girl."

30. Thomas W. Evans, "A History of the Firm," *Mudge Rose Guthrie Alexander & Ferdon: Alumni Directory 1994*, p. 33. One account of Mitchell's law career placed this moment after his graduation from law school, but before his admission to the bar. Yet Mitchell once said he was "the youngest lawyer in the firm" at the time, suggesting he had both graduated *and* been admitted to the bar; see Lyle Denniston, "He's No 'Gang-Buster' Type," *Washington Evening Star*, December 31, 1968, and James B. Stewart Jr., with Joan Kenyon, "Bond Counsel: New Race for the Riches," *The American Lawyer*, November 1979.

31. Paul R. Lusignan, "Public Housing in the United States, 1933–1949," *Cultural Resource Management* 25, 1 (U.S. Department of the Interior, 2002).

32. Stewart and Kenyon, "Bond Counsel." Elsewhere, Mitchell recalled the judge dismissing the program as "a

New Deal dan-fangled idea"; see Denniston, "He's No 'Gang-Buster.'"

33. Gilbert Hahn, *Notebook of an Amateur Politician: And How He Began the D.C. Subway* (Lexington Press, 2002), pp. 43–44 (passion); Mitchell-Reed, interview, May 5, 1992; J. Robert Mitchell, interview, February 26, 1998.

34. George J. Marlin and Joe Mysak, *The Guidebook to Municipal Bonds: The History, The Industry, The Mechanics* (American Banker/Bond Buyer, 1991), pp. 22–25 (sour); William A. Madison, interview with author, June 6, 1993.

35. Francis Maloney, interview with author, June 22, 1993.

36. Stewart and Kenyon, "Bond Counsel"; Evans, "A History"; Denniston, "He's No 'Gang-Buster'"; Milton Viorst, "'The Justice Department Is an Institution for Law Enforcement, Not Social Improvement,'" *New York Times Magazine*, August 10, 1969. Evans erroneously reported that Mitchell made partner in 1940.

37. Mitchell-Reed, interview, May 5, 1992; Clyde Jay Jennings, interview with author, August 1, 2002.

38. Denniston, "He's No 'Gang-Buster'"; MACT 252; Brenton Harries, interview with author, November 3, 1994; Robert Shogan, *A Question of Judgment: The Fortas Case and the Struggle for the Supreme Court* (Bobbs-Merrill, 1972), pp. 16–17 (archangels).

MORAL OBLIGATIONS

1. Helen Dudar, "Man in the News: John Mitchell Indicted," *New York Post*, May 12, 1973.

2. Moore later served, from August 1989 to September 1992, as U.S. Ambassador to Ireland.

3. Richard Reeves, "Nixon's Men Are Smart but No Swingers," *New York Times Magazine,* September 29, 1968; Don Bertrand, "Two County Men May Be in Nixon Cabinet," *New York*

Daily News, November 17, 1968; Milton Viorst, " 'The Justice Department Is an Institution for Law Enforcement, Not Social Improvement,' " *New York Times Magazine,* August 10, 1969. See also the family history written by Mitchell's niece; Dan Rather and Gary Paul Gates, *The Palace Guard* (Warner Books, 1975), p. 250; and Theodore H. White, *Breach of Faith: The Fall of Richard Nixon* (Dell, 1975), p. 115.

4. Letter to the author from Alyce N. Guthrie, April 18, 1995. Another account claimed Kennedy reported to Mitchell "during training," but Kennedy's training long preceded Mitchell's; see Evans, "A History of the Firm."

5. William Safire, "Watch What We Do," *New York Times,* November 14, 1988.

6. Author's transcript of *The Robert K. Dornan Show,* [aired] October 17, 1971, UCLA Film and Television Archive (combat role); CI [Hunt], January 16, 1991; E. Howard Hunt, interview with author, January 26, 2003.

7. Log Book[s] of the USS PT 536, 5 June 1944–30 September 1944 (in Mitchell's hand); 1 October 1944–31 December 1944 (Mitchell's hand); 1 January 1945–31 May 1945 (in Mitchell's hand until April 18); Log Book[s] of the USS PT 541, 1 April 1945–31 July 1945; 1 August 1945–4 December 1945; Memorandum from Commander Clark W. Faulkner to Commander in Chief, United States FLEET, May 10, 1945, Subj.: War Diary—June 1944 to December 1944 (Inclusive)-Forwarding of; Office of Naval Records and Library; and Memorandum from Commander Clark W. Faulkner to Commander in Chief, UNITED STATES Fleet, July 2, 1945, Subj.: War Diary—Month of June 1945–Forwarding of; Office of Naval Records and Library, National Archives.

8. Letter to the author from Russell Addeo, September 27, 1994; Russell Addeo, interview with author, January 10, 1995; John Bonham, interview with author, September 6, 1995; Thomas Wardell, interview with author, September 6, 1995; Adam Mancino, interview with author, September 10, 1995; John Duersteler, interview with author, July 19, 2003; Emery Lewis, interview with author, July 19, 2003; E. C. "Duke" House Jr., "Ron 37 PT Boaters Harvey and Mitchell," *The PT Boater* 53, 1 (Spring 1998); Barry C. Weaver, ed., *Awards and Casualties of the United States PT Boat Service in World War II* (Orders and Medals Society of America, 2000), which contained no entries for Mitchell; and the Guthrie letter, April 18, 1995, which stated flatly: "Mitchell did not receive any medal or award for PT service."

9. Madison interview.

10. MACT, 252.

11. Letter to Glen Moore from Francis X. Maloney [cc'd to the author], April 27, 1999 (peer); Joe Alex Morris, *Nelson Rockefeller: A Biography,* (Harper, 1960), pp. 284–88; Peter Collier and David Horowitz, *The Rockefellers: An American Dynasty* (Holt, Rinehart, 1976), pp. 270–73.

12. Cary Reich, *The Life of Nelson A. Rockefeller: Worlds to Conquer 1908–1958* (Doubleday, 1996), pp. 534–36, 833.

13. Ibid; WCHC (earnings).

14. The $2 million figure first appeared in Stewart and Kenyon, "Bond Counsel." It was repeated in David Harrop, *Paychecks: Who Makes What?* (Harper, 1980), p. 119.

15. Ashman and Engelmayer, p. 32; Morrison interview; Ken and Peggy Ebbitt, interview with author, October 11, 1993; Mitchell-Reed, interview, November 22, 2003; McLendon, *Martha,* p. 60; Rod Nordland, ed., *The Watergate File* (Flash Books, 1973), p. 16 (amicable). The final agreement also required Mitchell to maintain a six-figure insurance policy

with Bette as its beneficiary. Immediately after the divorce, Mitchell paid $25,000 in alimony, a figure that grew the following year to $53,000. By 1972, Mitchell had paid at least $386,542 to his ex-wife; see *Elizabeth S. Suyker v. John N. Mitchell*, New York State Supreme Court (Nassau County), [filed] April 12, 1967, WCHC.

16. Outside of the Watergate scandals, the question of how and when the Mitchells met occasioned more dispute than any other area of Mitchell's life. Profiling Martha at the height of her fame, the *New York Times* placed the date in 1957, but switched it, after her death, to 1954; see Nan Robertson, "Martha Mitchell: Capital's Most Talked-About," *New York Times*, May 1, 1970, and John T. McQuiston, "Martha Mitchell, 57, Dies of Bone-Marrow Cancer," *New York Times*, June 1, 1976. *Newsweek* reported the couple met "at a dinner party" during Martha's separation from her first husband, which lasted from May 18, 1956, when Clyde Jennings moved out of his and Martha's Stuyvesant Town apartment, to August 1, 1957, when a court in Dade County, Florida, granted their divorce; see "Washington's Own Martha," *Newsweek*, November 30, 1970; McLendon, *Martha*, p. 59; Agreement between Clyde Jennings Jr. and Martha B. Jennings, July 1, 1956; and Final Decree of Divorce and Custody, *Martha Beall Jennings v. Clyde Jennings, Jr.*, Circuit Court, 11th Judicial Circuit, Dade County, August 1, 1957.

Martha's authorized biographer claimed a mutual friend, a television executive, arranged a blind date by telling Martha, who was still married, that his pal Mitchell was "terribly unhappy and needs some cheering up." The TV man and his mistress supposedly accompanied John and Martha on their first date, at a French restaurant in Greenwich Village in 1956 (that same night, after spiriting Martha to his Park Avenue pied-à-terre for a nightcap, Mitchell reportedly told Martha he would marry her, adding, "Your problems are my problems"); McLendon, *Martha*, p. 57. Martha's other biographers asserted, without elaboration, only that she met Mitchell "at a party in 1957"; see Ashman and Engelmayer, *Martha*, p. 32.

Jill Mitchell-Reed thought it was not a mutual friend, but her father's Wall Street chum, Roald Morton, who introduced him to Martha; see Mitchell-Reed, interview, February 23, 1992. Another intimate of Mitchell's thought he met Martha when hiring her as his legal secretary, while two others independently recalled her being an airline stewardess Mitchell met on the road; see J. Robert Mitchell, interview, February 26, 1998 (secretary); and Marv Segal, interview with author, October 23, 1997, and Jerris Leonard, interview with author, October 14, 1999 (stewardess). Law partner Bill Madison was adamant that Mitchell "picked [Martha] up" when his commercial flight, bound for Memphis in "1953 or '54," was diverted to Little Rock; see Madison interview (asked to name Mitchell's greatest mistake in life, Madison replied: "Taking that plane to Memphis that landed in Little Rock"). Martha's cousin, Ray West, recalled meeting Mitchell for the first time in early May 1956, prior to the date Martha's first husband vacated their apartment; see McLendon, *Martha*, p. 57.

Martha herself told *Time* in 1969, "I first met John in New York about 15 years ago," leading the magazine to conclude, erroneously, that the two "met on a weekend in New York in the early '50s and were married several months later"; see "The Warbler of Watergate," *Time*, December 5, 1969.

The most reliable fact on the subject is the Mitchells' verified date of marriage: December 19, 1957. That this came only eleven days after Mitchell's divorce from Bette suggests strongly that his affair with Martha commenced while he was still married to his first wife.

17. McLendon, *Martha*, pp. 24–54; Ashman and Engelmayer, pp. 32–33; Clyde J. Jennings Jr., interview with author, July 23, 2002.

18. Brenton Harries interview.

19. Winzola McLendon, "The Amazing Martha Mitchell," *Look*, July 28, 1970; Louis M. Kohlmeier, "A Velvet Glove," *Wall Street Journal*, August 5, 1970; Sheila Moran, "Mitchell: Recluse on Central Park South," *New York Post*, February 19, 1974; Thomas W. Evans, interview with author, April 23, 1992.

20. Robert H. Connery and Gerald Benjamin, *Rockefeller of New York: Executive Power in the Statehouse* (Cornell University Press, 1979), pp. 259–60.

21. MACT, 253–54; Delfiner and Rudy, "The John Mitchell Story."

22. Ibid., 254, 299. Mitchell himself disliked the term "moral obligation." "I don't know whether that accurately describes it," he said in 1975. "I think it could be described more as a legislative appropriation aspect of the obligation." See also Gerald Benjamin and T. Norman Hurd, eds., *Rockefeller in Retrospect: The Governor's New York Legacy* (Nelson A. Rockefeller Institute of Government, 1984), p. 86. Also providing the state's backing was the approval of the bond offering by the state comptroller, as mandated under the law that created HFA.

23. "New York State Bills Creating 2 New Agencies Signed by Rockefeller," *The Daily Bond Buyer*, April 22, 1960; MACT, 256–61; and Collier and Horowitz, *The Rockefellers*, p. 469.

24. *Daily Bond Buyer*, November 1984.

25. Record of these offerings, and of the retention of Caldwell, Trimble, and Mitchell as counsel for them, can be found in issues of *The Daily Bond Buyer*, 1960–67, passim. See also letter to John N. Mitchell from Robert F. Muse, March 11, 1970, JMRC; Maloney letter, op. cit.; and Benjamin and Hurd, *Rockefeller in Retrospect*, p. 85.

26. J. Anthony Lukas, *Nightmare: The Underside of the Nixon Years* (Bantam, 1977), p. 6 (wink); Morrison interview (kingmaker); "The Sharp New Line on Antitrust," *BusinessWeek*, June 21, 1969.

27. "A Conversation with John Mitchell: Moral Obligation Bonds, the Industry's Old Days, and More," *The Bond Buyer*, September 26, 1991 [reprinting previous interviews with Mitchell, including one from November 1984, from which this exchange was taken].

28. Stephen Grover, "Cabinet Enigma: New Attorney General Poses Question Marks on Antitrust Rights," *Wall Street Journal*, January 17, 1969 (emphasis added).

29. Denniston, "He's No 'Gang-Buster' " (honor), and Richard G. Kleindienst, *Justice: The Memoirs of Attorney General Richard Kleindienst* (Jameson, 1985), p. 41 (invariably); and Closing document, Re: Perkins to Mitchell/Sunset Lane, Rye, N.Y., September 30, 1964; and Closing Statement, Sale of Premises, Sunset Lane, Rye, N.Y., by John N. Mitchell and Martha B. Mitchell to Peer T. Pedersen and Lucy S. Pedersen, March 28, 1969, WCHC. On two occasions when he purchased property in Connecticut, lots of nine and twenty-one acres, respectively, contracts show Mitchell paid the seller a total of one dollar. The documents leave unanswered how else, if at all, Mitchell recompensed the sellers; see Contract between William D. Mewhort and

Charlotte W. Mewhort, Norwalk, and John N. Mitchell and Martha Beall Mitchell [undated]; and Contract between Ruth E. Boski, Norwalk, and John N. Mitchell and Martha Beall Mitchell [undated; c. March 3, 1961], WCHC.

30. Lewis H. Lapham, "The Attorney General Has Heard It All Before," *Life*, February 13, 1970; author's transcript of *Here's Barbara*, WJLA-TV program, [aired] December 4, 1969, WHCA, Tape No. 3545, NARA.

THE HEAVYWEIGHT

1. William Ruckelshaus, interview with author, March 8, 1994.

2. "Martha Mitchell: Dream Is Gone," *Newsday*, February 19, 1974; and Nixon Mudge Rose Guthrie Alexander & Mitchell Partnership Agreement, December 31, 1966, WCHC. Displeased at not being named partner in the new firm, Trimble was bought off at considerable expense. He received annual payouts tied to the average earnings of the new firm's partners, with Mitchell himself making up the difference if his annual earnings exceeded the average of the firm's top three earners. Nixon biographer Jonathan Aitken claimed Mitchell, burning with "eagerness to gain proximity to a future president," took a 60 percent salary cut to "fit in with the remuneration structure" at Nixon Mudge. Likewise Tom Evans claimed in 1992 that Mitchell "was making twice as much as the other senior partners; he came here [to Nixon Mudge] and took what amounted to a 50 percent cut, but within a couple of years, he was making more money than he had been." In fact, Mitchell's tax returns show his salary actually *grew* 10 percent after his first year with the new firm, and *58* percent by the second; see, Aitken,

Nixon: A Life (Regnery, 1993), p. 333; Thomas W. Evans, interview with author, April 23, 1992; and WCHC.

3. Joseph C. Goulden, *The Superlawyers: The Small and Powerful World of the Great Washington Law Firms* (Weybright and Talley, 1971), p. 225; and McLendon (1979), *Martha*, pp. 67–68.

4. Kleindienst, *Justice*, p. 40 (beaten); HN, April 24, 1969 (DDE); The President's News Conference of August 24, 1960; "Transcript of Nixon's News Conference on His Defeat by Brown in Race for Governor of California," *New York Times*, November 8, 1962; Thompson, *The Nixon Presidency*, p. 370 (Hess); and William Safire, *Before the Fall: An Inside View of the Pre-Watergate White House* (Belmont Tower, 1975), pp. 263–64. Estimates of the vote margin in 1960 vary somewhat, with sources as disparate as the Associated Press, the Republican National Committee, *Congressional Quarterly*, and the Clerk of the House of Representatives releasing figures ranging from a low of 111,803 votes to a high of 119,450; see Theodore H. White, *The Making of the President 1960* (Atheneum, 1961), p. 422. Subsequent scholars supported the Nixon camp's cries of foul play; see Stephen E. Ambrose, *Nixon*, Volume I, *The Education of a Politician 1913–1962* (Touchstone Books, 1987), p. 606 ("Charges of fraud in Texas and Illinois were too widespread, and too persistent, to be entirely without foundation"), and Seymour Hersh, *The Dark Side of Camelot* (Little, Brown, 1997), pp. 132–34.

5. Beth Fallon, "Black-Letter Day for Two Former VIPs," *New York Daily News*, February 20, 1974.

6. Don Oberdorfer, "Mitchell's Power Still Unmatched," *Washington Post*, April 19, 1970, and Safire, *Before the Fall*, p. 263 (heavyweight); Odle interview, (teacher); Gerald S. Strober and Deborah Hart Strober, *Nixon: An Oral*

History of His Presidency (Harper-Collins, 1994), p. 294 (Santarelli).

7. Frank van der Linden, *Nixon's Quest for Peace* (Robert B. Luce, 1972), p. 33.

8. Bruce Oudes, ed., *From: The President, Richard Nixon's Secret Files* (Perennial Library, 1990), pp. 11 (end tables), 335 (wines), passim (the press).

9. CI, October 24, 1987 ("Milhous"); and van der Linden, *Nixon's Quest*, p. 35 (emphasis in original). In fact, Mitchell's name was added to the firm's shingle four years *after* Nixon's was.

10. Viorst, " 'The Justice Department.' "

11. Jack Landau, interviews with author, December 2 and 16, 1993, and January 12, 1994 (shower); CI, January 5, 1988 (mystified), December 15, 1987 (grandson); Henry Kissinger, interview with author, March 30, 1995; and letter from Jerris Leonard to the Friends of John Mitchell, January 10, 2002 (protected).

12. H. R. Haldeman, interview with author, September 26, 1993; Richard Nixon, *The Memoirs of Richard Nixon: Volume 1* (Warner, 1979), pp. 326–27.

13. Denniston, "He's No 'Gang-Buster.' "

14. Stephen C. Shadegg, *Winning's a Lot More Fun* (Macmillan, 1969), p. 109.

15. Evans interview.

16. Jules Witcover, *The Resurrection of Richard Nixon* (G.P. Putnam's Sons, 1970), p. 210.

17. Jeb Stuart Magruder, *An American Life: One Man's Road to Watergate* (Pocket Books, 1975), p. 58.

18. Leonard Garment, *Crazy Rhythm: My Journey from Brooklyn, Jazz, and Wall Street to Nixon's White House, Watergate, and Beyond* (Times Books, 1997), p. 119; Thompson, *The Nixon Presidency*, p. 110.

19. Garment, *Crazy Rhythm*, pp. 119–20. Garment's chronology was confused. He claimed the "Mitchell moment" occurred in Nixon's office "late in 1967," with the men's room proffer coming a few weeks later, at the black-tie dinner; however, Garment also said the dinner was held to celebrate the merger of the Nixon and Mitchell law firms, which occurred January 1, 1967.

20. Leonard Garment, interview with author, March 13, 1992.

21. Grover, "Cabinet Enigma" (news conference); Denniston, "He's No 'Gang-Buster' " (bare, hidden, publicity).

22. Ken Adelman, "You Do What Needs to Be Done," *Washingtonian*, April 1988.

23. Rowland Evans Jr. and Robert D. Novak, *Nixon in the White House: The Frustration of Power* (Vintage, 1972), p. 27 (emphases in original); Oberdorfer, "Mitchell's Power," carried a slightly different version of Mitchell's blunt soliloquy.

24. Relman Morin, *The Associated Press Story of Election 1968* (Pocket, 1969), pp. 135–36.

25. Kleindienst, *Justice*, p. 48.

26. SSC, VII: 2890.

27. Eleanora W. Schoenebaum, ed., *Profiles of an Era: The Nixon/Ford Years* (Harcourt, Brace, 1979), p. 261 (near-genius); SSC, VII: 2872; Verne A. Stadtman, "The Centennial Record of the University of California" (University of California Press, 1967).

28. Thompson, *The Nixon Presidency*, p. 76; KI, February 9, 1988.

29. KI, February 9, 1988 (S.O.B.); Schoenebaum, *Profiles of an Era*, p. 184; John Ehrlichman, *Witness to Power: The Nixon Years* (Pocket Books, 1982), pp. 2–22.

30. Ehrlichman, *Witness to Power*, pp. 56–57; Kleindienst, *Justice*, p. 48 (carefree); Robert Mardian, interview with author, August 2, 1993 (crowd).

31. *CBS Morning News*, October 6, 1966 (Robert F. Kennedy); Theodore H. White, *The Making of the President 1968* (Atheneum, 1969), p. 138.

32. Witcover, *The Resurrection*, pp. 311–13 (EI Supremo); Herbert G. Klein, *Making It Perfectly Clear* (Doubleday, 1980), pp. 12–13. Klein also recalled (pp. 12–13) groggily taking a call in his villa at midnight and hearing "a woman . . . screaming into the phone, demanding to speak to John Mitchell. The tone was so high and the words so distorted," he continued, "that I was embarrassed to have answered the phone. . . . That was my midnight introduction to Martha Mitchell."

33. Goldman, "Mr. Law-and-Order"; Nixon, *RN*, pp. 382–83.

34. Klein, *Making It Perfectly Clear*, p. 29 (thorough); Lewis Chester, Godfrey Hodgson, and Bruce Page, *An American Melodrama: The Presidential Campaign of 1968* (Literary Guild, 1969), p. 458; Harry S. Dent; *The Prodigal South Returns to Power* (Wiley, 1978), p. 95.

35. Chester, Hodgson, and Page, *An American Melodrama*, pp. 461–63; Dent, *The Prodigal South*, pp. 97–98.

36. "Nixon Said to Bar Southerners' Bid: Shuns Pledge on Choosing Conservative for Ticket," *New York Times*, August 7, 1968 (consistent); and Glen Moore, "Richard Nixon: The Southern Strategy and the 1968 Presidential Election," in Leon Friedman and William F. Levantrosser, eds., *Richard M. Nixon: Politician, President, Administrator* (Greenwood Press, 1991), pp. 285–97.

37. Hal Bruno, interview with author, February 25, 1994; Kleindienst, *Justice* p. 55; Peter Flanigan, interview with author, October 28, 1993 (no emotion); Nixon, *RN*, pp. 384–85.

38. Nixon's acceptance speech was reprinted in Richard M. Nixon, *Six Crises* (Pyramid, 1968), pp. v–xvi.

39. Hubert H. Humphrey, *The Education of a Public Man: My Life and Politics* (Doubleday, 1976), p. 437.

40. Nixon, *RN*, p. 395.

41. A. James Reichley, "Elm Street's New White House Power," *Fortune*, December 1969; White (1969), *The Making of the President*, p. 363. Mitchell's analysis proved correct: For every vote lured from Wallace, the Nixon campaign lost a vote to Humphrey; see Robert D. Behn, ed., *The Ripon Society: The Lessons of Victory* (Dial Press, 1969), pp. 139–40.

42. Fred LaRue, interview with author, August 4, 2003; Morin, *The Associated Press Story*, p. 193.

43. Witcover, *The Resurrection*, p. 366, and UMS 4570 ($34 million); Goldman, "Mr. Law-and-Order" (austerity); Chester, Hodgson, and Page, *An American Melodrama*, p. 612 (mechanical, hardware).

44. Shadegg, *Winning's a Lot More Fun*, p. 240; Morin, *The Associated Press Story*, pp. 194–95. When Senator Abraham Ribicoff (D-CT) criticized the Chicago police from the podium, host Mayor Richard J. Daley reportedly shouted at Ribicoff: "Fuck you, you Jew son of a bitch, you lousy mother-fucker, go home"; see *U.S. v. Dellinger, et al.* (69 CR 180).

45. Shadegg, *Winning's a Lot More Fun*, p. 240; Morin, *The Associated Press Story*, pp. 194–95. Viorst, " 'The Justice Department' "; Reichley, "Elm Street's New White House Power."

46. Witcover, *The Resurrection*, p. 444; Morin, *The Associated Press Story*, pp. 194–95; Adelman, "You Do What Needs to Be Done."

47. Nguyen Cao Ky with Marvin J. Wolf, *Buddha's Child: My Fight to Save Vietnam* (St. Martin's, 2002), pp. 290–91.

48. Anna Chennault, *The Education of Anna* (Times Books, 1980), passim; William Bundy, *A Tangled Web: The Making of Foreign Policy in the Nixon Presidency* (Hill and Wang, 1999), pp. 37, 549ff. Another account suggests Nixon introduced Chennault to John Mitchell in 1967; see Anthony Summers, *The Arrogance of Power: The Se-*

cret *World of Richard Nixon* (Viking, 2000), p. 299. Finally, Bui Diem wrote the meeting took place not in Nixon's apartment, but at his campaign headquarters; see Bui Diem with David Chanoff, *In the Jaws of Victory* (Houghton Mifflin, 1978), p. 237.

49. It is unclear whether Chennault was wiretapped, followed, or both. J. Edgar Hoover's definitive biography reported the FBI director nixed the idea, fearing disclosure "would put [the FBI] in a most untenable and embarrassing position"; see Athan Theoharis and John Stuart Cox, *The Boss: J. Edgar Hoover and the Great American Inquisition* (Bantam, 1990), p. 453n. Deputy Director Cartha "Deke" DeLoach told the Senate Watergate committee, in previously unpublished testimony, that Chennault was placed under physical surveillance for "several days"; see SSCEX, Cartha D. DeLoach, October 3, 1973. DeLoach later told the Church Committee the FBI wiretapped both the South Vietnamese embassy and Chennault's telephone; see the committee's Final Report, Book II, p. 228n. Still later, DeLoach said only the embassy was bugged, but in 1998, he renewed his claim that electronic surveillance was also placed on Chennault; see Bundy, *A Tangled Web*, p. 551n. Only one author has claimed Mitchell was tapped; see Aitken, *Nixon*, p. 365.

50. Chennault, *The Education of Anna*, pp. 190–91; Thomas Powers, *The Man Who Kept the Secrets: Richard Helms and the CIA* (Pocket Books, 1981), p. 253.

51. Nixon, *RN*, p. 411; White (1969), *The Making of the President*, p. 438.

52. Nixon *RN*, p. 412 (irritated). Estimates of the vote margin in 1960 vary somewhat, with sources as disparate as the Associated Press, the Republican National Committee,

Congressional Quarterly, and the Clerk of the House of Representatives releasing figures ranging from a low of 111,803 votes to a high of 119,450; see White, *The Making of the President 1960*, p. 422. Subsequent scholars supported the Nixon camp's cries of foul play; see Nixon, p. 606 ("Charges of fraud in Texas and Illinois were too widespread, and too persistent, to be entirely without foundation") and Hersh, *The Dark Side of Camelot*, pp. 132–34.

53. Garment, *Crazy Rhythm*, p. 142.

54. Morin, *The Associated Press Story*, p. 196; Nixon, *RN*, pp. 412–13 (Chapin).

55. Nixon *RN*, pp. 412–13; Strober and Strober, *Nixon*, p. 295 (tear).

56. "People," *Time*, April 15, 1974; Don Bertrand, "Two County Men May Be in Nixon Cabinet," *New York Daily News*, November 17, 1968. The *Washington Post* reported Mitchell was a registered Independent before merging firms with Nixon; see Don Oberdorfer, "Justice," *Washington Post*, December 12, 1968.

57. Mitchell-Reed, interview, February 23, 1992.

58. Jennings, interview, August 1, 2002.

59. McLendon, *Martha*, pp. 69–75.

60. Tom Ottenad, "Was Saigon's Peace Talk Delay Due to Republican Promises?" *Boston Globe*, January 6, 1969, and Judith Viorst, "Anna Chennault: Washington's Own Fortune Cookie," *Washingtonian*, September 1969, both quoted in Summers, *The Arrogance of Power*, p. 519; Seymour M. Hersh, *The Price of Power: Kissinger in the Nixon White House* (Summit, 1983), p. 22 (concerned).

61. WH memorandum from Peter M. Flanigan for John N. Mitchell, [no subject], October 2, 1969; FG 17 WHCF, DOJ, Box 1, NARA.

62. HN, February 25, 1969 (underlining in original).

63. HN, April 12, 1971 (high-level), May 18, 1971 (finesse).

64. Summers, *The Arrogance of Power*, p. 306.

65. Safire, *Before the Fall*, pp. 88–91; John Lehman, interview with author, March 3, 2001.

66. E-mails from [a confidential source] to the author, January 21, 2003, 6:16 p.m.; and Wednesday, January 22, 2003, 3:25 p.m.

67. Rowland Evans and Robert Novak, "Due to the Typical Mitchell Caution, Nixon Didn't Embrace Labor Chiefs," *Washington Post*, October 28, 1968 (golden opportunity); Evans and Novak, "Mitchellism," *New York Post*, November 24, 1969; and Evans and Novak, *Nixon in the White House*, pp. 27, 56 (fatal).

68. Richard Kleindienst, interview with author, April 21, 1992; Behn, *The Ripon Society*, pp. 139–52; Strober and Strober, *Nixon*, p. 54 (Chapin). Nixon benefited from a drop in voter turnout: Only 60 percent of eligible voters cast ballots, down from 69 percent in 1960 and 64 percent in 1964, with the decline "especially noticeable in the largest cities."

69. Bertrand, "Two County Men" (autonomy); CI, September 27, 1988 (debates); Viorst, " 'The Justice Department' " (lean, temper); "The Sharp New Line," *Business Week*.

LAW AND ORDER

1. Ruckelshaus interview.

2. Nixon, *RN*, p. 420.

3. Ehrlichman, *Witness to Power*, p. 57n; author's transcript of Nixon-Frost interview (aired September 8, 1977).

4. CI, August 9, 1988 (Disneyland); "Fighting Crime in America: Exclusive Interview with Attorney General John N. Mitchell," *U.S. News & World Report*, August 18, 1969 (twenty-six); Schoenebaum, *Profiles of an Era*, p. 443

(fat). Appearing on *The Dick Cavett Show* in 1970, Mitchell said he was "not really surprised" when Nixon chose him to be attorney general. "I think the suggestion was made quite a number of times, about twenty-three, as I recall, and we were just in disagreement as to who should be the attorney general," Mitchell said. "But it finally turned out that he wanted me, and so I'm there." Herb Klein cut in: "I remember, as a matter of fact, John resisted that suggestion." "Twenty-three times, I think it was, Herb," Mitchell insisted; see Makay and Brown, *The Rhetorical Dialogue*, pp. 37–57.

5. Garment interview, March 13, 1992 (emphases in original); Nixon-Frost interview; Morrison interview; Harries interview; McLendon, *Martha*, p. 75; Deborah Gore Dean, interview with author, March 10, 1992.

6. Kleindienst, *Justice*, p. 61.

7. "Attorney General: John Newton Mitchell," *New York Times*, December 12, 1968 (pragmatic); Oberdorfer, "Justice" (take-charge).

8. Denniston, "He's No 'Gang-Buster.' "

9. Harris, *Justice*, p. 121.

10. FBI statistics reprinted in Robert W. Peterson, ed., *Crime and the American Response* (Facts on File, 1973), pp. 6–12.

11. Jerry Antevil and William Twaddell, "He'll Wiretap to Fight Mob, Mitchell Tells Senators," *New York Daily News*, January 15, 1969 (should be used, easy time); John P. McKenzie, "Mitchell Backed by Senate Panel," *Washington Post*, January 15, 1969 (capacity, fine, isn't likely, Ervin); Harris, *Justice*, pp. 122–24.

12. Jack Hushen, interview with author, December 30, 1993.

13. HN, March 10, 1970; April 15, 1970; July 15, 1970.

14. Craig Smith, "Mitchell Vows to Fight Crime 'On All Fronts,' " *Staten Island Advance*, January 22, 1969 (balding).

15. Author's transcript, NT, Nixon-Haldeman, Conversation No. 3–199, White House Telephone, May 13, 1971, 5:45 p.m. to 6:06 p.m., NARA (hell of a lot); letter from William Rehnquist to the author, June 29, 1993 (more than one) and William Rehnquist, interview with author, October 20, 1993.

16. HN, January 23, 1969; The President's News Conference of January 27, 1969. Except where noted, all quotations from the Public Papers of the Presidents are taken from John Woolley's and Gerhard Peters's exhaustive online database, *The American Presidency Project*, accessible at www.presidency.ucsb.edu.

17. Except where noted, all citations of Nixon-Mitchell anticrime legislation are based on *Congressional Quarterly Almanac, Vol. XXV, 1969* (Congressional Quarterly, 1970), pp. 687–722 and *Congressional Quarterly Almanac, Vol. XXVI, 1970* (Congressional Quarterly, 1971), pp. 208–19, 545–51.

18. Harris, *Justice*, p. 163; Sidney E. Zion, "Hard Line by the Administration," *New York Times*, July 27, 1969.

19. *60 Minutes*, CBS News program, [aired] March 18, 1969; "Where War Against Crime Is Being Won: Interview with Attorney General John N. Mitchell," *U.S. News & World Report*, March 22, 1971.

20. "Remarks on Signing the Organized Crime Control Act of 1970," October 15, 1970. The Senate voted to repeal the "no-knock" provision of the drug laws four years later; see *CBS Evening News*, July 12, 1974.

21. Malcolm S. Forbes, "That's Always the Way It Is for John Mitchell," *Forbes*, October 1, 1971.

22. UPI report, "Mitchell Reports Gain in Crime War," *New York Times*, January 20, 1971.

23. Forbes, "That's Always the Way."

24. *CBS Evening News*, March 28, 1973. Although Mitchell advocated expanded wiretapping powers, the Nixon administration between January 1969 and March 1971 employed court-authorized electronic surveillance on only 309 occasions, 80 percent of them involving gambling or narcotics. These installations resulted in more than 900 arrests, more than 500 indictments, and more than 100 convictions. Even in national security cases, the administration placed 747 wiretaps, 115 fewer than Lyndon Johnson's, and only 165 more than John F. Kennedy's—an impressive fact given that Nixon's presidency lasted more than two-and-a-half years longer than Kennedy's. Moreover, the Nixon administration, according to figures released by President Ford's attorney general, Edward Levi, made only 163 national security room-microphone installations, 29 fewer than Johnson's administration, and 105 fewer than Kennedy's; see David Wise, *The American Police State: The Government Against the People* (Random House, 1976), p. 145n.

25. Forbes, "That's Always the Way."

26. "Where War Against Crime Is Being Won," *U.S. News & World Report*.

27. "Attorney General Mitchell: The Tide Is Turning Against Crime," *Nation's Business*, June 1970 (hand).

28. AOP, 128; Kleindienst, *Justice*, p. 64; Kleindienst interview.

29. Erwin Griswold, interview with author, June 28, 1994.

30. Baker, *Conflicting Loyalties*, p. 11.

31. Author's transcript, NT, Nixon-Haldeman, Conversation No. 534-12, Oval Office, July 1, 1971, 1:38 to 2:05 p.m., NARA (better off, repels); author's transcript, NT, Nixon-Ehrlichman, Conversation 137-12, Camp David, August 13, 1972, 9:53 to 10:02 a.m. (didn't want).

DAYS OF RAGE

1. DOJ transcript of Mitchell press conference in Indianapolis, Indiana, October 16, 1970; FBIM.
2. Peter Fleming, interview with author, December 17, 1991 (raising hell); Morrison interview (bastards).
3. HN, February 14 and 21, 1969; March 3, 1969 (emphases in original).
4. Harris, *Justice*, pp. 172 (hard-line, evidence, component), 175 (forefront).
5. Spencer Rich, "Mitchell Urges Crackdown on College Rioters," *Washington Post*, May 2, 1969 (imprisonment, legitimate, there shall be); Marjorie Hunter, "Mitchell Opposed to New Laws on Student Unrest," *New York Times*, May 21, 1969 (into the hands); Kirkpatrick Sale, *SDS* (Vintage, 1974), p. 541 (detention camp).
6. With the severance of Seale's case, the indicted men became known as the Chicago Seven.
7. Harris, *Justice*, p. 63 (intense); Nancy Zaroulis and Gerald Sullivan, *Who Spoke Up: American Protest Against the War in Vietnam, 1963–1975* (Doubleday, 1984), p. 249 (hound, malicious); Judy Clavir and John Spitzer, *The Conspiracy Trial* (Bobbs-Merrill, 1970), pp. 147–71 (fascist pig liar); "Indicted Chicago 8 Ask Mitchell to Quit Over Wiretapping," *New York Times*, June 16, 1969. The Chicago Eight branded Mitchell's argument "shocking, lawless." In June 1972, the U.S. Supreme Court held it unconstitutional to wiretap domestic groups without a warrant; see *U.S. v. U.S. District Court*, 407 U.S. 297 (1972). Asked about this years later, Mitchell noted "the other circuit courts had sustained the power and we assumed the Supreme Court would. . . . But I wasn't personally involved in it"; see KI, February 9, 1988.
8. Rennie Davis, interview with author, May 9, 2004; Jonah Raskin, *For the Hell of It: The Life and Times of Abbie Hoffman* (University of California Press,

1998), photo insert (boxing gloves). On the Chicago Seven–inspired riots at the Watergate—an incident whose obscurity is curious, given the severity of the clashes and the later prominence of the targeted building—see "1,000 March to Watergate in '7' Protest," *Washington Evening Star*, February 19, 1970; Lance Gay, "March on Watergate Rebuffed," *Washington Evening Star*, February 20, 1970; Carl Bernstein and Paul Valentine, "145 Arrested in March on Watergate," *Washington Post*, February 20, 1970; Myra MacPherson, "Security 'Wonderful' for Watergate Area," *Washington Post*, February 20, 1970; "Police Bar March on Mitchell Home," *New York Times*, February 20, 1970; B. D. Colen, "Watergate Residents Happy," *Washington Evening Star*, February 21, 1970; "Backers of 'Chicago 7' Obtain Rally Permits," *Washington Evening Star*, February 21, 1970; Woody West, "Underground Newsman to Fight Charge," *Washington Evening Star*, February 21, 1970; and Dana Beal and Steve Conliff, eds., *Blacklisted News, Secret History: From Chicago '68 to 1984* (Youth International Party Information Service, 1983), pp. 444–45. Riot officers may have been swifter to attack in this case because of Mitchell's residency at the Watergate: "Reporters who had covered similar protests here," observed the *Washington Evening Star*, "said that police seemed more impatient and rougher in handling the demonstrators yesterday than in the past."
9. "Fighting Crime in America," *U.S. News & World Report*; Sale, *SDS*, pp. 543–44; Seymour M. Hersh, "Underground for the C.I.A. in New York: An Ex-Agent Tells of Spying on Students," *New York Times*, December 29, 1974 (profiles).
10. Beacon Hill Revolutionary Action Group, "The Knock at the Door," [undated leaflet c. 1969], reprinted in

Mitchell Goodman, *The Movement Toward a New America* (Alfred A. Knopf, 1970), p. 580 (culture); Raskin, *For the Hell of It*, p. 182 (darkened, menacing); *CBS Evening News*, May 4, 1971 (dictatorship); William Ayers, interview with author, May 8, 2004; Billy Ayers, Bernadine Dohrn, Jeff Jones, and Celia Sojourn, eds., *Prairie Fire: The Politics of Revolutionary Anti-Imperialism* (Communications Co., 1974), pp. 23–30; Sale, *SDS*, pp. 544–45.

11. CCT, 127–31. Apart from the FBI's efforts to "penetrate and disrupt the Communist Party USA and white hate groups," COINTELPRO operations were "apparently not reported to any of the attorneys general in office during the period in which they were implemented," concluded Attorney General William B. Saxbe and FBI Director Clarence M. Kelley in November 1974; see Noam Chomsky in Nelson Blackstock, *COINTELPRO: The FBI's Secret War on Political Freedom* (Vintage, 1976), pp. 4, 212n2. In 1975, at the hearings of the Senate's Church Committee, which investigated domestic spying abuses, Mitchell told Senator Walter Mondale there were "areas in which the Bureau was not fully accountable to me"; this led Senator Walter Huddleston to ask if COINTELPRO was among them. "From what I know about it," Mitchell answered, "yes, sir." Former FBI agent M. Wesley Swearingen stated in a 1980 deposition that although COINTELPRO "had been 'officially' discontinued [by Mitchell] in April 1971 . . . agents continued to carry out the program's objectives"; see Ward Churchill and Jim Vander Wall, *The COINTELPRO Papers: Documents From the FBI's Secret Wars Against Domestic Dissent* (South End Press, 1990), p. 334n25. On the FBI's surveillance of Mitchell, see Alexander Charns,

Cloak and Gavel: FBI Wiretaps, Bugs, Informers, and the Supreme Court (University of Illinois Press, 1992), pp. 112, 184n4. "No other information about this interception has been made public," wrote Charns. "The FBI claims the ELSUR [electronic surveillance] log concerning John Mitchell is still classified."

12. TPOP, 203n (off the hook); *CBS Evening News*, August 31, 1973. A former member of the Seattle underground argued Mitchell triumphed over the antiwar left only *inadvertently*, by conferring "martyrdom" on the notoriously ineffective Yippie leaders Abbie Hoffman and Jerry Rubin: "Mitchell ultimately achieved his goal in a backwards way: He destroyed the New Left by handing the keys to the asylum over to its worst lunatics." See Walt Crowley, *Rites of Passage: A Memoir of the Sixties in Seattle* (University of Washington Press, 1995), p. 135.

13. Ayers interview; *CBS Morning News*, November 6, 1973 (kung fu); "The Rise and Fall of Mr. Law and Order," *Newsweek*, April 30, 1973.

14. FBI memo from Mr. Mohr to Mr. Tolson, March 26, 1969, Subject: Protection of the Attorney General (white girls); FBI memo from Mr. Mohr to Mr. Tolson, April 2, 1969, Subject: Protection of Attorney General (racial demonstrations); FBI memo from Mr. Mohr to Mr. Tolson, April 3, 1969, Subject: Protection of Attorney General; FBI memo from Mr. Mohr to Mr. Tolson, April 4, 1969, Subject: Protection of Attorney General (delayed), all in FBIM; Bobby Seale, *Seize the Time: The Story of the Black Panther Party and Huey P. Newton* (Random House, 1970), pp. 428–29.

15. Tom Wells, *The War Within: America's Battle Over Vietnam* (University of California Press, 1994), pp. 304–35, 627n66 (face up, bring the war

home, attack the beast, off the pig); Rudd interview; Susan Stern, *With the Weathermen: The Journey of a Revolutionary Woman* (Doubleday, 1975), pp. 234 (idiot), 255 (capitalists), 351 (shut up).

16. Wells, *The War Within*, p. 338.

17. "Look at It: America 1969," *New Left Notes*, August 1969, reprinted in Harold Jacobs, ed., *Weatherman* (Ramparts Press, 1970), p. 174 (tens); William Ayers, *Fugitive Days: A Memoir* (Beacon Press, 2001), pp. 166–69 (couple hundred, sank, running, turning back); Wells, *The War Within*, p. 367 (Dellinger); Sale, *SDS*, pp. 603–9 (kill or be killed, mangled, October 8 statistics); Jeremy Varon, *Bringing the War Home: The Weather Underground, the Red Army, and Revolutionary Violence in the Sixties and Seventies* (University of California Press, 2004), p. 82 (cumulative statistics).

18. Wells, *The War Within,* p. 462 (psychopaths); Joseph Volz, "FBI Break-ins Bring Mitchell Back to Court," *New York Daily News,* October 29, 1980 (testimony); Lapham, "The Attorney General Has Heard It All Before" (Leninists, run the show, stuck, second-act, penalties). Mitchell's testimony came at the trial of W. Mark Felt and Edward S. Miller, two former FBI officials convicted of having ordered five illegal break-ins, in 1972 and 1973, at the New York and New Jersey homes of Weather Underground sympathizers. In April 1981, President Reagan granted both men "full and unconditional" pardons. In May 2005, Felt was identified as "Deep Throat," the Watergate-era source for *Washington Post* reporter Bob Woodward; see Woodward, *The Secret Man: The Story of Watergate's Deep Throat* (Simon & Schuster, 2005). Even after the identification of Felt, important questions about Woodward's Watergate-era reporting,

and its many references to Deep Throat, remained; see James Rosen, "The FBI Informant," *Weekly Standard,* August 29, 2005. Mitchell's appearance in the Felt case, in which ex-President Nixon also testified, marked the former attorney general's first return to the federal courthouse where he had been convicted and sentenced in the Watergate cover-up trial.

19. Thomas F. Parker, ed., *Violence in the U.S., Volume 2: 1968–71* (Facts on File, 1974), p. 190. Asked about the "dog" threat in 2004, Ayers dismissed it as "macho rhetoric": "Harming Mitchell or [bombing] the Watergate complex . . . never occurred to us, I don't think."

20. Robert Walters, "U.S. Expected March Violence," *Washington Evening Star,* November 18, 1969.

21. WH intelligence memo no. 2 from TCH [Thomas C. Huston] to John Ehrlichman, October 30, 1969; WHSF—SMOF, JDE Subject file, Intelligence—Memoranda—Huston, NARA.

22. "Mitchell Asserts Militants Lead Coming Protest," *New York Times,* November 3, 1969 (destroy); Rowland Evans and Robert Novak, "Liberals Capitulate to Extremists, Reds Dominate 'Peace' Movement," *Washington Post,* November 12, 1969 (dominated); Kleindienst, *Justice,* p. 73 (fall offensive).

23. Richard Harwood and Warren Unna, "Hill Doves to Join Mobilization Rally," *Washington Post,* November 11, 1969 (McGovern); Clayton Fritchey, "Nixon Men Conjure Faceless Enemy," *Washington Evening Star,* November 14, 1969.

24. John Dean, "The Other Side of the Demonstrations," in Lynda Rosen Obst, ed., *The Sixties* (Rolling Stone Press, 1977), pp. 290–93 (blasé, nuisance, annoyed, backs, stopped); see also Philip Hirschkop, interview with

author, May 15, 2004 ("He had his own agenda," Hirschkop said of Dean, adding, "He didn't answer to Mitchell, I'll tell you that") and "Mayor Helps Break Stalemate on Mass March," *Washington Post*, November 12, 1969. Dean later acknowledged he sided with the protesters because "many times, I thought they had a good point"; see SSC, IV: 1446.

25. FBI memo from J. P. Mohr to Mr. Tolson, Subject: Protection of the Attorney General, November 10, 1969; FBI memo from J. P. Mohr to Mr. Tolson, Subject: Protection of the Attorney General, November 12, 1969, both in FBIM; Kleindienst, *Justice*, p. 69 (Action Plan).

26. Richard Harwood and Warren Unna, "Hill Doves to Join Mobilization Rally," *Washington Post*, November 11, 1969 (28,000, readiness); Carl Bernstein, "9,000 Troops Poised for Antiwar Trouble," *Washington Post*, November 13, 1969 (thoroughly); *The Fire Next Time* [Weatherman newspaper], November 21, 1969, in Jacobs, *Weatherman*, p. 275 ("pig marshals").

27. "Mitchell Decries Johnson 'Deception,'" *New York Times*, November 12, 1969; John P. MacKenzie, "Mitchell Lays Distrust in U.S. to LBJ," *Washington Post*, November 12, 1969. Discussing Mitchell's claims about the disingenuousness of the Johnson White House, reporter Paul Niven told the attorney general: "I know many people who were *in* that administration who agree with you"; see "The President's Men," PBS program, [aired] December 4, 1969, WHCA, Tape No. 3545, NARA.

28. Richard Harwood, "War Protest Walk Begins on Quiet Note," *Washington Post*, November 14, 1969; Mary McGrory, "If It's Violent, It'll Be Just a Mockery," *Washington Evening Star*, November 14, 1969 (drums).

29. Richard Harwood, "Militants Break Peace as War Protest Grows," *Washington Post*, November 15, 1969 (Spock); "Huge Throng Masses in Protest," *Washington Evening Star*, November 15, 1969 (petitions, insoluble); Paul Hoffman, *Moratorium: An American Protest* (Tower, 1970), pp. 160–63 (Wizard, smash the state, someone).

30. Harwood, "Militants Break Pence" (eviction, full-fledged); William Greider, "Rubin: 'It's Like Peace Is Respectable,'" *Washington Post*, November 16, 1969 (rocks); "Gas Routs Night March on Embassy," *Washington Post*, November 15, 1969 (restrained); THD, 108 (estimate, photo count); Richard Harwood, "Largest Rally in Washington History Demands Rapid End to Vietnam War," *Washington Post*, November 16, 1969 (ignored, white); Robert Walters, "U.S. Probes Protest Violence, Weighs Anti-Riot Prosecution," *Washington Evening Star*, November 19, 1969 (breach); Kleindienst, *Justice*, p. 73.

31. "Protest Has Many Forms: Slogan, Signs . . . and a Cross," *Washington Post*, November 16, 1969; THD, 107 (strange, unreal); "Police Tear Gas Disperses 6,000 at Justice Dept.," *Washington Evening Star*, November 16, 1969 (Seale, Minh); William Chapman, "Thousands at Justice Dept. Gassed in Radicals' Assault," *Washington Post*, November 16, 1969; Caleb S. Rossiter, *The Chimes of Freedom Flashing: A Personal History of the Vietnam Antiwar Movement and the 1960s* (TCA Press, 1996), p. 197; Hirschkop interview; Jerris Leonard, interview with author, May 23, 2004; Robert Walters, "Officer J.V. Wilson Patrols His Beat," *Washington Evening Star*, November 16, 1969; Paul Delaney, "Mitchell's Wife Says He Likened Protest to 'Russian Revolution,'" *New York Times*, November

22, 1969. Rossiter recalled seeing Martha Mitchell on the balcony as well; he is probably mistaken. The *Evening Star* spotted Mitchell, Kleindienst, and "a handful of aides," but made no mention of Mrs. Mitchell. Members of the Yippies also claimed to have spotted the attorney general's wife on this occasion; however they also claimed, falsely, that the mob "broke every window" at the Justice Department. See Beal and Conliff, *Blacklisted News*, pp. 2, 43. For another eyewitness account of this clash, see Larry Grathwohl and Frank Reagan, *Bringing Down America: An FBI Informer with the Weathermen* (Arlington House, 1976).

32. "Police Tear Gas Disperses 6,000 at Justice Dept.," *Washington Evening Star*, November 16, 1969 (White House, fumes); "Protest Has Many Forms: Slogan, Signs . . . and a Cross," *Washington Post*, November 16, 1969; THD, 108 (Krogh); Stanley I. Kutler, *The Wars of Watergate: The Last Crisis of Richard Nixon* (Knopf, 1990), p. 79. (Ruckelshaus).

33. Landau interview, January 12, 1994.

34. Wells, *The War Within*, p. 398 (Gallup); Sale, *SDS*, p. 622 (depression).

35. Address to the Nation on the Situation in Southeast Asia, April 30, 1970.

36. Parker, *Violence in the U.S.*, pp. 161–62; Wells, *The War Within*, p. 421; Zaroulis and Sullivan, *Who Spoke Up*, p. 319.

37. FBI 302 form of interview with [redacted] by SA [redacted], [conducted and filed] May 16, 1970 [I] (hard-core) and FBI 302 report of interview with [redacted] by SA [redacted], [conducted] May 16, 1970, [filed] May 17, 1970 (My God). The most exhaustively researched account of the killings at Kent State is William A. Gordon, *The Fourth of May: Killings and Coverups at Kent State* (Prometheus Books, 1990); see also

James Rosen, "About Kent State: Shades of Watergate?" *New York Newsday*, May 4, 1995.

38. Parker, *Violence in the U.S.*, p. 166 (credible, likelihood); "Justice at Kent State?" *New York Times*, August 18, 1971.

39. William Lineberry, "Richard Nixon's Ten Days," *Newsweek*, May 18, 1970 (political difficulty); HN, May 3, 1970 (emphasis in original); and Rosen, "About Kent State."

40. Charles W. Colson, *Born Again* (Chosen Books, 1976), p. 37 (grim-faced); Leonard interview, May 23, 2004.

41. DOJ summary of FBI reports on Kent State [undated, c. June 21, 1970], reprinted in its entirety in I. F. Stone, *The Killings at Kent State: How Murder Went Unpunished* (New York Review, 1970), pp. 60–104; FBI 302 report of interview with [redacted] by SA [redacted], [conducted] May 15, 1970, [filed] May 18, 1970 (M-1s). In only one case did a Guardsman admit shooting a specific individual: Sergeant Lawrence Shafer told the FBI he shot Joseph Lewis Jr., the victim standing closest to the Guardsmen—sixty feet away—because Lewis made an obscene gesture at him. Yet investigators had only these statements, not firm ballistics evidence, to prove Shafer shot Lewis. Moreover Shafer was the only Guardsman injured seriously enough on May 4 to require medical treatment; see also Gordon, *The Fourth of May*, pp. 33, 63.

42. HN, May 4, 1970 (sniper, Rhodes), May 6, 1970 (effective, brainstorm, reconciliation [emphases in original]), May 8, 1970 (conciliatory).

43. EN, May 21, 1970 (totalitarianism); HN, May 16, 1970 (lines drawn, just as well), May 20, 1970 (anti-student, offensive), June 16, 1970 (teeth, the public).

44. John P. MacKenzie, "Deaths Sickened, Saddened Mitchell, He Tells

Students," *Washington Post*, May 10, 1970.

45. "Mitchell Eyes Prosecution by U.S. in Kent State Case: Apparent Violations of Federal Law," *Akron Beacon Journal*, July 29, 1970, cited in Gordon, *The Fourth of May*, pp. 67, 196n13; FBI memo to W. C. Sullivan from C. D. Brennan, Subject: Unknown Subjects: Fire Bombing of Army ROTC Building . . . , May 5, 1970 (sabotage); FBI Teletype to SAC, Cleveland from FBI Director, May 5, 1970 (conspiracy); File No. 98–46479. J. Edgar Hoover wondered whether the ROTC fire was the work of "SDS or other militant New Left" groups.

46. Gordon, *The Fourth of May*, pp. 65–75 (knock down); HN, October 17, 1970 (emphases in original). It incensed Hoover that the Justice Department did not file federal charges against any KSU students. When an assistant attorney general notified Hoover of this decision, the FBI director scrawled on the memo: "The usual run around by the do nothing Div[ision]"; see DOJ memo to Director from J. Walter Yeagley, Subject: [Redacted]; Peter Charles Bleik [*sic*]; Douglas Charles Cormack; Rick Felber; Thomas Graydon Foglesong; [Redacted]; Jerry Rupe; [Redacted]; Sabotage; Sedition; Civil Rights— Federally Protected Activity; Destruction of Government Property, June 15, 1970.

47. Unsigned FBI memo for the record, Subject: Memorandum from Will Wilson, Assistant Attorney General, Criminal Division, Department of Justice, to Director, Federal Bureau of Investigation, [filed] June 19, 1970; Helen Kennedy, "Nixon Wanted City to Suffer for Snub," *New York Daily News*, October 18, 1996 (request, assured); see also *New York Law Journal*, October 18, 1996.

48. Thomas R. Hensley, *The Kent State Incident: Impact of Judicial Process on* *Public Attitudes* (Greenwood Press, 1981), p. 101. The existence and text of Ehrlichman's memo were first reported by NBC News in 1978. The earlier memorandum by Nixon, to which Ehrlichman alluded, has not surfaced.

49. WH memo for John Ehrlichman from H. R. Haldeman, [no subject], January 28, 1971, WHSF—SMOF, H. R. Haldeman, Box 196, NARA.

50. EN, January 28, 1971; see also Rosen, "About Kent State."

51. Ken Clawson, "No U.S. Action Likely on Kent," *Washington Post*, March 21, 1971. In December 1973, following the revelations of Watergate and continued public pressure, the Justice Department reversed itself and empaneled a federal grand jury in the case. Assistant Attorney General J. Stanley Pottinger emphasized that the move reflected no judgment on Mitchell's conduct. In March 1974, eight Guardsmen were indicted for violating the students' due process rights; eight months later, all eight were acquitted. Likewise, the jury in a 1975 civil suit filed against the Guardsmen and public officials by the victims' families found in favor of the defendants. That verdict was later overturned by a higher court, prompting a second civil trial in 1978–79. The case was ultimately settled out of court. The slain students' parents received $15,000 each and $75,000 for attorneys' fees; one paralyzed student received $350,000, while eight other wounded students received judgments ranging from $15,000 to $42,500. As part of the settlement, twenty-eight Guardsmen signed a statement "deeply regretting" the shootings, while still maintaining that "some Guardsmen . . . may have believed in their own minds that their lives were in danger." Charges against most of the twenty-five individuals indicted in Ohio for torching the ROTC build-

ing and other offenses were quietly dropped.

52. HN, September 9, 1970 (turn off); "Mitchell Assails 'Stupid' Students," *New York Times*, September 19, 1970 (emphasis added); Hunter S. Thompson, *Fear and Loathing: On the Campaign Trail '72* (Warner Books, 1983), p. 467; Milton Viorst, *Fire in the Streets: America in the 1960s* (Simon & Schuster, 1979), p. 543. A spokesman sought to douse the furor caused by Mitchell's attack on academia by issuing a weak nondenial ("comments attributed to the attorney general, apparently based on fragmentary and overheard conversations at a social gathering, are distorted and highly inaccurate"), but Mitchell more cannily resorted to humor, telling a university audience: "There are stupid students. I was one when I was in college"; see Martin Weil, "Collegians Given Views of Mitchell," *Washington Post*, September 27, 1970.

53. Author's transcript of *Issues and Answers*, ABC News program, [aired] August 2, 1970, WHCA, Tape No. 3810, NARA.

54. NARA transcript, NT, Nixon-Colson-Haldeman, Conversation No. 482–27, Oval Office, April 19, 1971, 6:12–6:32 p.m., NARA.

55. Ibid.

56. NARA transcript, NT, Nixon-Haldeman-Kissinger, Conversation No. 484–13, Oval Office, April 20, 1971, 1:13 p.m.–1:24 p.m., NARA (forget the law, secretaries [emphasis added]).

57. Beal and Conliff, *Blacklisted News*, pp. 409–10 (evangelist, closing); David Gelber, "The Weathermen's Solution Is Part of the Problem," *The Village Voice*, March 26, 1970, reprinted in Goodman, *The Movement Toward a New America*, pp. 593–94 (banks); FBI memo from M. A. Jones to Mr. Bishop, December 16, 1971, Subject: Attorney General's Press/

Conference, FBIM. Years later, Davis strongly denied advocating the closing of the Pentagon or the burning of banks; see e-mail to the author from Rennie Davis, July 30, 2004.

58. "Wild in the Streets: After Kent," in Beal and Conliff, *Blacklisted News*, p. 409 (boldest and costliest); Davis interview; Parker, *Violence in the U.S.*, pp. 211–13 (manual).

59. "Mitchell Expects Violence to Come," *New York Times*, April 25, 1971.

60. James Reston, "The Leaderless Rabble," *New York Times*, May 5, 1971 (personally); Wells, *The War Within*, p. 486 (plain); "Youths Mass in Potomac Park," *Washington Evening Star*, May 1, 1971; Fred Barnes, "10,000 Troops to Be Brought into Area," *Washington Evening Star*, May 2, 1971. As late as ten days before May Day, authorities were estimating crowds of only 4,000; see Kleindienst, *Justice*, p. 75.

61. G. Gordon Liddy, *Will* (St. Martin's, 1997), p. 144.

62. "Youths Mass in Potomac Park," *Washington Evening Star*, May 1, 1971 (abridging); Wells, *The War Within*, pp. 499–500 (370). The *Evening Star* reported 339 arrests. Williams eventually came round to Mitchell's political views, endorsing Ronald Reagan for president in 1980.

63. Linda Wertheimer, ed., *Listening to America: Twenty-Five Years in the Life of a Nation, as Heard on National Public Radio* (Houghton Mifflin, 1995), pp. 1–3 (scented, 318,000); "City Shutdown Foiled, 6,000 Protesters Held," *Washington Evening Star*, May 3, 1971 (normal).

64. Kleindienst, *Justice*, p. 77.

65. Wells, *The War Within*, pp. 500–12 (Halloween, ugly mobs); Beal and Conliff, *Blacklisted News*, pp. 412–13 (war zone, grotesque).

66. HN, May 3, 1971; WI [Ehrlichman], November 20, 1985 (overplay); "City Shutdown Foiled," *Washington Evening Star* (flowing).

67. Wells, *The War Within*, pp. 506–7 (broken); "2,000 March to Protest at Justice Dept.," *Washington Evening Star*, May 4, 1971 (power, pigs); *CBS Evening News*, May 4, 1971 (carnival); "The F.B.I. Homes in and Gets Its Man," *New York Times*, May 5, 1971 and "The FBI Muffles an Echo," *Washington Evening Star*, May 5, 1971 (Froines).

68. Kleindienst, *Justice*, p. 80 (arrest and release figures); "City Shutdown Foiled," *Washington Evening Star* (young, white); Beal and Conliff, *Blacklisted News*, p. 413 (lost the revolution). May Day cost Washington taxpayers $3.9 million, while a class action lawsuit filed by the American Civil Liberties Union later resulted in a $12 million judgment; see Wells, *The War Within*, pp. 503–13. Then assistant attorney general William Rehnquist told newsmen "qualified martial law" applied on May Day; see Woody West, "Justice Official Defends Procedure in Arrests," *Washington Evening Star*, May 6, 1971.

69. Fred P. Graham, "Mitchell Urges All Police Copy Capital's Tactics," *New York Times*, May 11, 1971; Wells, *The War Within*, p. 511 (polls); "The Mob and the Law," *Washington Evening Star*, May 5, 1971 (willfully, effectively).

70. Dana Beal, "I Remember Martha," *YIPster Times*, June/July 1976 (Free Martha); "How We Got Nixon Before He Got Us" (shatter); and "The Legacy of 1970" (joke), all reprinted in Beal and Conliff, *Blacklisted News*, pp. 43, 343, 445; David Sheff, "Timothy Leary," *Rolling Stone*, December 10, 1987; Davis interview; Ayers interview; Rudd interview.

THE COMEDOWN

1. FBI memo from J. P. Mohr to Mr. Tolson, December 17, 1969, Subject Protection of the Attorney General; FBIM.

2. *Newsweek*, September 8, 1969.

3. "Senate Bars Haynsworth, 55–45," *New York Times*, November 22, 1969; "Senate Rejects Carswell by 51–45 Margin," *New York Times*, April 9, 1970; David Frost, *I Gave Them a Sword: Behind the Scenes of the Nixon-Frost Interviews* (Wm. Morrow, 1978), p. 157.

4. Jude Wanniski, "Disenchantment Over Mitchell Grows in Ranks of Republicans," *National Observer*, April 20, 1970; Rowland Evans and Robert Novak, "Mitchell Has Not Mastered His Job, Republican Senators Now Believe," *Washington Post*, April 20, 1970; "Mitchell Should Go," *Life*, April 17, 1970; Oberdorfer, "Mitchell's Power" (capital, blood).

5. THD, 109–10; Rehnquist interview; John Ehrlichman, interview with author, March 13, 1992; Kissinger interview; Haldeman interview.

6. HN, December 3, 1969; Oberdorfer, "Mitchell's Power."

7. Delaney, "Mitchell's Wife Says."

8. Dan Rather and Gary Paul Gates, *The Palace Guard* (Warner Books, 1975), p. 55 (gray-haired); Harriet Van Horne, "Tempering Justice," *New York Post*, November 24, 1969; "Mitchell Comments on Wife's Comments," *New York Times*, November 25, 1969; Associated Press, "Violence Top Peril: Mitchell," *New York Daily News*, November 24, 1969.

9. Fischer, "Warbler of Watergate"; "Eye Too, Eye Too," *Women's Wear Daily*, March 20, 1970. Many liberals likened Martha to Marie Antoinette; see Paul Healy, "Martha Always Says Mouthful," *New York Sunday News*, April 19, 1970.

10. Robertson, "Martha Mitchell"; McLendon, *Martha*, pp. 112–13.

11. White House memo from The President to Mr. Haldeman, [no subject],

December 1, 1969 [I and II], reprinted in Oudes, *From: The President,* pp. 74–76; McLendon, *Martha,* p. 109 (Dear Martha); Robert H. Phelps, "Comments Cost Mrs. Mitchell Her Office," *New York Times,* December 19, 1969.

12. UPI, "Mrs. Mitchell Called an Arm Twister," *Newsday,* December 9, 1969; Isabelle Shelton, "Mrs. Mitchell Tried to Twist Some Arms," *Long Island Press,* December 15, 1969; McLendon, *Martha,* pp. 112–13; UPI, "Mrs. Mitchell Won't Toe Designers' Fashion Line," *New York Times,* March 22, 1970 (nightgown). McLendon asserted, without substantiation, that Martha made the "arm-twisting" calls at Mitchell's behest.

13. Chennault, *The Education of Anna,* pp. 173–99; Isabelle Shelton, "Martha Mitchell Plays Role to the Hilt," *Long Island Press,* March 29, 1970 (Percy).

14. McLendon, *Martha,* pp. 121–22; Dorothy McCardle, "Women's Lib for Mrs. Mitchell?" *Washington Post,* April 13, 1970; Healy, "Martha Always Says Mouthful"; Robertson, "Martha Mitchell."

15. HN, April 11, 1970.

16. Myra MacPherson, "Press Aide," *Washington Post,* April 11, 1970; Healy, "Martha Always Says Mouthful."

17. McLendon, *Martha,* p. 123; Healy, "Martha Always Says Mouthful."; Isabelle Hall, "Martha's Mail: 10 to One in Her Favor," *Washington Post,* April 20, 1970. McCardle, "Women's Lib"; Judith Michaelson, "She'd Love to Go Back to the Kitchen," *New York Post,* April 25, 1970; Robertson, "Martha Mitchell"; Myra MacPherson, "Laughing Along with Martha," *Washington Post,* May 13, 1970. Ten of eleven letters supported Martha, the *Washington Post* reported. "I should have married someone like you," wrote a Tampa man. An Oregonian declared: "We need a lady like you for president—someone who will tell it like it is." But many resented Martha's outspokenness. "I can now understand why the Attorney General always has such a dour look," wrote a Minneapolis woman. "He probably has ulcers which you helped give him." A San Francisco woman clucked at "such a little mind in a big head," while a Dallas man asked: "Have you ever tried being quiet?"

18. THD, 149; HN, April 13, 1970 (emphasis in original). In annotations he added to his diary in the early 1990s, Haldeman wrote: "Martha's behavior was . . . due to both emotional and drinking problems. It was a source of embarrassment to both John and the administration. However, John was always patient with her."

19. HN, April 15, 1970 (talk to John), May 18, 1970. Haldeman's corresponding diary entry reads: "[The president] says Mitchell has to go unless he can solve the Martha problem"; see THD, 167.

WATCH WHAT WE DO

1. Makay and Brown, *The Rhetorical Dialogue.*

2. Mike Wallace and Gary Paul Gates, *Close Encounters* (Morrow, 1984), p. 130; Viorst, " 'The Justice Department' " (colored). Questioned closely about this passage, Wallace recalled: "I was stunned at his candor, not surprised especially to hear him say that . . . Bought doesn't necessarily mean money—well it does mean corrupted, but it doesn't necessarily mean cash; it means *quid pro quo.*" Did Shakespeare really kick Mitchell under the table? "Shakespeare knew the kind of reporter I was, and he wasn't absolutely certain that I would necessarily abide by the 'off-the-record' background lunch protocol that had been set up. I don't know that he kicked him, but it was more than a nudge."

See Mike Wallace, interview with author, October 26, 1997.

3. Hal Bruno, interview with author, April 13, 2002; confidential source interview with author (kike).

4. Peter Golden, *Quiet Diplomat: Max M. Fisher* (Cornwall, 1992), pp. 205–7; Yitzhak Rabin, *The Rabin Memoirs* (University of California Press, paperback ed., 1996), p. 165 (Rabin also recalled Mitchell saying in November 1972: "If you need a good campaign manager, I'm available!"). Ed Koch, then a Democratic congressman, also recalled that Mitchell, with help from Minority Leader Gerald Ford, "made it possible for *unlimited* numbers of Soviet Jews and non-Jews to enter the United States under refugee status known as 'parole status.'" "For that alone," Koch said, "[Mitchell] should receive some mercy, no matter where he has been consigned—purgatory or hell—for his misdeeds"; see letter from Ed Koch to the author, March 19, 1993 (emphasis added).

5. Nixon, *RN*, p. 543 (statistics); Harris, *Justice*, pp. 180–81; Viorst, "'The Justice Department'" ("Fink").

6. "Fighting Crime in America," *U.S. News & World Report*.

7. The President's News Conference of February 6, 1969. Mitchell's proposal to substitute legal action for funding cutoffs had long been advocated by John Doar, the assistant attorney general for civil rights under Presidents Kennedy and Johnson—and later Mitchell's cross-examiner at the House impeachment committee during Watergate; see Hugh Davis Graham, *The Civil Rights Era: Origins and Development of National Policy* (Oxford University Press, 1990), p. 320.

8. HN, February 17, 1969 (reign); John Robert Greene, *The Limits of Power: The Nixon and Ford Administrations* (Indiana University Press, 1992), p. 43; Leon E. Panetta and Peter Gall, *Bring Us Together: The Nixon Team and the Civil Rights Retreat* (J. B. Lippincott, 1971), pp. 61–73.

9. Grover, "Cabinet Enigma"; memo on Meeting with Attorney General John N. Mitchell, February 18, 1969, Box D61, Leadership Conference on Civil Rights Papers, Library of Congress; reprinted in Dean J. Kotlowski, *Nixon's Civil Rights: Politics, Principle, and Policy* (Harvard University Press, 2001), p. 28.

10. Graham, *The Civil Rights Era*, pp. 302–3; Jack Bass and Walter DeVries, *The Transformation of Southern Politics: Social Change and Political Consequence Since 1945* (Meridian, 1977), p. 29 (fool's gold); THD, 53 (emphasis in original); HN, April 15, 1969; Safire, *Before the Fall*, p. 237 (hundred years, intermarriage); Daniel P. Moynihan, *The Politics of a Guaranteed Income: The Nixon Administration and the Family Assistance Plan* (Vintage, 1973), p. 156; WH memo for [the] Secretary of Health, Education and Welfare from Alexander P. Butterfield, Subject: Note from the President, March 26, 1969; WHSF—SMOF, JDE Subject File, Desegregation, Box 30, NARA (forthright; emphasis in original); Ehrlichman interview (embarrassed); Leonard interview, October 14, 1999. In undermining Finch's standing with Nixon, the attorney general had inside help: At his suggestion, Robert Mardian, a Goldwater campaign veteran who worked the South and West for Nixon in '68 and owed his allegiances to Mitchell and Kleindienst, was named HEW's general counsel. "I didn't have a very comfortable time at HEW," Mardian later recalled, "because [Finch's aides] all referred to me, almost to my face, as Mitchell's spy"; see Robert Mardian, interview with author, August 2, 1993; Evans and Novak, *Nixon in the White House*, pp. 144; and Ehrlichman, *Witness to Power*, pp. 199–200.

11. Viorst " 'The Justice Department' " (hard-pressed); HN, February 17, 1969 (hit, too); Panetta and Gall, *Bring Us Together*.

12. Kotlowski, *Nixon's Civil Rights*, pp. 29–30.

13. HN, June 30, 1969 (emphasis in original); Kotlowski, *Nixon's Civil Rights*, p. 30 (record number). *Time* praised Mitchell for bringing "several important court suits that could hasten integration"; see "Nixon's Heavyweight," *Time*, July 25, 1969.

14. *Oregon v. Mitchell*, 400 U.S. 112 (1970); Michael Barone, "Nixon's America," *U.S. News & World Report*, September 20, 1999; Warren Weaver Jr., "Mitchell Urges a Wide Revision on Voting Rights," *New York Times*, June 27, 1969; Warren Weaver Jr., "Nixon Rights Bill Appears Doomed by a G.O.P. Attack," *New York Times*, July 2, 1969; "Excerpts From Statements by Mitchell and McCullough on the Voting Rights Bill," *New York Times*, July 2, 1969; *Congressional Quarterly Almanac, Vol. XXV, 1969* (Congressional Quarterly, 1970), pp. 411, 421–27; *Congressional Quarterly Almanac, Vol. XXVI, 1970* (Congressional Quarterly, 1971), pp. 192–93; Graham, *The Civil Rights Era*, pp. 346–65; Kotlowski, *Nixon's Civil Rights*, pp. 76–93.

15. "Sit-In at Mitchell's Office," *Washington Evening Star*, July 1, 1969; Associated Press, "Mitchell's Office Site of Sit-In," *New York Post*, July 1, 1969; "Nixon's Heavyweight," *Time*; Harris, *Justice*, pp. 193–94.

16. Reichley, "Elm Street's New White House Power"; Harris, *Justice*, p. 194.

17. "The President's Men," PBS; CI, August 13, 1986.

18. WH memo from Daniel P. Moynihan for John D. Ehrlichman, [no subject], November 25, 1969, WHSF—SMOF, JDE Subject file, Box 21, NARA (lawyer-like); Moynihan, *The Politics of a Guaranteed Income*, pp. 157–58.

19. Evans and Novak, *Nixon in the White House*, pp. 152–55 (public unrest); Panetta and Gall, *Bring Us Together*, pp. 253–62; Bass and DeVries, *The Transformation of Southern Politics*, pp. 29–30 (opposite); Warren Weaver Jr., "Nixon Missile Plan Wins in Senate By a 51–50 Vote," *New York Times*, August 7, 1969.

20. The President's News Conference of September 26, 1969.

21. Osborne, *The Second Year*, p. 22 (respect); Panetta and Gall, *Bring Us Together*, p. 302.

22. EN, February 7, 1970; HN, February 19, 20, and 27, 1970.

23. HN, February 27, 1970 (bullet, so be it); WH memo for the president from Bryce Harlow, Subject: Charlotte School Situation, February 11, 1970; POF, HW File, Box 5, NARA.

24. Evans and Novak, *Nixon in the White House*, p. 173; Statement About Desegregation of Elementary and Secondary Schools, March 24, 1970.

25. Robert Mardian, interview with author, September 14, 1993.

26. George Shultz, interview with author, April 29, 1996. In an uncharacteristic fit of peevishness, Shultz threatened to follow Agnew. "Shultz says if Mardian stays, he'll resign," Haldeman recorded; see HN, March 31, 1970. Both men stayed on.

27. George P. Shultz, *Turmoil and Triumph: My Years as Secretary of State* (Scribner's, 1993), p. 1046; and George P. Shultz, "How a Republican Desegregated the South's Schools," *New York Times*, January 8, 2003. As President Reagan's secretary of state, Shultz related the Mitchell story to Israeli prime minister Yitzhak Shamir, to illustrate how the Israeli-Palestinian dialogue could shift from "whether" to "how."

28. Leonard interview, March 17, 1992; Kotlowski, *Nixon's Civil Rights*, p. 37. Even George McGovern acknowledged in 1994: "Nixon was actually

pretty good on civil rights questions"; see Strober and Strober, *Nixon*, p. 114.

29. Robert R. Detlefsen, *Civil Rights Under Reagan* (ICS Press, 1991), p. 26.

30. *CBS Morning News*, July 23, 1973 (Vernon Jordan); Graham, *The Civil Right Era*, p. 320.

31. Kotlowski, *Nixon's Civil Rights*, p. 64.

32. Kleindienst interview. Nixon was also instrumental in the South's economic development. President Clinton's secretary of labor acknowledged that thanks to Nixon's revenue-sharing programs, the South's "population and share of the gross national product exploded"; see Robert B. Reich, "Without a Cause," *New York Times Book Review*, March 7, 1999.

ROBBING THE PRESIDENT'S DESK

1. SSCEX, W. Donald Stewart, February 19, 1974.

2. Landau interview, December 16, 1993 (emphasis in original).

3. Author's transcript, NT, Nixon-Kissinger, Conversation No. 17–132, White House Telephone, January 1, 1972, 2:43 p.m.–3:56 p.m., NARA (press conferences); Thompson, *The Nixon Presidency*, pp. 142, 204–5 (entirely trust, there goes Henry); Kissinger interview.

4. THD, 335–36 (gold standard); TPOP, 165 (MIRV). To author Len Colodny, Mitchell boasted of how Nixon persuaded the Soviets, in exchange for a corresponding American pledge, to abandon construction of a weapon system that Nixon, blocked by Congress, "couldn't have built anyway"; see CI, December 5, 1987. Mitchell also discussed with Colodny the attorney general's role in the Four Power Talks on Berlin, including the use of his own Watergate apartment, in February 1971, for secret strategy sessions. "I

think that there was a 'two-track' [back-channel policy] going on over in Germany, too," said Mitchell. He described Egon Bahr, an aide to West German chancellor Willy Brandt and a key interlocutor in the negotiations, as "a slippery character" who forced Nixon and Mitchell to "devise the program of getting Willy Brandt to act without Bahr closing it off"; see CI, July 10, 1986. Ken Rush, the U.S. ambassador to West Germany, also remembered the strategy sessions at the Watergate; see Thompson, *The Nixon Presidency*, pp. 338–39.

5. TPOP, 209–10. Richard Ober, the CIA official in charge of Project Chaos, rebutted internal complaints about its legality by noting that "members of the administration, including Dr. Kissinger and Attorney General Mitchell, have been briefed on this program."

6. Notes of interview with John Mitchell (May 8, 1985), 2:00 to 4:00 p.m. [by Robert Gettlin]. Mitchell told Gettlin the files showed President Kennedy had "smoked pot in the White House."

7. CI, August 17, 1986.

8. DOJ memorandum of meeting [by] J. N. Mitchell, Subject: Cambodia/South Vietnam, April 28, 1970, reprinted in its entirety in Henry Kissinger, *White House Years* (Little, Brown, 1979), pp. 1484–85. In his memorandum, Mitchell noted Kissinger "was leaning against . . . the use of U.S. forces in Cambodia."

9. Richard Helms handwritten notes, "Meeting with the President on Chile at 1525," September 15, 1970; reprinted in Peter Kornbluh, *The Pinochet File: A Declassified Dossier on Atrocity and Accountability* (New Press, 2003), p. 35.

10. Gettlin interview (devious); CI, March 8, 1985 (didn't like), April 19, 1988 (knock off).

11. Walter Isaacson, *Kissinger: A Biogra-*

phy (Simon & Schuster, 1992), pp. 209–10.

12. Haldeman interview.

13. Alexander Haig, interview with author, July 27, 2000 (Harvard faculty); CI, January 24, 1986 (Machiafucking-vellian, psychopath).

14. Isaacson, *Kissinger*, pp. 212–13, 789n2.

15. FBI memo for Mr. Tolson, Mr. DeLoach, Mr. Sullivan, and Mr. Bishop from John Edgar Hoover, [no subject], May 9, 1969, 5:05 PM, reprinted at HJC, VII: 143–45; TPOP, 91.

16. FBI Summary of Interview of John G. [*sic*] Mitchell [conducted May 11, 1973], [filed] May 12, 1973, reprinted at HJC, VII: 163–65.

17. Assistant FBI director William Sullivan told the *Los Angeles Times* he sent the wiretap records to the White House because he suspected the aging Hoover would use them to coerce Nixon and Mitchell into retaining him as FBI director. Sullivan called Hoover "a master blackmailer" who aimed "to keep Mitchell and others in line"; see Edward W. Knappman, ed., *Watergate and the White House*, Volume 1: *June 1972–July 1973* (Facts on File, 1973), p. 50. Robert Mardian, to whom Sullivan transferred the files, said Sullivan warned him the Kissinger taps "would destroy the presidency"; Mardian interview. Mitchell thought Sullivan "a little nuts" and accused him of "name dropping and wheeling and dealing" in a bid to replace Hoover; see FBI Summary of Interview with John G. [*sic*] Mitchell. At the same time, Mitchell shared Sullivan's concerns about Hoover's custodianship of the records: "Hoover is tearing the [FBI] apart trying to get at them," he told Nixon in October 1971. "Hoover won't come and talk to me about it. He's just got his Gestapo all over the place." Nixon agreed the records belonged "in a special safe"; see Anthony Summers, *Official and*

Confidential: The Secret Life of J. Edgar Hoover (G.P. Putnam's Sons, 1993), pp. 400–401. Later, Nixon disingenuously told Hoover's successor, Clarence M. Kelley, in June 1973: "That an officer of the Bureau would suggest that Edgar Hoover would blackmail the attorney general or the president of the United States—I just couldn't believe it. And I don't believe it today"; see author's transcript, NT, Nixon-Kelley, Conversation no. 933-5, Oval Office, 10:05 a.m. to 10:35 a.m.

18. Ruckelshaus's announcement is reprinted at HJC, VII: 285–86.

19. Letter to William D. Ruckelshaus from John N. Mitchell, May 17, 1973, reprinted at HJC, VII: 166–67.

20. FBI memo for the attorney general from John Edgar Hoover, Re: Colonel Alexander M. Haig/Technical Surveillance Request, May 20, 1969, reprinted at HJC, VII: 194–95 (installed); FBI memo for the attorney general from John Edgar Hoover, Re: Mr. [redacted]/Technical Surveillance Request, July 23, 1969, reprinted at HJC, VII: 273 (higher authority).

21. FBI memo to Mr. Tolson from C. D. DeLoach, Subject: [redacted]/Request for Electronic Surveillance/By Attorney General and President, September 10, 1969, reprinted at HJC, VII: 243; FBI memo for the attorney general from John Edgar Hoover, Re: [redacted], September 10, 1969, reprinted at HJC, VII: 244.

22. FBI Letter from William D. Ruckelshaus to John N. Mitchell, May 24, 1973, reprinted at HJC, VII: 169–70. Ruckelshaus asked FBI handwriting analysts to authenticate Mitchell's signatures, and they did; see FBI memo to Mr. Conrad from C. F. Downing, Subject: Sensitive Coverage Placed At/The Request of the White House, May 18, 1973, reprinted at HJC, VII: 168.

23. SSC, IV: 1626–27.

24. WSPF memo from Frank Martin to the file, Re: Interview of John Mitchell [conducted December 14, 1973], [filed] January 4, 1974; RG 460 WSPF *U.S. v. Mitchell* (Jencks)—Mitchell. Asked during his testimony before the House impeachment committee why "regular order" was not followed in the re-authorization of the wiretaps, Mitchell could only demur: "I can't answer that question after this period of time. I have no recollection as to the discussions involved other than the basic authorization with respect to the concern that [Nixon] had over national security. I was not privy or knowledgeable of all of the discussions that the people in the White House may have had with the director of the FBI"; see HJCW, II: 199. Mitchell found it hardest to explain the tap that most reflected his involvement: the physical surveillance placed on his youthful nemesis, John Sears.

25. "Questions About Gray," *Time*, March 5, 1973.

26. HJC summary of John Mitchell interview [conducted] July 7, 1974, [drafted] July 8, 1974; RG 460 WSPF *U.S. v. Mitchell* (Jencks)—Mitchell, NARA.

27. Ovid Demaris, *The Director: An Oral Biography of J. Edgar Hoover* (Harper's, 1975), p. 277. Kleindienst later expressed bitterness that Mitchell had misled him about the wiretaps. "This was the only aspect of my relationship with John Mitchell that I found [him] less than forthright, candid, and direct," Kleindienst said. "He always maintained to me that . . . he had nothing to do with it; and it turned out, in later years, that he did"; see Strober and Strober, p. 96.

28. CI, April 13, 1987 (emphasis added).

29. Letter to Ruckelshaus from Mitchell; DOJ letter to Hon. J. W. Fulbright from Elliot L. Richardson, September 12, 1973, reprinted at HJV, IV [*White House Surveillance Activities*], 200–201; *CBS Evening News*, May 16, 1973 (massive leaks); Isaacson, *Kissinger*, p. 223; Frank Jackman, "Nixon's Liability in Tapping Upheld by the Top Court," *New York Daily News*, June 23, 1981; Morton Halperin, interview with author, March 24, 1994. Halperin and Hedrick Smith, one of the wiretapped newsmen, filed civil suits against Mitchell and Kissinger—and in Halperin's case, ex-President Nixon—charging invasion of privacy. *Halperin v. Kissinger*, for which both Mitchell and Nixon gave depositions, dragged on for almost a decade. In 1981, the Supreme Court deadlocked over whether to uphold a lower court's assessment of damages against Mitchell and Nixon; Chief Justice Rehnquist recused himself from the case. Ultimately Mitchell was dropped as a defendant and the case settled—with no damages paid—when Kissinger sent Halperin a public apology. Anthony Lake, another wiretapped aide, asked Kissinger for a written statement affirming that Lake never violated any security clearances and acknowledging that the wiretapping program was wrong. When Kissinger refused, Lake sued his former boss; the case ended in January 1989, when Kissinger sent Lake a "Dear Tony" letter. Characteristically, Kissinger laid blame elsewhere—specifically on Mitchell, who had died two months earlier. "It was Attorney General Mitchell's view that such techniques were within the president's powers," Kissinger wrote.

30. Schoenebaum, *Profiles of an Era*, pp. 369–71; Haig interview (opposite [emphasis in original]).

31. Hushen interview, December 30, 1993. Reporter Sanford J. Ungar placed Laird's call on Sunday morning; professor David Rudenstine at one point dated it "late Saturday night or Sunday morning" yet elsewhere stated flatly that Mitchell "heard

about [the Sunday article] from Laird the previous day." Hushen, however, was certain the call came Sunday morning, before Mitchell had read the paper; see Sanford J. Ungar, *The Papers and the Papers: An Account of the Legal and Political Battle Over the Pentagon Papers* (Dutton, 1972), p. 108, and David Rudenstine, *The Day the Presses Stopped: A History of the Pentagon Papers Case* (University of California Press, 1996), pp. 69–71.

32. Except where noted, this study's treatment of the Pentagon Papers case draws on Ungar, *The Papers*; Rudenstine, *The Day the Presses Stopped*, which drew on unpublished segments of the Papers and on a 1988 interview with Mitchell; and two indispensable collections of White House tape transcripts published online after 2001, the first by the National Security Archive, at www.gwu.edu/~nsarchiv, the second by Daniel Ellsberg, at www.ellsberg.net.

33. H. R. Haldeman with Joseph DiMona, *The Ends of Power* (Dell, 1978), pp. 154–55. Historians must treat this book with caution, for Haldeman later discounted it as more his coauthor's product than his own, published at the wrong time (when Haldeman was entering prison), for the wrong reasons (to stave off creditors), and overly simplified for the reading public. Based on extensive taped interviews with Haldeman conducted in 1976–77, DiMona's second draft, Haldeman recalled in 1993, "was so much better than the original draft that I didn't realize how bad it was still. . . . So I agreed to let it be done, and it was a bestseller, and I made a lot of money on it, and it solved my problem at that time. But it created another problem, which is that it doesn't say what I want it to say in the way I wanted to say it."

34. Kissinger interview.

35. Laird denied so advising Mitchell; see Rudenstine, *The Day the Presses Stopped*, p. 82.

36. National Security Archive transcript, NT, Nixon-Haldeman, Conversation 519–1, Oval Office, June 14, 1971, 8:49 a.m.–10:04 a.m. (damn Jew); National Security Archive transcript, NT, Nixon-Mitchell-Ziegler, Conversation No. 521–9, Oval Office, June 15, 1971, 3:45 p.m.–4:30 p.m. (Ellstein); HN, June 29, 1971 (the Jew). Nixon's anti-Semitism was somewhat misplaced in Ellsberg's case. The latter was, by his own account, "raised fanatically" in Christian Science, educated at an Episcopalian school, and married in Cambridge's Christ Church. Leading a wholly secular life since the mid-1960s, Ellsberg has visited a synagogue only once in his life, to lecture about the Pentagon Papers; yet, despite all this, he has always, and proudly, identified himself as a Jew. "My parents always said we're Jewish, but not in religion," said Ellsberg. "I grew up thinking of myself as Christian, anyway. . . . Nixon could care fucking less whether you went to church or whatever. I was a Jew and I am a Jew. By his definition, I'm 100 percent a Jew, as I would be under Hitler's"; see Daniel Ellsberg, interview with author, March 13, 2004.

37. Author's transcript, NT, Nixon-Mitchell-Kissinger, Conversation No. 532-23, Oval Office, June 30, 1971, 2:55 to 3:07 p.m. (destroy); author's transcript, NT, Nixon-Haldeman-Kissinger, Conversation No. 534-2, Oval Office, July 1, 1971, 8:45 to 9:52 a.m. (Hiss case, good lawyer, destroying, play this game).

38. Author's transcript, NT, Conversation No. 534-12, op. cit. (better off); HN, July 1, 1971 (see it clearly).

39. "I learned about it from [John] Dean somewhere along the way," Mitchell recalled shortly before he died; see CI, April 15, 1988. In July 1974, however, Mitchell said he learned about

the Ellsberg break-in from either "Dean or Mardian." After the Watergate arrests, Mitchell told House investigators, "Mardian and Dean ... met with Liddy and Liddy informed them of the Ellsberg break-in." In fact, Dean was not present for Mardian's debriefing of Liddy, thus making it likelier that Mardian, not Dean, informed Mitchell of the Ellsberg break-in. Mitchell also told investigators that, once informed, he discussed the break-in with Haldeman and Ehrlichman, but "consciously avoided" raising it with Nixon; see HJC summary of John Mitchell interview [conducted] July 4, 1974 [filed] July 5, 1974; RG 460 WSPF *U.S. v. Mitchell* (Jencks)—Mitchell, NARA. After the break-in was publicly disclosed, in the spring of 1973, Ellsberg's lawyer, Leonard Boudin, wrongly told Federal District Judge Matthew Byrne the crime "was the product of a political espionage operation by ... John Mitchell"; see *CBS Morning News*, May 1, 1973. Two days later, President Nixon privately suggested likewise, even though he knew full well Mitchell had opposed the Plumbers' creation. "Hunt did work on the Ellsberg case," Nixon told Kleindienst, "and that was one of the main things they were working on, you know, through our dear friend John Mitchell"; see author's transcript, NT, Nixon-Kleindienst, Conversation No. 911-2, Oval Office, May 3, 1971, 8:51 a.m. to 9:09 a.m.

40. HN, June 17, 1971 (hang FDR); author's transcript, NT, Nixon-Mitchell-Haldeman-Ehrlichman-Colson, Conversation No. 576-6, Oval Office, September 18, 1971, 10:40 a.m. to 2:05 p.m.

41. SSCEX, Gordon Strachan, July 12, 1973.

42. James Rosen, "Nixon and the Chiefs," *Atlantic Monthly*, April 2002.

43. Ernest R. May and Philip D. Zelikow,

eds., *The Kennedy Tapes: Inside the White House During the Cuban Missile Crisis* (Harvard University Press, 1997), p. 188; H. L. McMaster, *Dereliction of Duty: Lyndon Johnson, Robert McNamara, the Joint Chiefs of Staff, and the Lies That Led to Vietnam* (HarperCollins, 1997), passim; Deborah Shapley, *Promise and Power: The Life and Times of Robert McNamara* (Little, Brown, 1993), pp. 240–41, 428–33.

44. Melvin Laird, author interview, August 28, 1997.

45. Ronald H. Cole and Willard J. Webb, *The Chairmanship of the Joint Chiefs of Staff* (Joint History Office, Joint Chiefs of Staff, Washington, 1995); William F. Jasper, "Admirals Sound the Alarm," *The New American* 15, 7, March 29, 1999; *All Hands: The Bureau of Naval Personnel Career Publication*, July 1970, pp. 8–13; Schoenebaum, *Profiles of an Era*, pp. 449–51; Robert Buzzanco, *Masters of War: Military Dissent and Politics in the Vietnam Era* (Cambridge University Press, 1996), pp. 173, 182, 268.

46. Cole and Webb, *Chairmanship*; Schoenebaum, *Profiles of an Era*.

47. Elmo R. Zumwalt Jr., *On Watch* (Quadrangle, 1976), p. xiv; Chalmers M. Roberts, "American Power Margin Is Slipping," *Washington Post*, October 4, 1970; Richard Nixon, *RN: The Memoirs of Richard Nixon, Volume 2* (Warner Books, 1979), pp. 242–43 (crap); George Lardner Jr., "On Tapes, Nixon Sounds Off on Woman, Blacks, Cabinet," *Washington Post*, December 27, 1998.

48. Author's transcript, NT, Nixon-Haig, Conversation No. 17–28, White House Telephone, December 24, 1971, 5:01–5:08 p.m., NARA. "We had firm evidence," Haig recalled years later, "that the Russians and the Indians were colluding, that the Russians were urging the Indians to dismantle Pakistan. This was a regional Cold War issue"; see Haig, July 27, 2000.

49. Jack Anderson with George Clifford, *The Anderson Papers* (Ballantine, 1974), p. 281. Kissinger claimed his remarks were "taken out of context"; see Associated Press, "Column," January 5, 1972, 3:31 a.m. EST, in WHSF—SMOF, JDE Special Subject File, Box 37, Young Project, NARA.

50. SSC, VI: 2410 (very ability). Mitchell concluded the SALT leak came from "someone who was in the NSC meeting in the Roosevelt Room" at which the negotiating position was adopted; see WH memo for the record by David R. Young, Subject: Meeting on 7/28/71 at 9:30–10:15 a.m., [filed] July 28, 1971; RG 460 WSPF Plumbers Task Force, General File—Documentary Evidence, David R. Young White House Files, Box 10—Memoranda, Chronological David R. Young Folder, NARA.

51. Testimony of Rear Admiral Robert O. Welander, USN, before the Senate Armed Services Committee, February 21, 1974, HHBP; Len Colodny and Robert Gettlin, *Silent Coup: The Removal of a President* (St. Martin's, 1991), pp. 3–68, 279–439, 456 (Ellsberg syndrome). Prior to the release in October 2000 of the relevant White House tapes, which were published for the first time in Rosen, "Nixon and the Chiefs," *Silent Coup* offered the most comprehensive account of the Moorer-Radford scandal, adducing, as Kissinger biographer Walter Isaacson noted, "a wealth of detail . . . [and] much useful reporting and information" on the episode. Isaacson's *Kissinger* also treated the affair in depth, as did Seymour Hersh's *The Price of Power*—which, like *Silent Coup*, drew on interviews with Mitchell. In addition to testifying before the Senate Armed Services Committee in February 1974, Radford spoke at length to Hersh; Colodny and Gettlin; Jim Hougan, author of *Secret Agenda: Watergate, Deep Throat*

and the CIA (Ballantine Books, 1984); and journalist Richard Lamb, who profiled Radford in "Tale of the Shadow Chaser," *George*, October 1998.

52. SSC memo to Fred Thompson from Don Sanders and Howard Liebengood, Subject: Donald Stewart Interview, July 24, 1973, HHBP (deception). Stewart told the Senate Watergate committee he only "boxed," or polygraph tested, Radford on one occasion, and only questioned him over the period December 16–17; Radford, on the same day, told the Senate Armed Services Committee he was "interrogated almost daily" by the same individuals over "two to three weeks," including "several" polygraph tests; see SSCEX Stewart; and Testimony of YNI Charles E. Radford, USN, before the Senate Armed Services Committee, February 19, 1974, HHBP.

53. Lamb, "Tale of the Shadow Chaser."

54. In one forty-nine-day period from March to May 1971, Anderson published thirteen columns based on leaks of classified material, including articles reporting U.S. seeding operations over clouds in Indochina, aimed at increasing rainfall on the Ho Chi Minh Trail; the Pentagon's development of secret plans to mine Haiphong Harbor, not carried out until May 1972; and American wiretapping of the Saigon palace of President Thieu. Anderson's source for these columns was not Radford but Stephen W. Linger, an enlisted man in the JCS Digital Information Relay Center; see TPOP, 182–83, 472.

55. Rosen, "Nixon and the Chiefs." Citations for all Moorer-Radford tapes quoted here appear on p. 580.

56. Ehrlichman, *Witness to Power*, p. 277.

57. CI, April 28, 1986.

58. CI [Mary Gore Dean], October 6, 1987.

59. CI, May 30, 1986. "I've been talking

to Tom Moorer about a business transaction," Mitchell said. The two men served on corporate boards for separate companies engaged in what Mitchell called "a joint venture."

60. KI, February 9, 1988, April 11, 1988.

61. Ehrlichman, *Witness to Power*, p. 279. In later years, Kissinger downplayed the episode. "There were traditional cold warriors who were opposed to the détente policy, no question about it," Kissinger said in 1995; but he suggested there was never any animus involved. "Moorer was actually a friend of mine. Radford I barely knew—I didn't know. That was just a way for them of getting information about what we were doing. It wasn't aimed at me, it was aimed at the office." Yet in a contemporaneous discussion about the incident, in January 1974—surreptitiously recorded by Kissinger and declassified thirty years later—Kissinger spoke of "these people spying on me" and added: "I could never tell whether this was superbureaucratic gamesmanship, or something a little more sinister. My feeling is that, you know, bureaucratic empires always go up by knowing things. It got out of control. I mean it may have started as bureaucratic gamesmanship and it got out of control"; see State Department Telcon, Secretary Kissinger/Hugh Sidey, January 21, 1974, 9:50 a.m., at foia.state.gov.

62. The transcript of the Ehrlichman-Welander interrogation was published, for the first time and in its entirety, as an appendix in Colodny and Gettlin, *Silent Coup*.

63. CI, November 1985 (grabber, abandon), August 17, 1986 (crucial, different light). Mitchell believed Haig was Deep Throat; see Gettlin interview.

64. Years later, Haig remembered these calls differently: "The president said, called me, he said, 'Al, what is this? I've got *spies* in the NS-C? Is this the military trying to take over the gov-

ernment?' . . . I said, 'Hey, Mr. President, come on!' " See Haig interview (emphases in original). The tapes reflect no such conversation.

65. Ehrlichman interview.

CLOUD OF SUSPICION

1. WSPF transcript, NT, Nixon-Haldeman-Colson, Conversation No. 697–29, Oval Office, March 30, 1972, 12:47 p.m.–2:32 p.m., NARA.

2. Frank Carlucci, interview with author, February 8, 2001; Rehnquist interview; letter from William H. Rehnquist to the author, June 29, 1993; CI, August 17, 1986 (smart ass), January 24, 1987 (full of); John Dean, *Blind Ambition* (Pocket Books, 1977), p. 42; Charles Bartlett, "Kleindienst Withdrawal Weighed?" *Washington Evening Star*, March 14, 1972.

3. James R. Williamson, *Federal Antitrust Policy During the Kennedy-Johnson Years* (Greenwood Press, 1995), p. xi; Lester A. Sobel, ed., *Corruption in Business* (Facts on File, 1977), pp. 78–179.

4. Sobel, *Corruption in Business*, p. 178; Grover, "Cabinet Enigma."

5. WH memo for the attorney general from Alexander P. Butterfield, Subject: Notes from the president, March 25, 1969; WHCF FG J-L, Box 9 (agree, anti-business); and WSPF memo from Paul Hoeber to the file, Re: Office Interview with John Mitchell [conducted December 14, 1973], [filed] December 19, 1973; RG 460 WSPF *U.S. v. Mitchell* (Jencks)—Mitchell, both in NARA.

6. Viorst, " 'The Justice Department' " (rather aggressive); Mark Green, *The Closed Enterprise System: Ralph Nader's Study Group Report on Antitrust Enforcement* (Grossman, 1972), p. 100.

7. WSPF transcript (Conversation No. 697–29).

8. WH memo to The President from John D. Ehrlichman, Subject: Anti-Trust

Policy, April 28, 1971, reprinted at HJC, V: 830–31; EN, September 1, 1971.

9. Robert J. Schoenberg, *Geneen* (Warner Books, 1986), pp. 20–30; Anthony Sampson, *The Sovereign State of ITT* (Stein and Day, 1973), p. 72; Priscilla S. Meyer, "ITT: Emerging Contradictions," *Wall Street Journal*, March 22, 1972; Anderson and Clifford, *Anderson Papers*, p. 51.

10. DOJ memorandum for John Ehrlichman from Richard W. McLaren, July 30, 1970, reprinted at HJC, V: 147–52.

11. Green, *Closed Enterprise*, pp. 44–45; Anderson and Clifford, *Anderson Papers*, p. 64.

12. HJCW, III: 735; HJC, V: 138 (inappropriate).

13. WH memo for Richard McLaren from Tod R. Hullin, Re: Ehrlichman's meeting with Mr. Geneen, ITT, August 10, 1970; WHSF—SMOF, JDE Chronological File, Box 53, NARA. Compounding the insult was the fact that prior to his meeting with Geneen, Ehrlichman had requested from McLaren—and received—a detailed memo outlining the status of all three cases against ITT; see DOJ letter to Tod R. Hullin from Richard W. McLaren [with attached memorandum], July 30, 1970, at HJC, V: 147–52.

14. KCH, 540 (express), 562 (theoretical); 551 (rebuffed), 576 (no change); Anderson and Clifford, *Anderson Papers*, pp. 109–10 (academic exercise). Tom Casey, ITT's Washington-based director of corporate planning, wrote Charles Colson three days after the Mitchell-Geneen meeting with his own account—its source unstated—of what was said. "Mr. Geneen and the attorney general," wrote Casey, "both agreed that because of the recent changes in the tax law, the decision of the Accounting Principles Board and the depressed state of the stock market and economy, the merger wave was over and we would not see such happenings again"; see ITT letter to Charles Colson from Thomas H. Casey, August 7, 1970, at HJC, V: 663–64. One ITT lobbyist claimed, also without substantiation, that the corporation gave "heavy financial support" to Nixon's '68 campaign; see WH memo for John Ehrlichman from Colonel James D. Hughes, [no subject], September 19, 1969, at HJC, V: 142.

15. ITT letter from Ned [Gerrity] to Ted [Agnew], August 7, 1970, with attached memorandum, [no subject], August 7, 1970, at HJC, V/674–76; Jack Anderson, "Agnew and Connally Linked to ITT Fix: Secret Papers," United Feature Syndicate, March 17, 1973, MFC; EN, August 7, 1970 (Rumsfeld).

16. WH memo for the attorney general from John D. Ehrlichman, Re: The United States vs. [*sic*] ITT, September 17, 1970, WHCF Chronological File, Box 38, NARA (Ehrlichman also sent a copy to Colson). That ITT viewed Ehrlichman as more receptive than Mitchell is clear from a thank-you note the company's Bill Merriam wrote after he and Geneen met again with the White House aide on March 3, 1971: "[We] came away . . . with the thought that you understand our position perfectly and are sympathetic," Merriam told Ehrlichman; see Schoenberg, *Geneen*, p. 265.

17. *U.S. v. International Telephone and Telegraph Corporation* (1970), 324 F. Supp. 19–55, at HJC, V: 217–53.

18. Kleindienst, *Justice*, p. 90–96.

19. HJC transcript, NT, Nixon-Ehrlichman-Shultz, Oval Office, April 19, 1971, 3:03–3:34 p.m., at HJC, V: 312–45. Schoenberg, *Geneen*, claimed (p. 396) it was unclear how much time elapsed between the end of the Ehrlichman-Kleindienst call and the start of the Nixon-Ehrlichman-Shultz meeting, and guessed a few minutes;

yet in the HJC transcript Ehrlichman stated: "I just talked to [Kleindienst] about an hour ago."

20. HJC transcript, NT, Nixon-Kleindienst, Conversation No. 2–2, White House Telephone, April 19, 1971, 3:04 p.m.–3:09 p.m., at HJC, V: 346–48. The words "you son-of-a-bitch" and "Don't you understand the English language?" were purposely omitted by House stenographers who prepared the first transcript of this tape, for the House Judiciary Committee's impeachment hearings.

21. HN, April 19, 1971. Haldeman noted the time of this discussion as "1545," meaning eleven minutes after the president's session with Ehrlichman and Shultz had ended.

22. WSPF Hoeber memo (fucking Ehrlichman); Kleindienst, *Justice*, p. 92 (McLaren and Griswold); Kleindienst interview (follow this directive, take it easy).

23. HJC, V: 362; Griswold, *Ould Fields*, pp. 292–96.

24. HJC transcript, NT, Nixon-Mitchell, Conversation No. 485–4, Oval Office, April 21, 1971, 4:18–6:13 p.m., at HJC, V: 372–76. Almost a year later, Nixon mused: "ITT is a bad company, I suppose"; see WSPF transcript (Conversation No. 697–29); and Kleindienst, *Justice*, p. 93.

25. Brit Hume, *Inside Story* (Doubleday, 1975), p. 121; Schoenberg, *Geneen*, pp. 139–40; SJC transcript of interview of Dita Beard by Mike Wallace, *60 Minutes*, CBS News program, [aired] April 2, 1972, at KCH, 1641–44; David Fleming, interview with author, December 1, 2003; Brit Hume, Memo for record, February 24 [1972], MFC. Fleming remembered that Beard drank a quart of Old Crow whiskey a day.

26. KCH, 541 (could not and would not, repeated my desire), 544 (two minutes, same harangue, dinner table), 545 (shove off), 546 (sweet disposi-

tion, Nunn confirmed); Hume, *Inside Story*, pp. 159–60.

27. WH memo for The Attorney General from John D. Ehrlichman, [no subject], May 5, 1971, at HJC, V: 829.

28. Kleindienst interview (quite taken, anybody else); Kleindienst, *Justice*, p. 97 (McLaren was right).

29. DOJ memo for the deputy attorney general from Richard W. McLaren, Re: Proposed Procedure in ITT Merger Cases, June 17, 1971, at HJC, V: 550–52.

30. Letter to James O. Eastland from Howard J. Aibel, Re: Senate Committee on the Judiciary Hearings on the Nomination of Richard G. Kleindienst, April 7, 1972, at KCH, 1330–31; "Questions About a Cozy Relationship," *Time*, April 10, 1972; UPI, "McLaren Defends ITT Antitrust Pact," March 20, 1972; Griswold, *Ould Fields*, p. 296; Griswold interview. In 1995, ITT's board of directors agreed to dissolve the conglomerate into three separate industrial, insurance, and hotel/gaming companies; see Tony Jackson, "ITT to Split into Three Businesses," *Financial Times*, June 14, 1995.

31. KCH, 584 (pleading guilty), 577 (confirmation), 617 (largest divestiture).

32. Photocopies of Mitchell's handwritten letter of resignation, and Nixon's handwritten letter accepting it, are reprinted in Eric Hamburg, ed., *Nixon: An Oliver Stone Film* (Hyperion, 1995), pp. 342–44. For Mitchell's undated yellow-pad draft of his resignation letter, see JMRC.

33. UPI, "Senate Panel Unanimous in Supporting Kleindienst," *New York Times*, February 25, 1972.

34. Hume, *Inside Story*, pp. 1–18; Leonard Downie Jr., *The New Muckrakers* (Mentor Books, 1978), p. 158 (brash). In 1974, Hume published *Inside Story*, which remains the most thorough, though not an objective,

chronicle of the ITT scandal. Hume later spent twenty-three years as an ABC News correspondent, covering Congress and the White House. In 1996 he became anchor and Washington managing editor at Fox News, where the author has worked under him as a correspondent since 1999. Hume has neither sought, nor been asked, to contribute in any way to this book. Except where noted, all references to Hume's work on the ITT story are drawn from his book (pp. 107–254).

35. A photocopy of the original memorandum appears in HJC, V: 614–15 (emphases in original).

36. Griswold recalled: "Mitchell got [McLaren] out by getting him nominated and confirmed as a federal judge in about five days." Asked if this was Mitchell's compromise with the White House, Griswold replied: "Yes . . . It was surmised, but it was reasonably clear"; see Griswold interview.

37. Hume memo.

38. Letter to John N. Mitchell from Lawrence F. O'Brien, December 13, 1971, at KCH, 1662; DOJ letter from Richard G. Kleindienst to Lawrence F. O'Brien, December 13, 1971, at KCH, 120 (emphasis added).

39. Jack Anderson, "Secret Memo Bares Mitchell-ITT Move," *Washington Post*, February 29, 1972.

40. DOJ Statement by John N. Mitchell, February 28, 1972, at HJC, V: 632.

41. Jack Anderson, "Kleindienst Accused in ITT Case," *Washington Post*, March 1, 1972.

42. Jack Anderson, "Mitchell, ITT Try to Lie Way Out of Scandal; California Colleagues Say Mitchell Knew All; ITT's Statement Contradicts Evidence On Hand," Universal Feature Syndicate, March 3, 1972, MFC; Jack Anderson, "Contradictions Cited in ITT Case," *Washington Post*, March 3, 1972.

43. WSPF RG 460, U.S. Attorney File—

Documentary Evidence, Martinez-Mitchell, Box 31, NARA.

44. Robert Walters, "Was Mitchell Told of Fund? Reinecke Says Yes," *Washington Star*, March 3, 1972; Robert Walters, "Reinecke Urges GOP to Refuse ITT's Gift," *Washington Star*, March 4, 1972; KCH, 1495–1502.

45. Walters, "Was Mitchell Told"; KCH, 1501–16; Lawrence Feinberg, "Reinecke Briefed, Dean's Aide Says," *Washington Post*, July 18, 1974 (Mardian).

46. WH memo for H. R. Haldeman from Gordon Strachan, Subject: 1972 Convention Site, June 29, 1971, MFC.

47. Kleindienst interview; Kleindienst, *Justice*, p. 103.

48. SSCEX, E. Howard Hunt, July 25, 1973; SSC, IX: 3753–91.

49. Dan Thomasson, "Dita: Memo Is a 'Hoax,'" *Washington Daily News*, March 18, 1972; Dita Beard Statement, March 26, 1972, at HJC, V: 720–21; SJC transcript; KCH, 1641–44.

50. THD, 427; The President's News Conference of March 24, 1972.

51. Dean, *Blind Ambition*, pp. 43–51; UVM, 8118 (circus); HJCW, III: 525 (weighed in).

52. WSPF transcript, NT, Nixon-Haldeman, Conversation No. 697–15, Oval Office, March 30, 1972, WSPF Reference Transcript, RG 460, February 23, 1971–March 23, 1973, Box 1, NARA. Kleindienst's nomination was eventually approved by the Judiciary Committee and confirmed by the full Senate. He served as attorney general from June 1972 to April 1973, when he resigned under pressure during Watergate. In May 1974 he pleaded guilty to a misdemeanor charge that he had refused to testify "accurately and fully" before the Senate Judiciary Committee about Nixon's angry telephone call to him in April 1971. In so pleading, Kleindienst became the first cabinet officer convicted of a crime

since 1929. Special Prosecutor Leon Jaworski said the charges against Kleindienst carried "no implication" that Nixon's order to Kleindienst had been illegal. Kleindienst was sentenced to a month in jail and a $100 fine, both suspended; see Edward W. Knappman and Evan Drossman, *Watergate and the White House*, Volume 3, *January-September 1974*, pp. 134–65. As one observer has noted, Kleindienst, far from "refusing" to testify, actually *demanded* to testify, at the confirmation hearings reopened at his urging, *then* testified falsely. Many thought he received undue leniency, among them three WSPF staff attorneys who resigned in protest. Kleindienst returned to practice law in Arizona, where a state court tried him in 1981 on new perjury charges stemming from his representation of a client involved in a $23 million Teamsters' insurance transaction. Kleindienst was acquitted, but suspended for a year and fined $11,823; see Schoenberg, *Geneen*, pp. 278–80. He died in February 2000.

53. Anderson and Clifford, *Anderson Papers*, p. 108 (wearing); "Investigations: 'Fake'?" *Newsweek*, March 27, 1972 (cool); Mary McGrory, "The Philosopher," *New York Post*, March 15, 1972; KCH, 626 (grounds, cards).

54. KCH, 547 (locating), 568 (may have), 569 (wouldn't be, impression).

55. Ibid., 568.

56. Ibid., 1513 (Kennedy), 1535 (Fong).

57. The calls were entered on Mitchell's phone logs for May 21, June 2, and June 23, 1971; see WSPF Box 31.

58. Lawrence Feinberg, "Reinecke Told Prosecutors of Fatigue," *Washington Post*, July 19, 1974 (situation; volunteer; substantive); and Feinberg, "Reinecke Briefed" (coaching).

59. Lawrence Feinberg, "Reinecke Testimony Conflicts," *Washington Post*, July 20, 1974.

60. Knappman and Drossman, *Watergate*, pp. 129–35, 218; Schoenberg, *Geneen*, pp. 280–81. A third perjury count in Reinecke's indictment, relating to when he himself first learned of ITT's convention pledge, was dropped.

61. E. W. Kenworthy, "Watergate Jury Indicts Reinecke For Lies on I.T.T.," *New York Times*, April 4, 1974. Asked about his dealings with Reinecke by the Watergate special prosecutors, Mitchell claimed he did not recall if the lieutenant governor mentioned ITT's convention pledge. Financing was the RNC's job, Mitchell said, so he "did not care what ITT did with its money"; see WSPF, Hoeber memo.

62. KCH, 552.

63. WSPF, Hoeber memo.

64. Associated Press, "Mitchell Seen Escaping New Charges," *Washington Post*, March 28, 1975.

65. KCH, 633. Two weeks after Mitchell testified, Charles Colson sent H. R. Haldeman a memorandum in which Colson claimed he and Fred Fielding, the deputy White House counsel, had uncovered a handful of White House and ITT documents that "contradict Mitchell's testimony"; see WH memo to H. R. Haldeman from Charles Colson, Subject: ITT, March 30, 1972, at SSC, VIII: 3372–76. Informed of Colson's claim, Nixon said: "I don't want to see the damn memorandum on this thing. I don't want one floating around in here, this memorandum. It'll be in the *Washington Post* in a few days"; see WSPF transcript (Conversation No. 697–15).

The documents Colson cited included Ehrlichman's memos to Mitchell from 1970 and 1971 about "assurances" and "agreed-upon ends"— which, though embarrassing to Ehrlichman and the White House, had no discernible effect on Mitchell or the ITT case, and hardly proved malfeasance by Mitchell; and Ned Gerrity's 1970 "Dear Ted" letter to Vice President Agnew, in which the

ITT man claimed Mitchell had promised Harold Geneen he would "talk with McLaren and get back to Hal." Despite this secondhand account of what Mitchell supposedly told Geneen in private, no evidence ever surfaced showing Mitchell interfered with McLaren or "got back to Hal"; indeed, even the Beard-Merriam memo, dated almost eleven months after the Gerrity letter, lamented that ITT was still "suffering McLaren's mickey-mouse." The final document Colson cited against Mitchell was a 1971 memo from Herb Klein to H. R. Haldeman mentioning ITT's convention pledge, copies of which were sent to three other officials, including Mitchell; see WH memo for H. R. Haldeman from Herbert G. Klein, Subject: 1972 Convention Site, June 30, 1971, at HJC, V: 820. The Klein memo, Colson concluded, "put the AG on constructive notice . . . [of] facts which he has denied under oath." Confronted with the Klein memo, Mitchell's lawyer, Bill Hundley, aptly scoffed that he was "inclined to doubt that Mr. Mitchell read—or paid much attention to—copies of Herb Klein memos"; see James M. Naughton, "Rodino Indicates He Seeks Data on Nixon's Role in I.T.T. Case," *New York Times*, April 24, 1974.

The principal goal behind Colson's memo was not to provide an honest assessment of Mitchell's testimony—Colson made no secret of his loathing for Mitchell, and vice versa—but to sway the president against Mitchell's advice that the White House should continue supporting Kleindienst's nomination. Yet disclosure of the Colson memo in August 1973, during the Senate Watergate hearings, led many journalists to conclude, erroneously, that the ITT antitrust cases must have been fixed after all. "I must say, this makes the Dita Beard memorandum look a little

better," reported CBS News correspondent Neil Strawser; see *CBS Morning News* with John Hart, August 2, 1973. Brit Hume thought Colson's memo "explosive," and said it revealed the ITT "cover up" in the "starkest terms"; see Hume, *Inside Story*, pp. 239–54.

66. WSPF transcript, Conversation No. 697–29.
67. "Impeachment: ITT and Milk," *Washington Post*, July 20, 1974.
68. UVM, 8195.

PETTY THIEF

1. UMS, 5423.
2. Joseph Carragher, "Mitchell Opposes Jersey Casino Proposal; Speaks at Sears Testimonial," *Newark Star-Ledger*, March 13, 1971; Audrey A. Fecht, "Mitchell Zeroes In on Crime in N.J.," *Newark Evening News*, March 13, 1971; Charles Q. Finley, "Martha Sparkled, But Let John Speak for Himself," *Newark Star-Ledger*, March 14, 1971; UMS, 3153–54, 3910. Asked what he'd told Mitchell about Vesco prior to this event, Sears said: "I told him . . . that I had been given help by a friend who had been a contributor and who had come to my rescue, both during the campaign and after, to help me on the debt. . . . Mr. Mitchell prior to March of 1971 would only have known Bob Vesco, if he remembered him, as a person who had helped me out"; see UMS, 4093. Another attendee testified that after Mitchell's speech, Mr. and Mrs. Vesco approached the podium with Sears. "Harry and Mr. Mitchell and Mr. Vesco were talking as I was working my way across a crowded ballroom," Laurence Richardson testified; see UMS, 4235.
3. Arthur Herzog, *Vesco* (Doubleday, 1987), pp. 7–25; UMS, 5276 (namedropper); A. L. Eisenhauer and Robin

Moore with Robert J. Flood, *The Flying Carpetbagger* (Pinnacle, 1976), p. 248. Vesco once claimed he'd given $100,000 in 1968; see UMS, 2043, 3420.

4. Robert A. Hutchinson, *Vesco* (Praeger, 1974), pp. 2–8, 32 (federal regulators), 47 (offshore interest), 79 (chaotic); Herzog, *Vesco*, pp. 51–61.

5. UMS, 3176 (witch hunt), 3999 (fuse), 6958.

6. Letter to John N. Mitchell from Harry L. Sears, May 18, 1971, and letter to Harry L. Sears from John N. Mitchell, June 10, 1971, UMS, 3186, 3410–12 (no way of knowing), 7550–55 (Sears's letters, talked to Casey), 7771 (mollify).

7. Mitchell's office log for November 30, 1971, in WSPF Box 31; UMS, 3220–22, 8854–55. On some details, however, Mitchell's recollection differed from Vine's. Testifying before a federal grand jury in New York on March 20, 1973, Mitchell said Vine told him only that "they were looking into" the case, and that "when they found out, he would let me know." Before the grand jury, and later at trial, Mitchell said nothing about Vine's assertion that the jailing of Vesco was "warranted," nor did Mitchell mention his own inquiry about the potential usefulness of a certain local judge.

8. UMS, 3233 (some assistance), 3417 (small change), 4637–38 (Felt testimony), 7458–63 (looking), 7558 (forgotten), 7785 (Swiss matter); and FBI memo from H. A. Boynton Jr. to Mr. E. S. Miller, 6/21/73, Subject: John N. Mitchell/Securities and Exchange Act, FBIM. For his single phone call to Mitchell, Sears received an additional $5,000 from IOS; see UMS, 4089.

9. UMS, 3234–53a (get John Mitchell, do much good); Hutchison, *Vesco*, p. 38 (occasion).

10. EN, January 18, 1972; UMS, 3272,

5493. Mitchell said he never saw Ehrlichman's memo; see UMS, 7788–89.

11. UMS, 3286–91, 7562–65, 7813 (Mitchell denial).

12. Ibid., 5164–75, 5294, 7707–8. Mitchell's alleged perjury before the grand jury on this point appears at UMS, 7706–7. Not until his *second* grand jury appearance did Casey recall Mitchell having told him about the SEC's interference in Geneva.

13. UMS, 4646, 7567, 7790–91 (genesis), 8011 (misimpression); Hutchison, *Vesco*, p. 270. Felt recorded Mitchell's request in an internal FBI document: "Attorney General contacted Bureau this date stating he wanted U.S. ambassador in Beirut to know that Attorney General and the administration have the utmost confidence in the integrity of Robert Vesco, who is in Beirut at this time. You should immediately so advise the ambassador."

14. UMS, 3346–48, 7569–70.

15. Ibid., 3353–55.

16. Schoenebaum, *Profiles of an Era*, pp. 615–18; "Sketches of Four Men Indicted in Campaign Gift Case," *New York Times*, May 11, 1973.

17. UMS, 4264–70; Hutchison, *Vesco*, p. 237. Stans steadfastly denied he asked Vesco to make his gift in cash; UMS, 2046.

18. UMS, 4575–77 (see Mr. Vesco, sum and substance), 4625 (I stay away). Appearing before the grand jury on March 6, 1973, Hofgren testified Mitchell's admonition was both longer and more personalized: "Dan, stay away from it. It is being taken care of"; see UMS, 4618–19. At trial, Hofgren testified he told Stans about his run-in with Mitchell, and Stans replied: "Okay, we will take care of [the Vesco matter] in another way"; see UMS, 4575–77. On another point—what happened in Vesco's March 8 meeting with Stans—Hofgren initially told the grand jury he had not attended, then amended his

story both to acknowledge his presence and to assert, uniquely, that when Vesco complained about the SEC, Stans spontaneously, and successfully, arranged an appointment for Vesco with John Mitchell. Even Vesco's associate, Richardson, did not remember Stans doing this; see UMS, 4572–74, 4617, 7668.

19. UMS, 4283.

20. Ibid., 3429–31. At disbarment hearings before the Morris County Ethics Committee in April and May 1975, Sears was asked if he was unaware of the true purpose behind Vesco's contribution: "I am not trying to paint myself here as somebody who didn't, who was so naïve and so stupid as not to know [that] in Vesco's mind, he hopes he gets some attention"; see *In the Matter of Harry L. Sears, An Attorney at Law*, 71 N.J. 175, 364 A.2d 777, Supreme Court of New Jersey, September 30, 1976.

21. UMS, 3435–37 (few minutes), 5189–90 (in town).

22. Ibid., 3438–48, 5192.

23. Ibid., 4673–79, 4772 (grand jury testimony).

24. Ibid., 5707 (based on a telephone conversation), 8829 (Stans grand jury testimony), 7603 (hell, rationale). John Dean claimed Mitchell first learned about the use of the initials, and confronted Stans about it, at a meeting all three attended in New York. According to Dean, Stans's reply was, "Well, it is there and that's just the fact." Before the grand jury, Dean had testified he was "certain" this meeting occurred in "late September, October"; at trial he testified it was November 1. Mitchell was in New York from October 25 to November 14; see UMS, 5566, 5779–97; and WSPF, Box 31.

25. UMS, 7863 (emphasis added); Ralph Blumenthal, "Mitchell-Stans Jury Expected to Be Seated Today," *New York Times*, February 28, 1974. When they

were both in the cabinet, Stans replaced a consumer protection bill that Mitchell supported with a weaker version that made it harder for consumers to collect in class-action lawsuits; see Schoenebaum, *Profiles of an Era*, p. 616. Stans denied he and Mitchell seldom spoke. "That was a mistaken impression.... We were good friends, we were on good terms.... We were mutual victims, we thought, of an ambitious local [U.S.] attorney"; see Stans interview.

26. UMS, 3472–76 (deVescoization, a year, settle), 5833 (baby).

27. "Learning to Love Exile," *Time*, February 9, 1976; John F. Berry, "New Law May Hit Famous Fugitive," *Washington Post*, February 6, 1977; Stanley Penn, "Vesco Says He Won't Consider Request to Leave Costa Rica Until Suits Settled," *Wall Street Journal*, June 13, 1977; Herzog, *Vesco*, p. 199.

28. The text of the Figueres letter is reprinted in its entirety in Hutchison, *Vesco*, p. 369 (emphasis added); UMS, 3725.

29. Hutchinson, *Vesco*, photograph section; Eisenhauer, *Flying Carpetbagger*, photograph section.

30. UMS, 3612–13 (those bastards, there's no way, ITT), 4358–59 (get hold of Mitchell, angry).

31. Ibid., 3615–17 (devastating, interested), 7603–4 (recollection, quash, postpone).

32. Ibid., 3626–27.

33. Ibid., 3628–38 (happy, relieved, grateful, going to talk to John Dean), 3643 (can't expect), 4021 (additional), 7719–21 (grand jury, didn't talk to John Dean).

34. Ibid., 3749 (sure relieved), 7952 (fine).

35. Sobel, *Corruption in Business*, p. 163; David L. Yermack, "After Years on Case, Those Pursuing Vesco Still Make Careers of It," *Wall Street Journal*, September 13, 1984; Arthur Herzog, "The Vesco Myth," *New York Times*, June 23, 1995.

36. UMS, 3836–38 (dogfight, petty thief). Asked about Mitchell's characterization, Vesco sounded wounded and disbelieving. "That may very well have been something that Mitchell might have said," he told Walter Cronkite. "Whether or not John actually believed that or not, I don't know"; see *CBS Evening News*, April 1–2, 1974.

37. UMS, 9001 (nervous).

38. UMS, 7388–91 (Sprizzo).

39. UMS, 5456 (what the hell), 5480 (bastards, runaway, Kleindienst); WHT, 150. Mitchell denied telling Dean these things. Asked if he thought Wing and Rayhill had behaved like "little bastards," Mitchell deadpanned: "Quite the contrary. They were very polite and seductive." After Wing objected, provoking laughter from the courtroom, Judge Gagliardi—smiling—struck the word "seductive" from the record. "It doesn't call for any humor," he told Mitchell. "Your Honor, I am not smiling," replied Mitchell's attorney, Peter Fleming; see UMS, 7694–98; and D. J. Saunders and Theo Wilson, "Mitchell Claims Talks With the SEC Wasn't Improper," *Daily News*, April 16, 1974. Dean, meanwhile, admitted that while discussing these subjects with Nixon, he neither mentioned Mitchell's supposed request that Kleindienst be asked to intervene, nor ascribed the words "runaway grand jury" to Mitchell. Asked how Dean could have come to regard the grand jury as "runaway" other than by hearing as much from Mitchell, the former attorney general snapped: "I imagine he has a great imagination"; see UMS, 5606–7, 8030.

40. Author's transcript, NT, Nixon-Colson, Conversation No. 40-95, White House Telephone, June 13, 1971, 10:32 to 10:39 p.m. (didn't make, prosecuting); author's transcript, NT, Nixon-Connally, Conver- sation No. 948-12, Oval Office, July 11, 1973. 3:03 to 4:22 p.m. (crook, never met).

41. *CBS Evening News*, April 24, 1973.

42. Clare Crawford, "A Fiery Martha Mitchell Gives Her Side of the Split-Up with John," *People*, March 11, 1974.

43. "And the Mess Goes On," *Newsweek*, May 21, 1973; Will R. Wilson Sr., *A Fool for a Client: Richard Nixon's Free Fall Toward Impeachment* (Eakin Press, 2000), p. 112.

44. "A Connection Named Vesco," *Newsweek*, May 21, 1973; *CBS Midday News*, May 10, 1973; *CBS Evening News*, May 10, 1973; *CBS Evening News*, May 21, 1973.

45. One week later, the trial was moved to Courtroom 110, where atomic spies Julius and Ethel Rosenberg were tried; see Martin Arnold, "Mitchell and Stans Are Acquitted on All Counts After 48-Day Trial," *New York Times*, April 29, 1974.

46. Arnold H. Lubasch, "Mitchell, Stans Go on Trial Here," *New York Times*, February 20, 1974; UMS, 120–21.

47. *CBS Evening News*, September 11, 1973; Hans Zeisel and Shari Seidman Diamond, "The Jury Selection in the Mitchell-Stans Conspiracy Trial," *American Bar Foundation Research Journal* (1976: 151).

48. UMS, 1923–24.

49. Ibid., 1932 (heart), 1975 (crass).

50. Ibid., 1980–2003 (emphasis added). When Wing repeated the offense, during redirect examination of John Dean, it drew defense objections, but no mistrial motions; see UMS, 5681. Later, Gagliardi reprimanded Wing for similar remarks. "The government did not commit the crime that John Mitchell is charged with," Wing said during arguments in Gagliardi's robing room. "*Nobody* has committed those crimes," Gagliardi shot back. "[Mitchell] is presumed to be innocent. You, above all people, ought to be saying that"; see UMS, 7007.

51. Joseph M. Treen, "For Defense, They Chose Democrats," *Newsday*, March 17, 1974 (cracks); *CBS Morning News*, March 25, 1974; Daniel Wise, "Fleming, Master Litigator, to Seek Leaks," *New York Law Journal*, December 16, 1991; Fleming interviews.

52. UMS, 2007–19.

53. *CBS Morning News*, March 14, 1974.

54. "Casey at the Bat," *Time*, April 1, 1974. Two decades later, Wing argued Casey had been "less than candid under oath" in the Mitchell-Stans trial. "Many people have written many things about Mr. Casey since that time," said Wing, alluding to the Iran-Contra scandal, "that might support the fact that perhaps he wasn't always a truth-teller"; see John Wing, interview with author, September 27, 1997.

55. CI, August 9, 1988.

56. Dean, *Blind Ambition*, p. 354; Maurice Stans, *The Terrors of Justice: The Untold Story of Watergate* (Everest, 1978), p. 346.

57. *CBS Evening News*, October 19, 1973; UMS, 118; Wing interview; James Rayhill, interview with author, December 11, 1997.

58. UMS, 5455.

59. Joseph M. Treen, "Defense Tries to Discredit Dean With Use of Tape Transcripts," *Newsday*, March 27, 1974.

60. UMS, 5674 (Dean himself), 5264–65, 5738 (inconsistent), 5761–75 (razor's-edge questions). On the Nixon-Dean talk, see also WHT, 150.

61. "Mr. Dean," the judge advised early on during Fleming's cross-examination, "if you will listen to the question and respond to the question, that's what you should do." The next day, Dean provoked Gagliardi to sterner words: "Mr. Dean, I must caution you—you are aware of it by training—if you will listen to the question and answer the question directly, there will not be motions to strike and I will not have to instruct the jury to disregard it." There was a third offense ("Mr. Dean, I have cautioned you before, please answer the questions") and a fourth ("You know, Mr. Dean, it is very difficult when a lawyer has to strike an answer and has to ask the court to give instructions [to the jury], and I would ask you again to listen to the question and respond directly to the question") before the fifth engendered the judge's explicit threat of punitive action ("Mr. Dean, I don't want to reprimand you again, sir"); see UMS, 5529 (should do), 5549 (by training), 5613 (cautioned you), 5759 (very difficult), 5761 (use that date), 5788 (reprimand).

62. *CBS Morning News*, April 29, 1974; Marcia Chambers, "Jurors Couldn't Believe Federal Witnesses," *New York Times*, April 29, 1974 (often unbelievable). *CBS Morning News*, April 29, 1974 (reasonable doubt).

63. Joseph M. Treen, "Mistrial Ruled Out in Mitchell-Stans Case," *Newsday*, March 5, 1974 (surprise); Joseph M. Treen, "Now It's the Prosecution Who's on Trial," *Newsday*, March 25, 1974 (every prosecution witness); Fleming interview (jury wants); Fleming interview (always knew).

64. Fleming interviews.

65. UMS, 7527–29 (series, relented, somewheres).

66. Ibid., 7742–54.

67. Ibid., 7831–35.

68. Ibid., 7815 (in part), 7882 (three different), 7886 (bad notes).

69. Wing interview; Rayhill interview.

70. D. J. Saunders, "Charges Mitch, Stans Felt Above Law," *Daily News*, April 25, 1974 (chin); Joseph M. Treen, "Accusations Abound as Lawyers Sum Up the Mitchell-Stans Case," *Newsday*, April 25, 1974 (Fleming quotes).

71. Treen, "Accusations Abound"; Martin Arnold, "Both Sides Sum Up in Mitchell Trial," *New York Times*, April 25, 1974.

72. Stans interview.

73. Chambers, "Jurors Couldn't Believe."
74. D. J. Saunders and Theo Wilson, "Mitchell Jury Focuses on Memo to Don Nixon," *Daily News*, April 27, 1974; Martin Arnold, "Mitchell-Stans Jury Seeks 'Don Nixon Memorandum,'" *New York Times*, April 27, 1974; Martin Arnold, "Sears Testimony Studied by Jury," *New York Times*, April 28, 1974.
75. Arnold, "Mitchell and Stans Are Acquitted."
76. "Mitchell and Stans Found Innocent on All 18 Counts," *Daily News*, April 29, 1974; Arnold, "Mitchell and Stans Are Acquitted."
77. Joseph M. Treen, "At the Victory Party, Feeling No Pain," *Newsday*, April 29, 1974; Ida Libby Dengrove and Frank W. Martin, *My Days in Court: Unique Views of the Famous and Infamous by a Court Artist* (William Morrow, 1990), pp. 64–71. Dengrove said Mitchell "displayed remarkable control" as a witness, appearing "level-headed even under cross-examination"; off the stand, he was so flirtatious the ladies dubbed him "Mr. Twinkles." Dengrove also suspected that during court recesses, Mitchell was "tippling in the back room," adding "there were times . . . that he looked red-nosed and appeared to sway."

GEMSTONE

1. WHT, 773.
2. UMS, 7651–52.
3. Hougan, *Secret Agenda*, pp. 44–45 (*Triumph*); Gordon Strachan quoted in Notes of Seymour Glanzer from Interview with Jeb Magruder, April 14, 1973, RG 460 WSPF—WGTF, Investigative Files, *U.S. v. Mitchell* (Jencks), Magruder, Box 73, NARA (Hitler incarnate). "I, a qualified Israeli Defense Force paratrooper, would just as well you did not indicate you think I am a Nazi," Liddy told the author in 2004. Despite his undeniable obsession with the Third Reich, Liddy has taken pains to rebut unkind suggestions about his belief system. "I have absolutely no sympathy for Adolf Hitler and Nazism," he told *Playboy* in 1980. "Remember, German history spans thousands of years, and the twelve years of the Third Reich was [*sic*] no more than a historical aberration . . . a stain on German honor from which the country will take many years to recover. . . . [F]or Adolf Hitler and the psychopathic scum in the concentration camps who butchered babies on an assembly line because they were born into the wrong race, I have nothing but contempt." Some scholars have questioned whether the Third Reich was a "historical aberration" in German history, and, too, Liddy's characterization of European Jewry as a "race"—but his sincerity in condemning Nazism was genuine; see G. Barry Golson, ed., *The Playboy Interview, Volume II* (Perigee Books, 1983), p. 364 [originally published October 1980]; Daniel Jonah Goldhagen, *Hitler's Willing Executioners: Ordinary Germans and the Holocaust* (Vintage, 1997); e-mail to the author from G. Gordon Liddy, November 14, 2004.
4. Liddy, *Will*, pp. 180–83, 200. In previously unpublished testimony before the Senate Watergate committee, Dean said he had "no specific knowledge of telling [Liddy] a million dollar figure" but "may" have told Liddy he would get "whatever you need"; see SSCEX, John Dean, June 16, 1973. Testifying in public session, Dean said he had "no recollection" of "specifying a dollar amount"; see SSC, IV: 1442. Yet in his 1976 memoir, Dean recalled telling Liddy he could have "maybe half a million bucks . . . maybe more" for intelligence operations; see Dean, *Blind Ambition*, p. 71. Asked in a 1995 deposition whether he promised Liddy "half a million dollars for openers," Dean

wavered. At one point he said "there was no such discussion"; elsewhere, he claimed "no recollection of such a conversation" but added, "If it was said as a passing remark, it did not register with me"—a suggestion Dean paid his *own* words no heed. Finally, Dean allowed that he "might have said something to Gordon Liddy based on a question he had posed to me, 'What kind of budget do I have?' something to the effect that, 'A half-million-dollar budget.'" See *Maureen K. Dean and John W. Dean v. St. Martin's Press, et al.*, C.A. No. 92–1807 [hereinafter referred to as "DVS"], Deposition of John W. Dean [hereinafter "JDD"], September 13, 1995. Certainly the phrase "for openers" was a favorite of Dean's; he used it, in contexts unrelated to the Liddy meeting, to end a sentence in each of the first four days of his deposition.

5. Magruder, *An American Life*, pp. 14–56; DVS, Deposition of Jeb Stuart Magruder, August 29, 1995.

6. Liddy, *Will*, pp. 185–86; CI, July 29, 1988 (spend); HJC summary (July 4, 1974) (left the matter). In the HJC interview and elsewhere, Mitchell said the November 24 meeting marked his first encounter with Liddy. However, Liddy testified in a 1972 deposition that he first met Mitchell, perfunctorily, in 1969; see *CBS Morning News*, February 7, 1973. Dean claimed Mitchell and Liddy held a "passing discussion" of intelligence, during which Liddy promised he would "familiarize himself with the problems . . . and would develop a plan." According to Dean, Mitchell replied: "Fine, take him by to meet Magruder." Dean's account conflicts with that of the other men—who said there was no discussion of intelligence—and with logic itself: After all, the session was necessitated by Liddy's salary dispute with Magruder; thus Mitchell would not suggest anyone take Liddy to "meet" Magruder. See SSCEX, Dean.

7. Dean, *Blind Ambition*, pp. 7–16.

8. SSC, II: 491; CI, March 11, 1988 (artistically). On the January 27 and February 4 meetings in Mitchell's office, see the conflicting accounts of Dean, *Blind Ambition*, pp. 72–78; Magruder, *An American Life*, pp. 207–11; and Liddy, *Will*, p. 196–200. Magazine illustrators twice re-created the January 27 meeting: in *New York* (June 17, 1974) and *Time* (April 21, 1980).

9. Magruder recalled Liddy himself, prior to the January 27 meeting, boasting of having worked as an assassin for the FBI, and of having hanged one of his victims from a garage rafter; see Magruder, *An American Life*, p. 206. Told this, Liddy laughed and dismissed it as "utter fabrication"; see G. Gordon Liddy, interview with author, August 9, 2004.

10. Though Dean later tried to take credit for ordering Liddy to burn the charts, Mitchell and Liddy remained adamant the order came from Mitchell. For Dean's claim, see SSCEX, Dean; UVM, 2634; and Dean, *Blind Ambition*, p. 78. For Mitchell's and Liddy's accounts, see SSC, IV: 1612; UVM, 8030; Liddy, *Will*, p. 200; and Liddy interview. Magruder supported Dean; see UVM 4510.

11. Glanzer notes; SSCEX, Jeb Magruder, June 12, 1973. In fact, in the second version of the Liddy plan, the houseboat was dropped, but the call girls remained, as did the kidnapping of radicals; see Liddy, *Will*, p. 203. "[Liddy] had cut off all the horror aspects of it," Mitchell told the Senate, "and it had been reduced down, basically, to the electronic surveillance." Asked if "burglary and bugging" were again proposed, however, Mitchell said they were; see SSC, IV: 1844–57.

12. SSCEX, Dean (very late); UVM, 8032 (shortly); SSC, II: 789 (most). Elsewhere, Magruder said Dean entered "approximately fifteen minutes" after the others; see UVM, 4511.

13. SSCEX, Margruder. See also Lawrence F. O'Brien, *No Final Victories: A Life in Politics from John F. Kennedy to Watergate* (Ballantine, 1976) and Richard B. Trask, *Pictures of the Pain: Photography and the Assassination of President Kennedy* (Yeoman Press, 1994), pp. 44–45.

14. SSCEX, Magruder; SSCFR, 22. Magruder wavered on whether the safe-cracking idea arose in the first or second meeting, and whether it originated with Dean or Mitchell, neither of whom recalled it arising at all. The claim also conflicted with Magruder's own acknowledgment that Mitchell objected to Liddy's second plan because it was "still too broad in scope"; presumably if Mitchell was raising such objections, which tracks with others' recollections, he would not *also* have been proposing that Liddy study the feasibility of a burglary and safe-cracking mission in Las Vegas. Also, when Magruder first began plea-bargaining with federal prosecutors, on April 13, 1973, he claimed "there was mention of the Watergate offices of DNC as a [wiretapping] target . . . at both meetings" in Mitchell's office. Perhaps alerted that a different story was being told by John Dean, who had begun meeting with the prosecutors several days earlier, Magruder dropped this claim the very next day; see Glanzer notes, April 13–14, 1973. Glanzer's notes of April 14 showed Magruder saying "no targets" were discussed on January 27. See also SSC memo to Terry Lenzner from Marc Lackritz, Re: Meeting with John Mitchell [conducted] October 18, 1973, RG 460 WSPF, *U.S. v. Mitchell* (Jencks)—Mitchell, NARA.

15. SSCEX, Dean; SSC, III: 929–30; UVM, 2632–33. A White House aide recalled Dean confiding that "the Watergate location had not been mentioned" at *either* meeting in Mitchell's office; see SSC, V: 1944.

16. Dean, *Blind Ambition*, p. 79.

17. Liddy interview. Even Magruder agreed that Dean posed his objection not in moral terms, but so that "Mr. Mitchell could have deniability"; see UVM, 4513.

18. SSC, III: 1152–53 (more info); Magruder, *An American Life*, p. 227 (feelings); Glanzer notes (in which Magruder recalled Dean conveying "his interest in having Liddy continue"); AOP, 159 (primary season). Howard Hunt told the Senate Watergate committee, in previously unpublished testimony, that Dean was "instigating" Liddy to develop his intelligence plan; see SSCEX, E. Howard Hunt, December 18, 1973. Yet Dean later claimed he immediately took his profound moral concerns about Liddy and Gemstone to H. R. Haldeman, from whom he sought—and received—permission to disengage from Liddy altogether. Captured on tape speaking with President Nixon in March 1973, Dean said he had gone to see Haldeman "right after the [February 4] meeting"; testifying before the Senate, however, Dean changed his story, saying it had taken him "several days" to get an appointment with Haldeman. This change may have stemmed from the fact that Haldeman's office logs showed no meetings with Dean between February 2 and March 9. In *Blind Ambition*, Dean reverted to his first version, strongly implying he met with Haldeman immediately after the February 4 meeting. For his part, Haldeman initially accepted Dean's claims that they met shortly after the February 4 meeting, and that they had agreed Dean should steer clear of Liddy; ultimately, however, Haldeman came to believe Dean was, as Ehrlichman put it, "salting the mine"—laying an evidentiary trail for an event that never happened. The evidence shows, in any case, that Dean continued to exhibit an interest

in Liddy's covert projects; see SSC, III: 930; SSC, VII: 2719; SSC, VIII: 3035, 3098; WHT, 136, 230, 386; Dean, *Blind Ambition*, pp. 79–81; Haldeman, *The Ends of Power*, p. 28; and WSPF draft memo by George T. Frampton, Dean's Anticipated Trial Testimony—From The Beginning Up Until March 21, 1973, [written] July 22, 1974, RG 460 WSPF, NARA.

19. Colson, *Born Again*; J. Anthony Lukas, "Why the Watergate Break-In?" *New York Times*, November 30, 1987 (evil genius); "Excerpts from White House Tape of a Nixon-Haldeman Talk in May 1971," *New York Times*, September 24, 1981 (murderers); Raymond K. Price Jr., *With Nixon* (Viking Press, 1977), p. 30 (worst); AOP, 279 (Kennedy); Garment interview.

20. WH memo to the file by Charles Colson, Subject: Howard Hunt, June 20, 1972, reprinted at HJCW, III: 246–49.

21. Colson memo, June 20, 1972; SSC, II: 793 (O'Brien [emphasis added]). See also Liddy, *Will*, p. 211.

22. SSCEX, Magruder.

23. CI [Ehrlichman], December 9, 1988 (sinew); Douglas Martin, "Fred LaRue, Watergate Figure, Dies at 75," *New York Times*, July 29, 2004; LaRue interview, September 19, 1993 (best friend); author's transcript, NT, Nixon-Ehrlichman, EOB Office, March 16, 1973, 3:00 to 4:47 p.m. (eyes).

24. Magruder's grand jury testimony, at HJC, 1: 136–39 (emphases added). The official transcript reads "firm the projects," probably a stenographic error.

25. SSCEX, Magruder (emphasis added); *Samuel Dash, Chairman, et al., v. Hon. John N. Mitchell, Attorney General of the United States, et al.*, Civ. A. No. 3713–70, 356 F. Supp. 1292 (1972).

26. LaRue's grand jury testimony of April 18, 1973, at HJC, I: 134–35. See also SSC, VI: 2281, 2331; HJCW, I: 182–83; UVM, 6546–52; and LaRue interviews, September 19, 1993, and August 4, 2003. "Jeb repeatedly pushed Mitchell to agree to this," LaRue said in 2003. "He said he was under a lot of pressure from the White House and that he needed an 'okay' on it." However, this recollection contrasted with what LaRue told Senate investigators, who recorded, in a previously unpublished internal staff memorandum, that LaRue "does not remember much discussion about the plan, or strong advocacy of it by Magruder"; see SSC memo of Interview with Frederick [*sic*] LaRue, July 6–7, 1973, by Hamilton, Lenzner, Silverstein and Moore, Dictated by Jim Moore, July, 10, 1973, RG 460 WSPF Investigative Files, *U.S. v. Mitchell* (Jencks Material), Box 72, NARA. In this same interview, LaRue stated that his "impression after the meeting was that no decision had been made and that what he referred to as 'a Mickey Mouse operation' would be shelved." The following year, LaRue told House investigators, according to their previously unpublished internal memorandum, that LaRue "does not recall Magruder saying anything" after Mitchell deferred decision; see [HJC memo of] Interview with Fred C. LaRue, [conducted] April 9 and 10, 1974, [filed] April 10, 1974, RG 460—WSPF, Investigative Files, *U.S. v. Mitchell* (Jencks Material), Box 72, NARA. In this same session, four months before Nixon's resignation, LaRue said he had to "assume" Mitchell approved Gemstone at some other time, since Magruder would not have done so on his own. "LaRue thought perhaps Mitchell had postponed the decision because he did not want LaRue involved," the House staff reported. In later years, free from criminal repercussions, LaRue abandoned this notion, telling the author and others that Mitchell would have confided in him about any approval order.

27. LaRue interview, September 19, 2003

(lying); WSPF notes of George Frampton and WSPF memo to Files from George Frampton, Subject: Meeting with Jeb S. Magruder, July 25, 1973, RG 460 WSPF—WGTF, Investigative Files, *U.S. v. Mitchell* (Jencks), Magruder, Boxes 73 and 109 [respectively], NARA. Frampton's typed memo to the file recording Magruder's newly "triggered" recollections sometimes deviated from the handwritten notes that Frampton took during his re-interview with Magruder, changes that had the effect of making the witness's new statements conform more neatly with his earlier testimony. For example, where Frampton's notes had Magruder quoting Mitchell as having said, "Give him [Liddy] the money and get him out of our hair," Frampton's memo changed the quote entirely: "Well, let's give him this much and see what he can do with it." This was much closer to the language that Magruder, in his Senate testimony, had already attributed to Mitchell ("Let's give him a quarter of a million dollars and let's see what he can come up with"). Frampton's memo also had the effect of preserving some wiggle room for Magruder on his new claim that LaRue had somehow been distracted at the precise moment Mitchell gave the final order on Gemstone. Thus, where the prosecutor's notes showed Magruder affirmatively changing his story to say LaRue "went to the phone," location unspecified, Frampton's typed memo stated: "Magruder recalls that LaRue *may have* gotten up to take a phone call *in the other room* . . ." (emphases added). Indeed, although they relied heavily on Magruder's testimony at *U.S. v. Mitchell*, the WSPF lawyers found him a bit too eager to help them build their cases. Prosecutor Jill Vollner "complained often about his eagerness to tailor his story to the prosecutors' needs"; see Dean, *Blind Ambition*, p. 363. Mitchell's defense team had access

to Frampton's memo—but not to his notes.

28. SSC, IV: 1614–15; SSC, V: 1854 (practically).

29. HJCW, II: 188; HJC summary, July 7, 1974; UMV, 8035, 8149–50.

30. CI, July 10, 1986 (vehement, regardless), June 10, 1988 (hand), September 21, 1988 (Key Biscayne).

31. Christopher Lydon, "Nixon's Advice to Mitchell in April, 1972: 'Start a Fight Right Now,'" *New York Times*, July 12, 1974.

DNC

1. Price, *With Nixon*, p. 369.

2. SSCFR, 28–31; HJCFR, 56–60 (emphasis added). The House report also concluded that H. R. Haldeman "concurred in" Mitchell's authorization of the break-in.

3. Lukas, *Nightmare*, p. 256; Kutler, *The Wars of Watergate*, pp. 204, 275; Martin, "Fred LaRue, Watergate Figure." Among the Nixon biographers and historians who traced the DNC wiretapping to Mitchell were Ambrose, *Nixon*, p. 562; Summers, *The Arrogance of Power*, pp. 402, 411; Brodie, *Richard Nixon*, p. 549n60; Melvin Small, *The Presidency of Richard Nixon* (University Press of Kansas, 1999), p. 256 (who got Key Biscayne's date wrong); and Tom Wicker, *One of Us: Richard Nixon and the American Dream* (Random House, 1991), p. 681 (who blamed Mitchell and Magruder jointly). In a league of his own, however, was Aitken, *Nixon*, who found (pp. 334–35) that "with the establishing of the Nixon-Mitchell relationship came the first seeds of the later troubles of Watergate." Aitken, who conducted numerous exclusive interviews with the ex-president, continued:

The cynicism of mind, brevity of tongue, and ruthlessness in executing decisions that were Mitchell's trademarks became artificially stamped on the president-in-waiting. . . . By encouraging the macho side of Nixon he created an atmosphere in which bad judgments were too easily made. Nixon the hater; Nixon the profane; Nixon the furious; Nixon the unscrupulous player of hardball were demons in his nature which had surfaced comparatively rarely during the first fifty-four years of his life. By contrast, there was Nixon the idealistic, the thoughtful, the sensitive, the kind-hearted and the thoroughly decent son of Hannah. . . . It was the arrival of John Mitchell as the strong peer relationship in his life that began shifting the balance of these conflicting forces.

Yet while Aitken reckoned Mitchell "a bad influence, the Mephistopheles to Nixon's Faust," the Briton also found Mitchell's "reach was limited," that the Nixon-Mitchell alliance, though marked by "considerable mutual trust . . . never deepened into great mutual intimacy," and that while Mitchell "had a great deal to do with building Nixon up and bringing Nixon down . . . [he] did not have a lasting impact on those more personal characteristics that constituted 'the real Nixon.' " This analysis is both inherently contradictory and unsupported by the evidence. One cannot argue that Mitchell was the catalyst for Nixon's great psychic shift, from the kind-hearted "son of Hannah" to the mean-spirited character heard on the tapes, while arguing simultaneously that Mitchell exerted "no lasting impact . . . on 'the real Nixon.' " Moreover, most of Nixon's biographers, friendly and hostile alike, would likely quarrel with Aitken's observation that "Nixon the

unscrupulous player of hardball . . . surfaced comparatively rarely" before 1967. Asked if Nixon himself propounded this view of Mitchell's influence on him, Aitken said "the paragraphs . . . which suggest that Mitchell helped to bring out the dark side of President Nixon are my own interpretation"; see letter to the author from The Rt. Hon. Jonathan Aitken, M.P., May 3, 1995.

4. *Hearings Before the Committee on the Judiciary on the Nomination of Earl J. Silbert, of the District of Columbia, to Be United States Attorney for the District of Columbia, Ninety-third Congress, Second Session* (U.S. Government Printing Office, 1974), p. 65.

5. SSC, VI: 2441 (sophisticated); WH memorandum to H. R. Haldeman from Gordon Strachan, Subject: talking paper, April 4, 1972, H. R. Haldeman Alphabetical Name File, [Lawrence] Higby Subject File, Copies of Gordon Strachan Memos, Box 281, NARA.

6. SSCEX, Strachan; SSC, VI: 2503 (frequently). On Magruder's failure to tell Strachan explicitly that it was Mitchell who approved Gemstone, see SSC, VI: 2441–52.

7. Emery, *Watergate*, pp. 104–5; SSCEX, H. R. Haldeman, January 31, 1974 (rarely); SSC, VIII: 3180–81.

8. SSCEX, Magruder; SSC, II: 532–33, 697; SSC, IV: 1618; Lukas, *Nightmare*, pp. 195–96; Liddy, *Will*, pp. 214–15. Emery cast the Mitchell-Stans discussion as an opportunity for Mitchell to have "countermanded" the Liddy disbursements, and Mitchell's failure to do so as evidence he never "truly disapproved of Liddy's plan." This reading ignores the fact that Stans never specified the disbursements' purpose, and, too, Magruder's executive session testimony, which showed Mitchell expressing concern about Liddy's budgetary requests; see Emery, *Watergate*, p. 105.

9. UVM, 4147 (public record); Liddy, *Will*, pp. 188–220. Liddy's recollection

that the DNC's Watergate offices were never targeted in any of his original Gemstone proposals conflicted with Fred LaRue's memory that the plan reviewed at Key Biscayne had indeed specified the DNC. The discrepancy is perhaps explained by LaRue's recollection that Magruder's secretary typed up the Key Biscayne documents, which may have misrepresented Liddy's actual proposals.

10. E. Howard Hunt, *Undercover: Memoirs of an American Secret Agent* (G.P. Putnam's Sons, 1974).

11. Kurt Singer, "James McCord Was My Boss" (undated [1973], unpublished manuscript), BP Singer Features, Inc.; Jim Hougan, "The McCord File," *Harper's*, January 1980; Hougan, *Secret Agenda*, pp. 10–31; Schoenebaum, *Profiles of an Era*, p. 397; SSCEX, James McCord, March 28, 1973; Fletcher Prouty on *CBS Morning News*, April 2, 1973 (Dulles); Baldwin interview (fear, one of us).

12. Liddy, *Will*, pp. 217–20; SSCEX, McCord; FBI memo to Mr. Tolson from J. P. Mohr, Subject: Protection of the Attorney General, February 28, 1972, FBIM. In this heavily censored FBI document, McCord's name was blacked out, as was the word "intelligence"—the only redaction concealing something other than a name; but the context and typography make clear McCord was the speaker, and that he spoke of shifting to an intelligence role. Also suggestive of a "secret agenda" was the fact that just prior to the break-in, McCord, a man of meager personal finances, engaged in a series of transactions involving suspiciously large sums of money. The FBI later found that he opened a bank account on February 22 for a group called Dedicated Friends of a Better America, through which more than $90,000 passed before McCord closed it on April 17—still more than two weeks before Liddy recruited him

for the Watergate mission. McCord claimed Liddy asked him to join the mission on April 12; but Liddy's first conversation with Magruder about burglarizing DNC did not occur until "late April"; see FBI memo to the Attorney General from Acting Director, FBI, [Subject:] James W. McCord Jr./And Others/Burglary of Democratic Party/National Headquarters/ June 17, 1972/Interception of Communications, July 21, 1972, FBIM.

13. A veteran intelligence analyst reported leading CIA officials were "thunderstruck" by Nixon's establishment of his own spy apparatus; Nixon's men, in turn, "underestimated both the bitterness and the subtlety of the CIA hierarchs, and it is conceivable that the CIA arranged a trap at the Watergate." See Andrew St. George, "The Cold War Comes Home," *Harper's*, November 1973. CIA's deceptions hardly ended with Nixon; the agency's inspector general later disclosed that from 1986 to 1994, CIA sent to successive presidents and Pentagon officials almost 100 reports from foreign agents whom Langley "knew or strongly suspected" were controlled by Moscow; see "White House Fed Flawed Data by CIA," *Chicago Tribune*, November 1, 1995, and Tim Weiner, "Presidents Got 11 Tainted Reports, Senator Says," *New York Times*, November 10, 1995.

14. Hougan, *Secret Agenda*, pp. 20–25 (Ruiz-Williams); SSCEX, Felipe DeDiego, June 18, 1973.

15. SSCEX, Hunt, December 18, 1973 (emphases added).

16. CIA memo from [Richard] Helms to [redacted], Subject: Clarification of the Yeoman Story, December 4, 1973, CIA FOIA Case Number EO-1994-00130 (emphasis added).

17. CI, November 24, 1987 (knew more), February 27, 1988 (whole thing).

18. FBI report of SA William C. Hendricke Jr., [Subject:] Interception of

Communications, June 22, 1972 (Baldwin's education and employment); and FBI interview of Alfred Carleton Baldwin by SAs Angelo J. Lano and Daniel C. Mahan, [conducted] July 10, 1972, [filed] July 11, 1972, [hereinafter "BFBI"], both in RG 460, WSPF—WGTF Investigative Files—Witness File, Howard-Jablonsky, Baldwin correspondence, Box 105, NARA (security work, immediate need); *Los Angeles Times* transcript of interview of Alfred C. Baldwin III by Jack Nelson, October 3, 1972 (joke [hereinafter "BLAT"]).

19. BFBI; Itinerary for Mrs. John N. Mitchell, May 2–6, 1972, RG 460 WSPF, U.S. Attorney File, Documentary Evidence, Martinez, Eugenio—Mitchell, John, Box 31, NARA.

20. Baldwin, interviews August 19 and September 9, 1995 (Scotch); SSC memo of Interview with Alfred Baldwin by Bill Shure, [conducted] March 30, 1973, [filed] April 1, 1973 (reports, team), NARA.

21. Memo by Alan Galbraith [lawyer for Williams and Connolly], [Subject:] Interview with "Al" [conducted] August 26, 1972, [filed] August 28, 1972, NARA. Questioned closely on this issue twenty-five years later—after rereading his previous accounts to the FBI, the *Los Angeles Times*, and the Senate Watergate committee—Baldwin reaffirmed that McCord's surveillance of DNC began *before* the burglars' first successful entry there. "There's no doubt in my mind," Baldwin said, "there was [*sic*] conversations being monitored . . . either on the night of the twenty-fifth or on the twenty-sixth"; see Baldwin interview, September 9, 1995. Baldwin later repeated this under oath: "The Thursday, May 25th, the day I returned from Connecticut . . . that was the first conversation. . . . There had been an entry [into DNC] prior to my getting back from Connecticut"; see

DVS, Deposition of Alfred Baldwin, July 26, 1996.

22. BLAT (we can talk).

23. Walter Rugaber, "Watergate Trial Is Told G.O.P. Got Wiretap Data," *New York Times*, January 20, 1973 (gag order).

24. *Lawrence F. O'Brien v. James W. McCord, et al.*, Civil Action No. 1233–72, Deposition of John N. Mitchell, September 5, 1972; SSC, IV: 1619–20.

25. Liddy, *Will*, pp. 239–40. Reminded of the version in Liddy's memoir, Mitchell, less than two months before his death, asked caustically: "What the hell has he got that in his book for? Is that a figment of his imagination, or what—that he put that envelope on my desk?" See CI, September 21, 1988.

26. Magruder, *An American Life*, pp. 248–49; Glanzer notes (this idiot). Strachan denied seeing the wiretap data; see SSC, VI: 2451. However, on this specific point, the usually unpersuasive Magruder passed a polygraph test, and Strachan failed one; see HJCW, III: 102, and the previously unpublished WSPF memo to Files from Earl J. Silbert, Subject: Gordon Strachan, April 24, 1973, RG 460 WSPF—WGTF, Investigative Files, Defendant Files, Gordon Strachan, Box 124, NARA. John Dean testified that Strachan privately acknowledged having seen the logs; see SSC, II: 934 and SSC, III: 955. And Strachan's boss, Haldeman, told Nixon in April 1973 that Strachan had confided: "I stopped reading the synopses, and they were—we had 'em here"; see WHT, 382.

27. Glanzer notes; Ehrlichman-Magruder tape; SSCEX, Magruder; SSC, II: 797; Frampton notes and memo; Magruder, *An American Life*, pp. 248–49; UVM, 4521–24, 4819–21. Magruder told Ehrlichman that Mitchell thought the wiretap data "so bad he *picked up the phone and called Liddy*

28. SSC, IV: 1619.
29. Ibid., VI: 2360 (Mardian); SSC, VI: 2304 (LaRue).
30. Liddy, *Will*, pp. 236–37. Two decades later, Magruder confirmed Liddy's account; see DVS, Magruder deposition.
31. CI [John F. Rudy II], April 14, 1989, and April 28, 1989; DVS, Deposition of John F. Rudy II, April 11, 1996.
32. DVS, Deposition of John F. Rudy II, June 19, 1996.
33. WVL, I, Deposition of Alfred C. Baldwin III, July 28, 1997 (eight of ten); Baldwin interview, September 9, 1995 (sexual nature, arrangements). Baldwin, in 1995, also recalled McCord ordering him to patronize the Democratic lounge at Watergate and observe "senators leaving with any of the young girls." Both Oliver and his secretary, Ida Wells, have repeatedly denied they had anything to do with prostitution. Oliver declined to be interviewed for this book. As the Watergate break-in trial approached, E. Howard Hunt, exhorting his fellow defendants to plead guilty, warned burglar Bernard Barker that "things like accusations about prostitutes would come out at trial"; see WSPF memo to The File from G. Goldman, Subject: Interview of Bernard Barker, September 13, 1973, RG 460, NARA.
34. "U.S. Hints Blackmail as Motive in Watergate Case," *New York Times*, January 19, 1973. All known references to the conversations overheard on the DNC wiretaps aver to amorous or sexual content. Unsealed portions of the *U.S. v. Liddy* trial transcript show Judge Sirica was informed, in chambers on January 11, 1973, that Baldwin had overheard discussion of "Mr. Oliver sleeping with a woman in Greenville, Mississippi"; see UVL 981-982. Meeting with John Ehrlichman in April 1973, Magruder said the wiretap had picked up Oliver "calling girls in Mississippi, saying, 'Honey, I'll be down for the weekend' "; see author's transcript of recorded conversation between John Ehrlichman and Jeb Magruder, April 14, 1973, NARA. During Magruder's briefing, Ehrlichman scribbled: "Oliver— ph[one] . . . sex"; see SSC VII/2940. Ehrlichman then reported to Nixon that "what they were getting was mostly this fellow Oliver phoning his girlfriends all over the country and lining up assignations"; see WHT 382. Magruder told Watergate prosecutors the logs "dealt with Spencer Oliver's extra-marital affairs," specifically his relationship with a "Miss[is-sippi] girl"; see Glanzer notes op. cit. Ida "Maxie" Wells hailed from Mississippi. Magruder told the Senate the GEMSTONE logs recounted "very personal" conversations in which one party told another she had "a date tonight"; see SSCEX Magruder, op. cit. In his memoirs, H. R. Haldeman said he learned "the chatter about love" picked up on the GEMSTONE wiretap reflected "Maxie" and other DNC secretaries "calling boyfriends all over the country—and using vivid details"; see Haldeman (1978), op. cit., p. 174.
35. The mass of information purporting to link Maureen Dean to organized crime figures and prostitution is most exhaustively collected in DVS, Declaration of Leonard Colodny in Support of Motion for Partial Summary Judgment, [filed] December 16, 1996. This mammoth court filing runs some four thousand pages and features more than 700 exhibits: documents, photographs, interviews, depositions. Both John and Maureen Dean have denied that either had anything to do with prostitution activity. For the Deans' lengthy response to these charges, see DVS, Dean deposition; DVS, Deposition of Maureen K. Dean, August 30, 1996; and DVS,

"Plaintiffs John Dean's and Maureen Dean's Provisional Response to Defendant Leonard Colodny's Motion For Partial Summary Judgment," [filed] March 20, 1997. The Court never rules on the Motion because the case was resolved.

36. John Dean interview with author, August 6, 1999 (even aware).

37. SSC, IV: 1445 (disposition); Dean, *Blind Ambition*, pp. 30-35 (valued, upward, Hollander); SSCEX, Jack Caulfield, March 16, 1974; Tony Ulasewicz with Stuart A. McKeever, *The President's Private Eye* (MACSAM, 1990), pp. 246-63; Colodny and Gettlin, *Silent Coup*, pp. 106-7, 131; Kenneth Tapman interview with author, January 4, 2003. "As far as I was concerned," Ulasewicz wrote, "Dean was up to his sleek cheeks in the whole Watergate affair—before and after the break-in."

38. WH memo for H. R. Haldeman from John Dean, Subject: Counter Actions (Watergate), September 12, 1972, at SSC, III: 1177-78; WHT, 67.

39. Magruder, *An American Life*, pp. 117, 197–98; SSCEX, Magruder (countermanded); author's transcript, NT, Nixon-Haldeman, Conversation No. 888-4, Oval Office, March 27, 1973, 9:47 a.m. to 10:55 a.m. (clarified). See also *Common Cause, et al. v. Finance Committee to Re-Elect the President, et al.*, Civil Action No. 1780–72, Deposition of John W. Dean III, May 15, 1973.

40. Jeb Stuart Magruder, *From Power to Peace* (Word Books, 1978), pp. 13–15; CI [Magruder], February 8 and August 7, 1990.

41. DVS, Magruder deposition.

42. CI, August 31, 1988 (protecting Dean); CI [Magruder], February 8, 1990 (pocket), August 7, 1990 (involved).

43. CI, June 15, 1987. Presented with the rudimentary outlines of the call-girl theory in 1986, Mitchell found it "startling" but ultimately judged it "a scam," probably because the outline presented to him implicated his former personal assistant, Kristen Forsberg, in the Columbia Plaza scheme. Forsberg has denied any connection to prostitution activity; see CI, April 28, 1986 (startling); Proposal for an Investigation by Phil Stanford, March 1, 1986; letter to Len Colodny from Jerris Leonard, November 10, 1988 (scam); and Kristen Forsberg, interview with author, April 23, 1995.

44. WSPF Box 31. McLendon, *Martha*, pp. 2–4; UVM, 8351; SSC, VI: 2285, 2311.

THE NEEDLE

1. WHT, 214.

2. Magruder, *An American Life*, pp. 250–53; DVSCM Exhibit 494 (several, drunk).

3. Glanzer notes.

4. Magruder, *An American Life*, pp. 252–55 (emphases added).

5. UVM, 4534–35 (emphasis added).

6. UVM, 6826 (9:00, ten to fifteen); SSC memo of Interview with Frederick [*sic*] Cheney LaRue by Hamilton, Silverstein, Sanders, [conducted] May 9, 1973, [filed] May 14, 1973, RG 460 WSPF Investigative Files, *U.S. v. Mitchell* (Jencks Material), Box 72, NARA (go back into); SSC, VI: 2285–2315, 2330–31. LaRue's grand jury testimony of April 18, 1973, was read in open court; see UVM, 6831–33.

7. Arnold Rochvarg, *Watergate Victory: Mardian's Appeal* (University Press of America, 1995).

8. CI, September 14, 1988 (ridiculous); *O'Brien v. McCord*, Mitchell deposition; and UVM, 8175–76.

9. Liddy, *Will*, p. 251; Rochvarg, *Watergate Victory*, pp. 22–23.

10. Liddy, *Will*, pp. 251–53; Kleindienst, *Justice*, pp. 145–46; SSC, VI: 2353; SSC, IX: 3561; UVM, 5973–74. In

his memoir, Kleindienst made no mention of Liddy's confession that the arrested men had been working under him, and recalled telling Liddy: "John Mitchell knows how to find me. I don't believe he gave you any such instructions." Moore claimed it was he who interjected that Liddy's instructions had come from Magruder; he recalled Kleindienst replying: "You get hold of Mr. Mitchell and tell him if he wants to talk to me about this matter that he can reach me here at Burning Tree." See UVM, 5904–9.

11. SSC, VI: 2353 (amazed); Magruder, *An American Life*, p. 258; McLendon, *Martha*, pp. 2–4; Steve King, interview with author, February 8, 1992.

12. HJCW, I: 195; Dean, *Blind Ambition*, pp. 101–2; McLendon, *Martha*, pp. 6–7 (Gulfstream, rest, brothers); FBI memo to Mr. Kinley from J. E. Herington, Subject: Maxine Cheshire/ Syndicated Columnist/"The Washington Post," April 26, 1973, FBIM (Disneyland).

13. FBI report of interview of Stephen B. King by Special Agent Charles W. Harvey, [conducted] May 1, 1973, [filed] May 3, 1973, FBIM; Donnie Radcliffe, "Martha Mitchell: Two Long Years After Watergate," *Washington Post*, June 16, 1974 (Jesus Christ, lightning); McLendon, *Martha*, pp. 8–9.

14. FBI memo to ADIC from SA [redacted], Subject: Visit of Mitchell Family/Newporter Inn, June 18, 1972, [filed] April 25, 1973, FBIM; Clare Crawford, "Martha's Charges Flare Again," *Washington Evening Star and Daily News*, September 12, 1972; "Mrs. Mitchell Fears Plot to Tie Watergate to Husband," *New York Times*, March 28, 1973; Jack Anderson, "Martha: Night of the Needle," *New York Post*, June 5, 1973; McLendon, *Martha*, pp. 6–22; Ken and Peggy Ebbitt interview. Another Mitchell aide

lamented that Marty had a "horrible childhood"; see Landau interview.

15. Helen Thomas, "Martha's Ultimatum," *Washington Post*, June 24, 1972, and "Martha Is 'Leaving' Mitchell," *Washington Post*, June 26, 1972; Steve Brown, "John Smuggles Martha Out of Sight," *Daily News*, June 29, 1972 (helicopter); "Exeunt the Mitchells," *New York Times*, June 29, 1972; Jack Anderson, "Martha's Latest Telephone Escapade," *Washington Post*, July 1, 1972 (talked-about); McLendon, *Martha*, p. 21.

16. Marcia Kramer and William McFadden, "Martha Sobs: 'I'm Prisoner,' " *Daily News*, June 26, 1972; Tom Donnelly, "If She's the Answer, What's the Question?" *Washington Post*, May 11, 1973 (heroine); Helen Thomas, "Long after Watergate," *Long Island Press*, May 27, 1973 (spectrum), and *Dateline: White House* (Macmillan, 1975), p. 242 (patriotism, bucking); Charlotte Curtis, "Martha Mitchell Testifies in Civil Suit," *New York Times*, May 4, 1973 (Watergate case); William Reel and Henry Lee, "Martha Tells It Like It Is to Lawyers," *Daily News*, May 4, 1973; Shana Alexander in Donald W. Harward, ed., *Crisis in Confidence: The Impact of Watergate* (Little, Brown, 1974), p. 42.

17. *CBS Morning News*, August 29, 1973 (Quinn); author's transcript, NT, Nixon-Haig-Ziegler, Conversation No. 945-5, Oval Office, June 19, 1973, 11:04 a.m. to 11:17 a.m. (poor sick); Thomas, *Dateline* (class, no friend); and Thomas, *Front Row at the White House: My Life and Times* (Scribner, 1999), pp. 215–16 (she knows, God almighty).

18. Dean, *Blind Ambition*, p. 99 (note). Mitchell said the meeting in his apartment was "set up by Magruder"; see CI, March 29, 1988. Some have argued Dean misled investigators about the timing of his return from the Philippines, and his activities imme-

diately prior; see Colodny and Gettlin, *Silent Coup*, pp. 168–71.

19. Liddy, *Will*, pp. 255–57; SSC, V: 1852. Dean denied making such promises; see UVM, 3893–901; DVS, JDD.

20. Glanzer notes; Magruder, *An American Life*, p. 268; Hougan, *Secret Agenda*, pp. 188–89 (shag rug).

21. SSCEX, Magruder; SSC, II: 799–800 (emphases added); Magruder, *An American Life*, p. 267.

22. UVM, 4549–50 (stuck, detail), 4824–36 (office interview, grand jury, incriminating).

23. UVM, 8052–53; HJCW, II: 155; WHT, 685; Dean, *Blind Ambition*, pp. 99–102.

24. LaRue and Mardian clashed over the date of their interview of Liddy— LaRue claimed it was June 20, Mardian, June 21—and over who initiated the interview; see SSC, VI: 2286–87, 2357–58.

25. UVM, 8056–58, 8196–97; SSC, VI: 2363 (shocked). Mitchell told the House he was "quite certain" this discussion took place June 22; see HJCW, II: 176. LaRue was silent on whether Liddy's request for bail money was conveyed to Mitchell; see SSC, VI: 2288–89. Asked how Mitchell reacted to Liddy's litany of horrors, LaRue testified: "I don't recall any specific reaction. . . . Mr. Mitchell is not a person who demonstrates a great deal of emotion about anything."

26. SSC, V: 1827–34. Mitchell testified he coined the term "White House horrors" prior to June 1972. Elsewhere, he called them "the other little gems"; see UVM, 8197; SSC, IV: 1622. Asked once to define the White House horrors, he took evident glee in recounting them, the better to demonstrate his distance from them: "Well, let me see if I can recall all of them at this late stage. Certainly there was the Ellsberg psychiatrist break-in, there was the Dita Beard episode,

there were the Diem cables and there was the Brookings Institute [*sic*] situation. Oh, yes, I believe that there . . . had been wiretapping undertaken outside of the normal channels of the Federal Bureau of Investigation, and some miscellaneous investigations of Chappaquiddick, and I think that covers the basic elements of it"; see HJCW, II: 133.

27. Author's transcript, NT, Nixon-Haldeman, Conversation No. 344-6, EOB Office, June 20, 1972, 4:35 to 5:25 p.m. In a meeting that same day with Charles Colson, Nixon expressed skepticism about the motives of the arrested men, saying: "It doesn't sound like a skillful job. . . . If we didn't know better, [we] would have thought it was deliberately botched." As for the strategy to be pursued, Nixon told Colson: "At times, uh, I just stonewall it"; see Bob Woodward and Scott Armstrong, "Nixon Knew of 'Hush Money' Before Dean Meeting," *Washington Post*, May 1, 1977.

28. HJC transcript of Nixon's DictaBelt recording of June 20, 1972, at HJC, II: 310.

29. "White House Transcripts of 3 Nixon-Haldeman Conversations on June 23, 1972," *New York Times*, August 6, 1974. The White House transcript is more reliable than the special prosecutors', which omitted, for example, Haldeman's statement: "That's not an unusual development, and ah, that would take care of it"; see Hamburg, *Nixon*, pp. 405–10. On Dean's conception of the CIA plan discussed on the smoking-gun tape, and his false claim that Mitchell endorsed it, see Colodny and Gettlin, pp. 195–205; and CI [Haldeman] March 1989. "I don't know how [Dean] can deny that he fabricated the Mitchell involvement in his conversation with me on the morning of the twenty-third," Haldeman said.

30. Magruder, *An American Life*, pp.

265–75 (tough); SSC, IV: 1660 (knock-down, pretty low).

31. SSCEX, Dean; SSC, III: 945–46. Testifying before the House, Dean said he left the June 24 meeting with "the plan that had been given to me over at the re-election committee with Mr. Mardian and Mr. Mitchell, to check the CIA because they [sic] were competent to handle this"; see HJCW, II: 303.

32. CIA memcons by Vernon A. Walters, [no subjects], June 28, 1972 and June 29, 1972 [I and II], at HJC, II: 437–41 (glum); SSC, III: 946–48; *Inquiry Into the Alleged Involvement of the Central Intelligence Agency in the Watergate and Ellsberg Matters: Report of the Special Subcommittee on Intelligence of the Committee on Armed Services, House of Representatives, Ninety-third Congress, First Session, October 23, 1973* (U.S. Government Printing Office, 1973), pp. 18–19 (pressing, pleadingly, not clear). Mitchell later remarked bitterly on the way Dean had been "over there nosing around" with Walters: "I don't know whether he was representing John Dean, the CIA, or the White House or whom"; see CI, March 25, 1988.

33. SSCEX, Dean.

34. Schoenebaum, *Profiles of an Era*, pp. 336–37.

35. SSC, III: 950.

36. SSC, VI: 2566–67 (strongly, attorneys' fees, back me up); WH transcript of Ehrlichman-Kalmbach conversation, April 19, 1973, 4:50 p.m., at SSC, V: 2215. Ehrlichman on one occasion recalled Dean seeking permission to use Kalmbach and not mentioning Mitchell; see WHT, 399. Haldeman recalled how Dean, in March 1973, shortly before defecting to the prosecutors, began claiming that "at some point in 1972, he, at Mitchell's suggestion, had asked me if it would be okay for him to contact Herb Kalmbach to ask him to raise some such defense funds. . . . I do not recall such a request. . . . Dean has said that he checked with both Ehrlichman and me on this point, and at other times he has said only that he checked with Ehrlichman"; see SSC, VII: 2885.

37. SSC, V: 2097–99; HJCW, III: 537, 569. Dean claimed he told Kalmbach everything he knew about Watergate, but Kalmbach recalled that Dean told him next to nothing about it, and certainly never identified Mitchell as the authority behind the hush-money scheme; see HJCW, III: 682.

38. SSC, V: 2106–10; Renata Adler, "Searching for the Real Nixon Scandal: A Last Inference," *Atlantic Monthly*, December 1976 (tough and dangerous). Ehrlichman denied that Kalmbach asked him to vouch for Dean; see SSC, VI: 2568–71.

39. UVM, 8307 (never tried); CI, April 19, 1988 (know anything, fish); CI [Kalmbach], April 27, 1988.

40. WSPF draft memo, July 22, 1974.

41. Ibid. (underlining in original, emphasis added). On another element of Dean's hush-money story—a supposed meeting with Fred LaRue—Frampton found the encounter Dean described "apparently didn't take place," and concluded: "We probably would do well simply to omit Dean's testimony about this."

42. UVM, 2729–31 (hold, explore), 4019–21 (time to time, Kalmbach angle).

43. WSPF memo to Richard Ben-Veniste from Peter F. Rient, Subject: Material Discrepancies Between the Senate Select Committee Testimony of John Dean and the Tapes of Dean's Meetings with the President, February 6, 1974; letter to John J. Sirica from Charles Shaffer, Re: *United States v. John W. Dean, III*, Criminal Case No. 866–73, [written] July 28, 1974 (Ervin); both in RG 460 WSPF—WGTF, Investigative files—Witness File, Dean, Box 101, NARA. See also James Rosen, "Anniversarygate," *National Review*, July 14, 1997.

44. DOJ memo to Professor Archibald Cox from Earl J. Silbert and Seymour Glanzer, Subject: Contacts Between Prosecution of John W. Dean, III, from April 1 [1973] Up to Date, [filed] May 31, 1973 (center, gradual); WSPF memo to James F. Neal from Larry Iason, Subject: ["]What Dean told the Prosecutors (directly and through Shaffer)["], October 8, 1974 (deliver); DOJ memo to Earl J. Silbert from Seymour Glanzer, [no subject], June 12, 1973 (incriminating, inadvertent); WSPF memo to Files from Peter F. Rient and Judy Denny, Subject: Interview of Earl Silbert on August 31, 1973, [filed] September 6, 1973 (Kalmbach); all in RG 460 WSPF—WGTF, Investigative files—Witness File, Dean, Box 101, NARA.

45. Author's transcript, NT, Nixon-Haldeman, Conversation No. 343-37, EOB Office, June 26, 1972, 12:35 p.m. to 1:25 p.m.

46. Nixon, *Memoirs: Volume 2*, p. 138 (harm); THD, 478.

47. HJC transcript of Nixon-Mitchell-Haldeman meeting, June 30, 1972, at HJC, II: 514–16. The House version of this transcript appears far more reliable than the special prosecutors'; see WSPF Reference Transcript, RG 460 WSPF, February, 23, 1971–March 23, 1973, Box 1, NARA.

48. SSC, IV: 1665, 1674; SSC, VIII: 3165–66; HJCW, II: 136–38, 168–69; UVM, 8067.

OFF THE RESERVATION

1. Author's transcript of *The David Frost Show*, April 8, 1971, WHCA Tape No. 4265, NARA.

2. Jerry Greene, "Mitchell Gives Up Politics for Love," *New York Daily News*, July 2, 1972; Robert B. Semple Jr., "Mitchell Quits Post, Putting Family First," *New York Times*, July 2, 1972; George Lardner Jr., "Mitchell Resigns to Spend Time with His Family," *Washington Post*, July 2, 1972.

3. Author's transcript, NT, Nixon-Haldeman, Conversation No. 744-24/745-1, Oval Office, June 20, 1972, 3:28 to 4:22 p.m.

4. Ashman and Engelmayer, *Martha*, pp. 10–11.

5. Paul Hoffman, *Lions in the Street: The Inside Story of the Great Wall Street Law Firms* (Signet, paperback ed., 1973), pp. 111–15; Michael C. Jensen, "Mitchell and His Law Firm," *New York Times*, May 7, 1972; Robert B. Semple Jr., "Mitchell Relaxes in New Office Only 50 Paces from His Old," *New York Times*, July 8, 1972. The *Times* found "no known cases of blatant White House or Justice Department influence" in behalf of Mudge Rose clients, but such charges recurred frequently; see Hoffman, *Lions in the Street*, and Jon Frappier, "The Lawyers," in Steve Weissman, ed., *Big Brother and the Holding Company: The World Behind Watergate* (Ramparts Press, 1974), pp. 219–43. Martha Mitchell told Helen Thomas the move was "what I wanted"; see "Nixon Discusses Mitchell's Move," *New York Times*, July 3, 1972.

6. FBI report of interview with John N. Mitchell by SA's [*sic*] Daniel C. Mahan and Robert E. Lill, [conducted] July 5, 1972, [filed] July 6, 1972; UVM Government Exhibit 64; HJCW, II: 147 (slight variance).

7. Lukas, "Why the Watergate Break-In?" (key link); THD, 483–84. Dean claimed he advised Haldeman only that Magruder "be removed in a graceful manner that would not unduly jeopardize him"; see SSC, III: 951.

8. SSC, II: 802 (heat); Magruder, *An American Life*, pp. 271, 283, 294; Glanzer notes (volunteer). Magruder testified that Mitchell brought Magruder's offer of self-sacrifice to the White House, and that it was rejected there; see UVM, 4556–57. "I think

there were some takers," Magruder told the Senate, "but it was turned down"; see SSCEX, Magruder.

9. Author's transcript, NT, Nixon-Mitchell-Haldeman-MacGregor, Conversation No. 768-4, Oval Office, August 14, 1972, 9:55 to 10:42 a.m.

10. Magruder, *An American Life*, pp. 271–72.

11. SSC, IV: 1624–25; SSC, V: 1859 (Ervin).

12. SSC, III: 944–52; SSC, IV: 1358; WHT, 141 (totally aware); SSC, II: 803 (two hours); FBI memo to Mr. Long from C. A. Nuzum, Subject: James Walter McCord Jr., et al./Burglary of Democratic National Committee Headquarters, June 17, 1972/Interception of Communications, May 1, 1973 (eighty-three); FBI report [unsigned], Watergate—Events at Initial Stage of Case, June, 7, 1973; both in RG 460 WSPF—WGTF, *U.S. v. Mitchell* (Evidence Not Used), Ehrlichman Materials, FBI Internal Investigation, NARA; WH memo for Richard G. Kleindienst from John W. Dean, III, [no subject], September 17, 1970, RG 460 WSPF—CCTF #804, Hughes-Rebozo, John W. Dean Documents Received, Box 15, NARA; Magruder, *An American Life*, pp. 295–99. Dean claimed he read fewer than twenty reports "out of the eighty I received," and that he "did not sit in on every single [FBI] interview that occurred at the White House"; see SSCEX, Dean. At *U.S. v. Mitchell*, Fred LaRue testified he was present at a meeting of Mitchell and Dean where the latter "was given the assignment of trying to get copies of these [FBI] interviews [with CRP personnel] so that our attorneys could examine them"; but LaRue could only place the alleged meeting in "mid-July" 1972. On one other occasion—to House impeachment investigators—LaRue claimed to have *shown* FBI reports to Mitchell, but couldn't recall "what he passed on"; see UVM, 6660; and HJC memo of Interview with Fred C. LaRue by Dick Cates, Bernie Nussbaum, Bill White, and Bob Murphy, April 9–10, 1974, RG 460 WSPF Investigative Files, *U.S. v. Mitchell* (Jencks Material), Box 72, NARA.

13. Linda Amster, "Chronology 1968–1974: Events Leading to the Resignation of Richard M. Nixon," in *The End of a Presidency* (Bantam, 1974), p. 153 (was reported); UVM, 8122, 8318. Silbert later said Mitchell's use of the word "non-productive" stirred momentary "disturbance" in him, but he "never dreamed . . . a former attorney general of the United States would lie to the grand jury"; see George V. Higgins, "The Judge Who Tried Harder," *Atlantic Monthly*, April 1974.

14. Agis Salpukas, "2 Nixon Ex-Aides Among 7 Indicted in Raid in Capital," *New York Times*, September 16, 1972; WHT, 57–69; Joseph Lelyveld, "Earl Silbert, Soon to Be Sworn In as U.S. Attorney, Reflects on His Days as Prosecutor in Watergate Case," *New York Times*, October 16, 1975; Karlyn Barker and Walter Pincus, "Watergate Revisited: 20 Years After the Break-in, the Story Continues to Unfold," *Washington Post*, June 14, 1992 (severe). On Mitchell's showdown with Edward Bennett Williams, see *O'Brien v. McCord*, Mitchell deposition; Robert Pack, *Edward Bennett Williams for the Defense* (Harper & Row, 1983), pp. 3–14; author's transcript of "Watergate: Twenty-Five Years Later," American Bar Association symposium, June 1997; and Joseph A. Califano Jr., *Inside: A Public and Private Life* (Public Affairs, 2004), pp. 267–72. Califano claimed Mitchell "had to squeeze his thighs together to avoid wetting his pants," but Williams's cross-examination, while skillful, gave rise to no perjury charges.

15. Carl Bernstein and Bob Woodward, "Mitchell Controlled Secret GOP

Fund," *Washington Post*, September 29, 1972; Carl Bernstein and Bob Woodward, *All the President's Men* (Warner, 1976), pp. 107–12; *CBS Evening News*, October 19, 1972 (Harris poll). Two years earlier, when the *Post* publicly apologized for having misquoted him, Mitchell privately wrote Mrs. Graham: "Now you can see why I say the *Post* is the best paper in the country"; see Chalmers M. Roberts, *In the Shadow of Power: The Story of the Washington Post* (Seven Locks Press, 1989), p. 408. Nixon also used the expression "tit in the wringer"; see author's transcript, NT, Nixon-Haig-Ziegler, Conversation No. 917-44, Oval Office, May 14, 1973, 6:28 p.m. to 7:27 p.m.

16. WH transcript of Colson-Hunt conversation, November 13, 1972, at SSC, VIV: 3888–91. The Senate Watergate committee erroneously placed this call in "late November."

17. SSC, III: 969–70 (tell Mitchell); SSC, IV: 1658 (turned down cold); HJC summary, July 4, 1974; HJCW, II: 134–35, 233 (hell); UVM, 8084–85; Dean, *Blind Ambition*, pp. 157–58; SSCEX, Dean (no instruction). In executive session, Dean completely omitted the Metropolitan Club meeting; in his memoir, he claimed Mitchell listened to the entire tape.

18. SSC, V: 2111 (set fire), 2114 (most often), 2135 (primary); WSPF letter to Clifford Kaden from Thomas F. McBride, Subject: Herbert W. Kalmbach, June 5, 1974, RG 460 WSPF—CCTF, Townhouse File #807, Planning and Coordination, Investigative Correspondence, Box 1, NARA (fire).

19. SSCEX, Dean; SSC, III: 970, SSC, IV: 1649 (no control); HJCW, II: 232; UVM, 2933–40; THD, 543–44; Dean, *Blind Ambition*, pp. 159–62, 183 (ringmaster), 302 (concrete); SSC memo of interview with Kenneth Parkinson by David Dorsen, James

Hamilton, Donald Sanders, and Robert Silverstein, [conducted] June 2, 1973, [filed] June 4, 1973, at HJC, III: 427–29 (the prosecutors agreed on the date of December 1, using it in the *U.S. v. Mitchell* indictment). LaRue told the House he raised with Mitchell in September or October 1972 the possibility of using the White House fund to pay the Watergate defendants, and that Mitchell advised him to take the matter up with Dean; see HJCW, 1: 243. In his Senate testimony, Haldeman was always careful to say he was informed of the payments by Dean and "possibly also by John Mitchell"; see, for example, SSC, VII: 2885 and SSC, VIII: 3046. Haldeman also claimed he thought the payments were lawful deposits into a proper defense fund, a claim difficult to substantiate or refute. The tapes show that as early as August 1, 1972, he told Nixon, "Hunt's happy," to which Nixon replied: "At considerable cost, I guess?" "Yes," Haldeman said. "It's worth it," Nixon countered. "It's very expensive," Haldeman replied. "They have to be paid," Nixon concluded, adding: "That's all there is to that." The discussion marked Nixon's earliest—if only ex post facto—approval of the payments, eight months before the infamous "cancer on the presidency" meeting; but neither Haldeman nor Nixon made clear he understood the payments to be illegal. See author's transcript, NT, Nixon-Haldeman, Conversation No. 758-11, Oval Office, August 1, 1972, 11:03 a.m. to 11:58 a.m.

20. Seth S. King, "46 Aboard Jet Die When It Crashes on Chicago Homes," *New York Times*, December 9, 1972; and John Kifner, "Toll in Chicago Crash Rises to 45 as 2 More Bodies Are Found," *New York Times*, December 10, 1972. The formal investigation by the National Transportation Safety Board attributed the crash to

"pilot error," but charges of foul play persisted; see Barboura Morris Freed, "Flight 553: The Watergate Murder?" in Weissman, *Big Brother*, pp. 127–57. The pilot's last words, as preserved by the flight recorder, reportedly were "I'm sorry"; see *CBS Morning News*, September 28, 1973.

21. Goldman memo, September 13, 1973 (prostitutes); SSCEX, E. Howard Hunt, June 11, 1973 (son of a bitch, very bitter); SSCEX, E. Howard Hunt, July 26, 1973 (Colson hadn't attended).

22. McCord letters, at SSC, VIV: 3834–42.

23. SSCEX, Dean; SSC, III: 972–76, 1080, 1289; Dean, *Blind Ambition*, p. 203; SSC, IV: 1634, 1650 (Florida, anybody else), 1673 (fabrication); HJCW, II: 286; UVM, 2993–99. Judge Sirica instructed the jury in *U.S. v. Mitchell* that the phrase "on or about" a given date could encompass events up to *two months before or afterward*; see UVM, 10012. Speaking to Haldeman in May 1973, Nixon made clear he believed Mitchell was guilty on this score, saying: "Mitchell is the fellow that, you know, had the greatest stake there and he was telling them to promise the Goddamn clemency." But Nixon also remarked that Mitchell, "to his credit, never discussed it" with the president; see author's transcript, NT, Nixon-Haldeman, Conversation No. 167-10, Camp David, 12:26 p.m. to 12:54 p.m. Dean claimed in his public Senate testimony—but nowhere else—that in March 1973, shortly before the defendants' sentencing, Mitchell called and again urged that Caulfield be dispatched to see McCord. According to Dean, Caulfield came to Dean's office and exhibited, then destroyed, a diary McCord had kept, in which he had chronicled his previous contacts with Caulfield. Dean said he called Mitchell back and told him he "did not think

that it was very wise" for Caulfield to see McCord again; see SSC, IV: 1545. On this story, Mitchell was apparently never questioned.

24. Lukas, *Nightmare*, pp. 306–7; UVM, 2688, 3410, 3648 (crux), 4190, 4340, 4376–77; Dean, *Blind Ambition*, pp. 167, 180–81; SSC, IV: 1439, 1587–88; SSC, IX: 3739, 3751–52, 3790; Hunt, *Undercover*, p. 277 (operational); *Hearings Before the Select Committee on Assassinations, Assassination of President John F. Kennedy*, Deposition of E. Howard Hunt, November 3, 1978; Hunt interview, January 26, 2003 (self-preservation, incriminatory). Hunt recalled in 2003 that among the "incriminatory" entries in his notebooks was one reading: " 'Liddy said that John Dean had told him that there would be no problem of additional funding,' something like that." That Dean failed to mention his destruction of the notebooks during his lengthy testimony before the Senate Watergate committee he chalked up to simple forgetfulness; yet minority counsel Fred Thompson explicitly asked Dean what he knew about "certain documents or certain materials [that] had not been turned over to the authorities when [Hunt's] safe was cleaned out." Dean replied with a long, circumlocutory answer, only fleetingly acknowledging that questions remained about "where given items that were in the safe were located." This exchange occurred only 160 days after Dean—"the man with the memory," *Time* dubbed him—had completed the "sweaty act" of shredding the notebooks. Such testimony belied Dean's claim that "I always, in dealing with any of the investigators from either this committee or from the prosecutor's office, told them exactly what I knew"; see "And Where Is the Palace Guard?" *Time*, August 11, 1975. On the motion to suppress disclosure of the contents of the DNC

conversations, see Charles Morgan Jr., *One Man, One Voice* (Holt, Rinehart, 1979), pp. 217–27.

25. SSC, IV: 1631–32, 1649 (Mitchell); SSC, V: 2114 (most often); SSC, VI: 2291, 2297 (LaRue); HJCW, III: 561–62; UVM, 3012–13, 6615–66, 8307; CI [Kalmbach], April 27, 1988; Notes of Seymour Glanzer from Interviews with Fred LaRue, [undated—May 1973], May 10, 1973, May 16, 1973, and June 18, 1973, RG 460 WSPF Investigative Files, *U.S. v. Mitchell* (Jencks Material), Box 72, NARA; SSC memo, May 9, 1973, SSC memo, July 6–7, 1973; HJC memo, April 9–10, 1974; HJC summary, July 7, 1974. On LaRue's claims about the summary sheet and the appeals to GOP donors, Mitchell was apparently never questioned.

26. NT, Conversation No. 758-11 (Hunt); author's transcript, NT, Nixon-Haldeman-Ehrlichman, Conversation No. 819-2, Oval Office, December 11, 1972, 11:07 a.m. to 2:25 p.m. (handling, kill).

27. George Lardner Jr. and Walter Pincus, "Nixon Ordered Tapes Destroyed," *Washington Post*, October 30, 1997 (overseeing); "A Fateful Trial Closes a Sorry Chapter," *Time*, January 13, 1975 (key figure); AOP, xiv (Kutler); Frost, *I Gave Them a Sword*, pp. 200–202, 243; Ehrlichman, *Witness to Power*, p. 60 (countless, rambling); Martin Levine, "An Interview with John Ehrlichman," *Book Digest*, May 1982 (chewing, days).

28. Thompson, *The Nixon Presidency*, p. 138 (didn't know what the truth was, particular moment); HJCW, 1:103 (incoherence); HJCW, III: 356 (genuinely confused); Associated Press, "Nixon Ill-Informed, Magruder Says," *Staten Island Advance*, June 13, 1974; Dean, *Blind Ambition*, pp. 184, 201; CI [Dean], January 5, 1989. Mitchell's press aide assessed his boss's "intellectual capabilities" far differently: "He had a quasi-photographic memory. He could remember the statistics and quotes and throw them back, and because of this he could jump from one subject to another, and back again"; see Landau interview, December 16, 1993.

29. WHT, 137–47.

30. SSC, IV: 1631; SSC, VI: 2297–98, 2321–24; WHT, 132–81; HJC, III: 1120–33; HJCW, II: 128–32, 203, 262–63, 300; UVM, 8087–89; HJC summary, July 4, 1974; *Brief on Behalf of the President of the United States, Richard Nixon, to the Committee on the Judiciary, Ninety-third Congress, United States House of Representatives*, July 19, 1974, pp. 40–52. In all, between July 1972 and March 1973, the seven Watergate defendants, their families, and attorneys received $429, 500 in hush money.

THE BIG ENCHILADA

1. Author's transcript, NT, Nixon-Ziegler, Conversation No. 164-2, Camp David, April 28, 1973, 8:21 a.m. to 8:41 a.m.

2. WHT, 181–94; SSC, III: 1000; HJCW, II: 251; THD, 592.

3. THD, 605; WHT, 322, 510, 649; SSC, III: 1001; SSC, IV: 1394–95, 1650, 1663; SSC, VII: 2853; HJCW, I: 206; HJCW, II: 132, 165, 180, 251; UVM, 3211, 10015; SSCEX, Dean; Dean, *Blind Ambition*, p. 210.

4. HJCW, II: 251; WHT, 194–222; "Comparisons Between Passages in the White House and Committee Transcripts," *New York Times*, July 10, 1974. The first version of the infamous "stonewall" transcript, leaked by House staff members, appeared in the *Times* on June 21, 1973; it differed in significant respects from the final committee version, published July 10. Both differed, in turn, with the version prepared by White House counsel, who, among other things, had Nixon concluding not

with "save the plan," but "save it for them," a reading that made more sense in light of Nixon's overall thrust, which concerned the protection of aides, not a specific "plan." When the committee versions appeared, major news media downplayed or ignored Nixon's second, more exculpatory set of remarks: The *Washington Post*, for example, bannered the indistinct "stonewall" segment across its front page, burying the rest on an inside page, while *Newsweek* omitted the second segment altogether; see Price, *With Nixon*, pp. 281–82.

5. Walter Rugaber, "Watergate Spy Says Defendants Were Under 'Political Pressure' to Admit Guilt and Keep Silent," and "Remarks by Principals in Watergate Sentencings," *New York Times*, March 24, 1973; *CBS Evening News*, March 24, 1973; "Mrs. Mitchell Fears Plot to Tie Watergate to Husband," *New York Times*, March 28, 1973; Walter Rugaber, "McCord Reported to Link Mitchell to Bugging Plot," *New York Times*, March 29, 1973; SSC memo of Interviews with James W. McCord by Samuel Dash [and] Fred Thompson, [conducted] March 23 [1973], March 24 [1973] [and] April 13, 1973, [filed] May 9, 1973, RG 460 WSPF Investigative Files, *U.S. v. Mitchell* (Jencks), McCord, Box 77, NARA; SSCEX, McCord; THD, 595–96; author's transcript, NT, Nixon-Haldeman, Conversation No. 425-26, EOB Office, March 28, 1973, 8:50 p.m. to 9:09 p.m. (Good Lord); Knappman, *Watergate*, pp. 24–25.

6. SSC, IV: 1579, 1649; Dean, *Blind Ambition*, p. 212.

7. SSCEX, Magruder; Magruder, *An American Life*, pp. 338–45; SSC, IV: 1379; UVM, 4634–39. Magruder said his visit to New York was undertaken at Mitchell's request, a claim on which Mitchell was apparently never questioned. *The Haldeman Diaries* also suggests (p. 611) the meeting was Mitchell's idea, but the White House

tapes make clear Magruder had been angling for such a meeting; see WHT, 231, 253. In his Senate testimony, and again at *U.S. v. Mitchell*, Magruder said it was Mitchell's idea that they meet with Haldeman; yet in his book, Magruder depicted himself proposing the session with Haldeman.

8. SSCEX, Magruder; SSCEX, Dean; WHT, 229, 288, 514; SSC, III: 1006–7; SSC, IV: 1634; UVM, 3276–77, 4638; THD, 615–22; AOP, 262–79; Magruder, *An American Life*, pp. 342–43; Dean, *Blind Ambition*, pp. 222–25; CI, November 2, 1988.

9. WHT, 222–66, 279, 283–341; CI, November 3, 1987 (kettle).

A GREAT TRIAL

1. CI, May 19, 1988 (tarnished), July 1, 1988 (drag, picture).

2. Stans interview; Dean, *Blind Ambition*, pp. 236–47; WH memo for The Files [from John Dean], Re: Meeting with John Mitchell/ Washington, D.C. Law Office/Time: 1:00–2:20 PM/April 10, 1973, [filed] April 12, 1973, at SSC, III: 1308–10, SSC, IV: 1679–80. Asked about Dean's refusal to "wire" himself, Mitchell said: "I wish the hell he had, so we would have an accurate description of what took place, not just his recollection." Mitchell said Dean never divulged that he had begun cooperating with the prosecutors.

Operation Sandwedge was the first proposal for a CRP intelligence plan. Circulated by Jack Caulfield in late 1971—with John Dean's encouragement—it was rejected "out of hand" by Mitchell, who liked Caulfield but doubted his qualifications. Assigned once to protect Mitchell on a flight to Key Biscayne, Caulfield discovered upon touchdown that he'd left his gun inside the American Airlines lounge at National Airport. "That was the end of Caulfield, as far as I was concerned,"

Mitchell chuckled years later; see SSC, IV: 1444 and CI, May 19, 1988.

3. HJC transcript of Haldeman-Magruder telephone conversation, April 14, 1973, at HJC, IV: 709–15; WHT, 300 (guilty as hell), 340–43; UVM, 8123–25; HJC transcript of Mitchell-Ehrlichman meeting, April 14, 1973, at HJC, IV: 725–68. Asked later why he secretly taped Mitchell, Ehrlichman said he had employed the technique on a number of occasions, so "I would be in a position afterward to say exactly what happened." Asked if Mitchell and the others were aware they were being recorded, Ehrlichman answered sheepishly: "In the—in the main, no"; see *CBS Evening News*, June 6, 1973.

4. WHT, 243 (*60 Minutes*), 341–78.

5. SSCEX, Magruder; Magruder, *An American Life*, pp. 345–56.

6. THD, 618; LaRue interviews; Seymour M. Hersh, "Charges Likely," *New York Times*, April 19, 1973.

7. Denny Walsh, "Mitchell Retains Prosecutor's Friend," *New York Times*, April 20, 1973; William Hundley, interview with author, March 11, 1992; "Legends in the Law: A Conversation with William G. Hundley," *Washington Lawyer*, November 2001.

8. WHT, 733–49; *CBS Morning News* and *CBS Midday News*, April 19, 1973; Seymour M. Hersh, "Mitchell Now Says He Heard Bugging Plot Three Times in 1972, but Rejected It," *New York Times*, April 20, 1973; *CBS Morning News*, *CBS Midday News*, and *CBS Evening News*, April 20, 1973; "Ex-Attorney General Halted by U.S. Guard" and "Transcript of Mitchell's News Conference," *New York Times*, April 21, 1973; "Watergate: The Dam Bursts," *Newsweek*, April 30, 1973; "Text of Indictment"; UVM, 8126–29, 8202–6, 8334; "Mitchell Brief Says Silbert Warned Him in '73 of Indictment," *New York Times*, August 5, 1975. Daniel Schorr reported that Mitchell "admitted to the grand jury

that he authorized payment of legal fees and expenses for the Watergate defendants"—an assertion that was almost certainly false. While most of Mitchell's grand jury testimony remains sealed, he never admitted as much in any other forum, and the WSPF never cited such grand jury testimony at *U.S. v. Mitchell*.

9. Lynn Rosellini, "Prophetic Protestations," *Newsday*, April 22, 1973; *CBS Morning News* and *CBS Midday News*, April 25, 1973; *CBS Morning News*, April 27, 1973; Charlotte Curtis, "Martha Mitchell Testifies in Civil Suit," *New York Times*, May 4, 1973, and "Mrs. Nixon's Aide Disputes Mrs. Mitchell," *New York Times*, May 5, 1973; "Mrs. Mitchell Tells Nixon to Quit," *Newsday*, May 7, 1973; William Sherman, "Martha's Alive and Kicking," *New York Daily News*, May 14, 1973; *Newsweek* and *Time*, May 21, 1973; "Prisoner of Fifth Avenue," *Time*, June 25, 1973; "Excerpts from Kissinger's News Conference," *New York Times*, August 24, 1973 (orgy).

10. "Summer of Judgment: The Watergate Hearings," PBS program, [aired] July 27, 1983 (80 million); Gladys Engel Lang and Kurt Lang, *The Battle of Public Opinion: The President, the Press, and the Polls During Watergate* (Columbia University Press, 1983), pp. 62–93. On Ervin, see Kutler, pp. 256, 370–71; Nixon, *Memoirs: Volume 2*, pp. 289, 445–46; Paul R. Glancy, *Just a Country Lawyer: A Biography of Senator Sam Ervin* (Indiana University Press, 1974), pp. 161–99, 218, 236–44; Bruce Allen, *Fortas: The Rise and Ruin of a Supreme Court Justice* (Wm. Morrow, 1988), p. 407; Bill M. Wise, ed., *The Wisdom of Sam Ervin* (Ballantine Books, 1973); Herb Altman, ed., *Quotations from Chairman Sam: The Wit and Wisdom of Senator Sam Ervin* (Harrow Books, 1973); "And the Mess Goes On,"

Newsweek, May 21, 1973; AOP, 205; *CBS Evening News*, February 19, 1973 (Cronkite); and CI, September 29, 1988 (senile). On Dash, see SS-CEX, E. Howard Hunt, May 14, 1973 (early morning); *Dash v. Mitchell*, Tom Wolfe, et al., "How Has the Most Famous Third-Rate Burglary Affected Your Life?" *New York*, October 22, 1973; Clancy, *Just a Country Lawyer*, pp. 203–4; William V. Shannon and Stanley Tretick, *They Could Not Trust the King: Watergate and the American People* (Macmillan Publishing, 1974), pp. 70–74; George V. Higgins, *The Friends of Richard Nixon* (Ballantine Books, 1976), pp. 263–64; and Victor Lasky, *It Didn't Start with Watergate* (Dial Press, 1977), pp. 319–20. On Nixon's low opinion of Thompson, see George Lardner Jr., "Baker Says He Didn't Want Supreme Court Seat," *Washington Post*, December 19, 1998. By the early 1970s, 97 percent of American homes contained a television set, with one in three homes boasting two or more sets; see Edwin Diamond, *The Tin Kazoo: Television, Politics, and the News* (MIT Press, 1975), p. 13.

11. "Martha Belts a Reporter," *Daily News*, June 20, 1973; "Martha Meets the Press," *Washington Post*, June 21, 1973; McLendon, *Martha*, p. 281 (insults).

12. "Prisoner of Fifth Avenue," *Time; CBS Morning News*, June 27, 1973; "Lawyer Says Mitchell Won't Implicate Nixon," *New York Times*, June 29, 1973; *CBS Evening News,* July 2, 1973; Mary McCarthy, *The Mask of State: Watergate Portraits* (Harvest, 1975), p. 39 (Observer); McLendon, *Martha*, pp. 280–88; Sandy Hobbs Perk, interview with author, May 1, 1992. Mitchell met with the committee staff in executive session on July 9; but unlike Magruder and Dean, who were trading their testimony for lenient plea deals, Mitchell deferred ex-

tensive interrogation until his public session.

13. SSC, IV: 1601–36.
14. SSC, IV: 1636–52. At trial, Mitchell said his answer to Thompson related "solely to the motivation and rationale for the actions that I did take, [and was] not an affirmation of the recitation of events that Mr. Thompson had in his question"; see UVM, 8336.
15. SSC, IV: 1653–81, 1810–13.
16. WHT, 255; SSC, IV: 1500–03; SSC, V: 1869–92. The official Senate transcript of Mitchell's testimony contained numerous errors, including an inaccurate rendering of his "great trial" line; the version cited above was taken from a videotape.
17. Lang and Lang, *The Battle of Public Opinion*, p. 77; Diamond, *The Tin Kazoo*, p. 44 (Godfather); *CBS Evening News*, July 10–12, 1973; *CBS Evening News*, April 5, 1973 (Sevareid); Evan Drossman and Edward W. Knappman, eds., *Watergate and the White House*, Volume 2, *July–December 1973* (Facts on File, 1974), pp. 139–42 (editorials); McCarthy, *The Mask of State*, pp. 51–69; H. Dale Crockett, *Focus on Watergate: An Examination of the Moral Dilemma of Watergate in the Light of Civil Religion* (Mercer University Press, 1982), pp. 59–61; Plato Cacheris, interview with author, September 8, 1993.

BLEED FOR ME

1. *CBS Morning News*, April 5, 1974.
2. Russell Long, interview with author, May 10, 1996.
3. Harry Schlegel, "Martha: Let Mayor Switch," *Daily News*, March 8, 1971 (defender); "Washington's Own Martha," *Newsweek*, November 30, 1970 (liberated); Myra MacPherson, "Nixon Tells Martha to Keep Punching," *Washington Post*, May 27, 1970 (respect); Healy, "Martha Always Says

Mouthful" (strawberry); Michaelson, "She'd Love to Go Back" (charm). "I just resent this women's lib business," Martha reaffirmed; see *CBS Evening News*, March 1, 1973.

4. Thomas O'Toole, "Martha and the Moon Rocks," *Washington Post*, February 13, 1971; Shelton, "Martha Mitchell Plays Role" (river); "Mrs. Mitchell Assails Court's 'Nine Old Men,'" *New York Times*, April 22, 1971; "An Early Morning Interview with Martha Mitchell," *Washington Post*, February 20, 1971 (Barbara Walters); Schlegel, "Martha: Let Mayor Switch."

5. Michaelson, "She'd Love to Go Back" (ten to twenty, slaves); "The Southern Belle," *Washington Post*, May 24, 1970 (colored, Negroes); Kandy Stroud, "Between Bites with Martha," *Women's Wear Daily*, January 25, 1971 (Jewish race).

6. Michaelson, "She'd Love to Go Back" (sick); "The Southern Belle," *Washington Post* (wonderful); "Mrs. Mitchell Said to Have F.B.I. Guard," *New York Times*, July 14, 1970 (Canada); Associated Press, "Martha: 'The War Stinks,'" *Washington Post*, September 8, 1970; Thomas, *Dateline*, pp. 231–32.

7. Dorothy McCardle, "Just One of the Boys: Mitchell Party Hears High-Level Humor," *Washington Post*, March 8, 1971.

8. Jennings interview; WH transcript of Ehrlichman–[Martha] Mitchell conversation, WHSF—SMOF, JDE Subject File, 1971 telephone conversations, Box 28, NARA. Asked why Martha never prevailed on John Mitchell to get her son deployed stateside—a favor well within his power to perform—Jennings explained: "My feeling was that . . . I wasn't any better than anyone else. And if this [being sent to Vietnam] happened, it was meant to happen, and I didn't want anybody interfering with it. . . . So I remember going to Key Biscayne, and I got John Mitchell alone and I explained to him that I had orders to Vietnam, and that I felt I should go, and that I was concerned that . . . if my mother found out that I was going, that she'd stop it somehow. . . . I'd felt at that point that John Mitchell would be an understanding stepfather, given his World War II combat experience. . . . And he did understand, and he said he respected my decisions and he would make sure that he didn't tell my mother."

9. Ehrlichman interview.

10. Harries interview; Chennault, *The Education of Anna*, pp. 173–99; Maxine Cheshire with John Greenya, *Maxine Cheshire, Reporter* (Houghton Mifflin, 1978), pp. 152–58.

11. Confidential sources, author interview (pregnant, women, affair); William F. Buckley Jr., "John Mitchell, R.I.P.," *National Review*, December 9, 1988; J. Robert Mitchell interview.

12. Action for a Separation, New York State Supreme Court, *Martha Mitchell v. John N. Mitchell*, May 10, 1974 (cruel and inhuman); Affidavit of Stephan H. Peskin, New York State Supreme Court, January 28, 1975 (leadership, Watergate break-in and cover-up); both in WCHC.

13. Answer to Complaint, *Mitchell v. Mitchell*, February 27, 1975, WCHC (disregarded, justify, alcohol, unfit, harassment); letter to Susie Morrison from John Mitchell, [undated; late 1973], provided to the author by Morrison (sick). Martha denied Mitchell's accusations, arguing she was "in all respects a dutiful wife [who] maintained her home in a loving and devoted manner"; see Complaint Action for Separation, Index No. 33052/74, [undated; 1974–1975], WCHC.

14. Mitchell charged his belongings were "thrown into a heap on the floor of the foyer" of the Fifth Avenue apartment. Martha's lawyer lamely countered that

his client had merely "placed in the foyer [Mitchell's belongings] so they could be picked up"; see Affidavit of William C. Herman, August 12, 1975, WCHC.

15. Affidavit of Lloyd George Soll in *Soll, Connelly, and Marshall v. John N. Mitchell*, New York State Supreme Court, Index No. 15550–1974, [filed] January 3, 1976, WCHC; UPI, "Mrs. Mitchell Says Her Husband Left Her on Lawyers' Advice," *New York Times*, September 17, 1973. That Mrs. Mitchell had good reason to believe her marriage was soon to dissolve was evident from the *New York Times* headline of August 27, 1973—fifteen days before Mitchell walked out—that read: "A Friend Reports Mrs. Mitchell Plans to Ask Separation."

16. Affidavit of Richard Creditor, October 22, 1975, WCHC.

17. Affidavit of John N. Mitchell, August 18, 1975, WCHC.

18. Creditor affidavit (cut back); Affidavit by John N. Mitchell, October 1974, WCHC.

19. Mitchell affidavit, October 1974 (abused, largesse, changed, severe, sustain, expected, phone, dry cleaning, realty); Affidavit of Marvin B. Segal, October 30, 1974 (Amtrak, exorbitant), WCHC.

20. Segal affidavit. The $90,000 Mitchell had spent on lawyers' fees was, according to Segal, "over and above any legal fees paid" in his behalf by the Nixon campaign committee, which demanded Mitchell be acquitted on all criminal charges before it would cover any of his legal costs. Nor would Mitchell's lawyers cut him the slack of advancing his fees, claiming they were "prohibited" from doing so.

21. Creditor affidavit; Segal affidavit; Order of Hon. Manuel A. Gomez, Justice, Supreme Court of the State of New York, December 2, 1974, WCHC.

22. Handwritten note [no addressee]

from Martha Mitchell, attached to U.S. Individual Income Tax Return [1040] form, 1973, Martha Beall Mitchell; U.S. Individual Income Tax Return [1040] form, 1973, John N. and Martha B. Mitchell; letter to Martha Mitchell from William C. Herman, April 16, 1975; and letter to Marvin B. Segal from William C. Herman, Re: *Mitchell v. Mitchell*, April 28, 1975; all in WCHC.

23. Affidavit of Marvin B. Segal, February 1975, WCHC; Rhoda Amon, "Martha Mitchell: 'I'm Basically a Housewife,'" *Newsday*, March 9, 1975 (your fault).

24. Complaint Action for Separation, Index No. 33052/74, [undated; February 28, 1975], WCHC; McLendon, *Martha*, pp. 223–25. McLendon's claim generated significant press coverage; see, for example, "John Mitchell's Martha Tells All," *New York Post*, May 17, 1979. "John Mitchell never pulled any punches," the tabloid reported, "except, perhaps, for the one he threw at his late wife, Martha, knocking out one of her front teeth."

25. UPI, "Mrs. Mitchell Says Her Husband Left Her" (never had a fight). On Martha's altercation with Marty, see "Martha Admits Scuffling with Daughter at School," *New York Post*, December 12, 1974; and McLendon, *Martha*, p. 386.

26. Ernest Leogrande, "Off the Shelves," *Daily News*, September 17, 1975.

27. UPI, "Martha Mitchell Has Blood Disease," *New York Times*, October 6, 1975; Associated Press, "Doctor Reports Martha Mitchell Has a Malignant Bone Disease," *New York Times*, October 8, 1975; William Hines, "Martha Has Bone Cancer," *New York Post*, October 8, 1975; Donnie Radcliffe, "Flamboyant Martha Mitchell Dies at 57," *Washington Post*, June 1, 1976 (ribs, vertebrae).

28. "Aftermath: Martha Mitchell," *Wash-*

ington Post, April 18, 1976 (paying the bills); McClendon, *Martha*, p. 446 (ignore); Hundley interview (barred); Fleming interview.

29. "Aftermath," *Washington Post* (fractured); "Martha Has an Operation Here; Is OK," *Daily News*, April 21, 1976 (thin, weak); "Martha Mitchell," *New York Times*, April 21, 1976 (spirits).

30. Affidavit of Martha Mitchell, May 12, 1976; Affidavit of John N. Mitchell, May 17, 1976; Affidavit of Marvin B. Segal, May 17, 1976 (exacerbate), all in WCHC.

31. Order of Hon. Manuel A. Gomez, Justice, Supreme Court of the State of New York, May 20, 1976; "Notes on People," *New York Times*, May 21, 1976 ($36,000); letter to Linda Francis from William C. Herman, July 2, 1976; and letter to Catherine Foster from William C. Herman, July 12, 1976.

32. Harry Stathos, "Martha Mitchell, 57, Dies of Cancer," *Daily News*, June 1, 1976; Radcliffe, "Flamboyant Martha"; McLendon, *Martha*, pp. 422–23.

33. McLendon, *Martha*, pp. 427, 443–51; Dorothy McCardle, "Martha's Party at Blair House," *Washington Post*, November 20, 1970.

HANDS OF THE GODS

1. Author's transcript, NT, Nixon-Haig, Conversation No. 434-9, EOB Office, May 9, 1973, 6:35 p.m. to 8:26 p.m.

2. Drossman and Knappman, *Watergate*, pp. 80–84. Agnew formally acknowledged taking payments in 1967 "and other years," but denied they "in any way" influenced his official actions. Elsewhere he protested his innocence; see Aaron Latham, "Spiro Agnew Looks for a Good Time," *Playboy*, August 1977; and Spiro T Agnew, *Go Quietly . . . or else* (Wm. Morrow, 1980). In judging Mitchell "guilty" along with Agnew, Cazenovia College professor John Robert Greene cited a previously unpublished tape from April 14, 1973, featuring Nixon, Haldeman, and Ehrlichman. On the tape, Haldeman can be heard relaying the vice president's claim that Joel Kline, a Maryland businessman who pleaded guilty to numerous crimes before cooperating in the Agnew probe, had, at some unspecified time, visited Mitchell's office carrying "a bag of cash which he turned over to Mitchell and which . . . was allegedly involved in [Kline] receiving some very good government contracts." Greene, however, ignored Haldeman's prefatory remark that Agnew had told this story "to scare us into being worried about his case." Ehrlichman said only that he had heard the same story from David Shapiro, Charles Colson's lawyer; Nixon was incredulous: "I can't believe that John Mitchell would take money in his office." The truth emerged more than a year later, during a bench conference in *U.S. v. Mitchell*, when Mitchell's attorney told Judge Sirica: "Mr. Colson made an allegation to Mr. Ehrlichman that somehow Mr. Mitchell was taking kickbacks from a Baltimore contractor. Now when that was going to come out before the Ervin committee, Mr. Colson's lawyer, Mr. Shapiro, called me up and said, 'Oh, by the way, you know that information we passed on was entirely wrong' "; see UVM, 9804–05. Neither Agnew's memoir nor the definitive account of his case, by two *Washington Post* reporters, contained any such allegations against Mitchell; see John Robert Greene, *The Limits of Power: The Nixon and Ford Administrations* (Indiana University Press, 1992), pp. 166–87; Agnew, *Go Quietly*; and Richard M. Cohen and Jules Witcover, *A Heartbeat Away: The Investigation and Resignation of Vice President Spiro T. Agnew* (Bantam, 1974). Alexander Haig believed Agnew's downfall was part of a

"conspiracy" by the Democrats. "They already were in liaison with the Baltimore investigation," Haig said. "They saw the prospect of a converging double-impeachment, and the turnover of the government to the Speaker of the House [Carl Albert], a Democrat—and also a drunk." Haig recalled that when he was named chief of staff, in April 1973, Democratic lawyer Joe Califano warned: "Al, don't do it." Asked why, Califano replied: "Don't you know we have this guy? *We got both of 'em!*" Agnew's grand jury probe was not yet publicly known; see Haig interview.

3. Levine (decisive); Thompson, *The Nixon Presidency*, p. 144 (ticket); letter to the author from Spiro T. Agnew, March 20, 1993 (business); CI, July 10 and August 13, 1986 (decent). As his troubles grew, Agnew offered an olive branch to the news media, against which he was the first national figure, in November 1969, to raise the cry of liberal bias. "I do not apologize for the content of my early criticism," he said, "but I freely admit that it could have been stated less abrasively"; see *CBS Morning News*, May 3, 1973.

4. Richard Ben-Veniste and George Frampton Jr., *Stonewall: The Real Story of the Watergate Prosecution* (Simon & Schuster, 1977), p. 357; Ostrow, "Mitchell Offered to Take Cover-up Blame"; Emery, *Watergate*, pp. 487–92; James Neal, interview with author, May 20, 1992. Daniel Schorr reported that the government offered Mitchell a one-count plea, which he refused, and that he made an unspecified counteroffer, which the prosecutors refused; see *CBS Evening News*, February 27, 1974. John Dean claimed Mitchell was still plea-bargaining after Nixon resigned; see Dean, *Blind Ambition*, p. 363.

5. "The Watergate Indictments," *CBS Evening News,* [aired] March 1, 1974; Anthony Ripley, "Federal Grand Jury Indicts 7 Nixon Aides on Charges of Conspiracy on Watergate; Haldeman, Ehrlichman, Mitchell on List"; Bill Kovach, "Ruling by Sirica Imposes Silence on All Concerned"; and Linda Charlton, "The Scene in Sirica's Court: A Historic 13 Minutes," all in *New York Times*, March 2, 1974; "The Indictments," *New York Times*, March 3, 1974; *CBS Evening News*, March 9, 1974 (*Sieg Heil!*); Anthony Ripley, "7 Ex-Nixon Aides Plead Not Guilty to Cover-up Plot," *New York Times*, March 10, 1974; "The Trials of the Grand Jury," *Time*, March 11, 1974; Emery, *Watergate*, p. 489 (strategy); Leon Jaworski, *The Right and the Power: The Prosecution of Watergate* (Reader's Digest Press, 1976), p. 109; Ben-Veniste and Frampton, *Stonewall*, pp. 249–50; and Seymour M. Hersh, "Nixon's Last Cover-up: The Tapes He Wants the Archives to Suppress," *New Yorker*, December 14, 1992, which featured the first publication of Mitchell's arraignment photos, commonly known as "mug shots."

6. Letters to Susie Morrison from John Mitchell, [undated; 1973–74], provided to the author by Morrison.

7. William M. Blair, "Panel's Lawyers Query Mitchell," *New York Times*, July 6, 1974; HJCW, II: 113–217; *CBS Evening News*, July 10, 1974; Edward Mezvinsky, *A Term to Remember* (Coward, McCann & Geoghegan, 1977), pp. 164–65. Robert Novak later decried the "false conception . . . that the impeachment of Nixon was unbiased and nonpartisan. . . . The efforts by Chairman Rodino to get Nixon were very strong. Nixon made enough mistakes that he couldn't garner enough Republican support, but you can't imagine how much the Democrats hated Nixon—I think even more than Republicans hate Clinton"; see "Novak: You Say You Want a Revolution," *Hotline*, March 27, 2000.

8. UVM, Mitchell Motion for Leave to Depose Richard M. Nixon, and If Nec-

essary, for a Continuance and Unsequestration of Jury, December 4, 1974 (emphases added); Cacheris interview; Hundley interview. Hundley said he "probably" cleared the December 4 motion with Mitchell, who "gave me a pretty free hand" to criticize Nixon but recoiled from doing so himself. Hundley also subpoenaed the White House for documents and tapes; see *CBS Evening News*, September 13, 1973.

9. *CBS Evening News*, August 19 and 22, 1974; Knappman and Drossman, *Watergate*, p. 154 (Colson); Ben-Veniste and Frampton, *Stonewall*, p. 316; Silbert interview; WSPF memo to Mr. Cox from G. Goldman, Subject: Gordon Strachan, September 25, 1972 [*sic*; 1973]; WSPF memo to R. Ben-Veniste from G. Goldman, Subject: Status of Gordon Strachan, January 15, 1974; and WSPF memo to Henry S. Ruth Jr. from Peter M. Kreindler, Subject: Gordon Strachan, February 11, 1975, all in RG 460 WSPF—WGTF, Investigative Files, Defendants' Files, Gordon Strachan, Box 124, NARA.

10. UVM, 1–2610a; Dean, *Blind Ambition*, pp. 380–81.

11. UVM, 3206 (discern), 3579 (dates), 4063 (perfect), 3716–31 (throw, an objection), 3984–4007 (what he knows), 4100 (barred), 4401 (latitude), 5922 (forgot), 6028 (keep track), 6561 (maybe), 8101 (mocked); *CBS Evening News*, October 23, 1974; Higgins, *The Friends of Richard Nixon*; Philip B. Kurland, *Watergate and the Constitution* (University of Chicago Press, 1978), pp. 73–74; Renata Adler, *Canaries in the Mineshaft: Essays on Politics and Media* (St. Martin's Press, 2001), pp. 345–77. Examining Sirica's life and career more closely than any previous researcher, Adler uncovered the startling fact that the famous Watergate judge, a former boxer, was himself indicted in 1927 on charges of

tax evasion and conspiring to fix the famous Dempsey-Tunney "long count" prizefight; for unknown reasons, the case never went to trial.

12. UVM, 8092–110 (enlighten, cheap), 8141–44 (Mexico), 8177 (presume), 8216–48 (urge), 11,555–714 (Neal's closing argument); *CBS Morning News*, October 22, 1974; *CBS Evening News*, November 25–26, 1974; *CBS Morning News*, November 27–28, 1974; Lesley Oelsner, "Prosecution Ends Case in Cover-up; Defense Starts," *New York Times*, November 26, 1974; Lesley Oelsner, "Prosecutor Says Mitchell 'Stonewalled' on Cover-up," *New York Times*, November 28, 1974; Lesley Oelsner, "Jurors Hear Dean Termed Perjurer," *New York Times*, December 21, 1974; Lesley Oelsner, "Jury Hears Nixon Termed 'Maestro,' " *New York Times*, December 24, 1974; Lesley Oelsner, "Watergate Jury Receives Charge; Weighs Fate of 5," *New York Times*, December 31, 1974; "Excerpts from Sirica's Charge to Cover-up Jurors," *New York Times*, December 31, 1974; *CBS Morning News*, January 2, 1975 (first real); Ehrlichman, *Witness to Power*, pp. 313–14; Hundley interview; Neal interview; "Legends in the Law," *Washington Lawyer*; Tony Parkinson, interview with author, August 2002.

13. Lesley Oelsner, "Haldeman Tapes Played by Jury," *New York Times*, January 1, 1975; *CBS Evening News*, January 1–2, 1975; "The Watergate Verdicts," *CBS Evening News*, [aired] January 1, 1975; *CBS Morning News*, January 2, 1975; Lesley Oelsner, "Watergate Jury Convicts Mitchell, Haldeman, Ehrlichman and Mardian in Cover-up Case; Acquits Parkinson"; Marjorie Hunter, "Few Tears, a Bit of Anger as the Verdicts Are Read"; Ernest Holsendolph, "Aloof Jury Foreman: John A. Hoffar"; "Guilty" [editorial], all in *New York Times*, January 2, 1975; Muriel Dobbin,

"Mitchell, Haldeman, Ehrlichman, Mardian All Guilty of Obstruction of Justice; Parkinson Is Acquitted," *Baltimore Sun*, January 2, 1975; UPI, "4 Nixon Aides Guilty, 1 Acquitted"; "Nixon Silence Seen Basis for Appeals"; " 'Watergate 4' React to Verdict"; "Jurors Did Not Smile"; and "Watergate Jury: Mostly Black and Female," all in *Philadelphia Daily News*, January 2, 1975; "A Fateful Trial Closes a Sorry Chapter," *Time*, January 13, 1975; "Sirica, 88, Dies; Persistent Judge in Fall of Nixon," *New York Times*, August 15, 1992.

MAXWELL

1. Franz Kafka, *Selected Short Stories of Franz Kafka* (Random House, 1952), pp. x–xi.
2. Linda Charlton, "Dean, Kalmbach, Magruder Freed from Prison by Sirica," *New York Times*, January 9, 1975; "Magruder Says Prisoners Might Try to Kill Mitchell," *New York Times*, January 15, 1975; Lesley Oelsner, "4 Ex-Nixon Aides Lose Bid to Void Cover-up Verdict," *New York Times*, February 15, 1975; Lesley Oelsner, "Mitchell, Haldeman, Ehrlichman Are Sentenced to 21/2 to 8 Years, Mardian to 10 Months to 3 Years," *New York Times*, February 22, 1975; Robert E. Cuthriell, ed., *Historic Documents of 1975* (Congressional Quarterly, 1976), pp. 141–51; Federal Document Clearing House transcript of remarks by Pat Buchanan at American Conservative Union Dinner, October 24, 1995 (turn 'em down).
3. "19 on Airliner Killed in Crash at Nantucket" and "Gordon E. Dean Led A.E.C. 3 Years," both in *New York Times*, August 16, 1958; Maxine Cheshire, "John Mitchell: Renewing a 20-Year Friendship," *Washington Post*, March 22, 1975; Nick Thimmesch, "The Final Days of John Mitchell,"

New York, June 27, 1977; Mary Gore Dean interview; Hundley interview; Annie Groer, "Style with a Few Tales to Tell," *Washington Post*, January 27, 2005. One newspaper erroneously reported that Mitchell "quietly" married Mrs. Dean in a ceremony at Marwood on October 15, 1981: a complete fabrication. "I did not marry Mr. Mitchell," she said flatly. "Marriage never came up"; see Rosemarie Wittman Lamb, "Watergate 10 Years Later: Where Are They Now?" *New York Daily News*, June 13, 1982.
4. Lesley Oelsner, "Nixon Questioned About Watergate for a Grand Jury," *New York Times*, June 28, 1975; EN, July 8, 1972; notes of Robert Mardian on his conversation with Richard Nixon, October 14, 1976, provided to the author by Mardian.
5. Rita Delfiner, "Mitchell: 'Automatic' Disbarment Now," *New York Post*, January 8, 1975; "Mitchell Asks Hearing on Disbarment," *Washington Post*, June 10, 1975; Morris Kaplan, "Mitchell Is Disbarred in State for His Watergate Conviction," *New York Times*, July 4, 1975; "Mitchell Brief Says Trial Was Tainted," *New York Times*, August 2, 1975; "Prosecutors Allege Testimony by Nixon Was Not Necessary," *New York Times*, October 16, 1975; Lesley Oelsner, "4 in Watergate Appeal Say Sirica Barred a Fair Trial," *New York Times*, January 7, 1976; "John Mitchell Asks N.Y. to Practice Law," *Washington Post*, May 5, 1976; "Mitchell Loses Plea; He's Still Disbarred," *New York Post*, July 17, 1976; letter to John Mitchell from Ronald Reagan, August 27, 1976, JMRC; John M. Crewdson, "Mardian Conviction on Watergate Upset," *New York Times*, October 13, 1976; notes of Robert Mardian on his conversations with John Mitchell, January 27 and May 25, 1977, provided to the author by Mardian; "High Court Reported to Oppose a Review of Nixon Aides' Case," *New York Times*,

April 22, 1977; "Court Rebuffs Watergate Group's Bid to File Memo," *New York Times*, May 3, 1977; Lesley Oelsner, "Supreme Court Bars Plea by Ehrlichman, Haldeman, Mitchell," *New York Times*, May 24, 1977; "Mitchell and Haldeman Lose Plea on Sentences," *New York Times*, June 1, 1977; "Sirica Says Haldeman and Mitchell Will Probably Go to Jail June 22," *New York Times*, June 3, 1977; "Haldeman Joins Mitchell as Court Sets Prison Date," *New York Times*, June 7, 1977; Haynes Johnson, "One Last Flash for Mitchell, Haldeman," *Washington Post*, June 7, 1977; Thimmesch, "The Final Days"; "Supreme Court Disbars Mitchell and Ehrlichman," *Wall Street Journal*, November 1, 1977; Bill Gulley with Mary Ellen Reese, *Breaking Cover* (Simon & Schuster, 1980), pp. 240, 264–65 (compassion, covert); Mary Gore Dean interview; Baruch Korff, *The President and I* (Baruch Korff Foundation, 1995), pp. 119–22. Mardian's notes also contained some rare remarks by the ex-president on the "smoking gun" tape of June 23, 1972: "[Nixon] said it never was brought out that he and Haldeman were talking of 2 different things—He about the possible CIA involvement and Haldeman about hush money—Said 'You know that money was never paid.'"

6. Mardian notes; "John Mitchell to Serve Term at Ala. Prison," *Washington Post*, June 9, 1977 (LaRue); Fred Bruning, "Stone Walls Do Not Make Mitchell's Prison," *Newsday*, June 9, 1977 (despair, Maxwell Country Club); Joseph M. Treen, "The Attorney General Goes to Jail," *Newsday*, June 22, 1977 (when to eat, arrangements, elevator); Thimmesch, "The Final Days" (face jail, worries, flowers); Jon Bixby, "John Mitchell, Inmate," *Newsday*, July 28, 1977 (*The Godfather*, brief visit); Ronald James, "Sharing the 'Joint' with John Mitchell:

From Top Cop to Top Con," *Miami Magazine*, March 1979 (anxiety, rumors, king, cop, shiv); "Legends in the Law," *Washington Lawyer* (concerned, no-nonsense); Mary Gore Dean interview; Sandy Hobbs Perk, interview with author, May 1, 1992; Ken Ebbitt interview; Norman Carlson, interview with author, September 13, 1993; Korff, *The President and I*, p. 122; Martin Schram, interview with author, February 26, 1999 (slammer). Even in prison, Mitchell was not safe from death threats. Twenty days after his surrender, previously unpublished documents show, the FBI began investigating a phone call threatening to "assassinate John N. Mitchell if Mitchell does not commit suicide this week"; see FBI teletype from Mobile (62-0) to Director Routine, [Subject:] Unknown Subject, Anonymous Call from Individual Claiming to/Be President of the Impeachment and Assassination of Nixon/Federal Prison Camp, Maxwell Air Force Base, Montgomery/Alabama, July 12, 1977, FBIM.

7. *CBS Morning News* and *CBS Evening News*, June 22, 1977; "Haldeman Enters Jail in California; Mitchell to Begin His Term Today," *New York Times*, June 22, 1977; "Mitchell Enters Alabama Camp to Serve Term," *New York Times*, June 23, 1977; "John Mitchell Is Jeered as He Enters Prison," *Washington Post*; Dunne, "John Mitchell Jets to Ala."; "Nos. 24171-157 and 01489-163(B)," *Time*, July 4, 1977; Harry F. Rosenthal, "Mitchell Leaves Prison Friday: Is It Final Watergate Chapter?" *Staten Island Advance*, January 14, 1979 (personified); James, "Sharing the 'Joint'"; D. B. Green, "How Tough a Jew?" *The Jerusalem Report*, April 12, 1999 (Lansky); letter to Susie Morrison from John Mitchell, September 24, 1977, provided to the author by Morrison; "Legends in the Law," *Washington Lawyer*; Julia Wilkinson, "First Person Singular:

Plato Cacheris," *Washington Post Magazine*, January 12, 2003; Hundley interview; Harries interview; Anson, *Exile*, p. 214; Robert Lowell, *Little Man: The Life and Times of Meyer Lansky* (Little, Brown, 1992), p. 385. "I'm free, but look who's in jail now. Mitchell!" rejoiced Lansky, who playfully sent his bête noire a crate of Southern Comfort "with my best wishes."

8. "Mitchell, Haldeman Seek Shorter Terms," *New York Times*, September 17, 1977 (traumatic, sensitive); Ronald J. Ostrow, "Irked Haldeman, Ailing Mitchell Request Leniency," *Los Angeles Times*, September 17, 1977 (severest, mental, authorized by Mr. Mitchell, pockets); Anthony Marro, "Mitchell, Haldeman, Ehrlichman Win Reductions in Prison Terms" and "Excerpts of Statements to Judge Sirica by Haldeman, Ehrlichman, and Mitchell," *New York Times*, October 5, 1977 (tour, crippled, unfairness, penalty); "Mitchell Petitions Carter for Immediate Release," *New York Times*, October 20, 1977 (drugs, constant); Anthony Marro, "Mitchell to Get Furlough for Tests on Arthritic Hip," *New York Times*, December 21, 1977; "Mitchell Freed to Receive Hospital Cure for Arthritis," *Washington Post*, December 21, 1977 (painful, impaired); "Mitchell Must Undergo Surgery," *Washington Post*, January 14, 1978; "Mitchell 'Doing Well' in Hospital," *New York Times*, January 26, 1978; Jimmy Breslin, "Bell Rang 'Out' & Mitchell Got 4 Furloughs," *New York Daily News*, April 23, 1978; Cynthia R. Fagen, "Another Furlough for John Mitchell," *New York Post*, April 26, 1978; Richard Edmonds, "Mitchell's Fifth Prison Furlough Is a First," *New York Daily News*, April 27, 1978; Pete Hamill, "Mitchell, the Fabulous Invalid, Is Making Justice Ill," *New York Daily News*, April 28, 1978; "Legends in the Law," *Washington Lawyer*; Mitchell-Reed interview; Griffin Bell, interview with author, February 21, 1994. Breslin and Hamill were especially unmerciful during Mitchell's illness and furloughs. Breslin wrote that Mitchell "appears to be demonstrating further that our laws apply only to the poor and to those too stupid to retain connections somewhere in government," while Hamill, seemingly regretful that Mitchell "would not soon find himself sweating in a prison laundry, or stamping out license plates, or breaking brick in a quarry . . . humiliated by sadistic prison guards [or] gang raped," shrilly demanded that "somebody should bring him back to the slammer, where he belongs."

9. "Parole Examiners Hear Mitchell," *New York Times*, July 6, 1978; "John's Misery," *Staten Island Advance*, July 6, 1978; "Mitchell to Be Paroled After 19 Months in Jail," *Washington Post*, July 21, 1978; "Parole Panel Stonewalls Mitchell 6 More Months," *Staten Island Advance*, July 21, 1978; "Judge Denies Mitchell's Bid for Immediate Parole," *Los Angeles Times*, August 26, 1978; letters to Francis X. Maloney from John Mitchell, December 13, 1978, and January 13, 1979, provided to the author by Maloney; "Mitchell Again Given a Christmas Furlough," *New York Times*, December 17, 1978; *CBS Morning News* and *CBS Evening News*, January 19, 1979; "John Mitchell Leaving Jail, Last in Watergate to Exit," *Staten Island Advance*, January 19, 1979; "Mitchell, Last Watergate Prisoner, Is Freed on Parole," *New York Times*, January 20, 1979; Jack Bass, *Taming the Storm: The Life and Times of Judge Frank M. Johnson, Jr. and the South's Fight over Civil Rights* (Doubleday, 1993), pp. 276, 390–91, 487n; Harries interview; Leonard interview.

GHOST

1. E-mail to the author from Jill Mitchell-Reed, September 24, 2003.
2. Harries interview; WHT, 179; Anson, *Exile*, pp. 213–14; Richard Nixon, *In the Arena: A Memoir of Victory, Defeat and Renewal* (Pocket Books, 1991), p. 14.
3. WHT, 179 (the Mitchell subject); Nixon-Frost interview, September 8, 1977 (emphases added).
4. "Biographical Information on John Vincent Brennan, Major, United States Marine Corps," White House Press Release, February 1, 1969, NARA; *CBS Evening News,* February 11, 1982; *Global Research International, Inc. v. Ahmad Habbous, Pan East International and William Phalen,* Civ. Case No. 90–0695, U.S. District Court for the District of Columbia, [filed] March 26, 1990; Martin Tolchin, "Cameo Players in an '84 Arms Deal with Iraq: Nixon, Agnew, Ceauşescu," *New York Times,* June 1, 1990; "All the Ex-President's Men," *U.S. News & World Report,* June 4, 1990; "The Arming of Iraq," *Frontline,* PBS program, [aired] September 11, 1990; Maura Pierce, "John Mitchell Died Nearly Broke But Heirs Are Fighting Anyway," *The Washingtonian,* October 1990; *60 Minutes,* CBS News program, [aired] January 20, 1991; Sidney Blumenthal, "The Prime Republican," *New York Times,* November 24, 1991; Dan Fesperman, "Middleman Agnew Does It His Way," *Baltimore Sun,* March 7, 1993; CI, January 24, 1987 (impact), January 31, 1987 (Rio), June 5, 1987 (London), December 5, 1987 (Caymans); Jack Brennan, interview with author, March 9, 1992; Deborah Gore Dean interview; James Tully, interview with author, March 2, 1994; Stephen E. Ambrose, *Nixon: Ruin and Recovery, 1973–1990* (Touchstone, 1991), pp. 541–42; Adel Darwish and Gregory Alexander, *Unholy Babylon: The Secret History of Saddam's War* (St. Martin's Press, 1991), p. 153; Susan B. Trento, *The Power House: Robert Keith Gray and the Selling of Access and Influence in Washington* (St. Martin's Press, 1992), pp. 309–10; Joseph J. Trento, *Prelude to Terror: The Rogue CIA and the Legacy of America's Private Intelligence Network* (Carroll & Graf, 2005), pp. 290–310. When Global's connection to the Iraqis surfaced, on the eve of the Persian Gulf War, the news media painted it in sinister terms. The remarkable convergence of Saddam Hussein, Nicolae Ceauşescu, Sarkis Soghanalian, Nixon, Mitchell, and Spiro Agnew—who represented the Saudis in the uniform deal—delivered an irresistible storyline: *All the President's Men* meets *The Boys from Brazil.* But some got carried away. *60 Minutes* overstated the value of the deal by $100 million. PBS denounced "Richard Nixon and his friends supplying Romanian uniforms to Iraq," when in fact Nixon had nothing to do with the actual deal. Nixon biographer Stephen Ambrose hinted darkly, and without substantiation, that the deal bore some connection to the profitable sale of Nixon's New York town house to the Syrian government; a few paragraphs later, Ambrose conceded there was "no proof that Nixon did more than write a couple of letters for Brennan and Mitchell, who were men who had served him loyally and well, men to whom he owed many favors." And liberal essayist Sidney Blumenthal repeated the false claim about the Syrians.
5. John Kennedy, "John Mitchell Sued by Publisher," *Washington Post,* February 21, 1981; CI, May 5, 1988 (loves me), November 10, 1988 (Thimmesch); Mary Gore Dean interview; Hundley interview; Warren Burger, interview with author, August 25, 1994; Harries interview; Lawrence Knutson, interview with author, June 25, 2001 (gray); Publishing Agreement, Simon

& Schuster, Inc., and John N. Mitchell, July 21, 1975; Acknowledgment of Debt and Schedule of Repayment in *Simon & Schuster v. John Mitchell*, Supreme Court of the State of New York, County of New York, Case Index No. 3499/81, [filed] January 21, 1982; letter to Philip E. Taubman, Esq., from [unsigned—Simon & Schuster letterhead], Re: *Simon & Schuster v. John Mitchell*, March 18, 1988; Release and Accord and Satisfaction [by Simon & Schuster, dated] November 3, 1992, [filed] January 15, 1993; all in MPP. See also letters to Susie Morrison from John Mitchell, August 13, 1975, and September 25, 1975, provided to the author by Morrison; and letter to Steve King from John Mitchell [undated—July 1977], provided to the author by King.

6. Letter to the author from Tony Madison, August 6, 1993; e-mails to the author from Jill Mitchell-Reed, September 24, 2003, and November 25, 2003; Deborah Gore Dean interview; Jill Mitchell-Reed interview; Mary Gore Dean interview; Madison interview; J. Robert Mitchell interview.

7. "Pierce Resigns Position as Counsel at Treasury," *JET*, May 17, 1973; Philip Shenon, "Reagan Officials Got Big H.U.D. Fees, a U.S. Audit Finds," *New York Times*, April 29, 1989; Leslie Maitland, "Focus of H.U.D. Inquiry: A Woman of Influence and Ambition," *New York Times*, May 31, 1989; Debbie Howlett, "HUD Prober Not an 'Activist,'" *USA Today*, April 11, 1990; Martin Tolchin, "Grand Jury Indicts Ex-Aide to Reagan's Housing Chief," *New York Times*, April 29, 1992; Mike Brown, "Nunn Tied to Probe of HUD, Mitchell," *Louisville Courier-Journal*, June 26, 1992; "Ex-HUD Official Pleads Not Guilty," *New York Newsday*, September 14, 1992; Diana McLellan, "Deborah Gore Dean," *The Washingtonian*, October 1992; Matt Yancey,

"Former HUD Official Dean Wins Tactical Victory Before Conspiracy Trial," Associated Press, April 6, 1993; Pete Yost, "Dean Did Bidding of HUD Secretary Pierce, Lawyers Say," Associated Press, September 13, 1993; "Prosecutor Raps Former HUD Aide," *New York Daily News*, September 14, 1993; Pete Yost, "Former HUD Aide Singing About Boss' Political Deals," Associated Press, October 6, 1993; Michael York, "Dean Lays Blame on System at HUD," *Washington Post*, October 8, 1993; "Corruption Case Is Sent to Jurors," *New York Times*, October 22, 1993; Stephen Labaton, "Ex-Official Is Convicted in HUD Scandal of 80's," *New York Times*, October 27, 1993; "Ex-Housing Aide Gets 21 Months for Fraud," *New York Times*, February 26, 1994; Stanley Meisler, "Ex-HUD Aide Dean Sentenced to 21 Months," *Los Angeles Times*, February 26, 1994; David Johnston, "Former Housing Secretary Won't Be Charged in Investigation," *New York Times*, January 11, 1995; Susan Watters, "The Unsinkable Deborah Dean," *W*, December 1998; Groer, "Style with a Few Tales"; Deborah Gore Dean interview; *Audit of Section 8 Moderate Rehabilitation Program*, Office of the Inspector General, U.S. Department of Housing and Urban Development, [filed] April 26, 1989; Superseding Indictment, *United States of America v. Deborah Gore Dean*, United States District Court for the District of Columbia, Criminal [Case] No. 92–181–GAG [subsequently 92–181–TFH], [filed] July 7, 1992; Opinion, *United States of America, Appellee v. Deborah Gore Dean, Appellant*, United States Court of Appeals for the District of Columbia Circuit, [argued] November 15, 1994, [decided] May 26, 1995; Robert A. Diamond, ed., *The Supreme Court: Justice and the Law* (Congressional Quarterly, 1973), p. 107; Bob Woodward and Scott Armstrong, *The Brethren: Inside the*

Supreme Court (Avon, 1981), p. 475; Henry J. Abraham, *Justices and Presidents: A Political History of Appointments to the Supreme Court* (Oxford, 1985), p. 307; James C. Humes, *Confessions of a White House Ghostwriter* (Regnery, 1997), pp. 104–6; Haynes Johnson, *Sleepwalking Through History: America in the Reagan Years* (Norton, 2003), p. 180. A 1996 press release from the Office of Independent Counsel stated that in seven years of investigation, it had secured seventeen criminal convictions, more than $2 million in criminal fines, and the recovery of $10 million in low-income housing funds. Former secretary Pierce was spared prosecution after he acknowledged in writing that his own behavior "contributed to an environment" at HUD that fostered "improper and even criminal conduct."

EPILOGUE

1. "Present and Accounted For: Mitchell's Hanging," *Esquire*, May 1985 (emphases in original).
2. Larry Martz, "He's Back: The Rehabilitation of Richard Nixon," *Newsweek*, May 19, 1986; *CBS Evening News* [6:30 and 7:00 p.m. broadcasts] and *ABC World News Tonight*, November 9, 1988; Sari Horwitz and James Rupert, "John Mitchell, Nixon Official in Watergate Scandal, Dies," and Laurence Meyer, "John N. Mitchell, Principal in Watergate, Dies at 75" [early and late editions], all in *Washington Post*, November 10, 1988; Carolyn Skorneck, "Nixon Pal Mitchell Dies at 75," *New York Daily News*, November 10, 1988; "John Mitchell, Key Watergate Figure, Dies at 75," *Los Angeles Times*, November 10, 1988; James Rupert, "Mistake Didn't Affect Care of Mitchell, Officials Say," *Washington Post*, November

11, 1988; "John Mitchell and the Loonies," *New York Times*, November 12, 1988; David E. Rosenbaum, "John N. Mitchell Is Remembered as a Victim of 'Cruel Treatment,' " *New York Times*, November 13, 1988; Mary Jordan and Lynne Duke, "Farewell for a Friend," *Washington Post*, November 13, 1988; "John Mitchell Died Nearly Broke," *The Washingtonian* (October 1990); Remarks by Richard A. Moore at the Funeral Service for The Honorable John N. Mitchell, St. Alban's Church, Washington, D.C., November 12, 1988, provided to the author by Moore; CI, January 24, 1987 (heady), March 1, 1987 (Hall), November 9, 1987 (close), March 29, 1988 (ego), August 19, 1988 (Quayle), October 23, 1988 (Dukakis); Octavius Prince, interview with author, July 22, 2003.
3. HN, July 13, 1970 (Mafia); SSC, IV: 1603–5; UVM, 8021–135 (mildly, agreed); WH memo [to the president from Tom Charles Huston], [Subject:] Domestic Intelligence Gathering Plan: Recommendations, July 1970, reprinted at R. W. Apple Jr., ed., *The Watergate Hearings: Break-in and Cover-up* (Bantam Books, 1973), pp. 748–51; WH memo for Mr. Huston from H. R. Haldeman, Subject: Domestic Intelligence Review, July 14, 1970, at SSC, III: 1324; WH memo for H. R. Haldeman from Tom Charles Huston, Subject: Domestic Intelligence, August 5, 1970, at SSC, III: 1325–29; "The Price of Arrogance," *New York Times*, February 22, 1975; Gross, "Conversation with an Author"; Adelman, "You Do What Needs to Be Done"; Safire, "Watch What We Do"; William C. Sullivan with Bill Brown, *The Bureau: My Thirty Years in Hoover's FBI* (Norton, 1979), pp. 206–17; Theoharis and Cox, *The Boss*, pp. 412–43, 470–77; Fred J. Maroon, *The Nixon Years, 1969–1974: White House to Watergate* (Abbeville Press, 1999), p. 44 (Mrs.

Ky); Helms interview; Morrison interview.

4. Mitchell-Reed e-mail, September 24, 2003; William F. Mullen, *Presidential Power and Politics* (St. Martin's Press, 1976), p. 244; Emery, *Watergate*, p. 492 (my dear); Wilson Sr., *A Fool for a Client*, p. 56 (client); Mitchell-Reed interview (Kennedy); Deborah Gore Dean interview; Rehnquist interview; Landau interviews, December 2, 1993, and January 12, 1994.

NOTES ON SOURCES

LIST OF INTERVIEWS

Addeo, Russell C., via telephone, Belfast, NY, November 10, 1995

Agnew, Spiro T., via correspondence, March 20, 1993

Ayers, Bill, via telephone, Chicago, IL, May 8, 2004

Baldwin, Alfred C. III, via telephone, East Haven, CT, August 19, 1995

———, East Haven, CT, September 9, 1995

———, via telephone, East Haven, CT, September 10, 1995

Barker, Bernard, via telephone, Miami, FL, January 5, 1995

Barreaux, Ted, Washington, DC, February 26, 2004

Bennett, Robert F., via telephone, Washington, DC, May 11, 1995

———, via telephone, Washington, DC, May 26, 1995

Ben-Veniste, Richard, Washington, DC, July 7, 1995

Berg, Richard K., via telephone, Arlington, VA, August 28, 1993

Bogan, Carl, via telephone, New York, NY, March 29, 1994

Bonham, John, via telephone, Bellview, PA, September 6, 1995

Brasco, Frank, via telephone, Brooklyn, NY, February 22, 1994

Brown, Edwin C., via telephone, Alexandria, VA, July 20, 1995

Bruno, Hal, Washington, DC, February 25, 1994

———, Chesapeake Bay, MD, April 13, 2002

Burger, Warren E., Arlington, VA, August 25, 1994

Bush, George H. W., via correspondence, June 11, 1993

———, via correspondence, September 3, 1993

Butterfield, Alexander, via telephone, San Diego, CA, October 12, 1994

Cacheris, Plato, via telephone, Alexandria, VA, September 8, 1993

———, via telephone, Washington, DC, May 16, 2005

Caddy, Douglas, via telephone, Houston, TX, July 7, 1995

———, via telephone, Houston, TX, July 13, 1995

Carlson, Norman, via telephone, Stillwater, MN, September 13, 1993

Carlucci, Frank, via telephone, McLean, VA, February 8, 2001

Carter, Roy V., via telephone, Miami, FL, April 3, 1994

Casey, Mr. and Mrs. J. Doug, Rye, NY, June 3, 1993

Chapin, Dwight L., via telephone, East Hampton, NY, June 2, 2005

Choa, Gregory, via telephone, New York, NY, February 17, 1992

Coggins, William N., via telephone, Washington, DC, July 19, 1995

Cohen, William S., aboard Air Force One, October 18, 2000

Colby William E., via telephone, Washington, DC, January 20, 1995

Colodny, Leonard, Tampa, FL, January 22, 1992

Colson, Charles W., via telephone, Washington, DC, May 24, 2001

Corbin, Sol Neil, New York, NY, August 12, 1993

Cox, Archibald, via correspondence, December 3, 2003

Creditor, Richard, via telephone, Queens, NY, September 10, 1997

Crowe, William J., via telephone, Alexandria, VA, February 16, 2001

Davis, Gil H., Washington, DC, January 13, 2003

Davis, Rennie, via telephone, Boulder, CO, May 9, 2004

Dean, Deborah Gore, via telephone, Washington, DC, February 17, 1992

———, Washington, DC, March 10, 1992

Dean, Gordon, via telephone, Washington, DC, March 10, 1992

Dean, John W. III, via telephone, Los Angeles, CA, August 6, 1999

Dean, Mary Gore, via telephone, Potomac, MD, March 2, 1992

Denis, Richard, via telephone, Green Bay, WI, September 8, 1999

Dent, Harry S., via telephone, Columbia, SC, February 17, 1992

———, via telephone, Columbia, SC, March 2, 1992

Dorsen, David, via telephone, Washington, DC, December 2, 1997

Douglass, Robert R., New York, NY, June 30, 1993

Duersteler, John M., via telephone, Lockport, NY, July 19, 2003

Duval, Michael Raoul, New York, NY, November 5, 1992

Ebbitt, Mr. and Mrs. Ken, Bronxville, NY, October 11, 1993

Ehrlichman, John D., via telephone, Atlanta, GA, March 13, 1992

Elfin, Mel, via telephone, Washington, DC, November 9, 1993

Ellsberg, Daniel, via telephone, Berkeley, CA, March 13, 2004

Evans, Thomas W., New York City, April 23, 1992

Feinberg, Kenneth, Washington, DC, February 4, 2002

Feldman, Cary, via telephone, Bethesda, MD, December 8, 1993

Finch, Robert H., via telephone, Pasadena, CA, June 5, 1993

———, via telephone, Pasadena, CA, June 12, 1993

———, via telephone, Pasadena, CA, August 5, 1993

———, via correspondence, August 31, 1993

———, via telephone, Pasadena, CA, September 17, 1993

Flanigan, Peter M., New York, NY, October 28, 1993

Fleming, David, via telephone, Los Angeles, CA, December 1, 2003

Fleming, Peter, New York, NY, December 17, 1991

———, via telephone, New York, NY, May 3, 1998

Flemming, Harry C., via telephone, Washington, DC, March 4, 1992

Ford, Gerald R., New York, NY, January 25, 1994

———, via telephone, Rancho Mirage, CA, February 13, 2001

Gagliardi, Lee P., via telephone, New York, NY, July 21, 1993

Garment, Leonard, Washington, DC, March 13, 1992

———, via telephone, Washington, DC, December 6, 1999

Gentry, R. Charles, via telephone, Washington, DC, November 16, 1993

Gillenwaters, Ed, via telephone, Carlsbad, CA, November 26, 2003

Gould, Ruth, via telephone, Washington, DC, March 22, 1994

Graham, Fred P., New York, NY, October 8, 1997

Griswold, Erwin N., via telephone, Washington, DC, June 28, 1994

Haig, Alexander M., Washington, DC, July 27, 2000

Haldeman, H. R., via telephone, Santa Barbara, CA, September 26, 1993

Halperin, Morton, via telephone, Washington, DC, March 24, 1994

Harries, Brenton W., New York, NY, November 3, 1994

Helms, Richard M., via telephone, Washington, DC, February 2, 1995

————, via telephone, Washington, DC, February 9, 1995

Herman, William C., via telephone, New York, NY, February 10, 1998

————, via telephone, New York, NY, February 12, 1998

Hersh, Seymour M., via telephone, Washington, DC, June 13, 2002

Hickey, Robyn, via telephone, Washington, DC, March 2, 1995

Hirschkop, Philip, via telephone, Lorton, VA, May 15, 2004

Hixson, Sheila, via telephone, Washington, DC, January 30, 1995

Hougan, Jim, via telephone, Ashton, VA, May 11, 1995

Hundley, William G., Washington, DC, March 11, 1992

————, via telephone, Washington, DC, May 16, 2005

Hunt, E. Howard, Miami, FL, January 26, 2003

————, via telephone, Miami, FL, April 1, 2003

Hushen, Jack, via telephone, Cleveland, OH, December 7, 1993

————, via telephone, Gates Mills, OH, December 30, 1993

Huston, Tom Charles, via telephone, Indianapolis, IN, May 7, 1995

Jennings, Clyde Jr., via telephone, Lynchburg, VA, July 23, 2002

————, via telephone, Jacksonville, FL, July 27, 2002

Jennings, Clyde Jay, via telephone, Woodbridge, VA, July 25, 2002

————, Woodbridge, VA, August 1, 2002

King, Anita C., via telephone, Washington, DC, March 30, 1994

King, Peter, Washington, DC, January 16, 2001

————, via telephone, Washington, DC, September 16, 2003

King, Stephen B., via telephone, Milton, WI, February 8, 1992

————, via telephone, Milton, WI, February 23, 1992

Kissinger, Henry A., New York, NY, March 30, 1995

Kleindienst, Richard G., via telephone, Phoenix, AZ, April 21, 1992

Knutson, Lawrence, aboard Air Force One, June 25, 2001

Koch, Edward I., via correspondence, March 19, 1993

Kresky, Edward, New York, NY, August 31, 1993

Kunstler, William, via telephone, New York, NY, August 6, 1993

Kutler, Stanley I., via telephone, Madison, WI, February 17, 1992

Laird, Melvin R., via telephone, Fort Myers, FL, August 28, 1997

Landau, Jack C., via telephone, Alexandria, VA, December 2, 1993

————, via telephone, Falls Church, VA, December 16, 1993

————, via telephone, Falls Church, VA, January 12, 1994

LaRue, Fred C., via telephone, Biloxi, MS, September 19, 1993

————, via telephone, Biloxi, MS, August 4, 2003

Lauer, Elliot, New York, NY, December 17, 1991

Lefcourt, Gerald, via telephone, New York, NY, May 14, 2004

Lehman, John F., Williamsburg, VA, March 3, 2001

Leonard, Jerris, Washington, DC, March 17, 1992

————, Washington, DC, October 14, 1999

————, via telephone, Washington, DC, May 23, 2004

Lewis, Emery A., via telephone, Port St. Lucie, FL, July 19, 2003

Liddy, G. Gordon, via telephone, Oxon Hill, MD, February 4, 1992

————, Washington, DC, August 4, 1999

————, via telephone, Oxon Hill, MD, December 4, 2003

————, via telephone, Washington, DC, August 9, 2004

————, via correspondence, August 21, 2004

————, via correspondence, November 14, 2004 (I and II)

———, via correspondence, December 5, 2004

Long, Russell, Washington, DC, May 10, 1996

Lubasch, Arnold, via telephone, Scottsdale, AZ, January 19, 2004

MacIntyre, Pope, via telephone, Atlanta, GA, February 21, 1994

Madison, William A., via telephone, Scottsdale, AZ, June 5, 1993

Malek, Frederic V., via telephone, Washington, DC, March 12, 1992

———, McLean, VA, December 15, 2002

Maloney, Francis X., New York, NY, June 22, 1993

———, New York, NY, July 28, 1993

———, New York, NY, November 9, 1993

Mancino, Adam, via telephone, Meriden, CT, September 10, 1995

Mardian, Robert C., via telephone, Phoenix, AZ, August 2, 1993

———, via telephone, Phoenix, AZ, September 14, 1993

———, via correspondence, April 20, 1995

———, via correspondence, August 20, 1996

———, via correspondence, August 22, 2001

———, via correspondence, February 6, 2003

Margiotta, Joseph, via telephone, West Hempstead, NY, December 8, 1997

McCord, James W., Washington, DC, July 25, 1994

McLaren, Richard, Jr., via telephone, Chicago, IL, December 8, 2003

McNamara, Robert S., Washington, DC, May 1, 2002

Mitchell, J. Robert, via telephone, West Hempstead, NY, February 9, 1998

———, via telephone, West Hempstead, NY, February 26, 1998

———, via telephone, West Hempstead, NY, August 8, 1998

Mitchell, Marion, via telephone, West Hempstead, NY, December 19, 1997

Mitchell-Reed, Jill, Cold Spring Harbor, NY, February 23, 1992

———, via telephone, Cold Spring Harbor, NY, March 12, 1992

———, Cold Spring Harbor, NY, May 5, 1992

———, via telephone, Cold Spring Harbor, NY, December 19, 1996

———, via correspondence, September 23, 2003

———, via correspondence, September 24, 2003

———, Miami, FL, November 22, 2003

———, via correspondence, November 25, 2003

Moore, Powell A., Alexandria, VA, May 17, 1993

Moore, Richard A., Washington, DC, January 31, 1992

Morrison, Susie, Orlando, FL, January 16, 1992

Murphy, Paul, via telephone, Washington, DC, September 24, 1997

Neal, James A., via telephone, Nashville, TN, May 20, 1992

Nelson, Jack, via telephone, Washington, DC, July 7, 1995

Nesline, Rebecca Sutton, via telephone, Dover, DE, August 30, 1995

Odle, Robert C., Washington, DC, April 17, 1993

Perk, Sandy Hobbs, New York, NY, May 1, 1992

Peskin, Stephan, via telephone, New York, NY, July 16, 2002

Phillips, Kevin, via telephone, Bethesda, MD, December 23, 1993

Porter, Herbert L. ("Bart"), via telephone, Newport Beach, CA, May 11, 1993

Prince, Ocatvius, via telephone, Delray Beach, FL, July 22, 2003

Prouty, L. Fletcher, via telephone, Alexandria, VA, October 12, 1994

Rayhill, James W., New York, NY, December 11, 1997

Rehnquist, William H., via correspondence, June 29, 1993

———, Washington, DC, October 20, 1993

———, Washington, DC, May 21, 2001

Rinaldi, Charles E., via telephone, Rockville, MD, July 18, 1995

Ronan, William J., via telephone, West Palm Beach, FL, September 26, 1994

Ruckelshaus, William D., via telephone, Houston, TX, March 8, 1994

Rudd, Mark, via telephone, Albuquerque, NM, May 12, 2004

Rumsfeld, Donald H., the Pentagon, January 4, 2002

Sankin, Andrew C., Washington, DC, June 13, 1996

Santarelli, Donald, via telephone, Alexandria, VA, May 6, 1995

Scotti, Gavin W., via telephone, New York, NY, September 16, 1997

Sears, John P., via telephone, Washington, DC, January 31, 1994

Segal, Marv, New York, NY, October 23, 1997

Shirley, Marie, via telephone, Mission, TX, March 23, 2004

Shogan, Robert, via telephone, Chevy Chase, MD, November 30, 1993

Shultz, George P., via telephone, Stanford, CA, April 29, 1996

Shumway, deVan L., McLean, VA, September 27, 1993

Silbert, Earl J., via telephone, Washington, DC, May 30, 1995

———, via telephone, Washington, DC, May 31, 1995

Simon, William E., via telephone, New York, NY, January 17, 1992

Sporkin, Stanley, via telephone, Washington, DC, December 12, 2003

Stans, Maurice, Washington, DC, June 4, 1992

Strauss, Robert, via telephone, Washington, DC, May 9, 1996

Tapman, Kenneth, via telephone, Highland Beach, FL, January 4, 2003

Thurmond, Strom, via telephone, Washington, DC, April 3, 1996

Timmons, William E., via telephone, Washington, DC, July 10, 1995

Treen, Joseph M., Montclair, NJ, May 20, 1995

Tully, James C., via telephone, McLean, VA, March 2, 1994

Uhre, Lee Jablonsky, via telephone, Potomac, MD, April 17, 1995

Ulicky, Sybil Kucharski, New York, NY, April 25, 1995

Vine, Richard D., via telephone, Chestertown, MD, December 9, 2003

Wallace, Mike, New York, NY, October 26, 1997

Wardell, Thomas R., via telephone, Phoenix, AZ, September 6, 1995

Webster, William H., via telephone, Washington, DC, February 15, 2001

Wells, Ida ("Maxie"), via telephone, Clinton, MS, October 29, 1994

———, via telephone, Clinton, MS, December 19, 1994

Wemhoff, Dan, via telephone, Washington, DC, September 10, 1999

Wickham, Julie Schlessinger, via telephone, Lorton, VA, January 15, 1995

Wiebe, Richard, via telephone, Las Cruces, NM, September 13, 1994

Williams, Kristen Forsberg, via telephone, Washington, DC, April 23, 1995

Wilson, David G., via telephone, Washington, DC, January 6, 1995

Wilson, Malcolm, White Plains, NY, May 12, 1993

Wing, John R., Brooklyn, NY, September 27, 1997

Wolfe, Tom, New York, NY, November 4, 2004

Wooten, James, via telephone, Washington, DC, April 9, 2004

THE MOORER-RADFORD TAPES

Below are citations for the White House tapes relating to the Moorer-Radford episode referenced in the chapter "Robbing the President's Desk." First declassified and released in October 2000, their contents were first published by the author in an article entitled "Nixon and the Chiefs," published in the *Atlantic Monthly* in April 2002. All of these tapes are available at the National Archives' Nixon Presidential Materials Project in College Park, Maryland. All transcripts were prepared by the author. The author acknowledges a special debt to Mountain State University's Nixon Era Center, which provided a digitally enhanced version of the December 21, 1971, tape. The center's Web site can be accessed at www.nixonera.com.

NT, Conversation No. 639–30, President Nixon, John Mitchell, H. R. Haldeman, and John Ehrlichman, Oval Office, December 21, 1971, 6:07–6:59 p.m. [HRH and JDE enter at 6:09 p.m.]

NT, Conversation No. 640–3, Nixon and Haldeman, Oval Office, December 22, 1971, 9:48–11:02 a.m.

NT, Conversation No. 640–5, Nixon, Mitchell, and Ehrlichman, Oval Office, December 22, 1971, 11:03–11:33 a.m.

NT, Conversation No. 640–11, Nixon and Haldeman, Oval Office, December 22, 1971, 1:16–1:50 p.m.

NT, Conversation No. 641–5, Nixon and Haldeman, Oval Office, December 23, 1971, 11:37–11:53 a.m.

NT, Conversation No. 641–10, Nixon and Haldeman, Oval Office, December 23, 1971, 12:27–1:15 p.m.

NT, Conversation No. 310–19, Nixon, Haldeman, and Robert Finch, Executive Office Building, December 23, 1971, 3:00–4:40 p.m.

NT, Conversation No. 17–28, Nixon and Alexander Haig, White House Telephone, December 24, 1971, 5:01–5:08 p.m.

NT, Conversation No. 17–37, Nixon and Mitchell, White House Telephone, December 24, 1971, 5:33–5:39 p.m.

NT, Conversation No. 17–55, Nixon and Mitchell, White House Telephone, December 24, 1971, 11:17–11:22 p.m.

NT, Conversation No. 17–91, Nixon and Melvin Laird, White House Telephone, December 25, 1971, 11:45–11:46 a.m.

NT, Conversation No. 17–102, Nixon and Thomas Moorer, White House Telephone, December 26, 1971, 12:12–12:16 p.m.

NT, Conversation No. 310–30, Nixon and Haig, Executive Office Building, December 26, 1971, 12:16–1:43 p.m.

NT, Conversation No. 17–132, Nixon and Henry Kissinger, White House Telephone, January 1, 1972, 2:43–3:56 p.m.

INDEX

public opinion regarding, 335,
382, 394
sentencing of Watergate burglars,
Hunt and Liddy, 358–59
sentencing of Watergate cover-up
convicts, 440–42
sentencing reductions for Watergate cover-up convicts, 440,
459–65
U.S. v. Liddy, et al. See break-in
trial
U.S. v. Mitchell, et al. See cover-
up trial
Vesco affair and, 230, 241–43,
249–50, 256, 336–37, 381
Watergate Special Prosecution Force
(WSPF), xviii–xix, xxiii,
151, 216, 258, 273,
317–20, 330–31, 341,
342–43, 419–34
Wayne, John, 303
Weathermen
See Weather Underground
Weather Underground, xiii, 82,
85–88, 89
Weicker, Lowell, 391–93
Weiner, Lee, 80
Welander, Adm. Robert O., 169,
170, 171, 172, 175, 180
Wheeler, Gen. Earle, 166
White, Byron, 450
White House Special Investigations
Unit (the Plumbers),
163–64, 169, 175

Wicker, Tom, xiii
Wilkins, Roy, 129–30, 145
Williams, Edward Bennett, 332
Williams, Hosea, 108
Will (Liddy), 265, 290
Wilson, Bob, 201, 202, 203, 209
Wilson, Jerry V., 94, 109, 300
Wilson, John, 445, 461
Wilson, Malcolm, 7
Wilson, Will, 71
Wing, John, 239, 243, 248, 249,
250, 252–54, 255
Wiretapping programs of Mitchell
Justice Department, 80–81,
150–54
Witcover, Jules, 38
Witness to Power (Ehrlichman), 43
Woestendiek, Kay, 124
Wolfe, Tom, 113, 383
Woods, Rose, 488
Woodward, Bob, xxiv, 225, 488
World War II, xv, 15–18, 42, 43

Yablonsky, Judy, 384
Yippies, 80, 89, 92, 106, 112, 113
Young, David, 164, 175

Zaroulis, Nancy, 80
Ziegler, Ron, 117–18, 162, 488
Zoning laws, 144–45
Zumwalt, Adm. Elmo, 165, 167